Environmental Law and Policy in the People's Republic of China

環保與法律

鐸若題

ENVIRONMENTAL LAW AND POLICY IN THE PEOPLE'S REPUBLIC OF CHINA

LESTER ROSS AND MITCHELL A. SILK

Q

QUORUM BOOKS
NEW YORK • WESTPORT, CONNECTICUT • LONDON

Library of Congress Cataloging-in-Publication Data

Ross, Lester.
Environmental law and policy in the People's Republic of China.

Bibliography: p.
Includes index.
1. Environmental law—China. 2. Conservation of natural resources—Law and legislation—China. 3. Environmental policy—China. 4. Conservation of natural resources—Government policy—China. I. Silk, Mitchell A. II. Title.

LAW 346.5104′4 86-22503
ISBN 0-89930-204-1 345.10644
(lib. bdg. : alk. paper)

Library of Congress Catalog Card Number: 86-22503
ISBN: 0-89930-204-1

First published in 1987 by Quorum Books

Greenwood Press, Inc.
88 Post Road West, Westport, Connecticut 06881

Printed in the United States of America

The paper used in this book complies with the Permanent Paper Standard issued by the National Information Standards Organization (Z39.48-1984).

10 9 8 7 6 5 4 3 2 1

Copyright Acknowledgments

Grateful acknowledgment is given to M. E. Sharpe, Inc., for permission to reprint copyrighted material from *The Bad Earth* by Vaclav Smil (1984) and to incorporate into this book the entire special issue of *Chinese Law and Government*, vol. 19, no. 1 (1986) on "Environmental Law and Policy in China," edited by Lester Ross and Mitchell A. Silk with Deng Jianxu.

Frontispiece by Dora Fugh Lee, courtesy of the artist.

To our parents—David and Helen Ross, and David and Malka Silk—who never dreamed that taking their sons to Chinese restaurants would shape their careers; and in memory of Sol and Bertha Silk *zt''l*, and Max and Esther Friend *zt''l*.

Contents

Preface

China has slowly awakened to the environmental problem since the early 1970s. In 1972 China participated in the United Nations Conference on the Human Environment in Stockholm. Since then environmental planning and legislation have ranked high on the priority lists of officials concerned with legal reform and development.

Despite increased attention to the problem, many questions remain unanswered with regard to environmental law and policy in China. What are the basic policies and ideology guiding environmental protection work in China? What legal principles provide the basis for China's environmental scheme? Is there such a thing as environmental litigation in China? What direct governmental and party controls does China employ in regulating the air, water, marine resources, noise, and solid and toxic wastes? How does China go about protecting its land, forests, fisheries, grasslands, and wildlife? How do the Chinese enforce their environmental laws? How and in what forums are environmental disputes resolved?

The purpose of this study is to shed light on the actual workings and policy underpinnings of China's environmental administration. To achieve these ends we have allowed the Chinese to speak for themselves in presenting the views and, in a limited way, the actual practices of leading Chinese environmental policy makers, administrators, judicial personnel, and scholars. Given the factional nature of Chinese political culture, not all of the materials presented represent a consensus on a given point. At the very least, though, the reader will find all of the materials informative in one way or another. Where necessary and relevant we have added commentary to highlight various points raised by the Chinese.

We have selected the readings from numerous sources, including China's Communist party newspaper *Renmin Ribao* (People's Daily), influential ideological journals such as *Hongqi* (Red Flag), and a number of the legal and environmental periodicals which began or resumed publication in the early 1980s such as *Huanjing Baohu* (Environmental Protection), *Faxue Yanjiu* (Studies in Law), *Zhongguo Huanjing Kexue* (Environmental Sciences in China), *Huanjing* (Environment), *Zhongguo Fazhi Bao* (China Legal System Paper), and *Huanjing Fa* (Environmental Law). We have prepared most of the translations ourselves and, where adequate, have edited and included existing English translations of the Chinese materials. We have noted in the headings where government or other translations are used. We have taken the liberty to change punctuation, capitalization, word usage, and the like to render the translations more readable.

The editors' introduction summarizes the development of environmental law and policy in China, explains the interplay between law and policy in the environmental area, and points out flaws in the existing system. The book is then divided into seven parts. Part One offers a policy and legal overview and touches specifically on the basic principles of China's environmental law, environmental rights in China, and environmental litigation in China. Part Two deals with the regulation of the environment and focuses on air pollution control, water pollution control, the protection of marine resources, noise control, and solid and toxic waste control. Part Three discusses the conservation of land, natural resources, and wildlife and focuses on land use and planning; forest, fisheries, and grassland protection; and wildlife protection. Part Four treats enforcement means and mechanisms by explaining the concepts of economic incentives and disincentives for environmental protection, registration procedures, legal responsibility, and dispute resolution organs within the Chinese system. Part Five reports on numerous pollution cases that have been decided since the promulgation of the Environmental Protection Law (1979). The cases were all widely covered as model cases in the press and include one involving a foreign venture in the Shenzhen Special Economic Zone that was affirmed by the Supreme People's Court. Part Six presents all relevant laws and regulations. The two charts in Part Seven outline China's environmental legislative scheme and administrative framework.

We hope that this study will serve as a useful tool for scholars, policy formulators, and the investment community. First, the book reveals the extent of China's awakening to dangers to its environment and provides a systematic survey of the means by which it has managed these problems. The material reflects China's commitment, both as a developing and as a socialist state, to legality and environmental protection within the evolving international and national regimes of resource management and preservation. It should be of value to students of law and politics, economics, communist affairs, and contemporary China. Second, with the U.S. Environmental Protection Agency and related bureaus actively involved in government-to-government exchange with the People's Republic of China, the material should provide a basis for policy formulation, particularly in the areas of economic development and international environmental protection. Moreover, the actions of China, as the world's largest developing country, may signal future trends in environmental protection among other Third World countries. Last, we hope that the materials—especially the appendixes and cases—will provide useful guidance to foreign investors and legal counsel in planning ventures in China. Realizing that the bottom line to which counsel usually looks may tend to get lost in the depths of this book, we would direct the planner elsewhere for more practical guidance.[1]

The Chinese are notorious for undocumented references. Many of the scholars in this volume, for example, exhibited an impressive knowledge of foreign laws and cases but, for the most part, failed to include source citations to the materials. To fill the gap, we have attempted to cite all legal and other important materials referred to in the translated material. Our notes are followed by the designation [eds.] to signify that the editors filled in the citation. This task was frustrated in large part because we were dealing with references to foreign language sources rendered in Chinese. Furthermore, some foreign language legal sources were unavailable. We apologize for those few references that are still without citations.

We have included in the bibliography references not necessarily cited directly in the book but which should nevertheless be useful and important to the researcher. This is followed by a general index.

Note

1. *See* Mitchell A. Silk, "Investing and Doing Business in China: The Environmental Implications," in Michael J. Moser, ed., *Trade, Foreign Investment and the Law in the People's Republic of China*, 2d ed., Hong Kong and London: Oxford University Press, 1987; and the chapter on pollution control in Lester Ross, *Environmental Policy in China*, Bloomington: Indiana University Press, 1988; and Lester Ross and Mitchell A. Silk, "Curbing Environmental Pollution," *China Business Review*, no. 2 (1987), pp. 51–53.

Acknowledgments

We are grateful to a number of people who helped in the course of this study. We will attempt to name them all here in no special order of preference. Some names will inevitably be left off. Our apologies in advance. As always, we alone are responsible for the views presented.

Professor Michael Y. M. Kau (Brown University) and Douglas Merwin (M. E. Sharpe Publishers) suggested, encouraged, and actively supported expanding our *Chinese Law and Government* special issue on "Environmental Law and Policy in China" into this full-length book. Dora Fugh Lee has graced this volume with her calligraphy, which appears as the frontispiece. The Asia-Pacific Educational Fund and the East Asian Legal Studies Program of the University of Maryland School of Law offered generous financial assistance. The better benevolence of some gurus at Melnicove, Kaufman, Weiner, Smouse & Garbis (formerly Garbis, Marvel & Junghans) allocated limited assistance for the production of this book. A special thanks to them for support of this nonbillable matter. We express thanks also to James Dunton and Todd Adkins of Quorum Books for putting up with the problems encountered in the transnational production of this book.

The administrative burdens connected with the production of this book were great. LuAnn ("Hun") Marshall, Eileen M. Gretes, Kathleen ("Kinky") Montroy (University of Maryland School of Law), and Linda Schram (Melnicove, Kaufman, Weiner, Smouse & Garbis, Baltimore, Maryland, and Washington, D.C.) got this book into manuscript form. They deciphered page after page of chicken scrawl and dealt most formidably with the Pinyin romanization of Chinese. Andy Y. T. Sun, Esquire, Wei-cheng Wang, and Karen Brown Thompson found time amid their already taxing schedules to assist with some of the translations. LuAnn Marshall, Mrs. Chih-yu Wu (East Asian Legal Studies, University of Maryland School of Law), and friends at Melnicove, Kaufman, Weiner, Smouse & Garbis and Coudert Brothers offered other administrative assistance.

A number of friends helped to locate fugitive citations for various environmental laws and regulations of countries ranging from Albania to Zimbabwe and provided us with various materials related to Chinese and U.S. environmental law. They include James V. Feinerman (Georgetown University Law Center);

Dr. Takeo Nishioka, Dr. Giovanni Salvo, Dr. Connie Johnson (all of the Library of Congress); Nicholas V. Chen, Esquire; Professors Oscar Gray, Garret Power, Robert I. Keller, Marc I. Steinberg, and Nancy Long (University of Maryland School of Law); Jennifer Little and Dorota Dyman (National Council for U.S.-China Trade Library); Marc A. Cohen, Deng Jianxu (Shenzhen University). Maxine Grosshans, Richard Ducey, Esquire, and Dennis Guion went above and beyond the call of duty to track down some of the cites.

So many others provided the much-needed support and other assistance to see this project through. We thank in this regard Claudia Ross, Magdalene Wo, Larry Chi-leung Chung, Dr. Thomas W. Robinson, Irving A. Breitowitz, Moshe Rappaport, Shlomo Porter, Nicholas V. Chen, Kam-yau Cheng and family, and Robert Kirchner. Lester Ross also expresses his appreciation to the Committee on Scholarly Communication of the People's Republic of China of the National Academy of Sciences, which funded a research leave in China during which this manuscript was prepared, and the Institute of Environmental Management Science of the Chinese Research Academy of Environmental Sciences, which served as a congenial support unit during this period. Mitchell A. Silk expresses a special thanks to David I. Salem, Esquire, (and Sally) for their fine counsel and, above and beyond all others, to Professor Hungdah Chiu for sharing his collective wisdom and his unselfish and unyielding support of all my endeavors, making the law school experience just a bit more bearable, and for acting as the true Confucian role model and teacher.

Abbreviations

All E.R.	*All England Law Reports*
BFWH	Ministry of Urban and Rural Construction, Office of Environmental Protection (1983) *Guojia Huanjing Baohu Fagui Wenjian Huibian* (Compendium of Laws, Regulations, and Documents on Environmental Protection). Beijing: Zhongguo Huanjing Kexue Chubanshe.
CCW	Blaustein, Albert P., and Gisbert H. Flanz, eds. (binder) *Constitutions of the Countries of the World*. Dobbs Ferry, NY: Oceana Publications.
FBIS-*CHI*	Foreign Broadcast Information Service. *People's Republic of China: Daily Report*.
FGHB	*Zhonghua Renmin Gongheguo Fagui Huibian* (Compendia of Laws and Regulations of the People's Republic of China)
FLHB	*Zhongyang Renmin Zhengfu Faling Huibian* (Compendia of Laws and Decrees of the Central People's Government)
GGB	*Zhonghua Renmin Gongheguo Guowu Yuan Gongbao* (Gazette of the State Council of the People's Republic of China)
H	*Huanjing* (Environment)
HB	*Huanjing Baohu* (Environmental Protection)
HBYWX	*Zhonghua Renmin Gongheguo Huanjing Baohu Yanjiu Wenxian Xuanbian* (Collection of Research Materials Concerning Environmental Protection in the People's Republic of China)
HK	*Huanjing Kexue* (Environmental Science)
H.L.	*House of Lords* (Reporter for appeals from the English Court of Appeals, from the Scottish Court of Session, Inner House, in civil cases, from the Scottish Court-Martial Appeal Court, and from the North Ireland Court of Appeal)
HQ	*Hongqi* (Red Flag)
JFGXB	*Jingji Fagui Xuanbian* (Collection of Economic Laws and Regulations)
JY	*Jingji Yanjiu* (Economic Research)
Q.B.	*Queen's Bench Division* (Reporter for English trials in tort and contract and other commercial claims)
U.N.T.S.	*United Nations Treaty Series*
U.S.C.	*United States Code*
ZHK	*Zhongguo Huanjing Kexue* (Environmental Sciences in China)
ZL	*Zhongguo Linye* (Chinese Forestry)
ZZ	*Ziran Ziyuan* (Natural Resources)

1

Introduction

Before embarking on the survey of Chinese views on environmental law and policy, we will present background material on the development of environmental law and policy in China and the shortcomings and key problem areas in China's environmental administration. This introduction will treat, in brief, the experience of previous Chinese governments in the environmental area and the response of the People's Republic to the environmental problem. It will then analyze the interplay between environmental law and policy, general problems in defining and enforcing substantive and procedural environmental rights, and conflict resolution. Finally, it will note some shortcomings in China's legal system pertaining to the area of environmental law.

THE DEVELOPMENT OF ENVIRONMENTAL LAW AND POLICY IN CHINA

Like other ancient civilizations, China's history reveals considerable understanding of the need for ecological balance, rooted in the efforts of people centuries ago to survive and prosper in agrarian and pastoral societies. China's religious and philosophical traditions stressed the need for man to live in harmony with nature and be careful not to upset the delicate forces that sustained civilization. Indeed, the emperor's legitimacy, known as the ''Mandate of Heaven'' (*tian ming*), was signified in part by the absence of natural disasters. Conversely, floods, earthquakes, and other dislocations in the natural order were considered portents of misgovernment and could be used by subordinate officials to criticize the throne.[1]

The sensitivity of Chinese culture in this regard was a factor in the promulgation of a fair number of laws and edicts over the years with regard to the conservation of nature. The Qin, Tang, and Qing codes all contained provisions on logging, hunting, water conservation, and the like.[2] More recently, forestry and related issues were a focus of attention in the early Republican period, and even in the Jiangxi Soviet Republic and Communist-ruled base areas during the revolutionary civil war.[3]

Despite clear signs of an incipient environmental awareness in Chinese culture,

Chinese civilization was, on the whole, guided more by the need to satisfy basic economic needs than by higher values. Population growth and the introduction of exotic plants, like corn and sweet potatoes, adaptable to sloped-land farming,[4] reliance on wood for heating, charcoal, and even to manufacture ink,[5] as well as wartime destruction and the ebb and flow of civil authority all contributed to a notable decline in China's forest resource base over the centuries. This in turn had severe consequences in terms of soil erosion, sedimentation, and flooding. In other words, the best features of the great culture and the laws of the state were often of no avail even in an era of relatively primitive technology. The danger of environmental destruction would be magnified in the industrial era.

The People's Republic of China (PRC) has had to cope not only with environmental problems of the traditional sort involving man's interaction with nature—forest, soil, and water conservation and similar concerns—on a vast scale, but also with the environmental by-products of modernization. Although the PRC has had some notable accomplishments in flood control and on the conservation front in some regions, its record has generally been lacking. Pollution was left unattended, forestry resources developed at a slow rate, soil erosion worsened, wildlife was attacked with abandon, farm chemicals were used recklessly, and wilderness areas were exploited as rapidly as possible.[6]

Although the failure to mount a pollution control effort can be explained in part as a function of ignorance, there was no lack of effort with regard to the traditional environmental problems. The PRC in fact mounted a massive effort to "greenify the motherland," and numerous decrees and regulations were issued on forestry and similar subjects.[7] To some extent, policy performance suffered from technical shortcomings, like poor planting stock and insufficient funding. The major factor, however, involved the perverse consequences of China's socialist political economy. Operating on the basis of a Marxist-Leninist ideological perspective, the regime laid claim to most of the country's forests in the name of state property and then collectivized the remaining forests. This magnified the deficiencies of common property resource ownership and greatly reduced individual incentives to cultivate woodlands. Coupled with highly inequitable pricing and procurement policies and repeated policy changes, the result was chronic deterioration of the resource base in many parts of the country. Similar problems arose in other policy sectors as well, often magnified by a propensity to impose uniform policies across the entire country, regardless of natural variations. For example, fragile grasslands in northwestern China were extensively damaged in the 1970s when they were plowed up in an effort to make each area of the country self-sufficient in grain production.

Pollution control policy was largely absent. Borrowing the Stalinist big-push development strategy from the Soviet Union, China emphasized heavy industry in the 1950s to the virtual exclusion of more environmentally benign sectors of the economy. Even worse than the glorification of the steel and other heavy industries was the failure of the central planners to consider the environment when deciding where to locate industrial plants. This oversight resulted in the construction of many new facilities in Beijing, Lanzhou, and elsewhere in the hearts of cities, and upwind and upstream of population centers. This problem was, in turn, exacerbated by the requirement that each *danwei* (unit) provide housing for its own employees, a rule that led dormitories and apartment blocks to be built right inside factory compounds. When combined with the chronic inefficiency that has plagued command economies, the consequence was that most of China's cities and streams became hellholes of pollution. This was regarded as a positive sign of a thriving socialist economy, although living standards were rising at only a slow rate. One set of environmental standards was introduced in 1956 on a provisional basis and then promulgated on a revised basis in 1962, but it was based on Soviet industrial hygiene standards of the day and was both inadequate and widely ignored.[8] Even after environmental awareness rose in the West, little change occurred in Maoist China, which, to the extent that any attention was paid to the problem, insisted that pollution was an evil visited on the people of the world by venal capitalists and imperialists.

Things began to change in the 1970s. China participated in the United Nations Conference on Man and the Environment held in Stockholm in 1972.[9] Chinese participation was disruptive, but it did force formulation of a program that was announced at the first National Environmental Protection Work Conference in 1973.[10] In 1974 an Office of Environmental Protection was set up under the State Council to take charge of administration, under the guidance of the Leading Small Group on Environmental Protection. With the exception of some keypoint and pilot projects involving the improvement of water quality in Beijing's Guanting Reservoir and air pollution control in Shenyang, progress was generally slow in the mid–1970s.[11] This was, in part, because of the political turmoil surrounding the choice of Mao's successor and because of an inappropriate mix of policy instruments. At the time, China relied heavily on a creaky and gap-ridden central planning structure that guaranteed inefficiency, which is itself the major cause of pollution. This was supplemented by mobilizational campaigns that provided no more than episodic and single-faceted attention to complex matters (e.g., recycling wastes without figuring out how to reduce the generation of wastes in the first place).

Under the reforms initiated by Deng Xiaoping in the late 1970s, conditions have changed rapidly. The regime has emphasized speeding development by raising efficiency, relaxing the cumbersome planning and bureaucratic controls that had hobbled performance, and making the system more responsive to popular demands. A host of legislation has been promulgated, including articles in the 1978 and 1982 constitutions.[12] In 1979 the PRC passed its first draft Environmental Protection Law[13] and a Forestry Law.[14] The PRC has also promulgated specific laws and regulations on the regulation of water pollution[15] and marine resources[16]; the preservation of land[17]; grasslands[18] and fisheries[19]; mineral, water, and soil conservation[20]; and wildlife protection.[21] The main items appear in the Appendixes. The legislation has been accompanied by an expanded administrative structure, particularly in the State Bureau of Environmental Protection, and a shift in policy instruments. The regime has relaxed planning, giving enterprises an incentive to become more efficient. With regard to pollution as such, they have relied on a mix of regulatory controls (e.g., requiring construction and expansion projects to include an environmental evaluation, and imposing more comprehensive and stringent emission standards) and economic instruments, particularly effluent fees. Powerful industries like metallurgy and chemicals have been compelled to substantially increase their expenditures for pollution control, although there is a great deal still to be done. Meanwhile entrepreneurial talents have been enlisted in the struggle against traditional environmental problems by decentralizing responsibility for a large percentage of the afforestation and soil conservation programs down to households, which have been provided with greatly expanded property rights and material incentives, although they are still hampered by lingering fears of a policy reversal and the remaining restrictions on private land ownership and marketing.

THE INTERPLAY BETWEEN LAW AND POLICY

From a political point of view, it is particularly remarkable that support for pollution control and many other aspects of environmental protection has by and large remained firm regardless of shifts in the relative influence of contending leadership groups, notably the reformers versus the more conservative readjusters. This indicates that the policy enjoys a broad reservoir of support at the elite level, but changes in the legal system are also needed if policy is to be freed from the vicissitudes of factional competition. The stronger linkage between policy and law is in contrast to the Great Leap Forward and the Cultural Revolution eras, when politics or ideology was the determining factor in the decision-making process, signifying that the contemporary preferences of the dominant faction or supreme leader outweighed all other considerations. The post-Mao leadership realized that this style of governance introduced an unnerving degree of instability into a country traditionally characterized by the rule of leaders through the emulation of behavioral models, rather than rule by law. Therefore, Deng Xiaoping and other members of the post-Mao leadership have moved, albeit at an uneven pace, toward regularizing the policy process on the basis of legislation and reconstituting judicial processes in order to inject a greater measure of stability and predictability into society. In this respect China in the 1980s resembles, yet in some ways also transcends, China of the 1950s. These developments have affected environmental policy as well as other policy sectors.

In the most limited aspect, law has simply been used to provide a veneer of respectability for what are essentially partisan political purposes. The clearest example of this with regard to environmental policy concerns the obligatory tree-planting campaign which originated in 1981 as one component of the Communist party's controversial effort to ensure that orthodoxy, in the name of building a socialist spiritual civilization, was not abandoned in the course of economic modernization. For this purpose everyone between the ages of eleven and sixty-five was ordered to plant several trees a year "voluntarily," a policy with dubious and, at best, tangential benefits to a regime which has always been able to plant large numbers of trees but encounters great problems in ensuring their survival and maturation. In the past such a program would have been put into effect through a party or joint party and government decree, a type of policy formulation that remains prevalent. In keeping with the new tenor of the times, obligatory tree planting was delayed for several months, during which time quasi-legislative deliberations were conducted in advance of the next session of the National People's Congress, where a formal resolution was passed. In this instance the integration of law and policy amounted to little more than the legitimation of the party will through the mechanism of a state legislative body. Obligatory tree planting has proved to be an epiphenomenon or sideshow to the real world of forestry policy, while socialist spiritual civilization has itself been contained within loose confines, lest it disrupt modernization.[22]

If law played no more than an enlarged legitimating role in post-Mao China, there would be little need for concern with the place of law and judicial institutions in the policy process. In practice, however, it was recognized early on that decrees and circulars failed to adequately define the regime's policy goals and distinguish between desirable and undesirable behavior. Without statutes, or their equivalents, applicable to the entire society, each department or sector would feel entitled to define the national or social interest in its own way. Industrial- or production-oriented departments could confidently subordinate all other considerations to the overriding priority of satisfying the state plans' output goals. By contrast, regulatory institutions, like the environmental protection bureaucracy, could not function without the power to supervise and limit the actions of the production-oriented departments. The regulatory bodies required the backing of lawlike documents and authority in order to compel other state institutions to modify their customary forms of behavior involving the discharge of untreated wastes and other acts recently defined as socially undesirable.

The desirability of statutory backing became even more pronounced as the post-Mao economic reforms took hold.[23] These reforms generally relaxed the direct, often economically counterproductive controls of the party and the state over the economy. In their stead a more loosely regulated economy subject to guidance or indicative planning was introduced, and some segments of the economy gained substantial autonomy from the planning process altogether as elements of a market economy were introduced. So long as central planning was in place, senior officials could persuade themselves that social externalities and public hazards could be controlled by simply improving or tightening the planning process. By contrast, the market-oriented economy cannot encompass all social effects within the scope of market transactions, and governmental regulation becomes essential if externalities are not to be ignored. Legally defined regulatory powers thus became more important as economic controls were relaxed, given that the leadership showed a rising commitment to environmental protection.

Therefore, environmental protection has been among the most heavily legislated sectors of public policy in the post-Mao period. As early as 1979, within months of the historic Third Plenum, when Deng Xiaoping's policies gained ascendancy, the Forestry Law (for trial implementation) and, later that same year, the Environmental Protection Law (for trial implementation) were passed. The latter is a basic law within the Chinese legislative structure. That is, it seeks to define and elaborate on brief passages within the Constitution and create an organic basis for the promulgation of more specific laws and regulations. The Marine Environmental Protection Law, the Water Pollution Prevention and Control Law, and numerous regulations, many of them translated in this volume, are other examples of these more specific regulatory policy enactments. In each case the legislation is intended to extend the scope of governmental authority to subjects which were not clearly defined in the more basic laws, in order to give the regulatory agencies the authority to act and to inform the regulatees of their responsibilities in such matters.

PROPERTY AND PROCEDURAL RIGHTS

Although environmental law serves the principal purpose of expanding and defining the scope of regulatory authority with regard to the defense of social interests by enhancing the collective power of various state agencies vis-à-vis other state agencies, collective organizations, individuals, and foreign entities, it also defines the average citizen's rights and responsibilities. This has acquired special importance as a result of the post-Mao leadership's recognition of the contribution of material incentives and the profit motivation to economic growth. This is most apparent with regard to the commodity-based aspects of the environment like forestry and grasslands, where slow timber growth or production of stumpage has been a chronic problem. With the exception of an odd program like obligatory tree planting, which, as noted earlier, was adopted for political reasons and serves only a tangential role, there has been a pronounced shift away from honorific incentives and centralized management which proved to be both economically and ecologically inefficient.

Instead, the regime has elected to emphasize the devolution of usage-based property rights to households and groups of households within the collective sector and to relax marketing restrictions in order to give producers a fair return on their effort. These newly granted property rights and marketing freedoms did not at first arouse the hoped-for response among rural producers, who had become inured to policy instability. A brief policy relaxation would soon be followed by renewed collectivization, or profit-oriented activity would soon be condemned and persecuted in the name of cutting off "capitalist tails." Because forestry is a long-term production process, like other long-term capital investments, it was especially vulnerable to the risks of a policy reversal. As a result, rural producers at the outset tended to use their newly expanded rights to harvest what they regarded as a sudden windfall before the inevitable policy reversal took place.

As the section on forestry in this volume reveals, that reversal did not take place. The regime moved instead to stabilize policy and enforce property rights while setting restrictions on logging, in preparation for the subsequent enlargement of property rights and marketing freedoms. Indeed, the leadership was soon convinced that the reforms would work only by extending the period of leaseholds, granting a right of inheritance, and allowing a limited right to transfer or reassign property rights to other individuals. Only in this way could the regime hope to increase the output of forest products on a sustained-yield basis and, at the same time, enhance forestry's ecological functions.

The demarcation of property rights is less apparent with regard to pollution control, but here, too, the polluters have been granted some rights out of necessity. Rather than pretend that all pollution can be eliminated, or that all residuals can be converted into useful by-products (the misguided approach to waste control initially adopted by China in the early 1970s), the regime now seeks to create a regulatory climate defined by laws, standards, and incentives to reward desirable behavior. Polluters have the right to continue production if they satisfy the applicable emissions standards. When they are not in compliance they may instead be given only a temporary license to operate or be compelled to pay higher emissions fees until they attain the standards. So far there is no indication that China plans to establish pollution banks or similar systems to allocate pollution rights, measures which exceed the country's current technical capacity and arouse ticklish political questions involving the apparent approval of pollution. If the process of reform continues to advance, then it is not at all inconceivable that pollution rights will be auctioned, especially since the environmental protection agency, like all other regulatory bureaucracies, is feverishly at work trying to develop off-budget revenue sources.

CONFLICT RESOLUTION

The judicial system is also increasingly important as a conflict resolution and policy enforcement medium, although most conflicts continue to be resolved through less formal mediation mechanisms in which the precise determination of rights and liabilities is less important than achieving a solution acceptable to all parties within a context structured by law, social custom, and economic reality. For example, only two or three dozen of the 1,600 pollution-related conflicts that occur in Chongqing in a year are resolved in the courts. However, these are among the most intractable cases and help to define future conflict resolution principles, such as the emerging rules governing the admissibility of evidence regarding emissions.

With regard to less formal means of conflict resolution, the principal mediating organs are the local environmental protection bureaus and the pollution monitoring stations.[24] In recent cases the Chongqing bureau has mediated disputes involving air and noise pollution caused by brick and tile kilns newly constructed by rural farming collectives on land adjoining state properties and workers' residences. When called in to investigate the effects of the Baishulin Brigade brick and tile kilns on the Bashan Instruments Plant, after several years of mounting complaints, the bureau discovered sulfur dioxide levels more than ten times greater than state standards, noxious gases, and clogged drainage ditches. The kiln was clearly at fault and was ordered to be dismantled. The factory was ordered to pay the brigade 10,000 yuan once the factory had been dismantled—approximately two-thirds of the kiln's annual revenue or one-half of its construction costs. The latter payment was intended to smooth worker-peasant relations and facilitate the brigade's conversion to a more environmentally benign nonagricultural endeavor. It was necessitated by the high degree of autonomy now enjoyed by agricultural production units and made possible by the instrument factory's access to the state budget and off-budget funds. The monetary "damages" closely resemble a side payment by the victim to the polluter to persuade him to alter his behavior, of the form recommended by Coase in the name of socially efficient solutions.[25]

This same Chongqing bureau was faced with another case in 1984, when the Southwest Aluminum Fabrication Plant complained that construction of the Huaguo Shan Tile and Brick Plant was the cause of severe noise and air pollution, and that once completed and in operation, the new plant might endanger the state factory's overhead electric lines. An investigation, conducted promptly in this instance, by the bureau, along with related organs of government from the broader municipality and Baxian County where the parties were located, quickly concluded that the building materials plant had been improperly sited. The problem arose because peasant-run factories or small-scale factories, because of their small-polluter status, are largely exempt from the "three simultaneous points" (design, construction, operations) licensing process. The investigation also determined that the building materials plant site was chosen in part because of its proximity to the fabrication plant. It seems that one of the latter's branch mills had invested in the building materials plant to provide jobs for its own employees' children and other dependents, a major burden on all state enterprises in China. Consequently, the offending plant was ordered to be dismantled and relocated, but the parent aluminum plant was ordered to compensate the rural collective for its expenses, totaling 80,000 yuan.[26]

The problem of mediation becomes more complex when more than one source may be at fault. Interview data, as well as documentary sources, state that the mediator seeks to apportion the expenses among the various sources according to both their respective responsibility for pollution and each source's ability to pay.[27] The resulting formula is, at best, an approximation of justice, but it is said to be accepted by the parties in most cases.

There are increasing numbers of cases in the post-Mao period in which the results of mediation have proved unacceptable to one or another party, who then turn to the courts in hopes of gaining a more favorable settlement. Many of these cases involve disputes over the size of damage awards in compensation or civil matters. They are usually handled at the lower court level, but important cases may be tried by the intermediate courts, although there do not seem to be any specific regulations in this regard. Several such cases are reported in the article by Judge Wang Yinghuai reprinted in this volume, which discusses the procedures to be followed by a court when mediation fails.

More recently, Wenling County was the locale for the first publicly conducted environmental pollution case in Zhejiang provincial history. Four factories had been ordered to share the costs for compensating a fish hatchery for its losses when a fish kill occurred on the Beishen River, allegedly as the result of pollution. Three of the factories, including a cannery and an auto parts plant, denied any responsibility, while the hatchery complained that the award was insufficient. Three separate suits were filed by the cannery, the auto parts plant, and the hatchery, which the court consolidated for purposes of the trial. The court rejected the factories' pleas of innocence on the grounds that their testimony revealed ignorance of the applicable statutes, and their failure to monitor emissions rendered moot all claims that their emissions were not of sufficient magnitude to cause the fish kill. The court, therefore, sustained the original mediation findings, ordering the auto parts factory to pay 22,700 yuan and the cannery to pay more than 30,000 yuan in compensation to the hatchery. The hatchery was also unsuccessful in its effort to win a higher award, suggesting that a compromise solution was reached on the basis of the original award.[28]

Far more interesting has been the role of the judicial process in criminal matters. The courts, on the one hand, have tended to uphold the position of the regulatory agency in administrative actions. They appear to be moving in the direction of demanding positive exculpatory evidence on the part of the defendant before dismissing the suit brought against the culprit by the regulatory agency. This point is argued in one of the selections included in this book.[29] At first glance this point may seem trivial, since the procurator always has the upper hand in an authoritarian, if no longer totalitarian, regime. The distinction is relevant, however, when one realizes that in such cases the law is being used by one state agency against other state agencies, collectives, or other legal entities for regulatory purposes.

On the other hand the courts have excused individuals of criminal responsibility and civil liability for damages to the property of a polluter when they have been driven beyond forbearance by pollution after the regulatory authorities failed to respond. The editors have analyzed several of these cases elsewhere, and some examples are included in this volume.[30] Others can be cited as well. In Jiyuan County, Henan, the state-owned No. 531 Cement Plant disrupted agricultural production with its dust emissions from the time it began production in 1978. After years of complaints and demands for compensation got nowhere, Guo Hesheng and several other peasants locked the factory gate. A riot ensued when efforts were made to open the gate, and the Public Security Bureau arrested the ringleaders. After three weeks in detention the prosecutor decided against bringing charges, although the Public Security Bureau itself had criticized, and perhaps even physically abused, the defendants. Within weeks public security again arrested Guo and his associates, and this time they were given three-year sentences on charges of disrupting the social order. More than a year later, in September 1984, the county court reversed itself on realization that the state policy and the environmental protection law excused individuals for taking limited, emergency action in order to prevent a worse act from taking place.[31] At about the same time the Pujiang County Court in Zhejiang similarly vacated a one-and-one-half-year sentence against Ma Rongqiu for destroying production when he and other peasants ruined a noxious lime kiln operated by the nearby township of Zhongyu. In this case the provincial environmental protection bureau won the support of the standing committee of the provincial people's congress for a reversal, and the county court soon responded, since the courts are subordinate to the legislature.[32]

PROBLEMS

Although law now plays a much more central and generally positive role in the policy process, there are numerous problems that need to be addressed. The most basic is the simple weakness of the courts and the procuracy in terms of manpower and other resources. There are now only 20,000 lawyers in China.[33] Development is now under way, but it will be quite some time before these organs can be equipped to handle the workload that confronts them.

More important is the relationship of the judicial organs to the political system. China has traditionally been ruled by men rather than by law, and now it is ruled by the men and women who lead the Communist party. It is encouraging that the incumbents now give much more weight to the role of law, but it is also clear that the judicial organs remain subordinate to the will of the ruling elite. The judiciary, in other words, tends to act only after it has received orders to that effect from the party. This is most apparent in one of China's most important pollution control cases to date. It involved the persistent discharge of coal dust and fumes from Dock No. 41 in Wuhan, along the Yangtze River. The local residents complained repeatedly to the wharf management and municipal and port authorities that they were unable to open their windows or hang their clothes out to dry. But this was all to no avail. When the local residents resorted to direct action and sabotaged the dock in desperation, their leaders were promptly arrested. Politburo member, Party Secretary, and Senior Vice-Premier Wan Li read an internal press account of the incident and ordered an investigation. This quickly led to enforcement action against the polluter, the release of the protestors, and the subsequent enunciation of a limited right to self-defense even in cases involving the destruction of state property, an act often otherwise treated as counterrevolutionary.[34]

Similarly, Premier Zhao Ziyang and other leaders became personally concerned about rampant deforestation in the early 1980s, which posed a serious problem for forest conservation and threatened to discredit the new rural reforms. This led to several urgent directives tightening the regulation of logging before sales and distribution controls could be further relaxed. What is important to note in this regard is that the Forestry Law, just enacted in 1979 (and subsequently amended in 1984), was not in and of itself sufficient to generate the desired conservation-conscious behavior. Therefore, Zhao, in 1982, explicitly demanded that party leadership over the matter be increased at all levels and, moreover, that particular cases involving connivance by local officials be prosecuted. A wave of publicity would then be orchestrated around these cases to educate officials and the public alike. This is indeed what happened, although the problem of overlogging or liquidation of standing timber persists among people who are skeptical about the wisdom of undertaking long-term investments, albeit to a lesser degree than before the party leadership intervened.[35]

Chinese environmental officials repeatedly complain that their policies do not receive adequate support from local officials, many of whom fail to take violations of the law seriously, and thus allow unwanted behavior to persist.[36] Therefore, elite intervention is essential if local and bureaucratic obstruction of environmental pollution is to be overcome and if the conditions for effective policy implementation are to be established. In the longer term such direct intervention by the party may deprive judicial institutions of the aura of independence and competence they need to win popular trust. There is now a case being made in the legal literature, and presumably *in camera* as well, for the party at all levels to obey the law in its own long-term interest as well as that of the nation.[37] Such rule by law rather than by individuals—or, more precisely, by a combination of the two concepts—would involve procedural, and eventually substantive, modifications of the party's prerogatives to a degree that cannot be foreseen at this point in time.

Despite a flurry of legislative activity, the legislative structure remains incomplete. Many laws and regulations are still in process, including a revision of the Environmental Protection Law of 1979, an air pollution control law, a noise pollution control law, regulations for implementing the Marine Environmental Protection Law, regulations for implementing the Water Pollution Prevention and Control Law, methods for assessing effluent fees, methods for managing environmental protection on capital construction projects, an action outline for nature preserves, and updated standards for regulating pollution, ambient environmental quality, monitoring procedures, and listing endangered flora.[38] Although the basic laws and various decrees specify policy intent for the most part, their lack of specificity makes the regulatory authorities less confident of their ability to take action and makes the judicial organs more reluctant to accept cases involving these matters. For example, the Regulations on Soil Conservation Work included in this volume only have the status of regulations (*tiaoli*). Interviews with local conservation officials revealed frustration over their inability to take action against other governmental departments because the regulations have neither the status nor the enforcement power of a law (*fa*).[39] This reduces soil conservation's power to one of persuading the agriculture, communications, and other powerful ministries to adopt policies which may involve substantial costs. By contrast, local environmental protection officials insist that their effectiveness is greatly increased by their power to assess effluent fees or fine recalcitrant offenders, or both.

Other shortcomings involve the rights of defendants and the nature of the legal process itself. With the recent exception of the aforementioned cases involving victims of pollution who took direct action against the polluters, there are no reports of cases in which accused polluters were exonerated even when new regulations are enforced after the fact. There are, however, instances of successful appeals leading to the reduction of effluent fee assessments. This suggests that the polluters are at considerable jeopardy when sued by the local environmental protection agency, as the Shenzhen foreign venture case published here indicates. Without greater opportunity for defendants to prove their innocence, regulatory organs may well be tempted to abuse their authority by harassing or extorting payments from certain polluters, while at the same time their incentive to improve their monitoring capability and data base is lessened. Officials with the national Environmental Protection Bureau in Beijing acknowledge that irregular monitoring procedures and the lack of uniformity in assessment procedures is one of the biggest problems they confront in extending the concept of effluent fees and fines.[40]

Defendants are also at jeopardy because of the vagueness of the distinction between administrative and criminal law violations. The latter are nominally expected to involve more serious offenses, but the distinction is usually ill-defined, allowing the judicial organs wide discretion. The dangers are hinted at in the article by Zhu Zanping included in this volume. Zhu argues for a distinction in handling cases involving poaching or encroachment on the forestry rights of others or the state and marginal cases involving above-quota logging on one's own leasehold. Zhu fears that equation of the two will dampen producer interest in forestry, but the vagueness of forestry legislation, as well as the corresponding provision of the Criminal Law (Article 128), suggests considerable potential for abuse. Moreover, even administrative penalties may be severe in some instances. Administrative fines for the violation of pollution control laws can amount to tens of thousands of yuan.

PROSPECTS FOR THE FUTURE

Looking toward the future, other issues will have to be addressed. Conflicts between resource use and preservation have so far been minimal because of the low level of economic development and limitations on the freedom of expression. For the most part the regime has been able to embark on development projects without having to seriously reflect on the ecological and historical or spiritual consequences. The hundreds of nature preserves that have been established so far exist largely in name only and, in any event, are expected to coexist with substantial economic activity within their boundaries.

Conflicts over resource use are likely to become more salient over time as different scientific constituencies are organized and as the standard of living rises. The authorities will then have to specify more clearly the rules on resource use and development and to decide how much in the way of development opportunities they are prepared to forego in the name of less tangible, spiritual values.

Most fundamental is the continuation of the reforms themselves. One sees no fundamental conflict between the reforms and environmental quality. To the contrary, more efficient resource use and greater freedom of expression are essential to wise environmental management. However, the potential for true scarcity pricing of commodities like timber, water, and energy remains circumscribed by the economic dislocations they would engender. More important, the history of reform elsewhere in the communist world indicates that the political support base eventually erodes in the face of internal opposition and the technical complexity of the problem. Thus, as long as the reform constituency remains largely intact, economic development on a more environmentally sound basis than the People's Republic has known before will be a bright prospect.

Notes

1. William Theodore deBary et al., *Sources of Chinese Tradition*, New York: Columbia University Press, 1964, pp. 170–74.

2. *Han Fei Zi*, a compilation of essays by the Legalist philosopher Han Feizi (died 233 B.C.), notes that "under the law of the Yin dynasty (circa 1800 to 1200 B.C.), he who litters on public thoroughfares shall have his hand cut off." *See* Cai Shouqiu, "On the Character of the Environmental Protection Law," *Faxue Yanjiu* (Studies in Law), no. 3 (1981), p. 15. The English text of *Han Fei Zi* may be found in Burton Watson, *Han Fei Tzu: Basic Writings*, New York: Columbia University Press, 1964.

The Qin dynasty lasted roughly from 221 B.C. to 206 B.C. On environmental protection, the Qin Code included provisions forbidding cutting lumber in mountain forests in the spring, blocking up waterways, burning grass to be used as fertilizer unless in the summer, picking budding plants, poaching young animals, birds' eggs, and young birds, and killing fish and turtles with poison. Ma Xiangcong, "Preliminary Discussion on the Law of Environmental Protection," *Faxue Yanjiu* (Studies in Law), no. 2 (1979), p. 40. Excavations conducted since 1975 in Hubei province have unearthed portions of the Qin Code. The first of its eighteen chapters, *Tian Lü* (Law on Land), contains numerous provisions on environmental management and protection. *See* Shuihudi Qin Mu Zhujian Zhengli Xiaozu, *Shuihudi Qin Mu Zhujian* (Bamboo Writings from the Qin Tombs at Shuihudi), Beijing: Wenwu Chubanshe, 1978, pp. 24–29.

In this period there is also mention of environmental protection in the *Record of Rites of the Elder Tai* (circa first century B.C.). *See* M. Conway, "Asia: The Unnatural Rape," *Far Eastern Economic Review*, April 23, 1970, p. 21, *cited in* Leo A. Orleans and Richard P. Suttmeier, "The Mao Ethic and Environmental Quality," *Science*, vol. 170, no. 3962 (1970), pp. 1173–76.

The Tang dynasty lasted from A.D. 618 to A.D. 907. In the "Miscellaneous Articles" section of the Tang Code, there were provisions regulating, *inter alia*, the digging of pits (394), land use (including mountainsides and lake shores)(405), and the burning of fields and wilderness lands during the wrong season (430). W. Johnson, *The T'ang Code*, Princeton, N.J.: Princeton University Press, 1979, pp. 287–89.

The Tang administration also placed much emphasis on remedying the problem of deforestation. *See* S. Reidel, "The Incredible Journey: A Forester's Perception of China," *American Forest*, May 1981, p. 22; T. Tuan, "Our Treatment of the Environment in Ideal and Actuality," *American Scientist*, vol. 58 (1970), pp. 244, 248; Zhu, "China's Great Green Wall," *American Forest*, May 1981, p. 24; all cited in Bruce L. Ottley and Charles C. Valouskas, "China's Developing Environmental Law: Practices, Policies and Legislation," *Boston College International and Comparative Law Review*, vol. 7, no. 1 (1983), pp. 81–131.

The Qing dynasty lasted from A.D. 1644 to A.D. 1911. Numerous provisions in the Qing Code relate to environmental protection and conservation. *See* the relevant articles in "Land and Tenements" (such as §§97, 98), "Miscellaneous Offenses" (such as §376), and "Public Ways" (such as §§433, 434), *translated in* G. T. Staunton, *Ta Tsing Leu Lee*, Taipei: Ch'eng Wen Publishing Co., 1966 (reprint), pp. 103–105, 411, 471–73.

3. The Republic of China's regulatory arsenal includes the Forestry Law (1932, last amended 1972), the Water Conservation Law (1942, last amended 1974), the Air Pollution Prevention and Control Act (1975, subsequently amended 1982), the Water Pollution Prevention and Control Act (1974, subsequently amended 1983), the Waste Materials Clean Up Law (1974, subsequently amended 1980), and the Resource Control Law (1980). The Chinese texts are in Tau Baichuan et al., eds., *Liu Fa Quan Shu* (The Complete Six Codes), Taipei: San Min Publishers, pp. 1009–10, 1021–26, 1456–65. The English texts of the air and water pollution amendments, as well as the Executive Order of March 23, 1981, by the Ministry of Communications Governing Marine Pollution, Jianfa (70), Zi No. 6250, are in Fa Jyh-pin, "Legislation and Constitutional Interpretations of Human Rights in the Republic of China, 1982–83: An Overview," *Chinese Yearbook of International Law and Affairs*, vol. 3 (1983), pp. 87, 93–97. For recent developments, *see* Qiu Congzhi, "The Importance of Incorporating Environmental Protection Policy into the Law," *Lianhe Bao* (United Daily), December 16, 1985, p. 2.

On the Chinese Soviet Republic era, *see generally* W. E. Butler, ed., *The Legal System of the Chinese Soviet Republic*, Dobbs Ferry, N.Y.: Transnational Publishers, 1983.

4. *See* Ping-ti Ho, *Studies on the Population of China, 1368–1953*, Cambridge, Mass.: Harvard University Press, 1959.

5. *See* Edward Schafer, *Ancient China*, New York: Time-Life Books, 1967.

6. *See* Vaclav Smil, *The Bad Earth: Environmental Degradation in China*, Armonk, N.Y.: M. E. Sharpe, 1984.

7. During the PRC's early years, the government promulgated the following regulations: Measures Governing Land Requisition for National Construction (1953) in *FLHB*, Vol. 4, pp. 86–90; Provisional Measures on Highway Afforestation (1956) in *FGHB*, vol. 3, pp. 267–70; Provisional Program for Water and Soil Conservation (1957) in *FGHB*, vol. 6, pp. 433–38; Regulations Governing the Safety of Drinking Water (1959) in *FGHB*, vol. 10, pp. 410–16; Regulations on Forest Protection (1963) in *FGHB*, vol. 13, pp. 205–14.

8. The early pollution control standards were (101–56) Provisional Public Health Standards for the Design of Industrial Enterprises and (GBJ 1–62) Public Health Standards for the Design of Industrial Enterprises, which are both cited in Guo Li'ai, *Jianzhu Sheji Weisheng Shencha* (An Examination of Public Health Considerations in Architecture and Design), Harbin: Heilongjiang Kexue Jishu Chubanshe, 1985.

9. For coverage of China's participation in the 1972 Stockholm conference, *see* Jeannette Greenfield, *China and the Law of the Sea, Air and Environment*, Germantown, Md.: Sijthoof and Noordhoff, 1979, pp. 219–21; Julian Gresser, "The Principle of Multiple Use in Chinese Environmental Law," in Jerome A. Cohen, ed., *Legal Aspects of Doing Business in China*, New York: Practising Law Institute, 1983, p. 453. A summary of the Chinese position at the conference is in "China's Ten Cardinal Principles on Amending the 'Declaration on the Human Environment,' " *Peking Review*, vol. 15, no. 32 (1972), pp. 12–18.

10. *See* Jiang Bikun and Guo Rui, eds., *Huanjing Baohu Fa Jianghua* (Lectures on Environmental Protection Law), Zhangjiakou: Falü Chubanshe, 1980, p. 30.

11. On the Guanting Reservoir, *see Beijing Ribao* (Beijing Daily), August 17, 1985. On Shenyang, *see Huanjing Guanli* (Environmental Management), no. 1 (1984), pp. 3–12.

12. There are two articles regarding environmental protection in the 1978 Constitution. Article 6 provides: "Mineral resources, waters and those forests, undeveloped lands and other marine and land resources owned by the state are the property of the whole people." Article 11 provides: "The state protects the environment and natural resources and prevents and eliminates pollution and other hazards to the public." Chinese and English texts in Fang Chun-ie, Zhang Xin, Chou Ling Ling, and Choy Mei-pik, *Laws and Regulations of the People's Republic of China/Zhonghua Renmin Gongheguo Fagui Xuanji*, vol. 1, Hong Kong: Kingsway Publishers, 1982, p. 1; *Documents of the First Session of the Fifth National People's Congress of the People's Republic of China*, Beijing: Foreign Languages Press, 1978, pp. 125–72.

The 1982 Constitution likewise contains two provisions. Article 9 provides:

> Mineral resources, waters, forests, mountains, grassland, unreclaimed land, beaches, and other natural resources are owned by the state, that is, by the whole people, with the exception of the forests, mountains, grassland, unreclaimed land and beaches that are owned by collectives in accordance with the law.
>
> The state ensures the rational use of natural resources and protects rare animals and plants. The appropriation or damage of natural resources by any organization or individual by whatever means is prohibited.

Article 26 provides:

> The state protects and improves the living environment and the ecological environment, and prevents and remedies pollution and other public hazards.
>
> The state organizes and encourages afforestation and the protection of forests.

Texts in *The Constitution of the People's Republic of China*, Beijing: Foreign Languages Press, 1983; *Renmin Ribao* (People's Daily), December 5, 1982, p. 1.

13. The Chinese text can be found in *Renmin Ribao* (People's Daily), September 17, 1979, p. 2; *BFWH*, p. 38; and *HBYWX*, p. 32. The English is presented in Appendix A.

14. The Forestry Law was since amended in 1984. The Chinese text is in *Renmin Ribao* (People's Daily), September 23, 1984. The English is presented in Appendix K.

15. The Water Pollution Prevention and Control Law. The Chinese text is in *Renmin Ribao* (People's Daily), May 13, 1984, p. 3; *Xinhua Yuebao* (Wenxian Ban), no. 5 (1984), p. 63; *GGB*, no. 10 (1984), p. 307. *See* Appendix E.

16. The 24th Session of the Standing Committee of the Fifth National People's Congress promulgated the Marine Environmental Protection Law (MEPL) on August 23, 1982. The MEPL came into effect on March 1, 1983. The Chinese text is in *Renmin*

Ribao (People's Daily), August 25, 1982, p. 3, *reprinted in Falu*, no. 8 (1982), p. 68. *See* Appendix F.

Three sets of regulations have been promulgated under the MEPL. The first two are the Regulations of the People's Republic of China on Prevention of Marine Pollution from Vessels and the Regulations of the People's Republic of China on Marine Environmental Protection from Oil Exploration and Exploitation. They were promulgated by the State Council on December 12, 1983. The Chinese texts are in *GGB*, no. 1 (1984), p. 6; *Zhongguo Fazhi Bao* (China Legal System Newspaper), January 13, 1984, *reprinted in Xinhua Yuebao* (Wenxian Ban), no. 1 (1984), p. 75. *See* Appendixes G and H. For commentary, *see* Edward J. Epstein, "China's New Pollution Laws," *Petroleum News*, March 1984, p. 11; Edward J. Epstein, "Pollution Law Laid Down," *China Trade Report*, March 1984, pp. 4–5; "Marine Environmental Regulations Promulgated," FBIS-*CHI*, January 11, 1984, pp. K19–20; "New Pollution Rules," *China Trade Report*, March 1984, p. 75; "New Rules in Drive to Reduce Sea Pollution," *China Daily*, January 13, 1984, p. 1. The State Council more recently, on March 6, 1985, promulgated the Regulations of the People's Republic of China on the Control of Marine Dumping. The Chinese text is in *GGB*, no. 9 (April 10, 1985), p. 222–27. *See* Appendix I.

17. The State Council promulgated the Regulations Governing the Requisition of Land for State Construction on May 14, 1982. Note also the Interim Provisions of the Shenzhen Special Economic Zone for Land Management and similar local regulations. *See* Appendix N.

18. The Grasslands Law was adopted by the Eleventh Session of the Sixth National People's Congress Standing Committee on June 18, 1985. The text is in *Renmin Ribao* (People's Daily), June 19, 1985, p. 2. *See* Appendix R.

19. The Fisheries Law was passed by the Fourteenth Session of the Sixth National People's Congress Standing Committee on January 20, 1986. The text is in *Zhongguo Fazhi Bao* (China Legal System Newspaper), January 22, 1986, p. 2. *See* Appendix Q.

20. The State Council promulgated the Regulations on Soil Conservation Work on June 30, 1982. The text is in *BFWH*, July 6, 1982, pp. 101–109. *See* Appendix P.

21. The PRC has issued a number of regulations on wildlife protection. *See, e.g.*, State Council Circular on the Stringent Protection of Endangered Wildlife, in *BFWH*, April 13, 1983, pp. 214–16. *See* Appendix S.

22. This program is analyzed in Lester Ross, "Obligatory Tree Planting: Campaign Implementation in Post-Mao China," in David M. Lampton, ed., *Policy Implementation in Post-Mao China*, Berkeley and Los Angeles: University of California Press, 1987.

23. The major elements of these reforms include the introduction of a largely household-based agricultural contract-guarantee system instead of people's communes, a general decentralization of the market with market mechanisms taking the place of central procurement and distribution monopolies, and heightened foreign trade and investment. *The China Quarterly*, no. 100, 1984, is devoted to an analysis of the Chinese economic reforms. For background, *see generally* A. Doak Barnett, *China's Economy in Global Perspective*, Washington, D.C.: Brookings Institution, 1981; Chu-yuan Cheng, *China's Economic Development: Growth and Structural Changes*, Boulder, Colo.: Westview Press, 1982; Jan Prybyla, *China's Economy: Problems and Policies*, Columbia, S.C.: University of South Carolina Press, 1981.

24. Their mediation functions are distinct from those of mediation committees which handle 90 percent of China's civil disputes. *China Daily*, December 31, 1985.

25. Chongqing Environmental Protection Bureau, "An Environmental Pollution Con-

flict Under Special Circumstances,'' *Zhongguo Huanjing Guanli* (Environmental Management in China), no. 1 (1985), p. 39. Ronald A. Coase, "The Problem of Social Cost,'' *Journal of Law and Economics*, vol. 3 (1960), pp. 1–44. Local officials explain that state enterprises are expected to compensate the polluter for some or all of his costs when there are extenuating circumstances or the polluter, especially a rural industry, cannot afford to reinvest in an environmentally more benign industry.

26. Chongqing Environmental Protection Bureau, ''An Environmental Pollution Conflict Caused by Improper Site Selection,'' *Zhongguo Huanjing Guanli* (Environmental Management in China), no. 1 (1985), p. 40.

27. Interviews conducted by Lester Ross with local environmental officials in Chongqing, Neijiang, and Zigong in 1986. Protocols available on request.

28. *Zhongguo Huanjing Bao* (China Environmental Paper), November 6, 1985. It has been argued, however, that only general governmental relief, as opposed to compensation by the polluter, is required when the latter acts rationally and prudently. Liu Honglin, ''Some Issues That Should be Addressed When Handling Environmental Pollution Disputes,'' *Faxue Jikan* (Jurisprudence Quarterly), no. 3 (1985), pp. 37–39.

29. *See* the Suzhou pollution case in Part Five.

30. *See* Lester Ross and Mitchell A. Silk, ''Post-Mao China and Environmental Protection: The Effect of Legal and Politico-Economic Reform,'' *UCLA Pacific Basin Law Journal* (1986).

31. *Zhongguo Huanjing Bao* (China Environmental Paper) January 26, 1985.

32. Id., January 12, 1985.

33. *China Daily*, November 14, 1985.

34. *See* Ross and Silk, *supra* note 30. An account of the case is translated in Part Five. *See also* ''Important Instructions by Comrades Hu Yaobang and Wan Li Regarding an Incident Involving Conflict over Environmental Pollution,'' n.d., in Ministry of Urban and Rural Construction and Environmental Protection, *Environmental Work Bulletin Compendium*, Beijing: Zhongguo Huanjing Kexue Chubanshe, 1984, pp. 133–38.

36. *Chinese Agricultural Yearbook 1983*, pp. 211–12; ''Comrade Zhao Ziyang's Talk on Halting Reckless Logging,'' October 8, 1982, in *Important Forestry Work Documents*, no. 8 (1982), pp. 6–9. The Forestry Law enforcement has been greatly expanded. The forestry police now number more than 30,000, and there are also 5,000 procuratorial and judicial personnel involved in law enforcement. More than 50,000 cases were investigated in 1985. *Zhongguo Fazhi Bao* (China Legal System Paper), January 29, 1986; *China Daily*, October 3, 1985.

36. *Zhongguo Huanjing Bao* (China Environmental Paper), June 22 and 25, 1985.

37. Cao Nanping, ''A Preliminary Discussion of Law's Restriction of Policy,'' *Faxue Pinglun* (Jurisprudence Review), no. 4 (1984), pp. 8–12.

38. Qu Geping, ''Strengthening Environmental Management,'' no. 6 (1985), pp. 2–5.

39. Interview by Lester Ross with Sichuan soil conservation officials in 1985. Protocol available on request.

40. Interview by Lester Ross with environmental protection officials responsible for planning and standards in 1986. Protocol available on request.

Part One
A General Introduction to Environmental Protection in China

The evolution of public policy in China can be traced through conferences and meetings convened by various Communist party, governmental, and other bodies. These sessions differ along various dimensions: authoritativeness (the higher and more exclusive the convenor and the attendees, the more authoritative the conference); scope (focus on a broad range of issues, or on a single policy problem or sector); and content (development of broad policy outlines or principles, or the drafting of specific policies and regulations).

Major policy departures are usually dependent upon a reconfiguration of the political balance within the Communist party. Changes in factional alignments and strength facilitate the modification or abandonment of previous policies and the introduction of policy innovations. Conversely, political stability fosters policy continuity, although this sometimes results in rigidity at the expense of essential flexibility. Senior party officials engage in factional maneuvers to increase their influence.

Once a favorable political balance exists, factional leaders encourage the proposal of favored policies while junior officials seize the opportunity by tailoring their own proposals to the newly fashionable political trend. Conversely, those factions on the sidelines try to avoid purges while simultaneously gathering data in order to mount a challenge to the majority faction(s) at a propitious occasion.

Once general policies have been formulated, they must be codified in the form of directives, circulars, laws, regulations, or other formats. The bureaucracies and other institutional interest groups seek to shape this stage of the policy process in accordance with their own interests, both in terms of the substance of the policies themselves and the choice of implementation instruments. For example, increased stress on regulation tends to elevate the status of regulatory agencies at the expense of production-oriented bureaucracies. Similarly, the deemphasis on central planning in the post-Mao era has enhanced the power of the localities and enterprises vis-à-vis the central government.

In China environmental policy has been heavily shaped by two major conferences—the First and Second National Environmental Protection Work Conferences. The first took place in 1973, about a year after the Stockholm

Conference on Man and the Environment and amidst a political thaw that had briefly emerged in the aftermath of the Cultural Revolution. The rise of pragmatists in the factional competition enabled enlightened officials to steer China onto an environmental protection track, although progress in the next several years was very limited. Environmental protection was hampered by continuing political instability and a lack of full appreciation for the time and resources needed to carry out the new policy.

The second conference was convened in the winter of 1983–84 and was an occasion for the summing up of experiences acquired in the previous decade, as well as an opportunity to authorize further advances. One very important theme was the strong political consensus that had emerged over the years in behalf of environmental protection, with reform-minded and relatively conservative leaders alike defending the proposition that economic development and the enhancement of environmental quality must proceed in tandem rather than with the latter lagging behind the former. At the same time there was strong appreciation for the fact that environmental protection presented a series of complex problems that required a sustained commitment, in terms of manpower and funding, oriented toward socioeconomic as well as physical factors.

The evolution of policy can also be followed through the writings of policy analysts and junior officials. Although less authoritative than policy directives or statements by senior officials, the authors are frequently the beneficiaries of patronage by senior officials. During the Cultural Revolution era senior officials sponsored contending groups of polemicists to engage in factional combat by the pen rather than the sword, although some of the latter also occurred. Nowadays writers emphasize the analysis of current problems instead of engaging in abstract arguments in the guise of abstruse allegories. This rise in candor has occurred in part because there is greater tolerance for a diversity of views within the bounds of the allowable spectrum. The sponsors encourage writers to present proposals and allow them to be subjected to some scrutiny before adoption, thus reducing their risk should the policies prove deficient or too controversial.

Several innovations in environmental law and policy were proposed beginning in the late 1970s once it had been established that class struggle was no longer the dominant social contradiction and that different forms of ownership and management could be allowed to coexist under socialism. Analysts endorsed price reform, arguing that irrational and unresponsive planners' prices had encouraged waste and overconsumption of natural resources. More realistic prices would discourage waste and thereby reduce pollution while simultaneously encouraging stepped up production of renewable resources. Similarly, the prevailing property rights structure with its dogmatic insistence upon state and state-influenced collective ownership and management was criticized. More flexible arrangements based upon management by contract and the separation of crop and land ownership in agriculture were also designed to encourage the production of renewable resources. With regard to pollution control, planners placed an emphasis on imposing semiautomatic penalties for pollution in the form of effluent fees for discharges in excess of allowable standards in order to give polluters or their parent agencies stronger incentives to reduce pollution.

Paralleling these economically oriented proposals were calls for increasing the role of law as part of the post-Mao return to normalcy. As recognition grew that even partially conflicting interests enjoyed legitimacy, law was needed to provide the ground rules for behavior and, in an increasing number of cases, to provide the means for the resolution of disputes. Society's right to a safe and clean environment was asserted even if it conflicted with the demands of state-assigned production plans. A sharp increase in legislative activity was recommended in accordance with international practice and in recognition that improvement in environmental quality is predicated upon providing regulators and economic actors with greater certainty and clearer requirements. In this fashion policy and legal developments combined to substantially reshape environmental policy.

Part One serves to provide a general backdrop for the parts to follow by presenting an overview of environmental policy and law in China. Ma Hong, President of the Academy of Social Sciences, Vice-Premier Li Peng, and Qu Geping, China's leading environmental official, begin Chapter 2 by outlining the goals of China's environmental program and highlighting current problems with the environment and environmental protection. Liu Wen, a leading policy formulator, and Zhou Fuxiang explain the relationship between economic development and environmental protection within the context of Chinese socialist economics and the various economic means which aid in ensuring progress toward enhancing environmental quality.

The remainder of Part One deals with the status, general principles, and selected fundamental issues in Chinese environmental law. In Chapter 3 a judge sitting on the Hubei Provincial High People's Court and two leading academics explain the general principles guiding environmental law, discuss the status of environmental law within China's emerging legal system, and outline the general legal scheme employed to protect the environment. The three remaining articles present analyses of three important and more refined issues in environmental law. Chen Lihu addresses the need for implementing local legislation that reflects local conditions. Cai Shouqiu then discusses the concept of environmental rights. Cheng Zhengkang concludes with an enlightening exposition of environmental litigation with specific reference to the resolution of environmental disputes before the courts and administrative bodies of China.

2

Policy Overview

Ma Hong (1984) "Strive to Improve Our Country's Environmental Protection Work"

HB (February), pp. 4–6; and (March), pp. 2–5. Translation, with permission, from *Chinese Law and Government*, vol. 19, no. 1 (1986), pp. 12–29.

The problem of the environment is a major problem confronting all countries of the world today. It poses a challenge to China as well as other countries and is closely linked with many other problems. In my work and my contact with foreign friends, I have acquired much information concerning environmental protection. This information tells us clearly that environmental protection is a major problem of strategic importance in our country's socialist modernization endeavor. Whether or not this problem can be solved satisfactorily has a direct bearing on our future and on whether we can smoothly achieve the magnificent goal of building a strong modern socialist country with Chinese characteristics. Therefore, environmental problems must be given ample attention and dealt with in real earnest.

As we know, environmental problems are complex. Here I would like to give my superficial views on the questions of understanding the functions of the environment and consciously engaging in environmental protection, paying attention to historical experience and strengthening environmental protection work, making clear the goals of environmental protection and perfecting the [environmental quality] index system, and taking practical measures to do a good job of environmental protection.

UNDERSTANDING THE FUNCTIONS OF ENVIRONMENT AND CONSCIOUSLY ENGAGING IN ENVIRONMENTAL PROTECTION

The "environment" we usually talk about in environmental protection refers to the environment in a broad sense. Its scope is extensive, extending from the top of the atmospheric troposphere, which is about ten kilometers above the surface, to the entire surface layer of the earth, which is about five kilometers deep. Its meaning is different from the "environment" mentioned in ecology.

Here the "environment" refers to the specific mutual relations between things, not the things themselves. When we talk about an environment, there must be a specific thing acting as the center, while the space, conditions, and situations around it are its environment. The "environment" referred to in ecology has living beings as its center. Living beings include animals, plants, and micro-organisms, and the lifeless conditions around them are their environment. This refers to the air, water, heat, and light in nature as well as to the space composed of all kinds of organic and inorganic elements. In other words, the environment mentioned in ecology refers merely to the material factors other than living beings. It does not include living beings and is exclusive of them. On the other hand, the "environment" mentioned in the environment of mankind, environmental science, and environmental protection refers to the space that is filled with all kinds of living and lifeless matter other than man but has man as its center.

Why should we take man as the center in studying the environment? Not only is man the master of the earth and the most lively and active element on the surface of the earth, but also man studies the environment with the aim of seeking coordinated development between himself and the environment. It is thus clear that the "environment" referred to in environmental science includes not only lifeless matter in nature, but all things other than man as well.

From the perspective of systems engineering, man's environment is a colossal, complicated system. In studying the environment with man as its center, we mainly study the relations between man and the environment in this system and the laws governing these relations, as well as the interactions, through the flow of matter and energy, among the physical, biological, and socioeconomic systems that constitute the environment and the laws governing these relations. To be specific, all movements of the environmental elements of the physical system are independent of organic life, including those of the lithosphere, atmosphere, hydrosphere, and continental glaciers. The biological system is composed of all auto-regenerating organic systems, including the smallest micro-organisms, organic communities, and the ecological system, all of which constitute the biosphere. The socioeconomic system comprises man's economic system, social system, political system, and information system, and man controls its input, output, and structure irrespective of their scale. Each of the three macro systems [physical, biological, and socioeconomic] has its own internal structure and functions. At the same time, there is an exchange of materials and energy, or interaction, between these systems. It can be said that environmental science refers to a science that studies the structure and functions of all the environmental systems, their interactions, and the laws governing them as well as how to make use of these laws in study.

What kind of relationship exists, then, between man and nature, or between the physical system and the biological system mentioned above? This can be seen from the reproductive process of human society. Marxist economic science tells us that the economic reproduction process is invariably interwoven with a natural reproduction process. Labor is not the only source of the use value or material wealth it produces. Labor and nature together constitute the source of all wealth. Nature provides labor with materials and labor turns the materials into wealth. It also points out that labor is primarily a process between man and nature, a process in which man, by his activities, gives rise to, readjusts, and controls the material transformation between man and nature. In other words, the entire process of reproduction of human society, including the process of economic reproduction and the process of natural reproduction, is closely integrated and interwoven with the transformation of matter and energy between man and nature and conducted in endless cycles. The eco-environmental system itself has an important function—to make self-adjustments, to conduct routine operations, and to maintain a relatively stable, dynamic equilibrium between man and his ecological environment. But this function has a limit, beyond which it cannot be performed normally and the system is disrupted. For this reason no element in the eco-environmental system can be increased or reduced without limit.

In the process of economic reproduction, man incessantly draws raw materials from nature, puts them into the process of reproduction, and, through labor, turns them into necessary products. At the same time he constantly discharges into the natural environment residues generated in production, distribution, circulation, consumption, and other processes of economic reproduction, as well as the residues of daily life while participating in the natural circulation of material and energy. To ensure a smooth process of economic reproduction, as far as regenerative resources are concerned, the amount of raw material drawn from nature must not surpass nature's reproductive ability; otherwise, it will lead to the disruption of the circulation of matter and energy in nature and the depletion of natural resources. Furthermore, the wastes discharged into the natural environment must not exceed nature's capacity; otherwise, it will lead to the deterioration of environmental quality. This explains why the process of economic reproduction is closely related to the process of natural reproduction. The latter is the foundation of the former, while the former is the main factor affecting the latter. To promote material and spiritual civilization, man develops the economy on a large scale and, correspondingly, draws from and adds to the environment on a large scale. He incessantly extracts raw materials from nature to put them into economic reproduction and produces all kinds of refuse in the course of economic reproduction, which he discharges into nature. The scale, scope, and depth of this complicated interaction increase day by day with the rapid growth of the forces of social production and the tremendous progress of science and technology. Thus the process of economic reproduction cannot be maintained smoothly unless it follows the economic laws and the laws of nature, that is, the eco-economic laws; otherwise, it will disrupt the structure and functioning of nature's ecological equilibrium, ruin the environment, and, in turn, impair economic growth. This is the dialectical relationship of the unity of opposites between environmental protection and economic development, forces which are interdependent and restrict and promote each other. We should correctly understand and handle this relationship and consciously make a success of the work of environmental protection.

PAYING ATTENTION TO HISTORICAL EXPERIENCE AND STRENGTHENING ENVIRONMENTAL PROTECTION WORK

The world today is confronted with two kinds of environmental problems. First, there is the industrial and environmental pollution of cities. Second, there is the agricultural and ecological disruption of rural areas. Generally speaking, most developed countries are faced with the former problem, while the developing countries mainly face the latter. China is a developing country with a backward economy and low level of production, but it is afflicted with both kinds of environmental problems.

Today our country is suffering from serious environmental pollution. Environmental pollution not only gravely endangers people's health, but also has caused huge economic losses.

The lessons drawn by industrialized countries from environmental pollution are worthy of our study. First, the increase in pollution is faster than the growth of industrialization. Second, both the harm caused by pollution and the effect of controlling it extend over a long period of time. This means that macroscopically there is a long period of time from the discharge of polluted matter until the appearance of its harmful effects and from the control of these pollutants to the eventual elimination of their harmful effects. In other words, it is only when certain harmful effects of pollution have been discovered that people begin to take measures to control it, and the pollution may have worsened before the construction of the system for pollution control is completed. Thus the failure to take preventive measures and adopting measures of control only after the harm has been done will land one in a passive position and compel one to pay a high price.

Third, the capacity of the environment is limited. That is, the natural ecological system has limited capacity for absorbing the discharge of human activities and turning it into materials useful, or at least not harmful, to living beings in other forms. When polluted materials are discharged on a sufficiently large scale, the natural absorbing mechanism may reach the saturation point. Consequently, the refuse of human civilization can accumulate in the environment and bring about environmental pollution. We do not know exactly the limit of the earth's capacity for absorbing a particular pollutant, much less its capacity for absorbing a conglomeration of polluted materials. However, we know that there is such a limit and that environmental pollution in many areas has gone beyond it.

Fourth, pollution control is very expensive. To avoid the disruption of the ecological system, it is necessary to have measures to bring pollution under control. Of course, strict pollution control does not necessarily mean the complete elimination of pollution. It is difficult to eliminate all pollution. This is because of technological as well as economic restrictions. Economically, the expense of pollution control rises sharply with increasingly strict standards for pollution discharge. According to calculations in the West, the operational cost of factories not allowed to discharge any organic wastes would be 100 times greater than the operational cost of factories allowed to discharge 30 percent of their organic wastes. This figure is not necessarily reliable, but has certain reference value.

Likewise, the situation of ecological disruption in our country should also be given the closest attention. Everyone knows that a striking manifestation of ecological disruption is the destruction of natural resources. The destruction and waste of natural resources in our country is serious. For example, our forest resources have dwindled considerably in the thirty-odd years since the founding of the People's Republic. It should be mentioned in particular that the present state of China's forest resources falls far short of the needs of national economic development. The contradictions between the supply and demand of timber, firewood, pulp, and other forest products are sharp. As a result, the annual consumption of forest resources far surpasses their annual growth. Moreover, these contradictions in the supply and demand of timber occur on the basis of a low level of timber consumption. With the advance of modernization and the rise of people's living standards, the demand for timber will increase enormously. Unless effective measures are taken, the contradictions between supply and demand will sharpen.

The waste of water resources is also conspicuous. In agriculture the irrigation rate, on the one hand, is rather low, while, on the other hand, in many irrigated areas the volume of water used is several times higher than what is needed because of the lack of accessories in irrigation equipment, serious seepage and percolation, and flood-type irrigation. In industry the water recycling rate is low, with a few cities as high as 50 percent while most cities recycle only 20 to 30 percent, far below levels in the advanced world. In addition to the problem of the volume of water, there is the problem of the quality of water. The discharge volume of China's industrial wastewater and urban sewage exceeds 30 billion tons annually, most of which is directly discharged into waterways untreated. This results in serious degradation of the water quality and further reduces the utilization rate of water resources that are by no means abundant to begin with.

Similarly, the pollution and exploitation of land resources is also serious. Owing to the pollution of cultivated land by wastewater and materials discharged by industrial enterprises (including those owned by communes, production brigades, and production teams), the country's grain output is reduced by 5 million tons annually, about two-thirds of the average annual increase of grain output over the three decades and more since the founding of new China. Irrational land development and utilization, deforestation, and destruction of grasslands have led to land degradation and desertification. China has become one of the countries in the world with the most serious soil erosion. The loss of nitrogen, phosphorus, potassium, and other plant nutrients by soil erosion every year amounts to the country's total annual output of chemical fertilizers. The economic loss is staggering.

The waste of land resources is also shocking. Generally speaking, when factories, railways, airports, and so forth are built on land, the economic effect of the land is raised. This is a road we must follow to achieve industrialization. However, we must give our attention to another aspect—that due to lack of unified land management. Many construction projects have taken up too much land and more land has been requisitioned than used, prematurely requisitioned, or even requisitioned and not used. In many cases good land is used where poorer land would serve the purpose. Such situations exist everywhere. China's cultivated land per capita is merely 0.1 hectare, less than one-third of the world average. With the expansion of the scale of capital construction, continued population increase, and the withdrawal of part of the steep, sloping fields and desertified land from cultivation for the purpose of afforestation and animal husbandry, the area under cultivation will continue to drop while new land reclamation is limited. Therefore, strict control on the loss of cultivated land has become a pressing task.

The developed countries of the world have begun to pay attention to the correct handling of the interrelationships among population, natural resources, environment, and development. They believe that aside from political and social factors, this is a question of paramount importance that has a bearing on whether their national economies can develop in a healthy and durable manner.

As far as understanding is concerned, the root cause of our country's environmental pollution and ecological disruption lies mainly in the fact that in construction, we have paid attention only to the growth of production to the neglect of ecological equilibrium. We have set our eyes on immediate interests and overlooked long-term interests. We have failed to deal correctly with the relations between the development of production and environmental protection and have thus committed careless errors that have polluted the environment, impeded development, and damaged things, which amounts to killing the goose that lays the golden eggs. We should draw lessons from these things, follow the laws governing eco-economic development, and tackle this as an important matter in our country's socialist modernization process.

MAKING CLEAR THE GOALS OF ENVIRONMENTAL PROTECTION AND PERFECTING THE INDEX SYSTEM

The Twelfth Congress of the Chinese Communist party has set clear-cut objectives for China's economic and social development by the year 2000—while steadily working for more and better economic results, to quadruple the gross annual value of industrial and agricultural production, to raise the people's standard of living to a well-off level, and to build socialist material civilization and spiritual civilization. All of these have something to do with environmental and social outcomes. Poor environmental results mean that the environment is polluted or disrupted, and this will surely impair economic growth and reduce economic results. If environmental pollution and ecological disruption are not strictly controlled, the objective of "quadrupling" cannot be achieved. Even if we manage to achieve it with an [extraordinary] effort, pollution will result in disaster and the people will not allow this to happen. A good standard of living includes a better material and cultural life for the people as well as improvement of the environment. It goes without saying that socialist material and spiritual civilization should include a clean, beautiful, and quiet environment. As Comrade Li Peng stated clearly in his report, China's environmental protection target by the end of this century is as follows: strive to solve basically the problem of environmental pollution throughout the country; restore natural ecology on the whole to a sound state of recycling; bring about a clean, beautiful, and quiet environment for production and life in city and country; and make the environmental conditions of the whole country in the main suit the development of the national economy and the people's improved material and cultural life. This requires that the quality of the environment in cities improve markedly, the pollution situation of most older enterprises be basically brought under control, the serious pollution of key river systems and marine areas be fundamentally improved, and the eco-environment be in the main in a good state. When these targets are realized, the demands of the national economy and social development on natural resources will be basically satisfied and the improvement of people's material and cultural life to a well-off level will be facilitated.

Environmental protection is closely linked with the general strategic objective and presents a strategic problem itself. At the Economic, Scientific, Technological and Social Development Strategy Symposium held recently by the Technical Economics Research Center of the State Council, there was general interest in the question of environmental protection, and many comrades put forward constructive views. For example, taking into consideration economic, social, and environmental results, some comrades set forth a pattern of development with Chinese characteristics which stresses comprehensive planning and overall balance of social production, people's lives, and environmental ecology; coordinated development of economy, science, technology, and society; and adherence to the four cardinal [political] principles. This pattern of development aroused general interest because there cannot be genuine development if we have only the growth of economic output value without betterment of the people's standard of living and improvement of the environment. Genuine development includes sustained growth of the national economy, a general rise of the people's standard of living, and steady improvement of the eco-environment.

A number of scholars in Western countries have raised questions about the gross national product (GNP) index, which takes only economic growth as the gauge to measure the level of development. They are of the opinion that it does not include all results of social labor, does not touch on the factor of environmental pollution and the effects of ecological disruption, nor does it consider whether the distribution of income is rational, and therefore, it cannot reflect the requirements of modern society. For many years China has adopted the gross value of industrial and agricultural output as the index for development. It reflects the production scale and growth rate of the two major production departments of industry and agriculture and facilitates the study of the material ties and proportionate relations between industry and agriculture. However, it does not include the results of labor of other material production departments aside from industry and agriculture. Moreover, because the calculations are made by means of the factory method, many factors are double-counted, and thus the index cannot precisely mirror the actual scale of the growth of the national economy. More important, it lacks a results index and a quality index and does not take into consideration the effects of environmental pollution and ecological disruption, and thus cannot fully reflect the basic aim of social production in a socialist society. Therefore, both at home and abroad, people are making exploratory studies in the hope of setting up an integral, scientific index system that can comprehensively reflect the level of economic and social development to promote the healthy growth of the economy and the society. In their study of the development and utilization of the land resources in Xishuangbanna, comrades of the Yunnan Economic Research Institute recently put forward an index system that includes indexes for production, living standards and ecology and takes into consideration the economic, social, and environmental effects, as well as social production, people's lives, and environmental ecology. It does not require complicated mathematical calculations and is handy to use. It has satisfactorily overcome some of the shortcomings of the GNP index and the gross industrial and agricultural output value index.

To be specific, this index system is composed of a production index, a [quality of] life index, and an ecology index. The gross index, called the comprehensive index for economic and social development, is composed of these three indexes plus their weights. These indexes can be called the comprehensive index, the production index, the life index, and the ecology index for short. The production, life, and ecology indexes are also composed of a number of specific indexes plus weights. The weight of various indexes is fixed in accordance with the position and role of that index in the national economy and social development—in other words, according to its importance. Let us suppose the production index of a certain place in a certain year is 1.11. This means that it has actually fulfilled the plan by 111 percent, or overfulfilled the plan by 11 percent. However, the life index and the ecology index are not so good, being 0.8 and 0.7, respectively. In other words, they have fulfilled the plan by 80 percent and 70 percent each. Suppose we set the weights of production, life, and ecology as 0.4, 0.3, and 0.3, respectively, in accordance with the degree of importance of the three kinds of indexes: the weighted production index is $1.11 \times 0.4 = 0.444$, the life index is $0.8 \times 0.3 = 0.24$, and the ecology index is $0.7 \times 0.3 = 0.21$. Thus the actual comprehensive index for economic and social development is the sum total of the three figures, or 0.894. This signifies that although the production plan may be overfulfilled, the life and ecology plans were not met, and consequently, the comprehensive index for economic and social development is only 89.4 percent and the total social effect is not terribly satisfactory. This line of thinking gives us some food for thought. Whether such an index system can be established and whether it is worthwhile to enrich and perfect it and popularize it for application remain to be seen. I suggest that the authorities concerned continue studying whether this indexing system can be established and whether or not it is worth improving and extending.

TAKING PRACTICAL MEASURES TO DO A GOOD JOB AT ENVIRONMENTAL PROTECTION

To succeed at the great causes of preventing and controlling environmental pollution, maintaining ecological equilibrium, promoting economic progress, and benefiting future generations, we must continue to increase the understanding by the whole society, particularly the leadership at all levels, of the importance of environmental protection work so that in practical work they can correctly understand and handle the mutual relations between economic development and environmental protection, act according to economic laws and ecological laws, and conscientiously carry out the principles, policies, decrees, and regulations concerning environmental protection. This is clear to all. Here I would like to set forth my views on three questions: why environmental protection has to rely on scientific and technological progress; why it is necessary to strengthen the study of environmental science; and why it is essential to incorporate environmental protection in the state plan and ensure necessary funds and materials.

Environmental Protection Must Rely on Scientific and Technological Progress

I share the view that to realize environmental protection in our country, reliance on scientific and technological progress should be one of the most important methods. In other words, the solution of China's environmental problems should be mainly realized by adopting relevant new technologies. This is a good, economical method that yields fast results. In our effort to quadruple our country's gross industrial and agricultural output value by the end of this century, scientific and technological progress will account for 50 percent of our success. What will be the proportion of contributions to be made by scientific and technological progress in the success of environmental protection? We should ponder this question.

To make environmental protection rely on scientific and technological progress, it is necessary to adopt technical economic policies that are favorable to the development of the economy and the protection of the environment. Attention must be given to this question, whether in the deployment of productive forces, or in the readjustment of the distribution of production, or in the technological transformation of industry and agriculture, or in the shaping and growth of new industries in an effort to achieve simultaneous economic, social, and environmental effects.

At a relevant meeting convened recently, discussions were held on which of the four strategies was to be selected to develop China's productive forces. In light of historical experience we cannot adopt a strategy of "imitation," which calls for following in the footsteps of another country. Nor can we adopt the "overtaking the advanced" strategy, which requires that in a relatively short period of time we catch up with or surpass the developed countries in the main aspects and even in all fields. Nor can we adopt once again the "closed economy" strategy, which requires "self-reliance" in everything and discourages and even rejects the adoption of advanced foreign technology. Rather, we should adopt a "creative" strategy, which requires that, in accordance with the state and the actual conditions of our country, we should make full use of every favorable opportunity to adopt all kinds of new, advanced technologies in the world which suit our needs. Many countries in the world are enthusiastically discussing new developments in world industry, marked by such new technologies as microprocessors, genetic engineering, lasers and optical fibers, new materials, and new energy sources. This heralds the message that at the end of this century and the beginning of the next, extensive application of new technologies which have already made a breakthrough, or are going to make breakthroughs, will bring about a new leap in productive forces and will correspondingly lead to changes in the set-up of production, social structure, and people's way of life. We must study this situation earnestly and seize the opportunity, meet the challenge, and do a better job in all endeavors of our socialist modernization. The work of environmental protection should also be included. To meet the situation in which world technologies and industries are advancing by leaps and bounds and new changes take place day by day, we should work out a special policy of flexible response and set up a sound management system so that we can rapidly master the newly developed technologies needed by our country, which we can adopt and use to make a success of our economic construction and our environmental protection work.

Our environmental protection work should be based on our needs and capability to adopt the new technologies that have emerged in the new industrial developments around the world. For instance, the developed countries are gradually transferring certain labor-intensive and seriously polluting industries to the developing countries. At the same time they are carrying out technological innovation and technical transformation of the capital-intensive iron and steel industry, chemical heavy industry, and automobile industry, centering on automation, energy saving, and nonpollution of the environment. Meanwhile they are actively setting up and expanding technology and knowledge-intensive industries that cause little or no pollution. In the face of this we should, in conjunction with the technical transformation of old enterprises, actively adopt state-of-the-art technological products, such as microprocessors, to strengthen enterprise management, economize on natural resources and energy, control the discharge of wastewater, waste gas, and slag, and reduce environmental pollution. For a number of backward small factories with outdated equipment in Shanghai, once computers are installed in key places, they can rapidly raise the quality of their products, cut down material and energy consumption, reduce the discharge of waste materials, and increase economic, social, and environmental results. Furthermore, genetic engineering technology, which is another hallmark of new developments in world production, can allow cereal plants to obtain nitrogen-fixing functions through bacteria grown in their roots and through the plants themselves to provide nitrogen fertilizer for the plants. Moreover, indications in foreign countries show that this technology can turn maize from an annual plant into a perennial plant. If this proves successful and is popularized, it will be of great practical significance for the development of agriculture, conservation of energy and raw materials, water and soil conservation, and maintenance of the eco-environment.

Strengthen the Study of the Science of Environmental Protection

Many major problems facing the world are enormously complex and transcend many fields. In most cases they cannot be solved by relying on only one science or profession. Only by integrating many branches of learning can a correct answer be found. Environmental protection is one such problem because it involves natural science, engineering technology, and social sciences. Only by relying on the theoretical guidance of these branches of science and the close cooperation and joint exploration and study by scientists in these fields can all kinds of environmental problems emerging in our country's socialist modernization be solved smoothly. For this reason close cooperation, comprehensive study, and joint efforts to tackle key problems by natural science workers, technical engineering personnel, and social science workers has become a feature of our time. I fully agree with the view expressed by Comrade Li Ximing [then Minister of Urban and Rural Construction and Environmental Protection] that the science of environmental science is a weak link in our country. The science of environmental control itself is also a comprehensive branch of learning involving economics, law, and sociology. The current situation is that among those who engage in research in economics, law, and sociology, few people undertake research in the science of environmental control and many theoretical and practical problems in the science of environmental control involving these branches of learning have not been studied comprehensively and deeply, and thus still have no satisfactory answers. Therefore, I fully agree with the proposal that natural science workers, technical engineering personnel, and social science workers should be actively organized to jointly engage in environmental forecasting and planning and the study of important technical economics environmental policies; and that comrades in environmental protection departments on all fronts who have studied natural science and engineering should be encouraged to devote themselves to learning some relevant social sciences, including management science, economics, law, and sociology. Similarly, comrades engaged in social science research and those in management departments should make an effort to acquire relevant knowledge in natural science and engineering. Through joint efforts by various quarters, China's environmental control will surely be raised to a new level in both theory and practice in the not-too-distant future.

To build a strong, modern socialist country with Chinese characteristics, it is essential to master economic and natural laws, to have long-term strategic insight, to view the situation as a whole, to strengthen foresight, and to overcome blindness. In accordance with the instructions by leading comrades of the party's Central Committee and the State Council, we are organizing the start of a forecast study, "China in the Year 2000." This study is aimed at realizing the strategic objectives set by the Twelfth Party Congress, to provide reference materials based on scientific information to enable various regions, professions, and undertakings to work out development plans and, by publicizing the image of "China in the Year 2000," to encourage people of the whole country to strive for the realization of the party's magnificent program. Under the personal guidance of Comrade Li Ximing, much work has been done, considerable progress has been made, and initial results have been achieved in the research work on "China's Environment in the Year 2000," which is a branch topic of "China in the Year 2000." I hope those comrades who are participating in this research project will make continuous efforts, strive to complete the task of forecasting at the earliest possible date, and produce high-quality and high-level results of scientific research as a contribution to our country's environmental protection work.

Incorporate Environmental Protection in the National Economy and Social Development Plans at All Levels, and Ensure Necessary Funds and Materials

China is guided by a socialist-planned economy. On the one hand various undertakings, particularly important projects, cannot be carried out smoothly unless they are incorporated in plans. On the other hand our planned economic system has a high capacity to intervene in the economy. If the plan conforms to economic and ecological laws, it can bring about a sound cycle of national and social development. Conversely, if the plan does not conform to the requirements of ecological and economic laws, it will bring about a vicious cycle for national economy and social development, disrupt the eco-environment, and damage economic and social development. Therefore, we must attach importance to the question of incorporating environmental protection in our plans and ensure the necessary funds and materials.

Because we did not have sufficient understanding and paid inadequate attention to environmental protection in the past, many engineering projects failed to incorporate environmental protection facilities during the building phase. This is an important reason China has serious environmental problems today. We must earnestly draw lessons from this and make conscientious efforts to strengthen environmental protection work, check the trend of deterioration of the environment in a planned way, and improve the quality of the environment in key places. We can envisage that by the year 2000, both in industry and in the urban environment, we can control the discharge of pollutants. This, combined with some treatment measures, will cause air pollution, water pollution, and other major pollution problems to be reduced considerably. In the natural environment the rate of forest cover will be increased from the present 12.5 percent to around 20 percent. Soil erosion and desertification will be basically brought under control. Wild animals and plants, particularly precious and rare ones, will be effectively protected and enabled to propagate. The exploitation and utilization of natural resources will be, in the main, appropriate and rational. And the disrupted agricultural ecological environment will be restored and developed considerably, forming an agricultural ecological system with a sound cycle. With efforts by all sectors, this can be achieved. We must follow the relevant instructions of the party's Central Committee, and in drawing up plans and distributing funds, we must have environmental protection in mind and ensure that necessary funds and materials are made available through proper channels.

Comments

In his address to the Second National Environmental Protection Work Conference, Ma Hong, president of the Academy of Social Sciences, revealed considerable insight into the goals and direction of environmental policy in China. Ma stressed the interrelationship between economic development and environmental protection which necessitated raising the priority of environmental protection with regard to the budget and planning processes, which is now being realized, albeit at levels still regarded as inadequate by virtually all environmental specialists. Ma's approach reflects a strong appreciation for systems analysis and indicator construction, which are attractive tools for policy makers trained in Marxist dialectics and engineering. There is, unfortunately, a serious danger that excessive trust will be placed in the ability of politically trustworthy (or any other kind of) technocrats to forecast, design, and engineer anything so complex as social development, particularly when political and scientific discourse are circumscribed by official policies.

Li Peng (1984) "Protecting the Environment Is a Major Task Facing China"

Xinhua Yuebao (January), pp. 70–73.

The State Council's decision to convene the Second National Environmental Protection Conference conveys the Party Central Committee and State Council's strong concern for environmental protection work. China has already entered a new historical period, with the whole party and the whole people all following the course set by the Twelfth Party Congress to struggle for the creation of a modernized socialist country. From the beginning of this new period, we must pay careful attention to environmental issues. If environmental issues are properly handled, we can both accelerate the realization of the "Four Modernizations" and pass prosperity on to our descendants. I have opinions on five points that I would now like everyone to ponder:

PROTECTING THE ENVIRONMENT IS A FUNDAMENTAL NATIONAL POLICY IN CHINA

The environment is one of the biggest problems facing the world, especially the advanced economies and China. For a long time we were ignorant about this problem and failed to accord it sufficient recognition.

The natural environment is the foundation of human existence. Mankind would be unable to survive without sunlight, air, water, soil, forests, and other biological and mineral resources. For a rather long time in the past, when global population was small and human capacity to exploit natural resources on a large scale was limited, humanity's impact on the natural environment was not too great. But the great increases in human population and the rapid development of the forces of production have created the potential for large-scale construction and creation with an ever-expanding scale of exploitation directed against natural resources. Under the circumstances improper actions can easily destroy the natural environment and the ecological balance. This is why we have an environmental problem that is growing progressively more critical.

In addition to grasping industrial and agricultural production, national defense, and science and technology, we also must properly solve two pressing problems when we undertake socialist construction: population and the environment. By now the population problem has already received heavy emphasis, but the environmental problem has yet to generate sufficient concern. Environmental pollution and destruction of the ecological balance are continuing to worsen. Industrial pollution, for example, has already spread from the cities and rivers to the towns and villages. If this situation is not quickly reversed, not only will the development of agriculture and industry and the realization of the Four Modernizations be thwarted, but people's health will also be impaired. We must have good environmental conditions and a sound natural ecology in order to modernize. If we should neglect environmental protection work now, by the end of the century environmental pollution and ecological deterioration may become a problem as intractable as population is in China today. What we absolutely must not do is behave like moths, which destroy their own homes and basis for future existence. Therefore, environmental protection is a strategic task and a critical policy in modernizing China.

It is wrong to hold the attitude that pollution is the inevitable accompaniment of modernization, for that leaves us in a state of complacency and inaction. Ours is a socialist country in which the purpose of developing production is to bring prosperity to the people. So long as we take advantage of the superiority of the socialist-planned economy and formulate appropriate policies, we are fully capable of escaping the pollution and public hazards that have arisen in capitalist countries. We should have complete confidence in this. We must connect environmental protection work to the achievement of the targets for struggle set at the Twelfth Congress, the building of socialist material and spiritual civilization, enhancing the superiority of the socialist system, and realizing the great ideal of communism. Only in this way can we have a correct appreciation and unified ideological formulation for performing environmental protection work well.

ECONOMIC CONSTRUCTION AND ENVIRONMENTAL PROTECTION MUST ADVANCE TOGETHER IN TANDEM

We must handle the relationship between economic construction and environmental protection in the course of achieving the Four Modernizations. As economic construction gradually advances, the scale of industrial production grows, and with it the scale of pollution. As agriculture develops, the intensity by which agricultural resources are exploited also expands. Meanwhile China's population continues to grow. All of these place enormous pressure on environmental protection work. If we fail to act properly, environmental pollution and destruction will worsen further and environmental quality will continue to deteriorate. Right now there are among us some officials who enthusiastically grasp production and construction, for which their activism is praiseworthy. But when they grasp production few think about environmental protection, which is a one-sided attitude. We favor solving environmental pollution and ecological destruction in the process of economic construction, making economic construction and environmental protection advance together in tandem. Through environmental protection work we create a better environment, which enables people to work and live better. Meanwhile environmental protection guarantees and accelerates the development of economic construction. In general, this means that economic construction, urban and rural construction, and environmental construction must be planned together, carried out together, and advance in tandem, as well as work toward the integration of economic, social, and environmental interests. We must start out with this concept to guide us and actively prevent pollution, improve the ecology, expedite the Four Modernizations, and make the people prosperous.

We propose to struggle for the achievement of the following targets for environmental protection by the end of the century: work hard to bring pollution in China under basic control; basically restore a sound balance in natural ecology; create a clean, beautiful, and orderly production and living environment in cities and towns; and have environmental conditions basically improve in correspondence with the development of the national economy and the rise in people's material and spiritual living standards.

It is essential to set this kind of target to provide a clear direction for our work. To ensure the realization of this target, we must conduct work in a solid down-to-earth manner and must be particularly conscientious in planning environmental protection, setting practical demands for each stage, and, in particular, strengthening planned guidance in environmental protection. Planned guidance is particularly important in environmental protection work. For if agriculture, light industry, and heavy industry should fall out of balance, their proportion can be adjusted over a period of some years, but in the event of severe environmental pollution and ecological disruption, even decades may not be sufficient to restore balance. Environmental protection targets, demands, and measures have already been instituted in the Sixth Five-Year Plan, but they were not sufficiently practicable. The key is to make them more practicable in the context of annual plans; otherwise, master plans and five-year plans are merely empty talk. The State Planning Commission must firmly take hold of establishing overall balance in this regard and at the same time must organize and supervise the localities and departments in realizing overall balance. The localities and departments must incorporate environmental protection in their plans to quadruple production, in economic regional planning, and in urban and rural construction planning. Only after we put environmental protection on the planning track can we ensure that environmental protection and economic construction will advance in tandem and develop in a coordinated fashion and ensure the realization of the struggle targets for environmental protection.

MAKE THE RATIONAL EXPLOITATION OF NATURAL RESOURCES AND COMPREHENSIVE UTILIZATION THE BASIC POLICY FOR ENVIRONMENTAL PROTECTION

Environmental protection is a fundamental experience in China; that is, although we are intent on controlling pollution, we are even more determined to unify environmental protection and resource conservation. Because of our low level of science and technology, many factories suffer from outmoded equipment, backward technology, and poor management, with the result that large quantities of precious resources are discharged as the "three wastes" instead of being converted into wealth. This is a major reason for both the low level of economic returns from our enterprises and the occurrence of environmental pollution. In all aspects of economic construction and social development, we must promote resource conservation, the full utilization of resources, and the comprehensive utilization of industry's "three wastes" to make them reusable so we can both increase economic returns and protect the environment. Ecological imbalance also primarily stems from the blind exploitation of natural resources. Therefore, we can effectively control environmental destruction and ensure the full and sustained utilization of natural resources only if we simultaneously focus on the conservation and rational exploitation of resources. In the future all localities and departments must begin with this fundamental policy when setting economic and social development and environmental protection policies and measures, to better coordinate them.

The prevention and control of industrial pollution must be integrated with the technological renovation of enterprises. [We must] renovate outmoded resources and energy-guzzling technologies and operations, develop the comprehensive control of the three wastes, and reduce emissions of the three wastes. We have accomplished a good deal in this regard, especially in the metallurgical industry. Enterprises like Anshan Steel, Shoudu [Capital] Steel, and Shenyang Smelter, which were notorious polluters in the past, have integrated technological upgrading with the comprehensive utilization of resources, and thereby controlled air pollution.

China's energy structure is based on coal, which inevitably leads to air pollution, and thus, objectively speaking, exerts a negative influence on the environment. However, we can alter these negative factors and reduce the level of air pollution caused by coal so long as we carry out the correct energy policy and adopt appropriate technical measures. In the near term we must properly handle the issues of district heating, cogeneration of heat in factories and mines, town gas, and supplying low-sulfur coal for household use. In the long term we must go all out with regard to the comprehensive utilization and transformation of coal and take the path of coal chemistry and gasification. We should expand the role of coal washing, and wash high-sulfur coal before shipping it out. When constructing thermal power plants we must consider sulfur dioxide-removal technology. We must grasp experimental and research work for the removal of sulfur from coal gas, achieve a rapid breakthrough on the technological side, and work toward technological rationality and commercial practicality. Environmental protection departments at all levels must actively participate in setting energy policy because it is a major item.

The protection of the agricultural environment must be integrated with the rational exploitation and utilization of agricultural resources and the development of diversified management. We must focus full attention on the conservation of land, water, forests, grasslands, and endangered species. We should make rational use of agricultural resources to maintain ecological balance by tailoring land use—forest, fisheries, or animal husbandry—to natural conditions. Blindly draining lakes or destroying forests and grasslands to expand farmland, like a moth consuming its own habitat as was done in the past, must not be allowed to recur. Moreover, we must conduct large-scale tree and grass planting, restore vegetation, and strive to expand reusable resources. When we go about large-scale tree planting and afforestation, this is not simply to produce more timber, but also to protect the environment and create a well-balanced ecological cycle of benefit to both the present and future generations.

Pollution from some commune-operated industries is quite serious and must be strictly controlled within a short period. Those which can be adjusted should be adjusted and those which should be shut down should be shut down. We must be firm in closing down heavily polluting small-scale enterprises that manufacture products containing mercury, arsenic, or asbestos, that process kerosene, coal tar, or sulfur by indigenous methods, or that release large levels of radiation. Others, like small-scale paper and chemical plants, must be tightly controlled. Still others, like small-scale electroplaters and smelters, must be merged and centralized into electroplating and smelting centers that earnestly control pollution. We must step up research on high-potency, safe, and economical agricultural chemicals and stress the development of chemicals that quickly break down in the soil to reduce pollution from agricultural chemicals. All new, heavily polluting agricultural chemicals will be banned from production, import, and application. Highly toxic and persistent chemicals are not to be applied on vegetables, tea, fruit, tobacco, medicinal herbs, and other such crops. We must rationally apply chemical fertilizer, make full use of household wastes for fertilizer, and work toward scientific farming. To reduce the loss of vegetation, we also must solve the rural energy problem through locally appropriate measures, like small-scale hydroelectric power stations, methane pits, fuelwood plantations, and solar-heated stoves.

Shunde County in Guangdong has had good experience in protecting the agricultural environment. Through comprehensive planning, acting according to the overall situation, and protecting the ecology, agriculture has developed, peasant incomes are up, and environmental pollution has been controlled. The Ministry of Urban and Rural Construction and Environmental Protection convened a conference to exchange experiences there, and everyone evaluated it highly. This is the right track to take, and I hope everyone will follow it.

STRENGTHEN SCIENTIFIC MANAGEMENT OF ENVIRONMENTAL PROTECTION WORK

Environmental management is crucial. A great many of our environmental problems are related to our lack of environmental management or inadequacies in this regard. At this time, when our financial resources are strained and technological conditions are rather backward, it becomes even more important to address many environmental problems by strengthening management. Moreover, quite a few environmental problems can be solved by strengthening management without necessarily having to spend a lot of money. Some examples are rational geographical distribution and urban planning, rational resource development, control of urban noise, and prohibition of blind ecological destruction that arises from draining lakes and deforestation. These are all problems for which we can obtain visible results by strengthening management, without necessarily spending a lot of money. Beijing obtained quick results in reducing traffic noise by writing specific regulations on the honking of horns, with fines for violators. Many problems can be solved in this way so long as we practice earnest and stringent management. Therefore, at the same time that we grasp pollution control, we also must further strengthen scientific management of environmental quality, natural resources development, and pollution discharges. We have to adopt different management methods for different types of ecologies and different environmental problems. When we fix environmental protection plans and standards, we must both satisfy basic environmental quality requirements and make them correspond to national conditions with reference to China's technical economic level. We also must be demanding in management, and we definitely must do what should and can be done.

Future environmental protection must further carry out the policy of "prevention first and combining prevention and control." We must first focus on prevention and cannot wait until after the environment has been polluted and the ecology destroyed before improving controls. Large-scale capital construction and resource development items must, right from the outset, focus on environmental protection. They must include environmental evaluation as an important component in project feasibility studies and make sound arrangements for preventing environmental pollution and ecological destruction. Capital and material needs must be fixed and entered into development and construction plans. We must actively control already polluted and ruined environments. It will be much cheaper and the benefits will be realized sooner if we intervene promptly; if we wait, the expenses and damages will mount up. We must sincerely implement regulations on environmental protection funding that the state has already clarified. No excuses for failing to carry them out will be entertained; nor will it be permitted to divert the funds to other purposes. The control of environmental pollution principally depends on each enterprise's own resources, and the principle of "the polluter must control his own pollution" must be upheld. Enterprises that cause pollution should assume this responsibility. When the enterprise's parent ministry or bureau sets industrywide technological renovation plans, it must simultaneously arrange pollution control measures. Major control items that involve several industries, as well as comprehensive regional control projects, must be included in the state capital construction and technological renovation plans. We must follow the principle of "the developer must also do the protecting" with regard to the development and utilization of natural resources. We must use some economic instruments, like taxes and fees, to administer control and regulation and raise the effectiveness of environmental management.

The structure of environmental management must be strengthened. Because of important regional differences in environmental problems, not all management methods can be applied across the entire country. We must have planning and management provided on a locally appropriate basis by government at all levels, with overall arrangements and, moreover, the setting of keypoints for action. At the national level the Ministry of Urban and Rural Construction and Environmental Protection acts as the coordinating department on the environmental protection side and is responsible for overall management and doing a good job of environmental protection planning, construction, supervision, and inspecting. The State Planning, Economic, and Science Commissions and other coordinating bodies also must manage environmental protection work well in terms of their respective missions. The State Council's various economic departments must grasp production with one hand and the environment with the other and absolutely cannot attend to only one while neglecting the other. Management of natural resources is primarily the role of the Ministry of Agriculture, Animal Husbandry, and Fisheries, the Ministry of Forestry, the Ministry of Water Conservancy, and mining and marine departments. The control of industrial pollution must rely on the industrial and transportation departments. Each must do a good job of managing environmental protection work within their respective systems. Environmental protection work can develop in a comprehensive fashion only if we act as a single large family with a management system based on working separately but cooperating with one another. All areas and departments must strengthen the building of environmental protection structures, including those devoted to science and research and monitoring, in accordance with the relevant environmental protection laws and regulations. We are undertaking structural transformation to solve the problems of overmanning and inefficiency. Environmental protection is something new, with rather flimsy structures and assets that have to be strengthened. The various State Council departments and provinces, municipalities, and counties all must establish specialized environmental protection structures. Districts and townships also must have specialized environmental management personnel, on a full- or part-time basis. At the same time we must take close interest in the cultivation of talents in the environmental protection specialties by raising professional and technical levels to correspond to the requirements of environmental protection work as it develops.

We must strengthen the legal system for environmental protection. To merely talk about environmental protection's importance is not enough; we also need legal regulation. The building of China's environmental protection legal system has barely begun. In accordance with [Article 26 of] the new [1982] constitution's provision—"The state protects and improves the living and ecological environment and prevents and remedies pollution and other public hazards"—we must prepare in detail various environmental plans and accelerate the creation of an environmental legal system. Once we have law we must act according to the law. Judicial departments, environmental protection departments, and all economic departments must strengthen their coordination and jointly enforce the law. We must have a strong legal outlook, with everyone equal before the law, and must consciously operate within and according to the law.

FURTHER STRENGTHEN THE LEADERSHIP OF ENVIRONMENTAL PROTECTION WORK

All State Council departments and local governments must include environmental protection, a basic national policy that affects life and the realization of the Four Modernizations, on their daily agendas for major items and handle it resolutely and responsibly. Ministers, governors, mayors, and county magistrates all must be responsible for their department's or area's environmental protection work and personally conduct inspections and study, supervise work, summarize experiences, criticize shortcomings, and praise advances. They must personally handle prominent environmental protection issues and model pollution cases that the masses complain about vociferously. Environmental protection departments at all levels must submit annual reports to the party organizations of State Council departments or local governments on their department's or area's environmental protection affairs. Party organizations in departments and local governments must discuss environmental protection work once or twice a year. We must be good at selecting models, both good and bad. After a model has been chosen, praise or correct it with big banners to popularize it and educate the cadres and masses. Our cadres exist to serve the people, so those serving as governor or mayor should make their contributions to improving the environment. Departmental, provincial, and muncipal leaders were invited to this conference in the hope of raising everyone's concern for the environment, strengthening leadership over environmental protection, encouraging accomplishments, improving work, sincerely and continuously making progress, and working hard to create a new state of affairs in environmental protection work.

Comments

The Second National Environmental Protection Work Conference convened in December 1983, about ten years after its predecessor. The first conference indicated that China was beginning to realize the dangers of environmental problems, but its practical effects were limited. By contrast, the second conference was intended to boldly reaffirm that the central leadership continued to embrace environmental protection amid rapid economic growth and to develop realistic approaches to environmental management.

One of the vice-premiers who spoke at the conference, Wan Li, is generally placed among the strong supporters of economic reforms, while the other, Li Peng, whose speech is published here, is considered a more conservative supporter of planning and centralized controls. This follows in part from Li's training in the Soviet Union and is indicated in the fact that Li made only one mention of economic or market-oriented instruments in his approach while strongly emphasizing the need for planning, albeit in a more flexible form than rigid commandism. This indicates that there is controversy within China over the choice of policy instruments and that pollution and other problems can be seized on by different leadership groups to buttress their political positions. This potential is most apparent in the continuing pressure to enforce orthodoxy by combating "spiritual pollution" in the name of building a "[socialist] spiritual civilization" in which environmental protection plays a part. Nevertheless, the fact that both tendencies embraced environmental protection confirms that the issue will continue to enjoy political support no matter who occupies leadership positions, although the form may well vary.

In terms of practical solutions, Li stresses management as well as leadership. Li's strong support for improved management is obviously sensible, given the fact that much of pollution can be ascribed to inefficiency. This point was prominently emphasized at a 1982 conference on combining environmental protection with technological upgrading during the economic readjustment phase of modernization. (*See* Ministry of Urban and Rural Construction and Environmental Protection, Bureau of Environmental Protection, *The National Industrial System's Exchanging of Experiences on the Prevention and Control of Pollution Conference*, Beijing: Chinese Environmental Sciences Publishing House, 1982 [in Chinese]). It is generally less costly and more politically acceptable than installing non-production-oriented pollution controls without reference to production. Past experience, however, indicates that tight planning and efficient management in the economy are often inversely related, a conflict that Li's position does not adequately address.

Qu Geping (1983) "Basic Features and Key Lessons Regarding China's Environmental Problems"

HB (August), pp. 2–5.

Differences in national conditions lead to different environmental problems. If we are to recognize and solve environmental problems, we must begin by analyzing national conditions, seeking out the objective factors that cause environmental problems, and then formulate appropriate responses. Many advanced industrialized countries have proceeded in this fashion and obtained visible results. What, then, are the objective factors responsible for China's environmental problems, or in other words, what are the national characteristics of our environmental problems? This question requires serious deliberation. We must research China's national conditions first, while all industries are discussing their plans to build Chinese-style socialism as part of the plan to quadruple output [from 1980 levels] by the end of the century. Propelling China's environmental protection work forward so that it develops in conjunction with the national economy also requires study of China's national characteristics. I have prepared some remarks for study purposes. I feel that the national characteristics of China's environmental problems can be considered in terms of the following points.

1. Massive population places enormous pressure on the environment and renders the environment vulnerable to pollution damage. China's huge population places ever-increasing pressure and encroachment on the eco-environment. Most of our environmental problems are directly or indirectly related to demographics.

The high people-land ratio, which has been unfavorable for a long time in terms of arable land, forests, grasslands, water, and other resources, has become increasingly serious as the population has risen continuously. According to United Nations Environment Program (UNEP) sources, global arable land per capita equalled 0.31 hectare in 1975 but is predicted to decline to 0.15 hectare by the end of the century because of population increases, construction, and other factors. In the early 1970s each hectare of arable land supported 2.6 persons on average, but by the year 2,000 it will be 4 persons. In 1975 China had only 0.1 hectare of arable land per capita, and by 2000 it is expected to decline to 0.08 hectare, assuming a population of 1.2 billion. Each hectare of arable land, which supported 5.4 persons in the early 1950s, by 2000 will support 12 persons. We have much less arable land per capita than the world average, and the number of people we have to support is three times greater per unit arable land.

Lizhai Brigade in Xinyin Commune, Lanxi County, Zhejiang, came up with a vivid metaphor to describe the high population, land scarcity predicament. Their brigade's 93 hectares are like a boat and their 1,400 persons are its passengers. Since Liberation, arable land has declined by more than 13 hectares, equivalent to the loss of a large cabin, while population has doubled. Because the boat cannot get bigger, but the number of passengers is increasing year by year, the boat may capsize, drowning the passengers, unless they stringently control population growth.

Because of population pressure, food supply has been a big problem for a rather long time. With food supplies precarious, agricultural encroachment in the forests, grasslands, and fisheries, overgrazing, and overfishing have easily developed, and what was originally a fragile eco-environment quickly came under assault and destruction. This is a major threat to China's environment.

This characteristic is serious in heavily populated developing countries but is absent in advanced industrialized countries.

Industrial development is the activist way to raise living standards and put large numbers of people to work. As industry develops, the urban population grows. Even at a relatively low 3 percent annual rate of increase, the urban population will rise to 200 million by the year 2000, giving China the world's largest urban population. Such a large mass of people concentrated in cities will further increase urban environmental pressures and aggravate already serious environmental pollution problems.

2. China's industrial structure dominated by medium- and small-sized enterprises, especially the development of rural and neighborhood industries, adds additional pressure to the environment. In 1981 more than 90 percent of our more than 380,000 industrial enterprises were medium or small sized. These enterprises' technology and plants are usually rather backward, waste a lot of raw materials and energy, and are often irrationally distributed, posing a severe danger of pollution. Moreover, rural industries have developed rapidly in recent years and now number in excess of 1 million. Neighborhood industries also have expanded quickly in the cities. This has a positive impact by employing surplus labor in the cities and accelerating the prosperous development of the national economy. However, the pollution danger has become more serious and harder to control because the number of enterprises is too large and they are located haphazardly, have irrational product lines, are lacking in terms of technology and equipment, have poor management, and overconsume raw materials and energy. In addition, most are completely lacking in pollution control measures. Because this situation is seldom found abroad, we can say that this is an environmental problem unique to China. It gradually spreads pollution from the point to the plane and from the city to the village.

3. China's energy is primarily produced from coal, posing a severe threat to the environment. Coal accounts for more than 70 percent of our energy structure. A coal-based energy structure is extremely unfavorable for environmental protection. Coal is a dirty fuel in comparison to oil, natural gas, or hydroelectricity and releases large volumes of soot, harmful substances, and cinders when burnt. Widespread air pollution in China's cities and industrial districts is largely due to coal combustion. To eliminate these harmful substances requires rather complex technology and equipment and large capital investments. One after the other, some advanced industrialized countries have promoted the substitution of oil for coal to reduce coal-induced air pollution. China cannot carry out such a conversion at this point and for quite some time to come cannot appreciably alter its coal-based energy structure.

The rural household energy shortage is serious in China. Each year more than 400 million tons of plant stalks are burnt, but this still cannot meet the needs for household energy, while resulting in the destruction of vegetation. A grave environmental problem facing us today is that primitive methods of chopping down trees for fuel, uprooting grasses, and burning straw not only have low heat efficiency and destroy a source of agricultural nutrients for farming, but they also erode the soil, desertify the grasslands, and seriously damage the agricultural ecology and natural environment.

4. Because of our backward economy, China will be unable to spend a lot of money on pollution control in the years ahead. Pollution control and preserving ecological balance requires large expenditures as well as appropriate policies. It is estimated that secondary treatment of polluted water alone will require an investment of more than 30 billion yuan. I am afraid that this will rise to 100 billion yuan if we include the control of industrial and urban air pollution. Such large investments in the environment far exceed China's financial capacity. This difficulty will be with us for a long time to come. This characteristic rules out the adoption of a big-ticket approach such as that used in some developed countries involving centralized waste treatment. We must discover a Chinese way to raise money and control pollution.

These points are one of China's basic conditions, that is, the widespread and long-term environmental problems facing China. Although these factors are unfavorable in an objective sense, that does not mean that the environment will inevitably be polluted and destroyed. Studying national conditions is for the purpose of identifying objective problems to devise appropriate policies for the purpose of winning long-term victories and avoiding setbacks.

In the past thirty years we have adopted several policies and measures compatible with our national conditions, enabling us to gain some notable accomplishments, principally involving the following.

The agricultural eco-environment has been improved. In the past thirty-odd years we have done extensive capital construction work in water conservancy involving dikes, embankments, polders, and reservoirs; transformed saline land; expanded irrigation; and built shelterbelts, thereby reducing our vulnerability to natural disaster and enabling agricultural production to forge ahead.

Urban environmental public health shows impressive changes. "Speaking about public health and loving cleanliness" have already become customs. Many serious communicable diseases, like plague, smallpox, venereal disease, Kala-azar, relapsing fever, typhus, and typhoid fever, have already been eradicated or greatly controlled, the incidence of some common and epidemic diseases has been greatly reduced, and the mortality rate has fallen from 25 per thousand in the early post-Liberation period to 6.2 per thousand. Average life span has risen from around thirty-five before 1949 to about sixty-nine. The level of health among the Chinese people has greatly increased.

The comprehensive utilization of waste products from industry and society has greatly expanded, converting environmentally dangerous substances into resources and conserving large quantities of raw materials and energy. Between 1962 and 1980 120 million tons of discarded materials were procured and distributed in society with a gross output value of 24.6 billion yuan, not only reducing pollution and improving the environment, but also aiding industrial and agricultural production and creating wealth.

In general, however, we lack deep and systematic research on the national character of our environmental problems, leading to a series of errors in policy. We have paid a heavy price for incisive lessons. What lessons should we learn?

1. The development of agricultural production must be conducted in accordance with the laws of nature, and we must work hard to create a sound ecologically balanced system. Because we ignored the laws of nature in favor of slogans, one-sidedly took grain as the key link, inappropriately promoted farming on sloped land and converted lakes into paddies, and blindly allowed farmland to encroach into forests, pastures, and lakes, large-scale erosion and desertification and climatic changes occurred that seriously damaged the agricultural ecological balance.

Because of illegal reclamation and reckless felling, our already inadequate forests were further depleted, causing eco-environmental degradation in some areas. Forest cover in Sichuan has fallen from 20 percent in the early 1950s to 13 percent, where rainfall in forty-six counties has declined by 10 to 20 percent, with once-rare springtime droughts now commonplace. Extremely heavy rainfall in the summer of 1981 caused hundred-year floods in eighty-three counties.

Grasslands are a major barrier to desert expansion as well as the natural base for developing animal husbandry. Since 1958 China has experienced four high tides of destroying the grasslands for farming, reclaiming about 6.7 million hectares but destroying the already fragile ecological balance in pastoral areas. Coupled with overgrazing, our grasslands have retreated by more than 51 million hectares and the grass production capacity has fallen by 30 to 50 percent. Because of the destruction of grass cover, the deserts have advanced unimpeded, creating a grave environmental problem.

About 1.3 million hectares of lakes have been converted into farmland. Lake Dongting, known as the 800 li [one li = one-third mile] lake, has shrunk by 37 percent through enclosures and sedimentation. The blind reclamation of lakes has caused severe ecological damage in some areas and a series of difficulties for economic development.

These all indicate that violation of the laws of nature and rapacious resource exploitation not only hampers forestry, animal husbandry, and fisheries production, but also prevents grain production from growing. This then leads to a downward environmental spiral in which poverty begets more reclamation and reclamation leads to worse poverty.

Agriculture is a biological production process whose chief object is living plants and animals. This production process is influenced and regulated by environmental factors like sunlight, temperature, water, climate, and soil. This means that we must operate according to the laws of nature and integrate the exploitation and utilization of natural resources with their protection and conservation and create a materially powerful and beneficial cyclical system, to enable farming, forestry, animal husbandry, and fisheries to develop continuously in a comprehensive fashion.

2. Urban development must have a master plan, respect ecological balances, and create a favorable environment to live and work in. Pollution and environmental destruction in China are prominently revealed in the deterioration of urban environments. Levels of dust, sulfur dioxide, and other harmful components in city air are high. Many cities and districts south of the Yangtze River now show signs of acid rain, revealing a new aspect of air pollution. About 85 percent of urban wastewater is discharged untreated, seriously polluting surface water, groundwater, and urban lakes in many of our cities, with water quality declining on a widespread basis. The noise danger in many cities also is serious, impairing people's work and rest.

There are many causes of urban environmental deterioration. First is the lack of a comprehensive master plan in urban construction. For a long time construction in many cities ignored the needs of environmental protection by one-sidedly emphasizing the conversion of consumer cities into producer cities and making cities self-sufficient entities. We always emphasized industrial development, especially heavy industry, to the extent that internationally renowned scenic and historic centers like Beijing, Hangzhou, Suzhou, and Guilin also were engaged in the large-scale development of major polluting industries. The result was a loss of control regarding each city's special nature, scale of development, structure, and geographical distribution. Urban environments became seriously polluted and degraded as the cities all grew in size, with various departments growing in disorderly fashion in an irrational pattern of development.

Irrational industrial distribution is a major cause of pollution. For example, Suzhou's city district is only 14 square kilometers large but is home to 480 factories. The chock-a-block clustering of residential neighborhoods, factory neighborhoods, military posts, and parks and scenic areas pollutes the entire city with industrial emissions. This is the situation not only in Suzhou, but in most large and medium-sized cities as well.

The irrationality of energy utilization is another cause of pollution. Supplying residential areas with high-ash and -sulfur coal for household use creates uncontrollable pollution, with black smoke pouring out of thousands of homes. Moreover, heat is unevenly delivered, boilers are backward, and the heat efficiency rate is low with high levels of pollution. In sum, modernized large-scale production and densely concentrated population centers contrive to rely on backward, small peasant-style energy utilization methods.

Cities are highly concentrated centers for population, economic activity, and science and culture. They are multifunctional and complex, multilayered ecosystems. If we only consider such a system's economic functions while ignoring its ecological functions, we will create major environmental problems and impede the development of the economic functions. This is a profound lesson. If we are to solve environmental problems, we must begin by strengthening urban planning, go all out to rectify the irrational geographical distribution, and implement economic and technological policies that raise both economic and environmental efficiency.

3. Industrial development must be concerned with rational geographical distribution and adopt pollution control measures during the construction process. We lacked comprehensive planning in economic development for a long time, especially with regard to environmental protection, making irrational industrial distribution decisions. Moreover, most factories were built without pollution control technology, creating grave pollution problems. In 1981 air emissions included more than 42 million tons of harmful substances, and we generated 30.3 billion tons of wastewater, 80 percent of which was industrial. Every year we emit 430 million tons of industrial slag, totalling more than 5 billion tons over the years and occupying 400 square kilometers of land.

Industrial pollution produces large economic costs. Although we still lack overall statistics, we can analyze survey data from the Xiangjiang valley in Hunan. There the economic cost of industrial pollution equals 1.56 percent of the gross value of industrial and agricultural output. If this figure is extrapolated to the country as a whole, the cost to the nation is 12 billion yuan annually, which in fact is on the low side. Survey data from the European Economic Community show that pollution frequently results in costs totalling more than 3.5 percent of gross national product, and yet their production technology and environmental standards are higher than ours. Consequently, China's economic costs arising from pollution cannot be lower than theirs. This requires that we fully emphasize environmental statistical work, increase our study of environmental economics, and adopt the concepts of benefit-cost analysis.

The incidence of diseases resulting from industrial pollution, such as respiratory diseases, fluoride poisoning, mercury poisoning, lead poisoning, and cancer, have demonstrably increased. Industrial pollution has steadily increased the incidence of conflicts between industry and agriculture and between factories and residents, impairing social order.

Although China's industrial growth rate is not high, pollution is rather heavy. This is a major problem confronting the building of socialist modernization in China. In addition to a lack of clarity regarding the purpose of developing industrial production, there are other reasons industrial pollution is serious.

1. *Irrational geographical distribution of industry*. This is chiefly reflected in the fact that most of our industry is concentrated in forty large cities, which account for more than 65 percent of the gross value of China's industrial output, with thirteen major cities accounting for half of the country's industrial output. The continuing growth in urban size not only makes it hard to control pollution, but it also overburdens the supply of energy, water, transportation, and housing. Many polluting factories are located upwind, in densely populated neighborhoods, or in scenic and historic districts, further aggravating the pollution problem. Setting the industrial product mix without regard for each city's special

nature and environmental conditions makes it even harder to control pollution. Polluters located along rivers who treat water bodies as drainage ditches spread the problem of pollution further.

2. *Poor enterprise management*. Enterprise surveys reveal that 25 to 50 percent of the "three wastes' " overall volume can be attributed to resource and energy wastes arising from poor enterprise management.

3. *Backward production processes and outdated equipment*. Statistics show that 55 to 60 percent of our technology and equipment is obsolete, wasting materials and energy and then discharging large volumes of materials and energy back into the environment in the form of the three wastes, and thus are themselves sources of pollution. A survey of more than 200 enterprises in the chemical industry shows that only one-third of raw materials used in production is converted into products, while the remaining two-thirds is discarded as "three wastes" to harm the environment.

4. *Insufficient comprehensive utilization of materials and energy*. Most industrial wastes are not recovered for reuse. The industrial water recycling rate is only about 20 percent.

5. *Lack of necessary treatment measures*. Overall, 85 percent of industrial wastewater, 80 percent of industrial slag, and most industrial gaseous emissions are released back into the environment untreated.

Moreover, the large-scale development of rural and neighborhood industry has expanded the scope and intensity of pollution.

Earnestly summing up China's experiences and lessons in environmental protection and striving to avoid repetition of these kinds of mistakes in future economic and social development are key steps in ensuring the victorious advance of environmental protection work.

Comments

In this brief article Qu Geping, China's leading environmental official for many years, lectures his readers on the need for environmental protection with an extended recital of China's environmental shortcomings owing to misguided policies. Qu's remarks of necessity reveal a weak data base that is now being improved and include some scientific half-truths on subjects like climatic change. This is typical of Chinese officials who are operating on unfamiliar terrain. However, it helps them to dramatize the needs of their particular organization or policy mission in order to gain larger appropriations and political support. Qu's prescription is for improved planning to better reflect ecological and geographical conditions. Qu is head of the Environmental Protection Administration and secretary-general of the State Environmental Protection Commission.

Liu Wen (1980) "Some Remarks on Environmental Economics"

In Yu Guangyuan, et al., eds., *Lun Huanjing Guanli*, pp. 68–72. Translated in Joint Publications Research Service, *Worldwide Report: Environmental Quality*, no. 336 (February 4, 1982), pp. 20–24.

[Excerpts] The investigation and solution of environmental economic problems is attracting increasing attention. On a global scale, in the ten years since the

United Nations Environment Program held a conference on the human environment in Stockholm in 1972, observation and analysis of the changes in the human environment have made it clear that if environmental economic problems are ignored, the prospects of solving the entire human environment problem will not be encouraging.[1] This international organization has therefore determined to make "environmental economics" the number one topic in its 1981 Report on Environmental Conditions, ahead of such topics as "Utilization and Management of Renewable Resources: Underground Water" and "Toxic Chemicals and the Human Food Chain," which are usually considered more important. In China, after years of practice in environmental protection, it is also recognized with increasing clarity that environmental economics is "an important component of environmental science and an important scientific basis for effective environmental protection work."[2] Furthermore, after the 1978 National Science Conference, research topics on environmental economics have been incorporated into the national development plans for science and technology and economic science in a timely manner. All these developments indicate that in order to gain faster and better understanding of the environmental problem, people both here and abroad have made a big jump in ideological understanding and have entered a new realm in practical action as well. It is quite clear that technology and economics are the two indispensable elements in solving the environmental problem; avoiding the study and solution of the environmental economic problem is no different from abandoning the study and solution of the entire environmental problem. But even though environmental economics is so important and significant, it is, after all, only in the exploratory stage in China. In particular, if environmental economics is to become an independent academic discipline, the establishment of a complete body of theory and methodology is still awaiting the joint effort of experts, scholars, and all comrades interested in this work. In this article we present some rudimentary views on the tasks and topics in environmental economic research.

Environmental economics studies the intrinsic relationship between environment and the entire social economic process in order to protect and improve the quality of the human environment. It is an applied science belonging to the interface between natural science and social science. Its tasks are, using the basic principles of Marxist-Leninist political economy, the economics of the productive forces and dialectical materialism, and the scientific method of quantitative economics, combined with the practical experience of building China's modernization, to interpret the general economic laws of socialism as manifested in the realm of the environment and the unique economic laws in the environment; to provide the nation with a scientific basis for establishing environmental protection policies; to explore avenues and measures for protecting and improving the human environment by combining economics, technology, management, and the legal system; and to protect the health of the population and promote continued development of production in society.

In the beginning the production of items on which the human race based its existence and progress relied principally on manpower and animal power; some natural forces, such as wind and water power, were also used in fishing, hunting, and farming. Although there were threats of floods, wild animals, unpredictable weather, and onset of soil erosion, shrinking forests, and a deteriorating steppe, the effects on the environment, on the whole, were relatively minor and the conflict between development and environment was not acute. The discovery and use of coal brought changes: although, on the one hand, it greatly promoted the progress of production—for example, the transportation power of a steam locomotive burning one ton of coal is equivalent to that of a 10,000-strong labor force—on the other hand, the dust and hazardous gases, such as carbon monoxide and sulfur dioxide, generated in burning coal remain major pollutants of the environment even today. The other mineral resources subsequently developed all produced great quantities of the "three wastes"—liquid waste, gaseous waste, and solid waste—and gradually intensified the pollution of the environment. In the past few decades industrialization and urbanization have accelerated the deterioration of the environment. . . . China is a developing socialist state, and both the party and the government take environmental protection seriously. . . . On the whole, however, not only does the environmental problem in China remain unsolved, but it is not even under control; the situation continues to deteriorate. The treatment of old pollution sources is proceeding slowly and new pollution sources continue to appear; this remains a prominent problem in environmental protection. According to statistics collected in ten provinces and municipalities, including Beijing and Heilongjiang, waste water emissions in 1979 were 7 percent higher than they were in 1978 and in turn were 13 percent higher than in 1977; waste gas emissions in 1979 were 5 percent higher than they were in 1978 and, in turn, were 11 percent higher than in 1977; solid waste emissions in 1979 were 3 percent higher than they were in 1978 and, in turn, were 7 percent higher than in 1977. The fact that the three waste emissions increased annually was by no means accidental, but rather the penalty we paid for going against objective laws in our socialist construction process. If we wish to be set free of this penalty, we will have to change our customary behavior and conform to the requirements of those objective laws. This is no small step, as Comrade Mao Zedong once pointed out: "In terms of socialist construction, our entire party is inadequate in knowledge. For a period of time henceforth we should accumulate experience, work hard to learn and gradually deepen our understanding of its law through practice."[3] These laws include natural laws and economic laws.

The laws of economics are laws of economic movement. In a historical time series observation, there are laws that apply to all economic periods, several economic periods, or just one economic period; in a cross-sectional spatial observation there are laws that apply to the entire economic society, to several economic aspects, or to just one aspect of economy. The laws we wish to interpret in our study of environmental economics are only those that apply to the socialist historical period and are related to the environment. If these laws are to be used in an economic system on the environment in the era of socialism, the dominant rules, as in the entire national economy and in other fields, are still the basic economic laws of socialism.

The basic economic laws of socialism are manifested in the dialectical relationship between the development of production in society to satisfy the needs of society and the society's need to further stimulate production. In the words of Stalin, the main characteristics and requirements are to "use those methods based on high technology that make socialism continue to grow and improve in order to ensure the maximum satisfaction of the ever-growing material and cultural needs of the society."[4] This principle was proposed as a counterpart to the fundamental economic principle of capitalism, the law of surplus value. Their basic distinction is in the different goal of production. The goal of production in socialism is the maximum satisfaction of the ever-growing material and cultural needs of the entire society, and this is consistent with the goal of environmental protection. Furthermore, the people's needs can only be satisfied completely by combining the two. In other words, the needs of the people that we should satisfy are not merely the upgrading of the material and cultural enjoyment. We must also provide the people with a proper environment in which to live and work because, in the first place, a suitable environment itself is one aspect of the people's need. This point may be proved with a negative example: superior material enjoyment and colorful literature and arts notwithstanding, if a person has a terminal disease and is in extreme pain, how can his life be considered desirable and happy? Second, an agreeable environment is also an important condition for realizing the people's needs in other aspects. Engels discussed this point in his *Anti-Dühring*: "The first thing a steam engine needs, and the major need of every production department in a large industry, is clean water." The effect of an adverse environment is not limited to the pollution of industrial water; it erodes and undermines all the essential elements of production and eventually leads to the degradation of the quality and quantity of production. This invariably affects other aspects of people's lives as well. Hence creating a suitable environment for the people to live and work in is a goal of socialist production. Only when this point is clarified theoretically can we then proceed to establish scientifically the status and role of environmental protection in the entire reproduction process of the society and in the various departments of the national economy, and to promote the undertaking of the development of environmental protection in China.

Naturally, the task of studying environmental economics is not just elucidating the general economic principles of socialism and its manifestation in the environment; nor is it limited to grasping the complex and constantly varying environmental economic problems in order to sort out the particular economic principles unique to the environmental problem and encouraging people to recognize and respect these principles. More important, we must also find methods to apply these principles and help the public grasp them and conduct their affairs accordingly so that the theory can serve practice directly and be tested in practice.[5] For instance, people have recognized that the waste of resources (including energy sources) is an important cause of today's environmental pollution. According to reports, the average loss rate of mining mineral resources in China is as high as 40 to 50 percent. In addition, the waste in transportation, refining, processing, and utilization is even more alarming. One of the important causes of the waste of natural resources is the "noncompensatory" nature of their use. In order to eliminate the root cause of this wasteful phenomenon and change the use of natural resources from "noncompensatory" to compensatory, some countries are conducting research to seek solutions. Alan Cottrell, a member of the Royal Society of Great Britain, for one, believes that in order to restrict consumption and protect resources, they must be given a value in one way or another. Michel Crepeau, minister of environmental protection in the French government, went as far as to set up a "natural wealth assessment and accounting group" for this purpose. However, owing to differences in social conditions and point of view, we cannot hope to simply "import" their solutions to solve our problems. For example, Cottrell[6] believes that "in today's world conditions, the consumer value theory—including the intrinsic value of rare and scarce resources—is closer to reality than the production value theory." He even goes on to say such things as: "The economics of Marxism led to the waste of natural resources." We must insist on the precondition of Marxism-Leninism and Mao Zedong thought in the search for solutions that suit our socialist system to solve our problems.

Nevertheless, our insistence on Marxism-Leninism is by no means intended to limit ourselves to the existing books on Marxism-Leninism and to bind ourselves by some Marxist-Leninist viewpoints that are in vogue. Instead, we should liberate our thinking, explore boldly, and scientifically consolidate the new experience and new knowledge of mankind on the premise of Marxism-Leninism. . . . For example, in order to determine the value of natural resources, some of our environmental economics workers are now conducting new investigations on the Marxist-Leninist view of natural resource value. In the area of renewable resources, our comrades have published articles discussing the question of establishing a fee system for forest resources. Regarding nonrenewable resources, the Ministry of Geology briefed the central leadership on the question of mineral resource compensation, and comrades of the central leadership took this question seriously and believe that studies are necessary. Our determination of product price is made according to the requirement of the value principle and on the basis of the value. The value, in turn, is determined by the necessary labor and time the society has to spend in producing the product. For natural resources, however, if their prices are also to be determined by their value, then how will the value be determined? In our thinking, since they are naturally endowed and do not involve the labor and time of the society, their value cannot be determined on the basis of society's labor and time. Therefore, should their value be determined by their usefulness, amount of reserves, quality, distribution, the effects on the environment of their exploitation and utilization, and the degree of difficulty of preventing pollution? If so, we suggest that a "shadow price" be given to them. Then we can view the state-owned natural resources as fixed assets, and when they are developed and utilized, economic measures can then be taken to control their use and encourage conservation.

In short, to protect and improve the environment of the human race and to realize our complete rule over nature, we must strive to recognize and manage to use all the relevant objective laws. The understanding and application of economic principles and the relationship between economic laws and natural laws are fundamental tasks of our study of environmental economics.

Comments

Liu Wen is head of the Department of Environmental Economics at the Beijing Municipal Research Institute of Environmental Protection, one of the most active think tanks of its type in China, and concurrently vice-president (for economics) of the Chinese Society of Environmental Management, Economics, and Law. In this paper, presented at a conference on environmental management convened by the Society, Liu goes to considerable lengths to stress the importance of economic factors in environmental protection. The underpricing of raw materials and environmental goods by central planners was one of the most salient causes of environmental degradation in China because it encouraged waste and misuse, while discouraging replenishment. Elsewhere in this paper Liu explained that such behavior could not be condemned in the main because producers were simply following the dictates of the plan in making their production decisions. Thus two public goods, production and environmental protection, were in conflict, and it would not do to condemn or prosecute those who neglected the one in order to improve performance of the other. The need instead was for economic adjustments to signal enterprises what forms of behavior were preferred. For this purpose Liu and his associates are determined to see a more realistic pricing structure put in place on the basis of shadow prices, a familiar tool in planned economies, that would better reflect the costs of replacing natural resources and the damages caused by pollution. If China's price reforms continue to progress, however, it is conceivable that more market-oriented prices will be adopted for natural resources and environmental goods as well as other commodities. This should exert a broadly positive impact on most aspects of environmental management.

Zhou Fuxiang (1982) "Economic Policy and the Solution of Problems in Environmental Protection"

HQ, no. 13, pp. 27–30.

I

Environmental problems and economic policy are closely related. To protect the environment and natural resources while preventing pollution and other public hazards is an important principle for developing the national economy. But because this principle was not adequately carried out in earlier economic policy, China has had slow progress in terms of controlling environmental pollution and the destruction of natural resources.

Economic policy is expressed through national economic planning. The preparation of plans in the past failed to include environmental protection among the major production and economic planning norms, except for considering pollution control measures in large- and medium-scale construction projects as well as supplementary investments for pollution control in existing enterprises. The key links in capital construction, such as the distribution of industry and choice of factory locations, also were conducted without regard for environmental impacts. Because of such gaps in planning, the major aspects of the project tended to be emphasized first, while resource recovery or pollution control aspects were disregarded. With regard to natural resources, basically there was attention only to exploitation and utilization, while conservation and growth were ignored. Resource exploitation and utilization also were one-sided without regard for comprehensive approaches. Together these factors created imbalances between economic development and environmental protection.

To solve these problems, we first have to raise awareness among economic workers regarding the importance of environmental problems, treat them as an important component of the national economy, consciously coordinate relations between production and the environment, and operate according to the intrinsic, objective laws concerning environmental problems.

The environment—including natural resources like water, air, soil, flora and fauna, and minerals—is a resource that supports both human existence and social production, and thus is part of the forces of production. Social production ultimately involves drawing resources from the environment and processing them into materials needed by people for production and life. The development of production is, in large part, a function of the exploitable reserves of nonrenewable resources and the regenerative capacity of renewable resources. At the same time the production process involves consumption, as a portion of natural resources are converted into products while another portion becomes waste materials and is returned to the natural environment. Social production and consumption in this way consist of an exchange of matter and energy with the environment, enabling reproduction to develop smoothly.

So-called environmental pollution and destruction chiefly occur when (a) the rate at which social production extracts resources from the environment exceeds the rate at which resources can be renewed, reducing mineral reserves and destroying forest, soil, and water resources; and (b) the discharge of waste products exceeds the environment's assimilative capacity, polluting the air, water, and soil and disrupting the natural ecological balance. This is the natural world's revenge when economic development violates the laws of natural ecology. Environmental pollution and destruction injure human health and destroy society's renewable resource base, resulting in enormous harm to society. According to 1970s estimates from the advanced industrialized countries, social costs arising from pollution alone equal 3 to 5 percent of gross national product (GNP). This does not include the impact on production from the destruction of resources, which is far greater than the amount spent on controlling public hazards. It is not enough to treat environmental problems as merely a matter of social welfare or environmental public health because they are comprehensive problems that affect the economy, technology, and societal aspects of the national economy.

The issue of rationally utilizing economic resources is intimately related to the social system and goals of production. When analyzing the occurrence of environmental destruction in human productive endeavors, Engels noted two basic principles. First, people's knowledge of the laws of nature is inadequate, so they cannot accurately predict the near or long-term impacts of production activity on nature. Second, current production methods are the newest and most direct beneficial results of labor. In capitalist society capitalists develop production to garner maximum profits, and they only care about the most short-term and direct results without regard for rather remote natural and social impacts. They treat nature as a dumping ground for industrial wastes and wantonly plunder natural resources. As the scale of production expands, the level of environmental pollution and destruction worsens. China practices socialist economics and, as Engels said, can allow industry to spread throughout the entire country in accordance with the principles most suitable to its own development and the maintenance or development of other factors of production. When we make economic policy, so long as we focus on this problem and consciously use the planned economy to coordinate the relations between economic development and environmental protection, we can rationally develop natural resources and oppose the one-sided intensification of exploitation. If we adopt effective measures to protect the environment and natural resources in capital construction and production, we can gradually alter China's current state of pollution and environmental ruin.

How can we coordinate the relations between economic development and environmental protection?

1. Within the overall national economic balance, we must proceed by creating a larger balance between environmental protection, and production and construction. This balance encompasses (a) balance between the consumption of economic resources and their replenishment and renewability to ensure sustained resource yield; and (b) balance between the discharge of waste products and the assimilative capacity of the natural environment, to check the deterioration of environmental quality and protect the quality of human life.

2. Economic development's compliance with ecological laws should become a major component of the state's economic policy. This includes actively developing and applying no-waste, or low-waste, production processes, devising production processes that are ecologically compatible, the recovery and recycling of waste products, and so forth. Decisions concerning the geographical distribution of industry and industrial siting must include careful evaluation of environmental impacts, and production should be halted on all projects that will have major harmful impacts on the environment.

3. The upgrading of industrial technology must simultaneously consider pol-

lution control. We should eliminate or reduce the emissions of wastes and raise the utilization rate for materials and energy through technological upgrading.

4. Environmental protection norms must be included in the state plan and performance must be examined. All industrial and mining enterprises must include environmental protection in production management.

Of course, environmental protection and economic development have some contradictions. They are natural opponents, advancing together and regulating each other. Economic development necessarily creates pollution. The development and utilization of natural resources, at a specific point in time, is subject to scientific and technological limits and must inevitably deplete natural resources and destroy their reproductive capacity. Here there is a need for balancing short- and long-term interests and the interests of the part and the interests of the whole. We must sum up experiences, carry out cost-benefit analyses, and find the most economically rational coordination procedures. Meanwhile we must carry out scientific research to minimize pollution and environmental destruction.

II

Last year's [1981] State Council "Decisions on Strengthening Environmental Protection Work in the Period of National Economic Readjustment" pointed out that environmental protection work must be conducted in harmony with economic readjustment policies and measures. This is the point of departure for setting environmental policy.

Environmental pollution and destruction in construction have accumulated over a long time, so our task is rather arduous. The causes of pollution and environmental destruction, in addition to questions about ideology and economic management, include the following.

1. In most industrial and mining enterprises the level of production technology is backward, equipment is crude, the resource utilization rate is low, large volumes of valuable resources are not fully utilized and are instead regarded as waste products causing pollution. Looking at energy, the energy utilization coefficient is less than 30 percent, while the volume of smoke and dust emitted is many times greater than in other countries. The raw materials utilization rate in many chemical industry products is only 3:1. The consumption of water and electricity for many products runs many times higher than abroad. In agriculture the effectiveness of farm chemicals and chemical fertilizers is low, with only 14 to 15 percent of the benzahex [benzene hexachloride (666)] pesticide that is applied being effectively used, while the inefficient remainder poses the most danger to man and livestock. Moreover, most of the farm chemicals and chemical fertilizers applied on farms runs off into the environment, causing serious pollution.

2. The pollution danger is exacerbated by the disregard for urban planning and the geographically irrational distribution of industry. Some heavily polluting factories are located in densely populated and scenic or historically significant areas, or upstream of water intakes. For example, Suzhou, with a history of

2,400 years and home of gardens and ancient walls, has almost 500 factories crowded into an area of 28 kilometers. Moreover, twenty-one heavily polluting chemical plants are located in the urban district itself, ten printing and dyeing plants are in the city center, and three paper mills are upstream of water sources, resulting in a chaotic situation where residential, industrial, and scenic neighborhoods are jumbled together, clustering smokestacks and pagodas alongside each other. This seriously damages the natural ambience of this southern city located in a land of rivers and lakes.

3. Municipal infrastructure is backward. Fewer than half of 224 cities within the country are served by sewer systems. There are only thirty-seven sewage treatment plants in urban areas and less than 2 percent of urban wastewater is treated. The remaining 98 percent is discharged untreated, reducing fish populations and impairing the quality of drinking water. There are too few thermal power plants or town gas plants in large and medium-sized cities. The continuing increase in urban population and growth of cities has enhanced the dangers of urban air, water, and noise pollution.

4. Natural resources are destroyed and, moreover, environmental quality is adversely impacted by the environmental destruction caused by the irrational exploitation and utilization of natural resources, for example, chaotic mining practices, water conservancy projects constructed without regard for multiple uses, the blind enclosure and reclamation of lakes, groundwater mining, and overlogging.

In order to solve these problems we must go beyond raising knowledge and adopting essential management measures because we also need definite economic and material capacity. China's environmental protection must be based on reality by concentrating strength, using plans, focusing on key points, and proceeding by stages and categories. We cannot propose targets that exceed China's objective possibilities at the present moment; nor can we solely control already polluted environments or promote pollution treatment measures. This approach is both too expensive and too slow. We must combine environmental protection with enterprise reorganization and strengthened management and put an end to the spread of pollution by man-made causes. We must integrate our effort with the upgrading of technology to control the occurrence of pollution at its source. We must combine this with urban construction and renewal and adjust the irrational structure and geographical distribution of industry. We must combine environmental protection with the rational utilization of natural resources to sustain their regenerative capacity, and we must stress the preservation of ecological balance. In the course of economic development we must gradually improve the environment and promote sustainable economic development by protecting and improving the environment.

III

Environmental protection involves all departments, industries, and enterprises. The state shapes policy to lead departments and enterprises to consider the needs of environmental protection when conducting their own operations. In addition to studying macro environmental policy, from the micro side we also must study technical economic policies to prevent and control pollution and protect the natural environment, to gain the greatest environmental and economic benefit for the lowest cost.

Pollution Control Policy for Industrial and Mining Enterprises

Industrial and mining enterprises are the keypoints for pollution control. We must change the old approach of simply regulating already polluted environments by linking up with technological renovation to strengthen environmental management at the enterprise level, and eliminate or reduce the discharge of pollutants in the production process. This will help to control pollution at its source as well as increase economic returns and societal wealth. Pollution was bad at the Shanghai Gaoqiao Chemical Plant. Prior to 1978 they spent more than 3 million yuan to build four sets of wastewater treatment facilities but were still able to treat only 8 percent of the plant's industrial wastewater. After 1978 they strengthened management and made micro-level reforms, raising the plant's industrial wastewater treatment rate to 86 percent. Moreover, they recovered 2,000 tons of chemical raw materials and products from the wastewater each year valued at 3,400,000 yuan.

What policies can environmental departments apply to induce enterprises to combine production with pollution control? The Shenyang Chemical Industry Bureau carried out a policy of total effluent control in some plants on an experimental basis, conducting individual analyses of the production process for each product, calculating materials balances, and then setting overall pollution control targets for the enterprise. The experimental points show that this control policy can make the enterprise set control targets in terms of management, equipment, and technology for pollutants at every stage of the production process, and thus closely combine production management and environmental protection at the enterprise level. This experience must be further summed up, perfected, and disseminated.

Policy for Natural Resources Utilization and Protection

For a long time people regarded natural resources as an inexhaustible source of cost-free wealth and exploited them ruthlessly, resulting in an extreme waste of resources. I feel that environmental pollution actually consists of the consumption of air, water, and other resources, and so the polluter must assume the economic burden of rehabilitating the environment which he has polluted. In order to protect water, mineral, forest, and similar resources, the developers and users cannot exploit the resources free of charge, but must assume the costs of exploring for new resources and regenerating renewable resources. We can consider imposing a resource conservation tax or a mandatory resource renewability fund. The good points of such a policy are as follows: (a) it can prevent rapacious exploitation; (b) the rise in price for raw materials can induce the recycling of waste materials; and (c) it favors the regeneration of renewable resources. In recent years some cities have been collecting groundwater usage fees. With regard to surface water, some have imposed usage norms, with higher charges for above-norm consumption. Together these measures have strongly encouraged water conservation among enterprises, thereby protecting water resources.

Air Pollution Control Policy

In the past we relied primarily on upgrading boilers. The cities spent a good deal of money and achieved some results, but the results were really not too impressive in terms of the urban environment as a whole. In recent years some scientists and technical people have favored changing the fuel mix to solve the air pollution problem. China's resource inventory, however, dictates that coal will continue to be the principal fuel for a long time to come. Therefore, in the short term, it is not feasible to change the fuel mix or build thermal power plants or town gas plants on a large scale to improve air quality.

During the period of readjustment China's air pollution control policy should be predicated on fully raising the rate of efficient utilization for existing energy sources. There is enormous potential in this regard, including giving residential users first priority for supplies of low-sulfur and low-volatility coal, fully utilizing factories' surplus heat, linking boilers in series for heating, and rationally utilizing natural gas. If we can raise our energy utilization rate from the current 35 percent level to 50 percent, as in Japan, that would be equivalent to saving hundreds of millions of tons of coal, thereby reducing coal dust emissions by millions of tons and measurably reducing air pollution.

Fushun is an industrial city which wastes a great amount of energy. If the energy utilization rate there could be raised to 50 percent, coal consumption would be reduced by 1.1 million tons annually, with attendant benefits for Fushun's air quality. In recent years Fushun has integrated air pollution control with conservation, utilizing excess heat and recycling combustible gases in a big way, generating heat from power plants and industrial surplus heat, is currently constructing a system to use recycled water from power plants for district heating, and is getting ready to recover high heat value exhaust gases from oil refineries and mine shafts for residential use to basically eliminate smoke from cooking. After these measures are in place, hundreds of thousands of tons of coal will be saved and air pollution will be substantially reduced.

Water Pollution Control Policy

Quite a few scientists and technical people favor building wastewater treatment plants to reduce river pollution, but because such plants are expensive to build and industrial and residential wastewater cannot be separated, it is hard to obtain the ideal operating efficiency. Therefore, it is unrealistic to depend on the construction of large numbers of wastewater treatment plants to reduce river pollution during the period of readjustment. Many local surveys confirm that the causes of river pollution go beyond the discharge of sewage from industrial and residential sources in cities, and involve the reduction in streamflow.

For example, the discoloration and smell of the Huangpu River in Shanghai, pollution of the Songhua River in Jilin during the low-water season, and the increase in pollution of Suzhou's canals are all clearly related to the reduction in streamflow. The explanation for the decline in streamflow is complex but primarily involves excessive agricultural usage. Therefore, water pollution control policy cannot be based exclusively on treating pollution, but must be combined with the rational utilization of water resources—constituting rational utilization and comprehensive control through a unified plan. The utilization of water resources affects industrial, agricultural, transportation, and aquatic products departments and often transcends geographical boundaries, making it imperative that the government organize regional development or river valley-based plans to solve the problem in a unified fashion. With regard to reducing water pollution, the key term is water conservation. If industry institutes closed-cycle recycling on a large scale, raising the recycling rate, the rate of water consumption per unit product will decline by several fold to advanced [country] levels, and at the same time valuable resources can be recovered from the water before it is discharged.

Economic policy is the key step in environmental management. In recent years China has devised a policy to reward comprehensive utilization, and many provinces and cities have experimentally instituted a system of effluent fees for pollution in excess of state standards and fines for pollution incidents. The results of these trials demonstrated that these economic policies exert a decided stimulative role with regard to pollution control by enterprises, so we must enthusiastically sum up and disseminate these experiences. As the national economic reforms proceed in the future with an expansion of enterprise autonomy, we must study economic policy with regard to environmental protection at the same time that we practice environmental planning and management, in order to encourage enterprises to control pollution more actively and correctly handle the relations between the interests of the enterprise on the one hand and those of the state and the people on the other, to ensure that economic development and environmental protection advance in conjunction with each other.

Comments

This article, published in the Communist party's leading ideological journal, stands out for the extent to which it attributes pollution to inefficiency and then, in turn, prescribes economic instruments like resource consumption taxes and effluent fees as spurs to greater efficiency. Although written from the standpoint of a defender of the planning regime, its indictment of past deficiencies, coupled with recommendations for the future, indicates the extent to which planning has been redefined in the shape of the looser, more indicative process, relying more heavily on rational prices and economic levers. The article is also insistent, however, that the state will not spend nearly as much on environmental protection as most experts consider necessary, given the state of degradation in China.

3

Legal Overview

BASIC PRINCIPLES OF CHINA'S ENVIRONMENTAL LAW

Ma Xiangcong (1979) "Preliminary Discussion on the Law of Environmental Protection"

Faxue Yanjiu, no. 2, pp. 40–43. Translation, with permission, from *Chinese Law and Government*, vol. 19, no. 1 (1986), pp. 30–40.

THE EMERGENCE AND DEVELOPMENT OF ENVIRONMENTAL LAW

Scattered provisions of the law on environmental protection existed in ancient countries. For instance, China's Qin Code included provisions forbidding cutting lumber in mountain forests in spring, blocking up waterways, burning grass for fertilizer before the summer, picking budding plants, poaching young animals, birds' eggs, and young birds, killing fish and turtles by poison, and so on. To deal with smoke pollution, the British Parliament issued a proclamation in 1306, forbidding artisans and manufacturers to use coal when Parliament was in session. After the Industrial Revolution the problem of industrial pollution emerged. A number of industrialized countries enacted individual laws and decrees to deal with industrial pollution. For example, Britain promulgated its first Alkali Act in 1863,[7] the Rivers Pollution Prevention Act in 1876,[8] and the Public Health Smoke Abatement Act in 1926.[9] It was only after the 1960s, however, that the law of environmental protection gradually took shape as an independent branch of law. As a result of the scientific and technological revolution, industry in many countries, particularly the synthetic chemical industry, developed swiftly, the scale of production increased sharply, natural resources were grossly abused, the environment was ever more seriously polluted and disrupted by industry, ecology became unbalanced, general environmental pollution occurred in many countries, and a series of pollution incidents took place. For example, 4,000 persons died in four days in the poisonous fog incident that occurred in London in December 1952; tens of thousands of persons in Kyushu, Japan, were poisoned by eating rice bran oil containing poison in 1968. The serious pollution and ravage of the environment greatly jeopardized the health and life of the people and hampered the advance of industry and agriculture. Consequently, many countries had to adopt different scientific, technological, and economic measures to protect and improve the environment. To realize the aim of protecting the environment, a country must resort to legal devices to readjust various relations concerning environmental protection activities. Since the late 1950s many countries have successively enacted large numbers of laws and regulations on environmental protection. The law of environmental protection has gradually developed into an independent branch of law. . . .

The development of the environmental protection laws of many countries over the past two decades points to the following characteristics and tendencies:

1. All countries with developed industry and a sound legal system have rather perfect environmental protection laws. In addition to the institution of many specialized laws and decrees on environmental protection[10] in accordance with the objects of protection (e.g., land, water, the atmosphere, forest, grasslands, wildlife and plants, scenic spots) and the objects of control (e.g., noise, vibration, foul smell, radioactive materials, waste oil, refuse, land subsidence), quite a few countries have enacted comprehensive environmental protection laws to make all-around adjustment of environmental protection activities. Examples are Japan's Fundamental Pollution Control Law,[11] Bulgaria's Nature Protection Law of 1976,[12] the U.S. National Environmental Policy Act of 1969,[13] . . . Rumania's Environmental Protection Law of 1973,[14] and Hungary's Law on the Protection of the Human Environment of 1976.[15] Furthermore, more than a few countries have included provisions on environmental protection in their constitutions, elevating it to the high plane of constitutional protection.

2. The scope of the objects of legal protection has been expanding. Prior to the 1950s the objects of protection stipulated by law in many countries were merely natural objects with special scientific, cultural, or historical value, such as endangered animals and plants, rare natural vistas, and particular sites. The method adopted was often the demarcation of nature reserves and banning or restricting of economic activity therein. Although some countries provided for protection of land, water, forests, minerals, and other natural resources, the provisions were simple and only a few stipulations dealt with pollution by industries and refuse accumulated in people's daily lives. Since the late 1950s the laws of various countries have extended the scope of protection to land, atmosphere, water, forests, grassland, minerals, wildlife and plants, other natural resources, and the entire natural environment of the country as well as the naturalized environment created by man's own labor, such as canals, reservoirs, man-made forests, scenic spots, and historical relics. Some countries have listed cities and residential areas as special objects of protection. Meanwhile the manner and content of protection have been greatly enriched, with the stress laid on rational utilization and conservation of natural resources in the course of their exploitation, including enhancement of their regenerative capacity; the prevention

and control of pollution and the disruption of natural resources and environment by industrial discharges and refuse accumulated in people's daily lives; and the comprehensive control of pollution and protection of the environment.

3. Improve the environmental control system and strengthen environmental control. First, clearly define the tasks and duties of state organs at all levels and the duties, rights, and obligations of various enterprises and undertakings. Second, set up unified, special environmental protection organizations. For example, the United States set up the Council on Environmental Quality in 1969 as an advisory agency for the President and in 1970 established the Environmental Protection Agency as an executive organ of the government. Britain established the Department of the Environment in 1970. In 1970 France formed the Supreme Environment Committee, which has an advisory, coordinating, and supervisory nature, and in 1971 it set up the Ministry for the Protection of Nature and the Environment. Japan established its Environment Agency in 1971. In 1974 Hungary set up the National Environment Protection Committee as a coordinating, supervisory, and advisory organ, and in 1977 it set up the National Environment and Nature Protection Bureau as an executive organ. Rumania also has established an Environmental Protection Committee. There is a growing trend to stress the duties of all levels of state organs, enterprises, undertakings, and social organizations in the field of environmental protection as well as the need to set up sound, unified, specialized control organizations for environmental protection.

4. Environmental protection is a common problem facing all countries. In many cases it involves common interests that transcend the boundaries of states. Moreover, the relations between human society and nature are, to a great extent, decided by the objective laws of natural development. For these reasons there are many common grounds between various countries in environmental protection. Broad prospects exist for various countries to learn from one another's experience and lessons and enter into international cooperation.

ENACTING A SET OF CHINESE LAWS ON ENVIRONMENTAL PROTECTION IS A PRESSING TASK

Since the founding of the People's Republic of China, the Chinese Communist party and government have done much work in environmental protection. This includes work in the areas of land protection, soil improvement, and the transformation of deserts; taming the Huang (Yellow), Huai, and Hai rivers, dredging navigation routes and building water conservation projects; protecting forests and afforestation; preventing and controlling plant diseases and insect pests and eliminating locust plagues; restoring dirty, old cities; selecting a number of nature reserves to protect rare animals, plants, and natural landscapes and natural areas. The state has successively promulgated a number of rules and regulations, such as Measures Governing Land Requisition for National Reconstruction (1953),[16] Provisional Measures on Highway Afforestation (1956),[17] Provisional Program for Water and Soil Conservation (1957),[18] Experimental Measures for the Inspection of Domestically Grown Plants for Contagious Diseases (1957),[19] Regulations Governing the Safety of Drinking Water (1959),[20] and Regulations on Forest Protection (1963).[21]

With the growth of industry, the party and government raised the issue of preventing and controlling industrial pollution and comprehensive use of natural resources. In 1956, when the late Premier Zhou Enlai inspected the Anshan Iron and Steel Company, he gave the instruction that the work of ''removing the dust'' must be done well. In view of the lessons of environmental pollution in capitalist countries in the course of their industrial development, Premier Zhou stressed time and again in the early 1970s that it was necessary to do environmental protection work well while engaging in industrial construction. In 1972 the State Council put forward the principle of ''comprehensive planning and rational resource allocation, multiple use and the conversion of harmful substances to beneficial uses, reliance on the masses and collective action, protecting the environment and enrichment of the people's life.'' The first National Environmental Protection Conference convened in 1973, and a series of projects were carried out, including the establishment of environmental protection organizations at all levels and the formulation of the Regulations Concerning Environmental Protection and Improvement (tentative draft)[22] and the Provisional Regulations of the People's Republic of China on the Prevention of Pollution of Coastal Waters (1974).[23] However, the disturbance and sabotage of Lin Biao and the ''Gang of Four'' greatly affected work in environmental protection.

After the overthrow of the ''Gang of Four,'' the party and government attached great importance to the question of environmental protection. The General Principles of the Constitution adopted by the Fifth National People's Congress stipulates that ''the state protects the environment and natural resources and prevents and remedies pollution and other public hazards.'' In his report on government work delivered at the Congress, Comrade Hua Guofeng pointed out that ''to eliminate pollution and protect the environment is an important undertaking having a bearing on the health of the masses; we must attach great importance to this matter and work out decrees and regulations for environmental protection to ensure practical solution of problems in this connection.'' This is the urgent task set us by the party and the government. The decision to shift the stress of work to socialist modernization adopted at the third plenary session of the party's Eleventh Central Committee demands that we step up our tempo of work in this respect.

1. The enactment of the law of environmental protection is necessary for socialist modernization. To carry out socialist modernization, develop the national economy at a high speed, and promote broad and deep production, it is necessary to [follow the principles of] comprehensive planning and rational resource allocation and protection, facilitate their regeneration, prevent the disruption of ecological equilibrium, prevent pollution and other public hazards caused by industrial and agricultural production, and, when such hazards are unavoidable, adopt positive measures to bring them under control. Otherwise,

the progress of events will violate the basic purpose of socialist modernization and genuine socialist modernization will not be achievable. This is because pollution jeopardizes the health of the workers and staff, corrodes and damages factory buildings, equipment, materials, and products, affects their use value, increases production costs, and even brings about suspension of production. Pollution and disruption of the environment also leads to depletion of natural resources and brings disaster to agriculture, forestry, fishery, animal husbandry, and the entire national economy. We have paid a price in this respect and must make up our minds to solve this problem in a satisfactory way. While taking other measures, we must work out through legislative procedures all kinds of detailed regulations, set up various systems, and make conscientious efforts to readjust various relationships in regard to environmental protection.

2. The enactment of the law of environmental protection is necessary for the protection of people's health. China is a socialist state under the dictatorship of the proletariat, and all its activities are directed at benefiting the people. Article 11 of the [1978] Constitution of China provides that the state shall develop the national economy at a high speed, steadily increase the social productive forces, and gradually improve the people's material and cultural life. [Article 26 of the 1978] Constitution also requires that "the state protect the environment and natural resources and prevent and remedy pollution and other public hazards." Thus it solemnly proclaims that protection of the environment and natural resources is an important task of the state and an important component of the development of the national economy and improvement of the people's material and cultural life. To this end we must enact a series of laws and regulations to ensure its realization and ensure that the people will enjoy clean and good living and working conditions. China still does not have a developed industry, but the pollution of the natural environment, including the air, water, and land as well as the pollution of crops and foodstuffs, has become serious and is jeopardizing the people's health. The law and jurisprudence must play appropriate roles in changing this state of affairs.

3. The enactment of the law of environmental protection is necessary for running the economic activities of the state according to objective laws, maintaining ecological balance, and benefiting our posterity. Nature provides man with the place, conditions, and living materials for existence. Therefore, man must love nature, protect and improve his living conditions and integrate immediate interests with long-term interests. This is the objective law of interaction of human society and natural environment. Speaking of the dialectical relations between land utilization and land protection, Marx said: "Even the whole society, a nation, and all the existing societies put together are not owners of the land. They are merely the occupants and users of the land, and like a good patriarch, they must improve the land before handing it down to posterity."[24] Engels also offered the advice that we must not deal with nature as "the conquerors rule over alien nations," but must "learn how to understand the natural laws more

correctly and how to know the more immediate or long-range effect of our intervention in the habitual course of nature.''[25] Otherwise, we shall suffer from the revenge of nature.

It is particularly noteworthy that in some places in our country there are still numerous practices that go against natural laws. Wanton destruction of forests for land reclamation, opening up grasslands for cultivation, reclaiming land from lakes and sea, reckless hunting of wild animals, and collection of wild plants have gravely ravaged forests, grasslands, wildlife and plants, and natural resources such as water and minerals, created ecological imbalance in some areas, and brought about serious consequences. Take Heilongjiang Province for instance. With the Greater and Lesser Xingan Mountains for shelter, crops in the province suffered no drought in the past. But in the past few years wanton tree felling has resulted in dwindling forests and cases of drought have occurred. As a result of the reclamation of grasslands, 1.2 million hectares of land in the Yikezhao Banner of the Inner Mongolia Autonomous Region have been desertified. Wind and sand have pressed in on Beijing because grassland and forest vegetation in vast areas of the Northwest have been seriously ravaged. Unless we take effective measures to deal with this situation, serious ecological crises will be created, thus passing disasters on to future generations. We must do things according to the objective laws of interaction between human society and nature, legalize ecological requirements, and carry them out in all our economic activities and related work so as to maintain ecological balance and safeguard the interests of posterity.

EXPLORATION OF THE CONTENT OF LEGISLATION FOR ENVIRONMENTAL PROTECTION

The legislation of environmental protection has rich content and involves a wide scope. Environmental protection covers the protection of water, air, land, forests, grasslands, minerals, wild animals and plants, scenic and tourist areas, and other natural environments on which man's survival depends so that they are not polluted and disrupted by production wastes, foul smell, radioactive materials, radiomagnetic waves, refuse produced in people's daily lives, and other harmful materials; rational utilization of natural resources and ensuring their regeneration as well as prevention and control of noise, vibration, land subsidence, and other public hazards. All these activities and related social relations must be regulated by law. It is necessary to enact at the earliest date a comprehensive law of environmental protection to specify legally the objects, guidelines, policies, and basic principles of environmental protection; the duties, rights, and obligations of state organs at all levels, enterprises, organizations, and citizens in environmental protection; the fundamental requirements and basic measures for preventing and controlling pollution and protecting the environment and natural resources; and the system of environmental protection organizations and the legal responsibilities to be assumed when environmental protection laws are violated. On this basis a series of necessary special laws and detailed regulations of implementation can be worked out, such as the air protection law, water protection law, noise control law, land law, grasslands law, minerals law, marine law, and wildlife and plant protection law. Furthermore, corresponding laws of environmental protection should also be included in other related substantive and procedural laws.

We should draw on the good experience of other countries, but more important, we should value and sum up our own experience to enact a set of environmental protection laws that conform to the conditions of our country. In our view, the emphasis should be laid on the following areas.

1. Include the tasks of environmental protection in the national economic plan. The long-term planning and annual plan of the national economy should include environmental protection and specific targets; various localities, departments, factories and mines, and people's communes should include the tasks of environmental protection in their corresponding plans; all authorities, from the central down to the local levels, should make concrete arrangements and give assurances for the provision of funds, equipment, materiél, and labor for environmental protection. Only in this way can environmental protection work acquire a reliable basis and become an element in appraising the work of various enterprises and units.

2. Define the duties, limits of authority, rights, and obligations of all levels of state organs, organizations, enterprises, undertakings, and people's communes as well as environmental protection organizations at all levels in regard to environmental protection. It is necessary to understand the principle of "the polluter must control his own pollution" in a broad sense. Not only should an enterprise or undertaking be responsible for remedying the pollution it has created, but the higher level organization in charge should also be held responsible for the pollution and for environmental protection.

3. Strict measures must be taken against cases of serious pollution of the environment and exploitation of natural resources, and in some cases legal responsibilities should be investigated and affixed. The laws of various countries are placing greater stress on such responsibilities and are rigorously demanding compensation for losses, imposing fines, and investigating the criminal responsibility [of alleged offenders]. We should also adopt legislative measures to ensure that the losses caused by pollution and disruption of the environment will be directly linked to the vital interests of the pollution-causing units as well as their leading officials, persons directly involved, and workers and staff, and see to it that the measures be institutionalized. The law should provide that compensation for environmental pollution should not be included in production costs, and that investigations into economic, administrative, and even criminal responsibility be instituted against those responsible for the incidents. In addition, the law should provide for the procedures for handling such cases by the law enforcement agencies.

4. It is necessary to define the ways and means by which the masses of people and various social organizations participate in environmental protection activities

and carry out social supervision. Environmental protection is an undertaking for the whole people, and everybody must take a hand in it. A corresponding system should be set up legally to encourage and ensure their participation. It should be pointed out that it is certainly important to institute a perfect law of environmental protection, but it is also important to abide by and strictly enforce the law. While stepping up the effort to enact the environmental protection law, we must also increase education in the legal system to ensure that the law is observed and strictly enforced and that those who break the law are punished in the struggle to create a clean and good environment.

Comments

Ma Xiangcong of the Institute of Law of the Chinese Academy of Social Sciences herein justified the need for an Environmental Protection Law months before its promulgation in the fall of 1979. Ma based the need for such a law on the experiences of more advanced countries, primarily those with capitalist systems. Ma also implied that the Environmental Protection Law would serve as a basic law to govern forestry and other laws which had heretofore enjoyed a more autonomous existence. His concern primarily involved establishing a legal and more comprehensive policy structure in the post-Mao era, in contrast to the arbitrary and noncomprehensive policies of earlier years which had contributed to environmental degradation. Ma pays rather little attention to jurisprudence per se, although he argues that investigation of legal responsibility and awarding of compensation are essential instruments in environmental protection.

Song Qiping and Shao Boding (1984) "A Brief Talk on the Status and Fundamental Principles of the Environmental Protection Law of China"

ZHK, no. 3, pp. 45–49.

The status and basic principles of environmental law within China's socialist legal structure have been frequently discussed theoretical questions within Chinese environmental law studies in recent years. Correct understanding of these issues is needed both in environmental law education and in order to complete and strengthen the socialist legal system within environmental protection work.

I

The issue of environmental law's status in China's socialist legal structure really is a question of whether environmental law can be considered an independent branch of the law in China. There are differences of opinion on this issue. Those who hold an affirmative view clearly note that environmental law is an independent branch of the law. This perspective is mostly found in teaching materials at major schools. Although those who hold a negative view do not clearly deny that environmental law is an independent branch of the law, they have various ways of indirectly arguing that environmental law is not an independent branch, but rather is subordinate to other branches of the law. Some people say that environmental law ought to belong under administrative law because environmental protection's first order of business is strengthening environmental management, and management is always in a subordinate relationship. Other people say that environmental protection's basic goal is to protect the people's physical health. Because man and labor are inseparable, it is possible that environmental law should be included in labor law's structure. Indeed, the May 1980 volume *Selected Documents in Labor Protection* [*Laodong Baohu Wenjian Xuanbian*, eds.],[26] jointly edited by the All China Federation of Trade Unions, the State General Bureau of Labor, and the Ministry of Public Health, included a series of environmental laws, such as the Environmental Protection Law, Public Health Standards for Industrial Enterprise Design,[27] and Management Procedures for the Protection of Public Health in Work Involving Radioactive Isotopes.[28] This further intensified the viewpoint held by some people that environmental law is part of labor law.

Others feel that people are the ultimate victims of environmental pollution and destruction. Because the volume of litigation involving the clearing of obstructions or compensation for damages owing to environmental pollution is steadily rising, environmental law therefore must belong to civil law. There also are many people who look to Article 3 of the Environmental Law: "The term environment used in this law encompasses the air, water, land, mineral resources, forests, grasslands, wild plants and animals, aquatic life, places of historical interest, scenic spots, hot springs, resorts, and natural areas under special protection as well as inhabited parts of the country." Obviously, the environment encompasses natural resources and is an important component of socialist economic construction. Therefore, it is more appropriate to include environmental law under economic law. The section on economic law in Part One of *Faxue Cidian* [Dictionary of Legal Terminology], published in the post-Liberation period, clearly noted that economic law "generally incorporates industrial and agricultural management, the conservation of natural resources, environmental protection . . . "[29] Also, *Jingji Faxue* [The Study of Economic Law], published in May 1983, not only assigns a special section to "The Environmental Protection Legal System," but also states that "economic law coordinates many socioeconomic relationships that civil law cannot adjust such as economic relations under the plan, economic relations involving the management of environmental protection . . . , etc."[30] That is to say, the authors of this book place environmental law outside civil law and under economic law.

We feel that environmental law in China is a vitally important and independent branch of the law within the socialist legal structure. This conclusion was reached for many reasons.

First, for environmental law to become an independent branch of the law is an inevitable tendency in Chinese social development and is objectively determined by current socioeconomic circumstances. We know that all legal standards develop and are gradually perfected in the course of the social development of class society. Regardless of whether it was under slave or feudal society, in Chinese history all legal standards were mixed together in the same pot. There were no distinctions between criminal, civil, and marriage law, or between public and private law, let alone an independent environmental law. Environmental law did not become an integrated political concept and novel, independent branch of the law until after the surge in modern production, especially when people became aware of the pollution visited on the environment by modern production increases.

For example, China's industrial foundation in the early post-Liberation period was extremely weak. Although there was pollution to a certain degree at that time, it was quickly broken down by nature's own self-assimilative capacity. But China's industrial production has undergone an enormous transformation in the ensuing thirty plus years. In terms of the Sixth Five-Year Plan's targets for the national economy and social development, by 1985 the output of electricity will reach 362 billion kilowatt-hours, or 33.5 times 1954 output [output actually reached 370 billion kilowatt-hours in 1984, thus surpassing the target]; coal production will total 700 million tons, equal to 8.5 times 1954 output [by 1984 output reached 789 million tons]; steel production will total 39 million tons equal to 18 times 1954 output [output exceeded 43 million tons in 1984]; pig iron production will total 35 million tons, equal to 11.5 times 1954 output [production totalled 40 million tons in 1984]; concrete production will total 98 million tons, equal to 21 times 1954 output [production reached 123 million tons in 1984]; and pulp production will total 6 million tons, equal to 12.5 times 1954 output [this target seems to have been out of reach as production totalled only 5.14 million tons in 1984].

The general trend in industrial production has been movement from weakness to strength and from scarcity to availability. China now already has built an independent and rather comprehensive industrial structure. However, industry's rapid development took place without regard for prevention and control, resulting in terrible environmental pollution. Therefore, effective protection and improvement of the environment and placing environmental protection work on the socialist legal track are crucial strategic decisions and are necessitated by current economic and social development. Our conclusion is that the development of modernization requires environmental protection and environmental protection law. Moreover, Comrade Deng Xiaoping's remarks, such as "We must concentrate on enacting criminal and civil codes, procedural laws and . . . laws concerning . . . environmental protection,"[31] and the convening of the party's Third Plenum [December 1978], where it was emphasized that we must strengthen socialist democracy and the socialist legal system, further created favorable political conditions for environmental law to become an independent branch of the law.

Second, for environmental law to become an independent branch of the law is quite consistent with the goals of Chinese socialist production. The basic goal of socialist production is, in the words of Stalin, to "use technologically advanced measures to enable socialist production to continuously expand and become more perfect in order to ensure the maximal satisfaction of society's ever-expanding material and spiritual needs."[32] The environment, which includes natural resources, is part of the material base for socialist production and is a vital organic component of the process of building socialist modernization in which we are now engaged. Protecting the environment conserves the supply bases for all the raw materials needed in socialist production. It is naturally consistent with the goals of socialist production. We must also point out that the basic purpose of environmental protection is not merely the conservation of natural resources, but, more important, the protection of the masses' physical well-being. Therefore, we can definitely say that the emergence of environmental law is needed by the people and is their wish. As Marx said, it is a "conscious reflection of the people's will" and it "is formed along with the people's will and was created by the will of the people."[33]

Third, environmental law has already climbed on to the stage of social life and has a definite regulatory objective. This is to regulate the social relations that arise while protecting and improving the environment. This [goal] is not the same as economic law. It has already been more than 200 years since the French utopian socialist Voltaire presented the concept of "economic law" in 1755 in *On Natural Law*. However, its precise definition is still subject to widely varying interpretations around the world, and its status in different countries can be poles apart. The primary reason for this is that it lacks a clear or definable regulatory objective. Environmental law is quite different because it has a clear and positive regulatory objective. In this respect environmental law in the future will have a definite status in the legal structure relative to economic law.

Finally, environmental law's internal characteristics qualify it as an independent branch of the law:

1. Environmental pollution and destruction of the ecological balance ultimately amount to a threat and hazard to human health. Strict enforcement of environmental law directly benefits human health.

2. Environmental law is closely related to natural science. Rapid advances in modern science and technology bind together the social and natural sciences. Because environmental law is a social science, it is permeated with natural science. Natural science not only permeates particular environmental protection laws, but also colors the basic law in environmental protection. Various legal provisions reveal the organic melding together of social and natural science.

3. Environmental law rather obviously manifests society's public rights and interests. There are many victims when the environment is polluted and ecological balance is destroyed. Some pollutants have long incubation periods and are persistent, some creating hazards for generations to come. Some forms of pollution—air, stream, and marine—also can transcend national boundaries.

4. Environmental law is closely bound up with economic development because "production is the most practical activity."[34] Mankind continuously develops the economy through production, distribution, exchange, and consumption. Yet all of these activities impact on the environment and are influenced, in turn, by the environment. Therefore, many countries around the world regard environmental protection as the foundation and as an important aspect of economic development. Just like other branches of the law, environmental law originates in the economic life of society, but it has an even more direct and visible relationship with economic development.

5. Environmental law has a broad scope in terms of regulatory objects, the subject to be protected, and targets of prevention and control. Within a country it includes all sovereign territory, coastal waters, and airspace. For the world as a whole it touches on the entire globe and surrounding outer space. In terms of the social relations regulated by environmental law, they seem to touch every sector and individual in society. No other branch of the law has such a wide reach yet.

6. Environmental law is relatively stable and enduring in comparison with other branches of the law, especially in terms of [ambient] environmental standards, emissions standards, monitoring procedures, and analytical formulas. It has already been proven that in real life, under normal conditions, environmental law does not fluctuate in response to leftward or rightward shifts in social and political movements or changes in the ranks of the leadership. For example, we can say that the August 1973 "Some Regulations on Protecting and Improving the Environment"[35] was the model for the Environmental Protection Law of September 1979, with much of the former absorbed into the latter.

7. When investigating people's legal responsibilities, environmental law goes beyond traditional criminal and civil law. For example, most countries have a provision requiring the complainant in criminal cases to assume the responsibility for presenting evidence that a crime has taken place. A party must provide the justification when he defends his rights in civil cases. This is what is commonly referred to as the complainant's burden of proof. But in many countries the responsibility for presenting evidence in environmental law has begun to shift, or will shift, to the defendant. Similarly, the principle of responsibility for unintentional acts requires that a person's behavior be illegal, that harm must have arisen intentionally or unintentionally, and that there must be a causal relationship with regard to the intentional or unintentional harm, in order to charge someone with legal responsibility. This ancient principle passed down from Roman law seems to have been adopted by every country in the world. Some countries, however, when investigating legal responsibility under environmental law, have begun to apply the principle of implicit, strict liability, which departs from Roman legal conventions and carves out a new path. Although Chinese environmental law still lacks clear provisions on these two points, as a socialist country we must protect the masses' fundamental rights and interests. Therefore, we can anticipate an

inevitable movement with regard to shifting the burden of proof and applying the principle of strict liability.

These characteristics of environmental law in some or all respects are not found in other branches of the law. Therefore, environmental law cannot be subsumed by any other branch of the law. There can be only one conclusion: environmental law is an independent branch of the law.

II

The basic principles of environmental law are the guiding thoughts and behavioral criteria for formulating and implementing environmental law. They express the socialist nature of Chinese environmental law and distinguish it from environmental law in capitalist countries. Therefore, it is a vitally important, fundamental issue in Chinese legal studies. However, there are rather sharp differences on this vital issue. Some comrades feel that the basic principles of Chinese environmental law are "protecting the environment to benefit the people," "making overall plans and taking all factors into consideration," "combining prevention and control with prevention as the leading factor," "comprehensive planning, rational geographic distribution, and turning the harmful into the good," and "combining rewards and punishment." Other comrades include among the basic principles of environmental law "making plans to actively control existing sources of pollution. We must control, upgrade, merge, transform, or limit and, when necessary, suspend, shut down, or relocate operations which are very irrationally located, very wasteful of resources and energy, heavy polluters, and hard to control, and which arouse the masses' intense ire."[36] There are many differences among writers on the basic principles of environmental law.

We feel that the basic principles of Chinese environmental law should draw intensive guidance and discipline from policies and practices regarding environmental law under the revolutionary regime led by our party. They not only sum up more than thirty years of post-Liberation experience, but also should include some experiences in environmental protection work in the revolutionary base areas led by our party during the New Democratic [pre–1949] revolutionary period. They should emerge out of actual conditions, both reflect and guide reality, and be specific to environmental law. Naturally, we are not opposed to overlap and duplication. In this regard we feel that environmental law has five basic principles.

1. *The principle of unity between environmental and economic returns*. The highest purpose and fundamental guiding thought of Chinese environmental law is to promote socialist economic development and protect the people's health, as stipulated in Article 2 of the Environmental Law:

> The Law on Environmental Protection of the People's Republic of China undertakes to rationally utilize the natural environment and control and prevent pollution and damage to the ecology so as to create a clean and salubrious environment for people's life and

work, protect people's health, and promote economic growth in the interest of socialist modernization.

The final eight characters in the thirty-two-character environmental protection work credo are "protect the environment and benefit the people."

Looking at the issue from different angles, these all show that we must uphold the identity of environmental and economic returns. The State Council last year [1983] reiterated once again that we must uphold "the principle of identity between economic and environmental returns."[37] Some capitalist countries developed historically by single-mindedly pursuing high-speed growth and placing first priority on output value. Their disregard for environmental returns not only resulted in enormous econmic costs, but also brought great suffering to the people.

Our party and country are placing ever more attention on environmental protection and have obtained visible results. This is especially because "our Party now has a much deeper understanding of the laws of Chinese socialist construction and we have accumulated rich experience, which has greatly strengthened our consciousness and determination to carry out our correct policies."[38] We are fully capable of organically combining the two. When we make major decisions affecting the environment, we must both meet the actual needs of the present and consider long-term rights and interests. This requires that we include environmental protection work in the national economic development plan, make comprehensive and rational arrangements, and ensure the unity of environmental and economic returns. The real world, however, is highly complex, so people's understandings will never necessarily be identical. In China not all environmental and economic results can be unified, and some are moving in opposite directions. This requires that we resolutely uphold the highest purpose of our environmental law: "to protect the environment and benefit the people."

2. *The principle of combining prevention and control, with prevention as the leading factor*. In the modern world all countries emphasize environmental management regardless of whether they are socialist or capitalist. However, their management aims are different, and their management approaches vary. As Lenin said: "What capitalists care about is management for the purpose of exploitation, and how to use management to carry out exploitation."[39] Therefore, capitalist countries are inherently incapable of fundamentally controlling pollution and protecting the environment, not to speak of preventing the emergence of pollution. They inevitably take and will continue to take the route of first polluting and then controlling afterward. This is determined by the social system in capitalist countries, which is predicated on the private ownership of the means of production.

What of China? Here we need not hide the truth. At a certain time and a certain level we, too, took the tortuous path of first polluting and then controlling afterward. We are a socialist country, however, predicated on public ownership of the means of production and we practice socialist-planned economy. Our country's character determines that we will not continue to tread this tortuous path.

Moreover, we are economically rather backward in comparison to some other countries and for now do not have enough money to control pollution. Therefore, we must adopt the principle of combining prevention and control, with prevention as the leading factor. The "three simultaneous points" [design, construction, start of operations] system in China's environmental law as well as many specific laws, the environmental impact assessment and environmental impact report systems, and so forth, fully express the spirit of "taking prevention as the leading factor." The three simultaneous points system in particular is the fundamental measure to maintain ecological balance and prevent the environment from being damaged by new sources of pollution, is a strategic policy of profound significance, and is an important legal system for protecting the environment that first originated in China. Some people feel that it is a waste of effort to endorse prevention as the leading factor in areas that are already badly polluted. This kind of reasoning is inappropriate because the principle of combining prevention and control, with prevention as the leading factor, does not signify a weakening of control. However, new sources of environmental pollution and destruction will not develop if we genuinely strive for prevention, and we can then concentrate our resources on the control of existing sources of pollution.

3. *The principle of comprehensive utilization.* Marxist dialectics tells us that there is no such thing as a final waste product. Although human bodily wastes cannot be directly used by people, they are a top-grade fertilizer in agriculture. The Shanghai Biochemical Pharmaceuticals Plant extracted an expensive emergency drug for the treatment of cerebral angiomas from human urine, which is worth 1,000 times its weight in gold. What is a waste product today may become a valuable source of wealth tomorrow thanks to increases in the levels of knowledge and technology. What is a waste product here may be a raw material for production elsewhere. Marx therefore said, "All so-called waste materials can have important uses in specific lines of production."[40] As everyone says, everything emerges from reality. China is a large country whose economy is not entirely prosperous but has more than 1 billion persons. The biggest truth about China is that its people eat and build. Therefore, comprehensive utilization has active meaning for all factories, [government] organs, mass organizations, military units, schools, and individual citizens. It can not only create wealth for state and society, but also reduce environmental pollution, and thus is a way to kill two birds with one stone. Comprehensive utilization thus is both an effective and an active environmental protection measure and is a vital principle that Chinese environmental law must uphold.

4. *The principle of combining administrative supervision with supervision by the masses.* Article 8 of the Environmental Law provides that "all citizens have

the right to supervise, inform against, and accuse any departments or individuals of causing environmental pollution and damage.'' This is a vivid expression of our party's mass line in environmental protection work. Environmental protection relates to the entire country, to every unit and every individual. Supervision by the masses is not only an extremely important prod for environmental protection work, but also a sign of the masses being masters in their own house. However, because supervision by the masses is not sufficient, it must be accompanied by specialized organs. Articles 26 and 27 of the Environmental Law specify the supervisory functions of central and local environmental protection organs. Combining the two forms of supervision can exert enormous strength of decided significance.

5. *The principle of combining rewards and punishment.* Article 31 of the Environmental Law prescribes the rewards system, and Article 32 prescribes the punishment system. Having rewards and punishment and distinguishing between compensation and fines has far-reaching significance for mobilizing the activism of units and individuals for environmental protection. Experience in recent years proves that upholding the principle of combining rewards and punishments has yielded excellent results. It has not only stimulated units and individuals to do a good job in environmental protection work, punished behavior that violates the environmental law, and upheld proper order in environmental protection work, but also strengthened people's appreciation of the legal system in environmental protection work.

Although the last two principles also apply to other branches of the law, their content varies. Upholding the basic principles of Chinese environmental law will definitely yield even better results in the making and enforcement of environmental law in China.

Comments

This article makes a case for elevating environmental law to the status of an independent branch of the law. Written by a judge of the Hubei Provincial High People's Court, Economic Section, and a law professor from the same province, the article is a rather tendentious exercise based on so-called ''principles'' and ''inevitability.'' It appears to run counter to the views of more established legal scholars and policymakers, who regard environmental law as an emerging specialty that overlaps economic, administrative, and criminal law but is not an independent branch of the law per se. Nor is it clear what the behavioral consequences would be if environmental law required independent status. The authors, however, seem to be arguing that the standards for admissibility of evidence and burdens of proof would be lowered, thereby enhancing the state's regulatory capacity.

One may take issue with the authors' simplistic view of the impact that different social, political, and economic systems have on environmental protection. China, under two regimes, provides a model illustration. There have been substantial differences in environmental management between the collective Maoist regime and the decentralized Dengist regime. (*See* Lester Ross and Mitchell A. Silk, ''Post-Mao China and Environmental

Protection: The Effects of Legal and Politico-Economic Reform,'' forthcoming in *UCLA Pacific Basin Law Journal* [1986]).

Chen Lihu (1984) "Creating a Body of Local Environmental Civil Law"

H, no. 5 (May), pp. 28–29.

The Second National Conference on Environmental Protection Work pointed out that environmental management is vitally important, and it needs to be enforced further in light of our country's budgetary constraints and technological shortcomings. It is a correct policy, and I believe that it is necessary to perfect environmental protection legislation as soon as possible in order to push forward the task of environmental management in this country. Furthermore, to enhance local environmental protection legislation is one of the most important steps in fulfilling this task and the establishment of a nationwide environmental protection system.

First of all, environmental problems are clearly localized owing to differences in natural conditions and human activities. For instance, the emission of sulfur dioxide into the atmosphere poses an acidification problem in the cold and humid efflorescent soil regions where coniferous forests exist. On the other hand, it poses a solidification problem for arid and drought-prone calcium soil areas where plains or steppes are found. Furthermore, the self-assimilative capacity, dispersion, and method and degree of transformation of the pollutants vary according to the various natural conditions. For instance, it takes two days for [certain water pollutants] to dissolve in a tropical zone, two weeks in a temperate zone, a year and a half in temperatures below five centigrade, and several years when placed below zero degrees centigrade. It takes a shorter period in a tropical zone than it does in a frigid zone for inorganic heavy metals to be transformed into hydroxyl metals. Thus, for a pollutant, its major form of existence and the damage it causes will vary, depending on the time and place. In other words, the different composition, structure, development stage, and storage ability for soil elements and energy result in different stabilities, self-purification capabilities, and sensitivity to the soil. Because this country has such a vast and complicated landscape, with different types of weather, the distinctions among different regions become more obvious. It boils down to the fact that in terms of environmental protection and development, discriminatory and expedient treatments must be applied based on the region involved. Thus the rules of economics as well as of natural development must be followed. This also determines the fact that we must focus our attention on local environments and their management.

Second, we have just stepped-up our effort in environmental protection legislation. The Standing Committee of the National People's Congress has passed the Environmental Protection Law of the People's Republic of China (for trial implementation) and the Forestry Law of the People's Republic of China in 1979, and the Marine Environmental Protection Law of the People's Republic of China in August 1983. The new Constitution enacted by the Fifth Plenary Session of the National People's Congress has also provided that this country shall protect the environment and preserve the ecological balance. In accordance with the Constitution and other related laws, the State Council has promulgated some administrative regulations on environmental protection. The authorized agencies have also promulgated numerous ambient and discharge standards. Furthermore, many government departments and local authorities now have enacted related regulations within their respective sphere of jurisdiction. Other national laws also contain provisions with regard to environmental protection, such as the Criminal Law.

These accomplishments are still far from sufficient to satisfy society's actual needs. Land, mineral resources, water, the air, and grasslands are all important environmental components for the survival of man and national economic development. Yet a systematic and comprehensive legislative scheme on these aspects is still lacking. This eventually causes many scholars to call for the enactment of a land law, mineral resources law, water resources protection law, air protection law, grasslands law, and so on. Therefore, a tremendous legislative task now faces the National People's Congress and its Standing Committee. It would be unrealistic to ask them to accomplish this work at once. Thus if every local force can be mobilized so as to enhance local environmental protection legislation, the central government's current burden and pressures would be significantly reduced. There are other advantages to such a procedure. First, the vacuum left in environmental protection and management can be filled as soon as possible. Second, a national environmental protection system will be more easily established on the basis of successful local legislation.

Third, Comrade Mao Zedong pointed out that "[o]ur Constitution provides that the legislative power is to be centralized in the Central Government. However, under certain circumstances and functional necessity, local government could go ahead and draft its own charters, provisions and regulations to the extent that they do not defy the Central [Government's] policy. The Constitution holds no restriction on this." Article 100 of the new Constitution states:

> The people's congresses of provinces and municipalities directly under the Central Government, and their standing committees, may adopt local regulations, which must not contravene the Constitution, the statutes and the administrative rules and regulations, and they shall report such local regulations to the Standing Committee of the National People's Congress for the record.

Article 104 states:

> The standing committee of a local people's congress at and above the county level discusses and decides on major issues in all fields of work in its administrative area.

Article 107 provides:

> Local people's governments at and above the county level, within the limits of their authority as prescribed by law, conduct the administrative work concerning the economy, education, science, culture, public health, physical culture, urban and rural development, finance, civil affairs, public security, nationalities affairs, judicial administration, supervision and family planning in their respective administrative areas; issue decisions and orders. . . .

These provisions provide a solid basis for a local environmental protection legislative scheme. Local authorities and people's governments may now promulgate environmental protection rules and regulations according to local circumstances and needs. This is exactly in accordance with the socialist principles of legislation, in which principles and means are harmoniously combined. This is also beneficial in mobilizing activism with regard to local environmental protection.

Fourth, numerous examples exist in which other nations have adopted the means to enhance environmental management, protection, and improvement through localized environmental legislation. Those laws and regulations which govern air pollution in the United States were originally enacted and enforced by each state. The federal government did not finalize its plan on air pollution control until 1955, and Congress did not act until 1963, when the Clean Air Act was passed. Japan was once a place where "explosive public nuisances" took place. It once was even labeled the "public nuisances islands." But today it is considered one of the most advanced nations in the world in controlling and managing its environmental pollution. One of the fundamental measures Japan undertook in turning around its environmental condition was to enhance legislation, form a systematic policy, and empower local governments to deal with this problem. Based on national guidelines as well as local circumstances, local governments may lay down standards and rules even more stringent than those established by the central government. Through 1976, 802 provincial, county, municipal, and township governments had done just that. Japanese laws further require that each and every level of local government authority must apply any and every national environmental standard in its jurisdiction.

Experience in environmental protection work [in the past] has proved sufficiently that it is most beneficial and most necessary to enhance local environmental protection legislation. In order to reduce traffic noise, Beijing has specifically regulated the blowing of automobile horns and will fine violators. The results were immediately obvious. In 1982 Tongling City in Anhui Province promulgated noise control regulations. That year, after the regulations were enforced, the average absolute sound level in the downtown area dropped from seventy-four decibels to sixty-nine decibels, satisfying the mandatory national standard.

From a nationwide aspect we ought to recognize that local environmental legislation has yet to gain the emphasis that it should have received. It is still quite common to observe such phenomena as massive soil erosion, polluted tourist resorts, and the like. One major cause is that the legislation is not comprehensive enough. If every region and locality promptly regulated the laws based on its environmental character and condition and then strictly enforced the law, a significant improvement in the environmental management work of this nation would definitely ensue.

To legislate is not an easy task. A law must reflect the will of the general public and be realistic and plausible, or the authority of the law would eventually be jeopardized. It is, therefore, necessary to accomplish the following to perfect local environmental legislation.

1. Through environmental monitoring we must investigate in detail current local environmental conditions and the degree of pollution, to determine local self-purification capabilities and the sources and cause(s) of pollution.

2. Because the environmental problem is a social issue which involves political, economic, educational, and technological aspects, experts in both the natural and the social sciences ought to participate in the drafting of such legislation.

3. Each region should earnestly sum up environmental protection work in its region and absorb their successful experiences. Applicable methods used in foreign countries and other regions may also be adapted.

4. [The control and management of the] air and water should be the first priority, since they are the most important factors affecting human life.

5. The laws should be precise. Ambiguity and vagueness should be avoided, so that the legislation does not fall short of its goal.

6. Strict enforcement is needed once the rules and regulations have been promulgated.

Comments

Chen Lihu, a graduate of Wuhan University's law faculty and presently at Nanjing University, urges a more decentralized approach to environmental regulation in accordance with variations in local conditions and, although he does not say so explicitly, the post-Mao devolution of many governmental responsibilities to lower echelons of government. Chen also indicates that local diversity will actually enhance the quality of public policy by increasing the number and range of decision-making points, thereby fostering innovation. He does not, however, address local capabilities or migration of pollution across jurisdictions.

ENVIRONMENTAL RIGHTS IN CHINA

Cai Shouqiu (1982) "Preliminary Investigation into Environmental Rights"

Zhongguo Shehui Kexue, no. 3, pp. 29–39.

In the wake of the modern development of production and increasing environmental pollution, the human ecosystem faces a serious threat. The people of all countries are demanding the formulation and perfection of environmental laws in order to protect the environment and prevent further pollution. Consequently, the study of environmental rights has been brought to the fore. The concept of environmental rights includes both the rights of the nation and its legal entities and citizens to use and enjoy natural environmental conditions, and their duty to keep the natural environment from becoming polluted further. This article, through a comparison of the relevant regulations contained in the laws of various countries, makes a preliminary investigation into the general concept and specific meanings of environmental rights as well as the question of laws relating to them. I consider that although China's constitution also contains provisions on environmental protection, China should nevertheless incorporate, emphasize, and broaden the concept of environmental rights in the laws of China. This is an important guarantee for doing a good job in our country's work of environmental protection.

Because of the spread of environmental pollution, a whole series of new social problems have been created. Hence the modern social sciences have been presented with many new topics for study, one of which is the question of environmental rights. Based on the actual current situation of China's environmental protection work and the demands of the broad masses, and in the course of stepping up the establishment of a legal system determining the areas to be covered by environmental protection, solving the question of environmental rights in both its theoretical and practical aspects has already become a problem worthy of attention. This article investigates the problem in several aspects, as outlined below, in the hope of motivating comrades to study the problem more intensely.

THE EMERGENCE OF ENVIRONMENTAL RIGHTS

Environmental rights is a new concept made manifest by advances in living standards and societal production. It is the product of the continuous degradation of the human environment as well as the continuous strengthening of the work of protecting the human environment. The question of the environment in human society has undergone a process of development, and in different historical periods the question of the environment has had a different nature and different characteristics. This fact is reflected in the different ways in which it has been manifested in law. During the long period before the Industrial Revolution, owing to the low level of human productive forces, from the point of view of the situation as a whole the influence of human activity on the environment did not constitute a serious attack on the ability of the environment to purify itself. During this period the question of the environment was manifested principally in problems relating to the utilization of natural resources or in areas that had considerable influence on people's lives. In the law some scattered provisions appeared which had the effect of protecting a part of the environment. During the period between the Industrial Revolution and World War II, in the wake of the appearance of capitalist heavy industry, the level of the productive forces was continuously raised and the influence of human activity on the environment became greater and greater. The question of the environment during this period consisted mainly of concern over point source pollution and area pollution by the "three industrial wastes," which was reflected in law by the appearance of some specialized environmental protection laws as well as regulations of a purely local nature. During these two stages neither general nor specialized laws and regulations clearly phrased the general concept of environmental rights, while in the fundamental laws and constitutions of the various countries, there was even less in the way of a clear formulation of environmental rights. After World War II, and in particular during the Sixties and Seventies, industrial and agricultural production grew by leaps and bounds, bringing about the danger of polluting large areas, or even the entire world, and seriously threatening the human ecological balance, the safety of mankind itself, and the economic develoment of society, thus creating a great number of disputes on the subject of environmental pollution. According to some estimates and statistics, there is a tendency for the total quantity of pollutants to double every fourteen to fifteen years. In the Soviet Union losses caused by water pollution each year amount to more than six billion rubles. In the United States total losses through death, disease, and material losses caused by air pollution alone amounted to $25 billion. In the United States in 1972, 80 million persons, or 40 percent of the population, were harmfully affected by noise pollution and an additional 40 million face the danger of hearing impairment. In Japan in 1970 alone the number of cases of litigation involving environmental pollution harmful to the public welfare reached 60,000. For this reason some people in Western countries call our present age the "Age of Environmental Crisis" and refer to the questions of environmental pollution and the ecological balance as "ecological politics." At this stage the people's cry for the prevention of pollution and for environmental protection is louder than at any other period in history, with the result that it has led to the formation of the newly independent legal area of environmental law, and it is also during this stage that the concept of environmental rights has been proposed.

Faced with the harsh reality of environmental pollution, people gradually awakened to the realization that the natural environment that originally gave benefits to people without ever asking anything in return is now capable of bringing along a good many troubling, disquieting elements as well, and that endowed rights that people had considered as part and parcel of life itself, such as the right to breathe clean air, are now capable of being invisibly harmed and expropriated. As the "Human Environment Manifesto"[41] points out:

> Human beings on this planet, throughout the long course of their evolution, have had a great many hardships and difficulties. Only the rapid progress of science and technology and the use of countless methods and the attainment of forces on a historically unprecedented scale have enabled human beings to reach the stage where they can change their environment. The question of the environment in its original, natural state versus the environment as altered by man is exceedingly important for the right of human beings to enjoy well-being, and for other basic human rights—even the right of existence.

For their own welfare, people in great numbers have called on those who discharge pollutants into the environment to respect others' right to life and prevent the quality of the environment from being harmed by pollution. The polluters, however, proceeding from the traditional viewpoint, consider that discharging pollutants into the waterways, atmosphere, and open country that are not owned by any individual is not to be considered illegal or as infringing on anyone's rights; that engaging in economic activity, and consequently making a profit, is their right as determined by law; and that discharging pollutants is a necessary condition for exercising that right.

In this way two contradictory and conflicting views concerning social rights emerge. The victims of pollution want to seek redress through some legal measure, which would have the greatest coercive force. However, traditional constitutions and laws, although they have formulated a great number of fundamental rights, have nevertheless still not formulated people's environmental rights. This places the law in a weak, powerless position with respect to the polluters and in a condition of being unable to help the victims of pollution. For example, in 1960 a doctor in West Germany brought a case before Europe's Human Rights Commission to the effect that "discharging nuclear wastes into the North Sea is a violation of human rights." The Commission, however, on the grounds that the European Human Rights Treaty[42] did not contain any provision that guaranteed the cleanliness and healthiness of this environment, dismissed the case. Since then, at the European Environmental Protection Conference, a motion to add environmental rights to the existing list of human rights in the European Human Rights Treaty has been proposed many times, but it has never passed.

This circumstance has aroused the indignation and censure of a great many people. For example, the American scholar [Rachel] Carson, who some people abroad consider to have launched the modern ecological era, laments in her 1962 book *Silent Spring*:

> The present is also the age of industrial rule; in industry, it is difficult for the right to make money at any cost to be condemned. . . . If one says that the Bill of Rights makes no mention of the right of citizens to a guarantee that they will escape the danger of

being exposed to poisonous chemicals discharged by private individuals or public organizations, that is really only because our forefathers, due to limitations in their wisdom and foresight, had no way of imagining such problems.[43]

The *White Paper on Human Rights*, published by the Federation of Japanese Lawyers in 1967, cried out loudly and urgently that "public hazards violate human rights." Afterward, people in great numbers strongly demanded a clarification, through law, of the rights to be enjoyed by the state, the collective, and the individual in utilizing natural environmental conditions, as well as the duties they must fulfill to protect that environment. In this way environmental rights mounted the social stage known as the "Age of Environmental Crisis." By the end of the Sixties, under the powerful impetus provided by public opinion, environmental rights all at once became the central topic of study and discussion by environmental protection departments and legal departments.

Theoretical study and legislative work relating to environmental rights also developed rapidly and manifested itself primarily in two areas.

First, in the international arena, some international conferences on environmental protection one after the other passed manifestos of principle on the subject of environmental rights, and some academic conferences investigated deeply and broadly theories on environmental rights and exchanged their results. For example, at the International Conference on Public Hazards convened in Tokyo in March 1970, the fifth item (relating to environmental rights) in the "Tokyo Resolutions" passed by the conference raised the following request: "Of particular importance is our request that the environmental rights, to be enjoyed by all people, of not being harmed by factors injurious to health or well-being, and the right of the present generation to leave to their descendants an inheritance consisting of natural resources filled with natural beauty, be made basic principles of legal rights and defined as part of the legal system." The principles of the "Declaration on the Human Environment," passed by the United Nations Human Environment Conference convened in June 1972, clearly proclaimed: "Man has the fundamental right to freedom, equality and adequate conditions of life, in an environment of a quality that permits a life of dignity and well-being, and he bears a solemn responsibility to protect and improve the environment for present and future generations."[44] Hence the concept of environmental rights was brought up in such a way that both the rights and the duties of environmental protection appeared at the same time. At the International Scientific Conference on the Human Environment convened in Tokyo in November 1975, at the conference on law, the central topic of discussion was "human rights with respect to the environment"; the legal experts coming from the various countries engaged in an academic exchange on the question of environmental rights, and the magazine *Research on Environmental Law*, edited by the Japanese legal profession's Association for the Study of Problems Related to the Human Environment, published a special edition to present the findings.

Second, in some countries where the question of the environment was prominent, theoretical study and legislative work relating to environmental rights have been rather broadly developed. In Japan, specialized societies for the study of environmental rights, such as the Environmental Rights Society of the Osaka Lawyers' Association, appeared. Because the concept of environmental rights had already been proposed in law and had aroused the attention of Japanese from all walks of life, the preamble to the "Tokyo Municipal Public Hazard Prevention Ordinance" formulated in 1969 emphasized that "all residents of the city have the right to a healthy, safe and comfortable life, and these rights cannot, because of public harm, be indiscriminately encroached upon."[45] Following the promulgation of the "Tokyo City Government Public Hazard Prevention Regulations," the "Kawasaki Municipal Public Hazard Prevention Ordinance" formulated in 1972 in turn adopted the same stand on environmental rights.[46] In the United States, discussions on the general concept of environmental rights, its constitutional basis, and other questions of legal theory relating thereto sprang up in 1969. The establishment of the U.S. Environmental Law Institute and the theory of public trust proposed by University of Michigan professor Sax provided impetus to the study of environmental rights in the United States. In legislation, Section One of the U.S. National Environmental Policy Act[47] (passed in 1969 and later amended) made a detailed formulation of the rights and duties of the state and its citizens with regard to the protection of the environment. The third clause of this section emphasizes that "the Congress recognizes that each person should enjoy a healthful environment and that each person has a responsibility to contribute to the preservation and enhancement of the environment."[48] The appearance of the concept of environmental rights in certain laws and regulations dealing with environmental protection gradually influenced some nations' fundamental, great law—the constitution. In Switzerland, in June 1971, the content of the seventh item in the newly established Article 24 of the Swiss Constitution provided: "The Federation should adopt legislative measures to protect people and their natural environment from harmful or unpleasant encroachments, and the Federation especially should struggle against air pollution and noise pollution."[49] Because of this statement, and the stipulations in the constitution regarding the protection of forests, wildlife, and beneficial birds promulgated as early as 1974, Switzerland is considered to be the first nation to have incorporated environmental rights, or matters closely connected with environmental rights, into its constitution. By now the issues constituting the basic content of environmental rights have been clearly recognized in the constitutions of a good many countries.

Three conclusions can be drawn from the process by which the concept of environmental rights has emerged.

First, from the standpoint of the historical development of society, the proposition of environmental rights is the natural product of the development of the human environment problem, and there is a definite tendency in the development of the constitutions, environmental laws, and other related laws of the various countries to include environmental rights among the basic rights of nations and citizens, as a good example of social phenomena being produced by physical causes. The whole scope of environmental rights, therefore, has deep roots in the material life of human society. Although the development of the concept of environmental rights and the ways this development has been manifested in various countries have been exceedingly complex, nevertheless it has presented a course of development that is legally unified and being strengthened daily. Therefore, the science of law under a socialist system should study the question of environmental rights in the same way. This study should be guided by Marxism-Leninism and undergo a scientific analysis of the conditions under which the proposition of environmental rights was produced, as well as an accurate estimate of their usefulness, so that this foreign concept can be properly implemented in China and used to promote China's environmental protection work. It should not simply copy the specific stipulations of foreign countries regarding environmental rights.

Second, environmental rights remain a core issue in environmental law and the basis of environmental litigation. Environmental law embraces the entire scope of all laws which serve to adjust the various social connections arising out of the need for protection of the environment. The greater part of environmental rights as they relate to environmental law manifests itself in the two aspects of rights and responsibilities. Environmental law, then, based on these two aspects, expresses and defines the relevant social connections and, by means of the coercive power of the state, guarantees the legal forms necessary to implement them. The clearer and more concrete the laws of a country with regard to stipulations on environmental rights, the more complete the conditions for the further development of its system of environmental law and the securer the basis for that system will be. Environmental litigation is based on the relevant environmental protection laws, for the purpose of preserving the advantage of people enjoying a good environment, and is an important avenue for solving environmental disputes. Because the development of the concept of environmental litigation has already been promoted, if the concept of environmental rights is not clearly defined in law, it would be difficult to develop environmental litigation. Therefore, immersing ourselves in launching programs of study on theoretical questions relating to environmental rights is important for setting up a sound system of environmental law for our country, developing our country's environmental litigation, and solving environmental disputes.

Third, theory regarding environmental rights is in a developmental stage, and China's legal workers should make a contribution to a scientific theory of environmental rights. There are many theories and views regarding environmental rights, and many issues are still being debated. For example, at the conference in support of human rights held by the Japanese Lawyer's Association in Niigata, Japan, in September 1970, the theory of absolute environmental rights was proposed, the core of which was the concept of the "agreement of all inhabitants"; that is, any change in the environment must obtain the agreement of all inhabitants. This theory considers that environmental rights take absolute precedence over other factors, and that environmental rights should take the form of concrete rights to be heard in litigation. Another influential theory of environmental rights is called the guiding principle theory of environmental rights, or the explanatory theory of environmental rights. This theory considers that environmental rights are a stipulation based on guiding principles and are not necessarily connected with any direct, concrete right to be heard: it is rather that, in order that environmental rights may be realized for everyone, the constitution must be revised or great changes must be instituted in the legal procedures currently in force. From the standpoint of the course of development of environmental rights, these diverging and contending aspects are entirely natural. The establishment of many other fundamental rights has passed through such a stage. Determined and conscientious social science workers should not skirt this kind of divergence, but actively proceed with analysis and study of these aspects.

THE CONTENT OF ENVIRONMENTAL RIGHTS

The environmental rights discussed in this article are rights under the law, that is, the various rights and interests bestowed by the law on the principal parties, to be enjoyed by them with regard to the natural environment in which they live. Because environmental pollution is largely the product of the development of modern industry, traditional laws in the past either made no stipulation or were not clear about the concept of environmental rights.

Hence legal workers both in China and abroad have not come up with a unanimous viewpoint regarding the definition and content of environmental rights, and the stipulations regarding environmental rights in the legal literature of the various countries are also not completely alike. Under these circumstances there are two ways of proceeding with a study of environmental rights. The first is to proceed from the basis of a predefined, general concept and compare a scholar's definition against the complex legal provisions in effect in real life. The points that coincide could be recognized as representing environmental rights, and those that differ would not be accepted. Another would be to proceed from the basis of the legal provisions regarding environmental rights in the laws currently in force, synthesize them, and generalize from them the primary content of environmental rights, clarifying the general concept, nature, and meaning of environmental rights. In view of the fact that (a) a good many countries already have some stipulations on environmental rights in the various environmental laws and regulations they have promulgated; (b) many countries also have specialized stipulations on environmental rights in the various environmental laws and regulations they have promulgated; and (c) many countries also have specialized stipulations on environmental rights in their constitutions, I believe that if we want to clarify the general concept and meaning of environmental rights, the best method is to compare the provisions on environmental rights in the laws of the various countries. Because a constitution is a country's fundamental law, a comparative analysis of the stipulations on environmental rights in the constitutions of the various countries is even more important for our understanding of this question.

1. Environmental rights include three aspects—the environmental rights of nations, of legal entities, and of citizens—which together make up the unified whole of environmental rights.

In analyzing the stipulations regarding environmental rights in the constitutions of the various countries, there are generally three types, according to who enjoys the right of environmental protection.

The first are the nation's environmental rights. A country's natural environment is the area and material conditions which that country relies on for survival, including that country's sea lanes, airspace, and territory. Therefore, a country's environmental rights are universally given preeminence in the laws of various countries. From the standpoint of international law, countries are the subjects of international law, and a country's environmental rights consist of its right to engage in all actions in the exercise of the protection of its environment, and are a component part of a nation's right of sovereignty.

From the point of view of the internal laws of the various countries, a country's environmental rights mainly consist of the state's fundamental responsibility to protect the natural environment needed for the life of the people. For example, Article 110 of the Constitution of the Republic of Panama (1972) stipulates: ''Based on the situation of the national economy and social development, actively protecting the ecological environment—and preventing environmental pollution and the disruption of the ecological balance—is a fundamental responsibility of the state.''[50] Article 24 of the Constitution of the Republic of Greece (1975) stipulates: ''Protecting the natural and cultural environments is a responsibility of the state, and the state should lay down particular preventive or coercive measures.''[51] Regarding these responsibilities the constitutions of some countries make stipulations in comparative detail, while those of other countries do so according to more general principles. In comparing the relevant stipulations in the constitutions of the various countries, four principal aspects of a country's environmental rights appear: (1) the state's right of ownership over all publicly owned land, waterways, mines, and other natural resources is clearly stipulated, as in Article 14 of the Philippines constitution[52] and in the relevant provisions of the constitutions of Bulgaria,[53] Poland,[54] the German Democratic Republic,[55] and the Soviet Union[56]; (2) the scope of the natural environment to be protected by the state is clearly stipulated, as in Articles 75, 77, and 93 of the Constitution of the Kingdom of Thailand[57] and in the relevant provisions in the constitutions of Papua-New Guinea[58] and Bulgaria[59]; (3) it is clear that the state has the right to formulate all kinds of laws and regulations for the prevention and control of environmental pollution, as stipulated in Article 151 of the Constitution of the Republic of Algeria,[60] and in the relevant provisions in the constitutions of Switzerland,[61] Sweden,[62] Chile,[63] and Czechoslovakia[64]; (4) the state's right to guarantee that its citizens obtain a healthy living environment is clearly stipulated, as in Article 1, Section 18 of the Constitution of the Republic of Chile and in the relevant provisions of the constitutions of Yugoslavia,[65] Cuba,[66] Thailand,[67] and Hungary.[68] It is not by chance that the stipulations regarding the environmental rights of nations of a number of countries having different social systems, such as Greece,[69] Chile,[70] Bulgaria,[71] and Yugoslavia,[72] all appear in the name of the responsibility of the nation. This is because the natural environment is a fundamental condition for the existence of human society, while environmental pollution is an objective phenomenon that has followed in the wake of human economic activity. Therefore, the protection of the natural environment possesses a universal and long-term nature. The establishment of the environmental rights of nations is actually the outcome of the enrichment and development of the theory of the function of the state and theories regarding the state and laws.

Second, environmental rights are enjoyed by legal entities (i.e., government organs, organizations, factories, mines, and similar enterprises and units). For example, Article 31 of the Constitution of the Republic of Bulgaria (1971) stipulates: "Protecting nature and natural wealth, waterways, the atmosphere, the surface of the earth, as well as cultural remains, is the responsibility of state organs and enterprises, cooperative social groups, and social organizations."[73] Proceeding from the basis of the actual circumstances of environmental protection, it is not enough merely to stipulate the environmental rights of states and citizens. Because of the mobile nature of environmental pollution (the mobility of water and the atmosphere, the transmission of noise), as well as the development of modern means of communication, the small universe of the individual no longer exists. Also, because in modern social life citizens frequently appear in the form of definite organizations and groups, and environmental pollution is mainly created by factories, mines, enterprises, and units that discharge pollutants, environmental protection also generally manifests itself as a common issue of a group of people in the environment of a particular settlement. So the environmental rights of the legal entities which are intermediaries between the state and the citizens have the particular effect of forming a link between the former and the latter. Therefore, many countries place particular importance on the environmental rights of legal entities. For example, Soviet Russia's Nature Protection Law,[74] with regard to the protection of the soil, mineral resources, waterways, forests, and wild animals and plants, specifically and concretely enumerates the rights and duties of the legal entities, such as factories and mining enterprises, farms, and farming villages. Article 1 of Japan's Fundamental Pollution Control Law also sets out clear provisions regarding the environmental rights of enterprises.[75]

Third, environmental rights are enjoyed by citizens. Article 193 of the Constitution of the Socialist Federal Republic of Yugoslavia (1974) stipulates: "People have the right to a healthy living environment."[76] The reason the environmental rights of citizens have been included within the scope of the protection offered by constitutions and, moreover, the reason they are urgently demanded by the broad masses is because, first of all, in the wake of the development of modern means of production and modern lifestyles, a clean, comfortable natural environment has already become a fundamental condition for people to enjoy effective, continuous work and a healthy, happy life. The functions of the natural environment are, first, to provide human beings with a place for life, work, and rest and, second, to provide human beings with all the natural resources required to develop their material and spiritual lives. Without a clean, agreeable natural environment that is able to guarantee the continuous provision of all the natural resources needed for the people's material and spiritual lives, humanity will be without the means to continue to exist and develop. If a person's place of work and living is polluted or encroached on by large quantities of poisonous and harmful substances, noise, and bad odor, then it may be impossible to protect the conditions for that person's existence. Second, citizens' environmental rights are necessary conditions for the realization of their fundamental rights to property, labor, and existence, but they are not the equivalent of these rights. Before the environmental rights of citizens were clearly formulated, people frequently adduced other rights as the legal basis for protecting the well-being of the victims of pollution. For example, in the course of the litigation over Japan's Osaka Airport, presiding judge Taneo Sawani gave the following account: "In circumstances of this kind, residents whose lives are jeopardized have the right, according to Article 13 of the Constitution (regarding the right of citizens to life, liberty, and the pursuit of happiness) to demand that the government adopt certain countermeasures."[77] In fact, some countries have stipulated their environmental rights precisely from this point of view, as stipulated in Article 15 of the Constitution of the Socialist Republic of Czechoslovakia:

> The state is concerned about beautifying nature and having nature thoroughly protected, and with protecting the beautiful natural scenery of the motherland, in order to create an increasingly richer source for the sake of the happiness of the people's lives, and to create an appropriate environment for the sake of the health and rest of the laboring people.[78]

From this one decidedly cannot reach the conclusion that the right to work, the right to rest, and other rights can be substituted for environmental rights. In actuality each has its own conditions and course of origin and development, and each has its specific scope of application. The environmental rights of citizens already cover a considerably broad area. Moreover, they are gradually developing from the prevention and control of environmental pollution to demands for comfort with regard to the environment (including the degree of quiet, cleanliness, pleasantness, and comfort), thus causing environmental rights to develop gradually into the most basic of rights.

From this it can be seen that the environmental rights of nations, legal entities, and citizens are interconnected. Furthermore, each has its own particular effect and scope of application, among which the environmental rights of nations possess guiding significance, the environmental rights of citizens are the most basic, and the environmental rights of legal entities, although they are derived from the former two, nevertheless possess an important position in environmental protection work that cannot be overlooked. From the standpoint of the provisions of the constitutions of the various countries, some only stipulate the nation's environmental rights, some stipulate two or three kinds of environmental rights, some—in the provisions of various laws—separately stipulate the environmental rights of the nation, of legal entities, and of citizens, and some stipulate all three kinds of environmental rights in the same provision. For example, Article 20 of the Constitution of the Socialist People's Republic of Albania stipulates: "Protecting the land, natural resources, waterways, and air from being spoiled or polluted is the duty of the state, economic and social organizations, and all the citizens."[79]

2. Environmental rights include the two aspects of the right to enjoy the environment and the duty to protect the environment, and the two together form the scientific social proposition of environmental rights.

From the point of view of rights versus duties, the constitutions of the various countries generally have four types of stipulations regarding environmental rights. The first is environmental rights expressed by the specific term "rights." The second is environmental rights expressed by the specific term "duty." For example, Article 50 of the Constitution of the Islamic Republic of Iran (1979) stipulates: "In the Islamic Republic, it is the duty of the citizens to protect the living environment of the present generation and of our descendants."[80] Third are environmental rights expressed simultaneously by both specific terms, "rights" and "duty." For example, Article 66 of the Constitution of the Republic of Portugal (1976) stipulates: "All citizens have the right to enjoy a living environment in which their health will not be harmed; at the same time, they also have the duty to protect the cleanliness of the environment."[81] Fourth are environmental rights which are not expressed in the form of the specialized terms "rights" and "duty."

There is a viewpoint which considers that environmental rights indicates the right of citizens to enjoy a good environment and, moreover, firmly believes that only if the legal standard of the term "rights" has been clearly used in the sections and chapters of a country's constitution dealing with the basic rights of citizens can they accurately be called environmental rights, and that if the legal standard of using "duty" or some other term is used, they cannot be considered environmental rights. I consider that in studying and advocating environmental rights, to proceed from the basis of an understanding of the unity of rights and responsibilities would be much more beneficial and effective than to do so from the basis of separating rights and duties. Originally, rights and duties were distinct from each other. A person had the right to decide whether or not to exercise his own rights, but if he did not fulfill his duties, he would be punished by law. From this standpoint to speak of rights and duties as the same thing would not be proper. However, although rights and duties are distinct from each other, they are also connected. Marxism considers that "there is no right without responsibility, and there is no responsibility without right."[82] If rights are stipulated, then the corresponding duties are pointed out by implication, and if duties are stipulated, then one will have bestowed on others the right to demand that the persons concerned fulfill these duties according to the law. In law there is no great distinction between stipulating, after all, rights, duties, or a combination of the two, and what basis to proceed from is generally a matter of convenience. Because of the intrinsic characteristics of environmental pollution and environmental protection work, it is especially worthwhile for us to immerse ourselves in the study and discussion of how to formulate environmental rights. From the point of view of the actual situation of the stipulations regarding environmental rights in the laws of the various countries, the laws have definitely not followed the restrictions designated by any one jurist, but have realistically reflected the new circumstances of actual life in all their multiplicity. From the point of view of the position of environmental rights within the constitutions, some countries put them in the general principles section or the preface, others place them in the chapters and sections dealing with the basic rights and duties of citizens, and still others place them in the chapters and sections dealing with the country's social and economic system. From the point of view of the relationship between rights and duties, some countries use the two terms distinctly, while others do not distinguish between them. From the point of view of the direction of development, there is a tendency for the stipulation of environmental rights in the form of a unity of rights and duties to be accepted by more and more countries, laws, and legal workers and, moreover, to be reflected in the three aspects of environmental rights for nations, legal entities, and citizens.

In the area of international environmental law, Principle 21 of the Declaration on the Human Environment provides:

> States have, in accordance with the Charter of the United Nations and the principles of international law, the sovereign right to exploit their own resources pursuant to their own environmental policies, and the responsibility to ensure that activities within their jurisdiction or control do not cause damage to the environment of other States or of areas beyond the limits of national jurisdiction.[83]

This clearly states that a country's environmental rights include the two aspects of rights and responsibilities. The sections on the environmental rights of the nation in the constitutions of some countries also stipulate them in their two aspects of rights and duties. For example, because Articles 24 and 25 of the Constitution of the Federation of Switzerland stipulate the rights of the Federation with regard to the natural environment (for example, the right to utilize, supervise, and pass laws regarding the environment), they also stipulate the Federation's duties.[84] The environmental rights of legal entities in the same way include the two aspects of rights and duties. For example, because Articles 12 and 18 of the Constitution of the USSR (1977) stipulate the right of legal entities to utilize the environment, they also stipulate their duty to protect the environment.[85] With regard to the environmental rights of citizens, from the point of view of the provisions of the constitutions of the various countries currently in force, constitutions which stipulate environmental rights in the form of citizen's "duties" or simultaneously in the form of citizens' "rights" and "duties" are in the majority, while constitutions which stipulate environmental rights only in the form of citizens' "rights" are relatively fewer. This circumstance occurs because the right of citizens to enjoy a good environment and their duty to protect the environment are frequently interconnected. Moreover, the stipulation of the citizens' duty to protect the environment tends to assist in the realization of their right to enjoy that environment.

In sum, there are environmental rights in both the narrow and the broad sense. Environmental rights in the narrow sense generally indicate the environmental rights of citizens (i.e., the citizens' right to enjoy a good, proper natural environment). Environmental rights in the broad sense indicate, generally, the rights to be enjoyed and the duties to be assumed by all major bodies having some connection with the law (including natural people, legal entities, special legal entities—the state) with respect to the natural environment they exist in. That is, the state, organizations, groups, enterprises, and units such as factories and mines, as well as the citizens, all have the right to utilize and enjoy the natural environmental conditions they exist in. They also have the duty to protect the natural environment and prevent environmental pollution. Although the narrow and broad senses of environmental rights reflect the different points of view people have adopted toward the problem, as well as the different areas to be covered by environmental protection, nevertheless whether one proceeds from the point of view of study and theory or from the point of view of the requirements of the actual situation, the concept of environmental rights in the broad sense is more important and more valuable.

REGARDING CHINA'S LAWS AND ENVIRONMENTAL RIGHTS

We should be aware that the laws of China do have some provisions concerned with environmental rights. For example, Article 11 of the Constitution of the People's Republic of China (1978) stipulates: "The state shall protect the environment and natural resources and prevent and eliminate pollution and other hazards to the public."[86] This stipulation belongs in the category of the environmental rights of nations. And the Environmental Protection Law of the People's Republic of China (for trial implementation) more specifically concerns the rights and duties of the state, legal entities, and citizens in protecting the environment. For example, Article 2 of this law stipulates:

> The Law on Environmental Protection of the People's Republic of China undertakes to rationally utilize the natural environment and control and prevent pollution and damage to the ecology so as to create a clean and salubrious environment for people's life and work, protect people's health, and promote economic growth in the interest of socialist modernization.[87]

The phrase "so as to create a clean and salubrious environment for people's life and work" can be understood as the state's recognition of the "people's right to enjoy a clean and proper environment." In addition, other laws and regulations also stipulate rights and duties in certain environmental protection areas. For example, Article 7 of the Forestry Law of the People's Republic of China (trial implementation) (1979) stipulates: "Planting trees and creating forests, and caring for them, is the glorious duty and right of all the people of the nation."[88]

One can see from these laws that the standard of our country's laws on environmental pollution is not clear or complete enough. China's constitution only briefly stipulates the responsibility of the nation with regard to environmental protection and does not stipulate the rights and duties of organizations, groups, enterprises, units such as factories and mines, and citizens in environmental protection work. Although the stipulations in China's environmental protection law and other related laws and regulations regarding the responsibilities and duties in environmental protection work of the nation, units, and citizens are comparatively clear and complete, nevertheless they seldom deal with, or are not clear, regarding the rights of the nation, enterprises, units, and citizens to enjoy good environmental conditions. For this reason the question is not whether or not we want to stipulate the issue of environmental rights in our country's laws, but how to further revise, round out, clarify, and bring into prominence the question of environmental rights.

The "Resolutions Regarding the Revision of the Constitution and the Setting Up of a Committee to Revise the Constitution"[89] resulting from the Third Session of the Fifth People's Congress point out that, regarding the revision of the constitution, we must turn the matter over to all the people of all nationalities in the entire nation for discussion, in order to pool their wisdom and formulate a constitution that is adapted to the general duties and requirements of China in this new period of historical development. The revision of China's Environmental Protection Law is also in line with this guiding principle. On the basis of this spirit and in view of the present condition of the stipulations in China's laws regarding environmental rights as well as the actual needs of China's environmental protection work, I consider that in China's constitution we should, in a principled way, stipulate the rights and duties with regard to environmental protection work of the nation, units, and citizens. In civil law, economic law, and the various other laws relating to environmental protection, we should further clarify and make more specific the rights and duties of the three groups with regard to environmental protection. The reasons are as follows.

1. Because of the important effect of protecting the natural environment on China's Four Modernizations, it is necessary to clarify and emphasize environmental rights in our laws.

China has already entered a new period of historical development. The general duty of our party and nation during this new period of historical development is to unite all the people of the various nationalities in China so that they, with one mind and one heart, in a planned fashion and according to the proportionate representation of their numbers, can achieve greater, faster, better, and more economical results in developing our socialist economy and build a strong, modern, socialist country with a high level of democracy and civilization. Because China's natural environment and natural resources are the material basis for China's modernization project and constitute the place and the conditions under which the people of China will make a concerted effort toward building the Four Modernizations, they are closely connected with the speed and prospects of the Four Modernizations project. Because the establishment of a fine and proper work, study, and living environment is an important aim in the building of socialist modernization and an important aspect of being a strong, socialist, and highly civilized nation, it has a bearing on the immediate well-being of all the people of China. The current situation of environmental protection in China, however, is definitely not adapted to the requirements of the new period. Although we have done a great deal of work, environmental pollution continues to develop and has already become a new, important problem for the building of the Four Modernizations. More than 100 million tons of smoke and dust are discharged into the environment every year in China, along with 15 million tons of sulfur dioxide, making it one of the top countries in the world in terms of the quantity of pollutants discharged. Throughout our country each year more than 25 billion tons of polluted water, resulting from both industrial and ordinary use, are discharged, so that economic losses each year owing to water pollution alone amount to 5.5 billion yuan, a figure which is substantially equivalent to the amount lost through air pollution. The unchecked proliferation of pollutants constitutes a vast waste of our natural resources and energy sources. China's utilization rate for energy sources is only 28 percent, whereas the energy source utilization rate for the United States and Japan is more than 50 percent. Even if we raise our utilization rate to 40 percent, we will still be wasting 100 million yuan and several tens of millions of tons of fuel per year. With regard to the natural environment, over the past thirty years the desertification of land in China has increased by 60,000 square kilometers. Each year our forests are reduced by 2.5 million hectares. Because of soil erosion, each year we lose more than five billion tons of soil and with it an amount of nitrogen, phosphate, and potash fertilizer equivalent to the total quantity of chemical fertilizer applied by China's agriculture in a year; and the area of inland bodies of water has been reduced by seven percent [over the past thirty years] owing to the blind construction of farmland around lakes. All these factors have a far-reaching and serious negative effect on the development of China's industrial and agricultural production. If we want to solve these problems, it will be necessary to mobilize the forces of the state, legal entities, and all of the people, and for this it will be necessary to stipulate clearly in our national laws for the new historical period the rights and duties of the state, legal entities, and citizens regarding environmental protection. Otherwise, if the laws for the new historical period do not reflect the new period's problems, then the continuing development of environmental pollution will become a bitter result and a serious obstacle to the building of the Four Modernizations.

2. To round out the concept of environmental rights and bring it into prominence in our laws is an important guarantee of doing a good job in environmental protection work in China.

Because the factors creating China's environmental pollution are exceedingly complex, environmental protection is a synthesis involving many fields of study and many departments, and this means that the fundamental outlet for China's environmental protection work lies in implementing the party's mass line, relying on the masses, and having everyone get to work. Some of our comrades, however, are in the habit of engaging in a "fool's" policy, which has arisen from an unwillingness to accept the fact that socialist China has an environmental pollution problem, and afterward, when pollution became so serious that it could no longer be ignored, they tried to minimize it or gloss over it, with the result that they dare not bestow environmental rights on the masses for fear that once this is done, the masses will raise improper demands. This is one of the important causes of the backwardness of China's environmental protection work. Actually, environmental rights definitely do not imply the making of harsh demands regarding the environment that depart from reality. Along with the right to enjoy a clean environment, one also has the duty to protect the environment. Once the masses make the connection between the quality of the environment and their own immediate well-being, this will become a powerful social force for protecting the environment. In addition, environmental rights are the same as the right to democratic freedoms, the right to work, and the right to rest. In order to change programmatic, guiding principles into concrete principles that can be used as a basis for litigation, they must still go through the process of being subject to concrete, actual legal provisions. It is definitely not the case that, once possessing environmental rights, one can then lodge environmental complaints at will or make trouble without just cause. In actuality, clearly stipulating environmental rights in our laws is a means of regularizing the mass line in the party's environmental protection work in the form of a fundamental right of the people. This not only places on all levels of government the responsibility for safeguarding the people's environmental rights, but as a result also places the problem of environmental protection on the agenda of government work and, moreover, bestows on the broad masses the right to supervise all activities that cause environmental pollution and demand the improvement of environmental conditions. In this way China's environmental protection work will have a continuous forward impetus and legal guarantee.

3. Under our socialist system environmental rights are a necessary condition for the exercise of citizens' right to work, right to rest, and other fundamental rights. China's constitution, promulgated many times over, clearly stipulates many basic rights for our citizens, and this is a concrete manifestation of the

popular, democratic nature of socialist constitutions. For example, Article 48 of the Constitution of the People's Republic of China (1978) provides:

> Citizens shall have the right to work. The state, based on the principle of taking all factors into consideration, will make arrangements for the citizens to labor and take up occupations and, on the basis of increasing production, will gradually increase remuneration for labor, improve working conditions, strengthen labor protection and improve the collective well-being, in order to guarantee the citizen's enjoyment of these rights.

Article 49 stipulates:

> Workers have the right to rest. The state shall fix the times for labor and the systems for taking leave, and shall gradually expand the workers' material conditions for rest and recuperation, in order to guarantee the workers' enjoyment of these rights.[90]

From the point of view of environmental protection, these working conditions and labor protection measures indicate principally the protection of the workers' work environment. The material conditions for workers' rest and recuperation include the living environment in which the workers rest. Whether work environment or living environment, both are part of the natural environment on which people depend for their existence. Although requirements for the quality of a work environment differ according to whether the work is physical or mental, the quality of that work environment will always have an effect on a person's spirit and psyche, influence the worker's enthusiasm and creativity, and have an effect on the quantity and quality of the material and spiritual wealth created by the worker. As for the material conditions for workers' rest and recuperation, in addition to clothing, food, shelter, and transportation, fresh air and fine, agreeable surroundings with blue skies, clear water, and green shade trees are required, and this will have an effect on the preservation and renewal of their capacity for labor. One can see, then, that the citizens' right to work and right to rest are inseparable from the protection of the natural environment. If the work or living environment is seriously polluted, the workers are without protection during their work time and cannot get proper rest during their rest time, the workers' health and lives will be threatened by all kinds of polluting factors, and the workers' rights to work and to rest will become empty words. The situation of China's environmental pollution is still comparatively serious, and to one degree or another it has already had a negative effect on the exercise of citizens' rights to work and to rest. For example, noise pollution and the pollution of air and water resources in the cities of China are already problems urgently in need of a solution and have already had some negative effect on people's work, study, and rest. These problems are already arousing more and more the serious attention of the state and the people. Moreover, positive measures for their gradual solution are in the process of being adopted. However, once we have stated that we want to guarantee the citizens' exercise of their rights to work and rest and other basic rights, then we must clearly stipulate that citizens enjoy environmental rights. For this reason clarifying and emphasizing citizens' environmental rights is a problem urgently in need of a solution in China's law and a pressing problem that is close to the people's hearts.

Comments

This lengthy article is faithful to the statist tradition in communist countries and, to a lesser extent, the tradition of Confucian paternalism in the sense that the author prefers that rights be granted only in conjunction with commensurate duties or obligations and that the rights of the state are superior to those of its citizens. This is reflected in extensive references to the constitutions of Eastern European countries. However, it does represent progress, compared with the Maoist era, by acknowledging and codifying rights which were undefined and completely subject to arbitrary violation during the Cultural Revolution.

Cai's extension of the concept of rights to the environment raises a number of fundamental questions about the basic theory of environmental law in China. First, is there really such a thing as environmental rights per se? If so, how are environmental rights distinguishable from rights granted under general legal theories, such as nuisance under tort law? (*See* the relevant sections in Dong Lou, *Minfa Yuanze* [The Principles of Civil Law], Beijing: Falü Chubanshe, 1983). Second, Cai, who is on the law faculty at Wuhan University, delineates three holders of rights. In whom do these rights vest? Can citizens assert the rights of the state? If so, what are the implications? (*See* Lester Ross and Mitchell A. Silk, "Post-Mao China and Environmental Protection: The Effects of Legal and Politico-Economic Reform," *UCLA Pacific Basin Law Journal* [1985]).

ENVIRONMENTAL LITIGATION IN CHINA

Cheng Zhengkang (1983) "A Preliminary Investigation into Some Main Points of Foreign Environmental Litigation: A Brief Discussion of the Legal Regulations Governing Environmental Litigation in China"

ZHK no. 1, pp 71–76.

Environmental pollution has swiftly aroused strong concern in countries around the world because of its vast scale, great danger, and broad scope owing to industrial development, population growth, and urbanization. In just the past twenty years these countries have adopted a series of policies, corresponding to the actual circumstances of environmental pollution within their own countries, in order to prevent pollution from worsening and to gradually control existing pollution. The formulation of stringent laws and regulations governing environmental protection is one of the most important measures to prevent and control pollution.

Environmental protection laws in capitalist countries are just like their other laws; they are expressions of the will of the bourgeoisie and serve the bourgeois class. We must realize, however, that the people in these countries have waged a protracted, vast, and unyielding struggle against the bourgeoisie's evil rapacious plundering of the environment, shifting the danger of pollution on to others, and encroaching on the environment needed by the people for basic existence. This has inevitably compelled the bourgeoisie to take account of the object of this class struggle in their environmental protection laws and regulations, resulting in some regulations that favor the masses playing a role in environmental management and litigation. These regulations have led to rather substantial modifications in civil law, criminal law, administrative law, and litigation law in terms of theory and content, in response to the special nature of environmental protection law. This article seeks to present a cursory analysis of some special characteristics of foreign environmental protection law with regard to environmental litigation, for use as reference in China's future legislation on environmental protection.

EXPANSION OF THE RIGHT TO BRING SUIT

A major and critical characteristic of environmental litigation abroad is the expansion of the right to bring suit, also known as the broadening of standing to appear in court. It has two principal forms.

The Grant of the Right to Bring Suit in Certain Civil Matters Involving Illegal Behavior in Contrast to Traditional Civil Law Where No Such Right Existed

According to traditional civil law theory, one (or his guardian, legal representative, or agent) had the right to bring suit against a party causing an injury only when one's person or one's rights and interests suffered direct or indirect harm as a result of the other party's illegal behavior. Such civil litigation can be classified into suits to eliminate the danger, suits to gain recognition of property rights, suits to restore the status quo ante, and suits to win compensation for damages. According to this theory, there was no right to bring suit for injuries to property, person, or other rights and interests caused by another party unless the latter's behavior was illegal. It has already been demonstrated that this traditional theory is not conducive to environmental protection. It has therefore been increasingly disregarded in environmental protection laws and regulations. In Britain, scholars recognize that traditional common law cannot protect rivers, the air, the marine environment, or residential environments and cannot effectively punish those who violate environmental protection laws and regulations. Therefore, Britain has, over the past twenty years, stepped out of character and actively enacted a host of statutes governing environmental protection.

Britain classifies environmental pollution into two categories, private nuisances and public nuisances, with the only differences between them being the number of people injured (injury to three or more persons is defined as a public nuisance) and differences in the nature of the rights and interests injured by the illegal behavior in question (a private nuisance if only private rights and interests are injured and a public nuisance if the rights and interests affected are enjoyed as a member of the public). In the case of the *Attorney General v. P.Y.A. Quarries, Ltd.* (1957)[91] the court stated: "Any hazard that gravely impairs the comfort and convenience of the Queen's subjects is a public nuisance." In English law a public nuisance is a criminal law violation and any injured party can file suit in his own name against the party causing the injury; other parties who suffer indirect injuries can also file suit in their own name (however, under certain conditions a party suffering an indirect injury requires the approval of the prosecutor before he can file suit).

With regard to private nuisances, in the past Britain always relied on common law rules, but after realizing that this limitation on the people's right to bring suit did not promote environmental protection, private nuisances were reclassified into two categories. Some private nuisances affecting property and person continue to be treated as ordinary private nuisances, whereas other private nuisances are classified as statutory nuisances. For example, the Clean Air Act of 1956,[92] with regard to the removal of smoke and other pollutants; the 1960 Noise Abatement Act,[93] with regard to noise and vibrations; and the 1958 Refuse Act regarding dumping refuse in public places[94] all deal with statutory nuisances, and anyone can file suit against someone who violates these laws. For example, anyone who discovers someone else dumping refuse in a public place can file suit against the dumper even though he is neither the owner nor the tenant of the site. Therefore, with few exceptions, British citizens can bring suit against violators of the environmental protection laws.

Laws and regulations in the United States are basically similar to those found in England, although their provisions are a bit simpler, clearer, and more practical. For example, the 1971 [sic] Clean Water Act provides that, except under some special circumstances, any citizen can bring suit in his own name against anyone who violates environmental protection laws and regulations.

The rise of class action suits in the United States and Britain in recent years is especially noteworthy. This type of litigation was originally used as a means of consumer protection against manufacturers who misrepresented counterfeit products as real, thereby causing damages. Now class actions have been extended into the area of environmental litigation. Under traditional common law only those vested with "riparian rights" (i.e., the title of the lands adjacent to river banks) or "fishery rights" (i.e., by permission, the right to conduct fishing activities as a major source of income) could bring actions against those who polluted a river and caused damages to it. Under the class action theory, however, the entire class may bring actions against the infringer(s) as long as anyone within that class suffered from such pollution and the entire class thus had interests related to the tortious conduct. As such, interest groups could bring actions against the river polluters if they extend to the owners of the river or fishery in question the right to become members in the action. This will normally have a deterrent effect on the polluters/infringers because a class action is a more powerful and effective weapon than individual private action.

The expansion of citizens' right to sue has had a positive effect on the supervision of polluters, who are, therefore, placed in a disadvantaged position and forced to abide by various environmental laws.

Expanding the Scope of Those Subject to Suit

The expansion of the right to sue also provides citizens with standing to sue those who may not be sued under traditional legal theories. For example, in the United States, Section 505(a) of the Clean Water Act of 1977 provides:

> Except as provided in subsection (b) of this section, any citizen may commence a civil action—on his own behalf—against any person (including [i] the United States, and [ii] any other governmental instrumentality or agency to the extent permitted by the eleventh amendment to the Constitution) who is alleged to be in violation of (A) an effluent standard or limitation under this chapter or (B) an order issued by the Administrator or a State with respect to such a standard or limitation.[95]

English law provides that citizens may bring actions against those organizations whose function is obviously in furtherance of the public interest whenever such legal duties have not been performed.

Expanding the scope of those subject to suit, especially that citizens shall be able to bring actions against any and all levels within the government or the person(s) responsible for carrying out governmental functions, benefits the citizens and allows them to monitor the government in the enforcement of environmental protection-related duties and adherence to environmental laws.

China is a socialist country where every citizen enjoys sufficient democratic rights. Our environmental law has long provided that any citizen can bring an action against any governmental unit or individual for the pollution or destruction of the environment. However, because of the underdevelopment of administrative law, the lack of practices such as judicial review or supervision of administrative behavior, and the ill-defined responsibilities among various organizations, the question of whether citizens may sue government units for nonperformance of their duties or violation of laws with regard to environmental protection remains unresolved. Because this will eventually affect our country's environmental protection work, it is essential that we consider supplementing the body of administrative and environmental laws and adding corresponding regulations.

SHIFTING THE BURDEN OF PROOF

Under traditional rules the plaintiff who brought the action, be it civil or criminal, bore the burden of providing evidence to support each of his accusations.

In a tort action the plaintiff should provide at least the following four [types of] evidence: (1) the plaintiff has suffered damages; (2) such damages were caused by the defendant's conduct or act; (3) the fault is on the defendant (i.e., intentional or negligent tort); and (4) the plaintiff has fulfilled his duty of avoiding damages. A defendant will not be held liable unless all four of these requirements are met.

Such a requirement with regard to the burden of proof no longer serves its purpose in the protection of the environment and pollution victims. The reasons are as follows. First, there is no way for the plaintiff to "avoid" damage, since the development of industry and technology have made it quite impossible for the general public (including specialists in other disciplines) to understand which factory's or enterprise's facilities or equipment cause what kinds of pollution, not to mention the damages it would suffer therefrom. Second, it is virtually impossible for the plaintiff to determine whether or not the defendant is at fault because legally protected trade or industrial secrets are not supposed to be made public. Third, it is improper to have the plaintiff pinpoint a particular pollutant which causes damages because the plaintiff normally lacks the expertise to understand the quantity or density of a pollutant that will result in such an injury or damage. Fourth, it is improper to have the plaintiff prove at which stage or when the damages occur because in many situations the damages done to human health by a pollutant result from an accumulation of effects. Thus to require the plaintiff to bear the burden of proof in environmental litigation is virtually taking away the victim's right to sue and be compensated, which, in turn, encourages and aggravates pollution.

In light of this many countries now adopt the new rules in terms of burden of proof. For instance, in the United States, Section 3 of the 1970 Environmental Protection Act of the State of Michigan provides:

> When the plaintiff in the action has made a prima facie showing that the conduct of the defendant has, or is likely to pollute, impair or destroy the air, water or other natural resources of the public trust therein, the defendant may rebut the prima facie showing by the submission of evidence to the contrary. The defendant may also show, by way of an affirmative defense, that there is no feasible and prudent alternative to defendant's conduct and that such conduct is consistent with the promotion of the public health, safety and welfare in light of the state's paramount concern for the protection of this natural resource from pollution, impairment or destruction.[96]

Therefore, in such types of litigation the defendant bears the major burden of proof.

Some other nations also relieve some of the burden originally placed on the plaintiff. French law provides that it is only necessary for the plaintiff to prove that there is cause in fact between the pollution act and the damages in a pollution damage action, without further proving that the defendant was at fault. Luxembourg's law states that even if the plaintiff cannot prove that the defendant is at fault, he can nevertheless apply the Supreme Court's interpretation to bring an action for damages. It goes further by regulating that the defendant is liable for such damages that are beyond what a reasonable man may endure under the permissible limitations. Japanese law has, in effect, exempted plaintiffs' partial burden of proof, although it is not expressly stated so.

The law in China has yet to apportion the burden of proof. Thus litigation in this area must apply, for expediency's purpose, the related rules under civil or criminal procedure. But in civil procedure the rule is that the plaintiff bears the burden of proof (Article 55).[97] It is foreseeable that applying such a rule in environmental protection cases will cause many difficulties. Therefore, it is quite necessary to enact some special legislation in the area of environmental protection so that the development of environmental protection work and the protection of those victims' legitimate interests may be enhanced.

PRESUMPTION OF CAUSE (IN FACT)

When a judgment must be made in a tort case or when making a decision on [the issue of] guilty [or not guilty], the most important step is to determine the causal relations (i.e., a cause and effect relation exists between a particular act or conduct and a particular result). An accurate and justified judgment can be rendered only when such a causal relation is determined.

In environmental cases it is bound to be difficult in determining that a causal relation does exist between a certain tortious conduct and a certain damage because (a) for such a newly developed science as environmental science, people have yet to fully understand the character, migration, toxicity, and so on of various pollutants; (b) many damages result from an accumulative effect which takes a long time to be realized; (c) some pollution damages are the consequence of compound action by many pollutants. Thus it is quite difficult, if not impossible, to apply the same doctrine as in criminal or tort cases to the environmental cases in the determination of causal relationship. . . .

Currently there are not many environmental cases in this country. However, the issue of how to determine causal relations has been discussed not only in court judgments, but also in the process of administrative mediation or arbitration. Thus it is necessary to adopt and absorb such laws [on the determination of causal relations] that are based on epidemiology in environmental litigation and that are distinct from the determination of causal relations in general criminal or civil cases.

STRICT LIABILITY

Under the traditional view of civil law one has a cause of action against another party for the property, physical, emotional, or reputational damages resulting from the other party's tortious conduct. But, as stated previously in the discussion of shifting the burden of proof, the victim has the burden to prove that the tortfeasor's conduct was injurious (i.e., either with intent or negligence) and that the infringer would be held liable for the damages caused by his conduct if, and only if, he acted with intent or negligence. This is the system of "negligent liability."

With increased environmental litigation many nations gradually have come to realize that this "negligent liability" system is detrimental to environmental protection and incompatible with the character of environmental law. The majority of these nations have thus started to adopt and develop the "strict liability" system which already exists in civil law.

Take the examples of Britain and the United States. The courts basically adopted the "negligent liability" system in the 1960s but have abandoned it by moving toward the "strict liability" system in the 1970s (i.e., to apply the doctrine of *Rylands v. Fletcher*[98] laid down by the British court in 1868 to environmental litigation). In *Ryland*, plaintiff Ryland owned a mine and defendant Fletcher owned a reservoir located above the plaintiff's mine. In one particular incident the water pouring out from the defendant's reservoir flooded the plaintiff's mine, thereby causing damages. The court stated that "if a person brings, or accumulates, on his land anything which, if it should escape, may cause damage to his neighbour, he does so at his own peril. If it does escape, and cause damage, he is responsible, however careful he may have been, and whatever precautions he may have taken to prevent the damage."[99] This doctrine has since become accepted and followed in Anglo-American environmental law.

In the civil law countries environmental legislation has adopted, for the most part, another form of expression in their industrial development process. Under "exemplary liability" any citizen or organization whose activities involve high risk to the surrounding people (e.g., transportation organization, industrial enterprise, architecture and construction department, automobile owner) is liable for the damages done to these people unless it can be proved that such damages resulted from an act of God (force majeure) or the intention of the injured party.

Japanese law, however, even extends the principle of strict liability to situations in which an act of God (force majeure) occurred in that the court would only consider it as an element in determining the amount of the pecuniary damage.

Adopting such a strict liability system would induce industrial and mining enterprises to reinforce their management, prevent damages to others, and protect and assert the legitimate rights and interests of the injured party so that the task of environmental protection would be enhanced. Our environmental legislation has yet to resolve this issue. This can be seen just by looking at Article 32 of the Environmental Protection Law. On the other hand, the current civil procedure still adopts the "negligent liability" system in most cases. Therefore, further research in this area and the promulgation of corresponding rules are needed. I believe that, as a socialist country, the sole purpose for the development of production is to fulfill the people's ever-increasing material and cultural needs. Thus it should be our nation's policy to provide full protection from pollution for the injured party in a way that the capitalist countries cannot match. For the reasons stated earlier I advocate adoption of the "strict liability" system in environmental litigation. If, however, there are difficulties in the overall adoption of such a system, the "strict compensation" system should nevertheless be adopted; that is, the tortfeasors should still provide necessary compensation for the environmental pollution caused by nonintentional or nonnegligent conduct.

DUAL LIABILITY

Unlike the traditional principle of individual [natural person] liability, dual liability is a unique aspect of environmental litigation. In capitalist countries the principal liability is placed on the person who acted and supplemental liability is placed on the enterprise or other organization to which that person belongs. For instance, the Japanese Water Pollution Control Law provides that "the representative, agent, employee or other [authorized] personnel of a legal or natural person is liable for the violation of the previous four Sections in conducting the business for such legal or natural person. That legal or natural person should also be fined for such violations as provided by the pertinent Sections." The British Water Resources Act of 1963"[100] . . . provides that "if an illegal act of a certain cooperation group (such as a corporation) was the result of the agreement or between members of the board, managers, secretaries or other officials, such persons are subject to the trial and punishment for the crime done." In some of the socialist states it is stipulated that under certain circumstances the enterprise is subject to principal liability, while the actor(s), may, however, be jointly liable. For instance, the Polish Ministerial Conference Order of September 26, 1967, stated: "When judging the fine charged upon an enterprise or industry, the administrative or disciplinary liability should simultaneously be imposed upon those natural persons who are responsible [for the illegal act]."

The purpose in adopting such a dual penalties system is to force factories and industries to strengthen their environmental protection work, especially to have the leaders of those facilities strengthen factory management and supervision of their employees.

Article 32 of our country's Environmental Protection Law has actually provided a dual penalties system. Its enforcement, however, has encountered certain obstacles, since its content is too vague. It is, therefore, necessary to clarify this provision.

APPLICATION OF SPECIAL CRIMINAL LAW

Another character of environmental litigation is the application of specific criminal laws. Because environmental pollution seriously jeopardizes every country's economic development and social security, many countries have come to realize that it is insufficient to accomplish the task of environmental protection by administrative and civil laws alone, and that a special criminal law with deterrent, rehabilitative, and punitive characters should be adopted for the protection of the environment. This results in the development of criminal legislation and the application of such special criminal laws in environmental protection and litigation.

Because the criminal law in many countries was originally enacted at a time when environmental crimes were not serious, the crime of ''environmental pollution'' was not established. Environmental pollution gradually came to be treated as a crime and was included in many countries' legislation as a crime of ''harming the environment'' or ''public nuisance'' as pollution problems became aggravated and societal damages became more obvious. Many countries (e.g., West Germany and the Soviet Union) now propose to perfect their criminal law or penal code by adding the crime of harming the environment. The vast majority of countries, however, have enacted specialized laws which make harming or damaging the environment a crime before they revise the penal code, or add a provision in their existing environmental legislation that the violation or harming of such constitutes a crime.

It is fairly easy to discover, after a careful study of foreign environmental law, that there are many specific criminal laws in existence in foreign countries. [As a result,] quite a few violations that were excluded from criminal punishment are now subject to severer penalties, some attempted offenses which were overlooked in the past are now subject to prosecution. For example, in contrast to the past there is criminal liability imposed on those who illegally utilize an installation or facilities which are detrimental to the environment. The enactment of special criminal laws has a positive effect on environmental protection.

The Chinese Criminal Law does not provide for the crime of ''harming the environment.'' This is not because the crime does not exist in this country, but because there was not thorough consideration during the enactment of the Criminal Law in the first place. In the areas of environmental law, although there is a provision with regard to criminal penalties, practical experience in the past has proved that no criminal who harms the environment may be brought under control without the enactment of a specific substantive criminal law. In the past several years judicial practice has concurred with this opinion, and yet people tend to neglect one suggestion that has already been proposed: ''It is worth consideration to pass a supplemental law to the current criminal law.'' The gap illustrates that this issue has not been fully resolved, even though many specialized environmental laws were drafted. I therefore suggest that it is time to formulate a special criminal law on environmental crimes, but one which does not contradict the spirit of the Criminal Law.

Comments

Cheng Zhengkang, in this essay, makes one of the earliest arguments on behalf of strict liability as well as looser evidentiary procedures and broader standing to sue in environmental jurisprudence. This involves an elaboration and redefinition of the rights of citizens, including the right of citizens to bring suit against the government itself. Cheng, on the law faculty at Beijing University, builds his case on the basis of Western (bourgeois) jurisprudence, which is typical of Chinese legal scholars. If the Western ideas which he apparently embraces in this essay were fully applied in China, they would greatly alter the distribution of citizen rights and the nature of the relationship between citizen and state.

Notes to Part One

1. See the closing address by Dr. Mostafa Tolba, executive director of the United Nations Environment Program, at the Eighth Conference of the Governing Council held in Nairobi on April 29, 1980.

2. Li Chaobo, "Address to the National Academic Exchange Conference on Environmental Management, Economics and Law," February 25, 1980, Taiyuan.

3. Mao Zedong, "Talk at an Enlarged Central Work Conference" (January 30, 1962) in Stuart Schram, ed., *Chairman Mao Talks to the People: Talks and Letters, 1956–1971*, New York: Pantheon Books, 1974, pp. 158–87.

4. Joseph Stalin, *Economic Problems of Socialism in the U.S.S.R.* (Chinese version), p. 31. [The English version was published by International Publishers, New York, 1952, eds.]

5. Alan Howard Cottrell, *Environmental Economics: An Introduction for Students of the Resource and Environmental Sciences*, London: Edward Arnold, 1978, p. 6.

6. *Id.*, pp. 7–8.

7. The text is at 26 and 27 Victoria, ch. 124 [eds.].

8. The text is at 39 and 40 Victoria, ch. 75 [eds.].

9. The text is at 16 and 17 George V, ch. 43 [eds.].

10. For example, Japan has enacted more than two hundred laws and regulations governing environmental protection.

11. Law No. 132 (August 3, 1967). The text is in *Roppo Zensho* (The Six Basic Laws), Tokyo: Yuhikaku Publishers (1985) [eds.].

12. The text is at *Durzkaven Vestnik* (Official Law Gazette of the People's Republic of Bulgaria) (hereafter referred to as *D.V.*), no. 4 (June 16, 1967); amended, *D.V.*, no. 3 (1977), and *D.V.*, no. 39 (1978) [eds.].

13. The text is at 42 U.S.C. §§ 4321–4370a (P. L. 91–190) [eds.].

14. Law no. 9 on Environmental Protection, *Buletinue Oficial*, no. 91 (June 23, 1973) [eds.].

15. Law no. II of 1976 on the Protection of the Human Environment, *Magyar Közlöny*, April 1, 1976, p. 318 [eds.].

16. The text is in *FLHB*, vol. 4 (1955), pp. 86–90 [eds.].

17. The text is in *FGHB*, vol. 3 (1956), pp. 267–70 [eds.].

18. The text is in *FGHB*, vol. 6 (1958), pp. 433–38 [eds.].

19. The text is in *FGHB*, vol. 6 (1958), pp. 450–53 [eds.].

20. The text is in *FGHB*, vol. 10 (1960), pp. 410–16 [eds.].

21. The text is in *FGHB*, vol. 13 (1964), pp. 205–14 [eds.].

22. The text is in *HBYWX*, pp. 7–12 [eds.]

23. The text is in *JFGXB*, vol. 2, p. 501 [eds.].

24. *The Complete Works of Marx and Engels* (Chinese), vol. 25, p. 875.

25. *Selected Works of Marx and Engels* (Chinese), vol. 8, p. 518.

26. Beijing: Gongren Chubanshe [eds.].

27. *See id.* at pp. 158–88 [eds.].

28. *See id.* at pp. 194–210 [eds.].

29. Legal Dictionary Editing Commission, ed., *Faxue Cidian* (Dictionary of Legal Terminology), Shanghai: Cishu Chubanshe, 1979, p. 485 [eds.].

30. Economic Law Editing Group, *Jingji Faxue* (The Study of Economic Law), Beijiing: Qunzhong Chubanshe, 1983, pp. 267–89 [eds.].

31. Deng Xiaoping, "Emancipate the Mind, Seek Truth from Facts and Unite as One Looking to the Future" (December 13, 1978), in *Selected Works of Deng Xiaoping*, Beijing: Foreign Languages Press, 1984, p. 158 [eds.].

32. Joseph Stalin, *Problems in Soviet Socialist Economics* (Chinese edition), Beijing: Renmin Chubanshe, 1958, p. 30.

33. *Complete Works of Marx and Lenin* (Chinese edition), vol. 1, p. 184.

34. Mao Zedong, "On Practice," in *Selected Works of Mao Zedong* (one-volume Chinese edition), 1967, p. 259.

35. The text is in *HBYWX*, pp. 3–14 [eds.].

36. Fan Ming and Liu Bochun, "The Foundation and Direction of Environmental Management," in *Huanjing Guanli*, no. 2 (1983), pp. 3–6.

37. Some Regulations on Combining Technological Upgrading with the Prevention and Control of Industrial Pollution, February 6, 1983. The text is in *GGB*, no. 3 (1983), p. 87.

38. *Selected Works of Deng Xiaoping* (Chinese version), p. 371.

39. V. I. Lenin, "How to Organize Competitions," in *Selected Works of V. I. Lenin* (Chinese version), vol. 3, p. 395.

40. *Complete Works of Marx and Lenin* (Chinese version), vol. 25, p. 117.

41. This article's sections on the "Human Environment Manifesto" were translated from the "Six Laws on the Environment," published in Japan in 1979.

42. The treaty is at 213 U.N.T.S. 221 [eds.].

43. Translated from Chinese edition published by Kexue Chubanshe, 1979.

44. The text of the Declaration is in *Report of the U. N. Conference on the Human Environment*, U. N. Document A/CONF. 48/14, pp. 2–65. *See also International Legal Materials*, vol. 11 (1972), pp. 1416–69 [eds.].

45. Municipal Ordinance No. 97 (July 2, 1969), in *Roppo Zensho* (The Six Basic Laws), Tokyo: Yuhikaku Publishers, 1985 [eds.].

46. The Kawasaki Ordinances were not reported or have since been repealed. There is, however, mention of the Osaka Municipal Public Hazard Prevention Ordinances, Municipal Ordinance No. 1, March 11, 1971, in *id.* [eds.].

47. 42 U.S.C. §§ 4321–4370a (P. L. 91–190) [eds.].

48. This is Section 101(c) of the Act [eds.].

49. The text is in *CCW*, vol. 14 [eds.].

50. The text is in *CCW*, vol. 12 [eds.].

51. The text is in *CCW*, vol. 6 [eds.].

52. The text is in *CCW*, vol. 13 [eds.].

53. The text is in *CCW*, vol. 2 [eds.].

54. The text is in *CCW*, vol. 13 [eds.].

55. The text is in *CCW*, vol. 6 [eds.].

56. The text is in *CCW*, vol. 16 [eds.].

57. The text is in *CCW*, vol. 16 [eds.].

58. The text is in *CCW*, vol. 12 [eds.].

59. The text is in *CCW*, vol. 2 [eds.].

60. The text is in *CCW*, vol. 1 [eds.].

61. The text is in *CCW*, vol. 12 [eds.].

62. The text is in *CCW*, vol. 15 [eds.].

63. The text is in *Constitution of the Republic of Chile* (as amended), Washington, D. C.: Organization of American States, General Secretariat, 1972, [eds.].

64. The text is in *CCW*, vol. 4 [eds.].

65. *See Constitution of the Socialist Federal Republic of Yugoslavia*, Belgrade: Dopisna Delavska Universa, 1974.

66. The text is in *CCW*, vol. 4 [eds.].

67. The text is in *CCW*, vol. 16 [eds.].

68. The text is in *CCW*, vol. 7 [eds.].

69. The text is in *CCW*, vol. 6 [eds.].

70. The text is in note 63 *supra* [eds.].

71. The text is in *CCW*, vol. 2 [eds.].

72. The text is in note 65 *supra* [eds.].

73. The text is in *CCW*, vol. 2 [eds.].

74. Decree on the Intensification of Nature Conservation and the Improved Utilization of Natural Resources, No. 898 (December 29, 1972), in *Sabranie postanovlenii Pravitel'stva SSSR* (1973), no. 2, item 6, and translated in William E. Butler, ed., *Collected Legislation of the Union of Soviet Socialist Republics and the Constituent Union Republics*, Dobbs Ferry, N.Y.: Oceana Publications, looseleaf, III–1 [eds.].

75. Law No. 132 (August 3, 1967), in *Roppo Zensho* (The Six Basic Laws), Tokyo: Yuhikaku Publishers, 1985 [eds.].

76. The text is in note 65 *supra* [eds.].

77. This class action was decided by the Osaka District High Court on November 27, 1975. *See Hanrei Jiho* (Case Report Times), January 22, 1976 [eds.].

78. The text is in *CCW*, vol. 4 [eds.].

79. The text is in *CCW*, vol. 1 [eds.].

80. The text is in *CCW*, vol. 7 [eds.].

81. The text is in *CCW*, vol. 13 [eds.].

82. *Complete Works of Marx and Engels*, Ch. 16, p. 16.

83. *See* note 44 *supra*.

84. *See CCW*, vol. 15 [eds.].

85. *See CCW*, vol. 16 [eds.].

86. The text of the law appears in Appendix A [eds.].

87. The text of the law appears in Appendix A [eds.].

88. This law was amended in 1984. The revision appears in Appendix K.

89. The text is in *Zhonghua Renmin Gongheguo Di Wu Jie Quanguo Renmin Daibiao Dahui Di San Ci Huiyi Wenjian* (Documents of the Third Plenary Session of the Fifth National People's Congress of the People's Republic of China), Beijing: Foreign Languages Press, 1981, p. 156 [eds.].

90. The Constitution was revised in 1982. The corresponding provisions to Articles 48 and 49 of the 1978 Constitution are to be found in Articles 42 through 44 of the 1982 Constitution:

> *Article 42*. Citizens of the People's Republic of China have the right as well as the duty to work.
>
> Using various channels, the state creates conditions for employment, strengthens labour protection, improves working conditions and, on the basis of expanded production, increases remuneration for work and social benefits.
>
> Work is the glorious duty of every able-bodied citizen. All working people in state enterprises and in urban and rural economic collectives should perform their tasks with an attitude consonant with their status as masters of the country. The state promotes socialist labour emulation, and commends and rewards model and advanced workers. The state encourages citizens to take part in voluntary labour.

The state provides necessary vocational training to citizens before they are employed.

Article 43. Working people in the People's Republic of China have the right to rest.

The state expands facilities for rest and recuperation of working people, and prescribes working hours and vacations for workers and staff.

Article 44. The state prescribes by law the system of retirement for workers and staff in enterprises and undertakings and for functionaries of organs of state. The livelihood of retired personnel is ensured by the state and society. [eds.]

91. [1957] 2 Q.B. 169, [1957] 1 All E.R. 894 [eds.].

92. The text can be found at 4 and 5 Eliz. II, ch. 52 [eds.].

93. The text can be found at 8 and 9 Eliz. II, ch. 68 [eds.].

94. The text can be found at 6 and 7 Eliz. II, ch. 34 [eds.].

95. *See* 33 U.S.C. § 1365(a) [eds.].

96. The text is in Michigan Legislative Service Bureau, *Public and Local Acts of the Legislature of the State of Michigan* (Regular Session of 1970), Lansing, Mich.: Speaker-Hines & Thomas, 1971, pp. 390–92 [eds.].

97. The text is in *GGB*, no. 6 (1982), p. 207 [eds.].

98. L.R. 3 H.L. 330 (1868) [eds.].

99. *Id.* [eds.].

100. The text is in 11 and 12 Eliz. II, ch. 38 [eds.].

Part Two
Regulation of the Environment

Once the basic law with regard to pollution control—the Environmental Protection Law—was enacted for trial implementation in 1979, environmental protection officials moved to increase the number and specificity of statutes in order to expand and clarify legislative authority to take action against pollution. In all cases a rather lengthy process of drafting new legislation was involved, in which China's small corps of legal specialists joined environmental officials to review foreign legislation and prepare drafts for approval by the relevant bureaucracies, the Law Committee of the State Council, the State Council itself, the Legal Committee of the National People's Congress, and then the National People's Congress or its Standing Committee.

In view of its international importance and the fact that China is a signatory of the 1982 Law of the Sea Convention, which requires the enactment of domestic implementing legislation, it is not surprising that the Marine Environmental Protection Law was the first specific pollution control law to be enacted. Similar in substance to comparable legislation in other countries, it is nevertheless marked by questionable claims to jurisdiction over vessel sources of pollution in international waters that harm China's environment. This and the other statutes also share a distressing lack of detail in their stipulations, a fact that leads to substantial uncertainty over their application, which is further aggravated by the paucity of judicial interpretation. Readers will wish to compare the Chinese statutes with their counterparts in other countries and with the prescriptions offered in the following articles. It should be noted that several of the statutes, including the Environmental Protection Law, are in the process of revision, and that some statutes, like the air pollution control law, have yet to be enacted, although in some instances the government has issued many directives and standards. In other cases, like toxic waste disposal, the process has only just begun.

Part Two details the various legal regimes by which China regulates all aspects of its environment and controls the major types of pollution. Each chapter herein focuses on one type of pollution or environmental hazard and documents its present state and characteristics, notes the significance of enacting legislation in that area, and then explains the legal framework, proposed or in place, employed by China to control the situation. The chapters feature discussions on air pollution, water pollution, marine resource exploitation and pollution, noise pollution, and solid and toxic wastes by the eminent scholars Wen Boping, Song Diantang, Ma Xiangcong and Chen Zhenguo, Chen Lihu, and Shi Qing.

4

Air Pollution Control

Wen Boping and Song Diantang (1981) "On the Legislative Control of Air Pollution"

Faxue Yanjiu, no. 6, pp. 29–34. Translation, with permission, from *Chinese Law and Government*, vol. 19, no. 1 (1986), pp. 41–49.

THE PRESENT STATE AND CHARACTERISTICS OF AIR POLLUTION IN CHINA

China has done a huge amount of work and achieved considerable success in the control of air pollution. But the existing problems are still serious. China is one of the countries in the world with the largest amount of pollutants released into the air. Air pollution in the cities is particularly serious. In 1978 there were eighteen cities with grave air pollution. In 1979 the number increased to twenty-two. Statistics compiled for sixty-two cities in 1979 show that the floating dust content in the atmosphere of all these cities surpassed the state standard. The annual discharge of soot into the air from industrial furnaces and household stoves in the whole country exceeds 14 million tons and the average dustfall per square kilometer measures 1.5 tons, more than double the average of 0.7 tons over the earth's land as a whole. The amount of sulfur dioxide emitted into the air in the whole country each year is estimated to exceed 15 million tons, with an average load of 1.6 tons per square kilometer, 60 percent higher than the one ton average for the world as a whole. The discharge of huge amounts of pollutants has caused grave harm to man's health and industrial and agricultural production, which has aroused increasing attention.

Smoke emitted by burning fuel, waste gas and soot and dust released in the course of industrial production, and exhaust discharged by running motor vehicles form the major sources of air pollution in China. Of these, smoke emitted by burning coal is the severest, accounting for 70 percent and more; waste gas released by motor vehicles accounts for about 10.5 percent; and industrial waste gas, about 19.5 percent.

Enormous quantities of coal are consumed seasonally in China. About 30 million tons of heating coal are consumed [in the winter] in Northeast,

Northwest, and North China annually, more than double the amount consumed ordinarily. This is why pollution is particularly serious in the heating period. There are two peaks of air pollution; usually from six to eight in the morning and from six to eight in the evening. In the South all kinds of coal with high sulfur and dust content are consumed, and therefore the pollution is also serious.

LEGISLATION GOVERNING THE CONTROL OF AIR POLLUTION

Although our country has promulgated the Environmental Protection Law of the People's Republic of China (trial implementation), it is merely the basic law of environmental protection, containing only a number of provisions on general principles. It is necessary to enact a law for air pollution control, a law on protection against water pollution,[1] a law on noise and vibration control, and other special laws. We would like to set forth our superficial views and proposals on the enactment of a law on air pollution control.

Set Air Quality Standards and Revise the Standards for Pollutant Discharge

Without environmental standards it is impossible to evaluate the quality of the environment. There is no scientific basis to distinguish between observance and violation of the law. Work in environmental protection is thus without a clear-cut, specific target at which it can aim its endeavors. Whether scientific and comprehensive environment standards have been formulated is an important indication demonstrating whether a country's environmental protection work is on the right track.

China has not set forth any standards of air quality so far. In the past we used relevant provisions in the Health Standards for the Design of Industrial Enterprises[2] in place of air quality standards. Although they have played a great promotional role, these standards are not identical with the air quality standards in purpose and requirements. Generally speaking, the former imposes more stringent demands than the latter. Some provisions are too strict and do not fit the conditions in China. Therefore, new air quality standards should be instituted. The Standards for the Discharge of Industrial "Three Wastes" Gas[3] promulgated in 1973 for trial implementation no longer meet the needs of environmental protection work and should be revised as well.

Environmental standards include various environmental quality standards and discharge standards regulating all kinds of pollutants. Once promulgated, they became law. Enforcement of these standards means implementation of the law. Therefore, we must be cautious in formulating these standards. If the environmental standards are too lax, they cannot achieve the purpose or protecting and improving the environment. If they are too stringent, they will be infeasible because huge state investment will be required, or they will be seen as a mere formality, since the standards will generally not be attainable, and will thus become meaningless. Therefore, the enactment of environmental standards must proceed from actual conditions in China, with an ample scientific basis and taking into consideration both needs and possibilities.

EXERCISE CONTROL BY AREA AND CLASS, AND PROTECT KEY AREAS

China stretches across a vast territory, and there are big differences in the character, natural conditions, and population of various areas. It is thus necessary to control air quality by different areas and different classes.[4] The areas can be divided into three categories in accordance with their character, natural conditions, and population. The first category would include state-designated nature reserves, well-known tourist areas, scenic spots and historical sites, and state sanatoriums. The second category would include the national capital, important tourist cities, and areas with beautiful landscapes, scenic spots and historical sites, and sanatoriums designated by various provinces, autonomous regions, and municipalities directly under the central government, as well as cultural areas and densely populated areas in cities. The third category would include cities with a heavy proportion of industry and areas in which factories are concentrated. In accordance with the classification of areas, air quality standards should be divided into three classes. The first and second areas should be taken as key protected areas and special measures should be adopted, such as overall planning and rational distribution, strictly following the practice of completing environmental impact analyses as required by law and licensing for building factories and other systems to rigidly control the selection of sites of pollution-creating factories. At the same time strict pollution discharge standards should be set to ensure that air quality reaches the required standard.

GRASP THE MAIN CONTRADICTION, WORK OUT EFFECTIVE MEASURES, AND CONCENTRATE EFFORTS TO SOLVE THE MAIN CONTRADICTION

The basic task and means of preventing and controlling air pollution are to control the sources of air pollutants. The sources of air pollutants are closely linked with energy policy. An analysis of the volume of energy consumption in our country shows that coal constitutes a large proportion. Judging from the result of air pollution monitoring, we can see that burning coal is the main source of air pollution. One of the main aspects of China's energy policy is that at present and for a long time to come, coal will be our country's main source of energy and fuel. Therefore, the law of air pollution control should give prominence to the control and reduction of the pollutants engendered by burning coal and work out corresponding technological policies and measures.

As far as the seasons are concerned, the largest quantities of coal are consumed during the heating period in winter. Both the 1952 and 1962 smog incidents in London occurred in the heavy fog period of December. Northeast, Northwest, and North China, all of which have a heating period, are the areas in which the largest quantities of coal are consumed. This is why the heating period in those areas is the most likely period of occurrence of a London-type smog incident in China. Focusing on this key season and the key areas, we should work out specific effective measures to prevent the occurrence of major pollution incidents, such as adopting the emergency measures of restricting the total volume of pollutant discharges and changing the composition of fuel.

Saving energy and fuel is an important economic policy of our country as well as a positive measure to reduce air pollution. In view of this the law of air pollution control should also embody this policy and make corresponding provisions.

In grasping the main contradiction we should also consider the whole situation and make efforts to solve the secondary contradictions. [We] must also take appropriate prevention and control measures against the pollutants produced by other kinds of fuel, such as burning petroleum and diesel oil, and against the pollutants emitted by automobiles, trains, and other mobile pollution sources. An example would be to demand that the motor vehicle-manufacturing enterprises improve automobile pollution exhaust equipment.

SET UP AN AIR POLLUTION MONITORING NETWORK

Environmental monitoring is the primary source of information for environmental protection and an important basis for environmental legislation and its implementation. Great efforts should thus be made to strengthen this area. The law of air pollution control should provide that environmental protection monitoring stations at all levels check regularly into the development of air quality at key points in areas under their jurisdiction and make forecasts on the trends of air pollution. Environmental protection monitoring stations throughout the country should be instructed to unify the method of air pollution monitoring and put forward a development plan for setting up a network of air pollution monitoring stations and introducing automation and standardization. The plan should be carried out after examination and approval by the state.

The state should utilize low-interest loans and other forms of economic incentives to enterprises manufacturing air pollution monitoring instruments and should create conditions for the establishment of large-scale or specialized integrated enterprises.

The circumstances regarding environmental pollution should be made public. This is in the interest of securing the people's supervision of the environmental protection work and promoting the pollution prevention and control work by the masses. The environmental laws of both socialist and capitalist countries have stipulations in this regard. China's air pollution control law should direct the people's governments at all levels to prepare an annual report on the state of air quality and improvement measures to the people's congress of the same level.

CARRY OUT THE SYSTEM OF COLLECTING EFFLUENT FEES

The Law of Environmental Protection of our country provides that "[f]ees shall be assessed according to the amount and concentration of pollutants as stipulated by regulations on enterprises that discard more pollutants than the state standards permit''[5] The levying of effluent fees has provided enormous impetus to environmental protection work because the payment of such fees affects the production costs of an enterprise. Because production costs are linked with profit—that is, the comprehensive index reflecting the economic results of the enterprise—levying of effluent fees affects the economic interests of each worker and staff member. Experiments conducted by some provinces and municipalities have yielded impressive results.

The levying of effluent fees is a means whose aim is to urge the unit discharging pollutants to improve its environmental protection work. In collecting effluent fees attention should be given to the following points.

1. The starting effluent fee should be set low, just a little higher than the cost for operating the equipment required for controlling the pollutant discharge, and the fee can be increased progressively year by year.

2. Enterprises paying effluent fees should include the payment in their production costs. Institutions should include them in their operating costs. Effluent fees can thus be tied to profits, bonuses, and material benefits of the unit discharging pollutants.

3. The fees should be reduced for units that actively treat wastewater, waste gas, and industrial residues but have discharged pollutants above the limit because of inadequate technology. In regard to units that have idled or mismanaged control facilities and units that have been provided with funds and materials but have failed to carry out control measures on schedule, the fees should be doubled, and for some the fees should be increased progressively.

4. In principle, effluent fees should be used in environmental protection work, with the environmental protection and financial departments supervising their use. Those who violate this principle should be held responsible for their misdeeds.

5. The discharged pollutants mainly do harm to the area in which the unit discharging pollutants is located. Hence the fees should be levied chiefly according to region. After collection by the department in charge, the fees should be transferred to the environmental protection department according to regulations. Penalties for late payment shall be collected from units that fail to pay effluent fees on time. The law should stipulate that the fee-collecting departments have the right to notify the banks to transfer the fees directly to them.

LEGAL SANCTIONS

Those who violate the air pollution control law should be given administrative sanctions, civil sanctions, or criminal sanctions.

The chief means of civil sanction is compensation for losses. In addition to clear-cut provisions in the Civil Law of the People's Republic of China, which is being drafted, environmental protection laws, such as the law of air pollution control, can also include compatible supplementary provisions. All units which, in violation of the legal provisions, have jeopardized people's health and caused sickness, disability, death, or damage to public and private property because of their pollution of the air should bear the responsibility of compensation.

The payment of effluent fees does not mean that the unit discharging pollutants has obtained the right to pollute the atmosphere, and it should not make this an excuse for not paying compensation.

If two or more parties cause pollution hazards or damages, the parties concerned should bear joint responsibility. If the victim himself purposely causes harm or loss, or if he alone is at fault, he should not have the right to claim compensation.

Submitting evidence for damage compensation is a complex problem. This is because various kinds of harmful materials discharged by diverse air pollution sources do not exist independently in the atmosphere but are turned into compounds, aggravating their effects. Complex channels transmit the pollutants. It is difficult for the victim to submit evidence demonstrating a causal relationship between the infliction of the harm and the harm done. The laws of some countries stipulate that the defendant bears the burden of proof. For instance, the Law Governing Criminal Responsibility in Public Hazard Cases of Japan[6] stipulates: "If a person in operating a factory or an enterprise, discharges pollutants harmful to people's health and causes harm to the life or health of the public, and if it is considered that the harm is caused by the discharged pollutant, it should be assumed that the harm is caused by the pollutant discharged by that person." If the defendant denies the charge, he must submit evidence to show that the harm caused by the pollution was unrelated to his actions.

Furthermore, statutory limitations should also be set limiting the time during which one has the right to claim compensation for damages. The Air Pollution Control Law of Japan[7] stipulates: "If the victim or his legal agent does not exercise his right three years in succession after he becomes aware of the conditions of damage and the person who should bear the responsibility of compensation, the right to claim compensation for damages will be forfeited; the same holds true twenty years after the damage is inflicted." According to the conditions of our country, the time limit for exercising the right to claim damages should be one year. The provision "the same holds true twenty years after the damage is inflicted" does not fit in with China's conditions either.

Some culprits should receive administrative or criminal sanctions or, in addition to civil sanctions, administrative or criminal sanctions simultaneously, in light of the seriousness of the case or the extent of harm done to society.

In applying legal sanctions the following principles should be followed: (a) Strengthening the protection of key areas. For example, if the air pollution has done harm to nature reserves, tourist areas, scenic spots, historical sites, sanatoriums, the capital, important tourist cities, cultural areas, and densely populated areas in ordinary cities, those responsible should be severely punished. (b) Meting out light punishment for those guilty of unintentional crimes and severe punishment for those who have committed intentional acts. (c) Giving light punishment to those who have committed occasional offenses and severe punishment to persistent offenders.

Because most cases of environmental pollution involve contradictions among the people, legal sanctions should mainly be administrative (administrative punishment or disciplinary action) and civil, whereas criminal sanctions can only be used as a supplementary means. Criminal sanctions, however, should be meted out to a handful of persons who have committed gross crimes with serious consequences.

The Criminal Law of the People's Republic of China has not clearly defined a public hazard or pollution offense. Before the Criminal Law is revised, environmental protection laws such as the law of air pollution control can carry as supplementary articles stipulations as to how to investigate and affix criminal responsibility in pollution cases. When the Criminal Law is revised the articles mentioned can be incorporated into it.

Comments

Wen Boping, professor of law at the Chinese Academy of Social Sciences and author of a widely read textbook on environmental law,[8] and Song Diantang explain the model legislative framework for air pollution control in China. The scheme closely follows that of the United States. The competent authority would promulgate air quality standards to be met through regulating the quantity and quality of discharges. These standards, according to Wen and Song, who anticipated their promulgation in 1982, should be set by area and class. Wen and Song's scheme also envisions intensified monitoring and economic incentives for controlling air pollution. Wen and Song explain the role of civil, administrative, and criminal sanctions in carrying out the program. The authors' recognition of the fact that China's Criminal Law of 1979 did not include a pollution crime and their recommendation to incorporate such crimes in a future amendment are significant in that they represent a clear move away from reliance on imputing criminal responsibility by analogy.[9] The article fails to offer, however, any concrete suggestions on such critical issues as enforcement, the division of responsibilities between central and local authorities or between neighboring jurisdictions on issues like setting environmental standards, or the means by which deterioration can be prevented after achieving air quality standards.

5

Water Pollution Control

Wen Boping (1984) "On the Water Pollution Prevention and Control Law"

Faxue Yanjiu, no. 5, pp. 74–78. Translation, with permission, from *Chinese Law and Government*, vol. 19, no. 1 (1986), pp. 50–63.

The Water Pollution Prevention and Control Law of the People's Republic of China was adopted by the Fifth Session of the Standing Committee of the Sixth National People's Congress on May 11, 1984, and became effective on November 1 of the same year. This is another important environmental protection law proclaimed in the wake of the Law of Environmental Protection of the People's Republic of China (trial implementation) (hereafter referred to as the Environmental Protection Law) and the Marine Environmental Protection Law of the People's Republic of China.

SIGNIFICANCE OF FORMULATING THE WATER POLLUTION PREVENTION AND CONTROL LAW

Water is a precious natural resource. It is the spring of life, the blood of industry, and the lifeline of agriculture. Without water, men cannot live or engage in productive activities.

Water resources are not inexhaustible. China's surface waters total 2,630 billion cubic meters, and groundwater resources amount to 800 billion cubic meters. The country is fifth in the world in terms of total water resources, after Brazil, the Soviet Union, Canada, and the United States. But its annual runoff per capita is only 2,600 cubic meters, a quarter of the world average and lower than that of most countries. With the growth of industry, agriculture, and the cities, the country's water consumption has increased rapidly. Water shortages are now being felt in areas once abundant in water. The contradictions are particularly sharp in the water-short northern areas. Take Beijing for instance. Since 1973 there has been a daily shortage of more than 100,000 tons of water during the peak water-use season in summer, and at times the shortage comes to 170,000 to 180,000 tons. It is evident that protection of water resources has become a matter of utmost importance and urgency.

"Water pollution" refers to the changes in water's chemical, physical, biological, or radioactive properties because of the introduction of certain materials, which affect the use of water, harm people's health, disrupt the ecological environment, or cause deterioration in water quality.

In recent years, particularly since the promulgation of the Environmental Protection Law, the state has adopted a series of measures to control water pollution. In conjunction with the consolidation of industry and technical transformation, many factories, mines, and cities have completed a number of pollution control projects and increased control over newly built projects. However, with the development of industrial production and the growth of cities, the amount of polluted water discharged into rivers and lakes has steadily increased, water pollution is far from being brought under control, and in some places it has worsened. In 1983 the country's wastewater discharge reached 31 billion tons, of which industrial wastewater accounted for 77 percent and household sewage, 23 percent. Toxic and harmful materials discharged with the wastewater amounted to some 130,000 tons. On the other hand, China has only several dozen wastewater treatment plants in urban centers. Only 17 percent of its industrial wastewater and less than 10 percent of its household sewage are treated. Consequently, pollution is serious. About 12.7 percent of the main streams of big rivers are polluted and 55 percent of their branches, especially rivers in urban areas, are seriously polluted. Pollution of small and medium-sized lakes in urban areas is common. The pollution of groundwater is mainly concentrated in large and medium-sized cities and polluted water irrigation areas. In some areas water pollution has become serious.

Water pollution causes great harm. First, it affects the quality of drinking water, and thus jeopardizes people's health and safety. The serious pollution of the Huangpu and Songhua rivers has affected the drinking water quality of 13 million persons in Shanghai and Harbin, arousing strong reaction among the public. Second, it causes the death of fish and a decline in the quality of aquatic products. The country's freshwater fish catch in the 1960s dropped by 20 percent compared with that of the 1950s. In the 1970s there was a further fall of 25 percent compared with the 1960s. The falling trend has not ceased, and one of the main reasons for this decline is water pollution. Third, it affects industrial and agricultural production. Water pollution lowers the quality of industrial production and increases the energy consumption rate. The expenses of twenty cities in the country for softening hard water surpass 1.1 billion yuan. Irrigation of farmland with untreated industrial wastewater causes decreased crop production. About 628,700 hectares of farmland in the country now suffer from pollution by mercury, cadmium, and other heavy metals to varying degrees. People who eat the poisoned crops inevitably get sick or may even die from poisoning. Fourth, it seriously affects the building of scenic tourist areas and the growth of tourism. According to statistics compiled by Shanghai and six other cities, the economic losses caused by water pollution reach 2.7 billion yuan annually. The economic losses of the whole country caused by water pollution exceed 10 billion yuan a year. Water pollution has caused declining health of the people, and in areas where water pollution is serious, the incidence of diseases is usually high. In short, water pollution directly affects the progress of China's socialist modernization.

The promulgation of the Water Pollution Prevention and Control Law has provided a powerful legal guarantee for the prevention and control of water pollution and the protection of water resources. It is of great importance to the protection and improvement of the environment, maintaining ecological balance, ensuring people's health, and promoting the four modernizations. At the same time it marks a major step in the formulation of China's environmental protection laws and provides a great impetus to perfecting the system of our country's environmental protection laws.

CHARACTERISTICS AND MAIN CONTENT OF WATER POLLUTION PREVENTION AND CONTROL LAW

1. The Water Prevention and Control Law is China's first law dealing with prevention and control of water pollution. It applies to surface waters, such as rivers, lakes, canals, irrigation ditches, and reservoirs, as well as groundwater within Chinese territory. In other words, it applies to China's inland waters. The Marine Environmental Protection Law of the People's Republic of China applies to the prevention and control of the pollution of China's seas. The Water Pollution Prevention and Control Law and the Marine Environmental Protection Law are sister laws, and both are important components of the country's environmental protection laws.

The Water Pollution Prevention and Control Law plays a role of primary importance in our country's laws for inland water pollution prevention and control. Where laws and regulations concerning inland water pollution prevention and control promulgated in the past contradict the Water Pollution Prevention and Control Law, the latter will be taken as the official law for enforcement.

The tasks and purposes of the Water Pollution Prevention and Control Law area to "prevent and control water pollution and protect and improve the environment so as to guarantee the physical health of the people, ensure the effective exploitation of water resources, and promote the development of our socialist modernization."[10] In my view the phrase "promote the development of socialist modernization" is important because it is a statement of the purpose of the Water Pollution Prevention and Control Law. The formulation is comprehensive, far-reaching, and appropriate. The waters of scenic tourist areas, for instance, are part of the people's living environment. They lift one's spirit, relax one's mind, and nurture one's patriotic feelings. If these waters become polluted and ruined, it would affect the development of the socialist economy as well as the building of socialist spiritual civilization. Therefore, the Water Pollution Prevention and Control Law should aim not only at "promoting the development of the socialist economy,'' but also at promoting the advance of the entire socialist modernization, including the building of socialist spiritual civilization.

The work of water pollution prevention and control is highly comprehensive and involves wide areas. It requires the coordination and concerted actions of the departments concerned and the unified supervision and control of the organizations in charge. The Water Pollution Prevention and Control Law contains clear provisions in regard to the supervisory and control organizations: The environmental protection departments of the people's government at all levels are the organs that are in charge of exercising unified supervision and administration over prevention and control of water pollution. Navigation organs in the communications departments at all levels are in charge of exercising supervision and administration over the prevention of pollution from ships and boats. The water conservation administrative departments, public health administrative departments, geological and mining departments, municipal administrative departments, and the watershed protection organizations for important rivers of the people's governments at all levels should coordinate, in light of their own responsibility, with the environmental protection departments in supervising and administrating work related to the prevention and control of water pollution.[11]

Because water pollution prevention and treatment involves complex situations, this law can only set forth comprehensive and systematic provisions on important questions of the prevention and treatment work and cannot make specific regulations on all details of implementation. Thus Article 45 of the law stipulates: ''Detailed rules for the implementation of this law defined by the environmental protection department under the State Council will be submitted to the State Council for final approval.''

2. The Water Pollution Prevention and Control Law embodies the principle of ''integrating prevention and control with the stress laid on prevention.'' The Second National Environmental Protection Conference emphasized that in environmental protection work, the principle of ''integrating prevention and control with the stress laid on prevention'' should be enforced. The Water Pollution Prevention and Control Law has fully embodied this principle, particularly in the following major aspects:

(a) It brings prevention and control of water pollution within the bounds of the state plan. Article 3 of the Water Pollution Prevention and Control Law provides: ''The relevant departments of the State Council and the local people's governments at all levels must incorporate work related to the protection of the environment in our water areas in their plans and adopt relevant policies and measures to prevent and control water pollution.''

(b) It institutes and provides for the implementation of the aqueous ambient quality and pollutant discharge standards. The ambient quality standard is the maximum allowable limit for the existence of pollutants in waters, set to protect people's health, ecological equilibrium, and living environment. The pollutant discharge standard is a regulation aimed at controlling the discharge of pollutants so that the waters are up to the ambient quality standard. Both standards are important criteria in enforcing the law. The Water Pollution Prevention and Control Law has clear-cut provisions for the power of the state and the localities in determining the ambient quality standards and pollutant discharge standards, their legal effect, and their revision.

(c) It stipulates the principles of state control over the work of water pollution prevention and control and the basic control system.

(1) The principle of coordination between the prevention and control of water pollution and the control of water resources. The Water Pollution Prevention and Control Law provides that

> [i]n exploiting, utilizing, and readjusting, and allocating water resources, the relevant departments of the State Council and the people's governments at all levels should take all factors into consideration, maintain the rational discharge of the rivers, the rational water level for lakes, reservoirs, and groundwaters, and the natural purification capacities of the waters.[12]

(2) The principle of coordination between the prevention and control of water pollution and municipal administration and the construction of public utilities. The Water Pollution Prevention and Control Law states that "[t]he relevant departments of the State Council and the local people's governments at all levels must incorporate the protection of urban water sources and the prevention of urban water pollution in urban construction plans and build and upgrade drainage systems and sewage treatment facilities."[13]

(3) The principle of integrating the prevention and control of water pollution with the technical transformation of industry. The Water Pollution Prevention and Control Law provides that

> relevant departments of the State Council and the local people's government at all levels should rationally plan the distribution of industrial enterprises, carry out consolidation and technical transformation of enterprises that cause water pollution, adopt comprehensive measures to prevent and control water pollution, raise the recycling rate for water, rationally utilize our natural resources, and reduce the discharge of wastewater and pollutants.[14]

(4) The system of demarcating protected areas for important water-using units. The Water Pollution Prevention and Control Law provides:

> The people's governments above the county level can designate as protected areas sources of drinking water, bodies of water in well-known scenic spots, bodies of water important for fishing, and other bodies of water of special economic or cultural value and adopt measures to ensure that the quality of water in the protected areas satisfies the water quality standards formulated for their particular purposes.[15]

(5) The system of environmental impact analysis. The Water Pollution Prevention and Control Law stipulates that

[c]onstruction projects to be newly built, expanded, or renovated or other equipment to be installed over water surfaces which will directly or indirectly discharge pollutants into the water must observe the state's regulations concerning the administration of environmental protection.

In preparing an analysis on the environmental impact of a construction project, it is imperative to make an appraisal of possible water pollution by the project under construction and of its impact on the ecology, while formulating preventive measures. The analysis should be submitted to the relevant environmental protection department for its examination and approval in accordance with established procedures. The installation of pollution discharge outlets in water conservancy projects, such as canals, channels, and reservoirs, should first meet the approval of the relevant administrative departments of the water conservancy project concerned.

Before the construction project is put into production or use, its water pollution prevention and control facilities must be tested by the environmental protection department. If it should fail to meet the requirements, the construction project concerned may not be put into operation or use.[16]

(6) The system of pollutant discharge registration. The Water Pollution Prevention and Control Law provides that

[t]hose enterprises or other undertakings which directly or indirectly discharge pollutants into bodies of water should adhere to the regulations of the environmental protection department under the State Council; report to the local environmental protection department and register their pollution discharge equipment, their treatment facilities, and the categories, quantities, and concentrations of the pollutants discharged under ordinary operations; and provide the local environmental protection department with the relevant technical materials on the prevention and control of water pollution.

Any major changes in the categories, quantities, or concentrations of pollutants discharged should be promptly reported. The dismantling or failure to operate pollution treatment equipment should be reported in advance and approved by the local environmental protection department.[17]

(7) The system of paying effluent fees and additional effluent fees for discharges exceeding standards. The Water Pollution Prevention and Control Law provides that

[t]hose enterprises or other undertakings which discharge pollutants into bodies of water should pay effluent fees according to state regulations. In cases where the pollutants discharged exceed state or local standards, those enterprises or other undertakings should pay additional effluent fees according to state regulations and should be responsible for control and treatment.[18]

It is noteworthy that with regard to the payment of effluent fees, the provisions of the Water Pollution Prevention and Control Law are stricter than those of the Environmental Protection Law. The latter provides that where the amount of pollutants discharged surpasses the standard set by the state, "[e]ffluent fees shall be assessed according to the amount and concentration of pollutants'' and in accordance with regulations.[19] The effluent fees provided under the Water Pollution Prevention and Control Law are divided into two categories. One is the ''effluent fee,'' which requires that enterprises and institutions that directly or indirectly discharge pollutants into waters pay such a fee, even if the discharge does not exceed the standard set by the state or the locality. The other is an additional effluent fee for discharges exceeding standards, which requires that those who discharge pollutants exceeding the pollutant discharge standard set by the state or the locality assume responsibility for the treatment and control of the excessive pollutants and, during the period of treatment, pay the additional effluent fee for discharges exceeding standards.

The provisions set by the Water Pollution Prevention and Control Law are aimed at making better use of economic incentives to urge the polluting units to economize on the use of water and step up the treatment of pollutants.

(8) The system of setting a time limit for pollution control. The Water Pollution Prevention and Control Law provides that

> [t]hose units releasing pollutants which have caused serious water pollution should treat and control the pollution within a specified time limit.
>
> The time limit set for enterprises or other undertakings under the direct jurisdiction of the central government or provincial, autonomous regional, or municipal governments for treating pollution should be proposed by the environmental protection departments of the provincial, autonomous regional, or municipal governments and be submitted to the people's government at the same level for its decision. The time limit set for enterprises or other undertakings under the jurisdiction of people's governments at or below municipal or county levels should be proposed by the environmental protection departments under the municipal or county people's governments and will be submitted to the people's government at the same level for its decision. The unit discharging the pollutants should fulfill the task within the stipulated time period.[20]

(9) Compulsory emergency measures. The Water Pollution Prevention and Control Law provides that

> [i]n an emergency like the serious pollution of a source of drinking water or a threat to the safety of the water supply, the environmental protection department should report to the people's government at the same level and seek its approval for adopting compulsory emergency measures, including ordering the enterprise or other undertaking concerned to reduce or stop the discharge of pollutants.[21]

(10) The system of on-site inspections. The Water Pollution Prevention and Control Law provides that

> [t]he environmental protection departments under the people's governments at all levels and relevant supervisory and administrative departments are authorized to conduct on-site inspections of units discharging pollutants within the scope of their jurisdiction. The units under inspection must truthfully represent the actual conditions and provide the

necessary data. The inspecting organs are responsible for safe-keeping technological and business secrets of the units under inspection.[22]

(d) It clearly spells out a number of prohibitions. In preventing the pollution of surface water, restrictive provisions are set against various kinds of activities that might create such pollution. Strict limits are imposed on the discharge of toxic pollutants, radioactive materials, pathogenic agents, and oils. For instance, Article 21 provides that the discharge of oils, liquid acids, alkaline liquids or waste liquids containing toxic matter is forbidden. Article 26 provides that "[t]he discharge or dumping into bodies of water of radioactive solid wastes or wastewater containing high or medium levels of radioactive matter is prohibited. The discharge of low radioactive wastewater must conform to state regulations and standards concerning protection against radioactive materials." Article 28 provides that "[w]astewater containing pathogenic agents must undergo sterilization treatment, and discharge is allowed only when the wastewater conforms to relevant standards set by the state." Article 30 provides that the application of pesticides must conform to state regulations and standards concerning safe application of the pesticide. Controls must be strengthened in transporting and storing pesticides and in disposing of outdated pesticides in order to prevent water pollution. In preventing the pollution of groundwater, strict limitations are placed on the use of seepage wells, seepage pits, and fissures and limestone caves to discharge poisonous industrial wastewater and wastewater containing pathogenic agents.

3. The Water Pollution Prevention and Control Law was enacted on the basis of conscientious investigation and study of the conditions of China and extensive efforts to draw on the useful experience of foreign countries. The Water Pollution Prevention and Control Law Drafting Group was set up in June 1980. In the stage of drafting preparations, data on the basic situation concerning the prevention and control of water pollution were sorted out and a huge number of laws and important treatises on water pollution prevention and control in foreign countries were translated. Meanwhile members of the drafting group went separately to more than twenty provinces and municipalities, including Jilin, Heilongjiang, Guangdong, and Hunan, to make systematic investigations and studies. In the course of the drafting, views of the relevant departments of the State Council and various provinces and municipalities were repeatedly solicited and four major revisions were made before the Water Pollution Prevention and Control Law of the People's Republic of China (draft) finally took shape. Later, the Standing Committee of the National People's Congress examined and discussed it, and additional revisions were made.

In view of the fact that China has a vast territory and the conditions in different parts of the country vary greatly, the Water Pollution Prevention and Control Law adopts the principle of integration of the central and local authorities with the stress laid on the local authorities in regard to the management system of water pollution prevention and control. For example, with regard to the right to draft ambient quality standards, the law provides that the environmental protection department of the State Council is responsible for setting a national water environmental quality standard. At the same time it provides that the people's governments of various provinces, autonomous regions, and municipalities directly under the central authorities can work out supplementary standards for those items unspecified in the state water quality standards and report them to the environmental protection department of the State Council for the record. Concerning the power to draft pollutant discharge standards and their legal force, the law provides that the environmental protection department of the State Council should work out the "national standards for pollutant discharge in accordance with the national standards for water quality and the state's economic and technological conditions."[23] It also provides that

> [f]or those waters where the implementation of national pollution discharge standards cannot ensure the attainment of the environmental quality standards for water, the provincial, regional, and municipal people's governments may fix local pollution discharge standards that are more stringent than the national standards and shall report them to the environmental protection department of the State Council for the record.[24]

It further provides that the units that discharge pollutants into the waters where local pollution discharge standards are already in existence should carry out the local standards. In regard to the management system of water pollution prevention and control, attention is paid to the principle of suiting measures to local conditions, giving full play to the role of the local government regarding the demarcation of important watershed protection areas, the system of pollutant discharge registration, and the system of setting a time limit for pollution control.

All this shows that the Water Pollution Prevention and Control Law was enacted on the basis of conscientious, deep-going investigation and study of the country's conditions.

On the question of drawing on the experience of other countries, attention was paid to incorporating good experiences and measures of foreign countries while avoiding the practice of mechanical application. Many foreign sources stress that the policy of "laying stress on prevention" should be observed in water pollution prevention and control and strict measures adopted for the protection of drinking water. The Drafting Group earnestly drew on these important experiences. But taking into consideration the different conditions in China, it did not adopt all the methods now being used in other countries.

4. The Water Pollution Prevention and Control Law provides for clear-cut, strict legal responsibilities. The chapter on "Legal Responsibility" specifies administrative responsibility, civil responsibility, and criminal responsibility.

Administrative responsibility. Article 37 stipulates that warnings should be given to or fines imposed on those who have committed certain misconduct, such as refusing to report or making a false report on the items of registration concerning pollutant discharge as required by the environmental protection department of the State Council, and storing, piling up, discarding, dumping, or discharging pollutants or wastes in violation of the relevant provisions of this law.

It is noteworthy that in view of the fact that some pollutant discharge units refuse to pay effluent fees and the environmental protection departments have no means to compel them to pay, the article also provides that warnings can be served or fines imposed according to the seriousness of the case on those who fail to pay effluent fees or additional effluent fees for discharges exceeding standards in accordance with state regulations.

Article 38 provides for rigorous administrative punishment of those enterprises and institutions that have caused serious water pollution and have been given a time limit to bring their pollution under control but have failed to meet their compliance schedule. It states: "Those which fail to finish the [pollution control] work within the set time must pay two or more times the charges for disposal of excess pollutants as fixed by the state. In addition, a fine may be imposed on them according to the harm and losses incurred, or they may be ordered to suspend operations or to close down."

Article 39 provides for the "dual punishment" system—meting out punishment both to the unit that violates the law and to the persons responsible. It states:

> The enterprises or other undertakings which cause water pollution in violation of the provisions of this law shall be fined by environmental protection departments or by navigation administrative organs of the communications departments according to the harm and losses incurred. If a serious case occurs, the responsible persons shall be subject to disciplinary action by the unit where they work or by the higher authorities in charge.

Civil responsibility. The law provides for the implementation of the principle of strict liability. In other words, when water pollution causes harm, the causer, whether (or not) he is at fault, should bear responsibility for compensating the victim. Article 41 states: "Units which cause harm from water pollution shall bear the responsibility for eliminating pollution and for compensating the units and individuals which have directly suffered losses." It also states clearly that there are three exceptions: "A third party shall bear responsibility for losses incurred from water pollution which is intentionally caused or occurs through the negligence of the third party"; "Units in charge of the disposal of pollution bear no responsibility for any losses incurred from water pollution caused by the victims themselves"; "No responsibility shall be borne for any unavoidable losses from water pollution caused by unavoidable natural calamities when proper measures have been taken in a timely fashion" [Article 42].

Criminal responsibility. The law has more concrete, explicit provisions than the Environmental Protection Law. The latter law has only some provisions of principle in this regard. It states: "The leaders of units, those directly responsible, or other citizens who pollute and harm the environment so seriously as to cause people's deaths and injuries or heavy losses in agriculture, forestry, animal husbandry, sideline production, or fishery should be investigated for their administrative, economic, or even criminal responsibility.''[25] The Criminal Law does not have special clauses dealing with ''pollution crime'' or ''public hazard crime.'' It contains some clauses related to environmental protection which can be employed. Article 43 of the Water Pollution Prevention and Control Law supplements the Criminal Law. It provides: ''If a serious water pollution accident arising from a violation of the provisions of this law leads to grave consequences in terms of heavy losses of public and private property or heavy casualities, investigation shall be made into the criminal responsibility of the responsible persons in accordance with Article 115 or Article 187 of the Criminal Law.''

Moreover, in the chapter ''Legal Responsibility,'' there are explicit provisions supplementary to the procedural law.

Comments

This commentary reveals that the Water Pollution Law was intended to fill some important gaps in regulatory authority and practice: for example, the right of environmental protection departments to recommend emergency response measures; a permit system to provide regulators with basic information on the volume and content of discharges to facilitate environmental management, and the obligation for polluters to supply such information; the right of regulators to conduct on-site inspections—all of which had proved troublesome in the past. The impact of the law continues, however, to depend on how water quality standards are interpreted and enforced and how much money is made available for upgrading factories and wastewater treatment. A good deal has been done in the first instance with regard to major industries in recent years, but the country still faces a multibillion-dollar bill if even primary stage wastewater treatment facilities are to be constructed in major industrial and population centers.

6

Marine Resources Protection

Ma Xiangcong and Chen Zhenguo (1983) "On the Marine Environmental Protection Law"

Faxue Yanjiu, no. 2, pp. 51–56. Translation, with permission, from *Chinese Law and Government*, vol. 19, no. 1 (1986), pp. 64–78.

The Marine Environmental Protection Law of the People's Republic of China (hereafter referred to as the Marine Environmental Protection Law) adopted by the Standing Committee of the National People's Congress came into effect on March 1, 1983. This is an important law to strengthen the control of our country's marine environment and develop marine undertakings.

SIGNIFICANCE OF ENACTING THE MARINE ENVIRONMENTAL PROTECTION LAW

1. The sea takes up more than two-thirds of the earth's surface area and constitutes an important environmental element and treasure house of natural resources. It plays a multifunctional role in sustaining man's existence and promoting social progress. With the growth of the population, the advance of science and technology, and the depletion of continental resources, man's exploitation and utilization of the sea have rapidly developed in magnitude and depth. In the early 1960s a "sea fever" appeared in the world. After the 1970s it developed into all-around exploitation, utilization, protection, and control of the sea and its resources. Today marine undertakings play an increasingly important role in state and social life.

China has a favorable marine environment. It has a long coastline, good harbors, vast sea areas, numerous islands, a broad continental shelf, and abundant resources. Our country's offshore sea areas possess rich marine resources. China has the largest shallow sea fishing ground. According to incomplete data, there are more than 1,500 kinds of marine fish. China has 2 million hectares of coastal beaches fit for the development of marine breeding and other undertakings. Colossal quantities of mineral resources are deposited in sea areas under our country's jurisdiction, and the reserves of sea-bed petroleum and natural gas are plentiful. China has favorable maritime shipping conditions, having more than

700 large and small harbors, of which 20 large harbors are open to the outside world. Chinese ships travel to more than 100 countries and regions in the world. Meanwhile an increasing number of foreign ships visit Chinese harbors or pass through China's sea areas.

Furthermore, seawater can be used to extract salt and other chemical materials. Tidal energy and seawater thermoenergy and wave energy can be used for power generation. Coastal scenic spots, such as Beidaihe, Qingdao, Gulangyu, and Penglai, are excellent places for tourism, recreation, and rest.

The Chinese people are endowed by nature with a vast sea area and rich marine resources which are the basis for the development of our country's marine undertakings. For our country, which has a large population and huge consumption but small per capita land area, the exploitation and utilization of the sea are of particular importance. The exploitation and utilization of the sea do not take up any land and yield important energy, raw materials, and other socioeconomic benefits with comparatively lower investment. Therefore, promoting China's marine undertakings and making full and rational utilization of the marine environment and resources are of paramount importance and an important aspect in the country's socialist modernization drive.

As an ecological system, the sea has its inherent law of development. In exploiting and utilizing the sea, we must respect natural laws, carry out the work rationally. . . . While engaging in exploitation and utilization, we must pay attention to protection of the marine environment and resources. Proceeding from overall considerations and long-term interests, we must adopt effective measures to protect the marine environment and resources, prevent the sea from being polluted or damaged, and ensure that it can be used perpetually.

China is underdeveloped in marine undertakings. The existing problem is that, on the one hand, we have not made full use of the marine environment and resources. On the other hand, in exploiting and utilizing the sea, we have not fully realized the importance of protecting the marine environment and have done poor management work, with the result that our country's marine environment has been polluted and damaged. For instance, China discharges eight billion tons of industrial pollutants and household sewage into offshore waters annually. The pollution and damage of the sea has brought about many harmful consequences. Aquatic resources are damaged and their output has declined, the breeding areas have moved outward, fish are poisoned and unfit for consumption, fishing nets and other gear are discarded, certain kinds of fish have become extinct, and some fishing and breeding grounds are lying waste. The pollution and silting up of harbor areas have affected navigation. The worsening of the quality of seawater has adversely affected many bathing beaches.

There are many reasons why China's marine environment has not been rationally utilized and has been polluted and damaged. An important factor is the legal system, which lacks necessary rules and regulations and rigorous controls.

Since Liberation the Chinese government has done a lot of work and adopted many measures for marine environmental protection, including the enactment of a number of laws and standards. For example, in the field of protecting marine aquatic resources and fishing waters, the "Order on Trawler Fishing in Forbidden Areas in the Bohai, Huanghai, and Donghai Seas"[26] promulgated by the State Council in 1955 has some provisions on protecting marine life resources. To protect marine animals and plants, the "Regulations on Protecting the Breeding of Aquatic Resources"[27] promulgated by the State Council in 1979 include detailed provisions on the principles of gathering marine plants and catching marine animals, seasons and areas off-limits to fishing, and protection of the environment of the water areas. In 1981 the State Council decided to set up two protection areas for undersized fish, one in the Yellow Sea and the other in the East China Sea, and stipulated seasonal restrictions on fishing.

In the field of preventing the pollution of offshore waters, the "Provisional Regulations of the People's Republic of China on Preventing the Pollution of Coastal Waters"[28] promulgated by the State Council in 1974 clearly prohibited the wanton discharge of oils or oil mixtures and other harmful pollutants and wastes into China's coastal waters and laid down specific provisions for the discharge of pollutants by ships and coastal factories and mines. The "Tentative Standards for the Discharge of Industrial 'Three Wastes,' "[29] which went into effect in 1974, have provisions for controlling the discharge of the "three wastes" (wastewater, waste gas, and solid wastes) into the sea by coastal industries. In preventing pollution of the marine environment by ships, the "Regulations Governing the Transport of Dangerous Freight" published by the Ministry of Communications for trial operation in 1972, the "Regulations on the Supervision and Control of Ships Carrying Dangerous Freight" promulgated in 1981, and the "Regulations of the People's Republic of China on the Control of Foreign Ships"[30] approved and published by the State Council in 1979 all have corresponding provisions.

Proceeding from the desire to prevent and control the pollution of seawater, safeguard people's health, protect marine aquatic resources, maintain ecological balance, and ensure the rational exploitation and utilization of the sea, the Leading Group on Environmental Protection of the State Council made public in April 1982 the "Standards for Marine Water Quality,"[31] which sets standards for the quality of marine water in all sea areas under China's jurisdiction according to different categories.

Moreover, provisions for the protection of the marine environment are also laid down in comprehensive laws, such as the "Law of Environmental Protection of the People's Republic of China" (trial implementation), and other relevant legislation, such as the "Regulations of the People's Republic of China on the Exploitation of Offshore Petroleum Resources in Cooperation with Foreign Enterprises."[32]

The laws and regulations mentioned above have played a positive role in exploiting, utilizing, and protecting the marine environment, but they are rather scattered, unsystematic, and uncomprehensive. They make legal adjustments, and most are administrative rules. These laws have left unresolved many issues of principle concerning marine environmental protection. In particular, they fail to legally adjust the various important relations from the perspective of protecting the marine ecological environment in its totality. To promote socialist modernization, we must step up efforts to exploit, utilize, and protect the sea. This urgently requires that we perfect our legal system and tighten the control of the marine environment. The enactment of the Marine Environmental Protection Law is designed to promote the development of China's marine undertakings.

2. The enactment of the Marine Environmental Protection Law not only is aimed at protecting and rationally exploiting and utilizing China's marine environment and resources, but is of great significance for safeguarding our country's marine rights and the fulfillment of the international obligation of protecting the seas of the world. The world's seas are an organic whole. The sea area under the jurisdiction of each country is a component of the world seas. In regard to the sea area under the jurisdiction of a certain country, other countries can also use it, provided that they abide by relevant regulations. The pollution and damage to the marine environment come not only from one country, but also from its neighbors and international exchanges. The pollution of the seas of one country will rapidly spread to other seas and produce harmful effects there. Most of the world's oceans and their resources are the "common heritage of mankind." Accordingly, protection of the marine environment is in the interest of all humanity as well as a common cause of all countries of the world. The protection of the sea area by a littoral country is part of the cause in defense of all seas of the world.

With the development of marine undertakings, the international community has shown increasing interest in protecting the marine environment. Particularly after World War II, the United Nations and other international organizations concerned convened many conferences to discuss the problem of marine environmental pollution and adopted and concluded a series of international conventions designed to prevent marine environmental pollution.

The "Convention on the High Seas"[33] adopted by the First United Nations Conference on the Law of the Sea in 1958 made provisions to prevent pollution of the high seas by ships, pipes, prospecting and exploiting of seabeds, dumping of radioactive wastes, and carrying out radioactive activities. At the Third United Nations Conference on the Law of the Sea held from 1973 to 1982, marine environmental protection remained an important special subject for discussion. One section of the Law of the Sea Convention adopted by the conference deals specially with "Protection and Preservation of the Marine Environment,"[34] and other sections also have many clauses on marine environmental protection. In enacting the Marine Environmental Protection Law, China has the aim of exercising our country's legal rights and fulfilling our international obligations, safeguarding our marine rights, and defending the interest of the seas of the world.

3. In the past two decades many countries have steadily reinforced control of the marine environment and worked out corresponding marine environmental

protection laws to protect their own marine environments and safeguard their own marine rights and interests. Most of these laws are specific laws directed at specified objects of protection or certain pollution sources, such as preventing ship pollution, petroleum pollution, and the dumping of wastes and the demarcation of pollution prevention areas. Among them the largest number of laws are concerned with preventing oil pollution by ships. Besides, some countries have enacted laws and decrees concerning the dumping of wastes in light of the international conventions they have acceded to. To prevent pollution originating from outside their territorial waters, some countries have set up pollution prevention areas. Some countries have adopted laws and decrees restricting large oil tankers or nuclear-powered ships from passing through the seas under their jurisdiction. To protect certain sea areas, some countries have marked out forbidden zones. A number of countries have enacted all-around comprehensive laws of marine environmental protection.

The marine environmental protection laws and regulations of various countries apply not only to citizens and units of their own countries, but also to foreign citizens and units. While sailing in the sea areas under the jurisdiction of other countries, the ships of our country have to abide by the relevant regulations of the country concerned and will be sanctioned if they violate the regulations. On the other hand, as our country's marine environmental laws are imperfect and there are no clear-cut provisions on many questions, we do not have strict control over foreign companies and their ships sailing or engaging in other activities in sea areas under our country's jurisdiction, and thus are unable to properly handle in a timely manner the pollution and damage caused by them. As a result, our country always suffers undue losses. In this sense the enactment of the Marine Environmental Protection Law is necessary for the defense of our country's legal rights and interests.

CHARACTERISTICS AND CONTENT OF THE MARINE ENVIRONMENTAL PROTECTION LAW

China's Marine Environmental Protection Law was formulated based on a summation of the experience of our country's marine environmental control and consulting relevant provisions of international marine law as well as the successful experience of other countries. Its main characteristics and contents are as follows.

1. The Marine Environmental Protection Law is a comprehensive law of our country in the field of marine environmental protection. Different from the marine environmental laws enacted by our country in the past, this law is not designed to solve individual problems in marine environmental protection or to readjust social relations in a specific aspect. Proceeding from the perspective of protecting the entire marine ecological environment, it has made all-around stipulations for major problems with regard to marine environmental protection as a whole and carried out comprehensive readjustments of social relations concerned to achieve the purpose of protecting the marine environment and resources, preventing

pollution and damage, maintaining ecological balance, safeguarding people's health, and promoting marine undertakings. Its object of protection is the entire marine environment and the entire marine ecological system, including the quality of seawater, the coastal area, all kinds of living and nonliving beings in the sea, as well as the value of the sea in all spheres. It involves not just a certain kind of activity in man's exploitation and utilization of the sea, but all kinds of activities, such as the construction of coastal engineering projects; offshore exploration and exploitation for marine petroleum; fisheries and the fish-breeding industry; transport service; military operations; scientific research; recreational, sports, and tourist activities; the discharge and dumping of wastes in the sea. All kinds of social relations related to the protection of the marine environment arising from any activities conducted in China's sea areas are thus within the scope of regulation of the Marine Environmental Protection Law. It has provided basic measures and control systems to prevent and control pollution and damage to the marine environment caused by all kinds of activities and has defined the control organizations and the legal responsibility of illegal acts. It is an all-around, systematic, comprehensive law.

The comprehensive legal readjustment of marine environmental protection is designed to meet the needs of development of our country's contemporary marine undertakings. An outstanding feature of contemporary marine undertakings is their comprehensiveness. Man, with the aid of advanced scientific technology, now carries out comprehensive exploitation and utilization of the sea and gives full play to its manifold functions to meet his own needs in all spheres. The sea is an ecological system with inherent laws of development. Its internal structure, bountiful resources, and manifold functions are mutually connected and restrict and influence one another. The utilization of one part of the sea will have an effect on other parts of the sea. One kind of utilization of the marine environment will affect other kinds of utilization of the sea. The utilization of one marine resource will affect the utilization of other resources. Therefore, to protect the marine environment, it is necessary to adopt measures of comprehensive control, to make overall planning, unified control, and comprehensive readjustment of all kinds of activities that might cause pollution and damage to the marine environment. This is the task of the Marine Environmental Protection Law. Consequently, it represents a great step forward compared with the unitary laws that only readjust certain aspects of relations in marine environmental protection.

As a comprehensive law for marine environmental protection, the Marine Environmental Protection Law plays a leading role in various marine environmental protection laws and regulations. Accordingly, in case any past laws and regulations of marine environmental protection contradict the Marine Environmental Protection Law, the latter will override them.

As a comprehensive law that has to make all-around, systematic stipulations on major problems concerning marine environmental protection, the Marine Environmental Protection Law cannot have detailed specific provisions on all issues. Thus it is necessary to work out a series of more concrete provisions and standards in order to carry out this law. All the laws to be enacted and promulgated must follow the letter and spirit of the Marine Environmental Protection Law.

2. The Marine Environmental Protection Law clearly defines its objects and scope of application. As the sea is an integral whole, the marine undertakings, including marine environmental protection, have a complex, international nature. It is thus of great importance to define clearly the objects of the law and its scope of application while making legal readjustment. The jurisdiction of the state over the exploitation, utilization, and protection of the marine environment and its resources is not confined to the scope of the territorial waters declared by the state. The state also enjoys certain sovereign rights and jurisdiction over a certain width of sea area outside its territorial waters—the continental shelf sea area and the exclusive economic zone sea area. Hence the Marine Environmental Protection Law explicitly provides that this law applies to the inland seas, the territorial waters of the People's Republic of China, and all other sea areas under its jurisdiction.

The sea is a vital communication line in international contact. There are Chinese as well as foreign ships, platforms, airborne vehicles, submersibles, enterprises, institutions, and individuals engaged in different activities in sea areas under China's jurisdiction. Therefore, the Marine Environmental Protection Law clearly provides that "[a]ll vessels, platforms, airborne vehicles, submersibles, as well as all enterprises and other undertakings and individuals engaged in navigation, exploration, exploitation, production, scientific research, and other activities in the sea areas under the jurisdiction of the People's Republic of China shall comply with this law."[35] In other words, the objects of application of the Marine Environmental Protection Law also include foreign ships and corporations conducting activities in China's sea areas. China's contact with other countries is increasing day by day and its cooperation with foreign countries in the economic, technological, scientific, and cultural fields is steadily expanding. There are more and more foreign ships, platforms, and corporations engaging in all kinds of activities in sea areas under China's jurisdiction. The provision mentioned above is of utmost importance in protecting our country's marine environment and safeguarding our country's sovereignty and legal interests.

Moreover, owing to the movement of the sea itself, not only can the activities in the sea areas under a country's jurisdiction create pollution and damage to the marine environment, but activities in sea areas outside that country's jurisdiction can also cause pollution and damage to sea areas under the jurisdiction of that country. Consequently, the Marine Environmental Protection Law provides that the law also applies to the creation of pollution and damage to sea areas under the jurisdiction of the People's Republic of China by discharging harmful materials and dumping wastes in sea areas outside the country's jurisdiction.

3. The Marine Environmental Protection Law was enacted in light of China's actual conditions. It takes into consideration both the need to protect the marine environment and the possibilities of our country's current social, economic,

scientific, and technological conditions to ensure that all its provisions can be carried out effectively and produce the intended social effects.

First of all, it was enacted with the aim of dealing with practical questions in China's marine environmental protection. At present and for a considerable period to come, the pollution and damage to China's marine environment mainly come from the following sources: (a) Pollution and damage to marine environment by coastal construction projects. This mainly refers to the pollution and damage caused by building harbors and petroleum transport docks at the seashore, water conservation projects where rivers enter the sea, and tidal power generation projects; developing beaches; reclaiming land from the sea; digging up sand; and quarrying. (b) Pollution and damage caused to the marine environment by oil exploration and exploitation. This mainly refers to the pollution and damage caused to the marine environment by blasting operations in prospecting and by the leakage of oil and discharge of oils, oil mixtures, oil-polluted water and refuse, and other wastes in the course of drilling, exploration, oil extraction, and oil transport, and serious pollution and damage caused by blowouts. (c) Pollution and damage caused to the marine environment by land-based pollutants. This mainly refers to the pollution and damage caused by the discharge of all kinds of pollutants into the sea, the establishment of waste material stocking sites and treatment sites by coastal cities, enterprises, and undertakings, as well as the application of farm chemicals to coastal farmland. (d) Pollution and damage to the marine environment caused by ships. This mainly refers to the pollution and damage caused by oils, oil mixtures, refuse, and wastes discharged by ships lying at anchor in harbor or sailing along the coast, as well as that caused by accidents. (e) Pollution and damage to the marine environment caused by the dumping of wastes. This refers to the pollution and damage to the sea caused by the disposal of wastes or other harmful materials in the sea by ships, aircraft, platforms, and other transport vehicles.

To protect the sea from pollution and damage, it is necessary to control these sources causing pollution and damage to the marine environment. For this reason most provisions of the Marine Environmental Protection Law (involving requirements, measures, and systems for prevention and control) are directed at these situations.

The provisions of the system of marine environmental control are also directed at China's specific conditions. For a long time China's marine environmental control has been weak. The state has no competent authority to give unified leadership and exercise control of marine environmental protection work, and there was no clear division of functions and powers between various organizations related to marine environmental protection. As a result, many things become nobody's business, while for some other things each tried to dip his finger in the pie. Directed against this situation and with a view to strengthening state control over the marine environment, the Marine Environmental Protection Law clearly specifies the department in charge of the marine environmental work; defines the duties, functions, and powers of various organizations concerned;

stipulates their administrative powers; and establishes a management system with the Ministry of Urban and Rural Construction and Environmental Protection under the State Council in charge, with a division of labor and responsibility among the departments concerned and with the central government and various coastal provinces, autonomous regions, and municipalities assuming control at different levels. This management system conforms to China's realities and is in keeping with the characteristics of marine environmental protection. As the marine environment is a complete ecological system and we are exploiting and utilizing the sea in an all-around manner, it is necessary to have competent authorities to exercise unified control of the marine environment in order to maintain ecological balance. On the other hand, the sea has manifold functions, and we are exploiting and utilizing it in many fields. Consequently, protection must be conducted from many quarters, and no single department can monopolize the marine environmental control work. Thus, to exercise satisfactory control of the marine environment, it is necessary to have unified control and centralized coordination. It is also necessary to maintain a division of labor so that the departments concerned can carry out specific control work. In the past thirty years plus we have established a certain division of labor in marine environmental protection. The law has confirmed and made clear this division of labor.

Another important aspect of the Marine Environmental Law is its provisions on the legal responsibility for law violations. The features of the law in this respect are, first, the law has made clear distinctions between the three kinds of responsibilities: administrative responsibility, civil responsibility, and criminal responsibility. Second, it has stipulated procedures for investigating administrative responsibility and handling compensation disputes. Third, it has strengthened the authority of the department in charge.

Those who have caused, or may cause, marine environmental pollution and damage in violation of the law can be instructed to remedy the damage within a certain period of time, pay effluent fees, defray the expenses for eliminating the pollution, and compensate the losses suffered by the state and be given warnings or fined. This is their administrative responsibility, within which instructions for them to remedy the damage within a certain period of time, pay effluent fees, defray the expenses for eliminating the pollution, and compensate the losses suffered by the state are administrative restrictive measures, whereas warnings and fines are administrative punishments. The administrative department in charge determines administrative responsibility as provided by law. If the person concerned refuses to accept the decision, he can bring a lawsuit at the people's court within a certain time limit. For those who do not file suit within the statute of limitations and refuse to carry out the decision, the department in charge can ask the people's court to institute compulsory enforcement.

Those who have caused damage to other people and units by polluting and damaging the marine environment should compensate the victims for the losses. The victimized units and individuals have the right to seek damages from the party causing pollution damage. In regard to disputes over responsibility and the amount of damages, the law provides two procedures. One procedure authorizes the administrative department in charge to handle the dispute, and if the person concerned refuses to accept the decision, the dispute can be settled in accordance with the procedures provided in the Law of Civil Procedure of the People's Republic of China (trial implementation). The second procedure calls on the persons concerned to bring a lawsuit directly in the people's court to settle the dispute according to civil procedure. The former combines administrative procedure and civil procedure, whereas the latter relies purely on civil procedure. After the dispute arises the persons concerned can select either of the two procedures. This flexible provision is made on the basis of summing up our country's experiences in handling environmental disputes in recent years. Practice proves that this facilitates a prompt and equitable settlement of any dispute and effectively safeguards the legal interests of the state and victims.

For those who have polluted and damaged the marine environment and cause heavy losses to public and private property or cause the injury or death of people in violation of the Marine Environmental Protection Law, the judicial organs will look into the criminal responsibility of those persons who are directly responsible in accordance with the Criminal Law and the Criminal Procedure Law.

The principal party assuming administrative responsibility and responsibility of civil compensation can be an individual or a unit. The principal party assuming criminal responsibility can only be a natural person.

Administrative responsibility and civil liability are two types of responsibility widely applied in marine environmental protection. The Marine Environmental Protection Law clearly defines the two types of responsibility and procedures investigating responsibility and has strengthened the power of the administrative department in charge of the marine environment in this respect. This is of great importance for ensuring the implementation of the law.

4. The Marine Environmental Protection Law conforms to relevant international conventions. While stressing that the Marine Environmental Protection Law was enacted in the light of China's practical needs and capabilities, we must point out that the relevant provisions of this law are in complete agreement with the provisions of the relevant international conventions which China has acceded to or agreed with. This is also one of its special features. To protect the seas of the world and rationally exploit and utilize them, the international community has defined various regimes under international law, including the territorial waters system, the continental shelf system, the special economic zone system, the system of preventing pollution by ships, and the system regulating dumping wastes into the sea. In other words, to protect the marine environment and its resources, a number of principles which all countries must observe have been established. This is in their common interest. The marine environment under China's jurisdiction is a component of the oceans of the world. China possesses an inalienable jurisdictional right over its sea areas and has the right to set up its own marine environmental control system. However, in controlling

our own marine environment, we must also abide by relevant provisions that all countries must observe. Therefore, in enacting the Marine Environmental Protection Law, we have given ample consideration to generally recognized principles of international law and the provisions of the relevant international conventions to which China has acceded or agreed so that the provisions can be consistent. This is in the interest of the smooth promotion of our country's marine environmental protection work, the increase of China's contact with other countries of the world, and the common cause of mankind in exploiting, utilizing, and protecting the oceans of the world.

Comments

Ma Xiangcong and Chen Zhenguo provide an exhaustive analysis of China's Marine Environmental Protection Law (MEPL). They offer insightful background on China's experience in marine environmental protection leading up to the MEPL and the means by which the MEPL deals with the environmental dangers posed by coastal construction, offshore oil exploration and exploitation, vessel source pollution, and ocean dumping. Ma and Chen's contention that the MEPL conforms with recognized principles of international law in all regards raises questions. Compare the operational language regarding jurisdiction under Articles 2 and 26 of the MEPL with Article 211, sections 5 and 6, and Article 220, sections 5 and 6, of the 1982 United Nations Convention on the Law of the Sea in United Nations, *The Law of the Sea: United Nations Convention on the Law of the Sea with Index and Final Act of the Third United Nations Conference on the Law of the Sea*, U. N. Pub. Sales No. E.83 V.5 (1983), and Articles 4(2) and 9 of the International Convention for the Prevention of Pollution by Ships (MARPOL), in *International Legal Materials*, vol. 17 (1978), p. 546, and its 1983 protocol in D. C. Jackson, ed., *World Shipping Laws*, vol. 8, Dobbs Ferry, N. Y.: Oceana Publications, 1984, 12/Cov. Compare also Regulation 4 of MARPOL with Article 27 of the MEPL, and Article VII of the 1969 International Convention on Civil Liability for Oil Pollution Damage, 973 U.N.T.S. 0. Further, of what practical value is the MEPL in light of the limited number of vessels available for enforcement along China's expansive coast? On these questions, *see* Mitchell A. Silk, "China's Marine Environmental Protection Law: The Dragon Creeping in Murky Waters," *Review of Socialist Law*, vol. 12, no. 1 (1985), revised in *Occasional Paper/Reprints Series in Contemporary Asian Studies*, Baltimore: University of Maryland School of Law, No. 6 (1986). On the expansion of monitoring and enforcement capacity, see *China Daily*, December 27, 1985, and March 3, 1986.

7 Noise Control

Wen Boping (1982) "The Legal Regulation of Noise Control"

In Wen Boping, *An Introduction to the Law of Environmental Protection*, Beijing: Qunzhong Chubanshe, pp. 98–108. Translation, with permission, from *Chinese Law and Government*, vol. 19, no. 1 (1986), pp. 79–86.

Noise, known as "slow poison," poses many dangers. After working in a noisy environment (exceeding ninety decibels) for a long period, a worker will become hard of hearing and even deaf from the noise. Investigations show that in workshops where there is a great deal of noise, the incidence of workers suffering from deafness caused by noise reaches more than 50 percent and is sometimes even as high as 90 percent. Tremendous noise will cause headaches, tinnitus, insomnia, blood vessel spasms, abnormal secretion of digestive fluids, the weakening of digestive functions, and weariness of the whole body. This often leads to heart disease, high blood pressure, gastric ulcers, and neurosis. Noise exceeding 150 decibels may cause serious damage to the human body, leading to bleeding in the eardrums, deafness in both ears, delirium, insanity, shock, and even death.

Noise diverts one's attention, and hence is often the root cause of all kinds of accidents. It can reduce labor productivity, sometimes by 10 to 50 percent. Moreover, under the impact of extremely strong noise, sensitive instruments will not work, explaining launch failures in guided missiles and spaceships.[36] Ultrasonic noise will cause damage to buildings, such as cracked walls, fallen tiles, shattered windows, and crumbled chimneys. It may even cause damage to steel structures from "sound fatigue."

In Japan urban noise has become a serious social problem. According to investigations made by the Ministry of Education of Japan, more than 10 percent of schools have trouble holding classes because of noise. Some schools have been rebuilt as windowless buildings, using artificial illumination entirely. Noise is most harmful in slum areas. Some poor people need cotton in their ears to get to sleep. The number of lawsuits filed by urban residents who have no place to hide from the noise increases annually. Statistics show that there were some 8,000 cases of damage by noise and vibration in 1966. By 1971 the number had exceeded 22,000. In recent years the cases of public hazards arising from noise and vibration in the big cities in Japan have accounted for more than one-third of the total public hazard cases, and in some of the secondary industrial cities the ratio is as high as 65.2 percent.[37]

According to the results of investigation and research in many countries, traffic noise is the main source of environmental noise in cities, accounting for about 70 percent of the total. Investigations made in recent years by relevant scientific research units in China on traffic noise in Beijing, Shanghai, Tianjin, and other cities show that the number of vehicles and the volume of air traffic in these cities are far lower than in New York, London, Rome, and Tokyo, but their traffic noise is generally greater than that of these foreign cities. At the same time the noise level in China's textile, machine-building, metallurgical, shipbuilding, and petrochemical industries is generally high. There have been quite a few disputes between factories and residents because problems have remained unsettled over a long period of time. Noise caused by the building of construction projects and people in their daily life is also serious.[38] In big cities such as Shanghai and Beijing environmental protection units have received large numbers of letters from the masses complaining about noise pollution. In Beijing there were eighty letters from the masses complaining about noise and vibration in 1977, accounting for 31 percent of the total complaints. In 1978 there were 326 such letters, representing a fourfold increase and accounting for 40.2 percent of the complaints. By 1979 such letters had accounted for half of the total complaints. Some of the letters with 100 signatures said: "Workers have the right to rest. We get no rest in the midst of noise." Other letters said: "The roaring noise makes us restless. We have nowhere to escape from it." Eliminating the harm caused by noise has become a strong concern of the masses.

Judging from the history of the struggle against noise and vibration in foreign countries, we find that improvement of the situation will come invariably from strengthening the legal system in this field. To reduce urban noise, protect people's health, and enable the people to work, study, and rest quietly, it is essential to perfect the legal system in this respect. The enactment of an urban noise control law has become an urgent matter. . . .

SEVERAL PROBLEMS CONCERNING CHINA'S NOISE CONTROL LEGISLATION

China is urgently in need of enacting and promulgating an urban noise control law. In formulating this law, stress should be laid on solving the following problems.

1. *The administrative organs*. The control of urban noise should be conducted under the unified organization and leadership of the people's governments at all levels, with the environmental protection department in charge, with a division of labor and close coordination with the public security, communications, labor, industry, railway, and civil aviation departments and units of the armed forces.

2. *Environmental noise standards*. The state should set environmental noise

standards for urban districts as standards for appraising environmental quality as well as standards for controlling urban noise. In drawing up the standards, different demands should be set for different districts. The urban environment can roughly be divided into six categories:

(a) Special residential areas: residential areas that the local people's government has designated as requiring special peace and quiet, such as sanatorium areas and high-class guesthouse areas;

(b) Residential and cultural and educational areas: pure residential areas and areas where cultural and educational establishments and government offices are located;

(c) First-class mixed areas: areas where commercial enterprises and residential housing are mixed;

(d) Commercial center areas and secondary mixed areas: downtown areas where commercial enterprises are concentrated and areas where industrial and commercial enterprises and residential housing are mixed and where there is a small amount of traffic;

(e) Industrial clusters: industrial areas demarcated by the local government; and

(f) Both sides of main traffic roads where traffic exceeds 100 vehicles an hour.

The maximum decibels of noise allowed for each of the six categories of districts should be specified. The demarcation of the six categories of districts should be determined after discussion by the local environmental protection department and the urban construction and planning departments and be made public by the local people's government.

3. The following measures should be adopted to control traffic noise:

(a) Control of noise from motor vehicles. The use of all motor vehicles in cities must conform to the "Permissible Noises for Motor Vehicles"[39] promulgated on July 1, 1979, by the State Bureau of Standards Administration for trial implementation. All existing vehicles that do not conform to these standards should achieve conformity before a certain time limit; otherwise, they will not be allowed to operate. New motor vehicles should be examined according to these standards and driver's licenses [sic] will not be issued to those that do not meet the standards.

In entering city districts the drivers of motor vehicles must abide by traffic regulations, regarding times, route, and speed, and use their horns reasonably. The use of loud horns or horns making strange noises is forbidden. The horn noise must not exceed 105 decibels one meter in front of the vehicle.

Signs forbidding honking should be installed in sanatorium, cultural, hospital, and guesthouse areas. Drivers in such areas (with the exception of fire engines, ambulances, utility repair trucks, and police cars on emergency assignments) must not use their horns; where honking is necessary in other areas, they should reduce the number and duration of honks and must not use the horn continuously or over a long period of time. Honking to call at the door or to call for someone is forbidden. Use of sirens by fire engines, police cars, ambulances, and utility repair trucks is forbidden except in the performance of their duties. Without approval by the public security department, other vehicles are not allowed to have sirens. The departments in charge of public security and traffic and the units using cars should include noise control in the rules and regulations for vehicle control.

The entrance of tractors into cities should be severely restricted. Those that need to enter the city must have the approval of the public security department, which will issue passes.

In newly built residential areas and newly built or reconstructed traffic roads, the city planning, environmental protection, building design, and municipal engineering departments concerned should adopt measures to keep a certain distance between the residential areas and the traffic routes to prevent disturbance of residents by traffic noise.

(b) Control of noise made by trains. Stipulations should be made to require trains to strictly observe the "Regulations on the Technical Control of Railways" issued by the Ministry of Railways, which provide that unless there is an emergency, all locomotives entering the city boundary must use wind whistles; the use of steam whistles is forbidden. Motorized vessels should be equipped with silencers and, after entering urban districts, should sound whistles rationally to minimize noise. In city planning the route of trains passing through urban districts must be gradually changed. No newly built railway line will be allowed to pass through urban districts. For existing lines that pass through the city, the railway department should adopt comprehensive remedial measures for noise control.

(c) Control of airplane noise. For existing airfields close to the city, flying of airplanes over the city at low altitudes should be severely restricted. The airfield authorities should be responsible for moving the residents living within five kilometers of either end of the runway and within one kilometer of either side of the runway to areas of safety with state subsidies. New airfields must be built in places far away from the city, and the routes of airplanes taking off or landing should not pass over the city. Planes engaged in flight training must not make trial flights or circle over cities. The Civil Aviation Administration of China must promptly work out standards for airfield environmental noise. An airplane noise monitoring system should be set up at large international airfields in China, and fees should be collected from airplanes of any country whose noise exceeds the airfield noise standards.

4. The following measures should be stipulated for the control of industrial noise:

(a) Control of machinery and equipment. State noise standards should be drawn up for machinery, equipment, and electrical machinery that create noise and vibration. All products mentioned above produced hereafter must be examined by the department concerned for noise, and only those that conform to the state standards will be allowed to leave the factory. These products must have their noise level marked.

(b) Protection of residential areas. For factories (including neighborhood-run factories) located in areas in the fourth category—areas where industrial and commercial enterprises and residential housing are mixed and where there is a small amount of traffic—the equivalent noise level in a place one meter outside of the boundaries of these factories should not exceed sixty decibels during the day and fifty decibels at night. Those factories and enterprises that exceed such standards must take measures to make the noise conform to the standards; otherwise, they must move to other places. Factories and enterprises that exceed the Environmental Noise Standards for Urban Districts[40] will be enjoined from building, expanding, or renovating in special residential areas and in [ordinary] residential, cultural, and educational areas.

(c) The principle of the three simultaneous points. For all newly built, expanded, or renovated industrial enterprises, the engineering projects for the prevention and control of noise and vibration must be designed, constructed, and commissioned simultaneously with the main engineering project. Industrial enterprises now under construction that have not adopted noise prevention and control measures must adopt such measures in a definite time period. Otherwise, they will not be allowed to go into operation.

5. The following measures should be stipulated for the control of construction noise:

(a) All large building machinery used outdoors in urban districts which creates noise must be equipped with sound insulation or silencing facilities where possible. At places thirty meters from the boundaries of the construction site, the noise of the building machinery and equipment must not exceed seventy-five decibels in general and the noise of impact machinery, such as pile drivers and riveters, must not exceed ninety decibels.

(b) Setting state noise standards for construction machinery and equipment. The noise created by building machinery and equipment at the construction site must conform to the above standards.

(c) Protection of residential areas. The noise created by construction in residential areas at night (generally from 10 P.M. to 6 A.M.) should not exceed the Environmental Noise Standards for Urban Districts. Otherwise, the construction will be banned.

6. The following measures should be stipulated for the control of noise in public life:

(a) Control of loudspeakers. The installation and use of loudspeakers in urban districts and suburbs should be forbidden. Except for special public security vans, equipping propaganda vans with loudspeakers is forbidden. Where equipping of propaganda vans with loudspeakers or the use of loudspeakers outdoors is necessary, this must be approved by the local environmental protection department.

(b) Control of broadcasting. Broadcasts by various units for morning exercises and workbreak exercises should be made at low volume and should not affect neighboring units and residents.

(c) Control of sound equipment. When turning on their television sets, tape recorders, radio sets, musical instruments, and other sound equipment, the user units or families must keep them at an appropriate volume so that the sound level outside their property does not exceed the local Environmental Noise Standards for Urban Districts, and thus does not affect the quiet of the outside environment.

(d) Protection of special quiet areas. In the first and second categories mentioned earlier, no uproar should be permitted at night, and noise should not exceed the environmental noise standards for urban districts to avoid disturbing the residents when resting.

Comments

Wen Boping describes the aims of noise pollution control and initial Chinese efforts to draft legislation in this regard. Wen suggests setting noise standards at the urban district level and prescribes measures for controlling noises from both mobile and stationary sources (i.e., vehicles and factories). Compare these means with the provisions under the Federal Noise Control Act of 1972, 42 U.S.C. §4901 *et seq*. (Supplement 1973). Which is best suited to carry out Wen's scheme: the central, provincial, or municipal authorities? Why? How can Wen's regime deal with short, sudden, and, consequently, disruptive noise? Should national interests be taken into consideration (such as noise from military aircraft) when regulating noise in China? *See* the arguments presented in *United States v. Causby*, 328 U.S. 256 (1956), and *Griggs v. Allegheny County*, 264 U.S. 84 (1961), and judge whether the principles therein would apply in the context of the Chinese system. The Noise Control Law has yet to be promulgated, and some problems cited by Wen remain unresolved, but traffic noise has been sharply reduced in many areas through exhortation and fines.

8

Solid Wastes

Chen Lihu (1985) "On the Legal Regulation of Solid Wastes"

Faxue Yanjiu, no. 4, pp. 71–75.

The problem of solid wastes is the product of complex interaction among political, economic, social, and scientific and technological factors. To do a good job at managing solid wastes, we need policies and guidance by the state and must combine legislative, economic, educational, and technological approaches to solve the problem. Legislation on solid wastes is the concretization, specification, and systemization of the state's policy on the management of solid wastes and is the legal basis and an important force for developing the management of solid waste.

The Chinese government has long since paid attention to this problem and has issued a series of regulations. The 1957 Act of the People's Republic of China for Security Administration Punishment provides that

> a person who commits any one of the following acts interfering with public health or the clean appearance of cities shall be punished by detention of not more than three days, a fine of not more than six yuan, or a warning: . . . (2) In cities willfully piling things up, drying things in the sun, or cooking articles with a foul odor, in disregard of an order to stop; (3) Dumping rubbish or filth in the streets, disposing of animal carcasses in the streets, or urinating or defecating anywhere in the streets;. . . .[41]

In 1973 "Some Regulations on Protecting and Improving the Environment" (for trial implementation) noted that we must "work hard to improve production processes, and not produce or produce less waste gas, wastewater, and waste solids . . . [and] we must develop the comprehensive utilization of the three wastes when their emission is unavoidable."[42] The Circular of December 30, 1979, issued jointly by the Ministry of Finance and the Environmental Protection Leading Group of the State Council on Methods for Profit Retention with Regard to Products Developed Through the Control and Comprehensive Utilization of the Three Wastes by Industrial and Mining Enterprises,[43] made rather concrete regulations to encourage the comprehensive utilization of the three wastes.

These laws and documents have played a role that cannot be overlooked with regard to the management of solid wastes in China. However, we still do not have a systematic law governing the management of solid wastes, which greatly affects the development of solid waste management work. To explain the urgency of this matter and provide a legal foundation for China's solid waste management, we should quickly perfect the structure of environmental law. This essay is a discussion of how to use legal instruments to manage solid waste.

I

Solid wastes refer to certain wastes discarded in the course of production and life, which can be grouped into five categories based on their origin: mine wastes, industrial wastes, agricultural wastes, radioactive wastes, and municipal residential wastes, or municipal refuse. They are produced and increase as the level of production and the standard of living rise. Human production and life require the consumption of many materials and simultaneously generate large quantities of solid waste. Statistics show that the annual volume of solid wastes equals 3.9 billion tons in the United States and 300 million tons in Japan, and that garbage alone equals 30 million tons in England. Materials on this point show that China annually discharges about 500 million tons of solid waste, with the volume deposited so far totaling more than five billion tons. Every day Shanghai alone must dispose of 3,000 tons of construction debris, 4,600 tons of garbage, and more than 8,000 tons of human body wastes.

The volume of solid wastes in China has been rising continuously in accordance with economic development and population growth. The volume of solid waste in 1979 was 3.6 percent higher than in 1978 and 12 percent higher than in 1977. Statistics from concerned departments indicate that the volume of industrial wastes in 1981 totaled 430 million tons, of which only 80 million tons was comprehensively utilized.

These solid wastes pose a great danger. First, they occupy land and pollute farmland. Every 10,000 tons of solid wastes on average requires about 0.1 hectare. More than 400 square kilometers have already been diverted to the storage of solid wastes and mine tailings. Most industrial wastes are dumped in open fields or into rivers and lakes, where they raise the level of streambeds and swallow up and pollute farmland. Right now the area of farmland that has been polluted totals about 2.7 million hectares. In the past ten years there was a reduction of more than 5 million catties of food production in Shanghai because of pollution from solid wastes.

Second, water quality suffers. The pollution and destruction of water resources in China right now is serious. Many enterprises located alongside rivers and the seas have customarily dumped their wastes into the water. Power plants alone dump more than 5 million tons of ash into the rivers each year. Water quality has seriously deteriorated in some seaside cities where there is no place to put garbage except to pile it along the shore.

Third, the air becomes polluted. As soon as the wind picks up and the sun comes out, the fine powder and dust in the trash are blown into the air. In winds of force four or greater, powdered coal ash up to 1.5 centimeters in diameter can be blown as high as twenty to fifty meters into the air with visibility declining from 30 to 70 percent in the windy season and with the black winds making it impossible for vehicles and pedestrians in adjoining areas to venture out. The hazardous substances in solid wastes become a source of toxic air pollution through the effects of wind and rain.

Fourth, infections spread. Not only is more than 90 percent of China's human wastes and garbage not rendered harmless, but also the human wastes and garbage from both ordinary hospitals and infectious disease hospitals are mixed in with ordinary wastes and garbage, becoming a source of environmental pollution by casually spreading gastritis, dysentery, and viruses.

Fifth, solid wastes not only affect the beauty of the environment, but also large expenditures in labor and materials are incurred to dispose of them.

These are several reasons why the solid waste problem is worsening in China. We lack a management system and structure to plan the comprehensive utilization of these wastes, comprehensive utilization is inadequate, and people do not have a strong sense of environmental protection. All of these are related to legislation. Therefore, the preparation of laws regarding the management of solid wastes in accordance with solid waste management policy, through research of foreign legislation and summing up practice here in China, has already become an urgent matter. Foreign practice tells us that to manage solid wastes well and make rational use of solid wastes, we need legal instruments as well as scientific, technological, and economic measures. Without clear and specific laws and regulations on the management of solid wastes, it will be hard to prevent and reduce pollution and hazards from solid wastes. Although we already have promulgated the Environmental Protection Law, this is just the basic law for environmental protection and contains only elementary principles on the issue of solid waste management. We must quickly prepare a solid waste disposal law to protect human health, control environmental pollution from all angles, expedite economic development, provide a clean and comfortable environment for people to live in, and halt pollution from solid wastes.

II

The historical development of environmental protection law around the world shows early provisions for solid waste management. For example, Han Fei Zi reports that Yin [Shang] dynasty law called for cutting off the hand of anyone who dumped ash on public thoroughfares. Some people consider this the earliest legal provision prohibiting the careless disposal of garbage. We should point out [, however,] that solid waste management laws in ancient times consist of scattered articles. Not until the twentieth century did there appear special laws and regulations governing the management of solid wastes. In 1917 France promulgated a law governing the management of dangerous, unsanitary, and hazardous wastes. Italy, in 1941, passed a law regarding the disposal, transport, and treatment of solid wastes.[44]

The gradual perfection of solid waste management legislation did not occur until the 1960s and 1970s. This followed the great development of science and technology, the rise in people's awareness, and the steadily increasing gravity of the solid waste problem. At that time garbage was already seriously threatening the human environment in Japan's big cities. At a session of the Tokyo legislature the mayor said: "We are in a major war with garbage. If we are to keep garbage from burying us, we must destroy it. We must adopt emergency measures. The slightest delay will bring about inevitable consequences." In England solid waste pollution resulted in many cases of liver tract poisoning, and the cancer rate for residents of Swansea in Wales was 40 percent higher than the national average because of exposure to mine tailings, and 60 percent higher for residents of Cardiff. People thus call solid waste pollution the third pollution [after air and water]. So far the United States, Japan, West Germany, England, France, Sweden, and Belgium all have passed laws in different guises regarding the management and disposal of solid wastes.

Because solid wastes have become an international problem, it is essential that we rely on foreign legislation to solve it. Because of strict controls in many developed countries, their chemical industry departments must spend a lot of money to treat solid wastes. Businesses in some countries have shifted production or exported their wastes to countries with less stringent controls to avoid these costs, turning these countries into international garbage cans. Some countries and companies ship their wastes to other countries in the name of storage, but in reality this is dumping, thus transferring the hazard to the second country. Moreover, foreign companies operating in developing countries usually insist on maintaining the secrecy of their production processes, sometimes making it impossible for the developing country to know how much and what kinds of solid wastes have already been deposited on their territory. It is hard to imagine how developing countries can effectively regulate pollution from solid wastes under such conditions. Relevant international organizations have been concerned for sometime about these new problems and are engaged in the preparation of international laws and regulations on solid waste management. At the United Nations Environment Program Conference on Environmental Law convened in Montreal in October 1981, eleven urgent items were decided, of which the third was preparation of international principles and regulations regarding the transport, utilization, and disposal of solid wastes.

We should recognize that it is hard to subscribe to any other country's laws on solid wastes because of differences in the composition of their solid wastes as well as wide differences in topography and levels of scientific and technological development. Differences cannot be ignored even among countries in the same region, like Western Europe. Nevertheless, they still share many points in common. The following are the most prominent.

1. In most countries, like Japan, Sweden, and Belgium, solid wastes and other

wastes are all grouped together under the same legislation. The United States especially passed the Solid Waste Disposal Act of 1965,[45] the Resource Recovery Act of 1970,[46] and the Resource Conservation and Recovery Act of 1976 (RCRA).[47] Other countries, like West Germany and England, have separate laws governing garbage within the broad category of solid wastes.

2. They have clear definitions of solid waste and disposal. For example, Japan's Waste Disposal and Treatment Law[48] stipulates that wastes under the act include garbage, large pieces of trash, ash, slag, waste oil, waste acid, waste soda, animal carcasses, and other liquid or solid wastes. Under Japanese law wastes are categorized as ordinary wastes and industrial wastes. Industrial wastes refer to coal ash, coal slag, slag, waste oil, waste acid, waste soda, and other wastes produced by industrial and mining enterprises, with other wastes falling under the category of ordinary wastes. Similarly, RCRA in the United States stipulates that disposal of wastes includes discharge, storage, spraying, dumping, spilling, seepage, and discharging hazardous solid wastes into the water.

3. They stringently control pollution by wastes and put just priority on prevention. All countries in different ways and through different systems take preventive measures. The following systems are the main ones. First, a country must include provisions for waste disposal when preparing development plans. Second, a country must make a special waste disposal plan. Third, a country must establish a waste disposal permit system. Fourth, there must be an assurance system. For example, American law requires businesses under its scope to provide guarantees on economic and transportation instruments and other equipment to handle accidents. Concerning waste disposal and handling methods, the law also incorporates stringent controls and guarantees to ensure enforcement of these measures.[49]

4. They have a complete supervisory system. For example, West Germany's Solid Waste Disposal Law[50] stipulates that disposal of solid wastes is subject to the supervision of the responsible department. For example, when public safety requires action, the responsible department can conduct an inspection of waste disposal procedures in a closed-down facility. The owner of solid wastes and those responsible for its disposal must answer any questions from the supervisory department regarding management, equipment, procedures, and so forth. In order to inspect whether they are in compliance with the law's obligations, personnel from the supervisory department can make on-site inspections and can enter residences to prevent serious harm to public safety and order. The solid waste disposal managers must explain disposal procedures to the supervisory personnel, provide personnel, equipment, and records essential for the conduct of inspections, and allow the superviser to conduct inspections of waste handling and transportation methods, with the expenses to be borne by the regulatee. Moreover, the Netherlands, Belgium, and other countries have established national public health inspectorates.

5. They emphasize the role of liabilities in regulating solid wastes. Environmental science theory affirms that environmental problems have a strong regional

cast. No matter which waste management measures are selected, they all must recognize this point. Practice also proves that national regulations are incompatible with the use of uniform methods to handle wastes. Localities can use measures that are more locally appropriate and economically more efficient. Because they can refer to local topography, climate, population distribution, and production distribution, they can draw lessons from earlier accidents in order to prepare regulations appropriate to local conditions. Many countries fully emphasize local law.

6. They promote comprehensive utilization in a big way to reduce the volume of wastes. For example, France stipulates that wastes can be burned to use the heat for heating and electricity and that residential wastes can be converted to fertilizer. Relevant laws in West Germany stipulate that the volume of waste to be discharged must be reduced and that recycling must be encouraged. Before selecting a disposal method, you should first discover whether these wastes can be reused. The Solid Waste Disposal Act and RCRA in the United States are primarily intended to promote comprehensive utilization and convert resources into wastes.

7. They provide financial subsidies. For example, Japanese law stipulates that the state should subsidize various categories of local expenditures in accordance with policy provisions, necessary expenditures for maintenance and repair of garbage disposal facilities and disposal of human wastes, and expenditures for the disposal of wastes caused by natural hazards or other factors. To protect the human environment and enhance human health, the state should strive to provide essential fiscal subsidies and other assistance for maintaining and building most solid waste disposal facilities.

8. They penalize offenders. The law is the standard for man's behavior in society and has a compulsory character because it is created by the state. Any individual or organization who breaks the law must be penalized. In other countries there are three types of punishment for breaking solid waste laws: administrative, civil, and criminal. Rumania's Environmental Protection Law,[51] passed on June 20, 1973, is rather comprehensive, with provisions governing air, water, soil, waste, and noise, and stipulates that lawbreakers' disciplinary, material, civil, and criminal responsibility must be determined. Under Japanese law the maximum penalty for violating the waste law is imprisonment for one year or a fine of 500,000 yen. RCRA in the United States stipulates two kinds of penalties for violators of solid waste disposal laws, civil and criminal. Civil penalties call for fines of up to $25,000 a day, while the maximum criminal penalty is one year in prison. The Soviet Union stipulates severe economic punishment for units that cause pollution, with the responsible individuals facing criminal penalties in especially serious cases.

III

As previously noted, China urgently needs to prepare and promulgate a solid waste law and related laws. Many questions must be explored because this is a new task. I personally feel we should emphasize the following issues.

1. China has already promulgated the Environmental Protection Law, the Marine Environmental Protection Law, and the Water Pollution Prevention and Control Law, but legislation on solid waste also is a specialized segment of environmental law. Because of dissimilar environmental management factors, specialized laws and regulations are essential in legislation and in enforcement. We can agree that specialized environmental laws and regulations all must abide by the following principles: the need for unified plans to ensure coordinated development of the national economy and environmental protection; the need to integrate pollution and control with regard to preventing pollution and protecting the environment, with first priority on prevention; comprehensive utilization to turn the harmful into the beneficial; and pollution prevention and environmental protection must maintain a correlation between rights and obligations so everyone has responsibilities as well as rights. These principles are important principles of Chinese environmental law, principles that all citizens together must abide by, and they are an important foundation for making and implementing environmental law. Making a solid waste law is naturally no exception.

2. We must earnestly study foreign environmental law and absorb the experiences of foreign environmental legislation. Environmental problems exist everywhere to varying degrees. We should acknowledge that many countries started working in environmental law earlier and that their contents are more complete. Some laws already have been revised several times and gradually perfected. Some countries have already created their own environmental law structures which have been included in environmental law histories. To avoid errors and to prepare our own solid waste law as soon as possible, we should study relevant foreign laws for both content and form. It will make us better able to absorb the essence of foreign environmental law.

3. Borrowing or referring to foreign environmental legislation does not mean that we can base Chinese law entirely on foreign methods. We have our own national character. Our land is big and resources are bountiful. Our population is large and 80 percent agricultural. The country is not yet rich. Our scientific and technological level is still below that of the advanced industrialized countries. These are all factors that our legislation must take into account. We must act according to the danger that solid wastes pose for us and seek out the causes of this danger in order to perfect our law. Moreover, our people have gained a great deal of experience in the disposal of solid wastes, like establishing a recovery network for discarded materials and converting urban garbage into fertilizer by high-temperature composting. We should earnestly sum these up and consider whether they can be codified into laws and regulations.

4. With regard to the content of solid waste law, we depend on the following principles:

a) Regulations on waste disposal must be considered in urban and economic development planning, with the state, various departments, and enterprises all pitching in and coordinating their efforts.

b) State departments should not conflict with waste management policies and laws when making their own policies.

c) A solid waste registration system, a waste disposal permit system, an assurance system to control pollution from wastes, and an inspection system should be included.

d) Emphasis should be placed on improving production processes, reducing the emission of solid wastes, developing man-made ecological processes, and recycling. Wastes that cannot be recycled should be disposed of by their generator after being treated to applicable standards. We must provide funding for storage of wastes and control of hazardous pollution.

e) Standards and management rules for the environmental protection structure must be established. Environmental standards use numbers to express environmental quality and the boundaries and limits for controlling the emission of pollutants. The enforcement of pollution disposal laws and regulations is closely related to the implementation of waste emission standards. Without emission standards it would be hard to put waste laws into effect.

f) The rights and responsibilities of localities vis-à-vis the center in waste management should be clarified.

g) Legal responsibility should be clarified to avoid vagueness. These problems exist in both the forestry and the environmental protection laws—the first group of these kinds of laws—chiefly because they have unclear responsibilities and muddled regulations. This problem must be considered when making new laws. Regulations on legal responsibility should be made more appropriate. I personally feel that legal responsibility in waste legislation should lean to the stringent side, given present conditions.

h) Definitions are an indispensable aspect of a solid waste disposal law. In terms of enforcement and interpretation, this component is essential. When making a law, definitions should avoid inappropriate and vague formulations.

5. Environmental law is a comprehensive branch of the law as determined by the breadth and complexity of environmental protection. Solution of any environmental problem in terms of legal management requires the use of various legal and readjustment measures. Solid waste law is a component of our environmental legislation, so it must naturally be perfected with various legal and readjustment measures. To simply rely on some solid waste laws is not enough for management, and regulations also are needed in other laws, like the Urban Planning Law, Urban Beautification Law, Burial Law, Nuclear Energy Law, Public Health Law, Mining Development Law, Labor Protection Law, and Packaging Law, which should contain provisions relevant to wastes. Theory and practice both tell us that this is a feasible approach. Article 25 of the Water Pollution Prevention and Control Law already has regulations on the waste problem, and we should include essential provisions concerning waste disposal in the Factory Law, Land Law, Mineral Resources Law, and so on.

Comments

This discussion of the need for a solid waste management law is notable for several reasons. First, the stress on the need for such a law confirms that the planning process itself is incapable of satisfactorily addressing waste management issues. Therefore, the planning process must, to some extent, be bounded by statutory constraints if environmental quality is to be protected. Second, the author's rather broad canvas of foreign law primarily includes references to advanced industrialized countries in Western Europe, North America, and Japan. This reveals no concern for class or socialist analysis in addressing complex policy problems. References to other socialist countries are largely confined to the enforcement issue, where China's practices are similar to those of other statist, authoritarian regimes. Third, the author's criticisms of the dumping of solid wastes in Third World countries, coupled with a later reference to nuclear energy, may be read as a veiled criticism of China's inconclusive negotiations with West German companies to store European nuclear wastes in China. This sensitive source of foreign exchange is bitterly opposed by many Chinese intellectuals and environmental specialists.

9

Toxic Wastes

Shi Qing (1984) "Management of Toxic Wastes"

HB, no. 7, pp. 8–11. Translated in Joint Publications Research Service, *China Report: Science and Technology*, no. 40 (December 6, 1984), pp. 104–10.

The management of toxic wastes is the responsibility of the solid waste environmental management departments. Toxic wastes include poisonous, ignitable, corrosive, reactive, radioactive, and infectious solid, semisolid, and liquid wastes. If dumped carelessly or handled improperly, these wastes will not only cause inflammation, fires, and relatively noticeable pollution, such as water and atmospheric pollution, but also affect the soil and groundwater quality and result in serious problems. This is why it is acknowledged as a serious environmental problem throughout the world.

LESSONS DRAWN FROM OTHERS' MISTAKES

In the 1950s the Jinzhou Ferroalloy Plant stored some chromium slag. It was found, a few years later, that the water within more than seventy square li was polluted by hexavalent chromium and that 7 of nearby Zirantun's 1,800 wells could not be used. For this reason the factory invested 650,000 yuan to build some water supply projects for the peasants in the area and 3.6 million yuan to build a brick manufacturing workshop. However, the bricks manufactured still contained hexavalent chromium and could not be used regularly. Finally they spent another 4.6 million yuan to make a seepage-proof wall more than ten meters deep around the chromium slag pile. The base of the wall went down to the underground rock stratum, and thus the chromium slag was, comparatively speaking, firmly encased.

Yanshan General Petrochemical Plant's Xiangyang Chemical Plant drained a small amount of ethane into the sewer while overhauling its equipment. The ethane and the water flowed through the electric cables into the distribution room, causing a fire that burned the forty-square meter distribution room to the ground. More than 4,700 yuan was lost and three staff members and workers suffered burns.

In the 1960s soot laden with arsenic discharged by a mine in the antimony smelting process was stacked up in the open air for a long time. The soot seeped into a well with rainwater. As a result, 308 persons were poisoned, 6 were killed, and the well had to be closed off.

Nationwide, about 500 tons of arsenic, 500 tons of cadmium, and 50 tons of mercury a year disappear along with wastes in the smelting of nonferrous metal. Moreover, paints, coatings, rubber, plastics, batteries, pharmaceuticals, agricultural chemicals, solvents, oil, tar products, and so on, which are internationally determined to be toxic, are mixed with solid wastes and water without our knowledge and become present or potential hazards to the environment.

ENVIRONMENTAL MANAGEMENT OF TOXIC WASTES

Our country is formulating standards and legislation relating to the environmental management of toxic wastes. Here are some suggestions based on foreign experiences for the investigation of pollution sources, creating files and making preparations for comprehensive management before [China's] standards and legislation are officially issued:

Definition and Appraisal

Toxic wastes refer to wastes which can cause or result in death or disease, which, when managed improperly, can become present or potential hazards to the health of human beings or the environment. Various toxicities and appraisal methods are listed below.

Values for the Reference Chart of Definitions and Appraisal of Various Toxic Wastes

Toxicities and Suggestions	Appraisal Value
1. Ignitability: substance whose flashpoint is lower than a certain value; or which has the tendency to ignite with friction, moisture absorption, or spontaneous chemical changes; or which will generate heat during processing or manufacturing; or which will burn violently and continuously when lighted and cause danger during the management period.	USA ASTM code flashpoint lower than 60°C
2. Corrosiveness: wastes which when touched will cause visible damages or incurable changes to the tissue, or skin; or which will cause qualitative changes to substances or leakage to containers with which they come into contact.	Liquids with pH >12.5 or <2 whose corrosive rate for steel products exceeds 0.64 mm/yr under 55.7°C

Toxicities and Suggestions	Appraisal Value
3. Reactivity: unstable at standard conditions; causes violent chemical reactions very easily; reacts violently with water, or forms an explosive mixture or produces toxic gas, offensive smell; contains chloride or sulfide; causes explosive reactions even under normal atmospheric pressure and temperature; explodes when heated or when placed near catalyst; has instability with heat or mechanical impact.	
4. Radioactivity: wastes which can release rays with nuclear collision, whose radio isotope exceeds the maximum density.	Radium 226 (Ra226) density equal to or higher than 10 microcuries per gram of waste.
5. Soaking Toxicity: any of the pollutants extracted through fixed soaking or extracting methods which exceed provided standard values. Pollutants include: cadmium, mercury, arsenic, lead, chromium, selenium, silver, benzene hexachloride, methyl chloride, toxaphene 2,4 -D and 2,4,5, -T, etc.	100 times more than drinking water using USA EPA/EP experiment method.
6. Acute Toxicity: toxic wastes which when administering one dose to animals for experiment has smaller lethal dose/50 (LD50) than provided value.	United States administrative method: oral toxicity LD50 $\leq$ 50 mg/kg body weight, inhale toxicity LD50 $\leq$ 2 mg/l, skin toxicity absorption LD50 $\leq$ 200 mg/kg body weight
7. Aquatic Organism Toxicity: when using fish for experiments the density value (TLm96) is smaller than provided value.	TLm $<$ 1000 PPm (96 hrs)
8. Plant Toxicity:	Semi-suppression density TLm $<$ 1000 mg/l
9. Biological Accumulation: the enrichment of an element or chemical compound in an organism exceeds the environmental water, and shows positive when tested.	Positive
10. Hereditary Variation: the molecular changes in the DNA or RNA of mitotic or meiotic cells caused by poisonous substances result in serious carcinogenic, mutagenic and teratogenic effects.	Positive
11. Irritation: causes dermatitis.	Cause dermatitis $\geq$ 8 degrees

Listing and Filing

The determination of toxic wastes should be done through appraisal and experiments. The procedure is complex, however, and many factories and networks have difficulty carrying it out. Therefore, many countries make lists of toxic wastes according to accumulated experiences and issue them through legislative procedures so that producers, operators, and environmental controllers and other related departments can keep informed. Up to now the United States has determined 96 types of industrial wastes, West Germany 570 types, and Denmark 51 types. The lists will be continuously revised and enlarged to keep pace with technological development. For units which are equipped to carry out actual examinations and appraisal, or when there are questions and needs to be determined, the methods provided in technical standards should be used for appraisal determination.

Regulations and Standards

National as well as local environmental protection bureaus should formulate regulations (usually included in regulations for solid wastes) which cover technical standards for toxic substances, handling, storage, transportation, management, and so forth. The regulations are to keep producers, operators, and controllers informed and allow the public to inspect and execute them. Generally speaking, the requirements of technical standards for new and old enterprises should be different.

As the first step in the environmental management of toxic wastes, our country is formulating pollution control standards for agricultural waste residues, sludge, construction waste residues, nonferrous metal solid wastes, and chromium dregs.

Transportation is an important link in the environmental management of toxic wastes. Safe transportation should be guaranteed. So far our transportation departments have regulations for more than 6,000 types of harmful substances. However, the transportation link of toxic wastes is still a weak point. It is urgently required that environmental and transportation departments collaborate to formulate standards or regulations for toxic wastes.

Collection, Handling, Storage, Transportation, and Disposal

Toxic wastes should be packaged and labeled according to the standards and rules provided. The quantities, quality, toxic composition, whereabouts, items to be marked "caution" during handling, transportation, and the storage disposal process should be indicated on a card (called routing in West Germany—a tag system) so as to enable the safe transportation of wastes from the point of origin to the disposal point where they can be disposed of harmlessly.

Giving a definite, distinct indication of harmful wastes is a link in the specialized management of the wastes. The following [with accompanying symbols] package designs have been stipulated for some of the dangerous substances in our country:

∘ extremely poisonous substance (black ink on white paper)

∘ ∘ poisonous substance (black ink on white paper)

∴ corrosive substance (black ink on white paper)

∷ ignitable substance (primary red ink on white paper)

Harmful wastes should never be discharged into sewers or mixed with regular wastes. Different packing, storage, and transportation containers and tools should be used for wastes of different natures. The international experience in specially managing harmful wastes should also enlighten us on the control of water pollution and the solution of wastewater problems. To mix harmful wastes with solid wastes is a potential crisis for soil and groundwater. This is an issue that we have to take into serious consideration in future environmental management.

Pretreatment of harmful wastes usually will reduce their treatment and management expenses. Examples: compacting loose wastes can reduce their volume; burning organic wastes can reduce their weight; compacting, dehydrating, filtering, pressing, demulsifying, degreasing, and so on can reduce the costs of final treatment.

The ultimate aim of the environmental management of harmful wastes is to finally reduce the wastes to an innocuous state before discharging them into the environment. Innocuous treatment generally includes two categories. One of them is the control and management of pollution. The other is the development of comprehensive utilization of wastes, converting them into useful materials.

DISPOSAL METHODS FOR HARMFUL WASTES

When disposing of harmful wastes, the environmental benefits should be ensured and energy and materials should be retrieved as much as possible so as to achieve certain economic benefits. The following waste disposal methods are widely used throughout the world and are grouped according to their nature.

Secure Landfill Waste Disposal Method

This relatively easy method can be widely used to dispose of many kinds of harmful wastes. This is also often the final disposal method for the final products of wastes after burning, solidification, and biological or chemical processing.

Landfill dumps can be established on the land or in a valley. When selecting a landfill dump, detailed hydrogeological information should be first mastered so as to guarantee that the groundwater will not be polluted and that the disposal system is easy to manage. The dump should be made to be used for as long as possible and should be built in compliance with laws and regulations. When setting up a dump, the earthwork, investment, and the like should be reduced to the minimum.

The seepage rate of the natural or artificial lining between the bottom of the dump and the substratum of the soil should be less than 10^{-8} mm per second; the position of the substances to be filled at the bottom of the dump should be higher than the water table; the wastes dumped daily should be properly covered; discharge, collection, treatment, and monitoring systems should be set up for gases and liquids produced by the wastes dumped; rain and snow diversion equipment should be installed to keep them from seeping into the dumped wastes; and when the wastes reach a designed height, the dump should be sealed with clay and solidified.

Incineration Disposal Method

The incineration disposal method is appropriate for the disposal of organic wastes, such as tar, petroleum, rubber, plastics, and the like. Up to now many kinds of incinerators have been developed throughout the world. Examples are rotary kiln, multistage incinerator, fluidized bed incinerator, boiling incinerator, multiple-chamber incinerator, and ship-borne incinerator. Modern incinerators are installed with smoke- and gas-scrubbing equipment in order to prevent atmospheric pollution. Usually energy-retrieving equipment is also installed to retrieve combustible gases and vapors for generating electricity. Some incinerators can even transform incinerated dregs into construction materials. Generally the dregs are landfilled.

Solidification Method

This method, through chemical or physical measures, fixes or encloses wastes within a solid-body end product, thereby decreasing or eliminating the leakage of harmful elements.

1. Cement, silicate, and lime fixing method: Uses cement, silicate, and lime mixed with wastes to form a solid concrete mixture. This is suitable for treating inorganic toxic wastes such as washing tower sludge, heavy metal sedimentation sludge, and the like.
2. Thermoplastic method: Uses thermoplastics such a tar, paraffins, or polyethylene to mix with dry wastes and enclose them during the cooling process. This method is appropriate for treating organic toxic substances but not for treating organics, strong oxidants, and the like.
3. Organic polymer method: Uses one kind of monomer to mix completely with the wastes and transform the mixture into a polymer by adding a catalyst. This method is appropriate for treating toxic organics but cannot be used for treating acids and strong oxidants.
4. Chemical methods: Uses the principles of acid–base neutralization, oxidation reduction, sedimentation, and so on to decrease or eliminate the harmfulness of wastes.
5. Biological methods: Uses the biological degradation of various organics. Examples are the active sludge method, the soil cultivation method, the high-temperature compost method, and the aerobic and the anaerobic fermentation method.
6. Comprehensive method: Treats organic and inorganic mixtures by combining several kinds of techniques: for example, combine effective eluviation with incineration; microbiological degradation with ozone oxidation or with alkali metal reduction; cement kiln high-temperature baking with microwave treatment.
7. Well injection method: Uses abandoned pits for backfilling harmful wastes.

Many countries use this method because it not only disposes of a lot of waste at lower costs, but also facilitates land reclamation. A study on waste dumps carried out by the U.S. Environmental Protection Agency found that the well injection method is used more than the landfill method. However, wells which are not handled carefully have resulted in serious groundwater pollution. Therefore, when adopting this method, detailed hydrogeological information has to be mastered. Besides, the wastes to be filled should be treated to the degree permitted by the environment and the wells should be equipped with security measures and monitoring systems.

Comments

Toxic wastes pose a greater threat to the human environment than many other pollutants. This article represents China's awakening to the problem. The regulatory means suggested closely resemble those employed in the United States. Two facts are troubling, however. As a threshold issue, it is surprising that, given the threat of toxic wastes, China has yet to adopt a law or adequate standards in this area, and beyond that few scholars discuss the topic in the literature. Second, the scheme presented here is primarily concerned with the control and regulation of new wastes. It does not address the clean up of existing sites and the liability connected therewith. Officials responsible for toxic wastes are aware of the problem, however, and anticipate that regulations will be promulgated in 1987.

Notes to Part Two

1. China has, since this article was written, promulgated the Marine Environmental Protection Law (1983) and the Water Pollution Prevention and Control Law (1984). *See* related discussion in this volume [eds.].
2. The text is in *BFWH*, pp. 398–428 [eds.].
3. The text is in *BFWH*, pp. 453–62 [eds.].
4. This concept resembles areas designated for the prevention of significant deterioration of air quality under U.S. law. *See* Clean Air Act, 42 U.S.C. §§ 7470–7479 [eds.].
5. *See* Article 18 [eds.].
6. Law No. 142 (December 25, 1970). The text is in *Roppo Zensho* (The Six Basic Laws), Tokyo: Yuhikaku Publishers, 1985 [eds.].
7. Law No. 97 (June 10, 1968) in *id.* [eds.].
8. Wen Boping, *Huanjing Baohu Fa Gailun* (An Introduction to Environmental Protection Law), Beijing: Qunzhong Chubanshe, 1982.
9. Article 79 of the Criminal Law provides:

> A crime that is not expressly stipulated in the Special Provisions of the Law may be determined and punished according to the most closely analogous article of the Special Provisions of this Law, but the matter shall be submitted to the Supreme People's Court for approval.

China is one of the few countries which retains this principle. Most countries, including the Soviet Union, recognize that crime by analogy is in contradiction with general principles of law—*nulla poena sine lege* (no punishment without a preexisting prohibitory rule). At any rate most Chinese scholars and jurists advocate a restrictive use of this principle. *See* Li Yongyi, "On the Stipulation and Analogy of Offenses and Penalties,"

Faxue Yanjiu, no. 5 (1980), pp. 19–24. *But see* Zhou Mi, "Should Offenses and Penalties Be Stipulated or Analogized?" *Faxue Yanjiu*, no. 5 (1980), pp. 25–29.

10. *See* Article 1 [eds.].
11. *See* Article 4 [eds.].
12. *See* Article 9 [eds.].
13. *See* Article 10 [eds.].
14. *See* Article 11 [eds.].
15. *See* Article 12 [eds.].
16. *See* Article 13 [eds.].
17. *See* Article 14 [eds.].
18. *See* Article 15 [eds.].
19. *See* Environmental Protection Law (hereafter EPL), Article 18 [eds.].
20. *See* Article 16 [eds.].
21. *See* Article 17 [eds.].
22. *See* Article 18. This provision resembles §308 in the U.S. Clean Water Act. See Federal Water Pollution Control Act, 33 U.S.C. § 1318.
23. *See* Article 7 [eds.].
24. *See* Article 7 [eds.].
25. *See* Article 32 of the EPL [eds.].
26. The text is in *HBYWX*, pp. 295–96 [eds.].
27. The text is in *Renmin Ribao* (People's Daily), March 29, 1979 [eds.].
28. The text is in *HBYWX*, pp. 89–97 [eds.].
29. The text is in *BFWH*, pp. 453–62 [eds.].
30. The text is in *JFGXB*, vol. 1, p. 609. Statutory authority for the regulation of the marine transport of dangerous cargo was provided in the Marine Transportation Safety Law of 1983.

Article 32. Shipboard facilities for storing, loading and unloading, and transporting dangerous cargo must maintain reliable safety equipment and conditions, and be in compliance with state regulations governing the management and transport of dangerous cargo.
Article 33. When transporting dangerous cargo, all vessels must follow cargo declaration procedures set by the responsible organization. Only after approval has been issued will they be permitted to enter or exit the harbor and load or unload their cargo.

The Ministry of Communications is in the process of updating the 1972 regulations with a new document tentatively entitled "Regulations Governing the Shipment of Dangerous Cargo Along Waterways" that was drafted in 1983 but has yet to be officially promulgated. Also relevant is the Chinese translation of International Maritime Dangerous Goods, *Regulations on the Marine Transport of Dangerous Goods*, Beijing: Renmin Jiaotong Chubanshe, four volumes [eds.].

31. The text is in *BFWH*, pp. 355–56 [eds.].
32. The text is in *GGB*, no. 377 (March 25, 1982), pp. 70–74, and translated in *Beijing Review*, no. 8 (February 22, 1982), pp. 14–18.
33. 13 U.S.T. 2312; T.I.A.S. No. 5200, 450 U.N.T.S. 82, entered into force on September 30, 1962 [eds.].
34. The author is referring to Articles 192 through 237 of the Third United Nations Convention on the Law of the Sea [eds.].
35. *See* Article 2 [eds.].
36. See Fang Danchun, "The Harm of Noise and Its Control," *Beijing Ribao* (Beijing Daily), October 4, 1978.

37. See Kang Fu, "The Shaping and Development of the Public Hazard Law in Postwar Japan," *Waiguo Faxue* (Foreign Law), no. 3 (1981), pp. 27–30.

38. See "Chinese Cities Suffer from Serious Noise Pollution," *Renmin Ribao* (People's Daily), August 20, 1979, p. 2.

39. The text is in *BFWH*, pp. 500–508 [eds.].

40. The text is in *BFWH*, pp. 357–59 [eds.].

41. The text is in Department of Public Security, *Gongan Fagui Huibian* (Collection of Laws and Regulations on Public Security), Beijing: Falü Chubanshe, 1980, pp. 113–22. The English translation is in Jerome A. Cohen, *The Criminal Process in the People's Republic of China*, Cambridge, Mass.: Harvard University Press, 1968, pp. 215, 218–19, 221, 224, 227, 228, 230, 231, 232, 233, 235, 237, 250; Shao-chuan Leng and Hungdah Chiu, *Criminal Justice in Post-Mao China*, Albany: State University of New York Press, 1985, pp. 235–48 [eds.].

42. The text is in *BFWH*, pp. 8–14 [eds.].

43. The text is in *BFWH*, pp. 274–77 [eds.].

44. Law on the Collection, Transport and Disposal of Solid Waste, Law No. 366 of 1941, *Gazzetta Ufficiale della Repubblica Italiana* (Official Law Gazette of the Italian Republic, GU), no. 120 (May 23, 1941).

45. Public Law 89–272 (October 20, 1965) [eds.].

46. Public Law 91–512 (October 26, 1970) [eds.].

47. 42 U.S.C. §§ 6901–6987, [eds.].

48. Law No. 137 (December 25, 1970), in *Roppo Zensho* (The Six Basic Laws), Tokyo: Yuhikaku Publishers, 1985 [eds.].

49. *See e.g.*, 42 U.S.C. §§ 6922–6926 [eds.].

50. "Abfallbeseitigungsgesetz," *Bundesgesetzblatt* (Federal Law Gazette), vol. 1 (January 1977), p. 41 [eds.].

51. Law No. 9 on Environmental Protection, *Buletinue Oficial*, no. 91 (June 23, 1973) [eds.].

Part Three
Conservation of Land, Natural Resources, and Wildlife

The philosophy guiding China's management of natural resources has changed greatly in recent years, as the old insistence on ownership and management by the state or state-controlled collectives has been partially subordinated to other values. The older philosophy's deficiencies were widely noted in the post-Mao era. In fundamental terms, the weakness of producer incentives discouraged good management and efficient use of natural resources. Whatever virtues state ownership brought in terms of long-term continuity were negated by abrupt policy fluctuations marked by leftist upsurges, which led to the liquidation of standing timber and to other examples of short-sighted management. Consequently a series of reforms were introduced involving pricing, marketing, and the decentralization of management, although as a matter of principle land ownership has remained within the exclusive purview of the state and the collectives.

As this part reveals, however, the transition from one philosophy to another has not been smooth. High opportunity costs, capital and credit shortages, fears of a policy reversal, and subversion by lower-level officials acting as monopolists and tax barons have substantially weakened the impact of the reforms in forestry, animal husbandry, and long-term agricultural improvements. Stronger legal guarantees are needed to ensure the productive exercise of newly won management and marketing rights, which should eventually be extended to permit the formation of cooperatives and other voluntary combinations in order to take advantage of economies of scale.

Fugitive wildlife resources are subject to a different set of problems since for the most part they cannot be appropriated by individuals or enterprises for the purpose of long-term investments. Instead, they continue to be harvested and fall victim to poachers at levels in excess of their reproductive potential. There has been steady encroachment on natural areas for agricultural and construction purposes, including the drainage of wetlands. These are long-standing phenomena, but they have been aggravated in the post-Mao era by high prices offered for reptiles, herbs, and rare birds and mammals. In response lists of endangered species have been promulgated, endangered species protection criteria have been added to the construction project approval process, and harvesting and marketing restrictions have been imposed with regard to frogs, cranes, and other wildlife.

Violators have been arrested and prosecuted, and among them are local officials charged with condoning or participating in such activities. Still, stronger management and enforcement by state agencies as well as public education campaigns are needed to alleviate the problem.

Part Three treats the conservation of land, natural resources, and wildlife in China. Of major concern to investors is the amount of capital required to pay for the use of land where a venture is situated. Planning decisions have proven problematic in China as the calculation of land prices has for the most part remained a secret process, with the numbers amounting to final offers not subject to negotiation. In Chapter 10 Zhang Chunyin and Kong Min shed light on this issue in their discussion of the price of land and the payment of fees for land use in China's socialist economy. A lengthy chapter on forest protection follows, in which the noted jurist Zhang Youyu and Minister of Forestry Yang Zhong discuss the basic goals and principles and the implementation of the Forestry Law. Zhu Zanping and a commentator in the *People's Daily* highlight endemic problems with forestry protection in China. The final three selections explain the recently adopted Fisheries Law (Chapter 12) and Grasslands Law (Chapter 13) and describe the state of wildlife protection in China (Chapter 14). These should be read in conjunction with the relevant appendixes. The Mineral Resources Law was promulgated as this book went to press. The law appears herein as Appendix Y; it was, however, impossible to include commentaries.

10

Land Use and Planning

Zhang Chunyin and Kong Min (1984) "The Price of Land and the Payment of Fees for Land Use in Socialist Economy"

Jingji Yanjiu, no. 2, pp. 37–42. Translation, with permission, from *Chinese Law and Government*, vol. 19, no. 1 (1986), pp. 87–100.

The price of land and the payment of fees for the use of land are important issues confronting China's economic reform at present. Does land have a price in a socialist economy? Should the land user pay compensation for the use of the land? In other words, should he regularly pay a fee to the landowner for the use of the land? This is one of the main aspects of the relations of production to be studied by socialist political economy. It is of great theoretical and practical significance.

CHINA'S LAND PRICE AND THE HISTORY AND PRESENT CONDITIONS OF THE USE OF LAND SUBJECT TO COMPENSATION

Before Liberation, China was a semicolonial, semifeudal society. Land that was under private ownership was also a kind of commodity and had a price. At that time there were two kinds of land price: the appraised price and the market price. The former was the price used for taxation purposes and the latter, the price used in business transactions. The two were unequal in amount. Take Tianjin's land price, for example. When the War of Resistance against Japan had just begun, the market price of Quanyechang (the Tianjin Department Store) in the downtown French Settlement was three times higher than its appraised price. As the areas under the control of the Chinese government were not as safe as the British Settlement or the French Settlement, the market price of the land under the control of the Chinese government was lower than the appraised price. The prices of land in different sections of Tianjin city differed by wide margins. The appraised price of Quanyechang was more than 20,000 yuan per mu (15 mu = 1 hectare), while that of Balitai (in the neighborhood of Nankai University) was only 500 to 600 yuan per mu, a difference of some forty times.

In the early post-Liberation period, land in the rural areas was under private ownership and could be bought or sold, and some real estate in cities and towns was also under private ownership and could be bought or sold. Urban and rural land deals then roughly followed the pre-Liberation price levels. After 1952 free market land transactions were banned, but land in towns and cities retained its price, and the price bracket was determined according to the degree of prosperity and communications conditions [accessibility] in the land area. (In Tianjin, land prices were divided into twenty-nine grades.) Later repeated adjustments were made in land price brackets, but such prices were not prices for use in transactions, but were designed to facilitate taxation. They have been in use up until the present day.

In 1953 the Government Administration Council promulgated the ''Measures Governing Land Requisition for National Reconstruction,''[1] providing for compensation for the requisition of rural land and setting forth the principles and standards of compensation. The revised ''Measures Governing Land Requisition for National Reconstruction''[2] published by the State Council in January 1958 provide that when requisitioning land, the state should, as far as possible, replace it with state-owned or publicly owned land, and where such adjustment is impossible or where the production and livelihood of the requisitioned party are affected after the adjustment, the land-using unit should pay appropriate compensation. The compensation fee should be fixed jointly by the local government department, the land-using unit, and the party whose land is requisitioned. For land in general the gross output value of the past two to four years was taken as the criterion. Later, owing to changes in circumstances, particularly the ten-year chaos of the Cultural Revolution, the government no longer followed this practice. Exorbitant prices were asked in land requisition, and the compensation for the requisition of each mu of land ranged from several hundred to several thousand yuan. Later the price soared to tens of thousands of yuan—even 100,000 to 200,000 yuan. According to research conducted in the Beijing area at the end of 1981, in some cases the compensation for each mu of rural land in the suburbs of the city exceeded 200,000 yuan. A certain production brigade in the suburbs of Tianjin even asked for compensation of 10,000 yuan from the state for putting up one utility pole on its land. In some places the compensation paid by the state for requisitioning rural land went to the peasants. In some places the bank interest from the income earned by the peasants for selling a few fen (10 fen = 1 mu) of land equals the wages of a 17th-grade cadre. All of these situations are irrational. In 1982 the State Council promulgated the ''Regulations Governing Land Requisition for National Reconstruction,''[3] stipulating that the requisition of rural land by the state for capital construction could be compensated in the following five portions:

1. *Land compensation*. This is the compensation for the investments made on the land by the commune, the production brigade, and the production team over the years. It amounts to three to six times the annual output value of that piece of land. This income can only be spent on reproduction by the commune, the production brigade, or the production team and cannot be distributed among the commune members as personal income.

2. *Immature crops fee*. This is fixed in light of the concrete conditions of the immature crops on the ground when the land is requisitioned. The compensation is paid for only one season. No fee is paid for land where there are no immature crops.

3. *Structures and crop removal fee*. This is determined by the value and depreciation of the property on the ground.

4. *Labor force resettlement fee*. This fee is issued to the enterprise that helps to absorb the labor force from the requisitioned land as expenses to cover the placement and training of the labor force.

5. *New vegetable garden construction fee*. This is the sum paid when vegetable gardens in the suburbs of large and medium-sized cities are used. The fee is paid to the local financial authorities for the building of new vegetable gardens. Calculated in terms of these five items, the compensation in the suburbs of Tianjin is roughly 5,000 yuan per mu. Furthermore, in the actual implementation of these regulations, there are additional provisions, such as giving people on the requisitioned land priority in the recruitment of workers and changing their family members' household registration from rural areas to urban areas.

After the publication of the "Regulations Governing Land Requisition for National Reconstruction," many places failed to carry it out conscientiously. Some asked for excessively high prices, some engaged in endless haggling and shifts of responsibility, and some even unreasonably obstructed construction work, thus affecting the progress of the country's construction projects. In 1983 the State Council made public the "Circular on the Strict Implementation of the Regulations Governing Land Requisition for National Reconstruction."[4] The circular stressed that with regard to requisition and moving to other residences, laws should be observed and situations in which the state and the capital construction units are exorbitantly charged could no longer continue. The people's governments at all levels should handle land requisition as important work and enjoin the departments in charge to take good care of the land for construction use. The problems existing in the requisition of land should be solved in due stead. In particular, those land requisition problems that have remained unsolved over a long period and have affected construction projects must be solved one by one within a certain time limit. The circular also provides that those who violate the regulations and insist on excessively high demands should be criticized. Those who have misappropriated or spent compensation fees and resettlement subsidies should repay them, and those who have misappropriated the enrollment quotas of workers or the transfer of household registration from rural to urban areas should correct their misdeeds; necessary punishment should be meted out in serious cases. Those who take advantage of land requisition to instigate the masses to make trouble, to engage in extortion and blackmail, and obstruct the country's construction shall receive legal sanctions by the local people's government.

The payment of fees by joint ventures with Chinese and foreign investment for the use of land is a new question that has arisen in the past few years. In foreign countries expenses for land investment make up a large portion of an enterprise's expenditures. Foreign enterprises that have made investments in China naturally cannot use land without paying compensation. In 1980 the State Council published the "Provisional Regulations Governing the Use of Land for Construction by Joint Ventures Using Chinese and Foreign Investment."[5] The regulations point out that all joint ventures with Chinese and foreign investment should pay land use fees, be it for rural or urban land, for newly requisitioned land, or for land from an existing enterprise. The fees range from 5 to 300 yuan per square meter, of which the fees for the land in the suburbs of large and medium-sized cities should not be less than 10 yuan per square meter.

We are of the opinion that not only in requisitioning land must compensation be paid, but taxes or fees for the use of land must also be paid to the state treasury regularly. Back in the early post-Liberation period, the state had imposed a real estate tax as a source of financial income for localities. The real estate tax was collected based on different land prices. During the tax reform of 1973 the real estate tax which the enterprises should have paid was incorporated into the industrial and commercial tax, which was levied according to production output. In this way the tax was divorced from the amount of land used by the enterprise, so a land user actually uses the land without compensation. The remaining real estate tax is levied only on individual landowners, overseas Chinese, and housing management departments. During the present reform of the taxation system, some have proposed enacting a law governing land use taxation. This law would divide land into three grades—upper, medium, and lower—and assess tax according to the amount of land used—fixing the amount of the tax directly according to the area of the land used instead of levying the tax according to the price of the land.

THE ECONOMIC NATURE OF SOCIALIST LAND PRICES

The situation regarding land prices and payments for the use of land after Liberation shows that people do not understand the economic nature of socialist land prices, thus causing the confusion. In fact, we were following the practice of the Soviet Union in using land without compensation and avoiding the question of land price. The viewpoint that natural resources can be used free of charge has long been prevalent in the Soviet Union and has even been regarded as an indication of the superiority of socialism. Their theoretical basis is that Marx had said that things such as air, virgin land, natural grasslands, and wild forests can have use value but no real value until they become useful to man through labor. Actually this is a misinterpretation of Marx's statement. Marx merely said that virgin land had no value, but he never said that it had no price. In fact, in our country's actual economic life, compensation has always been paid when the state requisitions land or when land is transferred between units, be it rural or urban land. How do we explain this phenomenon? Some people may think that to ask for compensation in transferring land is an indication of departmentalism. But why is compensation generally requested when land is transferred and why has a certain proportionate relationship been gradually formed in numerous land deals? Apparently there must be something more profound and essential to it. Therefore, we believe that in socialist society land has a price and cannot be used without compensation. Here we would like to set forth our understanding of the economic nature of socialist land pricing for discussion with comrades.

Before making an analysis of the question of socialist land pricing, we would like to talk simply about our understanding of Marx's penetrating exposition of capitalist land pricing. In capitalist society, uncultivated land has no value, but this does not mean that it has no need for a price. Land price is a kind of monopoly price. As land is limited, the monopoly of the land by its owner makes it possible for him to rent out the land or levy a land tax. This determines that land has a price. On how to understand rent, Marx pointed out: "If there is a correct understanding of rent, it will naturally be realized first that rent comes not from land but from farm yield, namely, from labor, from the price of the product of labor (such as wheat), or from the value of the farm yield, from the labor thrown in to the land, not from the land itself."[6] Marx also closely linked up rent with land ownership. He wrote in *Capital*: "Pure legal land ownership will not create any rent for the land owner. But this ownership entitles him to refuse to allow others to manage his land until economic relations enable the use of the land to provide him with a surplus, whether the land is used in true agriculture, or other production purposes (such as building)."[7] This is a way of obtaining income without compensation by dint of ownership:

Land income − land input (consumption of means of production + wage paid to labor force) = pure output from the land.

Pure output from the land is divided into two parts: (1) rent, which goes to the landowner, and (2) surplus agricultural profit, which goes to the capitalist renting the land. In capitalist society, rent manifests itself in the relationship between the user and the owner of the land. A capitalist land user is different from the land user under the feudal rent system in that he also exploits laborers. The land price under capitalism is not the price of value but the capitalization of rent. Marx pointed out:

> Any given amount of monetary income can be capitalized, in other words, can be regarded as the interest of an imaginary capital. For instance, suppose the average interest rate is five percent, an annual rent of 200 pounds can be regarded as the interest on 4,000 pounds of capital. One can see at a glance that the purchase price or value of land formed by such capitalized rent, the same as the price of labor, is of an irrational category because land is not the output of labor and thus has no value. But on the other hand, behind this irrational form lies a kind of realistic relation of production. If the land purchased by a capitalist with 4,000 pounds provides 200 pounds of rent annually, then, the average annual interest of five percent he obtains from the 4,000 pounds is just the same as if he invests this capital on interest-yielding securities or lends it out directly at 5 percent

interest. . . . In fact, this purchase price is not the purchase price of the land, but that of the rent provided by the land, and it is calculated in terms of an ordinary interest rate.[8]

It is therefore clear that although no labor has been put into it, land (and all other natural resources) still has a price and is no exception to this rule. The price of land is in fact the price of the rent provided by the land, and it is calculated in terms of regular interest rates. The formula is:

Rent ÷ interest rate = land price.

In other words, the price of land is in direct proportion to rent and in inverse proportion to the interest rate.

As to the question of the economic nature of land prices in socialist economy, we have the following understanding. In the sector of the socialist economy under ownership by the whole people, the party that occupies, uses, and controls the land is separated from the owner of the land. State economic organizations only exercise the right to occupy, use, and control the land apportioned to them by the state while the state is the owner of the land. But in the sector of the socialist economy under collective ownership, the collective exercises the right to occupy, use, and control the land and the land also belongs to the collective. In other words, in the sector of socialist collective economy, the owner and the user of the land are one and the same. Under the circumstances where the owner of the land and the user of land are separated, we posit that the user cannot use the land without compensation but must pay the landowner regularly, or, to put it another way, he must pay rent to the owner of the land. In other words, in a socialist economy the relationship between the owner and the user of the land is not merely one of administrative subordination, but is, more important, an economic relationship. Under the conditions in the rural areas where the owner and the user of the land are one and the same, there cannot be the portion of the output that the user delivers to the owner as "rent," and thus there are no economic relations between the two. For example, it is not necessary to pay rent in the same production brigade. But after the introduction of the production responsibility system in agriculture, a delicate relationship emerges between the owner of the land (the actual owner formed by the commune, the production brigade, and the production team) and the real user of the land—the peasant. The peasant cannot use the land that is not his own without compensation, and thus should pay a certain amount for the land. This is perhaps the rent that we should have in our rural areas at present, and it does not go against Marx's basic doctrine that the birth of rent is the result of the separation of the ownership of the land and the right to use it. Similarly, this doctrine can be extended to other spheres of production, such as industry and commerce. The introduction of the responsibility system in these departments gives birth to differences in economic benefit between various economic units, whether it is between industrial enterprises or commercial enterprises. The area of the land used and the location of the land will inevitably make the cost of the products and the profit of the enterprises different. Thus paying a cost for the land used becomes entirely necessary. Just as one has to pay for the use of state funds in production, one has to pay for the use of land, and this cost should be different in different cases. If we admit that in a socialist economy the user of land should pay a cost (or pay rent) to the owner of the land, then there must be a price for the land. It is an economic relationship arising from the monopoly of the land. If we say that the question of land price arises only when the land is sold, then the state has to pay a cost when it requisitions land. It is actually a kind of requisition purchase. As to the economic phenomenon of large numbers of transfers of land ownership in town and country today (the actual phenomenon of selling and purchasing land), the costs in various forms paid in this kind of land "deal" can be regarded as an expansion of the form of requisition purchase, and consequently, a land price has taken shape. Another reason for the existence of rent and land price in socialist society is that socialism recognizes the difference in material benefit obtained by different people under an identical general interest. The actual existence of this difference enables the economic phenomenon to penetrate into all of our production activities. Although land does not create value, it brings differential material benefit. Thus the difference brought about by the non-labor force should be transformed into the benefit of the landowner so that the principle of "to each according to his work" can truly be manifested in a kind of equivalence in quantity (an equal amount of labor obtains an equal amount of goods, instead of obtaining goods by labor plus the forces of nature).

Marx said:

> Looking from the angle of a higher social economic pattern, private ownership of land by an individual, like the ownership of one person by another person, is preposterous. Even the whole society, a nation, and all the existing societies put together are not owners of the land. They are merely the occupants and users of the land and, like a good patriarch, must improve the land before handing it down to posterity.[9]

However, our understanding is that Marx referred to the situation in the higher phase of communism. This is not the current situation of our country's socialist economy. We still have the problem of separation of the ownership of land and the right to use the land. Consequently, the existence of the idea of rent in a socialist economy does not run counter to the doctrine of Marx. Socialist land price is not the price of value, but the purchasing price or rent provided by land. The existence of rent is the prerequisite for the existence of a land price.[10]

To make the question clear, the land we discussed earlier referred to uncultivated land. This means that, in our view, under the socialist system, even the uncultivated land has a price. In actual economic life, production has developed to a point where land is not only limited but there is also in fact hardly a piece of land on which the society has not invested some labor. In other words, land is no longer an endowment of nature. Under these circumstances the payment of land costs is all the more natural. This completely conforms to Marx's doctrine of the value of labor.

This is our understanding of the economic nature of socialist land price. We conclude that it is necessary not only to clearly provide in qualitative terms the socialist price of land, but also to study in quantitative terms the socialist price of land. The quantitative stipulations of land price in a socialist economy are strictly governed by law, more strictly than in a capitalist economy. This requires joint efforts by theoretical and practical workers for study and solution.

PROPOSALS ON THE QUESTION OF THE CALCULATION AND PAYMENT OF LAND PRICE IN THE REFORM OF THE ECONOMIC SYSTEM

In light of the situation mentioned, we are of the opinion that in the course of the economic reform, the following reforms can be considered in calculating land price and its payment.

Restore the Land Price System

For a long time China has put into practice a highly concentrated planned economy. The enterprise in reality possesses no right to exercise independent control over its funds, land, labor force, products, and most of its profits. In other words, the enterprise has not become an independent accounting unit in the true sense of the term, and naturally it is hard to implement the principle of material benefit. All trades and professions are making vigorous efforts to carry out the economic responsibility system and enforce independent accounting. Hereafter, all enterprises will be required to rely on their own profits to ensure expanded reproduction with their own production funds. Consequently, the land price system will become imperative. This is an important aspect to ensure that the enterprises do not "eat from the same big pot."

The "Regulations Governing Land Requisition for National Reconstruction"[11] promulgated by the State Council in 1982 provide that compensation should be paid on the basis of area when requisitioning rural land, while no compensation should be paid when requisitioning urban land. In the present economic reform, we maintain that in requisitioning urban land, like the requisition of rural land, the requisitioning unit should pay the landowner according to the land price. Only in this way is it possible for the price of buildings in capital construction, whether in cities or in rural areas, to be unified, to make cost accounting in housing construction more scientific, and to create conditions for the stipulation of rational rent in the future. We also believe that the prices of various grades of land can be fixed minutely in accordance with the conditions of the land, such as its abundance and location. In land requisition the calculation of land price uniformly according to area, whether it is good or bad land, or according to roughly divided grades will lead to unjustified economic inequality among land users.

Pay Regularly for Land Use

Just as an enterprise cannot use funds without compensation and must pay a cost, the enterprise or peasant household should also pay for the land it uses so that the expense can become a constituent factor in the prices of products. All resources (including land, production funds, labor force, and so forth) are merely conditions of production and do not form value themselves. It is the labor put into production that forms value. But natural resources are of importance to production. Labor is the father of wealth and land is the mother of wealth. Although natural resources do not turn into value during production, the difference in natural conditions will inevitably affect the efficiency of the labor put into production. For example, the quality of the land, its location, and whether the mineral resources are high grade or low grade all have something to do with the wealth created by labor. This kind of difference is usually called differential rent. The practice of paying for the use of land in a socialist economy has at least the following functions.

1. The use of land can be economized. China is a mountainous country. Seventy percent of the country is mountainous, 20 percent is water, and only 10 percent is farmland. The contradictions between the large population and limited land are striking. According to a rough estimation, China has only 1.6 billion mu of cultivated land, with an average of 1.5 mu per capita, and the size of the land is steadily decreasing. Over the past three decades capital construction has taken up about 100 million mu of land, accounting for one-sixteenth of the original farmland. The occupation of land by commune members for building houses and by the collectives in rural areas for setting up commune-run industries and, for example, brickyards has also become a serious problem. Thus the adoption of measures to economize on the use of land is an urgent task. Experience shows that the free use of land often leads to abuse of land and results in waste of this important but limited natural resource.

2. We can accurately assess the economic impact of the enterprise. Inclusion of land in the scope of economic accounting is an important step for economic accounting to develop in-depth. Aside from subjective factors, many objective factors also affect the successful or unsatisfactory management of an enterprise. The size of the land occupied and the quality of the land being used are important objective factors. These factors not only have a tremendous effect on agricultural production and mining, but also have a direct bearing on industrial production and business management. Some industrial enterprises possess narrow lots, which often cause difficulties for normal, continuous production. There are wide gaps in the volume of business and circulation costs between commercial enterprises located in small, out-of-the-way lanes and those located in downtown areas. If the use of land is free of charge, the inequality of various enterprises in the distribution of free land will find expression in economic inequality. The enterprises that occupy more of the free land will surely be in a favorable position economically. Therefore, paying a price for the use of land is by no means a

meaningless act, such as taking money from one pocket and putting it in another. It can drive the enterprise to use as little land as possible and to make full, effective use of the land occupied.

3. We can concentrate funds for the state. In the course of economic readjustment, the inadequate role played by certain economic mechanisms has brought about the situation of "rich people but poor state." In the past few years the national income increased steadily but the accumulation of funds delivered to the state dropped; the gross value of industrial and agricultural output increased steadily but state revenue declined. The practice of using land with compensation can ensure the concentration of more revenues in the hands of the state.

It must be explained here that payment for the use of land is only redistribution. This expense cannot be included in the cost of production, just as the payment for the use of funds and interest cannot be included in the cost of production. Otherwise, a mistake of principle will be committed in theory and harm will be done in practice.

Implementation and Payment of Land Price Should Be Closely Coordinated and Carried Out Simultaneously with Other Economic Reforms

Whether it is the land price, the real estate tax, or payment for the use of land, without the assurance of corresponding reforms in other fields, a good motive cannot achieve good results. For example, if the requisition cost is paid in one lump sum as a financial expenditure and is not included in the cost of product construction, counted as an increase in the value of fixed assets, or incorporated in the production cost of the house-using unit, there will still be people asking for or occupying more land. Even if the requisition expense is included in the cost of investment items and turned into value of fixed assets, it will be meaningless to calculate requisition expenses if the products of construction are not counted as commodities and are sold to the using unit at a certain price or appropriated by the using unit without compensation. What is more important, even though the enterprise has paid a land cost (or real estate tax), under the existing practice of sharing of profit, the paid land cost is regarded as a factor of "objective" effect, which only reduces the total profit and the sum of the profit retained by the enterprise. The result is that, on the one hand, the land cost is delivered to the state in the form of taxation (or payment). On the other hand, the profit to be delivered to the state is reduced in the form of profit retained by the enterprise. This will in no way affect the enterprise, which will continue to try to occupy more land by all ways and means. This demonstrates that unless various kinds of reforms are carried out simultaneously, simply implementing a land price and payment will not bring about the expected result.

Comments

This article is part of an ongoing effort by some Chinese scholars and policymakers to break the confines of Marxist orthodoxy and bureaucratic inertia and extend the application of market methods to land allocation and usage. They recognize that the practice of allocating land bureaucratically without annual charges has led to massive inefficiencies like large, sparsely filled office and factory campuses, low-income businesses occupying high-value sites, and extortionate backdoor land transfer deals. Zhang and Kong are less explicit on the remedy and at times appear to merely favor an additional state land use charge or real estate tax. As they indicate, however, such a limited move will not suffice. The clear import of their views is the need to somehow establish institutions to treat land as a commodity, subject to purchase and sale, after decades of rigorous controls that helped neither the economy nor the environment. Housing is now increasingly being put up for sale in the cities, but most people balk at the subsidized prices after having been raised in an extremely low-rent system, which provided inexpensive, albeit shabby, accommodations for most people.

Recent legislative developments with regard to land-use fees, coupled with the relevant provisions of the State Council's Provisional Regulations on the Encouragement of Foreign Investment, (October 11, 1986), in *Beijing Review*, October 27, 1986, pp. 26–28, promise to regularize the practice of setting land-use fees governing foreign investment. Representative local land use fee regulations include the Shenzhen Special Economic Zone Measures for the Implementation of Land Use Fees (October 25, 1985), in *Wen Hui Bao* (Hong Kong), December 6, 1985, p. 8; the Shanghai Measures for the Management of Land Use by Joint Ventures, in *Wen Hui Bao*, November 7, 1986, p. 4; and the Regulations on the Use of Land in the Xiamen Special Economic Zone (July 14, 1984), translated in *China Economic News*, April 15, 1985, pp. 1–2. For further discussion, *see* Mitchell A. Silk, "Investigating and Doing Business in China: The Environmental Implications," in Michael J. Moser, ed., *Foreign Trade, Investment and the Law in the People's Republic of China*, 2d ed., Hong Kong and London: Oxford University Press, 1987.

11

Forest Protection

Zhang Youyu (1984) "Report to the National People's Congress on the Forestry Law Revision"

Renmin Ribao (September 11), p. 2. Translation, with permission, from *Chinese Law and Government*, vol. 19, no. 1 (1986), pp. 101–4.

Zhang Youyu, vice-director of the Law Committee of the National People's Congress, reported to the Seventh Session of the Standing Committee of the Sixth National People's Congress on the result of discussions on the Forestry Law of the People's Republic of China (revised draft) on the afternoon of September 11. He said that the Law Committee met four times in August and September this year to discuss the revised draft of the Forestry Law and studied the suggestions from members of the Standing Committee of the National People's Congress as well as provinces, autonomous regions, and municipalities directly under the central government and the ministries concerned. The Standing Committee held that the draft was feasible in general, but it also suggested a few amendments to the draft.

When he referred to the disputes over forests and forestland ownership, Zhang Youyu said that, as stipulated by the draft, ownership disputes should be settled through consultation between the parties to the dispute under the supervision of the county people's government in the place in question. If consultation fails, disputes can be brought to the local people's court for adjudication. Forest or forestland ownership disputes between county or higher-level administrative divisions should be solved through consultation under the supervision of the next higher-level people's government. If consultation fails, the mediating people's government body can direct a resolution binding on the parties.

The Supreme People's Court, the Supreme People's Procuracy, the Ministry of Civil Affairs, and the Ministry of Agriculture, Animal Husbandry, and Fisheries feel that it is unfair that, according to the stipulations of the draft, some disputes can be taken to court while others cannot. They suggested the following amendment to the draft: Forestry and forestland ownership and usage disputes between units of ownership by the whole people, between units of collective ownership, or between units of ownership by the whole people and units of collective ownership should be settled by the people's governments of the county level or higher. Ownership and usage disputes over forests and forestland between individuals, between individual(s) and unit (s) of ownership by the whole people, or between individual(s) and unit(s) of collective ownership should be settled by the people's government at the county or *xiang* (township) level. A party to the dispute that disagrees with the people's government's decision may, within one month of receiving notice of the decision, appeal it in an appropriate people's court.

Regarding examination and approval of applications to use state-owned forestlands, Zhang Youyu said that, according to the draft, the use of forestlands for national construction requires the examination and approval of the Ministry of Forestry. The State Planning Commission, the Ministry of Urban and Rural Construction and Environmental Protection, and other organizations feel that this stipulation is inconsistent with that of the ''Regulations Regarding State Requisition of Land for National Reconstruction''[12] and would be difficult to comply with. They suggested that this article be amended as follows: Forestlands should not be used or their use should be minimized when surveying and designing roads, completing engineering projects, and exploiting mineral resources. When forestlands must be used or taken over, the acquisition or use must be done in accordance with relevant laws and regulations. Acquisition or use of tracts larger than a thousand mu [15 mu = 1 hectare] must have the State Council's approval.

Logging will follow a state-coordinated plan for timber production, according to Vice-Director Zhang Youyu. The felling of trees outside the plan shall be forbidden. The State Planning Commission, the State Materials Supply Administration, and other departments feel that since the state plan does not include timber for local capital construction, rural house-building, and fuel, many rural people would be in technical violation of the law, so the law is in fact not feasible. They recommended that the law be amended as follows: A unified annual timber production plan will be made by the state, and its extent will be stipulated by the State Council.

Some members of the Standing Committee of the National People's Congress and some local authorities feel, according to Zhang Youyu, that it is unreasonable to restrict peasants from felling trees around their own homes without permission from the authorities, and this stipulation is not favorable to stimulating their initiative for afforestation. Therefore, they suggested that rural residents should have the right to fell their own trees around their family plot or around their own houses without the need to apply for a permit from the authorities.

Zhang Youyu said that some members of the Standing Committee of the National People's Congress and local authorities are of the opinion that because, in quite a few places, people now pay too much attention to logging while neglecting afforestation, cuts are not being reforested and forests are becoming fewer and fewer. More importance should be attached to afforestation, and a policy of integrating felling with afforestation should be implemented. To reverse the current trend in some places of logging without planting, and to carry out the forestry construction policy of giving priority to afforestation, they proposed the addition of the following stipulations to the law's chapter on felling: logging units or individuals must reforest in the time allotted in the felling permit and the quantity of reforestation must be equal to or larger than the size of the cut. If they do not meet this target in the allotted time, the permit-issuing authorities can decide not to renew the permit until the target is fulfilled.

Some members of the Standing Committee of the National People's Congress and some localities also proposed that the Forestry Law clearly state that collectives or individuals shall be permitted to sign afforestation contracts. Therefore, they proposed the addition of an article to the draft that forestlands owned by the state can be contracted for afforestation by collectives or individuals, and that forestlands owned by collectives can be contracted for afforestation by individuals.

When referring to the problem of punishing cases of poaching and denudation, Zhang Youyu said that the Supreme People's Court, the Supreme People's Procuracy, and some provinces, autonomous regions, and municipalities directly under the central government feel that in some places there is an erroneous tendency of lightly punishing violators of the relevant laws. This is because quite a few cases are not being handled in accordance with the criminal law concerning poaching and denudation. It is really improper to sentence those who poach a large quantity of timber to a light sentence of less than three years' imprisonment. The Legal System Working Committee discussed this problem, together with the Supreme People's Court, the Supreme People's Supervisory Office, and the Ministry of Forestry. It believes that poaching of a large volume of timber can be punished according to the larceny stipulations in the Criminal Law. Therefore, they suggested that the following article be added to the chapter on juridical responsibilities: Those who poach or appropriate a large volume of woods owned by others can be held responsible for a crime according to Article 152 of the Criminal Law.

Comments

Zhang's report shows that different departments had concerns about the Forestry Law, some of which were addressed in the legislative process. These primarily involved inconsistencies with other policies and the strong cultural concern among many educated Chinese for tighter management of logging. In general, however, laws go through many in-house drafts before advancing to the Standing Committee, so the formal legislative process is of marginal substantive significance. However, this may change if the political and legal reforms proceed.

Yang Zhong (1984) "How to Implement the Forestry Law"

Zhongguo Linye, no. 12, pp. 2–3.

The Forestry Law of the People's Republic of China will take effect on January 1, 1985. *Banyue Tan's* [Fortnightly] reporter interviewed Minister of Forestry

Yang Zhong about some questions involving its implementation which he answered.

Q: What is the basic spirit of the Forestry Law?

A: The Forestry Law is one of China's major economic laws. Its purpose is already expressed in Article 1 under General Principles, namely, to protect, nurture, and rationally utilize forestry resources; accelerate the greenification of China's soil; enhance forestry's functions with regard to water storage and soil conservation, moderating the climate, improving the environment, and supplying wood products—to meet the needs of socialist construction and people's livelihood.

In comparison with the Forestry Law issued for trial implementation in 1979, this version already emphasizes stable ownership and usufruct rights with regard to forests, trees, and forestry land and protects the legal rights and interests of both producers and users. It also affirms that forestry construction must carry out the policies of taking silviculture as the foundation, practicing forestry conservation everywhere, going all out for afforestation, integrating logging and cultivation, and sustained yield. It strengthens economic support for forestry through long-term credits to finance afforestation by collectives and individuals and establishes a forestry funding system and other conservation-oriented measures. It sets more complete and more stringent regulations with regard to the management of logging and transport and introduces logging quotas and legal responsibilities. The Forestry Law incorporates the party and government's recent series of important instructions and reform measures regarding the promotion of forestry. It is a law that promotes forestry, that conserves forestry, and provides legal assurances for developing forestry in China.

Q: How should we correctly perceive the relationship between relaxing policies and tightening management?

A: On the one hand, we relax forestry policy to enliven the forestry economy. On the other hand, we regulate forestry by laws and strictly manage forestry resources. These goals are parallel. Relaxation is to mobilize the enthusiasm of the masses for developing forestry. Stringent management is to guard the basic interests of the state and the people. Forestry can develop rapidly only if we correctly combine the two. Some cadres and masses in the villages still are concerned that there will be a policy reversal. We should clearly explain to them that the relaxation of forestry policy and enlivening of the forestry economy conforms to the interests of the state and the people and will not be changed, and that the proper interests of operators are protected by law.

Q: What problems should we pay attention to when carrying out the Forestry Law's provisions on stabilizing forestry and forestland rights?

A: Stabilizing forestry and forestland rights and protecting the legal interests of owners and users is the basis for protecting and developing forestry and is the core of the Forestry Law. The Forestry Law has clear provisions regarding the confirmation and registration, issuance of certificates, conflict resolution, distribution of proceeds, and legal responsibilities regarding forestry and forestland ownership and usufruct rights. Major items in the course of implementation are as follows:

1. We must continue to do well the critical "Three Fixes" (stabilizing mountain and forestry rights, demarcating private hills, and setting up a forestry production responsibility system) work in forestry. The "Three Fixes" are essential to forestry development. Seventy-seven percent of counties and 82 percent of villages have basically completed the "Three Fixes." Most areas that have yet to finish the job are in remote mountains, where work is more difficult. All areas must actively create the conditions and overcome difficulties to do this vital job well.

2. We must energetically resolve conflicts over forestry and forestland rights. Such conflicts often result in the destruction of forestry resources and even armed conflict, impairing stability and unity. The relevant leading party and government organs should actively resolve these disputes in a stabilizing fashion in accordance with the provisions of Article 14 to bring order and tranquility to the forestry districts.

Q: What concrete provisions in the Forestry Law govern the legal rights and interests of peasants regarding afforestation, private hills, and contract guarantee wastelands?

A: In order to protect peasants' legal rights and interests in afforestation [Article 23 of] the Forestry Law provides:

> Trees planted by village residents around their houses and on their private plots and mountains are owned by them. . . . In the case of afforestation performed on a contract basis by collectives or individuals on afforestable waste mountains or lands owned by the whole people or by a collective, the trees planted after signing the contract are owned by the collective or individual contractor. When the contract has other provisions, the contract's clauses should govern.

These provisions show that the state encourages peasants to manage private and responsibility hills well. The law allows the contracting of state- and collectively owned afforestable wasteland for afforestation to collectives and individuals whose legal rights and interests are protected by law. The Party Central Committee has also clearly specified that "contract guarantee rights are inheritable and transferable." Short-term contracts can be extended to enable the contractor to realize an appropriate return during the contract period. We definitely must communicate this important policy to the peasants clearly to enable them to work and invest with confidence and develop forestry to create prosperity.

Q: Some areas now have combined responsibility hills and private hills into private hills, turning the two hills into one hill. Is this a proper work style?

A: This must be analyzed in concrete terms. We should allow this in some areas where wastehills are few and responsibility hills were first divided on an equal per capita basis, but the masses now demand that they all be converted into private hills. But in most areas responsibility hills were demarcated on the basis of actual conditions, according to ability, rather than on an equal per capita basis. Moreover, responsibility contracts were negotiated with the collective and publicly registered so they have public backing. At the same time there is wide divergence in investment and management after contracting. To merge the two hills under such conditions would violate policy and cannot be allowed. Article 23, Section 4, is clear about this and no one can casually alter the contracts.

Q: What is logging by quota? Why do we have to institute a logging permit system?

A: Forestry is one of the state's precious resources. Respecting the principles of not allowing timber consumption to exceed growth, strictly regulating logging volume, instituting logging quotas, and sustained yield are all important jobs for forestry legislation and are fundamental principles of doing forestry management well. Consequently, we must strengthen logging management. With the exception of logging by peasants on scattered sites or their own private hills and around their homes, any unit or individual logging forests and trees that he owns or manages must apply for a logging permit and log according to the provisions of the permit. When applying for a logging permit, you must specify in the document the logging site, area of cut, volume of cut, tree species, logging method, time frame, regeneration method, and species for regeneration. Departments issuing logging permits must not exceed the approved annual logging quota for permits or they will be violating the law. Those with direct responsibility [for violating the law] will be punished with administrative sanctions or even criminal liability in accordance with Article 35.

Q: What will happen to existing township [forestry conservation] compacts once the Forestry Law takes effect?

A: The Forestry Law is forestry's basic law and all logging, utilization, cultivation, planting, and management must abide by it. Relevant local and departmental regulations and local laws, including township compacts concluded by the masses, must be revised to conform to the Forestry Law. Those which conform to the spirit of the Forestry Law can remain in force, but those which are incompatible should be nullified or revised and definitely cannot be allowed to subvert the Forestry Law.

Q: Poaching and illegal felling should be handled under which laws?

A: Article 6 clearly responds to this. These provisions consist of two parts: One consists of administrative sanctions, like ordering compensation for damages, planting replacements for the missing trees, and fines in the case of minor infractions. The other includes criminal penalties or assigning criminal responsibility in the case of major infractions. [Two points] should be specifically noted here. First, administrative sanctions include provisions not only governing the severity of fines and replanting, but also stating that the amount of the fines exceeds the limits set in the Act of the People's Republic of China for Security Administration and Punishment. Fines for poaching are set at three to ten times the ill-gotten gain, and fines for deforestation, at two to five times the gain. Second, when the amount of poaching is large, it is provided that punishment will be applied according to Article 152 of the Criminal Law, which provides, in particularly serious cases, for a maximum prison sentence of ten years or more in fixed sentences or for indeterminate sentences and possible confiscation of property. This exceeds the maximum sentence of three years for poaching under administrative law.

Q: What special provisions of the Forestry Law apply to forestry production and construction in minority nationality autonomous areas?

A: One-third of forestland and almost two-thirds of reserves are found in remote areas populated by minority nationalities. It is extremely important to determine how to help the minority nationality autonomous areas to protect and develop forestry in accordance with local nationality conditions and characteristics. Therefore, Articles 7 and 41 provide for somewhat greater self-ownership rights and economic interests regarding forest exploitation, timber distribution, and the use of forestry lands in comparison with other areas. Moreover, so long as the basic principles of the Forestry Law are not violated, more flexible methods suitable to local conditions can be formulated and then applied after being approved in accordance with legal procedures. Minority autonomous areas should further relax forestry policy, accelerate development and construction in forestry districts, free up timber distribution channels, and expand the rights of self-management with regard to forestry products in accordance with this spirit and the central directive ''Helping Impoverished Areas to Rapidly Transform Their Conditions'' (1984), so that the peasants can get a bigger return and we can reach the goal of making the mountains and the people prosperous by developing forestry.

Comments

The didactive interview format is often used to clarify ambiguity present in policy. Minister Yang, who appears to be a strong supporter of the reforms, uses this occasion to explain how the Forestry Law was revised since the trial implementation version was promulgated in early 1979. Essentially, the earlier version was issued at the outset of the reform period, just two months after the decisive Third Plenum was held in December 1978, during which time Yang was a provincial official in the reform pacesetting province of Sichuan. Consequently, the earlier version stressed the inviolability of state and collective forestry holdings while paying short shrift to households, and thus failed to anticipate the extent to which the rural reforms would weaken the collectives and enhance the rights of households. The new version better reflects the changes introduced since the Third Plenum, although it, too, tends to lag behind events. Despite Yang's disclaimer, private and responsibility hills have been combined in many areas.

The purpose of these reforms, of course, is to stimulate forestry development, which had been seriously handicapped by leftist excesses and rigid central planning. The potential for development, however, is still restricted by prohibitions on the private ownership of land, the recent historical legacy of policy impermanence, and exploitation by local officials—all of which induce the rural populace to liquidate standing timber and invest the proceeds in non-forestry-related activities. The quota, or ''single ledger,'' system was introduced in 1984 to establish a comprehensive logging and regeneration balance to prevent overfelling, but it paradoxically undercuts much of the reform potential by giving forestry and local government bureaucrats the authority to decide who can log what, where, when, and how. It is not easy to envision how these overarching controls can be successfully joined with the decentralized management introduced by the reforms, although somewhat tighter policing is essential in the transitional period. If regulation and relaxation prove to be more contradictory than Yang claims, forestry development will face a clouded future.

Zhu Zanping (1984) "Discussing the Internal Motivation to Cultivate Forests in the Collective Forest Areas of South China"

Nongye Jingi Wenti, no. 11, pp. 36–39.

Sustained yield is the goal of forest management. The decline of forest reserves is a widespread and serious problem in the collective forest areas of the South. The cause of the decline in forest reserves cannot be simplistically ascribed to overcutting, but rather requires an overall and historically based analysis from a developmental perspective. If we regard overfelling as the dominant aspect of the contradiction and adopt a policy of reduced harvests, this will inevitably impair the delivery of timber for building the Four Modernizations and meeting the needs of the people. This is unacceptable. We can reverse the trend for forest reserves to decline only by adopting measures to mobilize the activism of the woodsmen to cultivate forests in a big way. We can reverse this trend and see an increase in reserves only by studying and devising strategic policies to develop forestry in the collective forest areas of the South on the basis of this fundamental concept and by working hard to create resources.

What is the main reason forest cultivation cannot keep pace in the collective forest areas of the South? Past analysis of this question focused on three items: leadership inattention, insufficient funding for silviculture, and low timber prices. These three points are, without a doubt, important factors. However, the key factor is afforestation for whom? For a long time this question has not been adequately resolved, so forest cultivation has been short on internal motivation.

The main force for managing forestry in the collective forest areas of the South is the peasant masses or woodsmen in these areas. The quality of forest management depends on the level of activism among the woodsmen. Looking back, we can see that forest reserves declined because logging activism was high but afforestation activism was low. Why were most woodsmen not enthusiastic about afforestation? This is because collective management for a long time was characterized by the "swarm-of-bees" style of production and the "uniform" style of distribution, which could not link the results of the woodsmen's labor to their material interests. The woodsmen basically were powerless to control the forests which they themselves had cultivated. Therefore, in most woodsmen's minds there was no sense of afforesting for themselves, with they themselves being the owners and enjoying the benefits, or we can say that this belief was weakly implanted. This inevitably produced a deviation among woodsmen who "depended on the mountains but did not cherish them, and used the forests without nurturing them," who were incapable of entertaining a conscious need and self-initiative to cultivate the forests.

There have been great accomplishments in man-made afforestation in the collective forest areas of the South since the founding of the People's Republic. These gains, however, appear to have been exclusively the product of pressure from administrative commands and the inducement of economic subsidies. Although the state has paid quite a price, the results from afforestation have been far from ideal because of the lack of self-initiative among the woodsmen.

It is absolutely correct to use the slogan "afforest for the revolution, create prosperity for one's children and grandchildren" to mobilize universal obligatory tree planting, but it is clearly insufficient to mobilize the woodsmen in large numbers to cultivate the forests. Because the woodsmen regard forest cultivation as a means of livelihood, any operator always regards his own personal interests as the object of his management. If woodsmen are powerless to control the forests which they themselves have cultivated or have no rights with regard to cultivating forests, they cannot manage their work with any self-initiative or activism. Next, I will sketch out a bit more clearly the changes in conditions which have occurred in mountain and forestry rights since the founding of the People's Republic.

During land reform we used expropriation without compensation to distribute the mountains and forests owned by the feudal landlord class to the woodsmen, making the latter the masters of the mountains and forests. Soon afterward, during cooperativization, we cooperativized the forests and trees on a discounted basis; that is, we took the mountains and forests originally owned by the woodsmen individually and made them the collective property of the cooperatives. These two fundamental changes did not damage the economic interests of the woodsmen who joined the cooperatives. Thus not only was there no decline in the woodsmen's activism to cultivate forests, but these changes also greatly accelerated the development of the forces of production in forestry. From this we can see that the low level of woodsmen's activism with regard to forestry cultivation is only partially related to instability in forest rights and frequent changes in policy, but this is not the full story.

Looking at the situation in the postcommunization period, we find the following.

1. No compensation was provided in the course of equalization. At one command all the mountains and forests belonging to the agricultural cooperatives became commune property. The reassignment of forestry rights without compensation signified no compensation for the fruits of other people's labor, which totally violates the socialist principle of to each according to his labor.

2. During the "Great Leap Forward" a big "communist wind" blew up to cut down the forests. This not only resulted in deforestation on a scale seldom

seen before in history, but the worst part was that this episode of destruction eroded the concept of cherishing and protecting the forests in people's minds, causing a spiritual loss that proved hard to remedy.

3. When the people's communes were restructured in the early 1960s according to three levels of ownership, with the production team as the base, the delimitation of mountains and forests was based on the principle of enhancing production and management rather than on the monetary value of stumpage at the time of communization. In actuality this was still another instance of redistribution without compensation. In many areas the structure of mountain and forestry rights became utterly chaotic, fomenting many property conflicts, which is a basic reason for the continuance of poaching and deforestation.

4. During the 1970s another wind sprang up in the collective forestry districts of the South to establish large numbers of logging and cultivating farms run by the communes and brigades. In many areas there was basically no respect whatsoever for the property rights and autonomy of the teams holding forestry rights. Because administrative force was relied upon and arbitrary demarcation and management decisions were made, logging took place at will without regard for reforestation.

5. Ever since the communes were formed, most areas in the collective forestry districts of the South have basically not instituted the policy of the owner enjoys the benefits with regard to timber revenue. Right up to now, some areas continue to equalize income from the sale of stumpage. For example, in addition to legal tax assessments and public accumulations, some areas continue to impose a 3:3:4 or 1:2:7 split on timber income between the commune, the brigade, and the production team. This, in actuality, is disguised infringement on timber ownership rights.

We can clearly see from the elementary issues discussed earlier that forestry rights instability and policy fluctuations are merely symptoms. The core of the problem is that forestry in the postcommunization period has been continuously buffeted by a "communist wind" that has gravely impaired the interests of forestry rights holders, depressing the willingness of most woodsmen to engage in forest cultivation.

If everyone knows that it is wrong in theory to blow up a "communist wind," why do we consciously, or unconsciously, continue to commit the same kind of mistake? Analyzing this in terms of cognition, the following are the major factors.

1. *A lack of clear understanding about the nature of the collective ownership system.* Although the collective ownership and ownership by the whole people at the present stage are both socialist forms of public ownership, they are different in concept. In China any unit owned by the whole people is a unit with only the right of independent management; it is not an independently owned unit. Therefore, any vertical change (centralization or decentralization) or horizontal change (splitting or merging) involves changes in the structure of management rights but not in ownership rights. Therefore, no issue of compensation for equal

value in rights and interests ever arises. In this sense, ownership by the whole people is a uniform concept.

But collectively owned units, regardless of size, are all independently owned units. Any vertical or horizontal change among such units involves a change in ownership rights and requires compensation for equal value in rights and interests. Failure to provide compensation indicates an infringement on ownership rights and can lead to destruction of the object subject to possession. In this sense, collective ownership is a composite concept. The stirring up of a "communist wind," arising from the failure to provide compensation for equal value for changes in mountain and forestry rights, was due to insufficient understanding of the distinction between ownership by the whole people and collective ownership, and originated in erroneous concepts like "change among collectives implies no change in essence."

2. *A lack of clear understanding about the special features of mountain and forestry ownership*. In the past we lumped together the terms "mountain land" and "forests" in the term "mountain forests" [*shanlin*], but actually mountain land and forests are two separate concepts. The long growth process of forests is a mark of distinction compared with agricultural crops. If we say that mountain land is a natural resource that requires no compensation when mountain and forestry rights are reassigned because mountain lands have no labor value (however, rights to it also should be compensated if we regard mountain land as having usage value), the forests are largely a product of labor, so any transfer involving their rights and interests deserves compensation. In the past some comrades did not clearly understand this special feature of mountain and forestry ownership and regarded the ownership system for mountains and forestry as identical to the ownership system for ordinary land. A lack of appreciation in policy for the distinction between mountain land and forests is another factor in the development of "communist winds."

3. *A lack of clear understanding of the concept of forest resources*. Standing forests include both man-made and natural forests. There is no doubt that man-made forests are a product of labor whose value should be expressed in prices. However, do natural forests also have value, and should it also be expressed in prices? Looking at the collective forestry districts of the South, there are almost no virgin forests that grow without any human intervention whatsoever. Present-day natural forests matured only with the help of some human management and protection. Moreover, after these natural forests are cut down, man-made regeneration or artificially assisted natural regeneration is essential. Therefore, all forests in the collective forestry districts of the South, whether man-made or natural, cannot be perceived as purely natural resources, but should be considered products of labor. The failure to clearly affirm this issue in theory and policy in the past was another pretext for stirring up a "communist wind" in some areas.

The Party Central Committee has already put forth a policy saying that there will be no changes for thirty to fifty years, or for a long time. This is an essential and correct step to calm people's feelings; however, we should realize that it is still hard to expiate misgivings about change among woodsmen with this "no-change" policy because "no-change" policies were also enunciated in the past but never sustained, and there were continuing fluctuations. We are currently building and perfecting forestry production responsibility systems and readjusting production relations, which are also in flux. As the forces of production develop in the future, the specific forms of forestry production responsibility systems will definitely see some changes. The question is not whether there will be change, but what kind of changes there will be. Changes can be good or bad. What the masses are afraid of is bad changes. They will be enthusiastic supporters of good changes. The profound changes that have taken place in Chinese villages in the past few years prove this point. Therefore, the point of departure for our policy research is not to convince the masses that there will be no change, but to overcome the masses' fear of change. The reason woodsmen have mental misgivings about change now, frankly speaking, is that they fear that another "communist wind" will be stirred up, damaging their rights and interests. Consequently, the key point in future changes is that we must abide by two basic policy principles.

First, we must uphold the principle of voluntariness and mutual benefit. That is, all changes must respect the masses' wishes, protect the masses' interests, and take place only if the masses want them. We definitely cannot use mass mobilizational methods to institute an "all in a row" wind or "one knife cuts all" kind of changes.

Second, we must uphold the principle of exchange for equal value. Any transfer of mountain and forestry rights among the workers involving collectives or individuals must include compensation for equal value. We cannot use exploitative methods, promote leveling, or stir up a "communist wind."

So long as we uphold these two basic policy principles, the woodsmen's mental reservations about change will gradually dissipate.

To sum up the previous analysis, we must adopt the following fundamental policies in order to arouse the woodsmen's activism for cultivating forests.

Fix Mountain and Forestry Rights and Resolutely Defend Rights

Any ownership right consists of rights and interests. Rights refer to the legal aspects of ownership, and interests refer to the owner's special interests. Only when the two are completely integrated, with the owner enjoying the benefits, is the ownership right genuine and effective. The constant changes in the collective structure for a long time have brought chaos to mountain and forestry rights in most areas, with unclear boundaries and rights common and without any way of defending rights and interests. In the past few years the "three fixes" in forestry [clarifying forestry rights, assigning private hills, and establishing a production responsibility system] have basically solved these problems in most areas, but in some difficult cases mountain and forestry conflicts have still not been satisfactorily resolved. We must continue to work hard on this mission and cannot let it slide.

There are two problems in defending mountain and forestry ownership rights that require urgent solutions: (1) we must resolutely correct the mistaken work style of excessive levies at every level and equalized stumpage revenue; and (2) we must resolutely root out the evil wind of poaching and deforestation.

When handling cases of poaching and deforestation, we cannot simply draw policy boundaries on the basis of quantity, but should stress qualitative analysis. Cases involving coercive and illegal feeling that trample on the owner's rights must be sternly dealt with, for only then can we protect the masses' activism for afforestation and forest protection. But disposal of problems involving excessive feeling that go against planned management requires careful discretion. This is because planned management of timber can only basically guarantee the needs of state construction and cannot satisfy the masses' demands in terms of livelihood. When the supply and demand contradiction in timber is extremely acute, the contradiction will be merely aggravated if we carelessly use legal means to combat excessive feeling, and we can inadvertently dampen the masses' activism for afforestation and forest protection. This kind of problem can be solved only gradually by developing production in a big way.

Promote Household Responsibility and Stimulate Unified Management

The countryside has instituted a household-based production responsibility system on the basis of upholding public land ownership. This has powerfully stimulated the development of agricultural production. Since agriculture and forestry in the collective forestry districts of the South generally share the same labor force which works part-time in both sectors, the establishment of a forestry production responsibility system also should take the household contract guarantee route.

We also should consider the special aspects of forestry production and cannot engage in mechanical copying or, especially, a "one knife cuts all" approach. In all cases where household management is suitable and the masses want contracting down to the household level, we should practice household or joint household contract guarantee systems. All hilly wasteland and scrub forests also can be designated as private hills on a long-term, no-change basis if the masses are willing. Scattered trees in the mountains can be transferred to individuals on a discounted or marked-down price basis, or the income can be later divided proportionately.

Some comrades worry that contracting existing timber forests to households will result in poaching and deforestation, a problem which requires careful attention while the woodsmen still have misgivings about policy. However, household management does not inevitably lead to poaching and deforestation. Although we may say that contracting the forests among households will result in their being cut down, leaving no one responsible for the forests will lead everyone to cut them down, which is far worse. Therefore, poaching and deforestation must, to be sure, be resolutely prohibited, but we cannot shrink from household contract responsibility on these grounds. The key is to explain policy clearly, select good methods, and work carefully.

Ownership to the Planter with Rights of Inheritance and Alienation

Some comrades feel that the policy of ownership to the planter with rights of inheritance and alienation is suitable only for private hills, not for responsibility hills, saying that because responsibility hills are contract guarantee in nature, the afforested timber must be jointly owned by the collective and the contractor. This conceptualization is mistaken because this policy refers only to forests as a product of labor, and not to the mountainous land, which is a collectively owned means of production. With the exception of obligatory tree planting [instituted in 1981], all other forms of afforestation must follow the policy of ownership to the planter with rights of inheritance and alienation. Responsibility hills differ from private hills only in terms of the length of time involved, management direction, product distribution, and the obligations assumed, not in terms of forest ownership.

With regard to alienation, there is an historical custom of selling seedlings. It is entirely correct to apply this same method of selling seedlings, and thus institute separate management for different stages of forestry's long growth process. This is because a manager's outlook and purpose can change during the decades-long management process. Only if we allow the managers to alienate the object of their activity (i.e., trees of different ages) for compensation of equal value can we exorcise their retrospective doubts and attract even more social labor and capital into forest cultivation, a form of production with an exploitative nature. If we only acknowledge ownership to the planter without allowing inheritance and alienation, the ownership to the planter policy will lack reliable guarantees, and this will hamper resolution of the big problem of who the woodsmen are afforesting for.

Planned Distribution as the Leading Factor, with Market Exchange Supplementary

Ever since Liberation, timber has always been governed by the planned distribution system, which has played a major role in guaranteeing the needs of state construction. However, applying a uniform planned distribution system with regard to logging, timber sales, sales prices, and other issues directly linked to the woodsmen's interests, with everything decided by the state and no autonomy for the woodsmen, does not help to arouse activism for cultivating the forests. Therefore, timber production in the collective forestry districts of the South ought to permit market exchange and floating prices under the conditions of working to institute "a single ledger" for logging [governing off-plan as well as planned timber] and assuming the fulfillment of the state's unified procurement requirements. At the same time the state can intervene in market regulation. At present many areas have closed the free markets in timber for fear that they incite poaching and deforestation, but actually timber market exchanges have not halted. To the contrary, speculative activity has increased and black market prices have risen even higher, becoming a playground for adventurers. Although this can reduce the level of felling to some degree, it will, at the same time, cost us by weakening the woodsmen's activism for afforestation and forest cultivation.

Adoption of these basic policies will bring out the innate capacity for cultivating forests in the collective forestry districts of the South. Naturally, this inner force is insufficient. We also need lots of reinforcement from outside, like strengthened leadership at all levels, an increase in funds for silviculture, higher timber prices, and technical services, all of which are essential if we are to advance. However, we need the inner dynamic before we can adopt these measures to enhance this preexisting capacity.

Comments

This article, published in the leading agricultural economics journal, offers a well-constructed explanation for the slow pace of development in forestry. Writing from the perspective of property rights theory, Zhu maintains that the failure to enforce property rights and make them alienable is the principle reason woodsmen have been reluctant to invest in forest management and is a major factor in the undervaluation of forest resources as well as poor growth and excessive logging. In effect, the author maintains that the key to forestry development lies in genuine decentralization, giving the producer greater autonomy to market his forest or woodlot and then dispose of it. Zhu's arguments in this regard and his endorsement of proposals to sell timber rights to immature timber (a surrogate for hedging in a context of policy instability) resemble yet transcend the views of many forest economists. They devise policy solutions in terms of property rights, material incentives, and marketing systems, which, in most instances, appear to bear little resemblance to past orthodoxies about the superiority of socialism, public ownership, and unified procurement and distribution. At the same time Zhu's constant reiteration of the phrase ''communist wind'' makes plain his fear that policy reforms remain vulnerable to a change in the political climate back toward command-oriented planning, and that all policies are hostage to the arbitrary whims of local powerholders whose commitment to the sanctity of property rights and equal exchange is generally flimsy at best.

Zhang Mingqing (1985) ''It Becomes Hard for Forest Cultivators to Realize Any Benefits When They Are Squeezed at Every Step Along the Way''

Renmin Ribao (February 27), p. 1.

How much in the way of material benefits can woodsmen expect to derive from the abolition of the unified procurement of timber? Just recently I conducted an investigation in two typical counties within the forestry districts of Fujian and discovered that the woodsmen there all must pay more than ten kinds of taxes and fees. What with various kinds of givebacks and deductions, they emerge with less than twenty yuan per cubic meter of timber, just 10 percent of the negotiated price.

Let us consider Jianyang County. For every cubic meter of miscellaneous [i.e., ordinary] pine the woodsman sells, he must pay (a) a 10 percent product tax, amounting to 16 yuan; (b) a 12 percent special products tax, equalling 19.2 yuan; (c) an 8-yuan contribution to the silvicultural fund (to support afforestation); (d) a 10-yuan contribution to the development fund (for construction in forestry districts); (e) a 1-yuan inspection and grading fee; (f) a 5 percent transfer fee at the railroad station, amounting to 8 yuan; (g) a 3- to 5-yuan loading fee at the railroad station; (h) a 3 percent handling fee for an industrial and commercial administration and management license, amounting to 4.8 yuan; (i) a 3 to 5 percent handling fee at the enterprise station, equaling 4.8 to 8 yuan; (j) a 5 percent freight charge, including food and drink for the workers, for transporting the logs from the skidding site to the train station, totaling 8 yuan; (k) a railroad station joint management fee of 17 yuan per cubic meter, calculated on the basis of 500 to 1,000 yuan per freight car [this is apart from the freight charge, but there will be no car available unless this charge is also paid]; (l) wages of 22 yuan to the loggers; and (m) an 18-yuan land or mountain price [i.e., stumpage fee] paid to the owner of the land. Together they add up to 145 yuan, leaving the woodsmen with 15 yuan.

The same situation exists in Youxi County. There the woodsman gets only a little more than 17 yuan, for he must fork over 142.4 yuan for various kinds of charges for every cubic meter that he sells.

At the provincial rural work conference convened in early February, cadres in the forestry districts were incensed at the way these sundry charges are skimming woodsmen, leaving them with only a pittance. The provincial forestry departments proposed the following criteria for improving taxes and fees: The product tax is to be paid at a 10 percent rate, while the special products tax is converted to 12 percent of the negotiated price; for every cubic meter of timber collect an 8-yuan silvicultural fund contribution and a 10-yuan forestry development fund contribution (to be used for building new roads in the forests); and allow township forestry stations to impose a small inspection and grading fee. With the exception of these items, no other department will be allowed to impose additional charges, regardless of the reason.

Those units that collect fees on a variety of pretexts all have real power. If you do not pay, then your timber will not be moved. Taking the railroad station joint management fee as an example, the party selling the timber cannot get space in freight cars unless he agrees to joint management with the railroad station. Otherwise, he will not get a freight car even if there is a freight car norm set under the plan. And once it has joint management, the railroad station joint management company will take 30 to 50 percent of the seller's income. This is called a squeeze. And there are two other ways that they squeeze you to death. First, as in Jianyang, they collect 500 to 1,000 yuan per rail car. Second, they charge 8 to 10 yuan per cubic meter of timber. All of these charges are exclusive of the freight charge, which is calculated on a tons-per-kilometer basis.

The Party Central Committee's policy of abolishing the unified procurement of timber is a great way to make forestry prosperous and stimulate the economy in forestry areas, but it will only work if everyone pitches in. It will be impossible to generate activism with regard to tree planting, afforestation, management of the forest areas, and timber management if the woodsman is skinned to the point that he is left without any material gain. Neither the state nor the people will benefit—the only beneficiaries will be those who fatten their wallets with illegally imposed fees. The responsible departments should firmly root out these irrational fees to ensure that the woodsman gets his due.

Comments

This graphic commentary, supported by the Mininstry of Forestry, reveals the structural problems encountered in many policy changes in China. In this case the central authorities approved a major relaxation of marketing controls in early 1985, after seven years of halting movement in this regard. Although hardly the final step needed to improve the terms of trade for forest cultivators, it would have broken the monopoly enjoyed by the supply and marketing cooperatives and the Ministry of Forestry with regard to timber procurement and, in most cases, resulted in higher producer prices for logs.

As the commentary makes clear, however, this reform was negated in many instances by a plethora of local government exactions, new local monopsonies, and demands imposed by transportation agencies. The central authorities responded slowly to this subversion of their policy, in part because some of the relevant bureaucracies may have favored a restoration of the old system and because many policy makers opposed the reforms as a cause of inflation. It was not until October 31 that the Party Center and the State Council cracked down on such exactions (''Circular with Regard to Banning the Imposition of Reckless Levies and Charges on the Peasants'') which plagued the entire rural economy.

Because local finances are greatly dependent on special levies for road construction, education, and other purposes, and transportation is both insufficient and usually controlled by a single railroad or navigation bureaucracy, it is far from clear whether the problems identified by Zhang will be cleared up. Indeed, one problem is that the Ministry of Forestry itself insists on imposing its own silvicultural and development fees even though these are not necessarily expended in the areas where they are imposed, and thus are a de facto tax of their own. Unless these problems are resolved, cultivators will remain unenthusiastic about investing their time and money in forest management.

12

Fisheries Protection

Editorial (1986) "Apply the Law in Promoting and Supervising Fisheries"

Renmin Ribao (January 22), p. 2. Translated in FBIS-*CHI* (January 30, 1986), pp. K7-K8.

Following the readjustment of the rural production structure and the raising of urban consumption standards, fishery production will occupy an increasingly important position in our country's national economy and in people's lives.

The promulgation and implementation of the Fisheries Law of the People's Republic of China has provided a legal guarantee for the rapid development of our country's fishery production. This is a major event in the history of our country's fisheries. For quite a long time, because of the lack of a good understanding of objective law in the fishery economy, we made a series of mistakes in our general and specific policies concerning fishery production. As a result, our country's fishery production has become a weak link in our national economy, and it has become more and more "difficult" for people living in both urban and rural areas to "eat fish." In rural reforms implemented in recent years, we have carefully reviewed experiences and learned lessons and have gradually corrected our guiding ideology for accelerating the development of fishery production; have defined production policies, economic policies, technological measures, and methods concerning the strengthening of protection and management of fishery resources; and have achieved remarkable successes in practice. The new Fisheries Law aims at encouraging, supporting, and promoting the further development of fishery production and at legalizing the general and specific policies, experiences, and methods proven to be correct in practice over the past few years, thus enabling them to become authoritative, stable, and continuous. This will exert a profound impact on the development of our country's fisheries.

Because in the past we failed to protect fishery resources effectively and manage fishery production strictly, coastal areas blindly increased the number of fishing boats and fishing nets, violated regulations concerning prohibited fishing zones and prohibited fishing seasons, and fished recklessly. In inland waters some people destroyed the ecological environment for fish by poisoning, using explosives, stealing, and rushing to catch fish. In order to protect national interests and the legal rights of fishery workers, the new Fisheries Law clearly stipulates specific disciplinary, civil, and criminal sanctions against offenders, which are not only essential for safeguarding social order, but also conducive to the further development of fishery productive forces.

The Fisheries Law of the People's Republic of China is a basic fishery law formulated after the founding of the People's Republic of China. It fully embodies the spirit of applying the law in promoting and supervising fisheries and the spirit of "relaxing, invigorating, and administering." The people's governments at various levels and the relevant fishery departments must carry out propaganda and education among the masses and take the lead in observing and conscientiously carrying out the new Fisheries Law. We believe that so long as the broad masses of cadres and people consciously observe the new Fishery Law, a new situation will surely emerge in our country's fishery production.

Comments

The new Fisheries Law is intended to establish a regulatory framework for the development of fishery production, which stagnated for more than a decade in the 1960s and 1970s, when fishing by individuals and production teams was considered a "tail of capitalism" and in conflict with the grain-oriented agricultural policy. Beginning in 1977–78, producers were given more autonomy but abused it in the absence of well-defined property rights to what is frequently a fugitive resource. This new law seeks to place the economic reforms on a sounder basis in accordance with the need to regulate those biological resources which share common property ownership aspects, although it will be quite some time before regulation becomes widespread and professionally run.

13

Grasslands Protection

Editorial (1985) "Earnestly Implement the Grasslands Law"

Renmin Ribao (June 19), p. 2.

The Grasslands Law of the People's Republic of China has been officially promulgated and is to take effect on October 1 this year. Thus we will have a law to follow regarding conservation and the development of grasslands. The implementation of the Grasslands Law will further bring the initiative of different circles into play and will surely give an impetus to the constant development of grasslands and animal husbandry.

Accounting for 40 percent of the total area of our territory and equal to 370 percent of our farmland, grasslands occupy an essential place in the country's natural resources.

With 100 million domestic animals of different kinds, pastoral areas every year supply the state with hundreds of thousands of draught animals, more than 1 million beef cattle, more than 10 million sheep, nearly 100 million jin of down, and some 10 million hides. These areas are of great importance to the country's economy and the people's livelihood. Grasslands are also natural reservoirs which can conserve water and soil, regulate the climate, and improve the environment. Distributed in minority nationality areas along the border, grasslands have an important bearing on the livelihood of the local people. Therefore, protection and development of grasslands play a role not to be ignored both in boosting the economy and strengthening unity among the nationalities. In light of the importance of grasslands, we can fully see how significant the formulation of the Grasslands Law is.

All economically developed countries in the world attach great importance to pressing on with the conservation, development, and scientific exploitation of grasslands by legal means and various measures. The very purpose of our country in formulating the Grasslands Law is to promote the conservation, management, development, and rational exploitation of grasslands, to preserve and improve the ecological environment, to develop modern husbandry, to boost the economy in minority nationality autonomous areas, and to meet the needs of socialist construction and the people's livelihood. It cannot be denied that in the past, particularly in the ten years of turmoil, many localities destroyed grasslands while reclaiming wasteland, randomly exhausted grassland resources, and raised unreasonably large numbers of livestock on grasslands with limited area, and have turned them into deserts. Such a situation, if it continues, will not only endanger the interests of our people now, but will also entail untold troubles for our later generations. Since the Third Plenary Session of the 11th CPC Central Committee, the vast number of cadres and the broad masses in pastoral areas have taken vigorous action to preserve and develop grasslands, exploit grasslands in a rational way, and promote grassland animal husbandry and have accumulated a lot of valuable experience. The past practices of grassland destruction have been changed considerably. Now the Grasslands Law sets in legal form the principles, policies, and measures that the party and the state have effectively implemented; and the experience has been proved successful by the masses' practice, provides legal protection for the ownership of grasslands and the right to use grasslands, and clearly stipulates the conservation, development, and reasonable exploitation of grasslands. Therefore, the Grasslands Law is to provide a stronger guarantee for the revitalization of grasslands and the development of grassland animal husbandry.

Only by resolutely observing and strictly enforcing the law can we make sure that all orders and prohibitions are faithfully carried out. Those who govern by law must know the law, and those who are governed by law must know the law as well. Our governments at all levels must make use of various lively forms to conscientiously publicize the Grasslands Law, helping the vast number of cadres and masses to thoroughly understand the law and apply it, so that the implementation of the Grasslands Law will become an earnest practice by the whole party, the whole country, and the whole people and that grasslands will be full of life and animal husbandry will develop prosperously throughout the vast territory of China.

Comments

As in the case of forestry, post-Mao policy favors increased reliance upon property rights and production contracts to raise productivity and enhance range management. Greater tolerance is also accorded the minority cultures that have traditionally favored beef, mutton, and dairy products in their diet and economy, in contrast to the Han or ethnic Chinese who prefer grain and pork. However, land remains in public ownership, which discourages capital improvements. Shortages of capital, credit, and expertise hamper management, and property lines are often subjects of dispute. Additional progress on solving these problems, as well as providing greater security of tenure, is required if there are to be further improvements in livestock production and range management.

14
Wildlife Protection

Editorial (1980) "Protect Wildlife"

Renmin Ribao (October 22), p. 2

Properly handling the protection of the natural environment and wildlife resources is a problem before us which demands serious attention. Early in the 1950s our country paid attention to nature protection work and achieved great success. However, because of sabotage by the extreme left line over a long period of time, some of our work was not done well. Indiscriminate trapping and hunting, reckless cutting and lumbering, excessive overgrazing, indiscriminate fishing, unchecked cultivation of virgin soil, and other equally serious phenomena resulted in many economically valuable and scientifically significant species reaching the brink of extinction. According to studies, the wild horse (Equus przewalskii), long-nosed antelope (Saiga tatarica), Xinjiang tiger (Panthera uncia), rhinoceros (Rhinoceros sondaicus), white-headed leaf monkey (Presbytis leucocephalus), hog deer (Axis porcinus), Oriental ibis (Threskiornis melanocephalus), white crane (Grus leucogeranus), Cabot's tragopan (Tragopan caboti), Swinhoe's pheasant (Lophura swinhoii), and ten other valuable bird and animal varieties are already extinct, and the giant panda (Ailuropoda melanoleuca), gibbon (Hylobates spp.), black and gold silky monkey (Rhinopithecus bieti), gray and gold silky monkey (Rhinopithecus brelichi), Hainan slope deer (Cervus eldi), tiger (Panthera tigris), wild elephant (Elephas maximus), wild camel (Camelus bactrianus), dugong (Dugong dugon), Chinese alligator (Alligator sinensis), and more than twenty other rare animal types are also approaching extinction. The pattern of engaging in the plundering of natural resources has led to an imbalance in the natural ecological equilibrium of some areas, serious soil erosion, severe desertification, and frequent disastrous drought and is having disastrous effects on national construction and the life of the people. We must strenuously appeal to the public, and quickly take effective steps to protect nature, to save all those kinds of wildlife resources which face destruction.

The establishment of nature preserves is a fundamental construct in undertaking nature protection, presenting a reasonable solution to the contradiction of protecting nature and utilizing nature. This is an effective measure for saving those types of living beings on the verge of extinction and protecting their ecosystems and will become the basis for conducting scientific research on wildlife resources, nature's historical legacy, and ecosystems. The proper administration and establishment of nature preserves have great significance in furthering scientific education, accelerating achievement of the four modernizations, advancing international scientific technological cooperation, and improving the circumstances of mankind's existence. At present the international cry in demand of nature protection grows stronger day by day, attaching special importance to the establishment of nature preserves. Our nation's nature protection work lags far behind that of many countries. In some countries the total area of nature preserves constitutes from 10 percent to as much as 20 percent or more of territorial area, and in most countries they constitute about 4 percent [of territorial area]. Our country's vast territory, with a variety of natural conditions and natural environments, abounds in wildlife resources, yet the total area of nature protection areas constitutes only 0.17 percent of territorial area. Even these few nature protection areas continue to suffer violation. This state of affairs cannot continue! We must earnestly augment our work on nature protection areas, not only by administering and constructing existing nature preserves, but also, in accordance with each area's natural environment, characteristics, and distinctive natural resources, by going a step further in carrying out the demarcation of preserves, gradually creating new nature preserves, and progressively forming a representative network of nature preserves.

Some comrades regard nature preserves as local economic development burdens. This is incorrect. When constructing nature preserves, it is not easy to see short-term economic results, but it will provide an abundance of material resources for long-term economic development, create a beautiful and comfortable natural environment for future generations, and conserve and develop valuable natural resources. We must handle well our present use of nature, and in the long-term maintenance of nature, we must integrate nature protection and economic development. Some nature preserves are suitable to the development of tourism and can greatly increase economic earnings by producing long-term benefits through short-term means. We must use a variety of methods to publicize to the masses the great significance of nature protection and disseminate knowledge about nature protection, especially educating those people in and around nature preserves to reach every household, in order to establish a prevalent societal practice of cherishing nature.

In the work of building nature preserves, we must pay attention to the handling of relations with the local peasants. We must consider three interests—those of the nation, the collective, and the individual—and under the premise of not destroying the natural environment and protecting wildlife resources, help the collectives to develop collective economies, increase income from sideline occupations, and resolve in a rational manner the problem of everyday use of timber as firewood. In nature preserves we must, under the leadership of the managing department, organize the local people in a planned way to participate in certain construction, management, and maintenance activities, definitely for pay. In short, we must be adept at employing economic measures to link closely the construction of protected areas with the vital interests of the local people so that the people feel that building nature preserves can enable them to profit economically and feel more mastery over and responsibility for nature preserves. . . . We must strengthen the legal system, and for those few who deliberately destroy nature preserve resources, taking into consideration the seriousness of the case, apply economic and legal sanctions, while also investigating leadership responsibility.

Nature preserves are the base for conducting scientific research on wildlife resources and natural ecosystems. To emphasize preserves we must set up an expert scientific research organization, allocating certain scientific research personnel. Related scientific research units and institutes must fully utilize the ongoing everyday scientific research and education activities of nature preserves. This is not only beneficial to the development of nature protection work, but also fosters and trains talented persons for the country's four modernizations.

Comments

This editorial illustrates yet another aspect of China's environmental program. The editorial reveals China's expanded recognition and its commitment to rectifying wrongs committed during the early years of the People's Republic and the Cultural Revolution, when many forms of wildlife were victimized by practices of exploitation, extermination, and destruction of habitat. For detailed coverage of wildlife protection in China, *see* Catherine E. Enderton, "Nature Preserves and Protected Wildlife in the People's Republic of China," in Clifton W. Pannell and Christopher R. Salter, eds., *China Geographer*, no. 12 (Environment), Boulder, Colo.: Westview Press, 1985, pp. 117–40.

Notes to Part Three

1. The text is in *FLHB*, vol. 4 (1955), pp. 86–90 [eds.].
2. The text is in *FGHB*, vol. 7 (1958), pp. 183–93 [eds.].
3. The text is in *BFWH*, pp. 89–100 [eds.].
4. The text is in *GGB*, no. 2 (1983), p. 61 [eds.].
5. The English text is in Owen D. Nee, Jr., *Commercial, Business and Trade Laws of the People's Republic of China*, New York: Oceana Publications, 1985 [eds.].
6. Karl Marx, "The Theory of Surplus Value," *Complete Works of Karl Marx and Friedrich Engels*, vol. 26, sec. 2, p. 158 [Chinese edition].
7. Karl Marx, *Capital*, vol. 3, People's Press, 1975, p. 853 [Chinese edition].
8. *Id.*, pp. 702–3.
9. *Id.*, p. 875.
10. Whether it is appropriate to use the term "rent" in a socialist economy is debatable. We might borrow this term for the time being. Our main purpose here is to discuss the economic relationship.
11. The text is in *BFWH*, pp. 89–100 [eds.].
12. *Id.* [eds.].

Part Four
Enforcement Means and Mechanisms

Means of enforcement or implementation can be divided into several categories: exhortational campaigns, administrative regulations and controls, economic incentives, and legal sanctions. The People's Republic of China historically has favored campaigns and administrative measures. Campaigns are mobilizational instruments organized by the Communist party itself, are relatively low-cost in terms of financing but require participation by large numbers of people, and echo China's traditional pattern of governance in which officials rule by setting models to be emulated by the populace. Examples include anticorruption, antirightist, anticrime, and public health and sanitation campaigns. However, campaigns have proven to be too simplistic and politically colored for most environmental policies. For example, planting trees without regard for cultivation resulted in poor survival rates, and emphasizing waste recovery as the solution to pollution problems slighted the potential for adjusting production processes and inputs to reduce the volume of waste products generated. Therefore, the post-Mao era has witnessed proportionally fewer, more tightly controlled campaigns than in past years. Campaigns remain prominent where large numbers of individuals are the direct source of a problem—birth control campaigns and litter cleanups can be viewed as responses to problems of this nature—or where more demanding approaches have yet to be approved. One result has been a reduction in the direct policy involvement of the Communist party, because its mobilizational talents are often considered counterproductive.

There have also been major changes in the use of administrative regulations and controls. Under central planning controls were rigidly imposed but primarily with regard to financial instruments and production planning. This pattern had to be adjusted in the more complex and decentralized post-Mao political economy in which enterprises were accorded greater autonomy in the interest of spurring modernization. This was particularly true for new regulatory concerns like environmental protection where the State Planning and old State Capital Construction Commissions were no longer capable of performing control functions satisfactorily. The new State Bureau of Environmental Protection moved to introduce new regulatory tools, such as environmental impact statements and discharge permits, to ensure that environmental factors were incorporated in the planning and production processes. Although these instruments have provided regulators with additional powers, regulators have been inclined to exercise them cautiously and to avoid overt conflicts with regulatees whose political influence exceeds their own. Environmental protection officials are handicapped by the frequent inability of regulated enterprises to comply with regulatory orders unless approval is first obtained from their parent agencies. Moreover, many regulatory actions cannot be taken unless local political leaders agree on them. A further problem is the limited opportunity for environmentalists and others affected by environmental issues to express their views politically; this deprives the environmental protection bureau of an important constituency. Regulators are thus forced to appeal to their superiors and local officials for support. This arrangement has not worked out as poorly as one might expect, however, because in recent years governors and mayors as well as central officials increasingly have embraced environmental protection as a priority, in accordance with party policy.

In order to give polluters more direct and effective incentives in the relatively relaxed post-Mao climate, economic or market-oriented pollution control instruments also have been introduced in the form of effluent fees. "The polluter must control his own pollution" (*shei wurang shei kongzhi*) is the principle invoked, thereby relating modern environmental economic theory with Chinese reforms which link rewards and responsibilities. Because the fees are generally set well below the marginal costs of pollution control, they cannot serve as an exclusive means of pollution control. However, they do provide an added incentive, which can be toughened by multiplying the fee level for pollution when recalcitrants are encountered. Moreover, most fee receipts are rebated to polluters who are cooperative; this encourages the formation of tacit coalitions between regulators and enterprises to influence parent agencies of the latter to provide additional funds for pollution control. Fees also provide regulators with some discretionary funds and can in principle be imposed without the need for approval by local government. Thus fees are more attractive to the environmental protection bureaucracy than fines, which more closely resemble administrative penalties.

Although there has been a noticeable shift toward the use of economic incentives and other regulatory instruments appropriate to a decentralized, quasi-market-oriented economy, the role of the public security organs and courts as enforcement agents has also been strengthened for several reasons. Criminal law specialists and others alarmed at the extent of negligent behavior of enterprises proposed clearer and more stringent sanctions against pollutors. From their perspective, the frequently invoked concept of crime by analogy is, in principle, inimical to the practice of law and, in reality, is rarely invoked for pollution-related offenses. It is, however, by no means clear that criminal prosecution can exert a major role in deterring unwanted behavior that arises in the course of legitimate behavior like factory production. Modification of the basic contours of administrative behavior and the political economy would appear to be a far more potent approach.

A second motive for strengthening the public security and related organs was to protect property during the difficult transition from tight state control to a looser structure involving less centralization. The forestry reforms in particular were gravely threatened by widespread deforestation originating from yet another change in ownership, which inevitably aggravated producer uncertainty. In these circumstances the regime was forced to increase sharply the presence of public security forces in forest districts. Had overlogging and violations of newly awarded property rights been allowed to continue unchecked, the resource base and investor incentives would have been seriously impaired, and political support imperiled. Similar problems arose with regard to fisheries, land management, and other policies.

Other legal specialists stressed the judiciary's role as an organ for resolving disputes that arose between the environmental protection agency and regulatees, and also among enterprises and individuals whose relationships increasingly were defined by contracts and informal arrangements rather than plans and commands. Although statistics on this subject are closely guarded, it is known that hundreds of environmental disputes occurred annually in the early 1980s in Shanghai alone. Often, such conflicts would result in work stoppages, sabotage of machinery, and other incidents carried out by aggrieved victims. Rather than simply suppress such mass protests, the regime accepted the legitimacy of many grievances and moved to conciliate the protestors by engineering solutions that were acceptable to both the victims and polluters and that avoided overly punitive judgments against most polluters.

Without a specialized organ devoted to conflict resolution, it would be much more difficult to reach mutually satisfactory solutions. Of course, the courts are far from truly independent or impartial; rather, they become colored by the prevailing political trend and tend to heed the preferences of local officials. In recent years, however, this has resulted in a greater willingness to accept environmental cases for trial and, often, a tendency to favor environmental quality over other interests on both policy and statutory grounds.

Part Four treats China's panoply of enforcement means and mechanisms. Two of China's leading environmental law scholars, Luo Dianrong and Deng Jianxu, discuss China's effluent fee system in Chapter 15. The entry in Chapter 16 calls for the implementation of a pollution permits system and outlines a model of such a system. The principles behind the determination and imposition of legal liability (civil, criminal, and administrative) on those who pollute or act in contravention of environmental laws or regulations are outlined in two articles in Chapter 17. The selections in Chapter 18 present arguments in favor of establishing specialized dispute resolution organs—both formal and informal—for settling environmental conflicts.

15

Economic Incentives for Environmental Protection

Luo Dianrong and Deng Jianxu (1980) "Industrial Effluent Fees and Preventing the Industrial 'Three Wastes'"

Renmin Ribao (September 16), p. 5. Translation, with permission, from *Chinese Law and Government*, vol. 19, no. 1 (1986), pp. 108–10.

The pollution created by the industrial "three wastes" is serious in China and the resulting harm is shocking. However, people often show a lack of understanding and fail to give it due attention. They can see at a glance that committing arson that destroys natural resources and putting poison in something that endangers people's lives are illegal criminal actions, and those responsible must be punished by law. But they do not necessarily see the discharge of pollutants and poison that similarly endanger people's lives and destroy natural resources as law violations. Thus it appears all the more important to enhance publicity for the "Law of Environmental Protection of the People's Republic of China" (for trial implementation); carry out the provisions of Article 16 of the law on controlling and preventing "pollution and damage to the environment caused by waste gas, wastewater, slag, dust, sewage, radioactive material, and other harmful matter, as well as pollution from noise, vibration, and toxic odors emitted from mining and industrial enterprises and found in urban life"; and make use of legal means to protect the environment.

The Law of Environmental Protection was enacted on the basis of the reality that China's environment is suffering from pollution and disruption and in light of the natural ecological law and the law of economic development. It clearly provides that it is the duty of the organizers and participants of production to protect the environment as well as the rights and obligations of all citizens in this respect. The tentative measures to collect industrial effluent fees and impose fines carried out in many places, and large, medium-sized, and small cities in China are designed to make the responsible units assume economic responsibility for polluting the environment, disrupting the ecology, and damaging natural resources and people's health. Industrially developed capitalist countries have generally set up rigorous ambient and emissions standards. They levy heavy taxes against factories that create serious pollution and even order such factories to shut down. As for factories that have solved the pollution problem satisfactorily, they may reduce their taxes, exempt them from taxation, and even subsidize them. The purpose is to force them, through economic means, to adopt effective measures for the alleviation and elimination of pollution. The responsibility of eliminating the consequences of pollution, such as the expenses for eliminating pollution and compensation for the losses of the victim, is invariably assumed by the party discharging the pollutants. In addition, for major pollution incidents, the party that discharges pollutants has to assume criminal responsibility. A case in point was the sentence of two years' imprisonment in Japan passed on the former manager of a nitrogen gas company and a related factory director for causing a pollution-originated disease. These measures have been instrumental in reducing industrial pollution in these countries.

In China the reform of the economic management system has yet to be carried out in some state-owned enterprises. The state still exercises control of their monetary matters, and all the profits they make have to be turned over to the government. Consequently, these enterprises do not have independent operations, and either to collect effluent fees from them or to impose fines on them would be of no avail, as the fees and fines they pay do not affect their material interests or the welfare of their workers and staff. With the reform of the economic management system under way, things have changed greatly. The enterprises have extended their decision-making power and have their own interests, rights, and duties. The payment of effluent fees and fines will inevitably lead to rising production costs and lower profits, thus affecting the interests of the enterprises themselves. The more serious the pollution, the greater the responsibility and the greater the expenses for the compensation of the pollution. This will directly affect the enterprise and the economic interests of its workers and staff and will compel the workers to concern themselves with the control of the "three wastes" for their own vital interests. For example, the chimneys of the locomotive section of the Bengpu railway subbureau in the center of Bengpu city had for a long time emitted black smoke, polluting the air in the area. Criticism from the masses and instructions from the municipal environmental protection office calling on the locomotive section to improve the situation fell on deaf ears. It was not until an effluent fee of 450 yuan was collected that the leadership of the locomotive section sent people to other places to buy dust removers and had them installed in mid-March this year. Since then the chimneys have ceased to emit black smoke. The introduction of effluent fees and fines in Suzhou, Jiangsu Province, and other places has yielded similar results.

Now it seems highly necessary to sum up the experiences in the collection of effluent fees and fines in various places and various big and medium-sized cities and, through certain legislative procedures, make the measures perfect and more authoritative so that they can be carried out strictly on an even larger scale.

Comments

Luo Dianrong and Deng Jianxu explain China's scheme of using economic deterrents to reduce, or at least control, pollution. China has also adopted economic incentives to encourage polluters to take appropriate control measures. For example, the State Planning Commission, the Ministry of Finance, and the State Council Environmental Leading Group issued a circular related to recycling and controlling the industrial "three wastes." The circular grants tax benefits for the installation of industrial "three wastes" controls and recycling technology. Although the amount of benefit is discretionary, query, however, whether a qualifying enterprise which bears no tax liability in the year in question will be allowed a rebate. *See* the treatment under the U.S. Internal Revenue Code in, e.g., 26 U.S.C. § 46. The text of the circular is in *BFWH*, pp. 254–59, and translated here. Furthermore, the Ministry of Finance and the State Council Environmental Protection Leading Group issued a joint circular which allows three- to five-year tax holidays and profit retention for revenues stemming from recycling. The text is in *BFWH*, pp. 274–77, and translated here. Will such subsidies have a noticeable effect on the environment, or is it likely that the economic benefit will be funneled into areas other than pollution control, given production demands? This is a major enforcement issue.

16

Registration Procedures

Shen Xin (1984) "On Implementing a [Pollution] Permit Process"

ZHK, no. 2, pp. 29–32.

Ever since the Environmental Protection Law was promulgated in 1979, China's environmental management has had a law to abide by. A management structure has been gradually put into place and perfected, creating an improved situation. However, one general problem remains outstanding—the Environmental Protection Law's legal effectiveness falls far short of other laws with regard to implementation.

Environmental protection organs charged with "implement[ing] the principles, policies, laws, and decrees of the state governing environmental protection and supervis[ing] their enforcement" are powerless. Most consult with the relevant department on responses only when major pollution incidents occur and mass indignation boils over. Although there are clear regulations governing the investigation of polluting enterprises, operations, and units and the enforcement of the "three simultaneous points" [design, construction, start of operations], there are no legally defined procedures so it is hard to stringently enforce them. Therefore, existing pollution sources cannot be satisfactorily controlled while new sources continuously proliferate, and while the capacity to regulate actively polluting enterprises and operations is declining. To focus on this point, I investigated seven municipalities, counties, and townships in four provinces; consulted relevant materials on environmental management methods from Japan, the United States, England, and other countries; studied relevant laws, regulatory systems, and management structures governing Chinese industrial and commercial enterprise management, foodstuffs sanitary management, and transportation management; and combined China's national characteristics and present state of environmental management. On the basis of the Environmental Protection Law and other relevant laws, regulations, and systems, I propose the institution of a specialized permit management law with regard to enterprises, operations, and units that pollute the environment for management and production in selected industries, which I discuss below in a multifaceted fashion.

THE NECESSITY FOR INSTITUTING A SPECIAL PERMIT MANAGEMENT LAW IN CHINA

Production activity that pollutes the environment brings pollution and hazards to society and the environment at the same time that it produces goods essential for human existence and development. Economic activity under socialism is for the purpose of satisfying the people's ever-increasing material and cultural demands to the maximum extent, so any behavior that endangers the people's rights and interests and health cannot be tolerated. Therefore, [Article 6 of] the Environmental Protection Law clearly stipulates that "[i]n selecting construction sites, making designs, carrying out construction projects, and embarking on production, all enterprises and other undertakings shall pay adequate attention to preventing environmental pollution and damage." Therefore, production activities by enterprises and other undertakings is essential to society yet must not create environmental pollution and damage.

Moreover, there is a distinction between polluting and nonpolluting production activity. A special permit management law will distinguish between the two and only permit activity leading to pollution under special conditions, and organs exercising this authority will be established to manage the permits in a manner similar to traffic management which has traffic police and observation posts, food products sanitation management which has inspection stations and epidemic prevention stations, and industrial and commercial management which has industrial and commercial management stations. Thus a special permit management law is an environmental management law to prevent pollution as authorized by the Environmental Protection Law and is an essential tool to control pollution through the law.

In terms of system of ownership, China's economy currently has three forms: ownership by the whole people, collectives, and individuals. Polluting enterprises, operations, and units that are owned by the whole people may be regulated according to Article 6 of the Environmental Protection Law, but the economic structure at present contains two parts, central enterprises and local enterprises. In the case of a new construction project, the local enterprise's parent bureau usually bases its approval on the basis of economic criteria with the approval process seldom involving the environmental protection department so enterprises can put money in command. Meanwhile central enterprises do not require local approval so the parent bureau's approval is decisive, often without the environmental protection department taking part in the process of securing necessary approval. In recent years, with the exception of some keypoint projects which have been strictly regulated in accordance with the Environmental Protection Law, the Environmental Protection Law remains for most other projects a shell.

For example, one county near Hangzhou mounted nine projects in 1982–83 of which seven have already entered production. Four of the seven are heavy polluters, but none were inspected by the environmental protection department. Some enterprises near Chongqing, in Sichuan, began four projects between 1981 and 1983—all of them polluters—but not one went through the environmental protection department's approval procedures. Environmental management and the prevention of pollution are societal [needs], and the Environmental Protection Law's regulations are entirely correct. But, for a variety of reasons, they have not been implemented because the authoritative organs lack specific procedures and there is no specific process of implementation. A special permit management law provides organs and procedures for enforcement in order to ensure the implementation of the Environmental Protection Law.

Meanwhile collectively owned enterprises and individual jointly operated enterprises are self-financing and self-designed when they start production. Some have a supervisory bureau (e.g., the local second bureau of light industry), while others are operated by communes, brigades, or even several households working together. Some merely need a business license from the local branch of the State Administration of Industry and Commerce to satisfy legal requirements, while those that originated as agricultural sidelines [some agricultural sidelines are only now in the process of being redefined as industrial rather than agricultural forms of production] do not have to comply with any procedures whatsoever. Any such project getting under way heretofore did not require involvement by the environmental protection department. Such enterprises represent a large proportion of new sources of pollution whose numbers have been rising in recent years. Moreover, the strengthening of environmental management work in big cities that is now under way has led some enterprises to shift operations to medium and small-sized cities, or even the countryside, through joint management or outside subcontracting.

For example, the Hangzhou Electroplating Factory moved its buffing mill to some production teams located in the West Lake Scenic District, creating air and water pollution in the district. Similarly, some factories in Shanghai dispersed their pollution to Tonglu County, in Zhejiang, and elsewhere, while Beijing's sources of pollution have been migrating to Hebei. Once these polluting enterprises fall under production teams (60 to 70 percent) or communes, environmental pollution becomes serious because they basically have no need to comply with the "three simultaneous points" procedures. For example, several households jointly operated a paper mill in a production team in the mountains of Guizhou, where they illegally procured bamboo from all around [at the time, the state monopolized the procurement of bamboo], destroying the mountains and forests and carelessly discharging the mill's effluent into the river. As far as 42 kilometers away, in the Lijia Bay stretch of the river, the river surface was covered with scum, the water was blackened, and all aquatic animals had disappeared. Enterprises like this are dispersed throughout the entire country in large numbers, causing serious pollution while operating without being subject to any management. Instituting a special permit management law will distinguish polluting enterprises from ordinary enterprises operating under routine management law in this complex structure of polluting enterprises. Reinforcement by the provisions of the Environmental Protection Law will place polluting enterprises that endanger the people's rights and interests and health under stronger controls.

INSTITUTING A SPECIAL PERMIT MANAGEMENT LAW WILL OPEN UP A NEW AND COMPREHENSIVE STATE OF AFFAIRS IN ENVIRONMENTAL MANAGEMENT

Developments to date in environmental management techniques have advanced industrial pollution control from the control of individual sources to regional controls. China's environmental pollution work has set up a policy based on overall planning, rational distribution, multipurpose utilization, changing harmful things into beneficial ones, relying on the masses, and engaging everybody in protecting the environment and benefiting the people. This signifies an overall management policy. However, the current situation in which the number of polluting enterprises is on the rise is not a function of this policy, but a situation in which everyone is responsible for themselves. The environmental protection structure terminates at the "three simultaneous points" phase, which itself is often unguarded, while overall planning, rational arrangements, and comprehensive utilization are not easily practiced. Instituting a special permit management law can convert management from a passive state to an active state, assure that permits are issued under the guidance of overall planning and rational geographical distribution and even create the essential conditions for comprehensive utilization and changing harmful things into beneficial ones. For example, making acid through the comprehensive utilization of the metallurgical industry's waste gases [especially sulfuric acid] both controls the steel mill's air pollution and saves having to build a special acid works. We can control the establishment of new sources of pollution in big cities, densely populated areas, and scenic and historical sites through the authority to issue special permits and can ban existing sources of pollution. Instituting a special permit management law can resolve the following issues in environmental management and create a new situation in terms of overall environmental management.

1. In accordance with the Environmental Protection Law and other laws, regulations, and systems, and in order to achieve comprehensive control, rational geographical distribution, and comprehensive regional control, the environmental protection organs can issue special permits to control the blind and unplanned proliferation of polluting enterprises and operations, especially new, self-financed sources that operate outside the state plan.

2. With a special permit management law we can prevent pollution before it occurs. Because no enterprise, operation, or unit will be allowed to engage in production activity of a polluting nature without first securing a special permit, we may strike at the passive management style now current in which the symptoms are treated but not the sources of the problem, and we will extricate ourselves from the present passive state in which management is not grasped until after pollution occurs.

3. With a special permit management law we can separate scientific research from management in environmental protection organs, concentrating even more strength on scientific research into environmental protection, while turning environmental management into a specialized form of management. In this way scientific research and management with regard to environmental protection will both develop further, overcoming the present state of chaos in which some environmental protection organs are rent by infighting.

4. Through a special permit management law we can avoid the construction of unneeded duplicate and polluting enterprises, shrink the capital construction front, and raise the rate of production efficiency in enterprises already equipped with controls, thus saving the state money. We can also exercise a profit-balancing role between enterprises whose costs are increased by pollution control expenditures and enterprises that sacrifice the environment because they operate without controls.

5. With a special permit management law we can make environmental management work more knowledgeable and put it on a planning management track. By registering and issuing permits to polluting enterprises, we can grasp the overall picture in a comprehensive fashion to facilitate including environmental management work in the plan, to create a foundation for the comprehensive monitoring of pollution, and to provide a reliable analytical foundation for regional control.

6. A special permit management law will facilitate the enforcement of deadlines for controlling pollution from existing enterprises and the effluent fees system. This will change the current state of passivity, in which there is no power to take action when polluting enterprises refuse to pay or delay payment of effluent fees. Under a special permit management law, only temporary permits will be issued during the time frame in which controls are to be installed, during which time effluent fees will be collected. Those enterprises which fail to install controls in the specified time frame or which refuse to pay their effluent fees will have their permits revoked. This will make the enterprise's production unlawful, compelling it to cease production in order to expedite controls.

7. Environmental protection work is strongly social in nature. It is now characterized by a form of divide and rule in which resources are dispersed and management appears to be weak and easily shunted aside. The institution of a special permit management law will enable management organs to use unified authority in order to practice unified management, resulting in uniformity of law enforcement, the unification of standards, and the division of responsibility for management—providing implementation with a direction and facilitating coordination. With unified permit procedures we will overcome the irresponsible state of affairs in the issuance of approval, in which some enterprises are concerned only about the rights and interests of the small collective, while infringing on society's interests.

8. A special permit management law will facilitate the comprehensive utilization and rational distribution of water resources, effectively protecting water resources from pollution, and will facilitate the protection of historical, scenic,

and densely populated areas, preventing the rise of pollution sources in such areas.

9. A special permit management law can expedite the transformation of polluting enterprises into nonpolluting enterprises, promote research and development of nonpolluting technologies, and promote the comprehensive utilization of energy and materials.

10. A special permit management law can fully enhance and scientifically make use of the environment's self-assimilative capacity, thereby reducing costs for pollution control. For example, building large-scale livestock enterprises in mountainous areas, or building basic food-processing plants, allows for the direct conversion of solid and liquid wastes into fertilizer for new uses. By contrast, building similar enterprises in big cities can create major public hazards and waste a great deal of resources.

11. A special permit management law will facilitate participation by the whole people in environmental management, making the correct response and resolution of disputes concerning environmental pollution, satisfying the masses' rational demands regarding environmental protection, and banning inappropriate sources of pollution.

A SPECIAL PERMIT MANAGEMENT LAW'S ORGANIZATIONAL STRUCTURE

A special permit management law is an integral component of environmental management, and its tasks of "implement[ing] the principles, policies, laws, and decrees of the state governing environmental protection and supervis[ing] their enforcement" [Environmental Protection Law, Article 26, Section A] are assumed by specific organs for implementation. The administration and professional activity of these organs are under the leadership of the local environmental protection organ, but they also must come under ministerial leadership on issues like river basin planning that have national implications, or that concern the uniformity of national policies. Provincial and subprovincial administration comes under the leadership of the provincial environmental protection bureau, while counties will only set up special permit management offices or stations. With regard to specific terms concerning management and enforcement of the special permit management law, there will be provisions governing the issuance and revocation of permits; the issuance of temporary permits and the imposition of effluent fees with regard to existing enterprises; fines for enterprises and other undertakings that violate the law and rewards for advanced units; and the supervision, management, and assessment of management fees with regard to polluting units.

THE BASIC CONTENT OF A SPECIAL PERMIT MANAGEMENT LAW

1. In accordance with the Environmental Protection Law, an environmental impact statement to be entered on a standardized form as a requirement for all projects that cause pollution.

2. The organization and approval of "three simultaneous points" items.

3. The unified planning and rational geographical distribution of polluting enterprises, with the issuance of special permits to be based on the environment's assimilative capacity and the provisions of laws governing the conservation of nature (specific regulations on the issuance of permits will be made in accordance with the Environmental Protection Law and other relevant laws, regulations, and systems).

4. The revocation of existing permits and the permits of enterprises whose pollution continues to exceed the standards, and handling of enterprises, operations, and units that fail to comply with the Environmental Protection Law (e.g., fines, orders to suspend operations and reorganize production, deadlines for installing controls, and the assessment of effluent fees).

5. The issuance of temporary permits, the setting of deadlines for installation of controls, the simultaneous assessment of effluent fees, organized inspection and approval at the expiration of the time allotted for installation of controls, and the final disposition of cases involving existing enterprises in accordance with actual conditions and relevant regulations (e.g., issuance of an extension subject to increases in effluent fees, revocation, etc.).

6. The handling of units that engage in pollution-causing production activity without securing a permit (e.g., fines, orders to suspend production, the investigation of legal responsibility, and administrative penalties).

7. Statistical summaries of relevant materials with regard to local environmental protection, and analysis of local environmental quality, to provide primary materials for environmental planning and scientific research and to play a role in the making and implementing of environmental plans.

8. The organization of relevant units (monitoring stations, management bureaus, and the environmental protection bureau) to conduct periodic or irregular inspections of polluting enterprises, operations, and units.

9. The role to be played in the investigation and disposition of environmental pollution accidents and specific provisions regarding dispositions and their findings.

THE PROCEDURES FOR ISSUING SPECIAL PERMITS

Polluting enterprises, operations, and units applying for permits should submit their applications to the permit management office for approval and simultaneously provide the environmental protection bureau with a copy. The permit management office shall organize the relevant units within a specified time frame for review, with the environmental protection bureau responsible for technical appraisal and the technical review in terms of regional planning (the permit management office is responsible for organizing this process). The enterprise can conduct design work and construction on receipt of a statement certifying compliance with standards after compliance has been ascertained. Before the start up of production operations, the permit management office will organize relevant personnel to inspect and approve the "three simultaneous points" report filed by the enterprise. A permit will be issued to those enterprises that are in compliance with the standards, which will thus become legal production units.

Existing enterprises applying for temporary permits must submit a statement specifying their plans to control pollution within a certain time frame, as well as an environmental impact statement. A temporary permit will be issued on certification of compliance with the standards. If the enterprise fails to satisfy the standards, then its effluent fees will be increased, while the deadline for installation of controls is extended. If the enterprise still fails to satisfy the standards after three inspections, it will be ordered to suspend operations while it installs controls within a specified time frame.

SOME PROBLEMS THAT MUST BE RESOLVED IN CONNECTION WITH THE IMPLEMENTATION OF A SPECIAL PERMIT MANAGEMENT LAW

1. With regard to structural reform, when implementing a special permit management law, the environmental management organ must be detached from the existing environmental protection organ, to become an organ for implementing environmental management.

2. With regard to expenses, some can originate from the management fees paid by enterprises that are awarded permits. The remainder must be obtained from other sources.

3. Issues involving the overlap between permit management work and judicial and financial work must be resolved.

4. The implementation of a special permit management law requires the preparation of relevant documents (e.g., regulations governing enterprise permits and the permit management system, articles governing relevant rewards and penalties, etc.). These must be approved by the relevant departments and conferences.

5. Some new problems must be solved because the special permit management law shatters the existing leadership structure governing environmental protection work within an enterprise and creates shared leadership by the existing parent bureau and the permit management office in its place. Some problems also will have to be resolved when a leadership structure is established for collective enterprises and enterprises jointly operated by individuals, most of which seem not to have anyone managing environmental protection. The establishment of an organ exercising authority requires the full support of all departments in society. There also are special problems to be resolved when creating a new organ via the governmental structure.

Comments

In many respects Shen's proposal resembles the basic concept of pollution permits pioneered in the West and is a positive development. Although the law he describes has yet to be enacted, provisions governing permits were incorporated in the 1983 Marine

Environmental Protection Law and the 1984 Water Pollution Prevention and Control Law. However, there are several questions regarding his proposal. First, can the environmental protection bureaucracy secure compliance from other, more powerful ministries? Second, can environmental protection handle the vast increase in paperwork that a permitting system entails, when it is already seriously overburdened and suffering from administrative shortcomings? Third, permitting properly would incorporate small- as well as large-volume polluters. However, will tighter regulation of the former choke off the dynamic rural and private industry sectors, which are becoming increasingly important components of the Chinese economy, and might permitting therefore be manipulated as a political weapon by conservative officials partial to the state-owned sector of the economy?

17

Legal Responsibility

Jin Ruilin and Cheng Zhengkang (1983) "An Analysis of Crimes Relating to Environmental Damage"

ZHK, no. 4, pp. 71–76.

In the drafting of various environmental protection laws in recent years, the implementation of the provisions of Article 32, Section 2, of the Environmental Protection Law of the People's Republic of China (for trial implementation)—the question of how to determine the criminal responsibility of those who seriously pollute and damage the environment—has been subject to much debate by those of divergent opinions. Some comrades believe that, in view of the extreme seriousness of environmental pollution and damage in our country, if strict legal measures are not adopted, this pollution and damage will be difficult to control. For this reason, these cadres argue that we must add environmental crimes to our criminal laws, and until these laws are formally revised and the revised regulations are clearly defined, provisions for criminal punishment should be incorporated into existing, separate environmental protection regulations, so that these regulations may be strictly enforced in order to effectively crack down on criminal environmental activities. Other comrades believe that "in order to avoid confusion, special provisions for criminal punishment should not be established in separate regulations which lie outside of the Criminal Law." And these comrades contend that "in China's legislation, there is no precedent for establishing special provisions for criminal punishment in separate regulations." In these debates the latter opinion has usually prevailed. The various individual environmental regulations merely copy the wording used in the Environmental Protection Law, which reads: "[offenders'] criminal responsibility will be determined according to the law." This type of general statement is not conducive to enforcement of the Environmental Protection Law and separate regulations; does not facilitate crackdowns on criminals who seriously pollute and damage the environment, and thus cannot uphold the proper sanctity of the law; and undermines the prestige of the socialist legal system. Currently, individual environmental protection regulations are being drafted in our country, and preparations are being made to revise the Environmental Protection Law. And at the

Third National Criminal Trial Work Conference criminal law comrades proposed all sorts of excellent recommendations on how to improve and supplement China's criminal legislation. Thus we must provide clear, theoretical answers to the following questions: Should the environment be given legal protection? Is there a need to protect the environment through criminal sanctions? Does the crime of damaging the environment exist? What is the definition of such a crime? What constitutes such a crime? What is the appropriate punishment? Do provisions exist in our country's criminal laws that could be applied to environmental crimes? Is there a need to improve our criminal legislation system as it relates to environmental crimes? What system should be adopted? What questions should we pay attention to in establishing criminal legislation relating to environmental crimes? And the like. Resolution of these problems will contribute to the development of China's criminal law, making it more comprehensive and systematic, and to the development of our country's young environmental law, facilitating the establishment of strict and enforceable environmental protection regulations that meet objective realities so that our environmental protection work will enter a new stage in legal development. This article presents some viewpoints on these questions.

THE ENVIRONMENT HAS ALREADY BEEN ACCORDED PROTECTION BY THE LAWS OF OUR COUNTRY BUT REQUIRES PROTECTION THROUGH CRIMINAL LAW

People have long come to believe that the essential elements of the natural environment are inexhaustible and do not belong to anybody, and therefore that the principle of occupancy—the prepossession of things that belong to nobody, a concept which in civil law is applicable to (monetarily) valuable property—is also appropriate for such environmental elements. According to this reasoning, occupants can use environmental elements freely and without compensation (except when strictly in violation of civil regulations, in which case the occupant should be held liable). This concept and this principle have posed a great threat to the natural environment. During industrialization, the capitalist pursuit of excessive profits has caused especially severe pollution and damage to the environment. Such activity has brought mankind unlimited harm. The broad masses have carried out a mammoth struggle against this behavior, which passes pollution onto them. During this struggle new legal theories have been presented—those of "public property" and "public trust"—according to which, the essential elements of the natural environment, such as air, water, sunlight, and scenery, as well as the environmental elements created by man, such as roads, shipping channels, and residential areas—all of which are things man cannot live without—are not "unowned property" which individuals can occupy, but public property belonging to the entire citizenry. The state is entrusted by the entire people with the authority to manage the environment, a legal relationship like that between a trustee and a trustor. The trustee is obligated to preserve the property entrusted to him by the trustor, and damage to said property constitutes a violation of the right of the trustor. Without the agreement of the trustor (the people), the trustee (the state) cannot arbitrarily take action on said property (the environment). Otherwise, the trustor may take legal action against the trustee for abuse of the trustor's position and for failure to fulfill the obligations of the trustee. At the same time trespass on common property is an offense against all common proprietors, and any one of these proprietors may represent the entire proprietorship and file suit against the trespasser. From these concepts has evolved the theory of "environmental rights," which means that citizens are entitled to live in clean and suitable environments. The people of many countries have engaged in long struggles to gain these rights, which were formally recognized in the declaration passed by the Conference on the Human Environment in Stockholm in 1972. Since then many countries have also provided for environmental rights in their constitutions or amendments thereto, making such rights basic rights, like those to liberty, the pursuit of happiness, and property. In the world today the environment has won legal protection in every country. . . .

Because the environment has come under the protection of our country's laws, the state, which represents the entire people in managing and protecting the environment, has the authority to adopt the measures necessary, including legal (such as administrative law, civil law, and criminal law), to the performance of that function. Our country's experience has proved that reliance on persuasive education alone, without adoption of the necessary legal measures, including punishment, is insufficient to protect the environment and natural resources. The problems we encountered in implementing the Forestry Law and other regulations are proof of this. Among the various legal measures, we should, of course, adopt those of administrative law first because in order to protect the environment, we must first strengthen state control. The most vigorous and effective method is to establish administrative laws and regulations that conform to conditions in our country, differentiate responsibilities, establish appropriate procedures, and set strict and clear punishments and rewards. This will facilitate determination of the responsibilities of the state, units, and individuals in the protection of the environment and natural resources and the formation of an environmental control network that is coordinated vertically and horizontally and that places environmental protection work under the overall control of the state. Then, we can apply civil law to protect the environment. The civil law concept of the system of ownership, trusts, trespass, exacting compensation for damages, and the obligation to exercise due caution are effective weapons in environmental protection.

We should also note that although civil law includes a procedure by which one may seek removal of obstructions and which can be employed to prevent pollution, the great majority of civil remedies—such as restitution to the status quo and compensation for damages—can be effected only after harm has actually occurred. This is contradictory to the principle of "an ounce of prevention is worth a pound of cure" in environmental protection work. Moreover, some serious destruction of the environment constitutes criminal behavior and exceeds the remedies of administrative and civil law. Thus we must employ special preventive, educational, and disciplinary criminal laws to protect the environment. And the state should use criminal law as an essential measure in the management and protection of the environment. Under present conditions the use of criminal law to fight pollution of and damage to the environment and natural resources will enable our country's environmental protection work to make great advances and will put an end to the situation in which criminals who damage the environment escape their legal responsibilities and in which victims lack strong and effective protection. Only when those who have no regard for law and order or concern for people's lives and who wantonly pollute and damage the environment receive their just and necessary punishment can the spread of environmental crimes be stopped, criminal elements be reformed, and the citizenry educated.

The use of criminal law to protect the environment has become an important question attracting the attention of the international criminal law and environmental law professions. The United Nations looks on the poisoning of the environment as an international crime. At the twelfth meeting of the International Criminal Law Conference held in Hamburg in September 1979 a special discussion of this question was conducted. And most countries already employ criminal law to protect the environment.

THE OBJECTIVE EXISTENCE OF ENVIRONMENTAL CRIMES, THEIR DEFINITION, AND THE ESTABLISHMENT OF THEIR EXISTENCE

What is a crime? Article 11 of our country's Criminal Law provides a scientific and complete answer to this question. A crime has three characteristics: (1) It is harmful to society; (2) it constitutes an offense, either intentional or negligent; and (3) it violates the criminal law and is subject to criminal punishment.[1] Some comrades analyze these three major characteristics mechanically, believing that, since only acts violating criminal law constitute crimes, those acts for which no clear provision exists in the Criminal Law thus are not crimes. Moreover, such cadres believe that outside the code, other laws cannot incorporate special provisions for criminal punishment. There are two major errors here: (1) these cadres have equated "criminal law" with the Criminal Law, a separate compendium of laws and regulations. This equation is inaccurate, for "criminal law" refers to all criminal legislation. And (2) the viewpoint these cadres maintain, "if not clearly specified in the law, an act is not a crime and therefore not subject to punishment," is equivalent in principle to *nulla poena sine lege*, no crime without a preexisting prohibitory rule, a theory advanced by the capitalist class in its struggle against feudalism during the eighteenth century. This theory is contrary to Marxism and has even been discarded by the capitalist class.

We should understand the three major characteristics of crimes on a comprehensive, scientific, and dialectical basis. Here, the harm suffered by society is decisive and is the basic characteristic of crimes. Whether or not such harm exists and, if it does, the magnitude of that harm are the keys to the determination of whether or not an act constitutes a crime. In analyzing an act we should first determine whether or not it is harmful to society, whether or not that harmfulness is serious enough to constitute violation of criminal law and warrant criminal punishment, and whether the act was deliberate or accidental. This is the approach we should take, instead of placing priority on ascertaining whether or not the act is defined as unlawful in criminal law and then determining the harmfulness. Thus, in deciding environmental criminality, we should first determine whether or not specific acts of serious pollution of and damage to the environment and natural resources are harmful to society. Then we should analyze the subjective factors relating to the perpetrators of such acts and the degree such harmfulness must attain before the acts warrant criminal punishment.

Let us take the case of Suzhou People's Paper Mill as an example.[2] The person held responsible in the case caused 28 tons of sodium cyanide solution to be spilled into the river, polluting a large area, killing many fish and clams, and endangering the health of the people. Is this type of behavior harmful to society? In the case of the Xingcheng County Water Company, a chlorine gas leak damaged nearby trees and crops and caused more than 100 persons residing at the Forestry Sanatorium (a convalescent area) to suffer acute poisoning. Does this type of behavior constitute harm to society? And does the illegal felling of trees in scenic and watershed forests, the destruction of scenic spots and historical sites, the indiscriminate catching of endangered wild animals, discharging large quantities of oil into the sea, dumping large quantities of wastes into the sea, dumping large quantities of wastes into rivers and lakes, the abuse of toxic and radioactive substances, emitting unbearable noises (or noise exceeding tolerable limits) which are harmful to human health, and the like constitute harmfulness to society? I believe that no one would deny that such acts harm society, and that they are clearly unlawful when they seriously pollute and damage the environment, endanger citizens' health or even cause injury or death, or cause severe private and public property losses. Whether deliberate or accidental, such acts obviously constitute crimes, and the persons responsible therefore should receive criminal punishment. Thus the crime of damaging the environment exists objectively, and to deny that existence on the basis of the fact that the crime is not so defined in the Criminal Law is erroneous in theory and harmful in practice.

When speaking of environmental crimes we refer not only to those that damage environmental elements that are monetarily valuable, such as land, forests, and wild animals and plants—but also to crimes that damage elements that are not so valuable but are particularly important to the lives of the people—such as air, water, sunlight, and peace and quiet—and natural scenery, which can only be computed in terms of cultural and enjoyment values.

In defining environmental crimes most people tend to include only those crimes that damage environmental elements that are tangible and monetarily valuable—such as the illegal harvest of trees and fish, animal and bird poaching, and destruction of historical sites—and ignore the crimes that affect air, water, sunlight, and natural scenery. Yet these elements are indispensable and form the major targets of environmental protection. And although the Criminal Law does not yet accord these elements such status, this lacuna represents a shortcoming in the law, which must be corrected, and cannot be employed as a basis for arguing that damage to such elements does not constitute a crime.

Environmental crime may be defined as the pollution and destruction of the environment and natural resources, either intentionally or negligently, causing severe damage thereto, endangering people's physical and mental health, or causing much public and private property loss.

The major elements that constitute environmental crime are as follows:

1. *The object of the crime:* violation of citizens' personal rights, environmental rights, public or private ownership and usufruct rights, etc., as a result of damage caused to the environmental elements defined in the Environmental Protection Law.

2. *The objective requisites of the crime:* pollution and destruction of the environment and natural resources, which causes serious damage to environmental elements, endangers the physical and mental health of citizens, or causes serious threats or damage to much public and private property.

3. *The subject of the crime:* the natural person who committed the crime and who should bear criminal responsibility according to the law and sometimes may also be a legal person (including factories, enterprises, government agencies, etc.).

4. *The culprit must have subjectively*, which means either intentionally or negligently, *committed an offense*. There is no criminal responsibility if the damage suffered is a result of irresistible force or unforeseen events.

Treatment of legal persons as subjects of crimes contravenes the traditional criminal law theory that only natural persons can be held so responsible. This point precisely underlines the special nature of environmental crimes. Fallacious is the notion that, since criminal law ignores the responsibilities of legal persons, environmental and other (such as commercial) laws also cannot consider legal persons subjects of crimes. We intend to discuss this issue further in another article.

Another important feature of environmental crimes is that they may cause injury to several objects at the same time and in such cases are hard to classify. We therefore believe that the "crime of damaging the environment" should be established as a separate type of offense.

VIEWS ON THE PROVISIONS IN OUR COUNTRY'S CRIMINAL LAW THAT RELATE TO THE ENVIRONMENT—CONCRETE CHARGES FOR ENVIRONMENTAL CRIMES AND APPROPRIATE PUNISHMENT

Our Criminal Law already contains some provisions relating to the environment, which, however, are dispersed under several categories. Examples are Articles 105, 106, and 115 of Chapter 2 (crimes endangering public security); Articles 128, 129, and 130 of Chapter 3 (sabotage against the socialist economic order); Article 156 of Chapter 5 (trespass); Articles 174 and 178 of Chapter 6 (disturbance of the administrative order of society); and Article 187 of Chapter 8 (misconduct in office). All these provisions undoubtedly have had a positive effect on environmental protection. However, because environmental protection is a new field in our country, we lack both legislative and judicial experience in this field, and existing laws obviously require further study and improvement. [Specifically]: (1) Many lacunae exist, and many serious environmental crimes, such as serious pollution of the atmosphere and of water, emission of high-intensity and sustained noise and vibration, wanton disposal of wastes that damage the environment, and destruction of the environment in residential areas, have not been made targets of criminal sanction. Thus the Criminal Law has played only a minor role in environmental protection. (2) Environmental provisions are not treated systematically under their own heading in the [Criminal] Law, but are scattered through several chapters. (3) Criminal punishments have not been taken into appropriate account. Perusal of the [Criminal] Law reveals that existing laws provide for relatively light punishment for environmental crimes, and such punishment is not commensurate with the harm caused by these crimes to society. Even worse is the fact that these laws do not treat acts that potentially may harm the environment as criminal offenses deserving punishment. Yet this latter consideration is exactly the point that should be emphasized in environmental protection and is like the theft of railway ties. Even if a train has not actually overturned, the offense should be punished when the theft reaches the point at which they may be caused to overturn. And such punishment should not be the same as that meted out for ordinary crimes of theft, that is, measured by the value of the ties stolen. This "germ of a crime theory" should be employed in environmental protection, for all acts that could lead to large-scale, serious environmental pollution and damage, and punishment should be meted out, as in the case of railway tie theft, in accordance with that potential harm. Moreover, in cases in which environmental crimes have already been accomplished, the resulting social harm and losses should not be assessed solely in terms of monetary value. Cultural and aesthetic values should also be considered. For instance, if either the welcoming pine of Huang Shan or the yulan magnolia of Tanzhe Temple is cut down, such a crime should not be punished according to the value of the lumber obtained from either tree. Similarly, the poaching of pandas, swans, and golden monkeys cannot be punished according to the value of these creatures' meat or skins or of the live animals themselves. Of course, it is difficult to evaluate and employ cultural and aesthetic values as bases for meting out punishment. However, this problem should not be used as an excuse to ignore these values, but as a spur to further study. Also, in cases of water and air pollution, we cannot use the substances (such as the 28 tons of sodium cyanide solution and the tank of chlorine gas) spilled, discharged, or leaked as bases for determining punishment, but should focus instead on the harm or loss incurred. We believe that we should address the aforementioned defects in the Criminal Law, undertake necessary revisions of the code, or adopt other measures in order to improve our country's criminal legislation for the protection of the environment.

We believe that "crimes of damaging the environment" should at least include (a) air pollution, (b) water (including inland waters and oceans) pollution, (c) emission of noise and vibration, (d) emission of malodorous odors, (e) soil erosion, (f) indiscriminate catching, killing, or picking of wild animals and plants, (g) destruction of forests, (h) destruction of grasslands, (i) destruction of mineral resources, (j) destruction of scenic spots and historical sites, (k) destruction of natural preserves, (l) destruction of specially designated natural scenery, (m) destruction of aquatic resources, (n) unlawful use of radioactive and toxic substances, (o) contamination of food and beverages, and (p) use of facilities and equipment potentially harmful to the environment.

Appropriate criminal punishment may be decided on the basis of the magnitude of the damage suffered by society. We believe that all punishments specified in the Criminal Law are applicable.

IMPROVE CRIMINAL LEGISLATION RELATING TO ENVIRONMENTAL CRIMES

In order to strengthen our struggle against the crimes of serious pollution to and destruction of the environment and natural resources, we believe that we must immediately improve our country's criminal legislation concerning environmental protection.

Our country's Criminal Law is not a formal code. We have only that and some special criminal laws and regulations. This in itself illustrates that our criminal legislation is still in the developmental stage. Using this as a pretext, some comrades argue: "Except for the Criminal Law, other laws and regulations (including environmental protection laws and regulations) lack the authority to incorporate provisions for criminal punishment." This interpretation is groundless. Since the founding of the People's Republic, in order to punish certain specially defined crimes, our country has promulgated specialized criminal laws and regulations. Even after promulgating the Criminal Law, our country has issued a number of special criminal laws and regulations, and our constitution does not stipulate that such laws and regulations cannot incorporate special provisions for criminal punishment. The problem lies in the fact that the notion that separate laws and regulations cannot (or lack the authority to) incorporate such provisions is generally accepted and has even been put into practice, which point is evidenced by the fact that the provisions were excluded from the Forestry Law and the Environmental Protection Law, which instead employed "criminal responsibility is to be investigated and affixed according to law" and similar wording. This notion will impede improvement and systematization of our system of legislation, and thus allow acts causing serious social damage to escape the punishment they deserve. The notion has already rendered some laws and regulations toothless, damaged the prestige of the socialist legal system, and caused dissatisfaction among the masses. Is this fact we face not a painful one? In addition, it should be emphasized that, even though the Criminal Law includes the "crime of damaging the environment," the breadth of social relationships covered by the code precludes detailed provisions concerning any one object of a crime. Thus we must still formulate, with reference to the codes, special provisions for criminal punishment and incorporate these into separate criminal and other laws and regulations, which we can then use to supplement and improve the code. For instance, the recent decision to crack down on serious criminal activities in the economic area supplements and makes more concrete the code's provisions concerning economic crimes. We believe that such improvements are especially necessary in environmental protection. One task facing workers in environmental and criminal law is to strengthen study of criminal legislation dealing with environmental crimes and, by supplementing and revising the Criminal Law, to formulate special laws to punish such crimes and special provisions for criminal punishment that can be incorporated into separate environmental protection laws, so that our country's legislation on environmental crimes can be systematized and our environmental laws and regulations, strictly enforced.

CONCLUSIONS

We have emphasized the role of criminal law in environmental protection because that role has thus far not been effective. It should be pointed out, however, that criminal law is neither the only means of protecting the environment nor a panacea. Attention should be given to the following problems.

1. Environmental pollution in our country is becoming increasingly serious, basically because of poor management, backward economic technology, and ineffective propaganda education. After all, criminal law is limited in effect, cannot eliminate the basic causes of environmental offenses, and has only limited deterrent force (including sanctions and educational influence). Overemphasis on criminal law will cause us to forget that we should adopt more administrative legal measures and adversely affect our environmental protection work. Therefore, the urgent task facing China's environmental legislative work is to formulate administrative laws and regulations for environmental control that accord with our country's conditions.

2. We should employ more administrative and less criminal punishment. By strengthening sanctions against minor offenders we can generally prevent serious environmental pollution. Thus we must employ more administrative punishment in handling minor crimes. Criminal punishment should be used only against those offenders whose crimes are serious, when circumstances are odious, when great harm has been done, and especially against offenders who seek petty selfish gain without regard for the consequences, thereby causing serious pollution, destruction of the environment, and major damages.

3. We must strengthen study of civil remedies, especially those having preventive and remedial effects, so that the civil law can play its proper role in the fight against pollution and destruction of the environment.

4. Standards of administrative, civil, and criminal responsibility for environ-

mental pollution and destruction must be studied, so that crime and punishment will be commensurate with each other.

Comments

Jin Ruilin and Cheng Zhengkang make the argument for imputing criminal responsibility for environmental crimes. The argument certainly makes sense in the context of "severe" or "serious" pollution cases. Jin and Cheng fail, however, to address such fundamental problems as who will make the determination of what is "severe" or "serious" and what standard is to be applied. Determinations such as these are essential to the maintenance of ordered society. Without them the system, in meting out punishment without clearly defined norms, will be operating without predictability. In refuting the arguments of *nulla poena sine lege* (no crime without a preexisting prohibitory rule) and the basic notions of notice and due process, Jin and Cheng merely invoke the tenets of Marxism. Compare Jin and Cheng's stance with the arguments presented in Rollin M. Perkins and Ronald N. Boyce, *Criminal Law*, 3d ed., Mineola, N.Y.: The Foundation Press, 1982, p. 11; *United States v. Cadiff*, 344 U.S. 174 (1952); A. Amsterdam, "The Void-for-Vagueness Doctrine in the Supreme Court," *The University of Pennsylvania Law Review*, vol. 109, no. 1 (1960), pp. 67–116.

He Ge (1983) "Legal Responsibility Issues in the Marine Environmental Protection Law"

Zhongguo Fazhi Bao (March 18), p. 2. Translation, with permission, from *Chinese Law and Government*, vol. 19, no. 1 (1986), pp. 111–14.

The Marine Environmental Protection Law of the People's Republic of China is the first Chinese law to strengthen marine environmental control and protect the marine environment as well as an effective weapon to combat all kinds of criminal activities that pollute and harm the sea environment. The implementation of this law is of great significance in preventing pollution of the sea, preserving the marine ecological equilibrium, rationally exploiting and utilizing marine resources, and promoting the all-around development of marine undertakings.

The pollution and damage of the marine environment comes from many sources, mainly from energy, ships, oil exploration and exploitation. Proceeding from the realities of our country and implementing the principle of "stressing prevention," the Marine Environmental Protection Law has codified concrete measures for the prevention and control of marine pollution and damage with prohibitions and obligatory stipulations. To defend the solemnity of the law and ensure the observance and execution of these measures, the law, in the chapter on legal responsibility, has made provisions of principle on the legal consequences of the illegal activities and legal sanctions to be meted out. Because the conditions and nature of the law violations are different, the legal responsibilities to be assumed are different. To be specific, they are divided into civil liability, administrative responsibility, and criminal responsibility.

With regard to the civil liability proceeding from protecting the interest of the victim and consulting international practice, the Marine Environmental Protection Law adopts the principle of a strict liability system. According to this principle, all those who have polluted and damaged the marine environment in violation of the provisions of the Marine Environmental Protection Law, whether they have done it on purpose or not, shall be responsible for compensating for the economic losses suffered by the victimized unit or individual. Only when the person concerned can prove that the pollution and damage are caused by an act of war, an irresistible natural calamity, negligence, or other wrongful acts on the part of the departments responsible for the maintenance of beacons or other navigational aids in exercising their functions, and after reasonable measures have been adopted in good time but without success can he be exempted from assuming the responsibility of compensation. The sum of damage compensation should, in general, include three portions: (1) the actual losses sustained by the victim, (2) the expenses actually paid or to be paid by the victim for the elimination of the pollution, and (3) the normal income lost by the victim because of pollution and damage. However, if an international agreement concluded or acceded to by China contains provisions on the responsibility of compensation, the case should be dealt with in accordance with the stipulations of the international agreement.

With regard to administrative responsibility, the Marine Environmental Protection Law provides that for those who have violated the law and have created or may create pollution and damage to the marine environment, the administrative department in charge can instruct them to remedy the pollution within a certain time limit, pay an effluent fee, pay the expenses for eliminating the pollution, and compensate the state for its losses. It also can serve warnings or impose fines on them. Here the compensation for the losses suffered by the state is not carried out as a civil responsibility, but is determined by the administrative department in charge as an administrative responsibility. Moreover, the administrative department in charge can also mete out administrative punishment to those who break the law and who have already polluted and damaged the marine environment. This provision is aimed at giving special protection to the sea area under the jurisdiction of the state and to national natural resources.

With regard to criminal responsibility, the Marine Environmental Protection Law provides that for those who have violated the law, polluted and damaged the marine environment, and caused heavy losses to public and private property or injuries or death, the judicial organ can look into the criminal responsibility of those who are directly responsible for the incident according to legal provisions. It is thus clear that one of the important conditions constituting a criminal offense is that the pollution and damage of marine environment has caused heavy losses to public and private property or injury and death. This is also the main hallmark that distinguishes criminal offenses from general illegal activities. However, as the Marine Environmental Protection Law has no specific provisions on what punishments are to be meted out and the Criminal Law also has no provisions dealing with crimes of pollution and damage to the marine environment, the judicial organs can only base themselves on the provisions of Article 79 of the Criminal Law and consult similar provisions of the Specific Provisions of the Criminal Law to pass sentences, but these sentences have to be reported to the Supreme Court for approval. Looking into the criminal responsibility of the offender does not relieve him or exempt him from assuming his due administrative and civil liability.

In the chapter on legal responsibility the Marine Environmental Protection Law makes specific provisions on the relevant procedure in settling civil liability and meting out administrative punishment as well as the mutual relations between the administrative departments and the People's Court. With regard to civil compensation disputes, the victimized unit or individual can directly bring a suit before the People's Court and can also ask the administrative department in charge to handle the case. If the victim does not accept the handling by the department in charge, the case can be settled in accordance with the provisions of the Law of Civil Procedure. In this way the administrative department can bring into full play its frontline role, solve large numbers of civil disputes, and reduce the pressure on the People's Court. As regards administrative punishment, if the party concerned does not accept the administrative punishment meted out by the department in charge, he can bring a lawsuit before the People's Court within fifteen days after receiving the decision. If he does not bring a lawsuit within the time limit and refuses to carry out the decision, the department in charge can appeal to the People's Court to force him to carry out the decision. Accordingly, the People's Court has the dual duty of examining whether the administrative department has legally enforced the law and supporting its correct handling of the disputes. In short, the administrative department and the People's Court should each do its duty, closely coordinate with and respect each other, work in concert, and jointly assume the responsibility of combating the pollution and damage of the marine environment in violation of the Marine Environmental Protection Law and contribute to the efforts to achieve a marine environment of good quality.

18

Dispute Resolution Organs

Deng Jianxu (1983) "Some Questions on Establishing Conflict Arbitration Organizations for Environmental Protection"

HB, no. 4, pp. 11–12.

Note: Recently, this magazine has received a series of letters from readers asking questions about the establishment of an arbitration agency for environmental protection. We have summarized these letters into four general categories and have invited Comrade Deng Jianxu of the Faculty of Law of Suzhou University to respond.

WHY PROPOSE AN ARBITRATION AGENCY FOR ENVIRONMENTAL PROTECTION WITHIN THE MINISTRY OF URBAN AND RURAL CONSTRUCTION AND ENVIRONMENTAL PROTECTION?

This was mainly proposed in view of China's present circumstances and urgent need to establish a rather authoritative specialized agency to handle pollution disputes. Some comrades suggest that an arbitration agency for environmental protection be set up independently of the environmental protection departments, under the jurisdiction of the Central Committee and various levels of local people's government. Other comrades suggest that environmental departments lead the way and organize arbitration agencies for environmental protection in concert with relative departments in charge of production. Of course, this is an academic question which it would be well to discuss, but the urgent matter is to establish an arbitration agency for environmental protection as quickly as possible in order to enforce the law strictly and accept and hear pollution dispute cases according to arbitration procedures. In recent years the volume of pollution dispute cases has been great. According to statistics from Shanghai in 1979, there were 339 disputes between plants and the masses. Eighty-one of these were conflicts and forty-nine caused partial shutdowns of production, with production stoppages totalling 668 days resulting in a 30.1 million yuan loss in output value, and involving more than 4,000 persons. In 1980, 212 factories and shops were involved in conflicts, with a loss of 3.56 million yuan. In 1982 there were 52 conflicts, stopping production for 232 days at a loss of 12 million yuan in output value. Recent statistics from the Shanghai Environmental Protection Bureau revealed that in 1982 there were clashes between the masses and the factory at thirty-five facilities, stopping production for ninety-five days at a loss of 3.76 million yuan in output value. Currently, pollution dispute cases are mainly handled through administrative means. Because the legal procedures are not complete, it is easy for the facts to be unclear, responsibility to be unclear, evidence to be insufficient, the quality of the cases to be low, and for cases to be withdrawn with waste of time, manpower, and resources. There have even been serious problems of putting the cart before the horse and the punishment not fitting the crime. Thus objectivity demands that an arbitration agency for environmental protection be established as quickly as possible. If an agency is established independently of the environmental protection departments, it will not conform to the spirit of the current vigorous streamlining of state agencies, and even if it is created, there is no knowing how long it will take. If an arbitration agency for environmental protection is organized by environmental protection departments and the relevant departments in charge of production, whether the departments in charge of production are willing to take on the mission is also a problem. Some of the departments in charge of production have not accepted the mission of mediation in disputes over economic contracts, so why should they bother with environmental pollution disputes. Thus establishing an arbitration agency for environmental protection within environmental protection departments best suits the actual situation.

DO ENVIRONMENTAL PROTECTION DEPARTMENTS HAVE THE AUTHORITY TO ARBITRATE ENVIRONMENTAL DISPUTES?

The authority to arbitrate means the authority to mediate and adjudicate a dispute between two parties. Environmental protection departments are state administrative agencies and functional departments of environmental protection. Their scope of responsibility has determined that they have the authority not only to arbitrate pollution disputes, but also to carry out administrative laws and regulations and punish individuals and units which violate environmental protection laws and regulations. Take, for example, warnings and fines. In fact, in exercising this authority, environmental protection departments have mediated and adjudicated a great many pollution disputes and punished individuals and units that have violated the law. Thus environmental protection departments have arbitration authority for pollution disputes. Just as one function of industrial and commercial management departments is to manage economic contracts, with their scope of responsibility determining their authority to mediate and arbitrate economic contract disputes, no one has the right to censure them for exercising this right.

IS THERE A LEGAL BASIS FOR ESTABLISHING ARBITRATION AGENCIES FOR ENVIRONMENTAL PROTECTION WITHIN ENVIRONMENTAL PROTECTION DEPARTMENTS?

We considered establishing an arbitration agency for environmental protection within the environmental protection departments on the basis of experience in economic and civil trials, because of the scope of responsibility of environmental protection departments, in light of China's actual circumstances. Neither the Constitution nor the Environmental Protection Law in force contains this stipulation, but socialist law is the summation of practical experience and the belief of the knowledge of objective things in the law and is not formulated by some "great thinker" locked up in his room. Take the Environmental Protection Law, for example. It was formulated and promulgated through thirty years of practice since the founding of the People's Republic of China. It is impossible to imagine that right after liberation, people could have drafted this law without any knowledge of environmental protection whatsoever. The law is the principle by which the state uses its authority to guarantee that people comply and to stipulate what people can do and what they cannot do. But the law in force does not stipulate that arbitration agencies for environmental protection cannot be established within environmental protection departments. Therefore, establishing an arbitration agency for environmental protection within environmental protection departments is not impermissible.

On the contrary, some comrades now want to formulate articles for environmental protection arbitration through legislative procedures to give them legal validity. This thinking does not conform to actuality or to the laws of people's understanding of objective things. If these "Articles" can be formulated, can it become "water without a source or a tree without roots"? Obviously, this will not do. I propose that the Ministry of Urban and Rural Construction and Environmental Protection first set up pilot arbitration agencies for environmental protection in specific areas throughout the nation and, through practice, summarize experience and formulate articles for environmental protection arbitration and then, nationwide, establish arbitration agencies for environmental protection. State industrial and commercial general administrative bureaus are now drafting articles for the arbitration of economic contracts and have proceeded this way.

WITH AN ARBITRATION AGENCY FOR ENVIRONMENTAL PROTECTION WITHIN AN ENVIRONMENTAL PROTECTION DEPARTMENT, WON'T THE ENVIRONMENTAL PROTECTION DEPARTMENT BE PARTIAL TO THE AGGRIEVED PARTY?

Environmental protection departments are administrative agencies of the state, represent the state in handling pollution disputes on the basis of facts and in accordance with the law, and cannot be partial to either party. In dealing with pollution cases the Suzhou Environmental Protection Arbitration Agency also frequently encountered instances when the aggrieved party wanted to take advantage of the opportunity to seek excessive compensation. Such unreasonable demands cannot be satisfied. For example, in 1981 twelve agricultural brigades and five fishery brigades from the suburbs of Suzhou declared that because pollution of a river caused diminished food production and death of fish and shellfish, they demanded that the polluting unit compensate them 531,200 yuan for their loss. In line with arbitration procedures, the environmental protection arbitration agency studied the case in detail, gathered evidence, and finally awarded the brigades 116,900 yuan, less than one-quarter of the amount demanded. Not only did this resolve the contradiction between the plant and the communes so that the loss of the aggrieved party was compensated, but the state also avoided unnecessary loss and maintained the legal rights and interests of both parties. If the parties think that the environmental protection arbitration agency is partial in handling cases, they may take the matter to court and this will more effectively guarantee that the pollution dispute case will be handled fairly and prevent partiality.

Comments

See comments after the next selection.

Luo Dianrong and Deng Jianxu (1982) "The Necessity of Establishing a Trial Court System for Environmental Protection"

HB, no. 1, pp. 3–4. Translation, with permission, from *Chinese Law and Government*, vol. 19, no. 1 (1986), pp. 115–18.

Since the promulgation of the Environmental Protection Law (for trial implementation), the tempo of China's environmental legislation has quickened and many relevant important laws are being drawn up. Aside from the parts that are concerned with economic law, civil law, criminal law, labor law, and administrative law, most of the laws on environmental protection have an independent legal form and are sufficient to form an independent branch of law. To enforce the environmental protection laws more effectively, to bring into full play the role of legal methods in environmental protection, and to strengthen the building of environmental law enforcement organs, we are of the opinion that the establishment of a trial court system for environmental protection is already ripe for discussion. We base this conclusion on the following reasons.

1. To ensure the enforcement of the law, it is necessary, in general, to set up corresponding enforcement organs for independent law branches. Environmental protection has its specific domain and objects of protection. Furthermore, the environmental protection law has its specific object of adjustment and sphere of jurisdiction and forms a complete system itself. The Environmental Protection Law promulgated by our country is a basic law, or mother law, in the field of environmental protection. Many special laws are being enacted on the basis of this basic law, such as the Air Protection Law, the Law on Protection against

Radioactive Pollution, the Law on Protection against Pollution of Waters, as well as numerous regulations promulgated under these specific laws. But without the building of corresponding law enforcement organs, these laws, however perfect they may be, will be without effect. Therefore, legislative work must proceed in tandem with the simultaneous establishment of law enforcement organs. Criminal law and civil law are special branches of law and have long had their own independent trial organs. Whether economic law should also become an independent branch of law is still subject to much debate, but corresponding trial organs and economic trial courts have already been established. Thus it is necessary to set up trial courts for environmental protection under the Supreme People's Court as well as the higher, intermediate, and basic-level People's Courts in large, medium-sized, and small cities. According to Articles 24, 27, and 31 of the "Organic Law of the People's Courts,"[3] the Supreme People's Court and the higher and the intermediate People's Courts may set up other trial courts according to needs. It is thus clear that the establishment of a trial court for environmental protection has a legal basis.

2. The establishment of trial courts for environmental protection stems from the necessity of practical work. Since the founding of the People's Republic, owing to a lack of understanding, defects in the management system, and other reasons, industrial pollution and the destruction of natural resources in our country have become serious. In the meantime disputes arising from environmental pollution have been steadily increasing. According to statistics compiled in Shanghai, there were more than 300 cases of disputes between factories and residents arising from industrial pollution in 1979. According to data compiled from January 1 to December 15, 1980, there were 2,400 complaints from residents about pollution expressed either in letters or in visits to the local authorities (including 180 visits), 212 factories and workshops were involved in the pollution disputes, and 14 were involved in incidents leading to a limited suspension of operations. In the summer of 1980 the economic trial court of the Higher People's Court of Shanghai directly intervened and helped the environmental protection department settle fourteen pollution disputes. In fact, the economic trial courts in a number of areas have assigned some of their staff members to handle only pollution cases. The establishment of environmental trial courts has thus become a necessity of objective development.

3. The establishment of environmental trial courts is also determined by the special nature of environmental problems. This can be seen from the following aspects.

a) The subject of rights and obligations under the Environmental Protection Law includes both legal persons (social organizations, enterprises, or undertakings with the capacity of a legal person) and natural persons (citizens), while the subject of rights and obligations under the economic law is the legal person and under the civil law is the natural person.

b) The objects of protection under the Environmental Protection Law are numerous. The object of legal protection under the economic law is public property and under the civil law, private property, while the object of legal protection under the Environmental Protection Law consists of both public and private property. These subsume the material environment and natural resources on which man depends for his survival and development. If the environment is polluted and natural resources are destroyed, many of them are hardly retrievable and even impossible to retrieve. Many of the losses are incalculable, and their consequences are difficult to foresee at present.

c) The Environmental Protection Law has a wide scope of adjustment. The sphere of adjustment of the economic law is mainly confined to the economic relations among societal economic organizations and between the societal economic organizations and state organs. The scope of adjustment of the civil law is mainly confined to property relations and personal incorporeal relations among citizens. The Environmental Protection Law adjusts all kinds of social relations engendered from the pollution and disruption of the environment, involving social relations in the political, economic, cultural, military, and other fields.

d) The means of procuring evidence in environmental pollution cases is different from that of procuring evidence in criminal cases in general. Environmental pollution cases depend on environmental monitoring, technical determination, and laboratory analysis. Thus the means of procuring evidence mainly relies on state environmental monitoring organs and technical forces.

e) Handling environmental pollution cases is generally rather difficult and the responsibility of the person concerned is hard to determine. Certain chemical materials discarded as useless may produce chemical changes when they come into contact with newly discharged chemical materials and become toxic materials, causing harmful consequences. Because such occurrences may involve several parties, and because certain consequences of pollution and disruption and their latent harm are hard to determine, and because the present monitoring forces are insufficient and technological means are backward, it is often impossible to get reliable pollution data in time, making it difficult to determine the economic and legal responsibility of the persons concerned and greatly increasing the complexity of the case and difficulty in handling it.

In view of the situation mentioned earlier, we believe that the establishment of a special trial arrangement for environmental protection meets the need of objective developments and practical work and conforms to the characteristics of the environmental judicial work. The establishment of such courts will be in the interest of studying, summing up, and exchanging experiences in handling environmental pollution cases and of raising the professional level of the personnel assigned to handle such cases, thus greatly raising the quality of work in this field. In light of the fact that industry is relatively concentrated in cities, environmental trial courts should be set up under the Supreme People's Court and in the higher, intermediate, and basic-level People's Courts in big, medium-sized, and small cities. In the counties and districts where factories and mines are concentrated, such courts can be set up according to actual needs.

Comments

Luo and Deng present compelling arguments for the establishment of a specialized trial court to handle environmental cases. Given present institutional weaknesses that afflict the judicial system, special environmental sections may be more of an extravagance than a necessity. The key to the problem may be found in a more vigorous and autonomous role of the economic trial sections of courts at all levels, coupled with less formal mediation and arbitration structures like those Deng lobbies for in the preceding selection.

The United States has established tribunals to handle disputes arising in specialized areas of the law, such as the Tax Court, the Court of International Trade, and the Bankruptcy Court. A factor overlooked by Luo and Deng is that enforcement and compliance schemes in an area of the law is also a substantial factor to be taken into account when considering the establishment of a specialized tribunal. On this and other considerations, see the discussion by the U.S. Supreme Court in the relevant parts of *Flora v. United States*, 362 U.S. 145 (1960), *modifying on rehearing* 357 U.S. 63.

Notes to Part Four

1. The three requirements to determine criminality under Chinese law are discussed in the following sources: Cao Zidian, "Questions and Answers on China's Criminal Law," *Beijing Review*, vol. 23, no. 25 (June 9, 1980), pp. 19–20; Falü Wenti Bianxie Zu, *Xingshi Falu Wenda* (Questions and Answers on Criminal Law), Shanghai: Zhishi Chubanshe, 1983; Tao Zijin, "On Fundamental Problems of the Characterization of Crime," *Faxue Yanjiu*, no. 4 (1979), pp. 29–33; Feng Ertai et al., *Falu Dawen Sibai Ti* (Four Hundred Questions and Answers on the Law), Shanghai: Xuelin Chubanshe, pp. 54, 56–64; Shao-chuan Leng and Hungdah Chiu, *Criminal Justice in Post-Mao China*, Albany, N.Y.: State University of New York Press, 1985, p. 124; Zhang Shangzhuo, *Zhonghua Renmin Gongheguo Xingfa Gailun* (The Essentials of the Criminal Law of the People's Republic of China), Beijing: Falü Chubanshe, 1981, pp. 67–132; Zhang Youyu and Wang Shuwen, *Faxue Jiben Zhishi Jianghua* (Lectures of Basic Knowledge in Law), Beijing: Zhongguo Qingnian Chubanshe, 1979, pp. 94–101 [eds.].

2. Suzhou Municipal Intermediate People's Court Opinion (79) Xingzi No. 26, translated here [eds.].

3. The text is in *Renmin Shouce, 1979* (People's Handbook, 1979), Beijing: Renmin Ribao Chubanshe, 1980, pp. 403–6. The English text is in FBIS, *Daily Report: China*, July 27, 1979—Supplement, pp. 20–27 [eds.].

Part Five
Cases

In keeping with both traditional and communist Chinese culture, violations of law and civil disputes are usually handled outside of court. Environmental protection officials claim that over 90 percent of their actions are accepted by the parties concerned, although they concede that their decisions take account of factors like the ability to pay fines or make restitution and also that political realities temper their independence. Of the remainder, the overwhelming majority are resolved through semiformal mediation involving the regulator, the polluter(s), and the victim(s).

In Chapter 19 Wang Yinghuai, a judge sitting on the Chongqing Intermediate People's Court, reveals the general principles applied by the courts when resolving environmental disputes. Yet formal court proceedings are infrequent and generally serve to uphold the judgments reached earlier by senior officials or regulatory agencies. Defendants are expected to prove their own innocence to an even greater extent than in other areas of the law because of the complexity and time lags involved in environmental cases. Although mitigating evidence may be provided, the revelation of technical and procedural deficiencies in the government's case appears to be an insufficient defense.

However, Chapter 20 includes cases which show how the political authorities have carved out a small basis for claims of self-defense by victims of pollution who resort to extralegal means in response to threats of pollution when the government fails to fulfill its proper regulatory functions. Saboteurs of coal handling equipment at Wuhan's Pier 41, a phosphate fertilizer plant and a cement plant in Henan, a Zhejiang lime kiln, a Beijing factory, and other polluters, have been cleared of all criminal liability in such circumstances, although it is unclear how wide the area of exception is, or when it can be invoked. It is nevertheless a novel application of the law, particularly in an authoritarian regime.

Chapter 20 reports on two landmark decisions related to environmental infractions. The first is the Suzhou pollution case, which was China's first major environmental prosecution after the promulgation of the 1979 Environmental Protection Law (for trial implementation). The second case, the Kaida case, marks the first time an environmental dispute involving a wholly owned foreign venture was adjudicated before China's courts.

19

General Discussion

Wang Yinghuai (1985) "[We Must] Actively Employ Legal Means in Handling Environmental Pollution Cases"

Chongqing Huanjing Baohu, no. 1, pp. 51–53.

Positive effects will be seen in such areas as enhancing the control of environmental pollution, rationally utilizing natural resources, maintaining the ecological balance, creating a cleaner and healthier living and working environment for the people, and promoting agricultural and industrial development as well as the socialist modernization program if the people's courts should expand their functions in economic litigation, publicly try environmental pollution disputes, and expand propaganda and education on environmental law.

Environmental pollution cases involve both criminal and civil tort liability litigation. They are relatively deeply involved in matters of policy and technology and are broader in scope and revolve around more complicated fact patterns [than regular litigation], and thus are more difficult [to handle]. Based on some of the environmental pollution cases we have handled, these cases mainly include the following aspects.

1. Certain enterprises or other undertakings excessively discharge wastewater (such as water containing metals, toxic wastes, hospital wastes, solid wastes, refuse, dust, etc.) which seriously pollutes the water, and thereby severely threatens drinking water quality or even, in some circumstances, kills massive numbers of fish. [For example, in one particular case] a paper manufacturing factory in Baxian, Sichuan Province, discharged effluent from its paper manufacturing process and created severe pollution in the local reservoir and massive fish and shrimp kills. The reservoir and nearby collectives brought an action against the factory for damages in the amount of 120,000 yuan in the Baxian People's Court. After investigation it was found that the defendant factory had not undertaken adequate management or protective measures and, as a result, should be held responsible for the damages. On the other hand, however, considering the difficulties and economic losses that might have followed if the factory were to have been shut down, the factory, after mediation at the People's Court, agreed to pay 20,000 yuan. The factory has also changed its product line after the

People's Government of Baxian County decided to settle this matter once and for all.

2. Certain enterprises or industrial units failed to take proper measure [to control] their toxic discharges, which resulted in severe losses of agricultural and forestry products owing to chemical pollution. For example, in the past the Chongqing Dongfeng Chemical Plant discharged sulfides, anhydrous hydrofluride (production of both of these has since been halted), and silicomagnesiofluorite (containing fluorine gas), and this seriously damaged agricultural and forestry production. Since 1975, in nearby Shapianba District, the Jinkou Commune has suffered continued losses in its farming and forestry crops because of the pollution. In 1980 the commune finally requested 44,537 yuan in damages. The factory would agree to only 15,000 yuan because it claimed that necessary [pollution control] measures had been applied since 1979 so as to mitigate the impact and that the production of sulfides and anhydrous hydrofluride had been halted. Although related government agencies had gone to great efforts to reach a compromise between the two, the case was still pending and had yet to be resolved. This court, after its investigation on the basis of the facts, concluded that according to Article 32 of the Environmental Protection Law (for trial implementation), the factory had caused large-scale damages and should, therefore, be liable for it. After further negotiations both sides finally agreed to the amount of 18,414 yuan in damages. No similar incidents have arisen since.

3. In order to preserve scenic resort areas, to assure a comfortable living environment and tourist sites, and [in furtherance of the goal of] strictly prohibiting pollution in such areas, we handled a park pollution case. The Chongqing Electric Meter Factory moved its facilities into the Nanshan Park Preserve in 1968. In the then politically anarchic tempest the reckless chopping and felling of trees and plants by the staff was quite serious and hydrochloric acid was carelessly handled. Other illegal incidents, such as building a kitchen and destructing a protective wall [in the park], further ruined the flowers and trees. The park brought an action against the electric meter factory. This court ruled that the factory and its employees should be liable for all the damages to the trees and flowers, according to the Forestry Law and the Environmental Protection Law, and that the illegally built kitchen should be dismantled and removed within the designated period of time. Later the [entire] factory was relocated so that further environmental pollution [in the area] was prevented and the entire park was preserved.

Just like handling other economic disputes, we insist that the principles applied to environmental pollution cases must be based on the facts and in accordance with the law. The substantive measures for achieving these ends are as follows.

1. Strictly enforce the law. In handling environmental pollution cases, regardless of the size of the units, their ownership (state or collective), rural or urban location, or central or local government administration, all are equal under the law, and [we must] strictly adhere to the Environmental Protection Law (for trial implementation) and related laws. Through handling environmental pollution

cases, [we may] publicize [the need for] "rule by law" so that each person solemnly adheres to the law, and the law is strictly followed in handling affairs.

2. Thoroughly realize the policy of stressing settlement on the basis of clarifying the facts and responsibilities. According to the related provisions of the Law on Civil Procedure (for trial implementation), after the court clerk receives the complaint and a duplicate, he or she should immediately notify the defendant to respond and have both parties present evidence. Meanwhile the investigatory personnel should carefully review all the litigation materials, conduct a thorough investigation, examine the actual site, conduct technical assessment and monitoring, collect evidence, analyze and research the case, distinguish between right and wrong, and, on the basis of clear liability, earnestly uphold and further [legal] principles, while entering into reasonable settlement negotiations. As a consequence, first, this would benefit both parties by teaching them a lesson, strengthen the need for timely control of the environmental pollution problem, act in furtherance of the development of production, and enhance the physical health of the people. Second, because, in most cases, both parties reside near each other and have frequent contact, such measures are beneficial in fostering unity and future interactions. Third, it would also be of great help for the enforcement of the settlement agreement. But in the rare situation where certain cases are not settled after numerous unsuccessful negotiations, a judgment [by the court] should be rendered as soon as possible so that the case may not remain unresolved for an extended period.

3. Liaison with the environmental protection department and concerned supervisory departments should be enhanced. Environmental pollution cases [normally] involve a wide variety of technical areas. Some require on-site inspections, others call for special monitoring assessment for scientific proof, and yet others require supplemental information from other governmental agencies so that the entire investigation process can be completed, the facts can be clarified, and a proper judgment can be rendered. Therefore, the enhancement of such links between the various agencies plays an important role in environmental protection.

Certain points need to be met in order to seriously and strictly enforce the environmental protection laws and reduce or prevent the occurrence of environmental pollution cases.

1. [We must] publicize such laws and regulations as the Environmental Protection Law (for trial implementation), the Water Pollution Prevention and Control Law, and the Regulations on the Protection of Aquatic Resources. Every business and other undertaking as well as the broad masses must clearly understand the great significance of environmental protection, and that it is one of our basic national policies in the building of socialist modernization. For every newly built, renovated, modified, or expanded construction project, before the project commences, the business or enterprise unit which proposes such construction must comply with [Article 6] of the Environmental Protection Law (for trial implementation):

While carrying out new construction or renovation projects, an environmental impact report shall be submitted first, and design work can be started only after such a report has been reviewed and approved by the department concerned. Facilities for preventing pollution and other hazards to the public must be designed, built, and put into operation simultaneously with the principal project. The discharge of all harmful materials shall be carried out in accordance with the standards prescribed by the state.

Those units that have already caused environmental pollution or other hazards to the public shall work out plans and bring them under effective control in accordance with the principle that whoever has caused the pollution must bring it under control, or they shall obtain necessary approval from the competent authorities for a change in the type of operation or seek relocation.

2. [We must] establish arbitration organizations within environmental protection agencies at all levels. In the past only administrative means were used to handle a large number of environmental pollution cases, and yet problems like the failure to follow legal procedures, misstating of the facts, malapportioning liabilities, and imposing improper penalties have emerged from time to time. Without binding statutory authority on the type of procedure to be followed and the scope within which it can be operated, it is relatively difficult to enforce the law. In particular, because the policy of ''reviving the domestic economy and opening up to the outside world'' has been carried out, industrial and agricultural production has constantly progressed, the legal system has developed satisfactorily, there has been a positive response to the public demand for a better [living] environment, and there has been a rise in the number of environmental pollution cases. Therefore, it is necessary to establish arbitral bodies to follow legal procedures strictly, fine those who deserve to be fined, compensate those who deserve to be compensated, and shut down those factories which deserve to be shut down. A codified law is also necessary in this regard. For any party who wishes to appeal a decision, he may bring suit in the People's Court within fifteen days from the date he receives the notice [from the arbitral organ] in order to protect his interests. A specific performance decree shall be issued by the court on application from the relevant environmental protection unit if the losing party does not appeal within the statutory limitations or does not comply with the [arbitration] decision.

3. For those who violate the related provisions of the Environmental Protection Law, the Water Pollution Prevention and Control Law, etc., and thereby cause a major environmental pollution incident from which major property loss or personal injuries result, the prosecuting authority should bring a public action in the People's Court and charge every possible criminal infraction under the related provisions of the Criminal Law or the Criminal Procedure Law.

4. In order to fully expand the positive function of the socialist legal system of environmental protection, the Economic Trial Court (of the People's Courts) should try environmental cases in accordance with the Law on Civil Procedure (for trial implementation) and related legal provisions once they are brought to the court.

In sum it is an important mission for the People's Court to actively use legal means in handling environmental pollution cases. All the matters must be handled strictly in accordance with the law in [all] environmental pollution cases in furtherance of the principles of following the applicable law, strict enforcement, and investigating all violations. This will ensure smooth development in the area of environmental protection.

Comments

Wang Yinghuai, a judge on the Economic Trial Court of the Chongqing Intermediate People's Court, presents an extremely useful general overview of the disposition and means of handling environmental pollution cases. The specific cases referred to offer a sampling of the actual condition and disposition of environmental pollution cases in the city of Chongqing, a polluted city indeed. Beyond that, and by far more important, Wang reveals some of the principles guiding judicial units in resolving environmental disputes. Wang also makes the argument for the establishment of a specialized arbitral organ along the lines proposed by Deng Jianxu in Part Four, on Enforcement Means and Mechanisms.

20

Specific Cases

Suzhou Trial of a Case Involving Heavy Responsibility for Serious Pollution of the Environment

Jiangsu Province, Suzhou Municipal Intermediate People's Court Opinion (79) Xingzi No. 26, reported in *Huanjing Fa Cankao Ziliao Xuanbian* (Selected Reference Materials in Environmental Law), vol. 5, pp. 344–50.

PROSECUTING AUTHORITY

SUZHOU MUNICIPAL PEOPLE'S PROCURATORATE

DEFENDANT

Name: Zhang Changlin; male; 39 years old; native of Yancheng County, Jiangsu
Family Origin: Worker
Class Status: Worker
Educational Level: Primary School
Address: 165 Xueshi Street, Suzhou
Detention Date: Since September 18, 1979
Date of Arrest: September 21, 1979
Occupation Before Arrest: Worker in the warehouse and shipping department of the Suzhou People's Chemical Plant of Suzhou

JUDGMENT

The defendant, Zhang Changlin, was a worker in the warehouse and shipping department of the Suzhou People's Chemical Plant. Before he left work and went on leave at 3:50 P.M. on September 12, 1979, he failed to ask his supervisor or fellow workers to fill in for him and close a valve through which liquid sodium cyanide (volume 30 percent), contained in a 150-ton storage tank, entered into an eight-ton measurement tank. After returning to the factory at 6:00 P.M. the defendant again negligently and recklessly failed to turn off the valve. Consequently, when the eight-ton tank was filled and overloaded, the overflow liquid cyanide ran through a hole seven centimeters wide and four centimeters high in the retaining wall and flowed into the nearby river until 7:00 the next morning, when other workers in the same factory finally discovered the incident and closed the valve. Approximately 28 tons of liquid cyanide were eventually discharged into the river. Although 10.8 tons of sodium sulfite was spread into and along the river for dilution purposes, serious damages resulted in massive fish and mussel kills at the municipal fish hatchery and in the waters and fishing ponds in some [nearby] communes in Wuxian.

In sum, the defendant, Zhang Changlin, has [through his conduct] caused the overflow of the liquid cyanide from the 8-ton measurement tank and, thereby, damages of more than 34,800 yuan to the factory. More seriously, such conduct has resulted in massive pollution of the river, causing massive fish and mussel kills and danger to human health. This constitutes grave liability.

Because the defendant has maintained a good attitude through this judicial process, pleaded guilty to all charges against him, and showed regret for what he has done, this court, taking into account all the elements involved in this case, hereby renders its judgment, in accordance with the law, by sentencing the defendant, Zhang Changlin, for a total of two years imprisonment.

(The sentence should run from September 18, 1979, to September 17, 1981.)

[The defendant] may appeal to the Supreme People's Court of Jiangsu Province within ten days, starting from the second day he receives this judgment.

October 30, 1979 (Seal of the Court)

APPENDIX—HOW WE TRIED A SERIOUS ENVIRONMENTAL POLLUTION CASE (THE SUZHOU INTERMEDIATE PEOPLE'S COURT)

A serious and well-publicized environmental pollution case took place in Suzhou on September 12, 1979. The facts are as follows: Zhang Changlin, a worker at the warehouse for dangerous products of the Suzhou People's Chemical Plant, before putting in overtime hours, requested an early leave for two hours (from 4:00–6:00 P.M.) so that he could go home and take care of his children. After the permission for leave was granted, at 3:50 P.M. Zhang Changlin, feeling that nothing would happen within that two-hour period, violated standard operating procedures by failing to report to his supervisor, and opened the valve through which liquid sodium cyanide contained in a huge 150-ton storage tank would flow into an eight-ton measurement tank. When he returned to work at 6:00 P.M., he went directly to another place to ignite the fuel oil and forgot to turn off the valve. Consequently, after the measurement tank was filled, a great amount of liquid cyanide overflowed, ran through a hole on the east base of the retaining wall, and discharged into the river until around 7:20 A.M. of the next morning, when Comrade Jiang Jizhou and others from the same factory eventually discovered the incident and closed the valve. The entire discharge lasted for thirteen hours. According to the appraisal, 28 tons of liquid cyanide (which is equivalent to 84 tons of solid sodium cyanide) flowed into the river and caused serious pollution to a large water area and massive deaths to fish and mussels and had a devastating effect on the local people's daily life and production. Based on the estimate of the Suzhou Hatchery, 130,000 fish fry alone were poisoned. After the incident occurred, the Office of Public Security investigated the incident, and the procurator filed a complaint, and we accepted and handled this severe case in an expeditious manner.

On October 27 of the same year we opened a public trial and rendered a judgment in which Zhang Changlin, the direct cause of the incident, was sentenced to two years' imprisonment in accordance with the law.

The reaction of the broad masses of cadres and people was: "The Court has in a timely and accurate fashion taken care of this serious environmental pollution case right after the Environmental Protection Law was promulgated. This is a live and vivid lesson [related to the application] of the Environmental Law." Some operators and supervisors who work at the units in which dangerous goods or products were handled said: "Zhang Changlin's case has fired the warning shot, and we should take care of our affairs [from now on] by self-consciously following the rules of the Environmental Protection Law."

And now, we would like to report to [all] cadres and comrades some of the basic lessons that we learned in handling this case.

Handle Cases in a Bold and Timely Fashion

Suzhou is an ancient and beautiful city known for its tourist attractions, and yet, in the process of industrialization, environmental pollution has become a serious problem because of a lack of experience and irrational industrial distribution, especially during the chaotic and disruptive era of Lin Biao and the "Gang of Four." The central and provincial [governments'] designation of Suzhou as a key point for the control of environmental pollution, the leading comrade from the provincial Environmental Protection Bureau personally supervising this task, the responsible person in the municipality assuming the role of the leader of the environmental protection leading small group, and the many meetings that were held all served to advance the development of environmental protection. Last September the first Environmental Protection Law of this country was officially promulgated and was well received by the masses. At just about the same time a serious and major incident in which a massive amount of liquid cyanide was discharged into a river from the Suzhou People's Chemical Plant took place. This immediately caused great concern and dismay among the people of the entire city as well as those of Wuxian County. Some even complained to the news agency. The event's appearance in *Guangming Ribao* [Enlightenment Daily] stirred strong public opinion. The Municipal Party Committee was concerned about this incident and sent Vice-Secretary Fang Ming to the scene in person to conduct an assessment, to hold a special meeting for research and study, and to instruct the public procurator to process this case speedily and severely according to the law.

The party group of this court at first had some doubt as to whether this case should be referred to the Economic Trial Court, since this court had just recently been established and so far only one member had presided on the bench. At that point we also realized that a great number of difficulties were in store if we were to handle this case properly. Yet we recognized that the outcome of this case had a direct bearing on the thorough enforcement of the Environmental Protection Law, and that this was also an excellent opportunity for the Economic Trial Court to gain experience. Therefore, we hoped to take the attitude of handling cases in a bold fashion, but yet be open to constructive criticism in handling this case in a positive way. Our request received great support and encouragement from the court's party organization, and we were able to organize and coordinate our force in a timely fashion, transferring an experienced clerk from the Criminal Trial Court to assist in the case. Soon after the incident occurred, owing to our aggressive and positive assessment at the scene, the interview of related parties, the examination of the file, and a timely understanding of the facts, we were able to basically clarify the causes, details, and results of the incident before it was brought to us by the procurator. The speed in organization and preparation was therefore increased. It took only eight days for us to conclude the case, thanks to the direct leadership of the court's party organization, close coordination with the public security and procuratorial authorities, and enthusiastic support from the environmental and chemical industry departments.

Repeatedly Examine and Accurately Ascertain the Facts

The facts related to criminality remain the basis for ascertaining the character [of a crime] and the corresponding penalty that is to be meted out. The key to a successful trial is the repeated examination of the facts by going to the actual scene of the criminal act so as to accurately ascertain [the character] of the crime.

First of all, we must examine the main cause(s) of the incident and then determine the type of criminal responsibility the defendant is to bear. [In the present case] the cause was that Zhang Changlin, the operator, violated operating procedure by opening the valve for liquid cyanide flow before the scheduled time without reporting this to his supervisor, that he left his work position for family and personal reasons without finding a substitute, and that he even forgot to close the valve on return to the factory. Because of his mental stupor and poor performance on the job, there was an enormous overflow of liquid cyanide, and as a consequence, a serious pollution incident resulted. It is obvious that Zhang Changlin directly caused this incident.

Second, we have examined the issue of the hole in the retaining wall. At the beginning, Zhang's case file indicated that this hole was left by [previous] construction. We feel that this is [quite] unreasonable, since leaving such a hole through which the pollutant might escape, as in the present case, is contrary to the basic purpose of the wall. Therefore, we have tried to determine the origin of this hole and its relation to the defendant's action. After six examinations and investigations we came to realize that the hole was not ''left behind'' when it was built in October 1978. Two channels connect the two liquid cyanide containers within the wall. Only cement was applied in the "slot" between the two pipelines, without the placement of brick. After a period of time, cracks started to develop and a little hole was created. Because cleaning was also part of his duties, Zhang Changlin not only failed to exercise [care] by filling the hole, but actually further enlarged the hole [and as a result] the chemical drained through this hole into the nearby river. This is how the 4 by 7-centimeter hole was created. It is also one of the major factors why the liquid cyanide flowed into the river. Zhang Changlin is, therefore, liable for the incident.

Third, one of the key points we looked into was the amount of liquid cyanide that was discharged into the river. The People's Chemical Plant calculated four separate quantities (8, 17, 28, and 29 tons). Which one is reliable? One method was to make an estimate based on the amount, velocity, and duration of the overflow. This method is unreliable because no definite figure was given on how wide the valve was opened, how fast the fluid flowed, and how long the overflow lasted. As a result, we ruled out such divergent figures as 8, 17, and 29 tons of overflow, which are considered to be unreliable estimates. Another method was to subtract the current quantity of fluid in storage and the quantity already used from the original quantity in storage to determine the amount that was lost. The resulting sum of 28 tons of overflow was much more plausible, and therefore was adopted [by the court] as the basis for its judgment.

Sodium cyanide is such a poisonous element that the consumption of only 0.1 g can kill a human. In order to dilute, neutralize, and sanitize [the pollution], 10.8 tons of sodium sulfite was poured into the river. The loss of liquid cyanide and sodium sulfite alone resulted in the direct loss of 34,888 yuan to the Suzhou People's Chemical Plant. Large water bodies in the suburban and urban areas of Suzhou and five communes in Wuxian were severely polluted and massive fish and mussel kills occurred all because of such a large overflow of liquid cyanide. Through such an examination it is certain that the conduct of Zhang Changlin has constituted a crime and he should be held criminally responsible.

Comprehensive Analysis and Substantive Treatment

[Normally] in a liability case there are complicated circumstances, broad scope, and multiple causes. When examining those elements we not only clarify the major cause, but also take into account secondary causes through comprehensive analysis and treat them respectively and substantively. Two main issues were resolved in this regard.

1. *The issue of economic compensation.* In economic cases this issue is more complicated and harder to resolve. . . . Owing to such serious damages, the Suzhou Hatchery and the Aquatic Products Bureau of Wuxian requested large sums for economic damages. They even requested that this figure be disclosed openly while this court was in session. However, because all effort was placed on preventing people from being poisoned, no data regarding the exact numbers of fish and mussels killed or the density of sodium cyanide in the river were

ever collected. Furthermore, it was not until one month and seven days after the incident that the case was finally brought to us. Therefore, no actual damages or figures raised by the injured units could be verified. In our judgment we bypassed the difficulties when deciding the actual figure of damages. In order that the compensation issue could be taken care of properly and that the trial be conducted in a smooth fashion, we conducted serious investigations and research, explained the situation [of this case] to the environmental protection and epidemic control units, unified our thinking, and worked together with them to demonstrate concern for the injured units. Under the principle of seeking truth from facts, and with regard for state, collective, and individual interests, after a [series of] negotiations the People's Plant [agreed to] pay a total of 105,000 yuan in compensation, thereby resolving this dispute.

2. *The issue of respondeat superior liability.* The pollution resulting from this incident was so serious that some people, including the provincial Environmental Protection Bureau, requested the further pursuit of criminal responsibility on the part of the factory leaders. After careful investigation and analysis, we discovered that factory management was in turmoil, rules and systems of operation were incomplete, and safety and production were, for the most part, ignored by the factory leaders. This state of affairs stems from the poisonous influence of Lin Biao and the "Gang of Four." For instance, there was no system that could be strictly enforced for the management and use of such severely toxic chemicals as liquid cyanide, and there was insufficient safety education given to the factory employees. It is, therefore, no wonder that such incidents have taken place so often in the past. Since 1973 there have been discharges of liquid cyanide on four occasions. Three of these four incidents resulted from the operator's leaving his work position without authorization. The leaders of the factory did not, however, take them seriously, nor did they adopt proper measures to deal with such problems. In order to prevent the liquid cyanide from overflowing, a retaining wall was erected around the liquid cyanide storage tank in October 1978. It did not pass inspection. Because there were no uniform security checks, the hole in the wall was not discovered and remedied. Furthermore, there were too few workers in the dangerous materials warehouses and they were poorly deployed. The failure of key leaders to attach attention to this matter after the incident took place, despite the fact that they managed to inspect the scene cursorily, and the failure of the supervisors to submit a report to their supervisory department and other concerned agencies served to delay the response for three hours. Accordingly, they should be held responsible for all the counts [against them]. Of the five factory leaders only two had served at their current job since 1977; the others had just recently been transferred [to this factory], and thus were relatively unfamiliar with the work involved. After a comprehensive and objective analysis [of the facts], we concluded that [those three] leaders committed mistakes and that their actions did not amount to criminal conduct. It follows that we proposed to the authorized departments that [these leaders] be

given serious education through self-criticism and be subject to certain disciplinary action, respectively, based on their individual responsibilities and attitudes. The general public also considered such a judgment fair and reasonable.

Hold Open Trials and Publicize the Legal System

Open trials, the backbone of trying cases, are necessary means for rehabilitating the criminal, educating the masses, and publicizing the legal system. It is also a good way of assessing trial work. With great support from the provincial and municipal [party] committees and related departments and after full preparations, this serious environmental pollution case underwent an open trial. More than six hundred persons from the leadership of the various municipal districts and bureaus and some industrial and mining enterprises attended the trial. The provincial and seven other municipal environmental protection departments also sent special representatives to attend. *Guangming Ribao* [Enlightenment Daily] also sent a special correspondent from Beijing to cover the case. Whether or not this trial is successful in effect depends on whether the person sitting on the bench grasps the key factors, makes clear distinctions, and strictly follows legal procedures to determine the principal facts of the crime. During the trial, we emphasized doing a good job of oral argument, and effectively availed the function of counsel. With the support from related departments, before the start of the trial we hired a technician who possessed knowledge of the chemical industry to serve as defense counsel. We also helped him to familiarize himself with the facts of the case and related legal knowledge. During the trial this counsel liberated his thoughts and sufficiently presented the reasons. He conducted a thorough analysis of the lax management system and disregard for safety and production in the factory. He pointed out that, in addition to the responsibility the defendant must bear, the factory leaders ought to be held accountable. He further laid out the facts to show that the defendant had, in the past, maintained a relatively good character and performance and asked the court to exercise leniency toward the defendant in its judgment. After sufficient oral argument we further clarified the causes of this incident, both subjective and objective, and the criminal responsibility and civil liability of the parties. After careful consideration we unanimously decided, in accordance with Article 32 of the Environmental Protection Law and Article 115 of the Criminal Law, to sentence the defendant, Zhang Changlin, to two years' imprisonment. Because the investigation was clear, the oral argument sufficient, and the final decision accurate, the defendant did not appeal after the judgment was announced. All those who attended the open trial unanimously considered that this was a relatively successful trial and everyone had learned a good lesson regarding the legal system.

Practice confirms that full trial proceedings are a way to propagandize the legal system. Conducting trials well is for the purpose of educating the people and preventing crime, as well as for correcting criminal acts. To expand the reach of propaganda and broaden its effectiveness, a clip from this public trial was broadcast across the entire province by the provincial television station. The municipal propaganda department made a special film, and the Suzhou radio station recorded events at the trial for later broadcast to the entire city. When the court, together with the municipal propaganda department, sponsored an exhibition on legal system education, we used the Zhang Changlin case as a model and held a special showing of the film on the public trial of Zhang Changlin. More than 400 units and collective organizations participated and more than 140,000 persons attended the exhibition, an average of more than 3,000 a day, including specialists sent from Yangzhou, Chanshu, and Xinghua prefectures to observe and make copies.

Advance Structural Reform and Promote Environmental Protection

This grave environmental pollution case was a bad thing, but bad things can be turned into good things when handled right. The public trial of Zhang Changlin had a big impact on Suzhou's people, giving them an incisive lesson and making the broad masses of cadres and people raise their understanding of the importance of strict legal discipline; strengthening their legal understanding; tightening the control of the "three wastes" with regard to implementing the Environmental Protection Law; advancing structural reform; and preventing environmental pollution. Comrade Gu Sumei of the chemical workshop at the Suzhou No. 2 Plastics Factory said that the Zhang Changlin case was a big lesson to her . . . on the need to prevent accidents. . . . Because leaders of the Chemical Industry Bureau raised their awareness, they gave added emphasis to environmental protection and made environmental protection and control of the "three wastes" key items in the three-year readjustment period [1981–83], strengthened management, made widespread inspections, and operationalized procedures. Leaders in many units absorbed the lessons from the Zhang Changlin case.

Comments

This may have been the first case tried involving enforcement of the Environmental Protection Law (for trial implementation). It involved a discrete incident of pollution, responsibility for which could be attributed to identifiable individual(s). It amounted to dereliction of duty or criminal negligence and was duly prosecuted under Article 115 of the Criminal Law as well as Article 32 of the Environmental Protection Law.

However, the conduct of the proceedings raises serious questions. The equipment operator, Zhang Changlin, was tried and convicted for actions which were clearly part of the normal course of events at his factory, where operating procedures were routinely ignored and obvious defects in construction were left unrepaired. Zhang was in part simply a victim of poor luck, although that as such is not admissible as a mitigating factor. There was strong reason to pursue the criminal responsibility of the factory leadership, as demanded by the environmental protection department, but this course of action was rejected by the court on the hazy grounds that the leadership was inexperienced and merely guilty of errors of judgment rather than of criminal acts. This is a vague defense, since the acts in question took place months and even years after at least two of the leaders had assumed their posts, although it surely takes cognizance of the post–Cultural Revolution chaos that afflicted most workplaces.

The case was also clearly more a vehicle for mass education than an effort to determine the guilt or innocence of Zhang Changlin. The trial bench was inexperienced and acted at the behest of the Party Committee in close collaboration with not only the procurator and the public security department, but also the propaganda department, strongly indicating the unsurprising conclusion that the outcome of the "trial" had been decided in advance. The defendant also lacked adequate and effective counsel. His representative's sole purpose seems to have been to plead for leniency, perhaps the best that he could have done, given his lack of legal training. The evidence in the case was spotty and subject to dispute, as well as a coverup by the chemical plant, but this does not appear to have been raised by the defense as a reason for throwing the case out.

It is by no means clear how effective the public educational value of the trial was. Its novelty and salience probably exerted some impact on the populace, especially those with similar workplace responsibilities. The impact is unlikely to have been lasting, however, in the absence of a more regularized system for judicial enforcement. What is important is that the higher leadership's support for environmental protection, in the nation as a whole as well as in major cities like Suzhou, has risen. Therefore, more money and attention are paid to environmental protection in the normal course of events by state factories than was the case in the past, although there is a great deal more to be done.

Qiu Guotang (1984) "Some Questions Involving Hong Kong Related Environmental Pollution Disputes"

Huangjing Fa, no. 2, pp. 18–22.

The *Shenzhen Special Economic Zone News* on July 22, 1984, reported that the Economic Section of the Shenzhen Intermediate People's Court had publicly tried an environmental pollution case against Hong Kong Kaida Enterprises, Ltd.,[1] in which Kaida was found guilty, fined H.K. $20,000, and ordered to control its pollution satisfactorily within a specified time frame. We recently toured Shenzhen and investigated the origins, progress, and disposition of the case, giving us food for thought. This was the first publicly held environmental pollution case in the Shenzhen Special Zone, and it was handled well, with great educational value, and satisfied the masses. Moreover, this case touched on many questions in environmental law, justifying our summing it up and explaining it in terms of legislation and theory. Now I will comment on some issues it involves from my own perspective.

THE ORIGINS, PROGRESS, AND DISPOSITION OF THE CASE

Kaida Enterprises, Ltd., was the first wholly owned Hong Kong enterprise in Shenzhen. In September 1981 Kaida reached an agreement with China's Business Solicitation Bureau[2] to build a factory in the Shekou Industrial Zone, involving a total investment of U.S. $16 million, with 1,100 employees, to produce plastic toys for the export market, primarily in Europe and the United States. When the agreement was negotiated the Business Solicitation Bureau was mainly concerned about economic development and attracting investment, while ignoring environmental protection and pollution. There were no provisions in the agreement concerning responsibility for pollution control and environmental protection. After the agreement was formally concluded, Kaida began to produce plastic toys in 1982. The production process involved mixing polyvinyl chloride with large quantities of dioctyl phthalate and other plasticizers, which, when combined at high temperatures, produce malodorous and toxic gases. The plant discharged these wastes without treatment into the atmosphere, seriously polluting the surrounding environment. Moreover, equipment in this factory was noisy, with sound levels ranging from 91 to 106 decibels, far exceeding state standards and seriously disturbing the environment. Not only did the plant workers' health suffer, but, moreover, nearby residents also were affected, creating discontent among nearby enterprises, other undertakings, social organizations, and the people, all of whom loudly demanded a stern response by government organizations.

The Shekou District Environmental Monitoring Station on many occasions before May 3, 1983, urged Kaida to institute controls and engaged engineering and technical personnel from the Guangzhou Municipal Environmental Protection Equipment and Technology Service Center, the Guangzhou New Technology Applications Research Institute, and other units to visit the site and consult on control methods. But the factory refused to heed their advice and continued to operate under the same procedures. Finally, on October 22, 1983, the monitoring station set a deadline for the installation of controls, but the company still refused to pay any heed and did not introduce any control measures. The monitoring station then brought suit on December 22, 1983, in the Shezhen Intermediate People's Court, demanding that Kaida completely control the pollution and pay compensation for all damages suffered. When the company was charged they denied any culpability under Chinese law, saying:

> Our agreement did not include any provisions for pollution control and environmental protection so we are not responsible. . . . Under Hong Kong regulations, the government is responsible for all pollution caused by factories. . . . The Shekou Environmental Monitoring Station has yet to provide us with legally admissible scientific test data and the relevant state standards. To accuse us of being noisy and smelly and polluting the environment baffles us. It is even harder for us to accept the need for us to invest US $40,000 in pollution control equipment, and it is infeasible for us to do it.

When the court accepted the case it realized that the key issues were whether the noise from the machinery and the gases emitted polluted the environment, and how to use legal instruments in the trial. So the court first conducted a penetrating investigation to develop a clear understanding of the case. According to the investigation, nearby enterprises and other undertakings, social organizations, and residents began complaining to the monitoring station in 1983 that noise from the factory machinery was so deafening that it infuriated people, and that the malodorous gases it emitted made people choke and develop breathing difficulties. Accordingly, they demanded that the environmental protection department order the factory to quickly introduce controls.

In response to the massive reaction and to clarify the circumstances concerning the disturbance caused by the noise, they invited the Guangzhou Municipal Environmental Monitoring Center, Guangzhou Municipal Environmental Protection Equipment and Technology Service Center, and the Guangzhou New Technology Applications Research Institute to each conduct on-site inspections. Test results showed that the noise levels were 70 decibels 30 meters away from the air compressor building; 87 decibels one meter away from it; and between 91 and 106 decibels in the mold-pouring shop. The state requires, however, that industrial noise levels not exceed 65 decibels during the day and 55 decibels at night, with a maximum of 85 decibels on the factory floor. Noise from the company's machinery was thus far in excess of state-mandated standards. To clarify the source of the malodorous gas, they invited the Guangzhou New Technology Applications Research Institute to test the gases emitted from the mold-pouring shop. Through spectral analysis the tests revealed that the principal production components were polyvinyl chloride, dioctyl phthalate, and other plasticizers. These materials are malodorous and release malodorous gases under heat. The source of the foul smell thus was determined to be untreated emissions of gases into the air from No. 36 molding machine.

Once it had completed its investigation and understood the case, the court convened to hear the case with both the plaintiff and the defendant represented by legal counsel. Having clarified the facts and hearing from counsel for both parties, the judge presented to the court the conclusions of the aforementioned scientific tests and determined that in the course of its operations, Kaida Enterprises, Ltd.'s noisy machinery and malodorous gases had seriously polluted the environment, impairing people's physical health. Finally, on the basis of Articles 6, 16, and 32 of the Environmental Protection Law (for trial implementation), Articles 2 and 13 of the State Regulations for the Management of Environmental Standards, and Article 20 of the Shenzhou Municipal Provincial Regulations for Environmental Protection, the court issued the following ruling.

1. Kaida Enterprises, Ltd., must satisfactorily control its pollution in accordance with relevant state standards and regulations by October 31, 1984, and would be allowed to resume production only after obtaining a license from the Shenzhen Branch of the State Administration of Industry and Commerce.

2. On receipt of this notice to control pollution by the specified deadline, Kaida Enterprises, Ltd., must not only adopt effective control measures, but, moreover, for this and every subsequent time the offense is repeated the company shall pay a fine of H.K. $20,000 to the state treasury.

3. Kaida Enterprises, Ltd., is responsible for all expenses of the Guangzhou New Technology Applications Research Institute, the Guangzhou Municipal Environmental Protection Equipment and Technology Service Center, and other units that conducted repeated on-site tests and for all court costs associated with this case.

After the judgment was entered, responses on all sides were intense, the masses were satisfied, and the results were favorable. On the basis of the objective facts the accused recognized his errors, acknowledged polluting the environment and breaking the law, and promised to comply with the court decision without appealing to higher levels.

SEVERAL ISSUES AFFECTING THE CASE

The Issue of Applying the Law in Environmental Disputes Affecting Hong Kong.

During the trial Kaida Enterprises, Ltd., insisted that "[our] agreement did not include any provisions for pollution control and environmental pollution so we are not responsible. . . . Under Hong Kong regulations, the government is responsible for all pollution caused by factories." This is related to the issue of applying the law in environmental disputes affecting Hong Kong. Which law shall be applicable when businessmen from Hong Kong and Macau invest, build factories, and engage in production that pollutes the environment, creates hazards, and causes disputes either in the Special Economic Zones or in the rest of the country? How should it be correctly applied?

Because environmental and pollution cases affecting Hong Kong are of a special nature, we cannot simply refer to cases affecting foreigners or domestic environmental pollution. Each has its own special characteristics whether in terms of subjective or objective legal relationships or in terms of the origins, transformations, and termination of legal relationships. One such characteristic is that one party in the dispute is a Hong Kong or Macau compatriot or a company or enterprise operated by Hong Kong or Macau compatriots. A second is that the pollution hazard causes damage to our society and citizens (i.e., our enterprises, other undertakings, social organizations, and residents' property and health) and that their behavior infringing on others' rights takes place in our territory. Because of these special characteristics governing environmental pollution disputes involving Hong Kong, we need clear concepts to guide us when applying the law in such cases.

The purpose of handling such cases and adjusting their relationships is to protect state sovereignty and the interests of the state, collectives, and individuals; to protect the environment and control pollution and other hazards to make the people prosperous; to protect the legal rights of Hong Kong and Macau businessmen, promote the economic development of the Special Economic Zones, and accelerate the realization of the Four Modernizations. Under the guidance of this set of thoughts, we should carry out the following principles.

The principle of state sovereignty. Protecting a country's natural, human, and ecological environments from impacts and destruction originating from abroad and preventing and combating pollution and other hazards involve a country's right to protect its environment. The right to protect a country's environment is equivalent in nature and significance to protecting the integrity of a country's territory and not permitting external aggression. The sovereign nature of a country's environmental rights is internationally recognized. For example, the Convention on Halting Ships on the High Seas recognizes that a state whose coastline is polluted by a ship belonging to another country has the right to halt that ship, even if it is on the high seas. Article 9 of the Environmental Protection Law states that "all foreign nationals and foreign aircraft, vessels, vehicles, materials, and living beings entering or transiting the territorial land, waters, and airspace of China must observe this law as well as other regulations and rules for environmental protection." Article 2, Section 2, of the Marine Environmental Protection Law stipulates that "all vessels, platforms, airborne vehicles, submersibles, as well as all enterprises and other undertakings and individuals engaged in navigation, exploration, exploitation, production, scientific research, and other activities in the sea areas under the jurisdiction of the People's Republic of China shall comply with this law."

These provisions fully explain the sovereign nature of environmental rights. State sovereignty is supreme within the country and has equal and independent status internationally. The so-called supremacy of rights within a country refers to the state's rights over all people and affairs in its sovereign territory and its jurisdiction over its own citizens while abroad (i.e., supreme rights over land and people). The so-called right of independence externally is the manifestation of state sovereignty in international relations and means that the state is completely independent and sovereign in the exercise of its rights and can expel any external interference. When handling environmental pollution disputes involving Hong Kong, in accordance with the principle of state sovereignty, we must make clear that Hong Kong and Macau are inalienable parts of China's sovereign territory, and that Hong Kong and Macau compatriots are Chinese citizens. So they and their companies and enterprises, when investing or doing business in the Special Economic Zones or elsewhere in China, should obey Chinese law, regardless of whether the state's superior rights over territory or people apply.

Kaida Enterprises, Ltd., of Hong Kong, which came to the Shenzhen Special Economic Zone to invest in a factory and engage in economic activity, should obey Chinese law and environmental protection laws to prevent and control pollution and protect the environment. If they violate the environmental protection laws and pollute and destroy the environment, their cases ought to be handled according to the provisions of Chinese environmental protection laws, following the principle of state sovereignty. Kaida Enterprises, Ltd., stated that "under Hong Kong regulations, the government is responsible for all pollution caused by factories . . . , [and] our side is not responsible." This argument is without foundation and completely mistaken. The company's claim that "our agreement did not include any provisions for pollution control and environmental protection, so we are not responsible" is also mistaken. A basic point in the protection of a state's sovereignty is that the negotiations and content of contracts must comply with the laws of the People's Republic of China. On the one hand, this means that the provisions and content of contracts must comply with the regulations of Chinese law and cannot incorporate any provisions that damage the rights and interests of state sovereignty. On the other hand, this means that when honoring a contract infringes on the rights and interests of state sovereignty and contradicts the laws of the state, even if the contract makes no provisions in this regard, we must proceed on the basis of protecting state sovereignty and economic rights and interests, obey the regulations of the laws of the state, and conduct trials by applying China's current laws.

The principle of equality and reciprocity. Under private international law the content of the principle of equality and reciprocity refers to equal status in civil law between parties from different countries or territories conducting civil transactions, who, in civil transactions of mutual benefit, must both benefit. The People's Court upheld the principle of equality and reciprocity in cases involving disputes over environmental pollution involving Hong Kong by determining that the interests and obligations of both parties to a contract must be reciprocal; that is, to protect both parties' legal environmental rights and interests equally, both parties assume equal obligations to protect the environment and prevent and control pollution and other public hazards.

When Hong Kong and Macau compatriots go to the special economic zones to invest and engage in mangement, they receive the state's legal protection and the state legally provides them with much in the way of preferential treatment so that they can create a sound working, living, and investment environment. On the other hand, they have the obligation to protect the environment and prevent and control pollution. If they violate environmental laws and pollute and destroy the environment, they should bear legal responsibility, just like domestic companies and enterprises, and bear legal penalties in the same way. To make excessive profits, some Hong Kong businessmen use their production and technological superiority to deceive us, in the name of protecting patents and production secrets, by moving more seriously polluting enterprises that have already been banned in Hong Kong into the Special Economic Zones. This seriously pollutes the environment, endangers China's posterity and the people's rights and interests, is illegal, and should be penalized under Chinese law.

In upholding the principle of equality and reciprocity, the People's Court also accorded Hong Kong and Macau compatriots rights and obligations equal to those of domestic companies and enterprises in the conduct of environmental court proceedings. Article 186 of the Law of Civil Procedure (for trial implementation) provides that "foreigners and stateless people have rights and obligations equal to those of citizens of the PRC when bringing suit or being sued in the people's courts. . . . Foreign enterprises and organizations, when bringing suit or being sued in the people's courts, have the right to sue and the obligation to be sued in accordance with the stipulations of this law." Inasmuch as foreigners have the status of citizens in civil proceedings, the civil affairs of Hong Kong and Macau compatriots and the affairs within the country of the enterprises and organizations that they operate have the same status. They ought to have a status in environmental proceedings equal to that of domestic persons and obey our laws just like compatriots within the country.

Carrying out the principles of sovereignty and equality and mutual benefit and applying Chinese law when handling environmental pollution disputes involving Hong Kong not only are in accord with the rights and interests of the state, the people, and Hong Kong and Macau compatriots and promote regular economic transactions with Hong Kong and Macau, policy relaxation, and the realization of the Four Modernizations, but they are also in accordance with international precedent. In laws allowing contractual relationships among foreign parties, when the generally used legislation, judicial precedents, and practices of different countries are in conflict, the norm is the law chosen to negotiate the contract under (i.e., the principle of "voluntary consent"). If the contracting parties did not select a legal system when negotiating the contract, courts generally rely on the standards of their own domestic laws to decide which law should be followed in the contract. But standards applied in different countries vary (e.g., domestic contract law, contracts subordinate to domestic law, contracts subordinate to the courts, etc.). The most common procedures in international law are domestic contract law and contract subordination to domestic law. Thus we should uphold contractual formation, effectiveness, interpretation, and compliance with Chinese law as the basis for economic contracts involving Hong Kong carried out in the Special Economic Zones under the zones' right to conclude contracts. When conflicts arise over contracts the cases can be decided in accordance with the forum chosen in the contract. When no choice of a legal system is found in the contract and no regulations on environmental protection and pollution control were included in the negotiations, for the People's Court to uphold the principles of deciding the case by applying Chinese law is in agreement with international custom and practice.

In the environmental pollution case involving Kaida Enterprises, Ltd., the Shenzhen Intermediate People's Court began with this guiding thought and carried out the principles of sovereignty and equality and reciprocity with reference to international precedent. In accordance with Article 33 of the Constitution and Articles 6 and 32 of the Environmental Protection Law, the court imposed a fine of H.K. $20,000 on Kaida Enterprises, Ltd., for illegal pollution of the environment and ordererd the introduction of satisfactory controls within the specified time frame. This was rational and legal and corresponded to international custom and practice.

The Issues of Evidence and Responsibility in Environmental Litigation

In this trial the accused pleaded that "the plaintiff never provided our company with legally admissible scientific testing data and the relevant state standards. To accuse us of being noisy and smelly and polluting the environment baffles us. It is hard for us to accept the need to invest U.S. $40,000 to install filtration equipment; to control pollution by the specified date is truly impossible." In other words, because the plaintiff failed to provide sufficient scientific evidence, they did not bear any responsibility in the matter. In litigation involving conflicts over compensation for damages from environmental pollution, who ultimately bears the burden of proof? All countries follow similar practices in this regard.

In accordance with traditional procedural regulations, when the complainant provides the accused with the list of his crimes, he has a responsibility to present evidence for the case he is advocating. In a case involving compensation for damages, the complainant must provide evidence of the following before the accused can be assigned the burden of compensation: (a) the damages suffered; (b) the damages suffered were produced by the actions of the accused; (c) the accused acted negligently; and (d) the complainant fulfilled his obligation to avoid losses.

However, this regulation which imposes the responsibility for presenting evidence on the complainant is fruitless and hard to satisfy in litigation involving conflicts over compensation for damages arising from environmental pollution, and is an impediment to environmental protection and the protection of human health for the following reasons.

1. Foreign investment brought into the Special Economic Zones chiefly involves advanced technology and equipment. The rapid development of industry and technology has already made it impossible for people to understand in detail the impacts of advanced production processes, equipment, and technology on the disclosure of pollutants. Therefore, how could the complainant be expected to know what harm to others was caused by pollution from factories and enterprises. The complainant could not avoid this problem.

2. Because the patents involved in advanced production processes and technologies are protected under law and are secrets that cannot be publicly disclosed, the complainant had no way of knowing whether the accused acted improperly. If Kaida Enterprises, Ltd.'s plastic toy production process and technology are advanced, and the company erects a barrier in the name of protecting secrets, the Shekou Environmental Monitoring Station and the residents would have no way of knowing whether the harm caused by said company's pollution was the product of negligence.

3. What harm could the company's noise and odors cause to human health and property? Could high concentrations and volumes of discharges cause these dangers? Again, it was hard for the complainant to make a clear case.

Therefore, it would be extremely difficult, and perhaps impossible, to demand that the complainant clearly prove that the damage was the result of pollution by the accused, and that pollution by the accused was the proximate cause of the damages. This would place the victim in an unfavorable position because, even if he had suffered damage and had a just case, he would be unable to maintain the suit because of scientific limitations that made it impossible to present evidence. Meanwhile, even if the evidence presented by the complainant or victim had the burden of proof, the polluter (in this case Kaida Enterprises, Ltd.) would not have to bear responsibility if the victim were unable to present sufficient evidence to support the proposition that the polluter had acted improperly. This would be equivalent to enabling the party who created the hazard to plunder natural resources and pollute the environment without regard for the grave consequences in terms of human lives and damage to the state.

Therefore, to protect the state's environmental rights, to protect the environment, to prevent and control pollution and other public hazards, and to better protect the rights and interests of victims, and in accordance with the special and complicated nature of compensation for damages arising from environmental pollution, it is absolutely necessary and appropriate in litigation involving conflicts over compensation for environmental damages that the burden of proof be borne by the accused or by specialized organizations engaged by the trial-hearing body. Environmental law in many countries currently stipulates that the accused bears the burden of proof on compensation for environmental damages. For example, the Michigan Environmental Law of 1970 provides that the enforcement authority need only present superficial evidence showing that the polluter has caused pollution, and that the burden of proof [to rebut] rests on the accused polluter. There also are some countries that excuse the complainant of responsibility for presenting some kinds of evidence; for example, France stipulates that in suits involving compensation for damages caused by pollution, the plaintiff need not present evidence that the accused was negligent. It is sufficient to demonstrate a causal relationship between the defendant's pollution and the actual damages.

In Chinese environmental jurisprudence, when the environmental protection departments or people's courts handle disputes over compensation for damages arising from pollution, they generally engage environmental monitoring stations or other scientific and research organs to conduct scientific tests on complex scientific questions for the purpose of providing scientific evidence.

When the Shenzhen Intermediate People's Court tried this case, it acted in accordance with China's environmental litigation-related judicial practice and experience, with reference to other countries' practices. It engaged the Guangzhou Municipal Environmental Protection Monitoring Center, the Guangzhou New Technology Applications Research Institute, and other units to monitor and test Kaida Enterprises, Ltd.'s noise and malodorous pollution and to provide scientific data to try the case of Kaida Enterprises, Ltd.'s pollution-related damages. The court determined the legal responsiblity of the accused, provided legally admissible scientific evidence, and issued a just judgment. The court's approach was both correct and in conformance with legal theory.

Comments

As the first instance of environmental litigation involving foreign investment, the Kaida Enterprises, Ltd., case is important. It clearly indicates that an investor may be held responsible for failure to adopt pollution control measures and held liable for any damages arising from pollution, even if contracts governing the investment made no provisions in this regard. Unless the contract states otherwise, suits may be filed in Chinese courts under Chinese standards regarding the admissibility of evidence, which leaves the defendant in a vulnerable position.

It is entirely reasonable for foreign investors to assume liability for the consequences of their actions involving, in this case, pollution. Moreover, it is also normal practice for new regulations to be introduced after a plant has been in operation in accordance with changing social tastes (i.e., grandfather clauses are not applicable). As the Kaida case reveals, suit may be brought for arbitrary reasons. Kaida was sued for excessive noise, but factory noise regulations are routinely exceeded in China. Its gaseous emissions were capable of causing discomfort, but clear evidence was not presented regarding the extent or severity of any resulting illness. The commentary does not discuss contributing factors, such as the degree to which factory workers failed to wear personal protective gear. Indeed, it appears that the original investigation was prompted by other factors, including labor disputes, and the status of proprietary information rather than by pollution alone.

Under the circumstances, foreign investors would appear to be well advised to incorporate pollution control provisions in their investment strategy in order to avoid unanticipated liabilities arising at a later date. For example, the Sino-American Food Products Company, a joint venture with Beatrice, was persuaded to install additional pollution controls at its facility in Guangdong after the original contract had been negotiated, with the American company financing all of the additional costs. Foreign investors also should be prepared to satisfy maximal ("primary" in the Chinese lexicon) standards because of the more demanding criteria applicable to new pollution sources. Such controls may well seem unnecessary and too expensive to foreign investors, who may be forced to substantially modify their original plans. For example, one American investor was prevented from installing an economical on-site steam generation facility to power a plant on flimsy pollution control grounds, even though Shenzhen itself suffers from a power shortage (*Asian Wall Street Journal*, August 2, 1985). Effluent fees and fines are also likely to be higher under the assumption that foreign investors are more accustomed to such economic instruments and can afford to bear higher costs than their domestic counterparts elsewhere in China. Therefore, foreign investors should anticipate environmental as well as other contingencies and factor them into their investment calculus in order to determine whether a project remains viable and in order to persuade Chinese partners to share pollution control costs. *See* Lester Ross and Mitchell A. Silk, "Curbing Environmental Pollution," *China Business Review*, no. 2 (1987) pp. 51–53.

The Special Economic Zones also are colored with political controversy, with different elements of the leadership in Beijing critical of them on ideological, economic, and other grounds. Pollution is another reason for some officials to criticize the zones. For the most part, however, the zones have been defended as a means to introduce cleaner and more efficient industry into China, so the zones have a positive impact on the environment. These benefits will be magnified when local environmental protection ordinances for all the zones are in place and are accompanied by master planning to guide the zones' development, a process which is now belatedly under way. For political as well as environmental reasons, however, defenders of the zones insist on tighter controls than are in place elsewhere in the country. For more discussion on this point, *see* Cai Shouqiu, "On Environmental Protection in the Special Economic Zones and Open Zones," *Huanjing Fa*, no. 2, (1985) pp. 1–13; Qiu Guotang, "Some Issues Involving Strengthening of the Environmental Legal System in the Special Economic Zones," *id.*, pp. 14–22; and

Guangzhou Environmental Protection Office, "Strengthen Environmental Management in Accordance with the Law, and Promote the Opening of Cities to Foreign Investment." *id.*, pp. 28–31ff.

Supreme People's Court Decision on the Environmental Pollution Case between the Shenzhen Municipal Shekou District Environmental Monitoring Station and Kaida Enterprises, Ltd., Hong Kong (1985)

Zhonghua Renmin Gongheguo Zuigao Renmin Fayuan Gongbao (Gazette of the Supreme People's Court of the People's Republic of China) (September 20), pp. 44–46.

PLAINTIFF

The Shekou District Environmental Monitoring Station, Shenzhen Municipality (hereafter referred to as the monitoring station)

DEFENDANT

Kaida Enterprises, Ltd., Hong Kong (hereafter referred to as Kaida Company)[3]

The defendant, Kaida Company, signed an agreement with the Shenzhen Special Economic Zone's Bureau of Business Solicitation in September 1981 to build a wholly owned factory in the Shekou Industrial District for the manufacture of various kinds of plastic toys, involving an investment of U.S. $16 million and the employment of a labor force of 1,200 for the manufacture of products with a ready welcome on the world market.[4] In February 1982, after the company had commenced regular production, its molding workshop produced malodorous and toxic gases which went untreated and were emitted into the atmosphere, making people choke and causing respiratory difficulties. Meanwhile noise from the machinery was so deafening it made people nervous. Neighboring enterprises and other undertakings, organizations, and residents, one after the other, remonstrated with the monitoring station, demanding that the government take stern measures to handle the problem.

In accordance with the masses' intense demands, the monitoring station on numerous occasions, beginning in early May 1983, exhorted the defendant to control its pollution and successively invited specialists, professors, and technical personnel from relevant scientific research units in Guangzhou to make repeated inspections of Kaida Company, suggested control plans, and offered to provide assistance with regard to pollution control, but the defendant rejected all offers. On October 22, 1983, the plaintiff issued a circular setting a deadline for the institution of control measures by the defendant. The defendant, however, continued to refuse to take effective control measures. Therefore, the plaintiff filed suit in the Shenzhen Municipal Intermediate People's Court on December 27, 1983, demanding that the defendant institute stringent controls on the above-mentioned gases and noise, satisfy state regulations and standards, and reimburse the plaintiff for all costs incurred with regard to the engagement of scientific and technical personnel specializing in environmental protection for the purpose of investigating this problem.

The defendant responded that before October 22, 1983, the plaintiff never presented the company with legally admissible scientific data regarding environmental pollution or the relevant state standards. . . . It was even harder for the company to accept the need to invest U.S. $40,000 to install a filtering system. It was simply impossible to meet the plaintiff's deadline of December 25, 1983, for the satisfactory control of pollution, and moreover, the molding workshop had already closed down before the expiration of the deadline.

Having accepted the case, the Shenzhen Intermediate People's Court made repeated investigations and determined the following.

1. With regard to the noise problem, state regulations limit worker noise exposure levels to 85 decibels per eight-hour work day and daytime noise levels to 65 decibels in industrial areas. However, workers in Kaida Company's molding workshop were exposed to noise levels ranging from a low of 91 decibels to a high of 106 decibels during their work days extending eight hours or longer. The daytime noise level within the compressor building was 87 decibels, also far exceeding state standards.

2. With regard to gaseous emissions, Kaida Company repeatedly refused to provide information on the physical and chemical properties of the raw materials used in its molding workshop. Only after the plaintiff engaged scientific and technical personnel to take samples on the production site and conduct spectrochemical analysis did the monitoring station determine that the principal components of the raw materials were polychloroethylene mixed with large quantities of phosphobenzenediformate-dicaprilate, which emit malodorous gases when combined under heat. The untreated waste gases produced by No. 36 molding machine polluted the atmosphere, causing air pollution. It was only in January 1984, after the suit was filed, that the defendant provided the plaintiff with foreign language material on the composition of the plastics, which on translation proved that the fatty acids in the plastics were odor forming.

The trial conducted before the Shenzhen Intermediate People's Court determined that Article 6 of the Environmental Protection Law of the People's Republic of China (for trial implementation) provides:

In selecting construction sites, making designs, carrying out construction projects, and embarking on production, all enterprises and other undertakings shall pay adequate attention to preventing environmental pollution and damage. While carrying out new construction or renovation projects, an environmental impact report shall be submitted first, and design work can be started only after such a report has been reviewed and approved by the department concerned. Facilities for preventing pollution and other hazards to the public must be designed, built, and put into operation simultaneously with the principal project. The discharge of all harmful materials shall be carried out in accordance with the standards prescribed by the state.

Those units that have already caused environmental pollution or other hazards to the public shall work out plans and bring them under effective control in accordance with the principle that whoever has caused the pollution must bring it under control, [or they shall obtain necessary approval from the competent authorities for a change in the type of operation or seek relocation].

However, the defendant not only failed to provide an environmental impact report or statement to the environmental protection department and failed to list the chemical composition of the raw materials used in production, but also demanded that the environmental protection department identify the sources and provide a quantitative analysis of the malodor, which was entirely unjustified. After the plaintiff, acting in accordance with the law, set a deadline for controlling pollution, the defendant did shut the machine down on Christmas Eve, December 24. However, the machine went back into operation in the period from January 3 to 13, 1984, resuming pollution. All of these acts by the defendant were illegal.

Consequently, acting in accordance with Articles 6, 16, and 32 of the Environmental Protection Law of the People's Republic of China (for trial implementation), the Shenzhen Intermediate People's Court ruled as follows:

1. The noise and odors emanating from the defendant's molding workshop must be fully controlled in accordance with state regulations and standards before October 31, 1984.

2. The defendant responded to the lawful circular issued by the plaintiff setting a deadline for the control of pollution by not only failing to adopt effective measures to control pollution actively, but also remaining in production and continuing to pollute. A fine of H.K. $20,000 is imposed for these illegal acts to be payable to the state treasury.

3. The defendant shall bear all costs, totaling 810 yuan, incurred when the plaintiff engaged relevant scientific and technical personnel to examine the defendant's factory on repeated occasions.

4. The defendant shall pay legal fees, which total H.K. $1,740.

After the verdict was delivered, the defendant complied with the court's orders.

The Judicial Committee of the Supreme People's Court, at its 232nd session on August 17, 1985, summed up the experience of the trial in accordance with Article 11, Section 1, of the Organic Law of the People's Courts of the People's Republic of China and determined that the Shenzhen, Guangdong Intermediate People's Court had strictly applied the Environmental Protection Law (for trial implementation) in its conduct of the trial, and that the verdict reached was correct, halting environmentally polluting behavior and protecting the people's health.

Comments

The Supreme Court upheld the verdict of the Intermediate Court in all aspects, despite questions raised by the defendant and possibly others regarding the quality of the evidence presented in court and the extent of the defendant's liability. It is significant, however, that the Supreme Court did review the case and publish its decision. This may foretell improvements in judicial procedure in future litigation, at least when foreign investors are parties in the case.

Jiang De and Qin Liwen (1983) "Chang Jiang [Yangtze River] Shipping Administrative Bureau Learns Lesson: Strong Emphasis on Environmental Protection Brings Preliminary Results"

Zhongguo Fazhi Bao (February 25), p. 1. Translated in Joint Publications Research Service, *China Report: Science and Technology* (June 11, 1984), pp. 142–43.

The Chang Jiang Shipping Administrative Bureau of the Ministry of Communications has learned a lesson from the incident that occurred at its Pier 41 in Wuhan Port. The incident involved environmental pollution, which aroused dissatisfaction among the masses. The bureau has changed its work style, earnestly studied and implemented the Environmental Protection Law of the People's Republic of China (for trial implementation), and brought environmental protection work into a new phase. Now the black "mushroom clouds" covering the unloading machines for the railroad coal hopper cars have started to disappear, and other powder, dust, and wastewater that pollute the environment are being treated.

Pier 41 at Wuhan Port is a special pier for the loading and unloading of coal and has two unloading machines for the railroad coal hopper cars. The old equipment used in the open air generated black "mushroom clouds" all around whenever the machines were in operation, seriously polluting the environment and causing residents near Pier 41 to fear to open their windows and relax in cool places outdoors in the summer. The residents repeatedly sent their views to the Wuhan Port Office and the Chang Jiang Shipping Administrative Bureau, demanding that the pollution problems be resolved. They were unable, however, to arouse the attention of the leaders of the two bureaus, and thus became dissatisfied. During the three days from July 5 to 7, [1982], some angry masses broke into Pier 41 three times while it was in operation. They forced a halt to the unloading of coal, smashed some equipment, and caused direct losses amounting to more than 11,000 yuan. After the incident, leading comrades of the Chinese Communist Party's Central Committee severely criticized the leaders of the Chang Jiang Shipping Administrative Bureau for neglecting the people's interests and for their bureaucratic work style.

The incident at Pier 41 and the criticism from the leading comrades of the Central Committee strongly shook the Chang Jiang Shipping Administrative Bureau. The bureau party committee convened three standing committee meetings to examine the bureau's bureaucratic work style. With the help of responsible comrades of the Central Committee and provincial and municipal leaders, the bureau has begun to understand that, for a long time, it had set production and environmental protection in conflict with each other. Whenever environmental protection was mentioned, the bureau would stress the importance of production tasks, the lack of funds to make improvements, poor technical conditions, and other reasons. The bureau lacked understanding of how to implement the Environmental Protection Law and of the importance of environmental protection to the people's vital interests, and the bureau turned a deaf ear to the voice of the masses. These actions indicated conclusively that there was serious bureaucratism in the bureau. After the bureau's understanding was enhanced, leading comrades of the party committees of the port office and shipping bureau went personally to the scene and assessed the situation, formulated measures to control pollution, and sent representatives to listen to residents' critical views and give explanations. Subsequently, the party committees also convened an on-the-spot meeting at Pier 41 on dust prevention work along the entire Chang Jiang and demanded that subordinate units learn a lesson from the smashing incident, change work styles conscientiously, earnestly implement the Environmental Protection Law, and do a good job in environmental protection work. The bureau party committee also decided to set new limits on organizational size, personnel, and funds, to strengthen the training of grassroots environmental protection personnel, and to place the same amount of stress on environmental work as it placed on safety. The bureau has organized its forces to examine coal, cement and phosphorus mine piers, and all sources of pollution; has formulated measures to treat those sources sequentially and in groups; and will ensure implementation of these measures by guaranteeing supplies of labor, material, and financial resources. In accordance with the relevant articles of the Environmental Protection Law, the bureau has also stipulated that all future capital construction projects will adhere to the "three simultaneous points." All projects without measures to protect the environment must not be allowed to start.

The change in leadership work style has brought about a new start in environmental protection work. After a half-year of effort, dust covers have been added to all coal unloading machines at Wuhan Port, antidust spraying equipment has been installed, and all coal yards have been equipped with high-pressure water guns. The control of powder and dust in major coal ports such as Nanjing, Yuxikou, and Zhicheng is under way. Many large ships that sail along the Chang Jiang have been equipped with oil-water separators, which have greatly reduced pollution of the river from engine wastewater.

Comments

This major pollution case reveals the changes that have taken place in environmental protection in the post-Mao era. Production units and other institutions, particularly those owned by the state, customarily paid little heed to any considerations other than fulfilling their state production plan. Efficiency and environmental protection were of little concern, especially in a case like this, where the polluter was under the authority of the central government but the victims were under the jurisdiction of other departments and local governments. A studied lack of concern and failure to take responsibility for any consequences outside the unit or even one's specific tasks is all too common in China.

In this case the problem became so severe during the summer months in Wuhan, one of China's "summertime furnaces," that the nearby residents took the law into their own hands to put the offensive facilities out of action. Naturally, the immediate response of the local authorities was to detain the alleged ringleaders who were *prima facie* guilty of counterrevolutionary activity under the 1951 Act of the People's Republic of China for Punishment of Counterrevolution, which was often interpreted broadly, and, of greater immediacy, many provisions of the recently enacted Criminal Law, such as Articles 105, 125, and 158.

In the past this would have probably been the end of the matter. However, leadership concern for the environment was on the rise as a result of heightened awareness of the consequences of untrammeled pollution and realization that popular concern over pollution was growing, as revealed by the thousands of incidents of popular protest taking place in isolated, unpublicized actions all across the country. It seems that some members of the leadership were looking to seize on one or more incidents in order to demonstrate the gravity of the situation and use them as publicity vehicles throughout the country. When Politburo member and Senior Vice-Premier Wan Li learned of the Wuhan case through an internal press account, he ordered an investigation which led to the exoneration of the victims and severe criticism directed against the polluter and local officials, who had failed to take action for years in apparent violation, since 1979, of the Environmental Protection Law (for trial implementation). For further discussion, *see* Lester Ross and Mitchell A. Silk, "Post-Mao China and Environmental Protection: The Effects of Legal and Politico-Economic Reform," *UCLA Pacific Basin Law Journal* (1986).

Deng Jianxu (1982) "A Song of Victory in Defense of the Legal System"

Shanghai Sifa (October), pp. 1–2.

The Zhuzhou Municipal Environmental Protection Office, in accordance with the Environmental Protection Law of the People's Republic of China (for trial implementation) and related laws and regulations governing effluent fees, beginning in April 1980 carried out the assessment of effluent fees from Zhuzhou municipality's seven industrial enterprises which exceeded the national standards for pollution emissions. The Zhuzhou Chemical Plant, according to the amount by which it exceeded pollution discharge standards, in April of the same year paid effluent fees in the amount of 79,000 yuan. From May on the plant refused to pay and from May to December altogether owed a total of 230,774 yuan in effluent fees. The Zhuzhou Municipal Environmental Protection Office pressed for payment many times but to no avail. If legally enforceable means were not used to handle this situation, the state of affairs would not only affect national revenues, but moreover, [it would have set a dangerous precedent and encouraged] industrial enterprises which pay fees on time to follow suit. This was extremely detrimental to the "protecting of the environment and natural resources, [and] prevent[ion and elimination] of pollution and other hazards to the public . . . [and] protection [of the] people's health, and promo[tion] of economic growth.'' Thus a suit was filed in the Zhuzhou Municipal Intermediate People's Court seeking the overdue fees.

Since the Zhuzhou Municipal Environmental Protection Office began to assess effluent fees in April 1980, the provincial Finance Department had ranted that financial revenues had decreased and public finances were in dire circumstances, and they did not consent to the Zhuzhou Chemical Plant's paying the fees. Certain leading provincial comrades also said at a meeting that effluent fees could temporarily not be paid. After the Zhuzhou Municipal Intermediate People's Court accepted this lawsuit, in accordance with accepted legal procedures, a copy of the complaint was served on the defendant unit. The Zhuzhou Chemical Plant received the complaint, and its representative went twice to the provincial Bureau of Chemical Industry, the provincial Finance Department, the provincial People's Government, and the Zhuzhou Municipal Finance Office and Tax Bureau to further demand support. The provincial Finance Department prepared written comments on the Zhuzhou Chemical Plant's report that unpaid pollution emission fees from 1980 could no longer be made up. In the course of the court investigation, concerned departments spoke on behalf of Zhuzhou Chemical Plant, asking the court not to accept the case, or to delay it. Thus was it ''tried'' or was it ''delayed''? This put the law enforcement units to the test. If ''delayed,'' the enforcement unit would have made concessions to avoid trouble, turned big problems into small problems and small problems into no problem at all, condoned that which law and discipline do not permit, tarnished the law's solemnity, diminished the law's authority, and failed to protect the people's legal interests. If the case were ''tried,'' then concerned departments, and even certain provincial leading comrades, would be offended. After discussion the comrades of the economic trial court reached a consensus and concluded that the people's court is a law enforcement organization and must strictly enforce the law and carefully investigate incidents of illicit conduct. Thus this case laid an ideological foundation for trying cases according to the law.

The judge trying the case, after completing prehearing preparations, then called the court to order to hear the case. Originally, both parties' representatives raised frivolous arguments in court.

The Zhuzhou Chemical Plant representative put forth three arguments in defense of the plant's nonpayment of effluent fees. First, he questioned the date when the Environmental Protection Law entered into effect. The representative felt that all other laws specify promulgation and implementation dates and indicate the specific year, month, and day when it comes into effect. The Environmental Protection Law says only that it ''is now promulgated'' and is for trial implementation, and thereby does not call for immediate implementation. Second, the representative challenged the legal authority of the documents issued by the Hunan Provincial Commission on Capital Construction concerning effluent fees. He pointed out that Article 26 of the Environmental Protection Law states that only the State Council environmental protection departments may formulate environmental protection regulations, and thus the authority to formulate regulations and effluent fees assessment standards, an authority which is not conferred on local environmental protection organs. Consequently, the question of the legal authority of the Hunan Provincial Commission on Capital Construction's document warrants consideration. Third, do the instructions and suggestions of Zhuzhou Chemical Plant's higher-level leaders and supervisory departments count? Should they be implemented? This question involves the organizational principle of whether the lower level obeys the higher level.

The Zhuzhou Environmental Protection Office's representative rebutted on four grounds. First, the Environmental Protection Law was adopted and promulgated under the principles of the National People's Congress, in which the state uses legal means to achieve the goals of environmental protection and eliminate the public harm of pollution, and it, like all other laws, possesses legal authority. Although the Environmental Protection Law is "for trial implementation" and does not specify a certain year, month, and day when it enters into effect, it still definitely cannot be understood as merely a promulgation that did not enter into effect. It can only be understood to mean that it entered into effect on the date of promulgation. Otherwise, promulgation of the Environmental Protection Law would have had no actual significance. Meanwhile trial implementation of a law, although somewhat different from implementation, also is merely an indication that the maturity of the legislation is slightly inferior to that of formally implemented laws, but does not differ from officially implemented laws in legal authority. If, during the trial implementation of a law, the contents are found to be not suited to actual conditions, legal procedures should be followed to modify and amend [the law]. This is common legal knowledge. Obviously, the Zhuzhou Chemical Plant had no argument with respect to the issue of the Environmental Protection Law's trial implementation period. Second, the Hunan Provincial Commission on Capital Construction's environmental document (80–12) "Circular Concerning Measures for the Trial Implementation of the Assessment of Effluent Fees in Hunan Province" was ratified and promulgated by the provincial people's government and is a concrete means to enforce the national Environmental Protection Law. According to provisions of the "People's Republic of China Local People's Congresses at All Levels and Local People's Governments Organic Law," Chapter 4, Article 35, Section 1, it has legal effect. In view of this, until such time as the provincial people's government proclaims in writing the revocation and annulment of the original documents and issues a new document, effluent fees should still be assessed according to the above-mentioned document. Third, since the Environmental Protection Law was adopted and issued by the National People's Congress, only the National People's Congress and its Standing Committee have the authority to amend or interpret it. No person or other body has the authority to alter national law. Instructions by higher-level leading comrades and suggestions by responsible supervisory organs are correct only if they assist the implementation of the law, but they cannot undermine the law. This is explicitly indicated in the Party Central Committee's September 9, 1979, Document 64. The Zhuzhou Chemical Plant may not follow the instructions of higher-level leading comrades or suggestions by responsible organizations not to pay effluent fees. Fourth, Article 18 of the Environmental Protection Law provides: "Effluent fees shall be assessed according to the amount and concentration of pollutants as stipulated by regulations on enterprises that discard more pollutants than the state standards permit." State standards to assess effluent fees represent an effective economic measure to promote control of the environment. The Zhuzhou Chemical Plant discharged great quantities of toxic gas and matter in the course of production, and some by far exceeded state standards, causing great harm to the people's health and crops. Conscientious implementation of the Environmental Protection Law and vigorous adoption of pollution control measures will eliminate the social effects of pollution and benefit the people. Numerous incorrect arguments as pretexts for not implementing the Environmental Protection Law as an excuse for not paying effluent fees are far off base. Abundant evidence of indifference to the law should cause judicial organs to instruct the assessment of past-due effluent fees in accordance with the law.

After the hearing and arguments the facts were clear, right and wrong were distinguished, and the court sustained the plaintiff unit's request. The defendant Zhuzhou Chemical Plant realized that justice was not on its side and agreed to pay the effluent fees. With the court mediating, the two sides successfully reached an agreement. The Zhuzhou Chemical Plant was to pay within five days all effluent fees in arrears. The plaintiff unit Zhuzhou Municipal Environmental Protection Office, according to relevant provisions, was to return to the factory seventy percent of the fees specifically for the purpose of controlling environmental pollution.

After winding up the case the *Zhuzhou Daily* published the result of the case on the front page, and the provincial radio station broadcasted the news. Related municipal departments and some industrial enterprises reported that the Economic Court of the Zhuzhou Municipal Intermediate People's Court had tried the case and upheld the law and had given expression to legal authority. They praised this as "a song for victory in defense of the legal system."

Comments

This is one of the earliest accounts we have regarding the assessment of effluent fees. Clearly a great deal of resistance was encountered when polluters were suddenly forced to pay for the costs of their pollution. In this case the court, evidently with the backing of the Hunan Provincial Commission on Capital Construction, upheld the legal authority of environmental protection departments to assess fees. The case also reveals how budgetary considerations influence policy. The industrial bureaucracies and financial departments were, for at least several years, reluctant to increase expenditures for environmental protection unless the government appropriated additional funds for this purpose. This left individual enterprises in a bind because they lacked funds for pollution control, which had suddenly become a priority item. Effluent fees are a way to pry money out of the industrial bureaucracies to fund pollution control in their subordinate enterprises, since up to 80 percent of the fees may subsequently be remitted to the enterprises for earmarked purposes. In this way fees may benefit subordinate enterprises as well as environmental protection; however, the ongoing urban reforms may weaken this coalition as enterprises become more autonomous in an economic sense.

Sun Xiangming (1984) "Is This 'An Incident of Counterrevolutionary Destruction'?"

H, no. 10, pp. 24–25.

Zhaoqiushui Brigade, Dalian Commune, in Shahe County, Hebei, adjoined the Shahe County Phosphate Fertilizer Factory. The phosphate fertilizer factory, from the time it went into operation in the spring of 1973, in the course of production discharged great quantities of vulcanized hydrogen, oxidized phosphates, and other toxic and pernicious gases, as well as toxic liquid wastes because of the lack of control technology for handling the "three wastes." This caused serious pollution of farmland. Two hundred mu [15 mu = 1 hectare] of fall crops could not be harvested, 300 mu suffered a seventy percent or greater reduction in output, and other members of the masses suffered different degrees of production decline. Moreover, this greatly endangered human health. The Zhaoqiushui Brigade on many occasions sent people to the factory, the commune, and the county to report damage from the situation, but all complaints were rejected.

There was widespread public indignation and ideological confusion among commune members with respect to this situation. On the evening of August 4, 1973, the peasant masses gathered at the brigade gate, demanding that the brigade take steps to control the situation. The brigade cadre reported many times to upper levels but to no avail. In response to the masses' strong and unanimous demand, and having no other recourse, late that same day someone was sent to pull the phosphate fertilizer factory's electricity switch in an expression of protest.

After this a special group established by the county committee to investigate the case denounced the act as "an incident of counterrevolutionary destruction" and immediately confiscated all of the brigade militia company's weapons. Branch [party] secretary Liu Yuhe and deputy branch [party] secretary Zhang Yunshu were arrested and expelled from the party. They were paraded through the streets of the entire county for seven days and were sentenced to three years' and seven years' imprisonment, respectively.

This decision of the Shahe County Committee met with great popular dissent. The Zhaoqiushui Brigade thought: "This event is a contradiction which occurs in production between industry and agriculture, it is a problem of industrial-agricultural relations, it is a contradiction among the people." For several years afterward appeals were raised many times requesting redress of this unjust case.

On February 3, 1979, the State Council Environmental Protection Leading Group sent a letter to the Hebei Provincial Environmental Protection Office asking for prompt handling of the Zhaoqiushui Brigade case problem:

> Regarding the Shahe County, Dalian Commune, Zhaoqiushui Brigade management committee's appeal of the decision on the 1973 shut off of electricity to the phosphate fertilizer factory owing to a failure to resolve the problem of pollution being designated "an incident of counterrevolutionary destruction": if this proves to be valid, the original disposition [of this case] was inappropriate, and should be redressed. From now on, when the appeal documents are transmitted to you, please conduct a new investigation jointly with other concerned provincial departments to learn the circumstances and reach the proper decision, and definitely inform us of results in the future by letter.

In accordance with the State Council's suggestion, the Hebei Provincial Environmental Protection Office, with the support of the Hebei Provincial Party Committee leadership, jointly formed an investigative group with the Hebei Provincial Court, Xingtai Prefectural Environmental Administrative Office and Court, and Shahe County Court. After the investigation they maintained that the facts of the case should be corrected and unanimously affirmed that the case was not "an incident of counterrevolutionary destruction" and that the judgments and punishment against the two comrades, Liu Yuhe and Zhang Yunshu, were inappropriate. They decided that the two comrades would be rehabilitated. They convened a mass meeting to publicly proclaim them not guilty and restored their party membership. In view of the fact that, while serving their sentences, Liu and Zhang both assigned their workpoint subsidies to the production team, the committee awarded Zhang 300 yuan and Liu 100 yuan as hardship allowances. At the same time the committee also pointed out that Liu and Zhang's shut off of the electricity to stop production at the factory was wrong.

It took six years for the unjust case of "an incident of counterrevolutionary destruction" finally to be redressed.

LEGAL ANALYSIS

Liu Yuhe and Zhang Yunshu in this case were convicted of the crime of counterrevolutionary destruction, separately sentenced to severe punishment, and paraded through the entire county. This is extremely shocking.

Article 10 of the People's Republic of China Act on the Punishment of Counterrevolution stipulates:

> Those who, with a counterrevolutionary purpose, commit any one of the following acts of provocation or incitement shall be punished by not less than three years of imprisonment; where the circumstances of their cases are major they shall be punished by death or life imprisonment:
>
> 1. Stirring up the masses to resist or to undermine the enforcement of grain levies, tax levies, public service, military service of the people's government, or other government orders;

2. Provoking dissension among the various nationalities, democratic classes, democratic parties and groups, people's organizations or between the people and the government;
3. Conducting counterrevolutionary propaganda and agitation and making and spreading rumors.

This provision is quite explicit and in the 1950s was widely publicized and known to all. Even during the ten-year period of great calamity [the Cultural Revolution], this regulation never was abolished or lost effectiveness.

Under ordinary circumstances, how does one determine whether people's conduct has a counterrevolutionary purpose? For example: a plot to subvert the government, betray the motherland, to organize, lead, or closely participate in a counterrevolutionary clique and other offenses, all indicate harboring of counterrevolutionary purpose. However, murder, bombing, arson, breaching dykes, cutting off electricity, and other offenses can stem from both counterrevolutionary purposes and other criminal purposes. This, then, demands careful analysis of people's actions in carrying out crimes, to find from people's behavior the individual experience, motives, consistent expressions, customary methods, particular environments, and specific circumstances to make a comprehensive judgment accurately determining criminal character. The accused must exhibit subjective counterrevolutionary purpose and objective counterrevolutionary behavior to be found guilty of a counterrevolutionary offense. The two are mutually integrated and closely related as a whole.

The original disposition of this case was erroneous. First, the two persons in the case, Liu and Zhang, were brigade party secretary and deputy secretary and, under normal circumstances, definitely did not harbor counterrevolutionary intentions. However, after the factory's discharge of waste and pollution caused the brigade's land to suffer damages, people were sent many times to the factory, commune, and county to make a report on the situation and ask higher authorities to resolve [this matter] promptly. This in itself is definitely not a counterrevolutionary plot motive. Second, after making many reports but to no avail, the masses reached the limits of their endurance. The brigade cadre mediated but to no avail and, under the masses' strong demand to protect the conditions of the people's livelihood, only then sent someone to pull the factory's electric switch, with the purpose of expressing protest. However, the investigative group organized by the Shahe County Committee, in the end, took a bureaucratic attitude toward the [incident] and took too drastic an action. By regarding it as "counterrevolutionary destruction" in deciding punishment, both the punishment and parading of the accused were completely without legal basis. We insist that for every issue we should try to reach a resolution according to the law. Of course, cutting off electricity to cause a halt of production is wrong, but how should this kind of "people's rebellion" be properly handled? Should we painstakingly investigate and handle cases according to the law? Or should we frequently and indiscriminately label people and randomly come down with a big stick, not distinguish between black and white, and render reckless judgments?

When a person is imprisoned not only one household is stricken, but a brigade meets with injustice as well. This is really something for people to ponder.

As for this unjust case, after the collapse of the Gang of Four, the party and the government decreed rehabilitation for wrongly misjudged cases. This should reasonably summon local legal departments to pay serious attention to these cases. However, it was delayed until after a February 1979 national directive, when an investigation was conducted to handle [the matter]. This was a serious dereliction of duty and means that the people principally responsible for the original investigation of this case also committed a crime which violates and scorns national law.

Comments

This case is symptomatic of the changes that have taken place in the post-Mao era regarding environmental protection. Whereas in earlier years the victims of pollution, like Zhaoqiushui brigade, typically found that their complaints fell on deaf ears, and that any direct action subsequently taken in desperation would leave them vulnerable to dire consequences, in the post-Mao era there is much greater concern for the environment. Citizens' protests are more likely to be heeded, and direct action may even be excused. This was particularly true in this case, where Liu and Zhang were considered victims of leftist misrule and subject to exoneration and rehabilitation on that basis alone. However, intervention by higher levels of authority was needed to overcome the objections to a reevaluation of the case imposed by the county officials, some of whom were assuredly implicated in the original miscarriage of justice.

"Environmental Protection and Economic Construction Must Develop in Tandem" (1984)

Renmin Ribao (May 31), p. 2.

Deputy to the National People's Congress and Zhejiang Provincial Environmental Protection Bureau Senior Engineer Wu Hongmei declared that "environmental protection and economic construction must develop in tandem."

Wu Hongmei stated that urban reform will certainly bring with it great economic growth, but under no circumstances can it cause pollution and still bring "great development." We should recognize that this issue still has not been taken seriously enough by every side. At present, the water pollution situation is extremely grave. It can be said that practically all rivers in urban areas are filthy and foul-smelling. Air pollution has also become progressively more serious, and acid rain is appearing in many areas of our country. In the wake of the vigorous development of energy resources, if strong measures regarding air pollution are not taken soon, acid rain will become even more formidable.

To destroy the environment is easy, but to restore it is not a task which can be accomplished overnight. Now, the Party Central Committee has already made environmental protection a basic national policy and has formulated the Environmental Protection Law. This is definitely on target. However, because a few leading departments do not implement the law, the government's environmental protection departments often encounter resistance and get nowhere when they exercise governmental authority. For example, the Jiaojiang Municipal Fireproofing Materials Factory, which produces asphalt bricks, emitted harmful odors in large volumes. The people who lived near the factory could not put up with the odors and informed the county environmental protection department. The environmental protection department handled things according to the law and ordered the factory to halt production. But the county [party] committee supported the factory, and the factory resumed production in the same manner as before. The situation is similar in the area of assessing effluent fees, where the fees are collected subject to the permission of the financial departments. Huzhou municipality has twenty factories which should annually pay effluent fees totaling hundreds of thousands of yuan. The municipal (party) committee members did not approve, fearing an adverse impact on municipal finances, and finally, the municipal committee reduced the fees to only 30,000 yuan every year. The leaders thwarted this, making the agency's work difficult to manage.

Wu Hongmei said that if we do not pay close attention to environmental protection work, at the end of this century the state of affairs regarding our country's environmental pollution and ecological destruction may resemble today's population problem, becoming difficult problems to solve.

Comments

Deputy Wu's plaint is a familiar one. Local authorities often fail to give sufficient weight to environmental protection because of the higher priority they attach to economic performance, budgetary concerns, and ignorance about the possible consequences of environmental degradation.

Environmental problems are also becoming more severe as the pace of economic development outraces control measures, particularly in such an economically dynamic province as Zhejiang. Jiaojiang, along the East China sea coast, and Huzhou, near Lake Tai, are in economic growth zones. Wu's ability to get press coverage is evidence of political support for his position, but it is not always easy to implement that concern. In Zhejiang itself an even more prominent case involving the location of a factory in a watershed conservation area in Wenzhou municipality, in violation of established procedures regarding water pollution control and the "three simultaneous points," received considerable press attention in 1985. See *Renmin Ribao* (People's Daily), July 19, 1985.

Notes to Part Four

1. Kaida's formal name is Hoithe (HK), Ltd., based on transliteration from the Cantonese [eds.].
2. The bureau's official name is China Merchant's Development Corporation, Ltd., under the Bureau of Communications [eds.].
3. *Supra*, note 1 [eds.].
4. *Supra*, note 2 [eds.].

Part Six
Appendixes

Appendix A

Environmental Protection Law of the People's Republic of China (for trial implementation) (September 13, 1979)

Translation, with permission, from *The Bad Earth* by Vaclav Smil, New York: M. E. Sharpe, Inc., 1984, pp. 231–38.

CHAPTER I. GENERAL PRINCIPLES

Article 1. This law is formulated pursuant to Article 11 of the Constitution of the People's Republic of China, which stipulates that "the state protects the environment and natural resources and prevents and eliminates pollution and other hazards to the public."

Article 2. The Law on Environmental Protection of the People's Republic of China undertakes to rationally utilize the natural environment and control and prevent pollution and damage to the ecology so as to create a clean and salubrious environment for people's life and work, protect people's health, and promote economic growth in the interest of socialist modernization.

Article 3. The term environment used in this law encompasses the air, water, land, mineral resources, forests, grasslands, wild plants and animals, aquatic life, places of historical interest, scenic spots, hot springs, resorts, and natural areas under special protection, as well as inhabited parts of the country.

Article 4. The work concerning environmental protection shall be done in accordance with the principles of overall planning, rational arrangement, multipurpose utilization, changing harmful things into beneficial ones, relying on the masses, and engaging everybody in protecting the environment and benefiting the people.

Article 5. The State Council and its subordinate departments as well as local peoples' governments at all levels must effectively protect the environment. While formulating national economic development plans, overall arrangements for environmental protection and improvement shall be made, and such protection and improvements shall be carried out conscientiously and in an organized manner. Necessary plans must be worked out to cope with any existing environmental pollution and other hazards to the public so as to eliminate them in a planned and gradual way.

Article 6. In selecting construction sites, making designs, carrying out construction projects, and embarking on production, all enterprises and other undertakings shall pay adequate attention to preventing environmental pollution and damage. While carrying out new construction or renovation projects, an environmental impact report shall be submitted first, and design work can be started only after such a report has been reviewed and approved by the department concerned. Facilities for preventing pollution and other hazards to the public must be designed, built, and put into operation simultaneously with the principal project. The discharge of all harmful materials shall be carried out in accordance with the standards prescribed by the state.

Those units that have already caused environmental pollution or other hazards to the public shall work out plans and bring them under effective control in accordance with the principle that whoever has caused the pollution must bring it under control, or they shall obtain necessary approval from the competent authorities for a change in the type of operation or seek relocation.

Article 7. In renovating old urban areas and building new towns, an appraisal of the possible impact on the environment of the industrial zone, residential area, public utilities, and green area shall be made on the basis of meteorological, geographical, hydrological, and ecological conditions. Overall plans shall be made to prevent pollution and other hazards to the public so as to build modern and clean cities.

Article 8. All citizens have the right to supervise, inform against, and accuse any departments or individuals of causing environmental pollution and damage; the said departments and individuals shall not resort to any retaliation.

Article 9. All foreign nationals and foreign aircraft, vessels, vehicles, materials, and living beings entering or transiting the territorial land, waters, and airspace of China must observe this law as well as other regulations and rules for environmental protection.

CHAPTER II. PROTECTION OF THE NATURAL ENVIRONMENT

Article 10. Land must be used rationally according to local conditions, soil improved and conserved, vegetation increased, soil erosion prevented, and land kept from hardening, salinizing, and becoming sandy waste.

To reclaim wasteland, to reclaim land for lakes or seas by building dikes, or to build large or medium-sized water conservancy projects, comprehensive scientific research must be conducted in advance, and effective measures of environmental protection and improvement must be taken to prevent damage to the ecosystem.

Article 11. The waters of rivers, lakes, seas, and reservoirs must be protected and a good quality of water maintained.

Aquatic life must be protected, developed, and rationally utilized, and destructive fishing and damage must be prohibited.

Water for industrial, agricultural, and daily use must be strictly controlled and economized, groundwater rationally exploited, and the drying up of water sources and surface subsidence prevented.

Article 12. In exploring mineral resources, comprehensive prospecting, evaluation, and utilization must be carried out, indiscriminate mining strictly prohibited, tailings and slag properly disposed of, and damage to resources and deterioration of the natural environment prevented.

Article 13. The state Forestry Law must be strictly observed, forest reserves protected and developed, forests rationally opened to use and properly tended and reforested; reclamation of wasteland by destroying forests as well as denudation must be strictly prohibited and forest fires prevented.

Afforestation must be vigorously promoted, with waste hills, wasteland, deserts, villages, towns, cities, and mining and industrial areas afforested.

Wherever possible, trees and grass must be planted on odd lots near plants, mining areas, schools, government offices, villages, roads, homes, and waters so as to turn the land into gardenlike fields.

Article 14. Forage resources must be protected and developed. Grassland building must be actively planned and carried out, grazing rationally carried out, the regenerative capacity of grasslands maintained and improved, the degeneration of grasslands prevented, the indiscriminate reclamation of land from grasslands strictly prohibited, and prairie fires prevented.

Article 15. Wild plants and animals must be protected, developed, and rationally utilized. Hunting and catching of valuable and rare wild animals as well as picking of valuable and rare wild plants must be strictly prohibited in accordance with the state regulations.

CHAPTER III. PREVENTION AND CONTROL OF POLLUTION AND OTHER HAZARDS TO THE PUBLIC

Article 16. Effective measures must be taken to prevent and control pollution and damage to the environment caused by waste gas, wastewater, slag, dust, sewage, radioactive material, and other harmful matter, as well as pollution from noise, vibration, and toxic odors emitted from mining and industrial enterprises and found in urban life.

Article 17. No enterprise or institution that may pollute the environment may be built near living quarters in cities and towns or beside protected areas of water, places of historical interest, scenic spots, hot springs, resorts, or natural areas under protection. As for those already existing, measures should be taken to control their pollution, to readjust them, or to remove them to other sites in a given period.

Article 18. New technology and methods of processing as well as new products that will eliminate or reduce pollution should be actively tested and adopted.

Enterprise management must be strengthened, production carried out in a civilized manner, and multipurpose utilization of waste gas, wastewater, and slag that may pollute the environment carried out so as to turn harm into benefit. Those enterprises that must discharge waste gas, wastewater, and slag must attain standards fixed by the state; those enterprises that do not meet state standards in this regard must take measures to control the pollution within a given period; and those that fail to reduce their pollution to state standards within the given period must limit the scope of their production.

Effluent fees shall be assessed according to the amount and concentration of pollutants as stipulated by regulations on enterprises that discard more pollutants than the state standards permit.

Article 19. Effective measures must be taken to eliminate smoke and dust from all smoke-emitting equipment, industrial kilns and furnaces, motor-driven vehicles, and boats and ships. Harmful gas should be reduced to standards fixed by the state.

Nonpolluting or low-polluting energy sources, such as coal gas, liquefied petroleum gas, natural gas, marsh gas, solar energy, and geothermal heat, should be vigorously developed and utilized. District heating supply systems should be actively promoted in cities.

Article 20. No rubbish or slag should be discarded into rivers, lakes, or seas. The discharge of wastewater should meet the standards fixed by the state.

Boats and ships must be prohibited from discharging materials containing oil or toxic substances as well as other harmful wastes into waters protected by state regulations.

Discharging of harmful or toxic wastewater through seepage pits or crevices as well as by solvent action or dilution should be strictly prohibited. Seepage of industrial wastewater should be prevented so as to ensure that groundwater is not polluted.

The sources of drinking water should be rigorously protected, and sewage as well as water-purifying facilities in cities should be improved step by step.

Article 21. Insecticides having high efficiency with low poisonous effects and low residual toxicity should be actively developed. Multipurpose controls and biological controls should be promoted, sewage irrigation rationally utilized, and pollution of soil and crops prevented.

Article 22. Control of industrial noise and vibration in cities should be strengthened. All machines, motor-driven vehicles, and airplanes that cause enormous noise and vibration should be equipped with silencers and vibration-proof devices.

Article 23. Airtight production equipment and methods of processing should be actively adopted at all units that cause harmful gas and dust to spread, and devices for ventilation, dust collection, air purification, and reclamation should be installed. The amount of harmful gas and dust in working areas should meet standards fixed by state regulations concerning industrial sanitation.

Article 24. Poisonous materials should be strictly registered and controlled. Leakage in the course of storage and transport should be prevented.

Radioactive materials as well as electromagnetic radiation should be strictly guarded and controlled in accordance with relevant regulations of the state.

Article 25. Pollution of foods in the course of production, processing, packing, transporting, storing, and selling should be strictly prevented. Examination should be strengthened, and those foods that do not meet the sanitary standards of the state should be strictly prohibited from being sold, exported, or imported.

CHAPTER IV. ENVIRONMENTAL PROTECTION ORGANIZATIONS AND THEIR RESPONSIBILITIES

Article 26. The State Council shall set up an environmental protection organization, and its main responsibilities are as follows:

A. Implement the principles, policies, laws, and decrees of the state governing environmental protection and supervise their enforcement;

B. Draft rules, regulations, standards, and economic and technical policies on environmental protection in coordination with the departments concerned;

C. Formulate long-term and annual plans for environmental protection in coordination with the departments concerned and supervise their implementation;

D. Organize unified monitoring and surveying of the environment, have a good grasp of environmental conditions and their developing trends throughout the country, and set forth measures for their improvement;

E. Organize and coordinate scientific research on the environment and the conduct of education in this regard in coordination with the departments concerned and actively popularize advanced experience and technology acquired at home and abroad in environmental protection;

F. Direct the environmental protection work of various departments under the State Council and of all provinces, autonomous regions, and municipalities directly under the central government; and

G. Organize and coordinate international cooperation and exchanges in environmental protection.

Article 27. The people's governments of all provinces, autonomus regions, and municipalities directly under the central government shall set up environmental protection bureaus. The people's governments of [other] municipalities, autonomous prefectures, counties, and autonomous counties shall set up environmental protection organizations according to their needs.

The main responsibilities of local environmental protection organizations are to check and supervise the implementation by various departments and units in the areas under their jurisdiction of the state principles, policies, laws, and decrees governing environmental protection; draft standards and rules for local environmental protection; organize monitoring and surveying of the environment; have a good understanding of environmental conditions and their developing trends in their areas; formulate long-term and annual plans for environmental protection in coordination with the departments concerned in their areas and supervise their implementation; organize scientific research on the environment and the conduct of education in this regard; and actively popularize advanced experience and technology acquired at home and abroad.

Article 28. The departments concerned of the State Council and of various local people's governments, big and medium-sized enterprises, and the institutions concerned shall set up environmental protection organizations according to their needs and shall be respectively responsible for environmental protection in their own systems, departments, or units.

CHAPTER V. SCIENTIFIC RESEARCH, PROPAGANDA, AND EDUCATION

Article 29. The Chinese Research Academy of Environmental Sciences, the scientific research organizations concerned, and institutions of higher learning should vigorously engage in research on the basic theories of environmental science, environmental management, environmental economics, comprehensive technology for environmental control, assessment of environmental quality, environmental pollution and man's health, rational use and protection of the natural environment, and other questions.

Article 30. Culture and propaganda departments should actively disseminate and conduct education in the knowledge of environmental science in order to raise the understanding and scientific and technological level of the broad masses in environmental protection.

Specialized personnel in environmental protection should be trained in a planned way. Education departments should open required courses or special studies on environmental protection in institutions of higher learning and write adequate information on environmental protection into textbooks for primary and middle schools.

CHAPTER VI. REWARDS AND PUNISHMENTS

Article 31. The state shall commend and reward units and individuals who have made noticeable achievements and contributions in environmental protection.

The state shall reduce or eliminate taxes or give pricing consideration for products of enterprises that use waste gases, liquids and solids as their main raw materials; and the profits of these enterprises shall not be turned over to higher authorities and shall be used for pollution control and environmental improvement.

Article 32. As for units that pollute and harm the environment and endanger people's health in violation of this law and other rules and regulations governing environmental protection, environmental protection organizations at various levels, with the approval of the corresponding people's governments, shall criticize, give warnings to, or assess fines on those units or order them to compensate for losses or stop production to bring pollution under control according to their individual cases.

The leaders of units, those directly responsible, or other citizens who pollute and harm the environment so seriously as to cause people's deaths and injuries or heavy losses in agriculture, forestry, animal husbandry, sideline production, or fishery should be investigated for their administrative, economic, or even criminal responsibility.

CHAPTER VII. SUPPLEMENTARY ARTICLE

Article 33. The State Council may formulate rules and regulations governing environmental protection in accordance with this law.

Appendix B

Chapter 35 of the Sixth Five-Year Plan (1982) and Chapter 52 of the Seventh Five-Year Plan (1986)

The Sixth Five-Year Plan of the People's Republic of China for Economic and Social Development (1981–1985), Beijing, Foreign Languages Press, 1984; *The Seventh Five-Year Plan of the People's Republic of China for Economic and Social Development (1986–1990)*, Beijing, Renmin Chubanshe, 1986.

CHAPTER 35. ENVIRONMENTAL PROTECTION

One major task of socialist modernization is to take care of our environment, exploit and utilize our natural resources in a rational way, and preserve a fine ecological environment. During the period of the Sixth Five-Year Plan the basic goals of environmental protection are to check the destruction of the natural environment, prevent the development of new pollution, energetically control the continued deterioration of the ecological environment, solve with a firm hand the problem of serious contamination, continue to improve the environments of a number of key cities with scenic spots for tourism, such as Beijing, Hangzhou, Suzhou, and Guilin.

1. We shall resolutely curb the destruction of the ecological environment and natural resources. We shall utilize land, water, and other natural resources in a rational way and prevent water loss and soil erosion and good land from being turned into sand deserts. In exploiting mineral deposits and developing forest resources, we must see that these resources and the environment are not damaged. All enterprises and undertakings, in selecting sites and designs, in construction and production, must strictly prevent the contamination and destruction of the environment. All newly built engineering projects, or those being expanded, as well as projects under major technical transformation, must submit a report on their effects on the environment and shall go ahead with the design only after examination and approval by the departments in charge of environmental protection and other relevant departments.

2. Pollution control devices must be included in the design of all new engineering projects, constructed simultaneously with the construction of the main project in accordance with the provisions of the State Council, and commissioned simultaneously with the main project. The disposal of harmful substances must be carried out according to the standards set by the state to avoid and eliminate new sources of pollution.

3. We shall harness pollution by the old enterprises by stages and in groups and work hard to raise our capacity to handle wastewater, waste gas, and industrial residue and

the level of comprehensive utilization of resources. Wastewater from factories and mines containing mercury, chromium, cadmium, phenol, or cyanide must be handled inside the factories, and if it is to be discharged into rivers, lakes, and seas, the levels of these poisons must not be higher than that allowed by the state. In some enterprises pollution is rather serious, such as the metallurgical, chemical, petroleum, transport, building materials, light, textile, coal, electric power, machine building, arms and nuclear industries. A number of large and medium-sized enterprises of these industries are expected to utilize energy resources and raw and other materials more rationally, so that the discharge of the wastewater, waste gas, and industrial residue and the noise in the factory zone are brought under control in accordance with state regulations and that the factory zone and production will meet the needs of a clean and healthy environment.

4. We shall check the deterioration of water quality at the Changjiang ferries, at its Chongqing, Wuhan, Nanjing, and Shanghai sectors, at Huanghe's Lanzhou, Loyang, and Jinan sectors, in areas of the Bohai, the Huanghai, the Songhuajiang, and the Huaihe, and in main harbors and gulfs. We shall protect the main sources of drinking water in various cities and the water quality of the Lijiang, the Dianchi Lake, the West Lake, and the Taihu Lake in the scenic and tourist spots.

5. We shall, through more rigid control of the environment and pollution, strive to effect in three to five years a marked improvement in the environment in famous cities with scenic spots for tourism, such as Beijing, Suzhou, Hangzhou, and Guilin. All provinces, municipalities, and autonomous regions should emphasize the work of improving environmental conditions and environmental protection in one or two cities within their jurisdiction and solve any serious problems of environmental pollution there.

6. We shall carry out regional planning for improving the natural environment and make rational arrangements for the proportionate relations between the exploitation and utilization of natural resources on the one hand and the protection and regeneration of these resources on the other. Within the [next] five years, ten natural nonforest areas will be added to the eighty-five that are currently under government protection.

The main measures for bringing about the above plans are:

1. To give sounder guidance to the planning of environmental protection and set up reasonable channels from which funds for this purpose can be drawn. All enterprises and undertakings as well as the departments in charge should set up specific environmental protection goals and targets in inspection work in this field as required by the state plan and make such arrangements in their annual plans–the work so arranged should be organized and carried out in a down-to-earth manner. Departments in charge of environmental protection shall intensify their supervision and checkup. Investments in installations for preventing pollution in capital construction projects as well as funds for antipollution measures in enterprises undergoing technical transformation should be included in the plans. Profits from the comprehensive utilization of the wastewater, waste gas, and industrial residue should be reserved according to state regulations for these enterprises to further pollution control. The fee for eliminating pollutants thus collected should be used specifically for tackling pollution and must not be appropriated for other purposes.

2. The various departments in charge shall draw up a general plan to combine the restructuring and reorganizing of enterprises, and their technical transformation with pollution control. In selecting schemes for the restructuring of enterprises and their technical transformation, we should take into consideration the best environmental results. Factories whose production technology is backward, which produce pollution with dam-

aging effects that are hard to eliminate, should shift to the manufacture of other products, amalgamate with others, or move to other places in a planned way. In doing this, shifting pollutants such as waste gas, wastewater, and industrial residue to the countryside is strictly prohibited. Simultaneous with notifying industrial and mining enterprises of their production targets, the departments concerned should also notify them of the requirements and targets for environmental protection and there shall be strict inspections to see if these targets and requirements are fulfilled. Industrial enterprises and departments in charge of these enterprises must act in accordance with the principle of "the polluter must control his own pollution" and take up the responsibility of pollution control.

3. We shall have unified planning and tackle the problem in a comprehensive way. We shall take engineering, biological, physical, and other technical measures as well as administrative, legislative, and economic measures and combine the exploitation and utilization of resources with measures to protect, cultivate, and transform these resources, paying special attention to gradually bringing about permanent and continued utilization of renewable resources. At the same time we shall extensively promote the comprehensive utilization of resources and their utilization through recycling to gradually make wastewater, waste gas, and industrial residue an industrial resource, thereby avoiding the waste of resources and destruction of the environment.

4. We shall intensify monitoring of the environment and research work on this subject. We shall work more attentively for the construction of environmental monitoring stations at different levels and strive to equip as quickly as possible the national station of environmental monitoring and sixty-four key stations in order to build up the operational capacity. During the period of the Sixth Five-Year Plan, we shall basically set up the Chinese Research Academy of Environmental Sciences and equip a number of key local research institutes. We shall further strengthen the leadership of research work in environmental protection and make necessary readjustments of existing environmental research institutions at the provincial and municipal levels and work out a division of labor among them. We shall bring into full play the role of the Chinese Academy of Sciences, institutes of higher learning, and the various departments doing research in environmental science. Knowledge of environmental science shall be popularized in primary and middle schools. The various specialties of science, engineering, agriculture, medicine, economics, and law in universities and technical secondary schools shall offer courses on environmental protection.

5. We shall prepare laws on environmental protection and enforce them. Departments of environmental protection at all levels shall, together with the various other departments concerned, constantly check on the implementation of the laws and regulations on environmental protection and conduct timely summaries of work. They also shall issue circulars discussing experiences in this field and the existing problems and circulars commending advanced units and criticizing backward ones. They shall also penalize offenders. At the same time we shall seriously supervise and check up on the work to prevent atmospheric pollution, water pollution, and noise pollution as well as the work of marine environmental protection and the work in nature preserves.

CHAPTER 52. ENVIRONMENTAL PROTECTION

Section 1. Basic Tasks

1. Prevent and control industrial pollution. All existing enterprises must strive to raise their ability to control the "three wastes" and their comprehensive utilization of resources

rate. Within five years we must strive to reduce the aggregate volume of pollutant emissions for mercury, cadmium, lead, arsenic, hexavalent chromium, cyanogens, and radioactive substances by 5 to 10 percent. By 1990 we shall have 50 to 70 percent of major pollutants attain their stipulated state emissions standards; the utilization [recycling] rate for steel slag, coal mine tailings, and powdered coal dust shall reach 50, 30, and 22 percent respectively; and the fly ash removal efficiency for the various kinds of thermal power plants shall reach levels of 90 percent or higher. All enterprises included in the state's keypoint [technological] renovation plan shall have their pollution control measures attain stipulated state standards upon the completion of renovation.

2. Protect water quality in rivers, lakes, reservoirs, and seas. Strive to make water quality in segments of rivers and large-scale water diversion channels in urban watersheds, as well as reservoirs and lakes, attain secondary state standards. Water quality in the Dukou, Chongqing, Wuhan, Nanjing, and Shanghai segments of the Yangtze River, the Lanzhou and Baotou segments of the Yellow River, the Jilin and Harbin segments of the Songhua River, and the Guangzhou segment of the Pearl [Zhujiang] River must show relatively noticeable improvement. Water quality in primary, secondary, and tertiary marine zones in coastal seas must attain stipulated state standards in accordance with their respective schedules and categories.

3. Protect the environment in keypoint cities. With regard to total suspended particulates in the urban atmosphere, the north shall basically attain tertiary standards while the south shall attain secondary standards. With regard to the recycling rate for water in use by industry, northern cities shall reach the 60 percent level and southern cities the 40 percent level. Water quality in drinking water sources shall attain secondary state standards. Noise levels in principal transportation arteries shall not exceed 70 decibels.

4. Protect the rural environment. Rural enterprises lacking the means to control the "three wastes" may not engage in production that pollutes the environment.

5. Protect and improve the ecological environment. Subject to financial and material capacity, increase the number of nature preserves and gradually create a complete and multifaceted national network of rationally distributed nature preserves, and gradually create a group of breeding areas and gene banks for endangered species. Simultaneously establish experimental points for ecological agriculture that are representative of different natural conditions.

Section 2. Principal Measures

1. Continue to enforce the principle of whoever has caused the pollution must bring it under control. The technological renovation, reconstruction, and expansion of existing enterprises must include pollution control as an important item. New construction projects must work toward the simultaneous design, construction, and start of operations for pollution control measures and the principal construction items.

2. Implement the policies of "putting prevention first, integrating prevention and control, and controlling pollution in a comprehensive way," encourage the comprehensive utilization of resources, eliminate heavily polluting goods within a specified time frame, and resolutely prevent the migration of pollution from cities to the villages and from large- and medium-scale enterprises to small-scale enterprises. Large-scale water conservancy, railroad, highway, port, and mining construction projects, and regional developments must carry out environmental impact assessments in advance and can only be built after they correspond to requirements.

3. Build and equip a state environmental monitoring network on the foundation of

existing keypoint monitoring stations; cities of various kinds also must basically build environmental monitoring networks. Unify monitoring methods, improve monitoring procedures, and raise the caliber of monitoring.

4. Gradually build and fortify environmental management organs and scientific research organs at various levels, further improve environmental laws, regulations, and standards, complete the information network, and strengthen statistical work. At the same time strengthen educational work in environmental protection in a big way, accelerate the training of personnel, and organize well scientific research and the tackling of difficult problems.

5. The state stipulates that the various funds earmarked for environmental protection must be guaranteed and used for their designated purposes and may not be diverted for other uses.

Appendix C

State Council Decision on Strengthening Environmental Protection Work in the Period of National Economic Readjustment (February 24, 1981)

BFWH, pp. 51–58.

The environment and natural resources are the building blocks for human life and provide the material for expanding production and making the economy prosperous. Proper management of our country's environment and the rational exploitation and utilization of our natural resources is a fundamental requirement for constructing a modernized country. For a long time, due to a lack of understanding of environmental issues and mistakes made in economic work, an imbalance arose between economic activity and environmental protection. Environmental pollution and damage to natural resources and the ecological balance in our country has now become a serious issue in national economic development for it affects people's lives and impedes production and construction. We must fully appreciate that protecting the environment is in the basic interest of all our people. During the period of national economic readjustment, in accordance with the Central Committee's important policies on further readjusting the economy and stabilizing the political situation, we must sum up various policies and measures on economic readjustment, earnestly carry out the Environmental Protection Law of the People's Republic of China (for trial implementation), and actively use all means to firmly grasp and do a good job on this work. For this purpose the following decisions are stipulated.

STRICTLY PROHIBIT THE DEVELOPMENT OF NEW SOURCES OF POLLUTION

During the process of contracting the scale of capital construction, capital construction departments and environmental protection departments must earnestly review ongoing construction projects. We should be resolute in terminating all projects that are irrationally distributed and very wasteful of resources and energy and that will cause grave pollution of the environment that cannot be effectively mitigated.

All new construction, renovation, and expansion projects must strictly implement the provision that ''[f]acilities for preventing pollution and other hazards to the public must be designed, and put into operation simultaneously with the principal project'' stipulated in the Environmental Protection Law of the People's Republic of China (for trial implementation). All newly planned large and medium-scale construction projects must submit an environmental impact report before the start of construction and not fix site selection or start construction until after the assessment has been submitted to and approved by the environmental protection department; otherwise, they will not be incorporated in the plan and no appropriation or loan will be provided. Any construction project that is incorporated in the state plan must ensure the inclusion of investment, equipment, materials, and personnel for environmental protection facilities; omission of these items is prohibited. No otherwise-complete construction project whose environmental protection facilities have not yet been completed can be approved and begin production; responsibility must be investigated in all cases where coercion is used to begin production. With regard to unearthing slack, innovative, and renovation projects, economic commissions at all levels should strengthen their management according to the Regulations on the "Three Simultaneous Points."

Construction by small-scale, rural collectives, and joint agricultural-industrial-commercial enterprises must also be rationally distributed and be in strict compliance with the Regulations on the "Three Simultaneous Points." The departments supervising the enterprises and the administration of industry and commerce departments must pay close attention, and the environmental protection departments must supervise and examine them.

FIRMLY GRASP AND SOLVE GLARING POLLUTION PROBLEMS

Cities and industrial districts must investigate and analyze their sources of environmental protection and, in accordance with their severity, institute controls in a planned and step-by-step fashion. We must first solve some serious pollution problems caused by factories and enterprises located in residential areas, watershed conservation areas, and tourist areas. Some factories and enterprises with obsolete production techniques that cause serious pollution hazards which cannot be effectively controlled must be closed, suspended, merged, or transformed in a planned manner according to actual conditions.

In order to lessen air pollution in cities, we must adopt technical economic policies that both conserve energy and protect the environment. Materials supply departments should do their best to provide low-sulfur and low-volatility coal for civilian use first. In urban planning and construction we should actively promote central heating and serial [district] heating, develop the use of coal gas in a planned manner, and rationally use liquefied petroleum gas. It is especially important that newly built industrial complexes, residential areas, and satellite towns should no longer use outmoded heating systems with separate boilers for each unit. We should continue to grasp the tasks of reducing smoke and dust and renovating boilers. From now on all new boilers with a capacity of more than one ton of steam must be equipped with mechanical combustion and dust control systems, while those smaller than one ton must also have effective smoke and dust reduction mechanisms. Otherwise, they will not be allowed to leave the factory.

Factories and enterprises and their supervising units must follow the principle of "the polluter must control his own pollution" and conscientiously assume the responsibility of pollution control. During enterprise reorganization we must establish responsibility systems and reward and punishment systems for environmental protection. Technological renovation stressing energy conservation must set important targets for pollution control and environmental improvement. When upgrading technology and equipment we should, at the same time, solve the problem of pollution. Existing pollution control mechanisms must be maintained in proper operating condition in order to enhance their effectiveness. We must shatter the boundaries between industries or adopt joint management methods to actively promote the comprehensive utilization of the "Three Wastes" [liquids, gases, and solids], in order to achieve the integration of environmental results, economic results, and energy conservation results.

We must use economic levers to induce enterprises to control pollution. We should assess a "pollution effluent fee" on those units whose discharge of pollutants exceeds national standards. For commodities produced through the comprehensive utilization of the "Three Wastes," we should adopt a policy of rewards and, in accordance with related regulations, implement tax reductions or exemptions and profit retention. With regard to environmental protection measures adopted by enterprises experimenting with the systems of "turning profits into taxes, independent accounting, and individual responsibility for profits and losses," we should give them an incentive by reducing or exempting them from paying charges for the retention of fixed capital.

HALT DAMAGE TO THE NATURAL ENVIRONMENT

Exploitation and utilization of natural resources must be in accordance with the objective laws of nature. Environmental protection departments at all levels must join with agriculture, forestry, water conservancy, aquatic products, transportation, marine affairs, geology, and urban parks departments to strengthen planning and management of the natural environment. We must now particularly halt the destruction of water and soil resources and forestry resources.

The exploitation and utilization of rivers, lakes, and groundwater must stress maintaining ecological balance. Large-scale water conservancy and water withdrawal projects in particular must not be constructed until after the environmental protection department has reviewed their impact on the environment. Blind lake-enclosures, narrowing of river channels, and excessive withdrawals of groundwater that do damage to water resources are prohibited. We should investigate the responsibility of anyone who violates these provisions.

We should do a good job of designating nature preserves and establish and expand nature preserves of various types, in order that our country's representative natural ecological systems, the native habitat of our rare fauna and flora, and important natural history sites and sites of scenic and historical significance are properly protected. All areas and departments should strengthen the construction and management of the nature preserves under their jurisdiction.

DO A GOOD JOB OF ENVIRONMENTAL PROTECTION IN THE CAPITAL CITY OF BEIJING AND IN HANGZHOU, SUZHOU, AND GUILIN

Beijing is our country's capital, so environmental protection work there should be at the country's forefront. The Beijing Municipal People's Government should earnestly carry out the central secretariat's four suggestions on the capital's construction, do a good job of planning urban construction and environmental control, organize and mobilize the masses, carry out various measures, and strive to bring about a conspicuous improvement in Beijing's environmental features within three to five years.

Hangzhou, Suzhou, and Guilin are famous scenic and tourist cities in China, so we definitely must protect them properly. The provincial, autonomous region, and municipal, people's governments concerned must treat the protection of these three scenic areas as an important task, make plans in accordance with the nature and special characteristics of these tourist cities, and practice strict management. They must adopt effective measures to prevent and control pollution, halt the destruction of natural features, and gradually restore damaged scenic spots.

The State Council's Environmental Protection Leading Group will join with the State Planning Commission, the State Economic Commission, the State Capital Construction Commission, the State General Administration for Urban Construction, and the State Bureau of Travel and Tourism to assist and supervise these four cities, particularly Beijing, to devise plans, actively implement them, and achieve results. People's governments of all provinces, municipalities directly under the central government, and autonomous regions must also grasp environmental protection work in one or two cities in order to improve the quality of the urban environment.

STRENGTHEN THE STATE'S PLANNING AND GUIDANCE OF ENVIRONMENTAL PROTECTION

Protecting the environment and natural resources is an important national economic task. All areas and departments must strengthen planning and guidance. We must do a good job of comprehensively appraising and exploiting our natural resources, making locally suitable arrangements, and rationally distributing the forces of production. Ours is a country of 800 million peasants, so the work of surveying agricultural natural resources and agricultural zoning is critically important; we must strictly abide by natural laws and fully utilize the results of surveys and zoning, carry out the readjustment in agriculture, and foster a benign cycle in ecological systems. At the same time, in the course of building the Four Modernizations, we should do overall planning on such issues as the distribution of industry, the dispersal of cities and towns, and the population distribution in order to create a favorable living and working environment for people. Environmental protection departments and economic research departments should organize and promote research on environmental economics and territorial economics. Those areas that possess favorable circumstances should strengthen the comprehensive investigation of natural resources within their jurisdictions. We should gradually create favorable conditions for planning and strengthening the management of work on the control, exploitation, and utilization of our country's territory.

People's governments at all levels, when preparing national economic and social development plans, must treat the protection of the environment and natural resources as important elements in the overall balance, conscientiously incorporate goals, requirements, and measures for environmental protection in their plans, and strengthen planning and management. Industrial and communications, agricultural and forestry, scientific research, and public health enterprises and other undertakings and their supervising units must all stipulate specific environmental protection goals and norms and incorporate them in their annual plans.

In order to comprehend environmental conditions and to provide a scientific basis for policies and plans and to strengthen environmental management, environmental protection departments and statistics departments at all levels must do a good job of environmental statistics work and gradually put statistical supervision into effect.

STRENGTHEN ENVIRONMENTAL MONITORING, SCIENTIFIC RESEARCH, AND THE TRAINING OF PERSONNEL

Environmental monitoring is the basis for developing environmental management and scientific research work. Environmental protection departments must firmly grasp the building of environmental monitoring stations at various levels and strive to promptly equip the national environmental monitoring station and the sixty-four provincial-level and keypoint city monitoring stations so that they can form an operational force. At the same time the environmental protection departments should take the lead to organize a monitoring force in all concerned departments and coordinate closely with them in order to form a national environmental monitoring network. They should gradually survey and clarify environmental conditions in each area and, in some regions and cities, institute an experimental environmental monitoring and reporting system and submit environmental quality reports periodically.

Environmental science is an important, newly formed, and comprehensive scientific field. We should organize research capability in the natural and social sciences, design a division of labor, and develop research on basic environmental theory and technical economic policies. At the same time, with regard to pressing environmental problems, we should conduct research on prevention and control technology and sum up and disseminate low-cost but effective technological findings. The scientific commissions at all levels should strengthen their leadership and provide support in terms of expenses and equipment. All provinces, municipalities directly under the central government, and autonomous regions must reorganize and readjust their environmental protection research structures, concentrate their forces to build up existing provincial-level institutions that possess favorable conditions, and enhance the specialized characteristics of each.

Environmental protection is a new undertaking which requires large numbers of talented people with professional knowledge. We should incorporate the cultivation of environmental protection personnel in the national educational plan. Middle and primary schools must popularize knowledge about environmental science. Science, engineering, agriculture, medicine, economics, and law departments in colleges and vocational secondary schools should set up courses on environmental protection. Colleges and vocational schools with favorable conditions should set up specializations in environmental protection. All regions and departments must include environmental protection education in cadre training. Environmental protection units at all levels must actively raise the professional and technical levels of their current personnel. We should strengthen propaganda on the Environmental Protection Law and knowledge of environmental science, in order to cultivate a good social atmosphere of "it is every one's job to protect the environment."

STRENGTHEN LEADERSHIP OVER ENVIRONMENTAL PROTECTION WORK

The State Council's Environmental Protection Leading Group and its office must, in accordance with their responsibilities stipulated in the Environmental Protection Law, formulate policies, implement laws and regulations, carry out planning and guidance and essential administrative intervention, strengthen comprehensive management over the entire country's environment and natural resources, and direct the environmental protection work of departments under the State Council and in the provinces, municipalities directly under the central government, and autonomous regions. We must earnestly sum up experiences gained while implementing the Environmental Protection Law of the People's Republic of China (for trial implementation) and formulate concrete environmental management regulations in order to create a legal standard that can be followed. Departments under the State Council must strengthen their leadership over environmental protection within their respective systems.

People's governments at all levels should regard environmental protection work as one of their important duties and conscientiously take charge of it. They should periodically discuss and inspect environmental protection work, solve practical problems, and conscientiously conduct management and protection of the environment and natural resources within their respective jurisdictions.

All areas and departments should sum up actual conditions in accordance with these directives, formulate concrete measures, and effectively carry them out.

Appendix D

State Planning Commission, State Capital Construction Commission, State Economic Commission, and State Council Leading Group on Environmental Protection Procedures regarding the Management of Environmental Protection in Capital Construction Projects (May 11, 1981)

HBYWX, pp. 76–81.

These procedures are issued in order to further strengthen the management of environmental protection in capital construction projects and in accordance with the Environmental Protection Law (for trial implementation) and relevant regulations governing capital construction.

Article 1. Construction units and the departments that supervise them are responsible for environmental protection in capital construction projects. When the planning and construction commissions at various levels review capital construction project feasibility study reports, planning responsibility documents, site selection reports, and preliminary designs, they should hold consultations with the environmental protection departments to ensure that the projects' environmental protection needs are decided in conjunction with other economic and technical issues. When preparing annual capital construction plans, the funding, equipment, and materials for environmental protection measures must be organized in conjunction with the main project. Within the limits of their authority to approve the planning responsibility documents for capital construction projects, central and local environmental protection departments bear appropriate responsibility for approval of environmental impact assessments and to supervise and inspect environmental protection in capital construction projects.

Article 2. The authorization of capital construction projects must pay full attention to rational geographical distribution to minimize their negative environmental impacts. In general, there will be no more large-scale industrial construction or expansion projects in large cities or in districts that are already severely polluted. It is forbidden to build environmentally polluting enterprises or other undertakings in urban residential areas, watershed conservation districts, historical or scenic districts, hot spring or sanatorium districts, or nature preserves.

Article 3. Capital construction projects must pay full attention to comprehensive resource and energy utilization and minimize their pollution emission levels. Facilities to prevent pollution and other public hazards must be designed, constructed, and started up simultaneously with the main project. After construction has been completed and production has commenced, pollution emission levels must satisfy national or provincial emission standards.

Article 4. Construction units and the departments that supervise them must not prepare their construction project planning responsibility documents until after the environmental impact statements have been prepared on the basis of the project feasibility studies and have undergone examination and approval by the environmental protection departments.

If major alterations with regard to scale, major product lines, production processes, or the construction site are made after the environmental impact assessment has been examined and approved, then a revised statement should be prepared and submitted to the original examining department for approval.

Expenses incurred by construction units and the departments that supervise them with regard to the preparation of environmental impact assessments shall be paid out of the funds allotted for feasibility studies (in 1981 the expenses will still have to be financed out of existing funding sources).

Article 5. The contents of environmental impact assessments for large and medium-sized capital construction projects are listed in the appendix. The construction units and the departments that supervise them shall decide, together with the environmental protection departments, how detailed environmental impact assessments have to be for different kinds of projects. As to environmental impact assessments for small-scale capital construction projects and construction projects sponsored by rural collective enterprises, urban neighborhood enterprises, and joint agricultural-industrial-commercial enterprises, provincial-level construction commissions and environmental protection bureaus can stipulate what is to be required in light of specific conditions, with an emphasis on simple requirements.

Article 6. In accordance with environmental impact assessments and opinions regarding their acceptability, site selection reports for capital construction projects should provide further evidence regarding the site's impact on the local environment.

Article 7. The preliminary designs for capital construction projects must include a chapter on environmental protection to ensure that the various measures specified in the environmental impact assessment and opinions regarding its examination and approval are carried out. The environmental protection chapter should clarify the rationale for how environmental protection was designed; the types and volumes of pollutants to be discharged, along with technology for treating them and the emissions standards they will satisfy; the types, construction methods, and operating procedures for all pollution control technologies; measures to be adopted to mitigate ecological disruption arising from resource development; greenification design; and cost estimates for environmental measures.

In accordance with the State Construction Commission's Regulations on the Preparation of Design Documents and Procedure for Their Approval, construction units and the departments that supervise them shall transmit the relevant portions of design documents to the environmental protection departments for their examination.

Article 8. During the construction process itself capital construction projects should pay heed to the surrounding environment to avoid unnecessary damage to the natural environment. After construction is completed all elements of the surrounding natural environment that were damaged during construction should be restored. During the construction process they should prevent or reduce dust, noise, and vibrations from polluting and endangering the surrounding residential areas.

Article 9. During the course of construction and trial operation the environmental protection departments can inspect the actual working of environmental protection measures. Construction units should provide them with active assistance and necessary materials.

Article 10. The examination and acceptance of completed capital construction projects must include participation by the environmental protection departments, which shall inspect the extent to which environmental protection measures were instituted as well as their effectiveness. No project will be accepted, nor will production be allowed to commence, in any project for which environmental protection measures were omitted or fail to meet regulatory requirements. Legal responsibility will be investigated whenever coercion is used to order the start up of production.

Article 11. The principles embodied in these procedures are also suitable for projects involving the unearthing of slack resources, innovation, or technical upgrading. Economic commissions at various levels must strengthen their management of environmental protection in such projects.

Article 12. When construction units and the departments that supervise them violate these procedures and cause damage to the natural environment, pollution, or other public hazards, they shall be responsible for paying compensation for the resulting damages and may also be fined by the environmental protection departments.

Article 13. With reference to these procedures, the provincial-level units can draw up procedures for the management of environmental protection in small-scale capital construction projects and capital construction projects sponsored by rural collective enterprises, urban neighborhood enterprises, and joint agricultural-industrial-commercial enterprises.

APPENDIX: ESSENTIAL ELEMENTS OF ENVIRONMENTAL IMPACT STATEMENTS FOR LARGE-SCALE AND MEDIUM-SIZED CAPITAL CONSTRUCTION PROJECTS

Environmental impact assessments for capital construction projects are for the purpose of protecting the environment. They involve project feasibility studies, comprehensive evaluations, and the comparison and selection of the best alternative, to ensure that projects are rationally distributed geographically, that they have rather minor negative impacts on the natural environment, and that any pollution and other public hazards that are created can be controlled.

I. The Scope of Capital Construction Projects Requiring the Preparation of Environmental Impact Assessments

1. All large- and medium-scale industrial capital construction projects that impact on the natural environment or whose pollution affects the quality of the surrounding environment.
2. All large- and medium-scale water control, mining, port, railroad, and transportation capital construction projects that impact on the natural environment and ecological balance.
3. Large-scale capital construction projects involving agricultural reclamation, the enclosure of lakes and polders, and logging.
4. Large- and medium-scale capital construction projects with major impacts on the habitat, development, and survival of endangered species.

5. Capital construction projects with major impacts on the various kinds of nature preserves and special geological and geomorphological sites with great scientific value.

II. The Basic Content of an Environmental Impact Assessment

1. The general features of the construction project
   a) project name and construction methods;
   b) nature of the project site;
   c) scale of construction (in cases involving expansion, reference shall be made to the scale of the original project);
   d) product lines and principal production processes;
   e) consumption volume and sources for major raw materials, energy, and water;
   f) the types, volumes, and disposal methods for liquid wastes, gaseous wastes, solid wastes, dust, and radioactive wastes;
   g) the plans, measures, and major technical principles to be used in waste recovery and reuse, comprehensive utilization, and waste handling;
   h) number of workers and staff and the geographical distribution of residential areas;
   i) the area of land to be occupied and the ways in which the land is to be used;
   j) development plans.
2. Environmental conditions in the surrounding area
   a) geographical location of the project (to be accompanied by a surface map of the location);
   b) physical, geomorphological features and climatic features of the surrounding area;
   c) mineral, forest, grasslands, fisheries, wildlife, and other features regarding natural resources in the surrounding area;
   d) nature preserves, scenic districts, historical sites, hot springs, sanatoria, and important political and cultural facilities in the surrounding area;
   e) the geographical distribution of existing industrial and mining enterprises in the surrounding area;
   f) the geographical distribution of residential areas, population density, and diseases endemic to the surrounding area;
   g) ambient air and water quality in the surrounding area.
3. The project's environmental impacts on the surrounding area
   a) potential geological, hydrological, and climatic impacts, preventive and mitigating measures, and unavoidable impacts on the surrounding area;
   b) potential impacts on natural resources, preventive and mitigating measures, and unavoidable impacts on the surrounding area;
   c) potential impacts on nature preserves, preventive and mitigating measures, and unavoidable impacts on the surrounding area;
   d) ultimate emission levels for various pollutants and the breadth and severity of their impact on air, water, and soil quality in the surrounding environment;
   e) the breadth and severity of noise and vibration impacts on surrounding residential area;
   f) greenification measures, including shelter forests and greenification of the construction site;
   g) investment estimates for those measures solely devoted to environmental protection.
4. Opinions on the technical economic evidence of the construction project's feasibility in terms of environmental protection.

Appendix E

Water Pollution Prevention and Control Law (1984)

Renmin Ribao (May 13), p. 3.

CHAPTER ONE. GENERAL PRINCIPLES

Article 1. In order to prevent and control water pollution and protect and improve the environment so as to guarantee the physical health of the people, ensure the effective exploitation of our water resources, and promote the development of socialist modernization, this law has been specially formulated.

Article 2. This law is only applicable to the prevention and control of pollution in the rivers, lakes, canals, water channels, reservoirs, and other bodies of water on and under the ground within the territory of the People's Republic of China.

The prevention and control of pollution in sea areas is governed by a separate law.

Article 3. The relevant departments of the State Council and the local people's governments at all levels must incorporate work related to the protection of the environment in our water areas in their plans and adopt relevant policies and measures to prevent and control water pollution.

Article 4. The environmental protection departments of our people's governments at various levels are the organs that are in charge of exercising unified supervision and administration over the prevention and control of water pollution.

The navigation administrative organs in the communications departments at all levels are the organs that are in charge of exercising supervision and administration over the prevention of vessel source pollution.

The water conservancy administrative departments, public health administrative departments, geological and mining departments, municipal administrative departments, and watershed protection organizations for all important rivers should coordinate, in light of their own responsibility, with the environmental protection departments in supervising and administering work related to the prevention and control of water pollution.

Article 5. All units and individuals have the duty to protect the water environment and are empowered to supervise and inform against any acts that pollute or undermine the water environment.

The units and individuals who have directly suffered losses caused by water pollution are entitled to demand that those who caused this pollution eliminate it and pay damages for their losses.

CHAPTER TWO. FORMULATION OF THE STANDARDS FOR THE QUALITY OF THE WATER ENVIRONMENT AND FOR THE DISCHARGE OF POLLUTION

Article 6. The environmental protection department of the State Council is responsible for setting national environmental [ambient] quality standards for water.

The people's governments of provinces, [autonomous] regions, and municipalities directly under the central government can stipulate local supplementary standards for conditions not covered by the national water environmental quality standards and shall report these supplementary standards to the State Council's environmental protection department for the record.

Article 7. The environmental protection department of the State Council stipulates national pollution discharge standards in accordance with economic and technological conditions.

For those waters where the implementation of national pollution discharge standards cannot ensure the attainment of the environmental quality standards for water, the provincial, regional, and municipal people's governments may fix local pollution discharge standards that are more stringent than the national standards and shall report them to the environmental protection department of the State Council for the record.

Wherever a local standard for the release of pollutants has been set for the discharge of pollutants in a body of water, this local standard for the discharge of pollutants should be enforced.

Article 8. The State Council's environmental protection department and the provincial, regional, and municipal people's governments should revise, at an appropriate time, the water environmental quality standards and the pollution discharge standards in accordance with the requirements for preventing and controlling water pollution and in light of the economic and technological conditions of the nation.

CHAPTER THREE. SUPERVISION AND ADMINISTRATION RELATED TO PREVENTION AND CONTROL OF WATER POLLUTION

Article 9. In exploiting, utilizing, readjusting, and allocating water resources, the relevant departments of the State Council and the people's governments at all levels should take all factors into consideration, maintain the rational discharge of the rivers, the rational water level for lakes, reservoirs, and groundwaters, and the natural purification capacity of the waters.

Article 10. The relevant departments of the State Council and the local people's governments at all levels must incorporate the protection of urban water sources and the prevention of urban water pollution in urban construction plans and build and upgrade drainage systems and sewage treatment facilities.

Article 11. The relevant departments of the State Council and the local people's governments at all levels should rationally plan the distribution of industrial enterprises, carry out consolidation and technical transformation of enterprises that cause water pollution, adopt comprehensive measures to prevent and control water pollution, raise the recycling rate for water, rationally utilize our natural resources, and reduce the discharge of waste water and pollutants.

Article 12. The people's governments at and above the county level can designate as protected areas sources of drinking water, bodies of water in well-known scenic spots, bodies of water important for fishing, and other bodies of water of special economic or cultural value and adopt measures to ensure that the quality of water in the protected areas satisfies the water quality standards formulated for their particular purposes.

Article 13. Construction projects to be newly built, expanded, or renovated or other equipment to be installed over water surfaces which will directly or indirectly discharge pollutants into the water must observe the state regulations concerning the administration of environmental protection.

In preparing an analysis on the environmental impact of a construction project, it is imperative to make an appraisal of possible water pollution by the project under construction, and of its impact on the ecology, while formulating preventive measures. The analysis should be submitted to the relevant environmental protection department for its examination and approval in accordance with established procedures. The installation of pollution discharge outlets in water conservancy projects, such as canals, channels, and reservoirs, should first meet the approval of the relevant administrative departments of the water conservancy project concerned.

Before the construction project is put into production or use, its water pollution prevention and control facilities must be tested by the environmental protection department. If it should fail to meet the requirements, the construction project concerned may not be put into production or use.

Article 14. Those enterprises or other undertakings which directly or indirectly discharge pollutants into bodies of water should adhere to the regulations of the environmental protection department under the State Council; report to the local environmental protection department and register their pollution discharge equipment, their treatment facilities, and the categories, quantities, and concentrations of the pollutants discharged under ordinary operations; and provide the local environmental protection department with the relevant technical materials on the prevention and control of water pollution.

Any major changes in the categories, quantities, or concentrations of pollutants discharged should be promptly reported. The dismantling or failure to operate pollution treatment equipment should be reported in advance and approved by the local environmental protection department.

Article 15. Those enterprises or other undertakings which discharge pollutants into bodies of water should pay effluent fees according to state regulations. In cases where the pollutants discharged exceed state or local standards, those enterprises or other undertakings should pay additional effluent fees according to state regulations and should be responsible for control and treatment.

Article 16. Those units releasing pollutants which have caused serious water pollution should treat and control the pollution within a specified time limit.

The time limit set for enterprises or other undertakings under the direct jurisdiction of the central government or provincial, autonomus regional, or municipal [directly under the central government] governments for treating pollution should be proposed by the environmental protection departments of the provincial, autonomous regional, or municipal governments and be submitted to the people's government at the same level for its decision. The time limit set for enterprises or other undertakings under the jurisdiction of people's governments at or below municipal or county levels should be proposed by the environmental protection departments under the municipal or county people's government and will be submitted to the people's government at the same level for its decision. The unit discharging the pollutants should fulfill the task within the stipulated time period.

Article 17. In an emergency like the serious pollution of a source of drinking water or a threat to the safety of the water supply, the environmental protection department should report to the people's government at the same level and seek its approval for adopting compulsory emergency measures, including ordering the enterprise or other undertaking concerned to reduce or stop the discharge of pollutants.

Article 18. The environmental protection departments under the people's governments at all levels and relevant supervisory and administrative departments are authorized to conduct on-site inspections of units discharging pollutants within the scope of their jurisdiction. The units under inspection must truthfully represent the actual conditions and provide the necessary data. The inspecting organs are responsible for safekeeping the technological and business secrets of the units under inspection.

CHAPTER FOUR. PREVENTION OF SURFACE WATER POLLUTION

Article 19. It is forbidden to build new outlets for wastewater in sources of drinking water, bodies of water in scenic areas, bodies of water important for fisheries, and bodies of water of particular economic or cultural value in protected areas. Outlets for wastewater to be built in the vicinity of protected areas must ensure that the bodies of water in the protected areas are not polluted

Regarding those outlets for wastewater in existence before the publication of this law, when the pollutants discharged exceed state or local standards, they should undergo treatment. If those wastewater outlets should damage sources of drinking water, they should be relocated.

Article 20. If an accident or some unexpected incident takes place in the unit discharging pollutants, with the pollutants released exceeding the normal amount of release, which causes or will possibly cause the accidental pollution of water, emergency measures must be adopted at once. A circular should be tendered to the units facing possible injury or damage from the polluted water, and the case should be reported to the local environmental protection department. In the case of accidental pollution caused by ships, a report should be made to the nearest navigation administrative organs for their investigation and handling.

Article 21. It is forbidden to discharge into bodies of water acidic liquids, alkaline liquids, or waste liquids containing toxic materials.

Article 22. It is forbidden to clean in bodies of water vehicles and containers in which oil or toxic pollutants have been stored.

Article 23. The discharge or dumping into bodies of water or directly burying in the earth of soluble toxic solid wastes containing mercury, cadmium, arsenic, chromium, lead, cyanide, yellow phosphorus, and other harmful substance is prohibited.

In places where soluble toxic wastes are stored, measures should be adopted to prevent leaking, leaching, and erosion.

Article 24. The discharge or dumping into bodies of water of industrial wastes, municipal refuse, or other wastes is prohibited.

Article 25. The deposition or storage of solid wastes and other pollutants on beaches or on slopes located at the lower reaches of rivers, lakes, canals, irrigation ditches, and reservoirs is prohibited.

Article 26. The discharge or dumping into bodies of water of radioactive solid wastes or wastewater containing high or medium levels of radioactive matter is prohibited.

The discharge of low radioactive wastewater must conform to state regulations and standards concerning protection against radioactive materials.

Article 27. When discharging heated wastewater into bodies of water, it is necessary to adopt measures to ensure that the temperature of the bodies of water conforms to the regulations governing the environmental protection of water to prevent thermal pollution.

Article 28. Wastewater containing pathogenic agents must undergo sterilization treatment, and discharge is allowed only when the wastewater conforms to relevant standards set by the state. Otherwise, the discharge of such wastewater is prohibited.

Article 29. When discharging industrial wastewater and municipal wastewater into agricultural irrigation ditches, it should be ensured that water quality in the irrigation areas located at the nearest points downstream conform with the standards governing the water quality for irrigating farmland.

When making use of industrial wastewater and municipal wastewater to irrigate farmland, it is necessary to prevent the pollution of soil, groundwater, and agricultural products.

Article 30. The application of pesticides must conform to state regulations and standards concerning the safe application of agricultural chemicals.

Controls must be strengthened over the transportation and storage of pesticides and the disposal of outdated pesticides in order to prevent water pollution.

Article 31. When boats and ships discharge wastewater containing oil and human wastes, they should abide by the regulations concerning the discharge of pollutants from boats and ships. When oceangoing ships enter inland rivers or ports, they should abide by the regulations governing the disposal of pollutants in inland rivers.

Residual oil and waste oil should be recovered, and releasing them into bodies of water from ships and boats is prohibited.

Dumping refuse into bodies of water from boats and ships is prohibited.

When boats and ships load and transport oily and toxic materials, it is necessary to adopt measures to prevent them from leaking in order to avoid water pollution stemming from the leakage of these goods.

CHAPTER FIVE. PREVENTION OF GROUNDWATER POLLUTION

Article 32. Enterprises and establishments are prohibited from making use of negative wells, sinks, cracks, or holes to discharge or pour into bodies of water wastewater containing toxic pollutants, sewage containing pathogenic agents, or other wastes.

Article 33. When there is no satisfactory impermeable layer, enterprises and other undertakings are not allowed to make use of ditches, holes, pits, or dikes to carry or store wastewater containing toxic pollutants, sewage containing pathogenic agents, or other wastes.

Article 34. When exploiting multilayer groundwater, exploitation should be carried out layer after layer, provided that the quality of water at various layers is greatly different. While exploiting the water, phreatic water which has been polluted should not be mixed in with the aquifer water.

Article 35. When carrying out underground projects, underground prospecting, and other mining activities, measures should be adopted to prevent groundwater pollution.

Article 36. When recharging groundwater by artificial methods, it should be ensured that the quality of groundwater is not impaired.

CHAPTER SIX. LEGAL RESPONSIBILITY

Article 37. Any persons or units which commit any of the following offenses violating this law will be warned or fined by the environmental protection organs or the navigation administrative organs of the communication departments, in light of the seriousness of the offense concerned.

1. The offense of refusing to register or providing false information in violation of the stipulations worked out by the environmental protection department under the State Council concerning the discharge of pollutants;
2. The offense of going into operation or production prior to the completion of water pollution prevention facilities or meeting the regulations and requirements on environmental protection set by the state;
3. Those who refuse to accept on-site inspection carried out by environmental protection departments or by the relevant supervisory and administrative departments, or those who employ deception during the inspection;
4. Those who violate the relevant regulations and rules defined in Chapters Four and Five of this law and those who store, deposit, discharge, dump, or drain pollutants and solid wastes;
5. Those who do not pay effluent fees or the additional fees for discharge of excessive amounts of pollutants as defined by the state.

Detailed rules for the methods and amounts of fines are specified in this law.

Article 38. Enterprises and other undertakings which cause serious water pollution must eliminate pollution within a stipulated time. Those which fail to finish the work within the set time must pay two or more times the amount of the charges for disposal of excess pollutants as fixed by the state. In addition, a fine may be imposed on them according to the harm and losses incurred, or they may be ordered to suspend operations or to close down.

Environmental protection departments determine the amounts of fines. Local people's governments issue orders to suspend the operations of enterprises or other undertakings, orders to close them down, and decisions to instruct them to eliminate pollution within a definite time. Orders to suspend the operations of an enterprise or other undertaking or to close it down must be reported to the State Council for approval.

Article 39. The enterprises or other undertakings which cause water pollution in violation of the provisions of this law shall be fined by environmental protection departments or by navigation administrative organs of the communications departments according to the harm and losses incurred. If a serious case occurs, the responsible persons shall be subject to disciplinary action by the unit where they work or by the higher authorities in charge.

Article 40. If the person concerned refuses to accept the action taken against him or her, that person may bring action in the people's court within fifteen days of receipt of the notice. If the person refuses to accept the action taken against him or her and does not bring action in the people's court within the set time, then the offices which imposed action may ask the people's court to force the person to accept the action.

Article 41. Units which cause harm from water pollution shall bear the responsibility for eliminating pollution and for compensating the units and individuals which have directly suffered losses.

With regard to the other parties concerned, disputes over responsibility or the amount of compensation may be handled through environmental protection departments or through navigation administrative organs of the communications departments. If the persons concerned remain dissatisfied by the decision, they may bring suit in the people's court.

A third party shall bear responsibility for losses incurred from water pollution which is intentionally caused or occurs through the negligence of the third party.

Units in charge of the disposal of pollution bear no responsibility for any losses incurred from water pollution caused by the victims themselves.

Article 42. No responsibility shall be borne for any unavoidable losses from water pollution caused by unavoidable natural calamities when proper measures have been taken in a timely fashion.

Article 43. If a serious water pollution accident arising from a violation of the provisions of this law leads to grave consequences in terms of heavy losses of public and private property or heavy casualties, investigation shall be made into the criminal responsibility of the responsible persons in accordance with Article 115 or Article 187 of the Criminal Law.

CHAPTER SEVEN. SUPPLEMENTARY ARTICLES

Article 44. The terms in this law are defined as follows:

1. "Water pollution" means that the nature of water changes in terms of its chemical, physical, biological, or radioactive properties because of the entry of certain materials. As a result, this affects water usage rights, harms the health of human beings, destroys the ecology, or causes degradation of the water.
2. "Pollutants" refers to items which may result in water pollution.
3. "Pathogenic pollutants" refers to certain pollutants which may bring about diseases, abnormal behavior, hereditary diseases, physiological deficiencies, organic deformations, or the death of living beings or of future generations because microbes enter their bodies directly or indirectly.
4. "Oils" refers to any kind of oils or their refined products.
5. "Water areas for fisheries" refers to spawning grounds, fish hatcheries, wintering grounds, the migration routes of fishes and prawns, and the habitat of fishes, prawns, shellfish, and aquatic plants.

Article 45. Detailed rules for the implementation of this law defined by the environmental protection department under the State Council will be submitted to the State Council for final approval.

Article 46. This law shall come into effect on November 1, 1984.

Appendix F

Marine Environmental Protection Law (1982)

Renmin Ribao (August 25), p. 3.

CHAPTER ONE. GENERAL PROVISIONS

Article 1. This law is hereby enacted in order to protect the marine environment and resources, prevent pollution damage, maintain ecological balance, safeguard human health, and promote the development of marine programs.

Article 2. This law applies to the internal seas and territorial seas of the People's Republic of China and all other sea areas under the jurisdiction of the People's Republic of China.

All vessels, platforms, airborne vehicles, submersibles, as well as all enterprises and other undertakings and individuals engaged in navigation, exploration, exploitation, production, scientific research, and other activities in the sea areas under the jurisdiction of the People's Republic of China shall comply with this law.

This law also applies to the discharge of harmful substances and the dumping of wastes done beyond the sea areas under the jurisdiction of the People's Republic of China but causing pollution damage to such areas.

Article 3. All entities and individuals having access to the sea areas under the jurisdiction of the People's Republic of China shall protect the marine environment and observe and report actions polluting and damaging the marine environment thereof.

Article 4. The relevant departments under the State Council and the people's governments of the coastal provinces, autonomous regions, and municipalities directly under the central government may, as the need to protect the marine environment requires, establish special marine reserves, marine sanctuaries, and seashore scenic and tourist areas and take corresponding measures to protect them. The designation of special marine reserves and marine sanctuaries shall be subject to approval by the State Council.

Article 5. The environmental protection department under the State Council is in charge of marine environmental protection in the whole country.

The state administrative department of marine affairs is responsible for organizing investigations, monitoring, and surveillance of the marine environment and for conducting scientific research therein, and it is in charge of environmental protection against marine pollution damage caused by offshore oil exploration and exploitation and by the dumping of wastes into the sea.

The Harbor Superintendency Administration of the People's Republic of China is responsible for overseeing, investigating, and dealing with the discharge of pollutants from vessels and for keeping under surveillance the waters of the port areas, and it is in charge of environmental protection against pollution damage caused by vessels.

The state agency in charge of fishery administration and fishing harbor superintendence is responsible for supervising the discharge of wastes by vessels in the fishing harbors and for keeping under surveillance the waters thereof.

The environmental protection department of the armed forces is responsible for supervising the discharge of wastes by naval vessels and keeping under surveillance the waters of the naval ports.

The environmental protection departments of the coastal provinces, autonomous regions, and municipalities directly under the central government are responsible for organizing, coordinating, overseeing, and checking marine environmental protection in their respective administrative areas and are in charge of environmental protection against pollution damage caused by coastal construction projects and land-based pollutants.

CHAPTER TWO. PREVENTION OF POLLUTION DAMAGE TO THE MARINE ENVIRONMENT BY COASTAL CONSTRUCTION PROJECTS

Article 6. Entities in charge of coastal construction projects must, before drawing up and submitting their construction plans, conduct scientific investigations of the marine environment, select suitable sites in light of natural and social conditions, and formulate and submit environmental impact statements in accordance with relevant state regulations.

Article 7. Measures must be taken to protect aquatic resources when building harbors and oil terminals, as well as water conservancy facilities and tidal power stations in estuaries. Dams to be built across fish and crab migration routes shall be provided with corresponding fish ladders.

Article 8. There shall be installed at ports and oil terminals facilities to receive and treat oil residues and wastes, oily water and other wastes, along with necessary antipollution equipment and monitoring and alarm devices.

Article 9. The development and utilization of tidelands shall be comprehensively planned and their regulation tightened. Strict control shall be maintained over land reclamation from salt marshes and other coastal filling projects and over sand and gravel dredging and excavating operations. As for projects that are definitely necessary, environmental impact statements concerning them must be produced on the basis of investigations and comparison of economic results and be submitted for approval to the environmental protection departments of the relevant provinces, autonomous regions, and municipalities directly under the central government. In case of large-scale coastal filling projects, such statements shall also be submitted to the environmental protection department under the State Council for examination and approval.

It is forbidden to destroy seashore shelterbelts, scenic woods, scenic rocks, mangroves, and coral reefs.

CHAPTER THREE. PREVENTION OF POLLUTION DAMAGE TO THE MARINE ENVIRONMENT BY OFFSHORE OIL EXPLORATION AND EXPLOITATION

Article 10. Enterprises engaged in offshore oil exploitation or their competent authorities shall, before drawing up and submitting their work plans, produce environmental impact statements including effective measures to prevent pollution damage to the marine environment and submit them to the environmental protection department under the State Council for examination and approval.

Article 11. In case of offshore oil exploration and other offshore activities involving operations with explosives, effective measures shall be taken to protect fishery resources.

Article 12. Oils used in the course of exploration and exploitation shall be put under strict control so as to prevent their leakage. Oil residues and wastes shall be recovered and are forbidden to be discharged into the sea.

Article 13. Oily water and mixtures from both mobile and fixed platforms for offshore oil exploration and exploitation may not be directly discharged into the sea. When discharged after treatment following recovery, their oil content may not exceed the standards set by the state.

Article 14. It is prohibited to dispose of oily industrial wastes from either mobile or fixed platforms for offshore oil exploration and exploitation into the sea. The disposal of other industrial wastes may not cause pollution damage to fishing grounds or waterways.

Article 15. When conducting offshore well testing, oils and oily mixtures may not be discharged into the sea, and the gases shall be thoroughly burned so as to prevent pollution of the sea.

Article 16. Offshore oil pipelines and oil storage installations shall always be kept in good condition, fulfilling the requirements against seepage, leakage, and corrosion, so as to prevent oil from running off.

Article 17. When exploring and exploiting offshore oil resources, appropriate anti-pollution facilities and equipment shall be available, and effective technical measures shall be taken to prevent blowouts or oil spill accidents.

Once a blowout or oil spill occurs, it shall immediately be reported to the state administrative department of marine affairs and effective measures shall be taken to control and eliminate oil pollution, and the entity concerned shall accept the investigation and handling of the case by the department.

CHAPTER FOUR. PREVENTION OF POLLUTION DAMAGE TO THE MARINE ENVIRONMENT BY LAND-BASED POLLUTANTS

Article 18. The discharge of harmful substances into the sea by coastal entities must be conducted in strict compliance with the standards for discharge and relevant regulations promulgated by the state or the people's governments of provinces, autonomous regions, and municipalities directly under the central government.

No additional outlet for discharging sewage is allowed within marine sanctuaries, aquacultural grounds, and seashore scenic and tourist areas. Those outlets already in existence before the promulgation of this law, the discharge of which is not in conformity with the state standards, shall be improved within a prescribed period of time.

Article 19. It is prohibited to discharge wastewater containing high-level radioactive matter into the sea.

Any discharge of wastewater containing low-level radioactive matter into the sea, when actually necessary, shall be carried out in strict compliance with the regulations and standards concerning protection against radiation.

Article 20. No medical sewage or industrial wastewater carrying pathogens may be discharged into the sea until it is properly treated and strictly sterilized, with the pathogens therein exterminated.

Article 21. The discharge of industrial wastewater and domestic sewage containing organic and nutrient matter into bays, semiclosed seas, and other sea areas with limited assimilative capacities shall be put under control so as to prevent eutrophication of the seawater therein.

Article 22. When discharging heated wastewater into the sea, measures shall be taken to ensure that the water temperature in the adjacent fishing areas meets the state criteria for water quality so as to avoid damage to the aquatic resources by thermal pollution.

Article 23. The use of chemical pesticides in coastal farmlands shall conform to the state regulations and standards for the safe use of pesticides.

Article 24. No entity may discard or pile up tailings, slags, cinders, refuse, and other wastes along seashores and beaches without the approval of the environmental protection departments of coastal provinces, autonomous regions, or the municipalities directly under the central government. Waste containment and treatment facilities installed in accordance with lawful permits along seashores and beaches shall have dykes erected to prevent the wastes from escaping into the sea.

Article 25. The environmental protection departments of the coastal provinces, autonomous regions, and municipalities directly under the central government and the river valley administrative departments shall strengthen regulation over rivers emptying into the sea and prevent them from being polluted so as to ensure the good quality of the water in the estuaries.

CHAPTER FIVE. PREVENTION OF POLLUTION DAMAGE TO THE MARINE ENVIRONMENT BY VESSELS

Article 26. No vessel shall discharge oils, oily mixtures, wastes, and other harmful substances into the sea areas under the jurisdiction of the People's Republic of China in violation of the provisions of this law.

Article 27. Any oil tanker of 150 or more gross tons and any other vessel of 400 or more gross tons shall be fitted with special containers for recovering residual and waste oils.

Article 28. Any oil tanker of 150 or more gross tons and any other vessel of 400 or more gross tons shall carry on board an Oil Record Book.

Any vessels carrying 2,000 or more tons of oil in bulk as cargo shall have a valid Certificate of Insurance or other Financial Security in respect of Civil Liability for Oil Pollution Damage, or a Credit Certificate for Civil Liability against Oil Pollution Damage, or hold other financial credit guarantees.

Article 29. The discharge of oily water from an oil tanker of 150 or more gross tons or any other vessel of 400 or more gross tons must be conducted in compliance with the state standards and regulations concerning vessel sewage discharge and be accurately recorded in the Oil Record Book.

Article 30. The discharge of hold washings and other residues by vessels carrying noxious or corrosive goods must be conducted in compliance with the state regulations for vessel sewage discharge and be accurately recorded in the Log Book.

Article 31. The discharge of radiocative substances from nuclear-powered vessels or vessels carrying such substances must be conducted in compliance with the provisions of Article 19 of this law.

Article 32. Vessels, when bunkering or loading and unloading oil, must observe operating instructions and take effective measures to prevent oil spills.

Article 33. Shipbuilding, repairing, scrapping and salvaging units shall be provided with pollution-prevention equipment and facilities. During operations, preventive measures shall be taken against pollution of the sea by oils, oily mixtures, and other wastes.

Article 34. In case pollution has arisen from an abnormal discharge of oils, from oily mixtures of other harmful wastes, or from the loss overboard of noxious or corrosive goods, the vessel concerned shall immediately take measures to control and eliminate such pollution and shall report to the nearest harbor superintendency administration for investigation and disposition.

Article 35. In case any vessel is involved in a marine accident which has caused, or is likely to cause, serious pollution damage to the marine environment, the Harbor Superintendency Administration of the People's Republic of China has the power to take mandatory measures to avoid or minimize such pollution damage.

Article 36. All vessels have the obligation to watch out for pollution of the sea. On discovering acts in violation of law or the occurrence of pollution, they shall immediately report to the nearest harbor superintendency administration. Fishing boats may also report to the nearest agency in charge of fishery administration and fishing harbor superintendence.

Article 37. In the event of pollution caused by vessels that navigate, berth, or operate in the sea areas under the jurisdiction of the People's Republic of China, officers from a harbor superintendency administration of the People's Republic of China shall board the vessel in question to examine and handle the case. Officers from relevant government departments authorized by the Harbor Superintendency Administration may also board the vessel to conduct examinations and report the results thereof to the latter for disposition.

CHAPTER SIX. PREVENTION OF POLLUTION DAMAGE TO THE MARINE ENVIRONMENT FROM THE DUMPING OF WASTES

Article 38. No entity may dump any kind of wastes into the marine areas under the jurisdiction of the People's Republic of China without the permission of the state administrative department of marine affairs.

Entities that need to dump wastes must file an application with the state administrative department of marine affairs, and only after a permit has been granted by the department can the said dumping be carried out.

Article 39. Entities that have obtained permits for dumping shall conduct it at the designated place, within the time limit, and in accordance with the conditions specified in the permit. Wastes to be dumped shall be verified by the certifying department after their loading. Wastes to be dumped by means of vessels shall be verified by the harbor superintendency administration at the port of departure.

Article 40. Entities that have obtained permits for dumping shall make a detailed record of such operations and present a written report to the certifying department thereafter. Vessels that have finished the said dumping must present a written report to the harbor superintendency administration at the port of departure.

CHAPTER SEVEN. LEGAL LIABILITIES

Article 41. In cases of a violation of this law that has caused or is likely to cause pollution damage to the marine environment, the relevant supervising departments prescribed in Article 5 of this law may order the violator involved to remedy the pollution damage within a definite time, pay an effluent fee, pay the cost for eradicating the pollution, and compensate the loss sustained by the state, and may give the said violator a warning or impose a fine on him. An involved party contesting the decision may file a suit with the people's court within 15 days of receipt thereof. If a suit is not filed and the decision is not carried out before the expiration of the period, the supervising department shall request the people's court to enforce the decision in accordance with the law.

Article 42. Entities and individuals who have suffered damage caused by marine environmental pollution shall be entitled to claim compensation from the party causing the said pollution damage. Disputes over the compensation liability and the sum thereof may be settled by the relevant supervising department. In case a party contests the decision, the matter can be settled either by resorting to the procedures specified in the Law of Civil Procedure of the People's Republic of China (for trial implementation) or by filing a suit directly with the people's court.

Article 43. In cases due entirely to the following causes, there may be exemption from liability for compensation if pollution damage to the marine environment cannot be avoided in spite of the prompt and reasonable measures taken:

1. act of war;
2. unpreventable natural calamities;
3. negligence or other wrongful act on the part of the departments responsible for the maintenance of beacons or other navigational aids in exercising their functions.

In case of pollution damage to the marine environment resulting entirely from the intentional or wrongful act by a third party, that party shall be liable for compensation.

Article 44. In cases of violations of this law resulting in pollution damage to the marine environment and causing heavy losses of public or private property or death or injuries to persons, those who are directly responsible may be prosecuted for criminal responsibility by judicial organs in accordance with the law.

CHAPTER EIGHT. SUPPLEMENTARY PROVISIONS

Article 45. For the purposes of this law:

1. ''Pollution damage to the marine environment'' means any direct or indirect introduction of substances or energy into the marine environment which results in such deleterious effects as harm to marine biological resources, hazards to human health, impediments to fishing and other legitimate activities at sea, impairment of the usage quality of seawater, and degradation of environmental quality.
2. ''Fishing areas'' means spawning grounds, feeding grounds, wintering grounds, and migration channels of fish and shrimps, as well as aquacultural grounds of fish, shrimps, shellfish, and aquatic plants.
3. ''Oils'' means all kinds of oil and their refined products.
4. ''Oil mixtures'' means any mixture with oil content.
5. ''Discharging'' means acts to release pollutants into the sea, including pumping, spilling, draining, spraying, and pouring.
6. ''Dumping'' means disposal of wastes or other harmful substances into the sea from vessels, airborne vehicles, platforms, or other conveyances, including the disposal of vessels, airborne vehicles, platforms, and other floating apparatus.

Article 46. When provisions in force concerning marine environmental protection contradict the present law, the latter shall prevail.

Article 47. The environmental protection department under the State Council may formulate detailed rules and regulations for the implementation of this law and submit them to the State Council for approval and put them into effect after such approval.

The relevant departments under the State Council and the standing committees of the people's congresses and people's governments of the coastal provinces, autonomous regions, and muncipalities directly under the central government may adopt concrete measures for the implementation of this law, taking into consideration the actual conditions prevailing in the department or localities concerned.

Article 48. This law shall come into effect as of March 1, 1983.

Appendix G

Regulations of the People's Republic of China on the Prevention of Marine Polution from Vessels (December 29, 1983)

Zhongguo Fazhi Bao (January 13, 1984), p. 2.

CHAPTER I. GENERAL PROVISIONS

Article 1. These regulations are specially formulated in order to implement the Marine Environmental Protection Law of the People's Republic of China, to prevent pollution of sea areas by ships, and to protect the ecological environment of the sea areas.

Article 2. These regulations are applicable to all Chinese-registered ships, foreign-registered ships, shipowners, and other individuals within the sea areas and harbors under the jurisdiction of the People's Republic of China.

Article 3. The organs in charge of the prevention of pollution of the environment of sea areas by ships are the harbor superintendencies of the People's Republic of China (hereinafter called harbor superintendencies).

CHAPTER II. GENERAL STIPULATIONS

Article 4. Ships in the sea areas and harbors under the jurisdiction of the People's Republic of China should in no case discharge oils, oil-based mixtures, waste materials, and other toxic substances in violation of the stipulations of the Marine Environmental Protection Law of the People's Republic of China and these regulations.

Article 5. No ship should discharge oils, oil-based mixtures, waste materials, and other toxic substances into the freshwater sea areas of ports near river mouths, special marine protection districts, and marine nature preserves.

Article 6. When incidents of pollution to sea areas caused by oils, oil-based mixtures, and other toxic substances from ships occur, measures shall be immediately adopted to control and eliminate the pollution, a written report made to a nearby harbor superintendency as quickly as possible, and the matter accepted for investigation and handling.

Article 7. In cases where accidents at sea by ships cause or might cause major damage from pollution to the marine environment, the harbor superintendencies have the right to compel the adoption of measures to avoid or reduce this damage from pollution, including compulsory sinking or towing of the ships. The ship causing the problem is to bear all the costs arising therefrom.

Article 8. When ships in the sea areas under the jurisdiction of the People's Republic of China themselves cause or discover facts of pollution to sea areas or conduct in violation of regulations by other ships, the matter shall be handled in accordance with the stipulations of Articles 36 and 37 of the Marine Environmental Protection Law of the People's Republic of China.

Article 9. Ships which require in-harbor hold washing operations must adopt safety measures to prevent pollution to the sea areas and apply in advance to the harbor superintendencies, and may proceed only after having received approval.

Article 10. In order to guarantee safe pilotage and docking of oil tankers and to prevent pollution of sea areas, the ballast tank water kept by all empty oil tankers entering harbors must not be less than one-fourth of the deadweight capacity of the oil tanker in question. In cases where an oil tanker does not keep sufficient ballast tank water according to stipulations, the harbor superintendencies should investigate the whereabouts of its ballast tank water and handle the matter in accordance with the circumstances.

Article 11. After oil pollution incidents or discharges of oil in violation of regulations have occurred, ships must not use oil-eradicating chemical agents to eradicate oil on their own authority. If they must be used, application by telephone or in written form shall be made with the harbor superintendencies in advance, specifying the brand name of the oil-eradicating chemical agents and the quantity and location where they are to be applied, and they may only be used after approval has been received.

Article 12. In cases where pollution incidents or pollutant discharges by ships in violation of regulations occur, the shipowners or the persons causing the problem on whom fines are imposed or who are required to bear the economic responsibility for items like removal and compensation must fulfill procedures regarding financial assurance or complete payment of the sums of money involved before the ships [will be allowed to] set sail.

Article 13. For ships carrying 2,000 tons or more of bulk oil cargo navigating on international sea lanes, in addition to implementing the stipulations of this act, the International Convention of 1969 on Civil Liability for Harm from Oil Pollution, to which China has acceded, is to be applied.

CHAPTER III. DOCUMENTS AND EQUIPMENT FOR THE PREVENTION OF POLLUTION BY SHIPS

Article 14. Documents for the prevention of pollution by ships:

1. Oil tankers of 150 or more gross tons, non-oil tankers of 400 or more gross tons, and ships carrying 2,000 or more tons of bulk oil cargo must be respectively equipped with the corresponding documents for the prevention of pollution by ships stipulated in Article 28 of the Marine Environmental Protection Law of the People's Republic of China;
2. Ships shall also be equipped with other pollution prevention documents demanded by the harbor superintendencies.

Article 15. With regard to oil tankers of 150 gross tons or more and non-oil tankers of 400 gross tons or more, the equipment for the prevention of oil pollution shall meet the following requirements:

1. Use of separate piping systems for polluted water from the engine room and for ballast tank water;

2. Be fitted with tanks for storing oil pollutants;
3. Have standard discharge connections installed;
4. Have oil and water separation equipment or a filtering system installed and satisfy the requirements that the discharged oil content of processed oil-polluted water does not exceed 15 milligrams per liter when oil-polluted water is discharged within 12 nautical miles of the nearest land, and that the discharged oil content of the processed oil-polluted water does not exceed 100 milligrams per liter when oil-polluted water is discharged beyond 12 nautical miles from the nearest land;
5. Ships of 10,000 or more tons, in addition to satisfying the stipulations of this article listed above, shall also install equipment for the monitoring and control of oil discharges;
6. Other pollution prevention equipment installed by ships shall meet the relevant state regulations regarding structural and equipment standards for preventing pollution by ships.

The pollution prevention equipment aboard ships currently in service that does not attain these requirements shall reach the stipulated requirements within three years after the promulgation of these regulations.

Article 16. Oil tankers of under 150 gross tons and non-oil tankers of under 400 gross tons shall be fitted with specialized containers for retrieving oil residues and waste oil. These containers shall have the capacity to discharge oil residues and waste oil to the recipient equipment at harbors and shall be equipped with the equipment stipulated in Clauses 3 and 6 of Article 15 of this act.

CHAPTER IV. FUELING OPERATIONS AND DISCHARGE OF OIL-POLLUTED WATER BY SHIPS

Article 17. When conducting fueling operations, ships must observe the following stipulations:

1. Before beginning operations, the pipelines and valves must be examined, preparations must be made, the drainage holes on the decks stopped, and the relevant valves opening into the sea closed;
2. The relevant equipment for fueling operations must be examined and brought into good condition;
3. Containers for collecting oil should be installed wherever overflow and leakage may occur;
4. Both parties, primarily the recipient, shall earnestly follow the contact signals decided through consultation by the oil supplier and the oil recipient;
5. During operations there should be sufficient personnel on duty; those who are on duty must stand fast at their posts, strictly carry out operational rules, keep informed on how the operations are progressing, and prevent oil from escaping and leaking;
6. When operations stop, the relevant valves must be closed;
7. When retrieving or disconnecting flexible oil hoselines, the flexible hoselines must be sealed in advance with self-contained baffles, or other effective measures adopted, to prevent the remaining oil in the flexible hoselines from backflowing into the sea;

8. Oil tankers shall make accurate entries regarding the fueling operations in the Oil Record Book; non-oil tankers shall make entries in the "engine logbook" or the record book of those on duty.

Article 18. If in the course of conducting fueling operations, incidents of oil escaping or leakage should occur, the ships shall adopt measures to remove the oil in a timely manner and prevent the spread of oil pollution and at the same time make a report to the harbor superintendencies. After the cause has been ascertained, a written report shall be prepared and the matter accepted for investigation and handling.

Article 19. When ships discharge pollutants, they must meet the Standards for Discharge of Pollutants by Ships of the People's Republic of China.

Oil-polluted water like that in ballast tanks and hold washing and engine room wastewater aboard ships entering harbors must not be discharged at will; it shall be collected and disposed of by the disposal facilities for oil-polluted water at the port. If the port lacks facilities for receiving and disposing of oil-polluted water, and oil-polluted water aboard the ships must be discharged, a written report shall be submitted to the harbor superintendencies in advance. After approval is received, the water is to be discharged according to the stipulated conditions and in the designated areas.

Article 20. Discharge of oil-polluted water from ships approved in accordance with Article 19 of these regulations must respectively meet each of the following stipulations:

1. General circumstances
   a) Within the approved areas;
   b) In the course of navigating, the instantaneous discharge rate is not to exceed 650 liters per nautical mile;
   c) The oil content of the polluted water is not to exceed 15 milligrams per liter;
   d) The oil and water separation equipment, the filtering system, and the equipment for monitoring and control of oil discharges are to be in normal working condition;
   e) During ebb tide.
2. The discharge of oil-polluted water from the engine rooms of oil tankers of 150 or more gross tons and non-oil tankers of 400 or more gross tons, in addition to satisfying items a, b, d, and e of Clause 1 above, shall also satisfy the following:
   a) Be beyond 12 nautical miles from the nearest land;
   b) The oil content of the polluted water is not to exceed 100 milligrams per liter.
3. The discharge of ballast tank water and the water from hold washing by oil tankers of 150 or more gross tons, in addition to satisfying items b and d of Clause 1 above, shall also satisfy the following:
   a) Be beyond 50 nautical miles from the nearest land;
   b) The total amount of oil discharged in each ballast voyage must not exceed 1/15,000 of the total amount of oil carried in the case of oil tankers currently in service, and must not exceed 1/30,000 of the total amount of oil carried in the case of new oil tankers.

CHAPTER V. CARRIAGE OF DANGEROUS GOODS BY SHIPS

Article 21. When ships carry dangerous goods that are inflammable, explosive, corrosive, toxic, or radioactive, they shall adopt essential safety and pollution-prevention measures. They shall display the stipulated signals, observe the Regulations on Supervision and Control of the Carriage of Dangerous Goods by Ships and the Regulations on the Transport of Dangerous Goods through Water Ways of the Ministry of Communications of the People's Republic of China and the Rules on the Transport of Dangerous Goods in International Seas of the International Maritime Organization, and prevent incidents that would lead to the loss, spillage, or leakage of dangerous goods polluting sea areas.

Article 22. When ships load dangerous or toxic liquefied bulk cargoes in harbor, the various stipulations of Article 17 of these regulations are to be implemented by reference.

Article 23. When ships load and unload dangerous goods that are toxic, corrosive, or radioactive in port, both the ship and the unit conducting the operation must adopt precautions to prevent the cargo from falling into the water. If incidents should occur, urgent measures shall be adopted to conduct retrieval and removal. In addition, a report is to be made to the harbor superintendencies immediately and the relevant units informed in a timely manner, so that measures may be adopted to prevent the occurrence of major harm.

CHAPTER VI. OTHER POLLUTED WATER FROM SHIPS

Article 24. Nuclear-powered ships and ships carrying radioactive substances must observe the stipulations of Article 31 of the Marine Environmental Protection Law of the People's Republic of China.

Article 25. With respect to the ballast tank water of ships arriving from ports suffering from epidemics, application shall be made to the public health and quarantine department to conduct sanitary treatment.

Article 26. Ships carrying toxic or corrosive goods, when discharging hold wastewater containing such substances, must satisfy each of the following criteria:

1. Within approved areas;
2. Twelve or more nautical miles from the nearest land, in waters of depths 25 meters or greater;
3. While underway at a speed of not less than 7 knots or not less than 4 knots for non-self-propelled vessels;
4. During ebb tide;
5. Solid residue materials must not be discharged into the sea area, but must instead be recovered for disposal;
6. Entries of the circumstances of discharge to be made in the "ship's log."

CHAPTER VII. REFUSE FROM SHIPS

Article 27. Refuse from ships should not be dumped into harbor waters. Ships carrying toxic goods and powdery bulk goods should not wash their decks and cabins at will in harbors or discharge residues into the harbors in other ways. If washing is truly required, application must be made in advance to the harbor superintendency for approval.

Article 28. In all cases where ships in harbors need to dump refuse from aboard the ship, they shall display the signal stipulated by the harbor and employ refuse collection vessels to collect and dispose of the refuse. In addition, they shall do the following:

1. The containers for storing and collecting personal refuse from the ships must have covers and must not leak, and dumping is to be conducted at regular intervals;

2. Waste matter from cabin padding and cleaning of the compartments and various types of solid refuse shall be dumped by the shipping service departments in ports; the ship shall submit applications in advance to the shipping service departments in ports and designate the types and quantities of the materials to be dumped;
3. With respect to that portion of refuse from ships containing toxic or other dangerous substances, the ship, in applying for dumping, must provide the names, nature, and quantities of these substances, and they are to be strictly separated from other refuse when stored.

Article 29. With respect to refuse from ships arriving from ports suffering from epidemics, application shall be made to the public health and quarantine department to conduct sanitary treatment.

Article 30. When disposing of refuse at sea, ships shall meet the following stipulations:

1. Plastic items must not be dumped into the sea;
2. Human and food waste matter from ships in particles smaller than 25 millimeters in diameter after compaction, may be discarded beyond 3 nautical miles from the nearest land; those that have not undergone compaction shall be discarded beyond 12 nautical miles from the nearest land.

CHAPTER VIII. USE OF SHIPS TO DUMP WASTE MATERIALS

Article 31. Any unit that needs to use ships to dump waste materials shall submit a certification document from the State Bureau of Oceanography or its agencies to the harbor superintendency of the harbor where shipment begins, and the ship's entry and exit documents will be handled only after verification. If the actual shipments are not found to be in conformity with the approved manifest, the entry and exit documents will not be processed.

Article 32. When a ship conducts the dumping of waste materials, the ship should make accurate records of the circumstances regarding dumping. After its return to the harbor, the ship shall make a written report to the harbor superintendency of the locality.

Article 33. Foreign-registered ships should not dump waste materials in the sea areas under the jurisdiction of the People's Republic of China, including the discard of ships and other means of flotation.

CHAPTER IX. SURFACE AND UNDERWATER SHIP REPAIR, BUILDING, SALVAGING, AND SHIP-BREAKING PROJECTS

Article 34. Ship repair, building, salvaging, and ship-breaking units shall all have sufficient pollution-prevention facilities and equipment. When working on ships on the surface or under water, precautions shall be taken to prevent the pollution of the sea areas by oils, oil-based mixtures, and other waste materials. The oil-polluted water from work on ships on the surface is to be handled in accordance with the stipulations of Articles 19 and 20 of these regulations.

Article 35. In districts where ship repairs and building operations on the surface are concentrated, barriers to contain oil shall be set up to prevent the spread of oil and paint strewn about on the water, and these shall be cleaned up in a timely manner. With regard to industrial refuse and other waste materials from ship repair and shipbuilding, the work units are to organize recovery and disposal. These items must not be discarded into the sea.

Article 36. When breaking ships on the surface, the dismantled objects should not be discarded into the sea. The hull and the oil tanks should not be dismantled on the surface, but must be towed to the shore for ship-breaking operations, and the oil residues should be recovered and disposed of.

Article 37. In cases where accidents involving ships occur at sea, or when ships are in danger of sinking, the crew, before leaving the ship, shall as much as possible close the valves for all piping systems serving the oil compartments (tanks) and close the air vents for the oil compartments (tanks), to prevent oil spills. In addition, the quantity of oil aboard and the positions of the air vents shall be clearly stated in the maritime reports.

Article 38. When conducting underwater ship-salvaging projects, measures shall be adopted to prevent the spread of oil pollution and the occurrence of additional pollution.

CHAPTER X. COMPENSATION FOR DAMAGES FROM INCIDENTS OF POLLUTION BY SHIPS

Article 39. In cases when a ship violates the Marine Environmental Protection Law of the People's Republic of China and these regulations and causes harm through pollution of the marine environment, the harbor superintendencies may order the payment of a fee for eradicating the pollution and compensation for the state's losses. If a party contests the order, he may bring suit in the people's court in accordance with Article 41 of the Marine Environmental Protection Law of the People's Republic of China.

Article 40. All cases of units or individuals who have suffered harm from pollution as a result of marine pollution caused by ships which require the handling of claims for civil liability are to be handled in accordance with the procedures stipulated in Article 42 of the Marine Environmental Protection Law of the People's Republic of China. Disputes concerning liability for compensation and the amount of compenstion may be handled by the harbor superintendencies through mediation. If a party contests the handling of the matter, he may bring suit in the people's court. Suit may also be brought directly in the people's court. Cases involving foreigners may also be resolved in accordance with arbitration procedures.

Article 41. All units or individuals who have suffered harm from pollution by ships which file claims for compensation with the harbor superintendencies shall as quickly as possible submit a report claiming compensation for harm from pollution to a nearby harbor superintendency. This report shall include the following items:

1. The time, place, scope, and object of the harm caused by pollution from ships and the meteorological and hydrological circumstances at the time;
2. A detailed list of losses caused by the harm from pollution (including aquatic resources and various implements), including the names, quantities, unit price, method of calculation, and the breeding and natural conditions;
3. An appraisal by the relevant scientific research department or signature by the notary organ in confirmation of the circumstances of the harm;
4. The original copies of documents regarding evidence of the harm caused by pollution, photographs of the relevant circumstances, and other documents and testimony relevant to claims for compensation are to be provided to the maximum extent possible.

Article 42. Units and individuals who have participated in eradicating harm from pollution caused by ships and which require payment for services involved in eradicating the pollution shall, after completing the work of eradicating the pollution, submit as quickly as possible a report demanding payment for eradicating the pollution to the relevant harbor superintendencies. This report shall include:

1. The time, place, and the records of the schedule or the extracts from the ship's log regarding the eradication of pollution;
2. The personnel, machinery, tools, and vessels used and the quantities, unit prices, and method of calculating the value of the materials eradicated;
3. The management expenses, travel expenses, and other relevant expenses incurred in arranging the eradication;
4. A report on the results and the circumstances regarding the eradication;
5. Other relevant evidence and testimonial materials.

Article 43. In cases where pollution incidents involving ships occur in sea areas under the jurisdiction of the People's Republic of China, they shall be reported as quickly as possible to the nearest harbor superintendency, and when the ship enters its next port, a report shall immediately be submitted to the harbor superintendency, and the matter accepted for investigation and disposition. The contents of this report shall include the time, the place, the scope, the meteorological and hydrological circumstances, the circumstances of the process, the measures used for recovery and eradication, and the causes and harm of the pollution from ships. In addition, relevant materials shall be submitted as an appendix.

Article 44. In cases where pollution incidents involving ships have occurred, those shipowners who demand an exemption from liability for compensation shall submit a report to the harbor superintendency. This report should be able to prove that the harm from pollution entirely satisfies one of the conditions listed in Article 43 of the Marine Environmental Protection Law of the People's Republic of China and that, despite the timely adoption of reasonable measures, the harm involving pollution of the marine environment was still unavoidable.

Article 45. Cases involving disputes over liability for compensation and the size of compensation awards for pollution caused by ships that are accepted and heard by the harbor superintendencies, on the basis of the investigation and discovery of the facts, may be mediated or handled in accordance with the results of the investigation.

CHAPTER XI. PENALTIES AND REWARDS

Article 46. In any case of a ship in violation of the Marine Environmental Protection Law of the People's Republic of China and these regulations that causes or could cause harm from pollution of the sea areas and harbor waters under the jurisdiction of the People's Republic of China, the harbor superintendencies may give warning or impose fines on the shipowners according to the seriousness of the case and the extent of harm from pollution.

Article 47. With regard to fines imposed on the shipowner, the maximum amount is RMB 100,000 yuan. However, in any of the following cases, the maximum fine is RMB 1,000 yuan:

1. The use of unapproved oil-eradicating agents on the basis of one's own authority;
2. Failure to maintain the Oil Record Book according to stipulations;

3. Nonstandardized entries in the Oil Record Book or falsified entries;
4. Obstruction of inspections by the harbor superintendencies.

With regard to the crew found to be directly responsible and other individuals, education shall be given and, in serious cases, fines may also be imposed, but the maximum amount of a fine should not exceed 20 percent of the base salary of the person in question.

Article 48. In cases involving the occurrence of pollution incidents or pollution discharges in violation of regulations by ships, after investigation and when the evidence is found to be conclusive, the matter is to be handled in accordance with stipulations regardless of whether there is an admission [of responsibility] or not.

Article 49. If a party contests the imposition of a disciplinary penalty, the matter is to be handled in accordance with the stipulations of Article 41 of the Marine Environmental Protection Law of the People's Republic of China.

Article 50. Individuals who, on their own initiative, report and expose pollution incidents by ships, actively provide evidence, or adopt effective measures to reduce harm from pollution with outstanding results shall be commended and rewarded.

Article 51. The fines imposed on the ships that caused the problem and the personnel who bear direct responsibility are to be turned over to the state treasury as special funds. With respect to monetary awards for the relevant personnel prescribed in Article 50 of these regulations, they are to be allocated from state finances after verification.

CHAPTER XII. SUPPLEMENTARY PROVISIONS

Article 52. The meanings of the following terms in these regulations are:

1. "Harbors" refers to the coastal ports and the ports near river outlets to the sea whose main function is for seagoing vessels to dock, including the water areas and the sea lanes within the limits of these port areas.
2. "Ships" refers to the motor-driven and non-motor-driven vessels of all types but not including the stationary and mobile platforms involving exploration and development of offshore petroleum.
3. "Oils" refers to oils of any kind and their refined products.
4. "Refuse from the ships" refers to the personal refuse of the crew, the slag, pads and materials used to partition the compartments, refuse from sweeping of the compartments normally generated by ships themselves during their shipping operations and production, and materials like discarded tools, rigging, and spare parts from machines aboard ships.
5. "Ships currently in service" refers to vessels in service before March 1, 1983.

Article 53. With regard to the control of foreign-registered ships, in addition to implementing these regulations, controls based on the principle of reciprocity with the ships' countries of origin may be practiced.

Article 54. The state fishing administrations and organs of supervision and control of fishing ports are to exercise the functions and powers of the organs in charge as stipulated in these regulations.

Article 55. With regard to the control and prevention of pollution within areas under the jurisdiction of the military and aboard military ships, the military environmental protection departments are to formulate separate specific stipulations in accordance with the Marine Environmental Protection Law of the People's Republic of China and these regulations.

Article 56. These regulations shall come into force on the date of promulgation.

Appendix H

Regulations of the People's Republic of China on Marine Environmental Protection from Oil Exploration and Exploitation (December 29, 1983)

Zhongguo Fazhi Bao (January 13, 1984), p. 2.

Article 1. These regulations are formulated for the purpose of implementing the Marine Environmental Protection Law of the People's Republic of China so as to prevent pollution hazards to the marine environment from offshore oil exploration and exploitation.

Article 2. These regulations shall apply to all enterprises, institutions, operators, and individuals engaged in offshore oil exploration and exploitation in the sea areas under the jurisdiction of the People's Republic of China, as well as to the fixed and mobile platforms and other related installations they use.

Article 3. The competent authority in charge of environmental protection in offshore oil exploration and exploitation shall be the State Bureau of Oceanography of the People's Republic of China, including its agencies, which is hereinafter referred to as "the Competent Authority."

Article 4. While drawing up an overall development program for an oil (gas) field, an enterprise or operator shall draw up a Marine Environmental Impact Statement and submit it to the Ministry of Urban and Rural Construction and Environmental Protection of the People's Republic of China. The said ministry shall, in conjunction with the State Bureau of Oceanography and the Ministry of Petroleum Industry, conduct a review of the statement and make a decision on it in accordance with the provisions concerning environmental protection in state capital construction projects.

Article 5. A Marine Environmental Impact Statement shall consist of the following items:

1. The name, geographical location, and size of the oil field;
2. The natural environment and condition of marine resources in the sea area where the oil field is located;
3. The types, composition, quantities, and methods of disposal of the wastes that need to be discharged in the course of exploiting the oil field;
4. An assessment of marine environmental impacts: the possible effects of offshore oil exploitation on the natural environment and marine resources in the surrounding sea area; their possible effects on marine fisheries, shipping, and other offshore activities;

and the environmental protection measures proposed to be taken to avoid and mitigate various adverse effects;

5. The ultimately unavoidable effects and the extent and causes thereof; and
6. Measures to prevent major oil pollution accidents, including, among others, the organizations designated for prevention, personnel, technology and equipment, and other communications and liaison.

Article 6. An enterprise, institution, or operator shall have the ability to meet emergencies with regard to the prevention and control of oil pollution accidents, work out emergency plans, and be equipped with oil-recovery facilities as well as oil enclosure and eradication equipment and materials commensurate with the scale of offshore oil exploration and exploitation in which it is engaged.

When chemical dispersants are used, their trademark and composition shall be reported to the Competent Authority for approval.

Article 7. The antipollution equipment for fixed and mobile platforms shall conform to the following requirements:

1. There shall be oil-water separators;
2. The production platforms shall have equipment for treatment of oily water, and the oil content of the discharged water after treatment through such equipment shall conform to the national discharge standards;
3. There shall be monitoring devices for oil discharges;
4. There shall be recovery facilities for residual and waste oils;
5. There shall be refuse-compacting equipment; and
6. The above-mentioned equipment and facilities shall be inspected by the vessels inspection agency of the People's Republic of China, certified to be up to standard, and then granted a certificate of their effectiveness.

Article 8. If the antipollution equipment of a fixed or mobile platform already used in offshore oil exploration and exploitation in the sea areas under the jurisdiction of the People's Republic of China before March 1, 1983, fails to meet the prescribed requirements, effective measures shall be taken to prevent pollution and to ensure that such equipment meets the prescribed requirements within three years after the promulgation of these regulations.

Article 9. Each enterprise, institution, or operator shall carry insurance or other financial guarantees in respect of civil liabilities for pollution damage.

Article 10. A fixed or mobile platform shall have an Antipollution Record Book printed in a form approved by the Competent Authority.

Article 11. Oily water shall not be discharged, either directly or in diluted form, from any fixed or mobile platform. When the water is discharged after treatment, its oil content must comply with the state standards concerning oily water discharge.

Article 12. Requirements for the control of other wastes are as follows:

1. Residual oil, waste oil, oil-based mud, oily refuse, and other noxious liquids or residues shall be recovered and are forbidden to be discharged or dumped into the sea;
2. The disposal of industrial refuse in large quantities shall be controlled according to

provisions concerning marine dumping, and small quantities of industrial refuse may not be dumped into fishing areas and navigation channels; and

3. When it is necessary to dump domestic refuse within 12 nautical miles from the nearest land, it must be compacted into pellets of less than 25 millimeters in diameter.

Article 13. When offshore oil exploration and exploitation necessitates dynamite explosions or other operations harmful to fishery resources in important fishing grounds, effective measures shall be taken to avoid spawning, breeding, and fishing seasons for those fishes and shrimps of major economic value. Such operations shall be reported in advance to the Competent Authority, and distinct signs and signals shall be given while operations are carried out.

On receiving such a report, the Competent Authority shall promptly inform the relevant units of the location and time of the operations.

Article 14. Offshore oil-storage installations and oil pipelines shall meet the requirements against seepage, leakage, and corrosion and be kept in good condition through regular inspection so as to prevent oil leakage accidents.

Article 15. In the event of offshore well testing, the oil and gas shall be thoroughly burned in a burner. Effective measures shall be taken to dispose of the oils and oily mixtures fallen into the sea during the testing and a truthful record be made of such disposal.

Article 16. In case pollution accidents such as oil spills or leakage occur during operations, the enterprise, institution, or operator involved shall take prompt measures to enclose and recover the oil so as to control, mitigate, and eradicate the pollution.

Major oil pollution accidents involving massive oil spills, oil leakage, and/or blowouts shall immediately be reported to the Competent Authority while effective measures are taken to control and eliminate the oil pollution, and the accidents shall be subject to investigation and disposition by the Competent Authority.

Article 17. The use of chemical dispersants shall be controlled in such manner as follows:

1. When an oil pollution accident occurs, a small amount of chemical dispersant may be applied to a limited amount of oil which is indeed unrecoverable, provided that recovery measures have been taken;
2. The amount of disposable chemical dispersant (including its solvent) used shall be separately prescribed by the Competent Authority in accordance with different sea areas and other conditions. The operator shall submit a report to the Competent Authority in pursuance of relevant provisions and may use the chemical dispersant only after permission is granted;
3. In an emergency case in which the oil spilled is unlikely to be recovered and may cause a fire or present a serious threat to the safety of human life and properties whereas, by using chemical dispersants, pollution can be mitigated and the consequences of the accident prevented from expanding, the amount of such dispersant to be used and the relevant procedures for report may be exempt from the restrictions under paragraph 2 of this article. However, the facts of such an accident and the use of chemical dispersants shall be reported in detail to the Competent Authority after the accident has been dealt with; and
4. Only the chemical dispersant approved by the Competent Authority may be used.

Article 18. The operator shall make a truthful and detailed account of the following circumstances in the platform's Antipollution Record Book:

1. The operation of the antipollution equipment and installations;
2. The treatment and discharge of oily water;
3. The disposal, discharge, and dumping of other wastes;
4. Oil pollution accidents involving oil spills, oil leakage, blowouts, etc. and their disposition;
5. Operations conducted with explosives;
6. The use of chemical dispersants; and
7. Other matters as may be stipulated by the Competent Authority.

Article 19. Enterprises and operators shall, within fifteen days after each quarter of the calendar year, submit a comprehensive report to the Competent Authority on the antipollution situation and pollution accidents of that quarter on a form approved by the latter.

The location of the fixed or mobile platforms shall be communicated to the Competent Authority without delay.

Article 20. Functionaries of and persons designated by the Competent Authority have the right to board any fixed or mobile platform and any relevant installation for the purposes of monitoring and inspection, including:

1. Collecting various kinds of samples;
2. Inspecting the provision, operation, and use of the antipollution equipment, installations, and materials;
3. Checking relevant documents and certificates;
4. Inspecting the Antipollution Record Book and relevant operation records and, when necessary, making duplicate copies and excerpts thereof and asking the person in charge of the platform to certify that these duplicate copies and excerpts are authentic copies of the originals;
5. Questioning the concerned persons about pollution accidents; and
6. Handling other relevant matters.

Article 21. Ships on official duty of the Competent Authority shall be distinctly marked. In exercising their duties, the functionaries and designated persons shall be dressed in official uniforms and carry identity cards.

The inspected party shall furnish consideration to such ships on official duty, functionaries, and designated persons, provide accurate information, and state the facts.

Article 22. Entities and individuals claiming compensation on account of pollution damage resulting from offshore oil exploration and exploitation may, pursuant to the provisions of Article 32 of the Environmental Protection Law of the People's Republic of China and Article 42 of the Marine Environmental Protection Law of the People's Republic of China, apply to the Competent Authority without delay to claim compensation from the party causing the pollution damage. The injured party shall submit a statement claiming compensation for pollution damages, which shall consist of the following items:

1. The time, place, and area of, and objects affected by the pollution damage caused by oil exploration and exploitation;
2. A list of losses attributable to the pollution damage, including articles, their quantities, unit prices, and the methods of calculation, as well as information concerning agricultural and natural conditions;
3. The document of appraisal by relevant scientific institutions or certification by a notary body with regard to the damage; and
4. The original document and evidence of the pollution damage, relevant photographs, and other documentary evidence and materials relevant to the claim for compensation, which shall be supplied to the maximum extent possible.

Article 23. When an entity or individual (except those with commercial contracts) considers it necessary to submit a claim for clean-up expenses incurred in the eradication of pollutants resulting from offshore oil exploration and exploitation and applies to the Competent Authority to handle the claim, it shall submit to the Authority a statement of claims for such clean-up expenses. The statement shall consist of the following items:

1. The time and place of and objects involved in each clean-up operation;
2. The manpower, machines, tools, vessels, and materials used in each clean-up operation and the quantities, unit prices, and their methods of calculation;
3. The administrative expenses, transportation expenses, and other expenses involved in organizing such a clean-up operation;
4. The results of and related information about the clean-up operation; and
5. Other relevant evidence and documents.

Article 24. When an enterprise, institution, or operator involved in a pollution damage accident owing to force majeure asks to be exempted from compensation liabilities, it shall submit a report to the Competent Authority. Such a report shall verify that the pollution damage has really resulted from one of the causes specified in Article 42 of the Marine Environmental Protection Law of the People's Republic of China, and thus was unavoidable in spite of the prompt and reasonable measures taken.

Article 25. When dealing with a dispute over the compensation liabilities or the sum to be paid for pollution damage from offshore oil exploration and exploitation, the Competent Authority may settle the case through conciliation on the basis of investigation.

In case a party rejects conciliation or contests the conciliation proposals by the Competent Authority, the matter may be dealt with in pursuance of Article 42 of the Marine Environmental Protection Law of the People's Republic of China.

Article 26. An enterprise, institution, or operator who has violated the Marine Environmental Protection Law of the People's Republic of China and the present regulations shall be ordered by the Competent Authority to remedy the pollution damage within a definite time, pay the clean-up expenses incurred in eliminating the pollution, and compensate the losses sustained by the state, and those who have discharged pollutants in excess of the set standards may be ordered to pay effluent fees.

Article 27. The Competent Authority may, in light of circumstances, issue a warning to or impose a fine on any enterprise, institution, operator, or individual who has violated the Marine Environmental Protection Law of the People's Republic of China or the present regulations.

Fines shall be divided into the following categories:

1. A fine of no more than RMB 100,000 yuan imposed on an enterprise, institution, or operator for causing marine environmental pollution.
2. A fine of no more than RMB 5,000 yuan imposed on an enterprise, institution, or operator for one of the following unlawful acts:
   a) failure to report a major oil pollution accident to the Competent Authority in accordance with relevant rules; and
   b) failure to observe the relevant rules in using chemical dispersants.
3. A fine of no more than RMB 1,000 yuan imposed on an enterprise, institution, or operator for one of the following wrongful acts:
   a) failure to provide an Antipollution Record Book as required;
   b) making irregular or false entries in the Antipollution Record Book;
   c) failure to report or provide information on relevant matters as required; and
   d) obstructing the above-mentioned functionaries or designated persons in the exercise of their duties.
4. An appropriate fine imposed on an individual directly liable according to the seriousness of his case.

Article 28. In case a party contests the sanction decided by the Competent Authority, the matter shall be dealt with in accordance with the provisions of Article 41 of the Marine Environmental Protection Law of the People's Republic of China.

Article 29. The Competent Authority shall commend and reward entities and individuals who, on their own initiative, have reported on or charged the concealment of pollution damage accidents occurring in oil exploration and exploitation by an enterprise, institution, or operator, or have provided evidence in that respect, or have taken measures to mitigate such pollution damage.

Article 30. For the purposes of these regulations:

1. "Fixed and mobile platforms" refers to the drilling vessels, drilling platforms, and production platforms, as well as other platforms mentioned in the Marine Environmental Protection Law of the People's Republic of China.
2. "Offshore oil exploration and exploitation" refers to such operations as offshore oil exploration, exploitation, production, storage, and transportation through pipelines.
3. "Operator" refers to an entity engaged in operations of offshore oil exploration and exploitation.

Article 31. These regulations shall come into force from the day they are promulgated.

Appendix I

Regulations of the People's Republic of China on the Control of Marine Dumping (March 3, 1985)

GGB, no. 461 (April 10), pp. 222–27.

Article 1. These regulations were drawn up to carry out the Marine Environmental Protection Law of the People's Republic of China, to strictly control the dumping of wastes at sea, to prevent damage from pollution to the marine environment, to maintain the ecological balance, to protect marine resources, and to promote the development of marine enterprises.

Article 2. "Dumping" in these regulations refers to the use of boats and ships, aircraft, platforms, and other means of transportation to dispose of wastes and other material at sea; to discard boats and ships, aircraft, platforms, and other man-made marine structures at sea; and to dispose of the wastes and other materials produced from the exploration and exploitation of seabed mineral resources and from marine processing activities related to exploration and exploitation at sea.

The discharge of wastes during the course of normal operations of boats and ships, aircraft, and other means and equipment involved in transportation is not included in "dumping."

Article 3. These regulations apply to the following:

1. Dumping wastes and other materials in the inland seas, territorial seas, continental shelf and other marine areas under the jurisdiction of the People's Republic of China.
2. Loading wastes and other materials in the inland ports or seaports of the People's Republic of China for the purpose of dumping.
3. Transporting wastes and other materials through the inland seas, territorial seas, and other marine areas of the People's Republic of China for the purpose of dumping.
4. Burning wastes and other materials in the marine areas under the jurisdiction of the People's Republic of China.

The wastes produced from the exploration and exploitation of offshore oil should be treated according to the Regulations of the People's Republic of China on the Prevention of Marine Pollution from the Exploration and Exploitation of Offshore Oil.

Article 4. The department responsible for the dumping of wastes at sea is the State

Bureau of Oceanography of the People's Republic of China and its agencies (hereinafter referred to as the "responsible department").

Article 5. The areas for dumping at sea are designated on the basis of a safe, economical, and scientifically rational principle by the responsible department which discusses the issue with related departments. They then are approved and confirmed by the State Council.

Article 6. A unit that has a need to dump wastes at sea should apply to the responsible department in advance, fill out an application form according to the prescribed format, and report the characteristics and analysis of the composition of the wastes.

The responsible department will examine and approve the application within two months after receiving the application form. It will issue a permit to those who are approved to dump wastes.

No unit, boat or ship, aircraft, platform, or other means of transportation may dump wastes at sea without a permit from the responsible department.

Article 7. Foreign wastes are not allowed to be transported to the marine areas under the jurisdiction of the People's Republic of China and dumped at sea. These include abandoned boats and ships, aircraft, platforms, and other man-made marine structures. Those violating the regulations will be asked by the responsible department to resolve the problem within a designated period of time, pay the clean-up fees, pay for the damages, and pay a fine.

Those dumping wastes at sea outside the marine areas under the jurisdiction of the People's Republic of China and causing damage from pollution inside the marine areas under the jurisdiction of the People's Republic of China will be treated according to Article 17 of these regulations.

Article 8. For the purpose of dumping, any ship, boat, or means of transportation that transports wastes through the marine areas under the jurisdiction of the People's Republic of China should report to the responsible department fifteen days before entering the marine areas under the jurisdiction of the People's Republic of China. At the same time the dumper must report the expected entry date to the marine areas under the jurisdiction of the People's Republic of China, the route, and the name, quantity, and composition of the waste.

Article 9. Foreign boats, ships, and platforms in the marine areas under the jurisdiction of the People's Republic of China which have a need to dump wastes at sea in the course of their exploitation activities at sea should follow the formulated process and apply for permits from the responsible department.

Article 10. A permit for dumping should clearly specify the unit to which the permit is issued, its effective date, and the quantity, category, and method of dumping of the wastes.

Permit issuance should follow the rules in these regulations and be strictly controlled. The responsible department can replace or cancel a permit in accordance with the changes in the marine ecological environment and the development of scientific technology.

Article 11. Wastes can be classified into three categories based on factors like toxicity, the content of harmful materials, and their impact on the ocean environment. The standards for the classification will be drawn up by the responsible department. The responsible department may revise the appendix according to changes in the marine ecological environment, the development of scientific technology, and the need for marine environmental protection.

1. In emergency cases when wastes and other material listed as material banned from dumping at sea in Appendix 1 (see Appendix 1) will, if disposed of on land, severely endanger the health of the population, then they will be allowed to be dumped in a designated area according to the required method, provided that it was approved by the responsible department and an emergency permit was obtained.
2. A special permit should be obtained before dumping wastes that are listed in Appendix 2 (see Appendix 2).
3. A general permit should be obtained before dumping wastes with low toxicity or nontoxicity which are not listed in Appendix 1 or Appendix 2.

Article 12. At the time of loading wastes, the unit obtaining permission to dump waste at sea should notify the responsible department for confirmation.

The confirmation should be processed according to the items listed in the permit. If the responsible department discovers that the actual items are not consistent with the contents listed in the permit, it shall order the loading process to stop, and in severe cases, it shall suspend or revoke the permit.

Those using boats and ships to dump wastes should notify the harbor superintendency administration at the port of departure or the closest port for inspection. If the harbor superintendency administration discovers that the actual load is not consistent with the contents listed in the permit, it should not issue a transit visa and should notify the responsible department without delay.

Article 13. The responsible department should supervise and monitor the dumping activities at sea and send an inspector along if necessary. The dumping unit should provide accommodations to the accompanying government functionary.

Article 14. Having obtained a permit to dump wastes at sea, the unit should dump the wastes at the designated area within the designated time period and following the conditions specified in the permit. It should fill out the dumping conditions form in detail on the spot and send the form to the responsible department according to the requirements indicated in the permit. The boats and ships, aircraft, platforms, and other means of transportation should be equipped with distinctive marks and signals and the conditions regarding dumping should be recorded in the logbook.

Article 15. The boats and ships, aircraft, platforms, and other means of transportation used may not be held responsible for compensation if they meet the conditions listed in Article 43 of the Marine Environmental Protection Law of People's Republic of China.

Those dumping wastes under conditions or in an area which is not indicated in the permit during an emergency in order to avoid danger or to save lives, should try their best to avoid or limit the damage from pollution caused by dumping and report to the responsible department afterward as soon as possible. The dumping unit and the beneficiary of the action or lifesaving emergency should make compensation for the damage from pollution it creates.

If damage from pollution is caused by a third party, the dumping unit should submit conclusive evidence to the responsible department. After confirming the evidence, the responsible department will order the third party to be held responsible for compensation.

If boats and ships, aircraft, platforms, and other means of transportation navigating or working at sea dump wastes because of unavoidable conditions, their owner should report it to the responsible department and the nearest harbor superintendency administration and recover and clean up the wastes as soon as possible.

Article 16. The responsible department should monitor the dumping area regularly, strengthen its administration, and avoid impairment of fishing resources and other marine activities. When a dumping area is discovered to be unsuitable for accepting additional wastes, the responsible department may decide to close it.

Article 17. The responsible department will order those who violate these regulations and cause environmental damage to marine ecology to resolve the problem within a designated period of time. They will pay the clean-up expenses, compensate the aggrieved party for losses caused by the act, and, depending on the seriousness of the case and the extent of damage from pollution, receive a warning or a fine of not more than RMB 10,000.

Article 18. The unit or individual requesting compensation for damages should submit a report requesting compensation for damages from pollution to the responsible department as soon as possible. The report should include the time, the place, and the area of this damage from pollution, a detailed list of the damages, a technical appraisal and notarized testimony, along with related original documents such as receipts, bills, and invoices, and photographs if possible.

Article 19. After the clean up the unit which is commissioned to do the clean-up job should submit a bill for the clean-up fee. The bill should include the time, place, manpower, machines, and boats and ships used in the job, the quantity, unit price, and method of calculating the value of material used in the clean up, the management fee, the transportation fee and other related expenses in organizing the clean up, the results and conditions of the clean up, and other related evidence and identifying materials.

Article 20. The criteria for the punishment of unlawful practices are as follows:

1. Those responsible for one of the following actions will receive a warning or pay a fine of not more than RMB 2,000:
   a) forging a waste inspection manifest;
   b) filling out the dumping conditions form without following the rules set in Article 14;
   c) failure to report promptly to the responsible department or harbor superintendency administration in a situation cited in Article 15.
2. When the actual content differs from that indicated in the permit, the party will, in severe cases, pay a fine of between RMB 2,000 and 5,000, and the permit will be suspended or revoked.
3. Those who fail to follow the provisions in Article 12 to notify the responsible department to conduct an inspection and then proceed to dump wastes without authorization will pay a fine of between RMB 5,000 and 20,000.
4. Those guilty of any of the following actions will pay a fine of between RMB 20,000 and 100,000:
   a) dumping wastes at sea without permission;
   b) dumping wastes without complying with the conditions and areas indicated in the permit. (This does not refer to the conditions cited in Article 15 of these regulations.)

Article 21. The responsible department may issue a warning and/or impose a fine to the person who is directly responsible for violating these regulations and causing, or possibly causing, damage from marine environmental pollution.

The judicial organs will investigate the criminal responsibility of persons who are directly responsible for violating these regulations causing severe financial loss or injury or death from polluting and damaging the marine environmental ecology.

Article 22. A party that contests the penalty issued by the responsible department may file suit in the people's court within fifteen days of receiving notice of the penalty. The responsible department will request the people's court to enforce the penalties against those who have neither filed suit nor paid the penalty.

Article 23. Those who report and expose any conduct that violates these regulations and causes damage from marine environmental pollution and who actively provide evidence on their own initiative or take effective measures to decrease the damage from pollution will be praised and rewarded.

Article 24. These regulations shall come into force on April 1, 1985.

APPENDIX 1. MATERIALS THAT ARE BANNED FROM DUMPING

1. Waste materials containing organic halogen compounds, mercury and mercury-containing compounds, and cadmium and cadmium-containing compounds, except those with trace amounts of the materials mentioned above or those that can rapidly decompose into harmless materials in seawater.
2. Strongly radioactive wastes and other strongly radioactive materials.
3. Crude oil and its wastes, petroleum-refining products, oil residues, and mixtures containing those materials.
4. Synthetic materials such as fishing nets, ropes, plastic products, and other materials which float or remain suspended on the surface of the sea, severely obstructing navigation, fishing, and other activity or endangering marine organisms.
5. Sewage sludge and dredging materials containing the materials mentioned in Sections 1 and 2 of this Appendix.

APPENDIX 2. MATERIALS THAT REQUIRE A SPECIAL PERMIT FOR DUMPING

1. Waste materials containing large amounts of the following materials:
   a) arsenic and its compounds;
   b) lead and its compounds;
   c) copper and its compounds;
   d) zinc and its compounds;
   e) organosilicon compounds;
   f) cyanides;
   g) fluorides;
   h) beryllium, chromium, nickel, vanadium, and their compounds;
   i) insecticides and their by-products not mentioned in Appendix 1.
   Harmless materials or those that can rapidly decompose into harmless materials in seawater are excluded.
2. Waste materials containing weakly radioactive substances.
3. Containers, scrap metal, and other massive waste materials, which are likely to sink to the bottom of the sea and severely obstruct fishing and navigation.
4. Sewage sludge and dredging material containing the materials mentioned in Sections 1 and 2 of this Appendix.

Appendix J

Circular of China's State Administration of Industry and Commerce concerning the Registration of Foreign Companies Undertaking Joint Exploitation of Resources and Contracted Projects in China (March 12, 1983)

Zhongguo Duiwai Jingji Maoyi Fagui Huiban (Collection of Laws and Regulations of China concerning Foreign Economic and Trade Relations) (1983), pp. ix, 100, 102.

In order to meet the demands of the development of China's foreign economic co-operation, the following temporary provisions, modeled on the methods of registration of joint venture enterprises with Chinese and foreign capital, have been set for the registration of foreign companies which have undertaken the joint exploitation of resources and contracted projects in China.

Article 1. Foreign companies which undertake joint exploitation of resources and contracted projects in China, including the foreign general contractor (hereinafter referred to as the foreign contractor), who has signed contracts with China's National Offshore Oil Corporation, and foreign branch contractors, who build contracted projects and provide service, shall be registered in accordance with these provisions.

Article 2. Foreign contractors shall be registered with China's State Administration of Industry and Commerce. For registration, the following documents shall be produced:

1. The document of approval issued by the State Council or by a department authorized by the State Council;
2. The contract signed by the foreign contractor and China's National Offshore Oil Corporation;
3. The foreign contractor's certificate for legitimate business operation and capital credit;
4. Application for registration signed by the board chairman of the foreign contractor (the content of the application should include business scope, name list, posts, and biographical notes of main resident personnel in China);
5. The list of foreign branch contractors, items and content of contracted projects, and a list of the principal resident personnel in China.

After verification and approval of the registration of the foreign contractor by China's State Administration of Industry and Commerce, a Business License of the People's

Republic of China shall be issued to the foreign contractor. The registration fee shall be charged according to the standard set for Chinese and foreign joint venture enterprises.

Considering that foreign contractors who take part in the joint exploitation of offshore oil will assume all risks themselves during the exploration period, their registration fee shall be determined on preferential terms, temporarily set at RMB 2,000. When commercial production commences, foreign contractors shall go through registration formalities again. The fee shall be charged according to the standard set for Chinese and foreign joint venture enterprises.

Article 3. Registration of foreign branch contractors shall be handled at local branches authorized by the State Administration of Industry and Commerce. For registration, the following documents shall be produced:

1. The contract;
2. The certificate of the related company under China's National Offshore Oil Corporation;
3. The application for registration signed by the board chairman of the foreign contractor (the content of the application should include business scope, items, and content of the contracted projects; name list, posts, and biographical notes of main resident personnel in China).

After the verification and approval of the registration of foreign branch contracts, the Registration Certificate for Foreign Enterprises Undertaking Contracted Projects in China (hereinafter referred to as the "registration certificate") shall be issued to foreign branch contractors. The valid period of the registration certificate is the same as the time limit of the contract. The registration fee shall be determined according to the standard set for Chinese and foreign joint venture enterprises.

Foreign branch contractors who undertake contracted projects and provide services in several provinces, municipalities, and autonomous regions simultaneously shall be registered at China's State Administration of Industry and Commerce.

Article 4. If the content of the items under registration changes, or if a foreign contractor ends his activities in China because of the expiration or termination of the contract, the foreign contractor shall go to the original registration office and go through formalities for the change or cancellation of the contract.

Article 5. The registration of overseas Chinese and Hong Kong and Macao corporations which take part in the joint exploitation of resources and undertake contracted projects shall be handled in accordance with these provisions.

This circular shall come into force on April 1, 1983.

Appendix K

Forestry Law (1984)

Renmin Ribao (September 23).

CHAPTER I. GENERAL PRINCIPLES

Article 1. This law is stipulated for the purpose of protecting, cultivating, and rationally exploiting forest resources, accelerating afforestation, and bringing the role of forests into full play in terms of storing water and conserving soil, regulating the climate, improving the environment, and supplying forest products to satisfy the needs of socialist construction and the people's livelihood.

Article 2. All those who fell, exploit, cultivate, plant, and manage forests in the domain of the People's Republic of China must abide by this law.

Article 3. The forest resources belong to the whole people, except for those owned by collectives as stipulated by law.

Local people's governments at and above the county level should compile records to register forests, trees, and forest land owned by the whole people and collectives, the forest trees owned by individuals, and the forest land used by individuals, and issue certificates after checking to affirm ownership and usage rights.

The legitimate rights and interests of the owners and users of forests, forest trees, and forest land are protected by law. No units or individuals are allowed to infringe on them.

Article 4. Forests are divided into the following five categories:

1. *Shelter forests*: forests, trees, and bushes whose principal purpose is shelter. They include watershed conservation forests, soil conservation forests, windbreaks and sand-stabilization forests, field and pasture shelter belts, coastal shelter belts, and road shelter belts.
2. *Timber forests*: forests and trees whose principal purpose is to produce timber, including bamboo forests, whose principal purpose is to produce bamboo.
3. *Economic forests*: forests whose principal purpose is to produce fruit, edible oils, beverages, condiments, industrial raw materials, and medicinal materials.
4. *Fuel wood forests*: trees whose principal purpose is to produce fuel.
5. *Special use forests*: forests and trees whose principal purposes are national defense, environmental protection, and scientific experimentation. They include national defense forests, experimental forests, seed trees, environmental protection forests, scenic

forests, trees at historical and archaeological sites, revolutionary memorials, and forests in nature preserves.

Article 5. Forestry construction carries out the policies of treating silviculture as the foundation, widespread forestry conservation, afforesting the land in a big way, integrating felling with cultivating, and sustained yield.

The state encourages the study of forestry science to raise the level of forestry science and technology.

Article 6. The state takes the following measures to conserve forestry resources:

1. Setting logging quotas, encouraging tree planting and afforestation, and the closing of hillsides to facilitate natural regeneration, and expanding forest cover.
2. In accordance with the relevant regulations of the state and local people's governments, providing economic subsidies or long-term credits to collectives and individuals for afforestation and cultivation.
3. Assessing silvicultural fees to be earmarked for afforestation and cultivation.
4. The coal industry, paper-making industry, and other industrial departments should provide a certain amount of funds in accordance with the output of coal, paper made from wood pulp, and other products to be spent exclusively for establishing pitprop and pulp timber forests.
5. Establishing a forestry (capital) fund system.

Article 7. With regard to forestry production and construction in nationalities' autonomous areas, the central, provincial, and autonomous region people's governments should, in accordance with state regulations governing the right of autonomy in nationalities' autonomous areas, give them greater decision-making power and economic benefits than other areas in forest exploitation, timber distribution, and the use of forestry funds.

Article 8. The supervisory department under the State Council responsible for forestry is in charge of forestry work throughout the country as a whole. The departments responsible for forestry work in local people's governments at and above the county level are in charge of forestry work in their respective areas. Township-level people's governments should assign personnel to be responsible for forestry work on a full-time or part-time basis.

Article 9. Afforestation and forest conservation are a citizen's bounden duty. People's governments at all levels should organize all the people to obligatorily plant trees and develop afforestation activities.

Article 10. Units or individuals achieving outstanding results in afforesting land, protecting forests, and managing forests should be rewarded spiritually or materially by people's governments at various levels.

CHAPTER II. FOREST MANAGEMENT

Article 11. The departments in charge of forestry work at various levels will manage and supervise the protection, utilization, and regeneration of forest resources in accordance with this law.

Article 12. The departments in charge of forestry work at various levels are responsible for organizing inventories of forest resources, establishing a recording system for forest resources, and understanding changes in the composition of resources.

Article 13. People's governments at various levels should formulate long-range plans for forestry work. State forestry enterprises and other undertakings and nature preserves should prepare forestry management plans in accordance with the long-range plans for forestry work and implement them after they have been approved by supervisory departments at higher levels. The departments in charge of forestry work should guide rural collective economic organizations, state agricultural and animal husbandry farms, and industrial and mining enterprises to prepare forestry management plans.

Article 14. Disputes involving ownership and usage rights of forests and forest land among units owned by the whole people, among collectively owned units, and between units owned by the whole people and collectively owned units will be handled by people's governments at and above the county level. Disputes involving ownership and usage rights of forests and forest land among individuals and between individuals and units owned by the whole people or collectively owned units will be handled by people's governments at the county or township level. The parties concerned may file suit in the people's court if they are dissatisfied with the people's government's handling of the case within one month after receival of the notice from the people's government. Until the disputes concerning the ownership and right to use forests and forest lands are resolved, no party is allowed to fell the disputed trees.

Article 15. When conducting survey and design work, repair and construction projects, and the exploitation of mineral resources, the occupation of forest land should be avoided or minimized. When forest land must be occupied or requisitioned, the cases should be handled according to the relevant laws and regulations. The occupation or requisition of forest land involving 2,000 mu (133 hectares) or larger areas should be reported to the State Council for approval.

CHAPTER III. FOREST PROTECTION

Article 16. The local people's governments at various levels should organize the departments concerned to establish forest protection organizations to be responsible for the work of forest protection; expand forest protection facilities in large forest districts according to actual needs in order to strengthen forest protection work; and encourage units with forests and in forestry districts at the grassroots level to conclude forest protection compacts, organize the masses to protect the forests, designate forest protection responsibility areas, and assign forest wardens on a full-time or part-time basis.

Forest wardens may be appointed by county or township people's governments. The main duties of forest wardens are patrolling the forests and halting activities that damage forest resources. Forest wardens have the right to ask departments concerned in the locality to handle cases involving damage to forest resources.

Article 17. Local people's governments at various levels should sincerely do a good job of forest fire prevention and fighting:

1. Designating forest fire prevention seasons. During these seasons, outdoor fires in forestry districts will be prohibited. The use of fire due to special circumstances must be approved by the people's government at the county level or the organ designated by the people's government at the county level.
2. Installing fire prevention facilities in forestry districts.
3. When a forest fire occurs, immediately organizing local army men, the masses, and departments concerned to fight the fire.

4. Those who are injured, disabled, or die while fighting forest fires will be given medical treatment and compensated by their own units if they are state employees. Non-state employees will be given medical treatment and compensated by the units where the fires started in accordance with the regulations of the relevant supervisory departments of the State Council. When the unit where the fire started is not responsible for the accident or absolutely lacks the capacity to assume the burdens (of medical treatment and compensation), the local people's governments will provide medical treatment and compensation.

Article 18. Departments in charge of forestry work at various levels are responsible for organizing the prevention and control of forest pests and diseases. Departments in charge of forestry work are responsible for designating quarantine objectives for trees and seedlings, setting up quarantine areas and protection zones, and conducting quarantine work for trees and seedlings.

Article 19. The destruction of forests for land reclamation and for quarrying and excavating sand and earth and any other acts that cause damage to forests are prohibited. The cutting of trees for fuel and grazing of livestock in young forests and special use forests is prohibited.

Those who enter forests and adjoining areas may not move or damage forestry markers without authorization.

Article 20. The department of the State Council in charge of forestry and the people's governments in the various provinces, autonomous regions, and municipalities directly under the central government should set up nature preserves and strengthen protection and management in those forest areas which are worthy of special protection, including typical forest ecological areas in different natural zones, forestry districts where rare species of animals and plants are found, and natural tropical rain forest areas.

Measures for the management of nature preserves will be formulated by the department of the State Council in charge of forestry and submitted to the State Council for approval before being put into effect.

Rare species of trees outside the nature preserves as well as the botanical resources of special value within the forest areas should be earnestly protected. No logging or harvesting of such trees and resources is allowed without the approval of the forestry department of the respective provinces, autonomous regions, or municipalities directly under the central government.

Article 21. The hunting of wildlife on the state protection lists in forestry districts is prohibited. If the hunting of such animals is required to meet special needs, it must be conducted in accordance with the relevant laws and regulations of the state.

CHAPTER IV. TREE PLANTING AND AFFORESTATION

Article 22. People's governments at all levels should draw up tree-planting and afforestation plans, and fix struggle targets to raise forest cover in their respective localities according to local conditions.

People's governments at all levels should organize all trades and professions, as well as residents of both urban and rural areas, to fulfill the tasks set in their tree-planting and afforestation plans.

The afforestation of afforestable waste mountains and lands owned by the whole people should be organized by the departments in charge of forestry and other supervisory departments. If the waste mountains and lands belong to collectives, afforestation work should be organized by the collective economic organizations.

Afforestation work along highways, on river banks, and around lakes and reservoirs should be organized by the various supervisory units concerned in line with local conditions. In industrial and mining areas, areas occupied by government organizations and schools, military bases, and (state) agricultural, animal husbandry, and fishery farms, the respective units should be responsible for afforestation. Afforestation of afforestable waste mountains and lands owned by the whole people or by the collectives may be undertaken by collectives or individuals on a contract basis.

Article 23. Trees afforested by units owned by the whole people should be managed by these units, and the revenues obtained from the trees should be distributed according to state regulations.

Trees afforested by collectively owned units are owned by these units.

Trees planted by village residents around their houses and on their private plots and mountains are owned by them. Trees planted by urban residents and employees in the yards of their privately owned houses are owned by these individuals.

In the case of afforestation performed on a contract basis by collectives or individuals on afforestable waste mountains or lands owned by the whole people or by a collective, the trees planted after signing the contract are owned by the collective or individual contractor. When the contract has other provisions, the contract's clauses should govern.

Article 24. Local people's governments should arrange the closure of mountains to grazing and other activities on newly afforested sites and other sites where closure is essential.

CHAPTER V. LOGGING

Article 25. The state strictly controls the annual volume of logging according to the principle that consumption of timber forests shall not exceed the growth increment. Annual logging quotas shall be set for each state-owned forestry enterprise or other undertaking, farm, factory, or mine in the case of forests and trees owned by the whole people, and for each county in the case of forests and trees owned by collectives. The quotas shall be put together by the forestry supervisory departments of the respective provinces, autonomous regions, and municipalities directly under the central government and, after examination and verification by the people's governments at the same level, submitted to the State Council for its approval.

Article 26. The state sets a unified annual timber production plan. The annual timber production plan shall not exceed the approved annual logging quota. The scope of the plan shall be defined by the State Council.

Article 27. The logging of forests and trees must observe the following stipulations.

1. In accordance with variations in conditions, mature timber forests shall be logged by selection cutting, clear cutting, or shelter-wood cutting. Clear cutting should be strictly controlled, and regeneration must be completed within the same year or the following year.
2. With regard to the shelter forests and special use forests, including national defense forests, seed trees, environmental protection forests, and scenic forests, only sanitation and regeneration-oriented felling are allowed.
3. The felling of trees in certain special use forests, on historical and archaeological sites and revolutionary memorials, and in forests in nature preserves is strictly prohibited.

Article 28. Logging must be preceded by an application for a logging permit, and logging must be conducted according to the stipulations listed in the permit. However, residents in rural areas require no logging permits to cut their privately owned scattered trees on their private plots and around their homes.

Permits for logging by state forestry enterprises and other undertakings, organizations, bodies, military units, schools, and by other state enterprises and other undertakings shall be examined and issued by the local departments at and above the county level responsible for forestry.

Permits for regeneration felling in railway and highway shelter belts and urban trees shall be examined and issued by the relevant supervisory departments.

Permits for logging by rural collective economic organizations shall be examined and issued by the departments at the county level responsible for forestry.

Permits for logging by rural residents on private hills and privately contracted but collectively owned woodlots shall be examined and issued by the departments at the county level responsible for forestry or the township and town people's government entrusted by them with this authority.

The sections above are applicable to the felling of bamboo forests for which the principal purpose is bamboo production.

Article 29. Departments in charge of examining and issuing logging permits may not exceed the approved annual logging quotas when issuing logging permits.

Article 30. When applying for logging permits, state forestry enterprises and other undertakings must provide survey and design documents on the areas to be logged. When applying for logging permits, other units must provide documents specifying the purposes of logging the sites, the mixture of species, stand conditions, the area to be logged, timber stocking, logging methods, and regeneration methods.

With regard to units whose operations in logging areas are in violation of regulations, the departments which issued the logging permits have the authority to revoke their logging permits and suspend their logging permits until the deficiencies have been corrected.

Article 31. Units and individuals who harvest trees must fulfill their reforestation tasks with regard to the area, number of trees, mixture of species, and time limits as stipulated in their logging permits. The reforested area and the number of reforested trees must exceed the area and number of trees that were felled.

Article 32. With regard to methods governing the management and supervision of timber in forest districts, the State Council will separately issue regulations.

Article 33. Except for timber distributed under the unified state plan, no timber is allowed to be transported outside of forest districts without a transport permit issued by the department in charge of forestry.

With the approval of the governments of the provinces, autonomous regions, and municipalities directly under the central government, timber inspection stations may be established in forest districts to inspect timber transport. Timber inspection stations have the authority to halt shipments of timber lacking transport permits or distribution approval from the department in charge of materials supply.

CHAPTER VI. LEGAL RESPONSIBILITY

Article 34. In minor cases of the poaching of a forest or other trees, the departments responsible for forestry shall order compensation for damages by planting ten times the number of trees poached and paying a fine totalling three to ten times the amount of the illegal gains. In minor cases of deforestation, the departments responsible for forestry shall order the planting of five times the number of trees removed and the payment of a fine totalling two to five times the amount of the illegal gains.

With regard to serious cases of poaching and denudation, criminal responsibility should be investigated and affixed according to the stipulations of Article 128 of the Criminal Law.

With regard to the possession of large numbers of poached trees, criminal responsibility should be investigated and affixed according to the stipulations of Article 152 of the Criminal Law.

Article 35. People who are directly responsible for issuing logging permits in excess of the approved annual logging quota or issuing logging permits beyond the bounds of their authority in violation of this law will be given administrative punishment. In serious cases where forests are gravely damaged, the criminal responsibility of those who are directly responsible will be investigated and affixed according to the stipulations of Article 187 of the Criminal Law.

Article 36. Those who forge or engage in the illegal sale of logging permits will have their illegal gains confiscated and will be fined by the department in charge of forestry. In serious cases criminal responsibility will be investigated and affixed in accordance with Article 120 of the Criminal Law.

Article 37. Departments in charge of forestry will order anyone who violates this law and causes damage to forests and trees through land reclamation, stone quarrying, gravel quarrying, the excavation of dirt, seed gathering, resin tapping, cutting firewood, or other activities to pay compensation for the damages caused and to replant one to three times the number of trees thus damaged.

Article 38. Units or individuals who engage in logging but who fail to fulfill their reforestation tasks in accordance with their logging permits will not be issued new logging permits by the department in charge of forestry until they have fulfilled their afforestation tasks. In cases of serious violations, the departments in charge of forestry work may issue fines, and those who are directly responsible may be given administrative punishment by their units or by their supervisory organs.

Article 39. If a party contests the fines imposed by the department in charge of forestry work, they may file suit in the people's court within one month of receipt of the notification to pay the fine. The departments in charge of forestry work may ask the people's court to enforce the fines if the violators do not file suit in the people's court within the prescribed period and refuse to pay the fines.

CHAPTER VII. SUPPLEMENTARY ARTICLES

Article 40. The department in charge of forestry work under the State Council will formulate measures for the implementation of this law, which will be put in force following approval by the State Council.

Article 41. In nationalities' autonomous areas where this law may not be fully applicable, the local autonomous organizations may formulate varying or supplementary provisions according to the principles of this law and the special characteristics of the nationalities' autonomous areas, and then submit them to the various provinces and autonomous regions, or to the Standing Committee of the National People's Congress for approval and implementation in accordance with legal procedures.

Article 42. This law shall come into force on January 1, 1985.

APPENDIX: ARTICLES OF THE CRIMINAL LAW CITED BY THIS LAW

Article 120. Serious cases of forgery and reselling of planned supply certificates to make money will be punishable by fixed-term imprisonment or detention of not more than three years. They can concurrently or exclusively be given fines or have their property confiscated. Ringleaders in the above-mentioned offense or those with particularly serious cases will be sentenced to fixed-term imprisonment of not less than three or more than seven years and can concurrently have their property confiscated.

Article 128. Those guilty of a serious violation of the Forest Protection Law [sic] and of illegally cutting and denuding forests will be sentenced to fixed-term imprisonment or detention of not more than three years and can concurrently or exclusively be given fines.

Article 152. A habitual thief or swindler or anyone who takes away a huge amount of public or private property by stealing, swindling, or plundering will be sentenced to imprisonment for not less than five years or more than ten years. In extremely grave cases the offender will be sentenced to imprisonment for not less than ten years or life imprisonment and may at the same time have his property confiscated.

Article 187. Any state functionary who inflicts heavy losses upon public property, the state, or the people due to dereliction of duty will be sentenced to detention or imprisonment for not more than five years.

[*Editors' note*: The regulations mentioned in article 40 were promulgated in 1986. See "Detailed Measures for the Implementation of the Forestry Law of the People's Republic of China," May 10, 1986, in *GGB*, no. 501 (May 30, 1986), pp. 454–58.]

Appendix L

State Council Emergency Circular on the Strict Prohibition of Reckless and Illegal Felling of Forests (December 5, 1980)

Translation, with permission, from *The Bad Earth* by Vaclav Smil, New York: M. E. Sharpe, Inc., 1984, pp. 227–28.

In many localities trees are being logged arbitrarily, and timber is being resold for profit. Our forest resources are being seriously sabotaged. It is necessary to take effective measures to curb this immediately. Therefore the following emergency circular is issued.

1. The people's governments at all levels must immediately check on the implementation of timber and bamboo production plans transmitted to lower levels by provincial and regional authorities. It is imperative to immediately stop the felling of trees not covered by the plan. In places where trees have been recklessly felled and forests seriously sabotaged, it is necessary to impound any timber, bamboo, and semifinished products felled and procured, pending investigation. Before the completion of clearances, nobody is allowed to continue felling trees. Violators should be punished as forest saboteurs.

2. The state monopoly on the purchase and marketing of timber and bamboo must be strictly practiced. Timber produced by state-run forestry units and communes and brigades in forest areas should be purchased and marketed by the Ministry of Forestry; bamboo should be purchased and marketed by departments designated by the provincial and regional people's governments. No other departments, organizations, bodies, plants, mines, schools, People's Liberation Army (PLA) units, or individuals are allowed to enter forest areas to fell, purchase, or process timber and bamboo. Those who have entered must leave immediately. All timber and bamboo free markets in forest areas must be closed. It is necessary to seriously reorganize all commune- and brigade-run timber-processing plants in forest areas.

3. If the jurisdiction over mountains and forests is not clear or is controversial, the local people's government should make great efforts to solve the issue by acting according to the principle of benefiting production and unity. Pending the settlement of the issue, no party is allowed to fell the trees. Those who deliberately create disputes involving the jurisdiction over forests, or who sabotage forests, must be punished.

4. It is necessary to strengthen timber logging and the management of timber transport in forest areas. State-run forestry units must fell trees in accordance with the timber production plan relayed by the state. With regard to logging in collectively owned forests, the county forestry administrative departments must first examine and approve it according

to the plan relayed by the state and to the related stipulations of the Forestry Law (draft) and issue logging certificates. No timber or its semifinished products in timber-producing areas can be transported out of a county without transport certificates issued by the county forestry administrative departments; nor can they be transported out of a province or an autonomous region without transport certificates issued by the provincial or regional forestry administrative departments. No railway, communications, or other transport departments are allowed to transport timber without seeing the certificates issued by the forestry administrative departments. Violators must be sternly dealt with, and forestry departments violating these stipulations must be severely punished.

5. People's governments at all levels must examine and handle cases of seizing, plundering, chopping, and stealthily felling trees, profiteering on timber and bamboo, and assaulting forest protection personnel. It is necessary to punish severely the criminals who sabotage forests and who kill or injure forest protection personnel. It is necessary to investigate and affix responsibility among those leading personnel who connive at, or support, the sabotage of forests and deal harshly with them.

It is hoped that this circular will be earnestly carried out by all provinces, municipalities, and autonomous regions and that the results of carrying out the circular will be reported to the State Council.

Appendix M

Central Committee of the Chinese Communist Party, State Council Decisions on Some Problems regarding Forestry Conservation and Forestry Development (March 8, 1981)

BFWH, pp. 156–68.

Forestry is an important element in the national economy. A developed forestry is one mark of a prosperous state, flourishing nation and civilized society. For a rather long period of history, China's forestry base has been weak and forest destruction extremely serious. Therefore, forest conservation and forestry development are extremely urgent strategic tasks in the process of building socialist modernization and must arouse the full attention of the whole party and the whole people.

Since the founding of the People's Republic, forestry construction has made some notable achievements under the leadership of the party and the people's government as a result of arduous struggle by the broad people and masses and forestry personnel. We have supplied the state with 9,800 million cubic meters of timber, effectively afforested 28 million hectares, and made important contributions to building socialism. However, forestry remains backward despite enormous efforts because of the scarcity of forests in the past, insufficient attention to forestry's importance, and ''leftist'' errors and influence on our work and guidance.

At present, the gravest problems are serious forest destruction, overfelling, insufficient afforestation, excessive consumption, and insufficient cultivation. This makes the contradiction between supply and demand over timber and forest products even acuter and further worsens the natural eco-environment. If we allow this state of affairs to continue to deteriorate, it will bring about unfortunate consequences for agricultural and livestock production and the people's livelihood and we will bequeath disasters to future generations.

The causes of these problems are the chronic failure to put forestry in a position of equal importance alongside farming and animal husbandry; unstable forestry rights and frequent policy fluctuations; insufficient funding for silviculture, irrational timber prices, and too many customers and too few users located in the forests; locally inappropriate actions in the forestry districts and failure to practice a diversified economy with forestry as the leading factor; forestry production overemphasizing felling and underemphasizing afforestation and failure to carry out the policy of taking silviculture as the foundation; uncoordinated timber management and chaotic structures, so that while one person afforests with his hoe, 100 others are chopping down trees with their axes; loose forest management and longstanding laxity in law enforcement and discipline. All of these seriously impair the activism of the masses and various sectors for afforestation, forest cultivation, and forestry conservation, impeding forestry development.

The following decisions are for the purpose of swiftly reversing the grave situation confronting forestry, resolutely halting reckless and illegal felling, genuinely conserving standing forests, stringently regulating felling, lowering resource consumption, further carrying out forestry policy, fully mobilizing activism in all fields, greatly developing afforestation and forest cultivation, and gradually moving forestry construction onto a healthy development track.

STABILIZE MOUNTAIN AND FOREST RIGHTS AND PUT INTO EFFECT FORESTRY PRODUCTION RESPONSIBILITY SYSTEMS

1. All state and collectively owned mountains and forests, privately owned trees and utilized forest land, and trees owned by other departments and units, the rights for which have been clarified, should receive recognition of this through the issuance of forestry rights certificates by the people's government at the county or higher levels to ensure that these rights will not be altered. Party committees and people's governments at various levels must quickly establish procedures and organize their forces to complete the task before next spring [1982].

In all cases where there are disputes over forestry rights, the relevant government should organize both parties to mediate a solution. When mediation is ineffective, it should submit the issue to the people's court for adjudication. No one is allowed to cut the trees in dispute before the conflict has been resolved, and anyone who violates this provision will be punished according to law.

2. In accordance with the needs of the masses, we must assign private hills (or wasteland) to commune members for tree and grass planting on a long-term utilization basis. The size of private hills and the procedures for assigning them will be set by provincial-level governments.

Trees planted by commune members on their homesteads, private hills, and other sites designated by the production team will be individually owned by the commune members ever after and can be inherited.

3. State forest farms and communes and brigades must earnestly put into effect forestry production responsibility systems in accordance with the spirit of the Circular on Some Problems in Further Strengthening and Perfecting Agricultural Production Responsibility Systems and by summing up the special characteristics of forestry production. In accordance with the principle of from each according to his ability, to each according to his work, we must closely link responsibilities and compensation and the interests of the whole with the interests of the individual. Commune and brigade collectively owned forestry ought to expand the specialized contract guarantee, unified production, and compensation production responsibility system. Contracts can be let with work groups, households, or individual workers. In close correspondence with afforestation and silvicultural results, they should put into place rational compensation, bonuses for above-norm production, and proportional division of income approaches. Specific approaches may vary, with the choice to be made on the basis of actual conditions, the mass line, and local suitability.

MANAGE TIMBER ON A CENTRALIZED AND UNIFIED BASIS

4. Provincial-level governments must stringently control logging volume in accordance with the principle that timber consumption must not exceed growth. State forestry

bureaus [administrations] and counties in forestry districts must determine rational annual cutting volumes for timber and bamboo in accordance with logging rotation needs. We must institute a nationwide ''single-ledger'' by including in the plan timber subject to unified distribution by the state, locally utilized timber, timber used by state forestry units and other departments themselves, etc. Annual logging plans for provinces and relevant state departments will be set by the State Planning Commission with the Ministry of Forestry to establish a comprehensive balance, consulting with the provinces, and then unifiedly assigning quotas to be met. Different levels in the system are not allowed to increase logging quotas or conduct logging outside the plan. Timber shall not be subject to negotiated procurement and sales.

The logging of state-owned forests will be unifiedly apportioned by the department supervising forestry in each province. With regard to the logging of collective forests, the county forestry administrative department shall issue logging permits. Logging of their own forest by other departments and timber logged by the collectives for their own use will require submission of an application to the county forestry administrative department in accordance with relevant provisions of the Forestry Law (for trial implementation—1979), which will issue logging permits. Those who log without permits will be penalized for destroying forests.

5. All timber produced by state forestry bureaus that satisfies state standards is subject to unified procurement by the state with the exception of those portions designated for self-use and approved for retention by the localities. The state will unifiedly procure 70 to 90 percent of timber produced by collectives in forestry districts that satisfies state standards, with the exact proportions to be set by the provinces. The state will not apply unified procurement to below-grade timber in the forestry districts or to timber produced by individual commune members.

6. Timber and semiprocessed products in the forestry districts are under unified management by the forestry departments. No other department or unit is allowed to enter the forestry districts for the purposes of logging, procurement, or processing. The timber supply and market sales system in consuming areas will not be altered.

All fuelwood, charcoal, wooden handles, wooden rods, and large quantities of wooden manufactures and semimanufactures needed by supply and marketing, light industry, foreign trade, and collective enterprises should be entered into the plan, with the forestry departments organizing production and providing the supply.

Timber-processing plants operated by the collectives in forestry districts and other units must undergo through reorganization. All plants producing low-quality–high-cost goods, which waste timber, or lack their own sources of timber must be resolutely closed down, suspended, merged, or made to change their line of production. Supplies for those that are allowed to continue in operation must be entered into the plan.

No free timber markets are allowed in the forestry districts of adjoining counties. With regard to below-grade timber produced by the collectives in forestry districts; timber retained by the collectives, including the collectives' share of timber from participation in state silviculture, production, and construction; and large quantities of manufactures and semimanufactures produced from them, the forestry departments shall act as the sales agent. Alternatively, with the approval of the forestry departments, producer and consumer districts can engage in mutual exchange of needed products under unified organization. With approval by the production brigade, the forestry departments also can act as the sales agent for individuals' privately owned timber.

The provincial people's governments shall determine whether or not to open free timber and bamboo markets in nonforestry districts.

ECONOMIC SUPPORT FOR FORESTRY

7. Timber prices in collective and state forestry districts shall be adjusted in a planned and orderly manner. Income from higher prices should be retained by the timber-producing units, and [governmental or other units] are not permitted to intercept that income. The precise arrangements shall be transmitted down by the State Materials Pricing General Administration and the Ministry of Forestry.

8. Establishment of a state forestry funding system. We must include in the forestry fund: state forestry investment, fiscal appropriations, bank credits, and the silvicultural and renewal funds withdrawn in accordance with regulations. Central and local forestry departments will manage the fund at different levels according to stipulated rights and limitations, using earmarked funds for earmarked purposes, and carrying unexpended funds over from one year to the next. All areas every year must strive to assign some local funds to the support of forestry. Local governments will assign to forestry development a portion of subsidized investment in the communes; subsidies to underdeveloped areas for the aid of old revolutionary base areas, minority nationalities areas, and the border areas; and bank credits for agriculture. The actual regulations governing the forestry funding system will be decided and carried out by the Ministry of Forestry together with the Ministry of Finance, subject to State Council approval. Current state investment in silviculture and forest industry and subsidies for collective afforestation will be controlled and utilized by central and provincial forestry and financial departments.

9. Appropriately increase the assessment rates for the forest cultivation and renewal funds in collective forestry districts and in state forestry districts (excluding Heilongjiang, Jilin, and Inner Mongolia) and broaden the scope for assessment of the forest cultivation fund. The Ministries of Forestry and Finance will decide on specific procedures.

10. Provinces that have yet to demarcate forestry counties and collectives must make clear decisions in accordance with actual conditions. In order to further put into effect the policy of forestry as the leading factor in forestry districts, we must rationally handle grain procurement and supply work in forestry counties and collectives. Those areas with a marginal grain surplus must have their grain quota stabilized. In areas which cannot achieve self-sufficiency in grain, procurement quotas should be reduced or supplies increased in order to ensure that the grain rations for the masses in forestry units do not fall below those in neighboring grain-producing districts.

THE COMPREHENSIVE UTILIZATION, CONSERVATION, AND USE OF SUBSTITUTES FOR TIMBER

11. We must comprehensively utilize logging, processing, and manufacturing residues from the forestry districts, make a big effort to manufacture wood panels, develop the processing of small pieces of wood and small quantities of materials, and develop artificial board production.

Right now, on a keypoint basis, we must do a good job of tapping the full potential, innovating, and renovating in existing timber-processing and comprehensive utilization plants to raise production capacity and product quality. In the future we must develop processing and comprehensive utilization in the forestry districts in a planned way. The comprehensive utilization of timber is light industrial in nature, and departments and localities must provide support in terms of funding, fuel, and initiative.

In order to compensate for timber shortages, we must develop timber conservation and substitution work in a big way. Departments that are major consumers of timber like coal, railways, and building materials should actively expand the work they have already accomplished in using metal for pitprops, concrete for railroad ties, and steel for doors and windows and continue to research and manufacture additional substitute products.

12. We must go all out to alter the custom of burning good timber in the forestry districts. Employees, the masses of commune members, organizations, military units, schools, and industrial and mining enterprises in the forestry districts all must switch to burning branches and straw for fuel. Where it is possible, coal should be substituted for wood, and biogas digesters and small hydropower stations should be developed to conserve large quantities of timber. We must use economic subsidies to encourage units and the masses in forestry districts not to burn good timber. We need an earmarked revolving fund with income derived from timber conservation to be recycled for use in this work. There is great potential here. With the Ministry of Forestry in the lead, the various departments should establish experimental points to sum up experiences, formulate programs, and gradually carry them out.

GRASP RENEWAL AND CONSTRUCTION IN FORESTRY DISTRICTS

13. In accordance with variations in forest functions, the provinces must press home the job of demarcating forest types in major forestry districts to determine management directions and measures for different forest types. Expand, in a planned way, shelter, fuelwood, economic, nature preserve, and other special use forests. We must resolutely adjust the timber production volume downward in overcut forestry districts and stabilize the production volume for a while to give them a chance to recover. We must accelerate development and construction in new forestry districts and grasp the cultivation of the next generation of forest resources. Meanwhile we must do a genuinely good job of forestry conservation and fire prevention and strictly prohibit deforestation for the purpose of reclamation.

14. We must resolutely carry out the policy of treating silviculture as the base and finally correct the mistaken work style of regarding log production as the center and overemphasizing logging while underemphasizing afforestation. We must truly unite forest industry with afforestation and cultivation in both thought and practice. The development of new forestry districts in the future must start with overall forest management, arranging production, construction, and investment for forest industry, and agriculture in a unified manner. With regard to reserve forestry districts where construction has yet to begin, the supervising enterprises must take close charge of construction and gradually introduce rational geographical distribution and management. Forestry departments must move in the direction of performing regeneration in the same year or the year after logging has taken place. Examination of forestry enterprises in the future must give first place to reforestation, afforestation, and forest cultivation and institute a close connection with enterprise profit retention and employee economic interests. Leadership responsibility must be assigned when these tasks are not fulfilled.

15. State forestry units must adopt diverse styles in accordance with local conditions to organize the collectives in forestry districts to participate in forestry conservation, afforestation, forest cultivation, logging, road maintenance, and other production and construction activities and provide rational compensation. The construction of new forestry enterprises ought to maximally attract the masses in the districts to participate in production and construction. We must take diverse routes to help the collectives and masses enjoy

benefits from developing forestry. But we cannot divide the state forests among the collectives to solve the problem of economic interests among the collectives and masses in the forestry districts.

16. State forestry districts in autonomous nationality areas must closely integrate forestry conservation and development with the economic interests of the autonomous nationality areas. With the approval of leading organizations at higher levels, they can adopt methods regarding the distribution of timber products and the sharing of profits that differ from those used elsewhere in the country, to give these areas greater autonomy and a bigger economic return. We must attract the local minority nationality masses to participate in forestry production and construction and actively cultivate forestry cadres and technical talent among the minority peoples.

17. Local governments and enterprises in forestry districts in Heilongjiang, Jilin, and Inner Mongolia must organize local educated youth to participate in forestry production and construction. They can organize them to utilize residues from logging, processing, and manufacturing and some of the culls to develop comprehensive utilization and the collective economy. The products will then be unifiedly procured by forestry enterprises in accordance with state or provincial regulations.

Collectively owned units in which educated youth are the leading factor must be accorded special tax reduction and abatement treatment in accordance with relevant State Council regulations regarding farms and factories operated by rusticated urban youth in village or suburban districts.

Necessary funding to make arrangements for educated youth in the forestry districts can be obtained through loans. The first source of funding should be retained profits of enterprises in the mountains. When this is insufficient, appropriate subsidies can be provided out of local finances with provincial approval or by shifting money between expenditure lines within the enterprise's operating capital.

18. Provinces must continue to do well the organization of unified forestry-industrial-commercial enterprises on an experimental basis, and areas in which conditions have matured may gradually diffuse this experience more widely.

DO AFFORESTATION AND FOREST CULTIVATION IN A BIG WAY

19. We must further implement the Instruction by the Party Center and State Council on Developing Tree Planting and Afforestation in a Big Way (1980) and uphold the policy of relying on the collectives as the leading factor in afforestation, actively developing state afforestation, encouraging individual commune members to plant trees, and mobilizing the urban and rural masses and all sectors of the economy to plant trees and afforest in a steadfast manner. We must proceed in a geographically and temporally appropriate manner, ensure both quality and quantity, ensure that trees that are planted survive and develop into forests, and put a stop to formalism and wasted effort.

Everyone has a responsibility for greenifying the motherland. Except for the old, the feeble, the sick, and the halt, all cadres, staff, students, and troops must participate for a few days each year in obligatory tree planting and afforestation labor. Leading cadres at all levels and all party and youth league members must go further and lead afforestation. We must demarcate responsibility zones by unit and set deadlines for the completion of greenification tasks.

All villages and collectives should designate appropriate working days on a locally suitable basis to be devoted to afforestation and forest cultivation.

Agricultural reclamation, water conservancy, railroad, and transportation departments should all regard afforestation and greenification as one of their department's production and construction assignments. Coal mining, paper manufacture, and other big enterprises that use timber as a raw material should put up some forest cultivation funds and establish forestry raw materials bases. All departments can plant trees and afforest on state-designated sites, with ownership going to the planter. They also can afforest on a joint basis together with forestry departments or collectives, dividing up the income proportionately.

Cities of all sizes should include afforestation and greenification in their urban construction plans; mobilize the masses to plant trees, grass, and flowers; beautify their appearance; improve the human environment; and establish responsibility systems.

20. Beginning this year, provinces, prefectures, and counties must prepare and carry out five-year plans for tree planting, afforestation, and increasing forest cover, set ten- and twenty-year struggle targets, and inspect the results of afforestation each year.

There is great potential for tree planting and afforestation, with quick results in farming districts in the plains and in the hills and, in forestry districts, on wasteland with favorable conditions. All areas should adopt forceful measures to quickly greenify these areas. In the high mountains with low population densities and poor transportation, we should primarily rely on closing off the hills to allow natural afforestation and on aerial seeding to develop forestry. Continue to tightly grasp the construction of the "three norths" shelterbelt system and fast-growth timber bases and, on a locally appropriate basis, develop different kinds of economic forests in a big way.

Areas short on fuelwood must give first place in tree planting and afforestation to developing fuelwood forests: designating sites and organizing the collectives, commune members, organizations, military units, factories and mines, schools, and farms to practice afforestation, with ownership going to the planter.

21. Scientific afforestation and forest cultivation raise afforestation quality. We must do a good job of technical training in afforestation and planning and designing, establish tree seed companies and seed management systems, promote seed bases and nursery construction, and cultivate superior planting stock. We must set up afforestation inspection and reward systems on a widespread basis. We must strengthen forest cultivation and the prevention of pests and diseases, actively develop cultivation, thinning, and the improvement of secondary growth forests, improve forest quality, and resolutely oppose the deviation of caring only about afforestation while ignoring management.

Forest cultivation must be included in forestry plans at all levels, gradually increasing funding levels and accelerating the rate of cultivation.

22. State forest farms must now grasp well tending and thinning. All areas should, to the maximum extent possible, provide funding support. Forest farms must regard forestry as the leading factor, practice diversified management, practice comprehensive utilization, and use short-term income to support long-term projects. While engaged in cultivation, state forest farms should not remit their income to higher levels in order to develop forestry through forestry income.

Where the conditions are in place, we should continue to develop the reorganization and consolidation of collective forest farms and specialized teams. Forest farms which are operated with land, labor, and capital requisitioned in the past from production teams must clarify mountain and forest rights and the procedures for proportionate distribution of income. Farms can be run on a joint basis, distributing income according to ownership shares. We must strengthen management, do a good job of labor compensation, open up avenues for production, and increase economic returns.

DEVELOP FORESTRY SCIENCE, TECHNOLOGY, AND EDUCATION

23. Forestry science and research must serve forestry production and construction. Scientific research, educational, and production units must coordinate their efforts closely and realistically solve the key technical problems affecting forestry production and construction. We must concentrate our strength and develop research on improved seeds, species selection, sand fixation, forest pathology, forest inventory skills, logging and regeneration methods, forestry machinery, the technical upgrading of forest industry, and forestry economic and technical policies. Meanwhile we have to do a good job of disseminating the results of our scientific research.

China is among the world leaders in the diversity of forest biota and has many economically valuable, but endangered, plant and animal species. We must strengthen in a big way the management of nature preserves and develop inventories, research, and the utilization of wild animal and plant species.

We must work hard to improve the working and living conditions of scientific and technical personnel and stabilize the forestry scientific and technological work force.

We must strengthen forest inventories and resource management. The provinces must quickly determine what the basic conditions of their forest resources are, do planning and design well, and provide a scientific foundation for forestry production and construction. We must build up our inventory forces for their purpose and improve our technology and equipment.

24. Strive to develop forestry education. Now we ought to concentrate our strength on running a group of forestry institutes and keypoint schools well and improving the quality of teaching. We must develop professional training at the college level and correspondence programs, strengthen and develop middle school forestry education, and cultivate a technical backbone for grassroots-level production units. We must emphasize the training of forestry employees and leading cadres at the county and commune levels in forestry districts. We must operate middle and primary schools in the forestry districts well. We must actively set the groundwork for converting some ordinary middle schools into forestry vocational schools. Meanwhile we must actively embrace general education about forestry and increase the forestry content in middle and primary school curricula.

STRENGTHEN PARTY AND GOVERNMENT LEADERSHIP OF FORESTRY

25. Party committees and governments at all levels must give prominent place to forestry and include it on their official daily agendas, and genuinely strengthen leadership. The principal leading cadre should become personally involved, and he must assign a responsible cadre to take charge. Forestry organizations at all levels must be strengthened. Units or individuals who do an exemplary job in forestry work should be praised and rewarded.

Resolutely carry out the Forestry Law (for trial implementation). Strengthen forestry legal education in a big way and establish mass-based forestry conservation organizations, systems, and compacts. We must include cherishing and conserving the forest as an important component of building a socialist spiritual civilization. Cadres at all levels, especially leading cadres, must strictly carry out and obey the law. We must differentiate the circumstances involving forest destruction and criminal elements who break the law. We should administer disciplinary punishment and, in serious cases, determine criminal responsibility according to the relevant provisions of the Criminal Law. The forestry districts must resolutely establish and strengthen forestry public security, procuratorial, and judicial organizations.

Forestry departments at all levels must delve beneath the surface, conduct investigations and research, improve leadership work style and work methods, genuinely strengthen ideological and political work, show concern about the living conditions of forestry employees and the masses in forestry districts, and fully mobilize their socialist activism.

Developing forestry is a long-term, century-long item in building socialism and improving nature. China is a big country with abundant resources, and it has a large population and a bounteous diversity of tree species and forest products. There is great potential for developing forestry. So long as the whole country and the whole people go all out to build prosperity in China, engage in bold struggle, enhance their revolutionary spirit of ''The Foolish Old Man Who Moved the Mountain'' and moreover do a good job of summing up the experiences and lessons of history, thoroughly root out the influence of ''leftist'' ideology, and continue to thoroughly carry out the line and policies decided since the party's Third Plenum [December 1978] the Party Central Committee believes that the backward face of Chinese forestry can indeed be gradually improved. China's forestry development has enormous potential and hope.

[*Editors' note*: This 1981 directive went far beyond the usual springtime mobilization of the masses to conduct afforestation. It instead tried to address some of the fundamental problems that are holding back forestry, and therefore has continuing significance. Most important, it reaffirmed the value of the production responsibility system introduced under Deng Xiaoping's leadership, which allows more flexible, decentralized, and profit-oriented ownership and management. The reiteration of support for the responsibility system was vital because it had been thrown into jeopardy by a wave of deforestation or liquidation of forest holdings that had occurred in 1979–1980, when hard-pressed woodsmen cut down many trees in order to capture income out of fear that the policies would change once again. Indeed, Appendix L, coupled with the shift in the political balance from reformers to more orthodox elements that same month, signaled a tighter, more law-and-order-oriented approach. However, the decisions make plain the leadership's support for the responsibility system which made it possible for the reform momentum to resume in a few years.

The directive identifies many other problems (e.g., a lack of educational and employment opportunities in forestry districts and funding shortages) but does little to remedy them. Its support for a Ministry of Forestry/State Materials Pricing General Administration monopoly in the forest products industry was counterproductive and later had to be relaxed. Its endorsement of an obligatory tree-planting campaign was an irrelevant side issue proposed to reinstitute a sense of ideological commitment among young people.]

Appendix N

Interim Provisions of the Shenzhen Special Economic Zone for Land Management (December 24, 1981)

China's Foreign Economic Legislation, vol. 1, pp. 233–39.

CHAPTER I. GENERAL PROVISIONS

Article 1. These Interim Provisions are formulated in accordance with the pertinent laws and decrees of the People's Republic of China and the Regulations on Special Economic Zones in Guangdong Province.

Article 2. All the mineral resources, waters, wasteland, arable land, hills and forests, and other sea and land resources within the limits of this special zone that have been exploited or are yet to be exploited shall be put under the centralized management of the Shenzhen Municipal People's Government in Guangdong Province; the Municipal People's Government may purchase, requisition, or nationalize the land according to developmental requirements and in compliance with the provisions of the relevant laws and decrees.

Article 3. The overall development plan of the special zone that has been determined must be complied with and carried out by all units and individuals. Without approval, no one may arbitrarily alter the topography of or landforms on the land within the limits of the special zone or privately encroach on the land or construct any type of structure.

Article 4. Any unit or individual requiring the use of land shall file an application with the Shenzhen Municipal People's Government and may use land only after obtaining approval and completing the required procedures; if any person who has not been granted permission negotiates directly for the use of land with the unit or individual that has been using it, the agreement they have signed shall be entirely null and void.

Article 5. The units and individuals that have been approved to use land shall have only the right to the use of the land and shall have no right of ownership. Overt and covert sales and purchases of land, as well as the renting out and unauthorized transfer of land, are forbidden; the development, use, and destruction of underground and other resources shall not be allowed.

Article 6. Compensation for land to be requisitioned and for civilian houses and other structures to be dismantled and rebuilt elsewhere to meet the requirements of development shall be handled in accordance with the pertinent provisions of the People's Republic of China and of the People's Government of Guangdong Province.

Article 7. Land development projects in this special zone shall be established with the investment of the Shenzhen Special Economic Zone Development Company, and foreign investment may also be absorbed for participation in such establishment. The income and expenditures involved in land development and utilization shall be arranged by the Special Economic Zone Development Company as part of a comprehensive plan.

CHAPTER II. THE MANAGEMENT OF LAND

Article 8. Investors who require use of land for the purpose of setting up factories or establishing other undertakings with their investment in this special zone may fill out land use application forms by presenting the documents of approval issued by the Shenzhen Municipal People's Government and the contracts, agreements, and other relevant data concerning their investment in establishing these undertakings. After approval by the municipal planning department and going through the procedures for paying the land use fee, land shall be allocated and delineated, and a Land Use Certificate shall be issued to them.

Article 9. Within six months after the Land Use Certificate becomes effective, the investor shall produce an overall blueprint for the construction of the project, the construction plan, and the plan for putting it into operation, and within nine months the ground shall be broken for construction according to the overall project plan. Otherwise, the Land Use Certificate shall be withdrawn and the funds already paid out shall not be refunded. The plan for putting the project into operation shall be completed as scheduled. If it cannot be completed on schedule, the plan can be appropriately postponed only after the investor has submitted relevant documentation and the original approving authorities have examined the case and confirmed that there are proper reasons for delay. The Land Use Certificate may also be withdrawn in case of a delay without good reason.

Article 10. After the investor has fulfilled the requirements for construction as stipulated in the contract and agreement, the project shall undergo final inspection and approval by the competent authorities before it is officially put into operation. Investors may not demolish, alter, or rebuild any existing structure within the confines of the land they use without the permission of the municipal planning department.

Article 11. Investors shall build structures within the confines of the land they use in accordance with the ratio of space allotted to buildings and parks and greenery stipulated by the municipal planning department; they may not arbitrarily enlarge or reduce such space.

Article 12. All structures built by investors within the confines of the land they use shall conform to our country's construction standards and fire prevention and safety requirements. Any structures that violate those provisions shall not be allowed to be put into operation or use. Anyone who puts a structure into operation or use without authorization and thus causes an accident shall make compensation for the losses incurred and bear the legal liability.

Article 13. Investors shall, within the confines of the land they use, carry out construction for the purposes stipulated in the contract or agreement, and they may not arbitrarily use the land for other purposes.

Article 14. Investors may not for any reason encroach on land outside the confines stipulated in the Land Use Certificate. If they need to enlarge the confines of the land in use, they shall go through the procedures as stipulated in Article 8.

CHAPTER III. THE TERM OF LAND USE AND LAND USE FEES

Article 15. The term of land use by investors shall be determined through consultation, based on the amount of the investment in the project they undertake to build and on actual needs. The maximum term shall be:

1. for industrial use, thirty years;
2. for commercial use (including restaurants), twenty years;
3. for commercial residential buildings, fifty years;
4. for educational, scientific and technological, and medical and health use, fifty years;
5. for tourist industries, thirty years;
6. for crop planting, animal husbandry, and aquaculture, twenty years.

If an investor wants to continue to operate on the land which it has used for the operation of this project after the expiry of the term stipulated, the agreement for land use may be renewed on obtaining the approval of the competent authorities in the special zone.

Article 16. Land use fees shall be computed and collected for all land used by enterprises financed exclusively by investors or by joint ventures with our side, whether it is newly requisitioned land or the site of an existing enterprise. The rates for the land use fee shall be determined by classification based on the conditions of different regions, the different lines of business, and the term of use. The rates per annum per square meter shall be (in Renminbi):

Land for industrial use, 10 to 30 yuan;

Land for commercial use, 70 to 200 yuan;

Land for commercial residential buildings, 30 to 60 yuan;

Land for buildings for tourism, 60 to 100 yuan; and

Rates for land for crop growing, animal husbandry, and aquaculture shall be negotiated separately.

The rates shall be subject to adjustment once every three years, beginning from the day these Interim Provisions are promulgated, and the margin of fluctuation shall not exceed 30 percent.

Article 17. Those who establish educational, cultural, scientific and technological, medical and health, or public welfare institutions in the special zone shall receive special preferential treatment in respect to land use fees. Projects involving exceptionally advanced technology and nonprofit projects may be exempted from payment of the land use fee.

Article 18. Procedures for payment of the land use fee: it may be paid in full in one lump sum within two years, free of interest; or it may be paid in annual installments at an interest rate of 8 percent per annum. In the event of price adjustments, the fee shall be paid according to the new rates.

Article 19. The above-mentioned provisions for the collection of land use fees shall apply to all the units that establish enterprises or other undertakings in the special zone.

CHAPTER IV. PUBLIC UTILITIES

Article 20. The public utilities that investors undertake to construct within the confines of the land they use, as stipulated in the contract or agreement, shall be built in accordance with the requirements of urban planning.

Article 21. Investors shall be responsible for building, within the confines of the land they use, facilities for the supply of electricity and water, drainage, sewage, gas pipes, and telecommunications equipment; the investors shall pay installation and extension fees for their connections with all types of mainlines outside the confines of their land.

Article 22. The discharge and disposal of residual substances, fumes, and wastewater [waste solids, gases, and liquids] within the confines of the land used by investors shall conform to the standards for discharge and requirements for disposal stipulated by the People's Republic of China, and they shall be subject to the inspection and supervision of the municipal environmental protection department and shall pay disposal fees as required.

Article 23. These Interim Provisions shall go into effect on January 1, 1982.

[*Editors' note*:] The Shenzhen interim regulations included herein are representative of the basic legal framework governing land use. Beginning in late 1984, a number of localities issued their own regulations, including the Shenzhen Special Economic Zone Measures for the Implementation of Land Use Fees (October 25, 1985), *Wen Hui Bao* (Hong Kong), December 6, 1985, p. 8. The Land Management Law (1986) printed in Appendix Z later set the legal framework for land management, land usage rights, and other subjects. The State Council's Provisional Regulations on the Promotion of Foreign Investment (October 11, 1986), subsequently promised to regularize the setting of land use fees for some categories of foreign economic enterprises.]

Appendix O

State Council Emergency Circular on Prohibiting the Encroachment onto Arable Land by Rural Housing Construction (April 17, 1981)

BFWH, pp. 86–88.

In recent years, after the improvement of rural economic conditions, housing construction in rural areas has entered a period of prosperity seldom seen since the founding of our country. This is an inevitable and desirable trend resulting from economic growth and rising peasant incomes. But because many areas lack overall planning and essential management of rural housing construction, the phenomenon of encroachment on arable land by rural housing and commune and brigade enterprises is serious. If this situation is allowed to continue to develop, serious consequences will arise. Governments at various levels must pay close attention to this matter and adopt effective measures immediately to stop it.

1. We must conduct comprehensive and thorough propaganda and education among the cadres and broad masses in rural areas, explaining, again and again, that land conservation is a matter of great strategic significance in our country. Although our territory is large, arable land is limited. The growth of population has sharpened the contradiction between limited land and a huge population. If we lose control over the use of arable land, it will not only affect the development of current agricultural production and the improvement of people's living conditions, but it may also bring about long-term and possibly irreversible calamities for future generations. Governments at all levels must not slight this critical problem which concerns people's long-term interests and the overall situation. We should educate cadres and the people in rural areas to correctly handle the relationships between the individual and the collective and between current and long-term interests; to be concerned about the overall situation; and to uphold collective interests, protect arable land, and conserve the use of land. We absolutely must not allow any individual or unit to make reckless use of arable land.

2. The use of land for rural housing construction must be subject to unified planning and rational distribution, with a stress on land conservation. Communes and production brigades in rural areas must make locally suitable arrangements and do a good job of planning housing construction, fully utilizing sloped land, wasteland, and the foundations of abandoned housing sites, to minimize the use of arable land. In order to conserve land use, we should choose appropriate architectural forms according to specific geographical conditions: in mountainous areas, housing construction should be aligned with the moun-

tains; on the loess plateau, we should promote the excavation of caves; in the suburbs of large cities and other areas with unfavorable population to land ratios, we should promote the construction of housing two or more stories high. Those communes and production teams which are constrained by natural conditions and really have to use arable land to build houses must obtain permission. The concrete methods of review and approval will be set by local governments based on local conditions.

3. We must once again emphasize that all land in the communes and production brigades is collectively owned. With regard to the land distributed to the members of communes and production brigades for residential use, agricultural (forestry) private plots, and contract guarantee farmland, the members of the collectives only have usage rights; they are not allowed to rent, sell, or reassign the land by themselves, nor are they allowed to build houses, dig graves, open mines, make bricks, etc., on contracted and private plot land. Some people mistake responsibility and contract guarantee fields for individually owned land to be used as one sees fit. This is wrong.

4. We must gradually improve the building materials for rural housing to reduce the amount of land used for brickmaking, curing, and firing. Adobe brick is still the main building material for housing, but this should be gradually reformed because brickmaking consumes lots of energy and ruins farmland. In some areas we can use compacted earth, stones, and twigs to make walls; where conditions permit we can use industrial slag to make silicate bricks, cinder blocks, and hollow-core concrete blocks.

5. Governments at various levels must conduct investigations of conditions regarding rural housing construction and land acquisition by commune and production brigade enterprises. Cases of reckless occupation of arable land for housing construction, forcibly occupying land without approval, and the extravagant use of land for housing construction will be severely handled. Land occupied but not used by commune and production brigade enterprises must be forcibly taken away.

At this moment, State Agricultural Commission and the State Commission on Capital Construction are organizing their forces to conduct investigations and research on policies and management problems regarding the use of land for rural housing construction. While carrying out this circular, governments at various levels are expected to promptly report relevant conditions, problems, and opinions to them, to facilitate comprehensive research so that they can formulate a more perfect regulation.

Appendix P

Regulations on Soil Conservation Work (June 30, 1982)

BFWH, pp. 101–9.

CHAPTER I. GENERAL PRINCIPLES

Article 1. The prevention and control of soil erosion and the conservation and rational utilization of soil resources are basic measures to transform the topography in mountainous, hilly, and sandswept districts; regulate the rivers; reduce the incidence of disasters caused by water, drought, and windblown sand, build an improved eco-environment, and develop agricultural production; and is a vital aspect of the effort to improve China's land. These articles are specially formulated to manage soil conservation work well.

Article 2. The principles of soil conservation work are equal weight to prevention and control, the integration of control and management, local suitability, overall planning, comprehensive control, and elimination of hazards to create benefits.

Article 3. Soil conservation work throughout the entire country is supervised by the Ministry of Water Conservancy and Electric Power. The National Soil Conservation Work Coordinating Small Group is established with the Ministry of Water Conservancy and Electric Power as the leading factor and with participation by the State Planning Commission, the State Economic Commission, the Ministry of Agriculture, Animal Husbandry, and Fisheries, and the Ministry of Forestry to strengthen coordination among the relevant departments, study how to resolve critical problems affecting soil conservation work within a fixed time frame, and manage soil conservation work well. Local people's governments at each level with responsibilities concerning the prevention and control of soil erosion should establish soil conservation work organs in accordance with actual conditions.

The responsibilities of soil conservation work organs are to implement the state's principles, policies, laws, and decrees regarding soil conservation; conduct soil conservation surveys, prepare soil conservation plans, and organize their implementation; supervise and inspect soil conservation work by relevant departments; organize and develop scientific research, the training of personnel, and propaganda work with regard to soil conservation; and provide good management and use of funds and materials devoted to soil conservation.

All river valley organs should take charge of soil conservation surveying, planning, and scientific research within their respective valleys and assist and promote soil conservation work by the soil conservation work departments at the provincial level within these respective valleys.

Soil conservation stations, agricultural technology extension stations, forestry stations, water conservancy stations, agricultural machinery stations, fertilizer stations, and grasslands stations are all responsible for assisting local collectives to do a good job in soil conservation work.

Article 4. People's governments at all levels in mountainous, hilly, and sandswept districts must include soil conservation work in their plans, strengthen leadership, unify planning, organize coordination, conduct propaganda and education, and mobilize the people to do this kind of work well. Water conservancy, agriculture, forestry, animal husbandry, agricultural reclamation, environmental protection, railway, transportation, industry and mining, electric power, and scientific research departments must establish close coordination, divide their responsibilities, and do a good job of soil conservation work with regard to their own departments. Propaganda and publishing departments must develop soil conservation propaganda work in a planned fashion, disseminate scientific knowledge about soil conservation, and raise the awareness of the cadres and the masses about the dangers of soil erosion and the importance of soil conservation.

Article 5. Under the guidance of the local people's government's comprehensive soil conservation plan, rural collectives and state agricultural, forestry, and animal husbandry farms should formulate specific soil conservation plans in accordance with the natural conditions of the locality and the masses' actual needs for production and life, and organize their implementation.

Article 6. The prevention and control of soil erosion must mobilize society's strength and rely on the masses' self-reliance. The state provides essential support in terms of funding and materials and should provide greater assistance in keypoint districts.

Planning departments at all levels should include soil conservation work in their annual national economic plans. Soil conservation funding provided by the state should be earmarked for specified purposes, and not be diverted to other uses. Soil conservation work departments and financial work departments at all levels should strengthen their management over funding and concentrate on making investments bear fruit.

CHAPTER II. THE PREVENTION OF SOIL EROSION

Article 7. The reclamation and cultivation of sloped land for farming is prohibited on slopes of 25 degrees or greater. People's governments at the provincial level can set lower limits on the reclamation of sloped land in accordance with local topography, soil conditions, the availability of arable land, and population density.

Article 8. Reclamation, excavation, and demolition are prohibited in severely windswept areas; landslide danger areas; mudslide danger areas; the banks of railways, highways, streams, and irrigation ditches; areas submerged by reservoirs; nature preserves; scenic districts; and historical and culturally important districts.

Article 9. Reclamation is prohibited in the hilly and gullied loess areas and the gullied plateau areas in the loess plateau country. The concerned provincial-level units should demarcate those areas as off-limits to reclamation in accordance with their specific circumstances.

Article 10. Reclamation is strictly prohibited when it involves deforestation, slash-and-burn farming, or the destruction of grasslands.

Article 11. All units or individuals reclaiming sloped land within the prescribed slope limits must obtain the approval of the local people's government and adopt soil conservation measures. Violators will be ordered to restore the land to forest or pasture.

State agricultural farms wishing to reclaim sloped land within the prescribed limits must seek approval in accordance with relevant state regulations. The reclamation plan submitted for approval must include soil convervation measures to be taken. Before such measures are approved, the opinions of the soil conservation work departments should be solicited. After approval has been granted, the soil conservation department will supervise their implementation.

Article 12. It is strictly forbidden to wantonly log the forests, damaging soil conservation. In accordance with state regulations, all requests to log forests must include regeneration and soil erosion prevention measures in the plans. The opinions of the soil conservation work departments regarding such measures should be solicited before these plans are approved. After approval has been granted, the soil conservation department will supervise their implementation.

Article 13. In order to prevent soil erosion, soil conservation measures must be adopted on sloped land when conducting site preparation and afforestation, when intercropping and weeding new forest plantations, and when rejuvenating tea oil, tung, and other groves of economic forests.

Article 14. When water conservancy, railroad, transportation, industry and mining, and electric power departments are engaged in construction and production in mountainous, hilly, and windswept districts, they should minimize damage to landforms and vegetation. They must take soil conservation measures when they excavate dirt, rock, and sand where soil erosion can occur. Discarded dirt, rocks, sand, and mine debris and tailings must be properly disposed of. They are not allowed to dump such material in streams and reservoirs. After the construction project has been completed, the unit that did the work is responsible for replanting and initiating essential engineering measures on the sites exposed by excavation in order to conserve soil resources.

All departments must include measures to prevent soil erosion in their construction plan and designs and production plans when submitted for approval. The opinions of the soil conservation department should be solicited before these plans are approved. After approval has been granted, the soil conservation department will supervise their implementation. Those projects in which soil erosion has already occurred must put controls into place within a limited time. Funding necessary for the control of soil erosion should be provided by the capital construction unit out of its capital construction investment budget. Production enterprises and units should provide funds out of their technological upgrading account or production development account.

Article 15. In accordance with local conditions, county-level people's governments in mountainous, hilly, and sandswept districts should organize the rural collectives and state agricultural, forestry, and animal husbandry farms in a planned manner to close off access to the mountains and stabilize the sands; cultivate forests and grasslands; practice rotational grazing; actively expand fuelwood forests, forage grasses, and green manure crops; break the traditions of uprooting grasses and tree roots, wantonly cutting trees for fuel, and overgrazing; and conserve vegetative cover.

Article 16. With regard to uprooting medicinal herbs; raising tussah silkworms; cultivating wood ear and mushrooms; firing up charcoal, bricks, and tiles; mining, quarrying, and other forms of sideline production by rural people's collectives, state agricultural, animal husbandry, and forestry farms and individuals in mountainous, hilly, and sandswept districts, the county people's governments must integrate production planning with the needs of soil conservation, formulate concrete procedures, and proceed in an organized manner under leadership to prevent soil erosion from occurring because of reckless excavation and dumping and the destruction of vegetative cover.

CHAPTER III. THE CONTROL OF SOIL EROSION

Article 17. The control of soil erosion in mountainous and hilly districts should be conducted in light of natural conditions in the area; taking the small watershed as the unit; practicing overall planning, comprehensive control, centralized control, and serial control; integrating vegetative and engineering measures; integrating control on the slopes with control in the gullies; integrating field projects with water storage, soil conservation, and tillage; integrating control with production and utilization; integrating the rights and interests of the present with long-term rights and interests; and by striving for efficiency.

Article 18. Sloped land outside the prescribed limits that is currently under cultivation should be handled differently, depending on the circumstances. Collectives with low ratios of people to arable land should actively build permanent farmsites on level land and moderately sloped land and raise yields to enable sloped land to be gradually restored to forests or pastures. It is obviously a problem for collectives with high ratios of people to arable land to restore sloped land to forests or pastures. In such cases deadlines should be set in accordance with the severity of the slope for building terraces or taking other soil conservation measures. On sloped land within the prescribed limits that is currently under cultivation, soil conservation measures like high-contour tillage, rotation between farming and grasses, and terraces [should be taken] to prevent and control soil erosion.

Article 19. Local people's governments should sum up the conditions regarding the implementation of agricultural production responsibility systems and adopt locally suitable and appropriate measures to organize the collectives and the masses to carry out soil erosion control tasks.

Collectives with big soil erosion tasks must carry out controls in a coordinated fashion by applying the principles of voluntarism and mutual benefit, the exchange of equal values, and setting rational burdens. The units that participate in control will jointly decide how management tasks are to be handled after controls are in place, how income is to be distributed, and how newly created farmland is to be used. Existing land ownership rights will not be altered.

Article 20. Rural collectives and relevant units should actively establish nurseries and seed bases to supply seedlings and tree and grass seeds needed for control.

Article 21. All units and individuals should take responsibility for controlling any soil erosion that arises from their production activities like reclamation, engaging in agricultural sidelines, quarrying, road building, water conservancy and hydroelectric construction projects, and logging. Local people's governments have the authority to supervise and inspect them and to impose deadlines for taking action to control erosion.

Article 22. With regard to soil conservation measures, whether of the engineering or the vegetative type, all areas must carry out management responsibilities, strengthen the management of conservation, increase efficiency, and fully develop soil conservation functions.

In accordance with the conditions affecting the conduct of soil conservation, rural collectives should impose responsibilities for the management of conservation. For some soil conservation measures they can still conclude conservation management compacts among the peasants and establish organizations needed for conservation management. With regard to soil conservation measures within their respective spheres, water conservancy, railroad, transportation, and industrial and mining departments and state agricultural, forestry, and animal husbandry farms should establish conservation management organizations or designate specialized conservation management personnel.

Article 23. No unit or individual is allowed to encroach on or damage soil conservation facilities, experimental sites, instruments, or equipment.

Article 24. Under unified planning by the state, local people's governments in the sandswept districts of northern, northeastern, and northwestern China should organize the rural collectives and state agricultural, forestry, and animal husbandry farms to plant shelter forests and grass in a centralized and interconnected pattern to check the wind and stabilize the sands. In other sandswept areas the local people's governments should adopt effective measures in a planned manner to control the windblown sand hazard.

Article 25. On grasslands and grassy slopes damaged by sand or which have retreated, herd sizes should be regulated in a planned manner in accordance with the land's natural carrying capacity, and [the local people's government] should practice rotational grazing, the seeding of forage grasses, the planting of shelter forests, and the restoration of natural vegetation to improve the pasturelands. In seriously eroded districts they should actively expand the planting of forage grasses, promote the fencing in of rangelands, and break with nomadic grazing traditions to restore natural vegetation.

Article 26. In districts where swidden farming and slash-and-burn agriculture are customary, the local people's governments should strengthen propaganda and education, assist in the building of permanent farmsites, and disseminate agricultural science and technology to pave the way for a gradual change in cultivation patterns to facilitate soil conservation.

During the fallow cycle, sloped lands should be planted in a timely fashion with forage grasses or green manure crops to expand vegetative cover.

CHAPTER IV. EDUCATION AND SCIENTIFIC RESEARCH

Article 27. The education, water conservancy, agriculture, and forestry departments should set up soil conservation specializations or courses in relevant colleges. Severely eroded provinces can establish soil conservation middle schools or set up soil conservation majors or courses in water conservancy, agricultural, and forestry middle schools, to train large numbers of scientific and technical personnel in soil conservation. Relevant courses in middle and primary schools should incorporate material on soil conservation.

Article 28. The Chinese Academy of Sciences; water conservancy, agricultural, and forestry scientific research departments; provincial-level soil conservation work departments; and river valley organs should strengthen leadership over their respective scientific research units concerned with soil conservation, earnestly expand scientific research on soil conservation, and, in a timely fashion, sum up and disseminate the results of scientific research on soil conservation.

Scientific research on soil conservation must closely correspond to reality in order to prevent soil erosion and develop production. While conducting research on soil conservation techniques, they should also strengthen basic theory and research on relevant social and economic aspects, to provide a scientific foundation for preventing soil erosion.

CHAPTER V. REWARDS AND PUNISHMENTS

Article 29. Units and individuals with exemplary performance in one of the following activities shall be commended and rewarded by people's governments at various levels in accordance with the magnitude of their merit.

1. Outstanding accomplishments in preventing soil erosion or managing soil conservation facilities.
2. Controlling soil erosion over the long term, with notable success in terms of high-speed and high-quality soil conservation and economic efficiency.
3. Actively breaking with the pattern of extensive, low-yield farming, with notable gains in soil conservation and developing agricultural, forestry, and animal husbandry production.
4. Significant discoveries, creations, innovations, or other significant contributions to scientific research on soil conservation.
5. Notable achievements in scientific research, education, propaganda and extension, or management of soil conservation.
6. Waging a resolute and successful struggle to alter behavior that damages soil conservation.
7. Showing notable enthusiasm for soil conservation work at the grassroots level for fifteen years or longer.

Article 30. Units or individuals who violate these regulations in one of the following ways should assume responsibility for paying compensation for the resulting damages. Administrative discipline will be given to the responsible persons in units and to individuals who cause disturbances. Criminal responsibility will be investigated for anyone who violates the Criminal Law.

1. Reclamation in violation of Articles 7, 8, 9, 10, or 11, or failure to take soil conservation measures when legally reclaiming sloped land, with serious aftereffects.
2. Failure to undertake regeneration or to adopt soil erosion prevention measures in violation of Articles 12 or 13, resulting in severe erosion.
3. Failure to adopt soil conservation measures in violation of Article 14, resulting in a soil erosion catastrophe.
4. Wanton excavation and dumping or damage to vegetative cover while engaging in sideline production, resulting in a soil erosion catastrophe.
5. Encroaching on or damaging soil conservation facilities, experimental sites, instruments, or equipment in violation of Article 23.

Article 31. All units and individuals have the right to inform against and make accusations regarding behavior that violates these articles. Units and individuals who have been informed against or are the subject of accusations must not retaliate against their accusers, and violators will be punished according to law.

CHAPTER VI. SUPPLEMENTARY ARTICLES

Article 32. People's governments at the provincial level may formulate practical rules and regulations in accordance with these articles.

Article 33. These articles shall take effect on the day they are promulgated [June 30, 1982, although not published until July 6].

Appendix Q

Fisheries Law (1986)

Zhongguo Fazhi Bao (January 22), p. 2.

CHAPTER I. GENERAL PROVISIONS

Article 1. This law is formulated for the purpose of strengthening the protection, cultivation, development, and rational utilization of fishery resources, developing fish breeding, and promoting the development of fishery production to meet the needs of socialist construction and the people's livelihood.

Article 2. This law must be observed in all fishing operations, including the cultivation and harvesting of aquatic animals and plants, in inland waters, on beaches, and in the territorial waters of the People's Republic of China as well as in all other areas under the jurisdiction of the People's Republic of China.

Article 3. The state implements a fishery policy which puts breeding in first place, while promoting breeding, catching, and processing, and lays particular emphasis on local conditions. People's governments at all levels are to incorporate fishery production in economic development plans and adopt measures to strengthen unified planning and comprehensive use of waters.

Article 4. The state encourages research on fishery science and technology, popularizes advanced technology, and promotes the development of fishery science and technology.

Article 5. People's governments at all levels shall give moral or material rewards to units and individuals who have achieved remarkable success in developing and protecting fishery resources, developing fishery production, and conducting research on fishery science and technology.

Article 6. The relevant administrative departments of the State Council are responsible for the nation's fisheries. Fishery administrative departments of people's governments at the county level or higher are responsible for fisheries in their respective administrative areas. Fishery administrative departments at the county level or higher may set up fishery supervisory and administrative organs in major fishery waters or fishing ports.

Fishery administrative departments of people's governments at the county or higher level and their subordinate fishery supervisory and administrative organs may designate fishery inspectors. Fishery inspectors carry out tasks entrusted to them by the fishery administrative departments and their subordinate fishery supervisory and administrative organs.

Article 7. The state shall exercise unified leadership regarding the supervision and administration of fisheries, with different levels holding different responsibilities.

Except for those sea areas and specific fishery resources and fishing grounds designated by the State Council to be under the jurisdiction of the Fishery Administrative Department of the State Council or its subordinate fishery supervisory and administrative organs, the fishery administrative departments of people's governments of provinces, autonomous regions, and municipalities under the central government that adjoin sea waters are responsible for the supervision and administration of marine fisheries in these waters.

Fisheries in rivers, lakes, and other waters are subject to the supervision and administration of fishery administrative departments of the relevant people's governments at the county level or higher, in accordance with administrative divisions. As for waters which extend across administrative regions, the relevant people's governments at the county level or higher shall, through consultation, work out administrative measures, or they shall be under the supervision and administration of fishery administrative departments of the people's government at the next higher level, or of their subordinate fishery supervisory and administrative organs.

Article 8. Foreigners and foreign fishing vessels must get approval from the relevant responsible department of the State Council to enter waters under the jurisdiction of the People's Republic of China to fish or carry out surveys of fishery resources. They must also abide by other relevant laws and regulations of the People's Republic of China. In cases where applicable treaties and agreements exist with the People's Republic of China, they shall by handled in accordance with these treaties and agreements.

In dealings with foreigners, the state fishery and fishing ports supervisory and administrative organs shall exercise authority over the supervision and administration of fisheries and fishing ports.

CHAPTER II. FISH BREEDING

Article 9. The state encourages units owned by the whole people, collectively owned units, and individuals to make full use of waters and beaches suitable for raising fish in order to develop fisheries.

Article 10. Local people's governments at the county level or higher may, in accordance with unified state arrangements for the use of waters, assign state-owned waters and beaches designated for fish breeding to state or collectively owned units for that purpose, issue them breeding licenses, and affirm their right of use. Waters and beaches owned by state units or owned by collectives, and those which are state-owned but used by collectively owned units, may be contracted to collectives or individuals to raise fish. Ownership and the right to use waters and beaches are protected by law, and no unit or individual is allowed to infringe on these rights.

Article 11. Those who [gain use of] state-owned waters and beaches to raise fish but let them lie idle for a year or longer without justification shall be ordered by the license-issuing organ to develop and make use of them within a specified time. Their licenses may be revoked if they fail to do so within the specified time.

Article 12. Disputes between state-owned units and collectively owned units over ownership and the right to the use of waters and beaches shall be resolved through consultation between the parties concerned. If the disputes remain unresolved after consultation, they shall be referred to local people's governments at the county level or higher. If the parties concerned refuse to accept the ruling of the relevant people's government, they may file suit in the people's court within thirty days of being notified of the ruling.

No party is allowed to disrupt breeding production before the dispute over ownership and usage rights regarding waters and beaches has been solved.

Article 13. The requisitioning of waters and beaches owned by collectives for state construction shall be handled in accordance with the Regulations Governing the Requisition of Land for State Construction. If state-owned waters and beaches and those rented to state-owned or collectively owned units to raise fish are requisitioned by the state for construction needs, construction units shall provide proper compensation.

CHAPTER III. FISHING

Article 14. The state encourages and supports the development of deep-sea fishing and rationally arranges fishing capacity in inland waters and offshore.

Article 15. Approval must be acquired from fishery administrative departments of the State Council for deep-sea fishing, which the state supports in terms of capital, facilities, technology, and taxes.

Article 16. Fishing licenses must be acquired from fishery administrative departments for inland waters and offshore fishing. Fishing licenses for large-scale trawling or purse net operations at sea are approved and issued by the Fishery Administrative Department of the State Council. Licenses for other fishing operations are approved and issued by the fishery administrative departments of the local people's governments at the county level or higher. However, these fishing licenses for operations at sea shall not exceed the limits set by the state for vessels, nets, and other fishing implements. Specific measures in this respect shall be formulated by the people's governments of the provinces, autonomous regions, and municipalities directly under the central government.

Fishing licenses may not be sold, rented, illegally transferred, or altered in other ways.

Article 17. Units and individuals who fish in inland or coastal waters must operate according to the types of operation, areas, seasons, and the amount of fishing tackle specified in their fishing licenses and abide by relevant regulations for protecting fishery resources.

Article 18. Fishing vessels manufactured, renovated, purchased, or imported must pass the inspection of the fishing vessel inspection department before being put into operation. Specific administrative measures shall be formulated by the Fishery Administrative Department of the State Council.

CHAPTER IV. EXPANSION AND PROTECTION OF FISHERY RESOURCES

Article 19. Fishery administrative departments of the people's governments at the county or higher level should work out a unified plan for waters under their administration and adopt measures to expand fishery resources. Fishery administrative departments of the people's governments at the county or higher levels may collect fishery resources development and protection fees from beneficiary units or individuals, and use the money exclusively for expanding and protecting fishery resources.

Measures for collecting fishery resources development and protection fees shall be formulated jointly by the State Council Fishery Administrative Department and financial departments. They shall go into effect after being submitted to and approved by the State Council.

Article 20. The use of explosives and poisoning of fish are prohibited. It is forbidden to catch aquatic products in an area where fishing is prohibited or during a season when fishing is prohibited, or to use prohibited implements or methods, or nets with a mesh smaller than the minimum size prescribed by law.

The fishery administrative department of the people's government at the county level or higher should decide on the specially protected aquatic resources, areas where fishing should be prohibited, seasons when fishing should be prohibited, fishing implements and fishing methods which should be prohibited or restricted, the minimum mesh size, and other measures for protecting aquatic resources.

Article 21. Catching the fry of aquatic animals with great cash value is prohibited. The catching of fry with great cash value or of aquatic animals carrying spawn for breeding or other special purposes must be approved by the fishery administrative department under the State Council or under the province, autonomous region, or municipality directly under the central government and must be carried out within prescribed areas and periods and under prescribed quotas.

It is necessary to adopt measures to protect the fry when using or diverting water from key areas where the fry of aquatic animals are under protection.

Article 22. A unit constructing sluice gates or dams in passages where fish, shrimps, and crabs swim which may lead to adverse effects on aquatic resources should build fish ladders or other ameliorative facilities.

Article 23. Departments in charge of fishery facilities concurrently used for regulating and storing waters or for irrigation purposes should decide on the minimum water level needed for aquatic production.

Article 24. Reclaiming land from a lake is prohibited. Reclaiming land from coastal beaches without the approval of the people's government at or above the county level is prohibited. Reclaiming land from major sites for fry and breeding farms is prohibited.

Article 25. Units carrying out underwater explosions, prospecting, or other construction works which may lead to adverse effects on aquatic resources should first consult the fishery administrative department under the people's government at or above the county level and take measures to prevent or minimize the damage to aquatic resources. The people's government at or above the county level should order compensation from those who have damaged aquatic resources.

Article 26. People's governments at all levels should, in accordance with the Marine Environmental Protection Law and the Water Pollution Prevention and Control Law, work out measures for protecting and improving the ecology of fishery grounds and for preventing and controlling pollution and should investigate the responsiblility of units and individuals that pollute fishing grounds.

Article 27. It is necessary to protect aquatic animals designatd as rare by the state. Catching such aquatic animals for a special purpose should be carried out in accordance with relevant laws and regulations.

CHAPTER V. LEGAL RESPONSIBILITIES

Article 28. Whoever blasts or poisons fish, catches fish in prohibited areas or during prohibited periods, uses prohibited fishing implements or methods, or catches rare aquatic animals listed by the state without approval will have the catch and illegal gains confiscated and will be subject to a fine, the fising implements will be confiscated, and the fishing licence revoked. When the circumstances are serious, it is necessary to investigate the criminal responsibility of individuals or units involved directly in the case in accordance with Article 129 of the Criminal Law.

Article 29. Whoever poaches or catches aquatic products or harms the breeding waters and facilities of others is to be ordered to pay compensation for the harm and be subject to a fine by the fishery administrative department or its subordinate fishery supervisory organ. When the circumstances are serious and the damage relatively large, it is necessary to investigate the criminal responsibility of individuals or units directly involved in the case, in accordance with Articles 151 or 156 of the Criminal Law.

Article 30. Whoever catches fish without obtaining a license, in accordance with the provisions of this law will have the catch and illegal gains confiscated and be subject to a fine. When the circumstances are serious, the fishing implements will be confiscated.

Article 31. Whoever contravenes the provisions of the fishing license concerning the type, site, time limit, and number of fishing implements will have the catch and illegal gains confiscated and be subject to a fine. When the circumstances are serious, the fishing implements will be confiscated and the fishing license revoked.

Article 32. Whoever unlawfully trades, leases, or transfers a fishing license will have the illegal gains confiscated and the fishing license revoked and will be subject to a fine.

Article 33. Administrative penalties prescribed by this law will be decided on by the fishery administrative department or its subordinate fishery supervisory organ. A concerned party who contests the administrative penalty may bring a suit before the people's court within thirty days of receiving the notice. The organ which has issued the penalty will request the people's court to enforce it after the party fails to either bring suit in court or comply with the penalty. A concerned party who continues to fish at sea must first comply with the penalty.

CHAPTER VI. SUPPLEMENTARY ARTICLES

Article 34. Detailed rules and regulations for enforcing the law are to be worked out by the Fishery Administrative Department under the State Council in accordance with the provisions of this law and will be put into force after being submitted to the State Council for approval.

The standing committees of the people's congresses of the provinces, autonomous regions, and municipalities (directly under the central government) should formulate measures for the implementation in accordance with this law and the detailed rules and regulations.

Article 35. This law goes into effect on July 1, 1986.

APPENDIXES. RELEVANT ARTICLES FROM THE CRIMINAL LAW

The Criminal Law Article related to Article 28 of the Fishery Law is as follows:

Article 129. Whoeover violates the laws and regulations on the protection of aquatic resources, catching aquatic products in an area where fishing is prohibited or during a period when fishing is prohibited, or using prohibited implements or methods to catch aquatic products, when the circumstances are serious, is to be sentenced to not more than two years of fixed-term imprisonment, criminal detention, or a fine.

The Criminal Law articles related to Article 29 of the Fishery Law are as follows:

Article 151. Whoever steals, swindles, or forcibly seizes articles of public or private property of a relatively large amount is to be sentenced to not more than five years of fixed-term imprisonment, criminal detention, or control.

Article 156. Whoever intentionally destroys articles of public or private property, when the circumstances are serious, is to be sentenced to not more than three years of fixed-term imprisonment, criminal detention, or a fine.

Appendix R

Grasslands Law (1985)

Renmin Ribao (June 19), p. 2.

Article 1. This law is formulated on the basis of the Constitution of the People's Republic of China in order to strengthen protection, management, and the building of grasslands; to rationally utilize, safeguard, and improve the ecological environment; to develop modern animal husbandry; to promote economic prosperity in nationalities autonomous areas; and to meet the needs of socialist construction and the people's livelihood.

Article 2. This law is applicable to all grasslands on Chinese territory, including grass-covered mountains and meadows.

Article 3. The Agriculture and Animal Husbandry Department of the State Council is in charge of the work of grassland management throughout the country, while agricultural and animal husbandry departments of local people's governments at and above the county level are in charge of the work of grassland management in their respective administrative areas.

Article 4. All grasslands are owned by the state, that is, by the whole people, with the exception of those that are owned by collectives in accordance with the law.

Grasslands owned by the people may be allocated to collectives on long-term leases. Grasslands owned by the whole people and collectives and grasslands owned by the whole people allocated to collectives on long-term leases may be contracted out to collectives or individuals for pastoral production.

Local people's governments at and above the county level should compile a register of grasslands used by units owned by the whole people and, on verification, issue certificates to confirm the right of use of the grasslands. People's governments at the county level should compile a register of collectively owned grasslands and of grasslands owned by the whole people that have been allocated to collectives on long-term leases and, on verification, issue certificates to confirm the right of ownership or use of the grasslands. The rights of ownership and use of grasslands are protected by law. No unit or individual may infringe on these rights.

Article 5. When, under special circumstances, such as natural disasters, temporary adjustments are deemed necessary in the use of grasslands, they should be effected by both sides through consultation on the basis of the principles of voluntariness and mutual benefit. When there is a need to make temporary adjustments in the use of grasslands involving more than one county, the county-level people's governments concerned may solve the issue by holding consultations.

Article 6. Any dispute concerning the rights of ownership and use of grasslands should be solved by the parties concerned through consultation and in the spirit of mutual understanding and mutual accommodation and that of achieving unity. If the parties concerned fail to solve their dispute through consultation, the case will be handled by the people's government.

Any dispute with regard to the right of ownership or use of grasslands owned by the whole people, between units owned by collectives, and between a unit owned by the whole people and another unit owned by a collective should be handled by the people's government at or above the county level.

A dispute concerning the right of use of grasslands between individuals, between an individual and a unit owned by the whole people, or between collectively owned units should be handled by the people's government at the township or county level. If a party disagrees with the handling or decision of the people's government concerned, he may appeal the case to the people's court within one month after receipt of notification. No party is allowed to destroy grasslands or any facility on grasslands pending solution of a dispute over the right of use of grasslands.

Article 7. The requisitioning of grasslands owned by collectives for national construction must be carried out in accordance with the Regulations Governing the Requisition of Land for National Construction. When grasslands owned by the whole people and grasslands allocated to collectives on long leases are requisitioned for national construction, appropriate compensation must be provided and proper arrangements made to help herdsmen in production and livelihood, in accordance with the Regulations Governing the Requisition of Land for National Construction.

When grasslands are temporarily used for national construction, they must be handled according to the Regulations Governing the Requisition of Land for National Construction [1982]. After the period allowed for the use of the grasslands expires, the unit that uses the grasslands should restore vegetation to it.

Article 8. Local people's government at all levels are responsible for conducting a survey of grassland resources in their respective administrative areas; drawing up a plan for the development of animal husbandry on grasslands and incorporating it in the economic development plan; strengthening protection, construction, and the reasonable utilization of grasslands; and improving the livestock-carrying capacity of grasslands.

Article 9. The state encourages scientific research on animal husbandry grasslands and the raising of scientific and technological levels of animal husbandry grasslands. The state encourages grass planting in rural, forest, and pastoral areas and in cities and towns to promote the development of animal husbandry and improve the ecological environment. The state protects the ecological environment of grasslands and prevents and eliminates pollution.

Article 10. It is necessary to strictly protect vegetation and prohibit land reclamation and damage to vegetation on grasslands. Grassland users who wish to reclaim small tracts of land must apply to the local people's government at or above the county level for approval. As for those who have reclaimed land and destroyed vegetation or caused soil erosion, the local people's government at or above the county level should set a time limit to close the land off and order those responsible to restore vegetation and restore the cultivated land to pastureland.

Article 11. Those who want to cut shrubs, uproot medicinal herbs and wild plants, scrape off alkaline soil, and collect farmyard manure can do so in designated areas after obtaining the consent of grassland users and reporting to the people's government at the township or county level for approval. They must see to it that whenever they dig sod they fill the pits back up with soil and preserve the vegetation. Cutting shrubs and uprooting medicinal herbs and other sand-fixing plants on waste grasslands, semiwaste grasslands, and desertified land are prohibited. Without the approval of the county people's government, no one is allowed to collect valuable or rare wild plants on grasslands.

Article 12. It is necessary to use grasslands rationally and to prevent grazing in excess of the grasslands' carrying capacity. If grassland desertification, grassland degeneration, or soil erosion is caused by grazing in excess of the grasslands' capacity, the grassland user should readjust the number of animals allowed to graze, plant additional forage grass, and restore vegetation. Man-made pastures should be managed in a better way, run rationally, utilized scientifically, and prevented from undergoing degradation.

Article 13. Local people's government at all levels should adopt measures to prevent and eliminate rodents and insect pests on grasslands and to protect beneficial birds and animals which feed on rodents and insects.

Article 14. Local people's governments at all levels should adopt measures to prevent and cure epidemic diseases among livestock and common human and livestock diseases. Those hunting for wild animals on grasslands should strictly observe the relevant regulations of the local people's government on preventing the spread of epidemic diseases.

Article 15. Those operating motor vehicles on grasslands should pay attention to protecting the grasslands. Where there are regular highways, they must operate motor vehicles on these regular highways. Those purchasing livestock should lead the livestock and allow them to graze along designated routes and must not compete with herdsmen for the use of grazing land and water sources.

Article 16. The prevention of grassland fires must be strengthened. It is necessary to carry out the policy of "integrating fire prevention with fire control, with fire prevention playing the dominant role," adopt the responsibility system in fire prevention, formulate a grasslands fire prevention system and pledge, and set a time period for grasslands fire prevention. During the grasslands fire prevention period safety measures should be adopted for the strict management of grasslands. When grasslands catch fire the masses should be rapidly organized to extinguish the fire. It is necessary to investigate the causes of a fire and losses caused, and handle the case in good time.

Article 17. Units or individuals who attain outstanding achievements in protecting, managing, and building grasslands and in developing animal husbandry on grasslands will be morally or materially rewarded by people's governments at the respective levels.

Article 18. When the rights of ownership or use of grasslands of a unit or individual are violated, the unit or individual may request the agriculture and animal husbandry department of the local people's government at or above the county level concerned to handle the case.

The agriculture and animal husbandry department has the power to order the violator to stop the violation and compensate for losses. The unit or individual whose rights have been violated may also file a lawsuit directly with the people's court.

Article 19. If a unit or individual reclaims grasslands in violation of this law, the agriculture and animal husbandry department of the local people's government at or above the county level has the power to order the unit or individual to cease reclamation and restore the vegetation. It may also fine the violator if the violation is serious.

Article 20. If a unit or individual cuts sand-fixing or other wild plants or excavates the sod on grasslands, thus damaging grassland vegetation in violation of this law, the township-level people's government or the agriculture and animal husbandry department of the county-level people's government has the power to stop the violation and order the violator to restore the vegetation and compensate for the losses. It may also impose a fine if the violation is serious.

Article 21. A litigant may file a lawsuit with the people's court within one month after being given notice if he disagrees with the decision concerning the fine imposed or compensation awarded by the agriculture and animal husbandry department of the local people's government or by the township-level people's government. If he does not file a lawsuit with the court with regard to the fine within the prescribed time, or fails to pay the fine, the agriculture and animal husbandry department of the local people's government concerned, or the township-level people's government, may request the people's court to enforce the fine.

Article 22. The agriculture and animal husbandry department of the State Council shall formulate rules for the implementation of this law on the basis of this law and submit these rules to the State Council for approval before they go into effect. The standing committee of the people's congress of an autonomous region or a province may formulate rules for the implementation of this law, in accordance with the principles stipulated in the Constitution of the People's Republic of China and this law and in accordance with local conditions, and report these rules to the Standing Committee of the National People's Congress for the record.

Article 23. This law shall go into effect on October 1, 1985.

Appendix S

State Council Circular on the Stringent Protection of Endangered Wildlife (April 13, 1983)

BFWH, pp. 214–16. Translation, with permission, from *Chinese Law and Government*, vol. 1, no. 1 (1986), pp. 105–7.

China has the greatest variety of wildlife of any country, accounting for more than 10 percent of all varieties. More than a hundred varieties of rare Chinese wildlife are known throughout the world, such as the giant panda (Ailuropoda melanoleuca), golden-haired monkey (Rhinopithecus roxellanae), Taiwan monkey (Macaca cyclopis), antelope (Budorcas taxicolor), white-lipped deer (Cervus albirostris), muntjac (Muntiacus crinifrons), Chinese river dolphin (Lipotes vexillifer), Yangtze River crocodile (Alligator sinensis), Chinese sturgeon (Acipenser sinensis), white sturgeon (Psephurus gladius), brown-eared pheasant (Crossoptilon mantchuricum), pheasants and quail (Phasianidae spp.), and black-necked crane (Grus nigricollis). There are, in addition, many varieties of rare, endangered wildlife, such as the Manchurian crane (Grus japonensis), Siberian white crane (Grus leucogeranus), Japanese crested ibis (Nipponia nippon), black stork (Ciconia nigra), swan (Cygnus spp.), Cabot's tragopan (Tragopan caboti), Chinese monal pheasant (Lophophorus thuysii), Reeves' pheasant (Syrmaticus reevesii), various kinds of gibbons (Hylobates spp.), leaf monkeys (Presbytis spp.), tufted deer (Elaphodus cephalophus), snow leopard (Panthera uncia), and wild camel (Camelus bactrianus). Wildlife is a precious natural resource in China. For many reasons this natural resource has, over a long period of time, faced the danger of depletion. Protection and rational utilization of this resource are of great significance in preserving the natural ecological balance, promoting scientific research, and developing the economy, culture, education, medicine, and public health. In the past few years incidents of hunting rare wildlife and seriously disrupting the habitat of these animals, as well as the illegal export of such animals and products made from them, have occurred in many places.

To resolutely check the above-mentioned violations of the law and to strengthen the protection and control of rare wildlife, the following circular is hereby issued.

1. Protecting rare wildlife is an important element in building a socialist spiritual civilization and material civilization and is a duty to be fulfilled by every citizen. The people's governments at all levels should attach great importance to this and should strengthen their leadership and enjoin the departments concerned to take effective measures and make conscientious efforts in order to do a good job in protection work. It is necessary

to step up publicity and education on the protection of rare wildlife in order to create a powerful public clamor, strive to make it known to every household, and strike roots in the hearts of the people, so that cherishing rare wildlife can gradually become a new social habit and virtue. To do this job well, all areas should, in connection with ''Cherish the Birds Week'' and the concrete conditions of each locality, concentrate publicity and educational activities in this field during this period of time.

2. Resolutely check the wanton capture and hunting of rare wildlife. It is necessary to strictly carry out the state and provincial-level regulations concerning the protection of rare wildlife. Illegal criminal activities of secretly hunting rare wildlife and buying and selling, trafficking, and exporting such animals and their products in violation of these regulations must be thoroughly investigated and punished according to law. It is necessary to seize on representative cases, handle them swiftly and severely, and publicize them in the press to educate the masses of cadres and people. At the same time those units and individuals who have achieved outstanding successes in protecting rare wildlife should be praised and rewarded.

3. All places should further tighten the management of the hunting economy and hunting rifles and traps. Without the approval of the department in charge under the State Council, no unit shall be allowed to produce or sell hunting rifles and shotguns. The state regulations on no-hunting areas and hunting seasons and methods must be strictly enforced, and violators must be punished according to the law.

4. Forbid the export of rare wildlife and wildlife products. In case of special export needs, it is necessary to follow strict examination and approval procedures according to state regulations and to receive an export permit from the Office for the Management of the Import and Export of Endangered Species of the People's Republic of China.

5. Strengthen scientific research on rare wildlife and develop in a planned way the work of observing wildlife resources and domesticating and breeding these animals. When there is a need to capture wildlife protected by state regulations for purposes of domestication, it is necessary to follow the procedures of examination and approval according to regulations.

6. Pay attention to protecting the habitat of rare wildlife. The main nesting and breeding areas for rare wildlife should be marked as preserves or no-hunting areas in accordance with state regulations, where control and construction should be strengthened. Order: All economic activities that affect the breeding and survival of endangered wildlife in their main nesting area should be banned.

This circular should be made known to all citizens to be effectively carried out.

Appendix T

Provisional Measures for the Assessment of Effluent Fees (February 5, 1982)

BFWH, pp. 278–83.

Article 1. These measures are set according to Article 18 of the Environmental Protection Law of the People's Republic of China (for trial implementation), which provides that "effluent fees should be assessed according to the amount and concentration of pollutants as stipulated by regulations on enterprises that discard more pollutants than the state standards permit."

Article 2. The purpose of the assessment of effluent fees is to promote the strengthening of operations and management by enterprises and other undertakings, the conservation and comprehensive utilization of resources, the control of pollution and the betterment of the environment.

Article 3. All enterprises and other undertakings shall implement the Provisional Standards for the Discharge of the Industrial "Three Wastes" and other relevant standards promulgated by the state. Where the people's governments of provinces, autonomous regions, or municipalities directly under the central government have approved and promulgated local discharge standards, enterprises and other undertakings in the relevant locality shall implement such local discharge standards.

Effluent fees shall be assessed on any enterprise or other undertaking that discharges pollutants in excess of the above-mentioned standards. With respect to other units that discharge pollutants, effluent fees shall be assessed for smoke and dust emissions from boilers.

Polluting units which pay effluent fees are not absolved from the responsibility of controlling pollution, compensating for damages caused, or other responsibilities as provided under the law.

Article 4. Polluting units should report and register with the local environmental protection departments the types, amounts, and concentration of the pollutants they discharge, [and] after examination and acceptance by the environmental protection departments or the monitoring units designated by such departments, [this information] shall be used as the basis for effluent fee assessment.

Article 5. The standards for effluent fee assessment shall be enforced in accordance with the provisions of the appendixes to these measures. With respect to individual large or medium-sized cities where industry is concentrated and pollution is especially severe, the standards for effluent fees assessment may be appropriately adjusted on approval by the Environmental Protection Leading Group of the State Council.

In the event that a polluting unit discharges two or more types of harmful materials from the same port in [its] wastewater, waste gas, or waste solids, calculation shall be based on the type for which the highest rate is assessed.

With respect to additional items in local effluent standards, the people's governments of the province, autonomous region, or municipality directly under the central government shall prescribe the standards for assessment with reference to the schedule attached to these measures.

Article 6. With respect to polluting units that still fail to attain the standards for emissions after payment of effluent fees, the standard for assessment shall be raised by 5 percent every year, commencing with the third year of such assessment. Any polluting unit that has attained the emission standard or has noticeably reduced the quantity and concentration of emissions through control and tighter management may apply to the local environmental protection department, which should halt or reduce the assessment of fees after verification through monitoring.

After the promulgation of the Environmental Protection Law of the People's Republic of China (for trial implementation), all new construction, expansion, and reconstruction projects and efficiency-minded innovation and renovation projects that emit pollutants in excess of the standards; as well as those that have treatment facilities for pollutants but which fail to operate them or remove them without authorization and whose emissions exceed the standards, shall be assessed at double the regular rate.

Each province, autonomous region, or municipality directly under the central government may make provisions for an increase or reduction of charges in accordance with the actual circumstances.

Article 7. Effluent fees shall be assessed monthly or quarterly. All polluting units, regardless of who they are subordinate to or owned by, shall pay their effluent fees at the designated bank within twenty days pursuant to the notice of payment issued by the local environmental protection department. In case of failure to pay within the prescribed period, a surcharge of one-tenth of 1 (0.1) percent shall be charged for every day in arrears.

Effluent fees from polluting units that are under the central government or provinces (including autonomous regions and municipalities directly under the central government) shall be paid to the financial organs at the provincial level. Other polluting units shall pay their effluent fees to the local financial organs. With respect to cities where enterprises under the central government and provinces are concentrated, the effluent fees may be paid to the local financial organs with the approval of the provincial people's government.

Article 8. Effluent fees paid by enterprises and units may be included in their production costs. With respect to the segment of their fees assessed at a higher rate, enterprises owned by the whole people shall include this segment as expenditures in their profit retention or enterprise capital funds; enterprises owned by the whole people which practice the "turn profits into taxes, independent accounting and assumption of sole responsibility for profits or losses" system and collectively owned enterprises shall include this segment as expenditures under profits after [income] taxes. Effluent fees paid by other units shall be paid principally out of the cash balance remaining after the completion of responsibility projects and out of extrabudgetary funds; in the event of insufficiency such fees may be included as expenditures under the units' business expenses.

Article 9. Effluent fees that are assessed shall be included in the budget as a fund for subsidizing environmental protection to be administered as earmarked funds outside the system of budgetary allotments.

Use of the environmental protection subsidization fund shall be unifiedly arranged by the environmental protection department in conjunction with the financial department. "Reserving special funds for special purposes," "collecting the funds before spending them," "not allowing expenditures to exceed income," and "no overspending or misappropriation" are principles which must be upheld. Any unused funds may be carried forward for use in the following year.

Article 10. The environmental protection subsidization fund should chiefly be used to subsidize key polluting units to control pollution sources as well as [to finance] comprehensive control measures for environmental pollution.

When adopting pollution control measures, any polluting unit should first use its own financial resources. In the event such financial resources are indeed insufficient, it may, after submission of a report for examination by its supervising department, apply to the environmental protection department and financial department for a fixed amount of subsidy out of the environmental protection subsidization fund. Such a subsidy generally shall not exceed 80 percent of the effluent fee payable by the unit concerned. Another possibility is to turn over 80 percent of the environmental protection subsidization funds to various supervisory bureaus to arrange for the subsidization of enterprises or other undertakings with regard to the control of pollution sources, under the supervision of the environmental protection department and the financial department. Units having the characteristics described in Article 6, Paragraph 2, shall not be subsidized.

Environmental protection subsidization funds may be appropriately used for subsidizing environmental protection departments in the purchase of monitoring instruments and apparatus. However, such subsidies may not be used by the environmental protection department to pay for its administrative expenses or for building offices, dormitories, or other non-business expenses.

Article 11. The environmental protection subsidization fund shall be allocated under the supervision of the Construction Bank.

Article 12. The people's governments of various provinces, autonomous regions, and municipalities directly under the central government may formulate specific measures for implementation on the basis of these measures.

Article 13. These measures shall be implemented as of July 1, 1982.

Effluent Fees: Standards for the Assessment of Effluent Fees

I. Waste Gases

Unit: Yuan (Rmb)

	Quantity Emitted In Excess of Standards (kilograms)	Concentration of Emissions in Excess of Standards (10 cubic meters)
Sulfur Dioxide, Carbon Disulfide, Hydrogen Sulfide, Flourides, Oxides of Nitrogen, Chlorine, Hydrogen Chloride, Carbon Monoxide	0.04	
Sulfuric Acid (Fog), Lead, Mercury, Beryllides		0.03-0.10
Glass Wool, Mineral Wool, Asbestos, Aluminum Compounds	0.10	
Coal Dust from Power Stations, Cement Dust	0.02	
Dust from Steel-smelting Furnaces, Other Dust	0.04	

Soot From Indus-trial and Heating Boilers	Multiple In Excess of the Standard	-4	4.1-6	6.1-9	9+
	Ringelman Density	Grade 2	Grade 3	Grade 4	Grade 5
	Fuel (tons) Fee Assessments	3.00	4.00	5.00	6.00

Note: (1) There shall be no assessments for smoke emitted by steam locomotives and other mobile sources of pollution for the time being.

(2) Effluent fees for waste gases from thermal power plants, and industrial and heating boilers shall be assessed in accordance with the standard for soot for the time being, and no fees shall be assessed on other harmful materials for the time being.

II. Waste Water

Unit: Yuan/Ton of Water

Nature or Name of Harmful Material	Multiple by which the Concentration Exceeds Standard				
	-5	5-10	10-20	20-50	50+
Mercury, Cadmium, Arsenic, Lead and its Inorganic Compounds, 6-Valent Chromium Compounds	0.15-0.20	0.20-0.30	0.30-0.45	0.45-0.90	0.90-2.00
Sulfides, Hydrocarbons, Evaporative Phenol, Cyanides, Organic Phosphors, Copper, Zinc, Flourine and Its Compounds, Nitrobenzene, Phenylalanine Type	0.10-0.15	0.15-0.20	0.20-0.35	0.35-0.60	0.60-1.00
Suspended Solids, COD, BOD, PH Value	0.04-0.06	0.06-0.10	0.10-0.15	0.15-0.20	0.20-0.30
Pathogens			0.08		

Note: For PH values outside the 6-9 range, every additional value above or below this range shall be calculated at a rate double that of the -5 base concentration, i.e., 0.04-0.06 yuan/ton.

III. Waste Solids

Unit: Yuan

Name of Harmful Material	Quantity Dumped or Discharged in Water Body (tons)	Quantity Deposited Under Non-Waterproof, Leachable Conditions (tons/month)	Quantity Deposited Without Special Facilities (tons/month)
Solids Containing Mercury, Cadmium, Arsenic, Chromium, Lead, Cyanide, Yellow Phosphorus and Other Soluble and Highly Toxic Substances	36.00	2.00	
Powdered Coal Ash from Power Plants	1.20		0.10
Other Industrial Solid Wastes	5.00		0.30

Note: (1) In addition to charging a fee, acts of discharging or dumping highly toxic solid wastes or depositing such highly toxic solid wastes under non-leachable conditions should be immediately stopped and the party responsible shall be ordered to take treatment measures.

(2) The item "powdered coal ash from power plants" shall only apply to coal burning power plants built and put into operation prior to the promulgation of the "Environmental Protection Law (for trial implementation)" without ash yards that have been discharging ash in water bodies. The standard for other industrial solid wastes shall be applicable to the discharge of powdered coal ash by other power plants (including the expansion of the above mentioned power plants).

(3) Solid wastes deposited in mine tipples, ash yards and special (including gangue) dump sites for solid wastes shall not be assessed for the time being.

Appendix U

Ministry of Finance and State Council Environmental Protection Leading Group Circular Related to Procedures Governing the Retention of Profits from Products Derived from Multiple Use of the "Three Wastes" in Industrial and Mining Enterprises (December 30, 1979)

BFWH, pp. 274–77.

In accordance with the spirit of Article 31 of the Environmental Protection Law (for trial implementation) and the Main Points of the Work Report on Environmental Protection transmitted by the Central Committee (Doc. No. 79, 1978), with regard to an incentive-based policy to promote the comprehensive utilization of the "three wastes" in a big way, the circular related to the retention of profits from products derived from multiple use of the "three wastes" on industrial and mining enterprises is as follows:

1. The three wastes in industry are truly a waste of energy and resources. Maximal utilization of energy and resources is a basic measure to eliminate pollution and protect the environment and is an important way to enhance the potential within industrial and mining enterprises and to increase production and save energy. The use of incentives is a major state economic policy intended to stimulate management of the three wastes and develop multiple use in industrial and mining enterprises.
2. The products produced by industrial and mining enterprises to eliminate pollution, control the three wastes, and expand comprehensive utilization with the exception of goods stipulated in the designs refer to products manufactured principally through the recovery and reuse of wastewater, gases, solids, and other residuals, such as:
   a) products made from industrial and mining enterprises, mine detritus tailings, crushed stone, powder, dust, sludge, and all manner of solid wastes;
   b) products made from industrial and mining enterprises, wastewater, acid, lye, oil, and other waste liquids;
   c) products made from industrial and mining enterprises' various waste gases and vapors;
   d) hot water, steam, and electricity generated from heat and pressure emitted from industrial and mining enterprises;
   e) goods produced from all other industrial and mining enterprises' polluting materials;
   f) goods produced from industrial and mining, municipal, and transportation refuse.

3. Enterprises should have separate accounting for the costs, gains, and losses from goods that are sold or used in-house which are products of multiple-use management of the three wastes. With the exception of the profits on products derived from use of the three wastes in new construction, renovation, and expansion projects that have received national capital investment funds (the profits from which must be remitted to the state and which neither the enterprise nor its supervisory department may retain), when goods (which are the result of multiple use) yield a profit after all gains and losses have been set off against each other, such profit may be retained according to the following conditions without regard to the source of capital, the scale of operations, or the amount of gains.
a) As set forth in the 1978 Circular of the Central Committee (No. 79) beginning on January 1, 1979, the profits of goods derived from multiple use in the first five years need not be turned over to the state.
As set forth in the 1977 State Council Environmental Protection Office Document No. 3, the profits of goods derived from multiple use in 1977 and 1978 need not be turned over to the state in the first three years respectively; the profits derived from goods produced by multiple use before 1977, which have already been entered into the fisc may not be refunded or reclaimed. However, when profits from such goods increase as a result of efforts after 1977, such profits may be retained for five years, beginning in 1979.
b) When profits are derived from an enterprise's use of its own funds to manage the three wastes, all such profits may be retained.
When profits are derived from joint investment by an enterprise and its supervisory department or from investment by the supervisory department, such profits shall principally be retained by the enterprise; where the department certifies a need, the department may retain no more than 30 percent of said profits.
c) Profits from goods derived from multiple use of the three wastes may be counted only once. Thus any profits resulting from the use of these products as raw materials for the production of other goods ought not be calculated therein.
d) The retention of profits from products produced from management of the three wastes shall be in accordance with the Ministry of Finance's regulations and may not influence examination of the fulfillment of planning norms in industrial and mining enterprises.
e) Retained profits from goods derived from management of the three wastes shall be approved by the enterprises' supervisory department and the financial department at the same level [as the enterprise]. Enterprises shall conduct themselves in a spirit of truthfulness and full disclosure and shall not distort or misinterpret the facts or hide profits that will influence financial revenues.

4. Profits from goods derived from management of the three wastes that are retained by industrial and mining enterprises or their respective departments shall continue to be used for management of the three wastes, improving the environment, and improving working conditions and may not be used for other uses. Profits not used in a given year may be carried over. Those enterprises that have completed their work involving management of the three wastes may not retain additional profits and must turn over said profits to the Ministry of Finance. Use of these funds shall be subject to supervision by the local financial and environmental protection offices.

5. Units and individuals that make outstanding achievements and contributions to en-

vironmental protection shall receive praise and rewards. The quality of an enterprise's multiple-use management of the three wastes shall be a factor in the awarding of bonuses and is to be unifiedly examined and evaluated by the enterprise.

Said bonuses shall be unifiedly drawn from the regular production bonus fund as set forth in the Regulations of the State Council 1978, No. 91. Profits from goods derived from multiple-use management of the three wastes may not be used for additional bonuses.

6. Reduction and exemption from taxes on the profits of goods manufactured principally through the management of the three wastes as raw materials shall follow the formula set forth in the Regulations of the State Council of 1977 (No. 144) regarding the management structure for the assessment of taxes.
7. This circular will take precedence in cases of conflict between this circular and earlier notices on the retention of profits from multiple use and the reduction and exemption from taxes issued by various localities and departments.

Appendix V

State Economic Commission Provisional Regulations on Issues concerning the Multiple Use of Resources (1985)

Translated in FBIS-*CHI* (October 15), pp. K16–19.

The multiple use of resources is a major technical and economic policy of great significance in rationally utilizing resources, increasing social wealth, achieving greater economic effectiveness, and protecting the natural environment. To arouse various enterprises' enthusiasm in making multiple use of resources, the following regulations have been drawn up to deal with the relevant issues:

1. To encourage enterprises to make multiple use of resources, the state adopts preferential policies for production and construction involving multiple use of resources.

Projects eligible for preferential treatment should be those covered by the Catalogue of Multiple Use of Resources attached to these regulations. The State Economic Commission may revise the catalogue in accordance with the actual needs.

2. No single unit should monopolize the multiple use of resources. Barriers between departments and trades should be removed. The state encourages and supports all enterprises, especially large and medium-sized enterprises, in diversifying their operations while undertaking one principal business.

3. The surveying and prospecting for mineral resources and constructing and renovating of oil fields and mines (including coal, metal, and other mines) with paragenetic and associated mineral deposits must adhere to the principles of "finding, evaluating, mining, and utilizing in a comprehensive manner," in accordance with the state's relevant laws governing mineral resources. The study of the feasibility of making multiple use of mineral resources should be intensified. The planning of a mine should include measures for making multiple use of resources. One major requirement of evaluating a mining enterprise is to judge its method of increasing the total recovery rate in the process of mining and dressing mineral resources.

An enterprise must follow the principle of combining pollution control and multiple use of resources. When building or renovating an enterprise that consumes large amounts of energy, projects involving recycling of residual heat utilizing differential pressure and gases generated by blast or coking furnaces and the recycling of water should be considered a major aspect in construction. As with projects for controlling environmental pollution, economically practical projects for making multiple use of resources should be designed, built, and put into operation simultaneously with the main project.

4. In making multiple use of resources, an enterprise should follow the principle of "he who invests shall reap the benefits." An enterprise should reap the profits derived from a project it builds with its own funds. Its supervisory department and the department that takes charge of the trade should support this policy and should not withhold part of the profits, impose fees, or appropriate the output.

5. The state will not distribute the products produced by a project built by an enterprise with its own funds for making multiple use of resources. Nor will the state deduct any amount of these goods from its supplies for the enterprise. The enterprise may market these goods, with the exception of such precious metals as gold and silver, which the enterprise cannot market by itself under state law. While planning a state-invested project, leeway for above-quota output [of goods produced by making multiple use of resources] should be made for the enterprise, and the enterprise can market the above-quota portion according to state regulations.

6. All enterprises should actively support other units in utilizing the unprocessed tailings, coal ash, and various types of slag and should not charge the user in any way. However, it may collet a fee from the user—in accordance with the principle that the interests of the raw material supplier should come after the interests of the unit that carries out multiple use of resources—for the use of processed tailings, coal ash, and slag, except for those resources that the state has prescribed otherwise. The supplier and user should sign a contract and act strictly on that basis.

When the slag, waste gas, and waste liquid an enterprise produces are listed under the state's mandatory plan, it should first ensure the needs of the plan before utilizing them itself and should not discontinue the supply of those wastes to those units with which it has reached agreement.

7. On the condition of not increasing the state's fuel supply, the power generated by an enterprise by means of residual heat, differential pressure, or fuel of low heat value will not be included in the state's distribution plan, nor will it be deducted from its supply quota. The enterprise may market the surplus power through its own network or request the power department to sell it through its large power grid.

The power department should support the incorporation of those power stations that generate electricity by connecting them into its large power grid. Those power stations that generate power by making multiple use of resources and that have already been incorporated into the large power grid may offset part of the power they receive from the grid with the amount of power they supply to the grid each month, and the amount of power they exchange with the grid should be calculated on an equal basis. When a station has surplus power to sell, it should request the power department to do so on its behalf through the power grid.

8. An enterprise may set prices for its products as mentioned in Section 5 above, except those for which the state has prescribed otherwise. According to relevant regulations, favorable prices shall be paid for the gold and silver sold by an enterprise or individual.

In principle, in purchasing the power a unit generates by making multiple use of resources, a power grid will set the price according to the power generation cost, plus the average amount of profit the local power grid makes. The power grid's charge for selling the power should include the cost of supplying power, the depreciation of the transmission cables, the power delivery tax, and a handling fee of 5 percent of the price it pays for purchasing the power.

9. When the products produced by a project an enterprise builds with its own funds are included in the State Economic Commission's Catalogue of Multiple Use of Resources,

their taxes may be reduced or exempted in accordance with the Regulations of the People's Republic of China for Product Taxes (draft). After the project has begun production, the workshop or the branch plant that is capable of handling its own accounting need not pay income tax or adjustment tax for a period of five years but should be solely responsible for its own profits and losses.

Products produced by a project built with state funds to make multiple use of resources should still pay product taxes, income taxes, and regulatory taxes in accordance with the state's tax law.

10. An enterprise should be primarily responsible for the funds it requires for making multiple use of resources. An enterprise that produces goods for export may use foreign capital. A project that benefits society but not the enterprise itself should be incorporated into the state plan and assisted accordingly. Specialized banks should extend credits to projects for making multiple use of resources that are unprofitable but produce the kinds of raw materials the state badly needs. The time limit for repaying the loans may be extended appropriately.

When an enterprise uses bank loans to build a project for making multiple use of resources, it should repay the loans with profits derived from the new project.

All the funds retained for the depreciation of equipment for making multiple use of resources may be retained by the enterprise for renewing the facilities for making multiple use of resources.

11. The technology as well as the equipment and materials needed for building a project for making multiple use of resources may be regarded as one of technological transformation, and thereby enjoy such favorable treatment as tax reductions or exemptions and priority allocation of foreign exchange.

An enterprise may retain a percentage of the foreign exchange earned from the production of goods for export by making multiple use of resources.

12. While departments concerned under the State Council will organize personnel to tackle major technical problems in making multiple use of resources, other departments and the local authorities may also purchase their needed technology in the market for scientific and technological know-how. An enterprise may also solicit bidding for its special needs and request research institutions or other scientific and technological organs in society to undertake their projects.

All regions and departments should organize technical diffusion teams to disseminate the knowledge for making multiple use of resources, to exchange experiences, to diagnose difficult problems, and to undertake technical contracts. Standardization departments should speed up the preparation of state standards for products produced through the multiple use of resources.

13. The state shall establish awards to commend those units and individuals who have contributed to the multiple use of resources.

All enterprises should strive to conserve water and increase the rate of water usage by recycling water and carrying out multiple use of water. Enterprises that successfully conserve water should be rewarded.

A mine has the right to use the land it has reclaimed by filling in the depression with slag, rocks, and coal ash. It may charge an appropriate fee if it sells the land to another unit.

14. All departments should support enterprises in order to promote the multiple use of resources. They should take the initiative in coordinating cooperation between various trades and regions.

15. The State Economic Commission is responsible for organizing, coordinating, supervising, and inspecting the nation's multiple use of resources. The economic commissions of various provinces, autonomous regions, and municipalities directly under the central government are responsible for organizing, coordinating, supervising, and inspecting the multiple use of resources in local areas. Without creating additional organs, relevant departments under the State Council should designate a unit to take charge of the routine work of overseeing the multiple use of resources.

16. The State Economic Commission is responsible for interpreting these regulations.

Appendix W

Provisional Regulations for Environmental Management in Foreign Economic Development Zones (March 15, 1986)

GGB, no. 500 (May 20, 1986), pp. 426–27.

1. These regulations are specially stipulated in order to strengthen environmental management in the foreign economic development zones, prevent and control environmental pollution and ecological destruction, ensure the people's health, protect and create a favorable environment for investment, and accelerate economic and social development.

2. The foreign economic development zones referred to in the regulations are the state-approved special economic zones, coastal development cities, and the coastal economic development zones.

All units and individuals engaged in production or management activities in foreign economic development zones must comply with these regulations.

3. The people's governments at various levels in the foreign economic development zones must uphold the policy of "putting prevention first, and combining prevention and control," and strengthen their work with regard to comprehensive environmental control. They should incorporate environmental protection in their local economic and social development plans; clarify their environmental protection goals, tasks, and measures; and organize their implementation.

4. The foreign economic development zones must conduct environmental impact assessments, do overall planning, and make rational arrangements while constructing new zones. All departments concerned must conduct construction in strict accordance with the requirements of the plans and arrangements.

Irrational arrangements currently existing in the foreign economic development zones should be gradually corrected in the course of urban reconstruction and industrial readjustment. Projects that pollute the environment may not be built in residential neighborhoods, watershed protection areas, sanitorium districts, nature preserves, scenic and tourist spots, archaeological and historical sites, or other specially protected areas. Existing projects must be corrected, adjusted, or relocated within a specified time period.

5. The people's governments of the provinces, autonomous regions, and municipalities directly under the central government where foreign economic development zones are located may formulate supplementary local standards for items which are not yet regulated by state environmental [ambient] quality standards; and they may formulate local pollutant emissions standards more stringent than state pollutant emission standards in cases where

enforcement of the state pollutant emission standards cannot ensure that the requirements of the local environmental [ambient] standards will be attained; and they shall report them to the state environmental protection department for the record.

Enterprises and other undertakings located within these zones must comply with local pollutant emission standards formulated in accordance with the above provision.

6. Technology and equipment imported from abroad into the foreign economic development zones must satisfy the requirement of being nonpolluting or low polluting. When items that cause pollution are imported, and when domestic controls for such items are unavailable, the corresponding environmental protection measures should be imported at the same time. All new construction, renovation, and expansion projects must work toward putting their pollution control measures into operation at the same time as the principal project items.

7. All units and individuals in the foreign economic development zones should clarify the duties and responsibilities of all parties concerned with regard to environmental protection and specify pollution control measures when signing economic contracts. No provision in violation of national or local environmental protection laws or regulations may be included in a contract.

8. In accordance with state regulations, units carrying out development and construction in the foreign economic development zones must submit environmental impact statements or lists and preliminary designs for the environmental protection items included in the construction project. After the project has been completed, they must submit an installation certification report for environmental protection measures.

Within forty-five days of the receipt of an environmental impact statement or list, or thirty days of the receipt of the preliminary design of environmental protection items or an installation certification report for environmental protection measures, the environmental protection department should issue its response. When a response is not forthcoming within the designated time period, a report that has been submitted shall automatically take effect.

9. Enterprises and other undertakings in foreign economic development zones that emit pollutants must submit applications to emit to the environmental protection departments of the local people's governments. If they factually report their pollutant emitting equipment, treatment measures, and the types, forms, volumes, and concentrations of pollutants emitted under normal operating conditions, they can engage in production or operations after their application has been approved and they have obtained discharge permit certificates. Should changes occur in the circumstances involving the emission of pollutants, they should promptly make a report to the environmental protection department of the local people's government.

Those which exceed state or local emission standards shall pay effluent fees for extending the standards in accordance with state regulations; those which discharge pollutants into bodies of water shall pay effluent fees in accordance with state regulations.

10. The environmental protection departments of the local people's governments in the foreign economic zones are responsible for organizing, coordinating, supervising, and inspecting environmental protection work in their localities. Units under supervision and inspection must factually represent the relevant circumstances and materials.

The environmental protection departments have the duty and the responsibility to safeguard the secrecy of the circumstances and materials represented by the units under supervision and inspection.

11. All units that violate these regulations and cause harm from pollution may be

ordered by the environmental protection departments of the local people's governments at various levels in the foreign economic development zones or other supervisory departments designated by the state to institute controls within a specified time period, assume the expenses for eradicating the pollution, and compensate for the damages; and they may be issued warnings or fines.

If a party involved in the case does not accept the judgment, he may file suit in the people's court within fifteen days of receipt of notification of the judgment. If a party does not file suit before the expiration of the time period and does not comply with the judgment, the environmental protection department or another supervisory department may petition the people's court for compulsory enforcement.

12. The people's governments of the provinces, autonomous regions, and municipalities directly under the central government where foreign economic development zones are located may stipulate procedures for implementation in accordance with these regulations.

13. These regulations shall take effect from the date of their promulgation.

Appendix X

State Planning Commission, State Capital Construction Commission, Ministry of Finance, and State Council Environmental Protection Leading Group, Some Regulations on Controlling the Industrial "Three Wastes" and Developing Comprehensive Utilization (April 14, 1977)

BFWH, pp. 254–59.

Elimination of industrial "three wastes" pollution and protection and amelioration of the environment is an important task. Party committees at all levels must include environmental protection work on their daily agendas of important items, strengthen leadership, mobilize the masses, and sincerely pay it close attention. We must fully enhance the superiority of the planned economy and sincerely incorporate environmental protection in the national economic plan. At the same time, we must rely on the masses and establish a system of essential regulations.

Acting in accordance with our great leader Chairman Mao's teaching that "comprehensive utilization is very important, and attention must be paid to it," in accordance with Premier Zhou's important instructions on protecting and ameliorating the environment, in accordance with the spirit of the State Council's *Guofa* 158 (1973) document and the Report on Strengthening Environmental Protection Work approved by the Central Committee, in order to accelerate the comprehensive utilization of the "three wastes," to prevent and control the dangers arising from pollution, to ensure the people's health, to strengthen the alliance between workers and peasants, and to develop industrial and agricultural production more, better, faster, and more economically, the following regulations are stipulated with regard to relevant issues:

1. All departments, districts, and industrial and mining enterprises and other units must act in accordance with our great leader Chairman Mao's teaching, enhance the activism of both center and region, smash through the boundaries separating industries, and implement the policy of letting one industry take the lead with management by many industries. Enterprises must rely on the masses and strengthen economic management, reform production techniques, undertake comprehensive utilization in a big way, and make the fullest effort to eliminate the "three wastes" during the production process. Those industrial "three wastes" that must be discharged shall be discharged in accordance with state regulations and standards. We must uphold the principles of doing everything in a self-reliant and thrifty way, and do a good job of controlling the "three wastes."

2. In order to prevent the emergence of new pollution, all enhancement and renovation projects that involve new construction, renovation, expansion, and the adoption of technological measures to increase production capacity that discharge the "three wastes" and pollute the environment must strictly implement regulations on measures to control the "three wastes," measures which include design, construction, and entering into operation at the same time as the main project [the "three simultaneous points"]. Otherwise, they shall not be allowed to be built or enter into operation. All projects currently under construction that lack measures must adopt supplementary items with the responsibility for arranging the required funds to be borne by the department that originally issues the approval. While an enterprise is engaged in renovation, expansion, or renewal, it should take measures to solve existing pollution linked to the renovation, expansion, and renewal items in one fell swoop. Planning departments, construction departments, and supervisory departments at all levels must sincerely and earnestly carry out the regulations on the "three simultaneous points" when formulating capital construction plans and examining and approving plan item statements and expanded preliminary designs. Any project that fails to include measures to control the "three wastes" and which has not received the approval of the environmental protection departments and the supervisory departments, shall not be incorporated into the plan by the planning departments, and the design departments shall not prepare designs, the urban construction departments shall not allocate land, the construction bank shall not issue credits, and the construction departments shall not begin construction. The circumstances involving the implementation of the "three simultaneous points" regulations for projects that have entered into operation during the year shall be reported each year by the construction and environmental protection departments to the people's governments at higher levels. With regard to units that failed to implement the "three simultaneous points" regulations and which caused environmental pollution through human action, their responsibility shall be investigated and they shall be severely dealt with.

3. The elimination of pollution and protection of the environment should constitute a norm to be satisfied by industrial and mining enterprises in terms of overall fulfillment of the state plan. At the same time that they arrange, inspect, and sum up production tasks, leading departments at all levels and industrial and mining enterprises and units should arrange, inspect, and sum up environmental protection work. A unit cannot be selected as an advanced unit if it fulfills the other norms in its plan but lets the "three simultaneous points" take their own course, fails to actively develop comprehensive utilization, fails to actively institute controls, pollutes the environment, harms the people's health, and fails to consider overall fulfillment of the state plan.

4. We must protect and rationally utilize the state's natural resources. With regard to the state's important resources like mines, forests, rivers, lakes, and seas, we must smash through the boundaries separating industries and undertake comprehensive utilization in a big way. It is not permitted to poach and denude the forests, squander resources, or pollute the environment. It is not permitted to treat rivers, lakes, and seas as sewers or refuse bins. Increases in industrial production must fully utilize "three wastes" resources. All products that can be manufactured by existing enterprises through the comprehensive utilization of the "three wastes" must be accorded priority in development. When the volumes of these products cannot satisfy demand, new construction projects shall then be considered. When new mines are prospected and exploited, they must practice multiple use in the mine and do a good job of comprehensive utilization.

5. Enterprises and units that contain pollution hazards must prepare control plans and implement them by stages and in groups.

When control of the "three wastes" and the development of comprehensive utilization requires new construction or the expansion of subsidiary enterprises, independent workshops or sections, or the complete technological renovation of the entire factory or workshop, the project items should be incorporated in the capital construction plan, and the necessary funds should be provided for in the capital construction plans of the various departments and districts.

With regard to routine technical measures undertaken to control the "three wastes" and develop comprehensive utilization, and measures to control the "three wastes" undertaken in conjunction with the renewal and renovation of existing fixed capital, the funds in general should be met out of the enterprises' retained renewal and renovation funds or the renewal and renovation funds accumulated at higher levels. The various departments and districts should stipulate a fixed ratio of their accumulated renewal and renovation funds for use in "three wastes" control and comprehensive utilization measures.

With regard to some "three wastes" comprehensive utilization items in medium- and small-scale industrial enterprises which require small investments, promise a fast payback, and which conform to the stipulations of the Provisional Methods for Extending Credits for Small-Scale Technological Measures, application for small-scale technological measures credits may be made.

Construction and maintenance expenses for municipal pollution treatment facilities shall be met out of the municipalities' capital construction and maintenance funds.

Funds for controlling the "three wastes" in collective enterprises should be met out of the enterprises' "public accumulation funds," "cooperative undertakings funds," or renewal and renovation funds.

6. "Three wastes" discharged by enterprises that pollute the environment which have yet to be utilized and controlled (by the original enterprises) but which can be utilized by other units in general should be supplied on a cost-free basis. With regard to "three wastes" that have been processed and treated, a treatment fee can be collected. Expenses for loading, shipping, and managing the "three wastes" in general should be borne by the unit making use of them. With regard to the treatment of the "three wastes," the supplier and consumer units must establish a fixed coordinative relationship. With regard to units that have already established fixed coordinative relationships, they shall act in accordance with their original agreements, which shall not be altered without the consent of both parties.

7. In accordance with the spirit of the State Council's *Guofa* 158 (1973) document with regard to "we must adopt a policy of rewarding comprehensive utilization" and the 1973 regulations of the Ministry of Finance's Finance and Taxation Document No. 53, products manufactured by industrial enterprises utilizing the "three wastes" for whom the payment of taxes with reference to this chapter poses definite difficulties may be given tax abatement or tax exemption treatment for a specified time period. Concrete measures shall be weighed and decided by the people's governments of the provinces, autonomous regions, and municipalities directly under the central government.

8. With regard to enterprises' "three wastes" control measures to eliminate pollution which make use of renewal and renovation funds, the products and losses for products manufactured through these processes should be separately calculated (the portion of profits obtained from their use as raw materials in the manufacture of other products

should not be recalculated). If there is a surplus after the profits and losses from such products have been balanced out, subject to examination and approval by the finance department at the same level, the surplus may be retained by the enterprise for a period of three years after the start of production for continued use in "three wastes" control, but may not be used for other purposes.

9. Enterprises containing a pollution hazard should actively adopt measures to control the "three wastes," quickly eliminate any danger to the surrounding environment and agriculture, and reduce compensation (payments) for "three wastes" pollution to the maximum extent possible. In the future, enterprises may not casually pay compensation for pollution without the consent of the local supervisory department, finance department, and environmental protection department.

With regard to mature techniques, workable measures, and technological renovation items that produce "three wastes" control results within one or two years, treatment expenses should first be met in full out of enterprise or higher levels' funds designated for renewal and renovation. Should these funds be definitely insufficient, the unmet portion may be included in the enterprises' nonoperational expenditures subject to examination by the supervisory departments and the environmental protection departments and following review and approval by the finance department at the same level, provided that the total does not exceed the sum of pollution compensation payments arising from this item during the previous three years.

10. Expenditures for the wages and welfare of personnel and for the professional activities of environmental protection scientific research and monitoring organs belonging to the environmental protection management organs at all levels shall be paid out of environmental protection operating expenses. Expenditures for environmental protection monitoring work performed by water conservancy, meteorology, and geology departments shall be paid out of their own departments' operating expenses. Expenditures for environmental protection science items that warrant incorporation in the scientific plans of various departments and districts should be met out of relevant operating expenses. Expenditures for environmental protection research and monitoring conducted by enterprises and units should be paid out of the enterprises' management expenses.

11. With regard to the steel, cement, and timber required for environmental protection capital construction projects, during distribution the materials supply departments should ensure that the volumes are not less than the norm for state 10,000 RMB capital construction projects. Any equipment that is required shall be unifiably incorporated into the materials supply management structure's distribution plan and be provided in this manner. With regard to material and equipment needed for control projects financed by enterprises out of their renewal and renovation funds, they should be met first by enhancing the potential within the enterprises themselves. When they cannot be provided in this way, they shall be separately met by unified arrangements made by the relevant supervisory departments and districts according to need. When individual districts face definite difficulties in the making of arrangements, the state's materials supply distribution departments shall deliberate and offer suitable supplementary assistance.

With regard to materials and equipment required by collective enterprises for "three wastes" control, the planning and materials supply departments in the various districts should provide suitable support.

After "three wastes" control items have formally been entered into production, the products manufactured from them together with the raw materials, fuel, and material that they require shall be separately incorporated in industrial, materials supply, and sales plans in accordance with the scope of state commodity management and materials supply channels. With regard to commodities manufactured from comprehensive utilization of the ''three wastes'' by various departments and districts, the planning and materials supply departments at various levels should give priority during distribution to the ''three wastes'' control requirements within their respective departments and districts.

12. With regard to the work force needed for projects involving ''three wastes'' control and comprehensive utilization which the enterprises themselves absolutely cannot meet, they should be incorporated in the plans each year and application made to the labor departments at various levels. After examination and verification, the labor departments should incorporate them in the distribution plans.

Appendix Y

Mineral Resources Law (March 19, 1986)

GGB, no. 496 (April 10, 1986), pp. 195–202.

CHAPTER I. GENERAL PRINCIPLES

Article 1. In accordance with the Constitution of the People's Republic of China, this law is specially stipulated to develop the mining industry; strengthen prospecting, exploitation, utilization, and conservation work with regard to mineral resources; and guarantee the present and future requirements for the building of socialist modernization.

Article 2. All prospecting and mining of mineral resources that takes place within the sovereign territory and seas under the jurisdiction of the People's Republic of China must abide by this law.

Article 3. All mineral resources are owned by the state. The state's ownership rights with regard to both surface and subsurface mineral resources shall not be altered when the ownership or usage rights with regard to the land to which they are attached are held by others.

The state guarantees the rational exploitation and utilization of mineral resources. It is prohibited for any organization or individual to seize or damage mineral resources. The people's governments at all levels must strengthen mineral resources protection work.

Prospecting for mineral resources must be lawfully registered. The exploitation of mineral resources requires application for and issuance of a mining permit. The state protects the inviolability of prospecting and mining permits and ensures that production and work order in production and work areas shall not be hampered or damaged.

Mining permits may not be bought and sold or rented, nor may they be pledged as collateral.

Article 4. State mining enterprises are the main force for the exploitation of mineral resources. The state ensures the strengthening and development of state mining enterprises.

The state encourages, guides, and assists the development of rural collective mining enterprises.

Through administrative management, the state guides, assists, and supervises lawful mining by individuals.

Article 5. The state practices compensation for exploitation with regard to mineral resources. In accordance with relevant state regulations, the payment of resource taxes and resource depletion charges is required with regard to the exploitation of mineral resources.

Article 6. The state exercises a policy of unified planning, rational distribution, comprehensive prospecting, rational exploitation, and comprehensive utilization with regard to the prospecting and exploitation of mineral resources.

Article 7. The state encourages scientific and technological research on the prospecting and exploitation of mineral resources, disseminates advanced techniques, and raises the level of science and technology with regard to the prospecting and utilization of mineral resources.

Article 8. Units and individuals with outstanding achievements in the prospecting, exploitation, and protection of mineral resources and in scientific and technological research should be rewarded by the people's governments at various levels.

Article 9. The State Council's departments in charge of geology and mining are in charge of supervision and management work with regard to the prospecting and exploitation of mineral resources throughout the country. The State Council's relevant departments in charge shall assist the State Council's departments in charge of geology and mining in carrying out supervision and management work with regard to the prospecting and exploitation of mineral resources.

The departments in charge of geology and mining of the people's governments of the provinces, autonomous regions, and municipalities directly under the central government are in charge of supervision and management work with regard to the prospecting and exploitation of mineral resources within their respective areas of administration. The relevant departments in charge within the people's governments of the provinces, autonomous regions, and municipalities directly under the central government shall assist the departments in charge of geology and mining at the same level in carrying out supervision and management work with regard to the prospecting and exploitation of mineral resources.

CHAPTER II. REGISTRATION OF PROSPECTING AND THE EXAMINATION AND APPROVAL OF THE MINING OF MINERAL RESOURCES

Article 10. The state exercises a unified registration system with regard to prospecting for mineral resources. The State Council's departments in charge of geology and mining are responsible for registration work with regard to prospecting for mineral resources. However, the responsibility for registration work with regard to the prospecting for mineral resources of specially designated minerals may be assigned by the State Council to other relevant departments in charge. The State Council shall stipulate the scope and procedures for the registration of prospecting for mineral resources.

Article 11. The State Council's organ for the examination and certification of mineral reserves or the organs of the provinces, autonomous regions, and municipalities directly under the central government for the examination and certification of mineral reserves are responsible for examining and certifying prospecting reports with regard to the opening, design, and utilization of mines, and shall transmit a response to the units within the stipulated time period. Until a prospecting report has been approved, it may not serve as the basis for opening or designing a mine.

Article 12. A unified management system shall be applied to the records and materials obtained from prospecting for mineral resources and to the statistics and materials regarding the reserves of various kinds of minerals, and in accordance with State Council regulations they shall be either compiled and transmitted or tabulated.

Article 13. The opening of state mining enterprises shall be separately approved by the State Council, the State Council's relevant departments in charge, and the people's governments of the provinces, autonomous regions, and municipalities directly under the central government.

With regard to state mining enterprises whose opening is subject to approval by the State Council and the State Council's relevant supervisory departments, the State Council's departments in charge of geology and mining shall conduct a review and add their comments and signatures to documents regarding the scope of exploitation and comprehensive utilization prior to approval, and after approval shall issue mining permits in accordance with the approval documents. Mining permits for specially designated minerals may be issued by the relevant departments in charge assigned by the State Council.

With regard to state mining enterprises whose opening is subject to approval by the people's governments of the provinces, autonomous regions, and municipalities directly under the central government, the departments in charge of geology and mining of the people's governments of the provinces, autonomous regions, and municipalities directly under the central government shall conduct a review and add their comments and signatures to documents regarding the area of exploitation and comprehensive utilization prior to approval, and after approval shall issue mining permits in accordance with the approval documents.

Article 14. The standing committees of the people's congresses of the provinces, autonomous regions, and municipalities directly under the central government shall stipulate procedures with regard to the examination, approval, and issuance of mining permits for the opening of rural collective mining enterprises, and procedures for the management of mining by individuals.

Article 15. The state exercises planned exploitation within state planned mineholdings, in mineholdings of major value to the national economy, and with regard to specially designated minerals for which the State Council has stipulated the application of conservation-oriented exploitation. No unit or individual may engage in their exploitation without the approval of the State Council's relevant departments in charge.

Article 16. Following the lawful demarcation of the area of state planned mineholdings, mineholdings of major value to the national economy, and mining enterprise mineholdings, the departments in charge of the demarcated mineholdings shall inform the relevant county-level people's governments for the purpose of issuing proclamations.

Any change in the area of a mining enterprise must be submitted to the original examination and approval organ for its approval and submitted to the organ that originally issued the mining permit for an additional review and issuance of a mining permit.

No unit or individual is allowed to enter and mine within the area of anyone else's mining enterprise's mineholding for which a mining permit has previously been obtained.

Article 17. The exploitation of mineral resources within the following districts is not allowed without the consent of the relevant departments in charge assigned by the State Council:

1. Within the perimeters of harbors, airfields, and national defense works and facilities.
2. Within a designated radius of important industrial areas, large-scale water conservancy works and facilities, and urban public works and facilities.
3. Within a designated radius along both sides of railways and major roads.

4. Within a designated radius along both sides of rivers, dikes, and dams.
5. State demarcated nature preserves, important scenic areas, and the sites of immovable, state protected, keypoint historical, cultural, and archaeological antiquities.
6. Other areas that the state has designated as off-limits for the exploitation of mineral resources.

Article 18. Closure of a mine pit requires submission of a mine pit closure report together with relevant materials on excavation projects, hidden hazards, land restoration and utilization, and environmental protection, which shall be submitted for examination and approval in accordance with state regulations.

Article 19. When rare geological phenomena and cultural artifacts are discovered in the course of prospecting or exploitation of mineral resources, they should be protected and the relevant departments should be promptly notified.

CHAPTER III. PROSPECTING FOR MINERAL RESOURCES

Article 20. Regional geological investigations shall be conducted in accordance with the state's unified plan. Reports and maps from regional geological surveys shall be checked and accepted in accordance with state regulations and provided to the relevant departments for their use.

Article 21. At the same time that the task of surveying principal minerals is completed, surveys of mineral resources also should issue preliminary comprehensive evaluations of their work areas, including geological conditions involving mineralization through paragenesis or minerals found in association with each other and ore bodies with industrial potential.

Article 22. The prospecting for ore bodies must include a comprehensive evaluation of all paragenetic minerals or minerals found in association with each other and having industrial value, and estimate their reserves. Any prospecting report that fails to include comprehensive evaluations shall not be approved. However, this does not apply to the prospecting for ore bodies separately designated by the State Council's planning department.

Article 23. When surveying and exploring special types of nonmetallic minerals, liquid, flammable, explosive, or soluble minerals that are easily damaged, and minerals containing radioactive elements, the survey and exploration methods stipulated by the relevant departments of the people's government at or above the provincial level must be followed, including the necessary technical equipment and safety measures.

Article 24. The original geological records and maps from mineral resources surveys, rock and mineral core samples, survey specimens and other physical specimens and materials, and survey markers of all types should be protected and preserved in accordance with the relevant regulations.

Article 25. In accordance with State Council regulations, reports on the exploration of ore bodies and other valuable survey materials shall be used on a compensation basis.

CHAPTER IV. THE EXPLOITATION OF MINERAL RESOURCES

Article 26. With regard to the opening of mining enterprises, the examination and approval organs shall examine the area of the mineholding, the mine design or exploitation plan, technical conditions affecting production, safety measures, and environmental protection measures. Approval shall be granted if the examination confirms that the requirements have been met.

Article 27. The exploitation of mineral resources must adopt a rational sequence of exploitation, exploitation methods, and ore dressing techniques. The mining enterprise's ore recovery rate, ore dilution rate, and mineral beneficiation and recovery rate should attain designed levels.

Article 28. At the same time that the principal minerals are being exploited, all other paragentic minerals or minerals found in association with each other and having industrial value should be unifiedly planned, comprehensively exploited, and comprehensively utilized while preventing waste. Effective preventive measures should be taken to prevent damage or destruction to mineral resources that temporarily can not be exploited, or that must be extracted at the same time but which temporarily can not be utilized, and to mine tailings that contain usable materials.

Article 29. The exploitation of mineral resources must abide by state regulations on occupational safety and public health and arrange conditions necessary for ensuring safe production.

Article 30. The exploitation of mineral resources must abide by relevant laws and regulations on environmental protection and prevent pollution of the environment.

The exploitation of mineral resources should conserve usable land. When arable land, grasslands, and forest lands are damaged during mining, the mining enterprises should adopt restoration and utilization, tree and grass planting, or other use-oriented measures on a locally suitable basis.

When the exploitation of mineral resources harms the production or lives of other people, responsibility for paying compensation should be assumed and essential rescue measures should be taken.

Article 31. Before building railways, factories, reservoirs, oil pipelines, power transmission lines, and other large-scale construction projects or complexes, the construction unit must acquire an understanding of the distribution of mineral resources and the conditions affecting their exploitation in the location of the construction project from the geology and mining departments in charge of the provinces, autonomous regions, and municipalities directly under the central government where they are to be situated. Important ore bodies may not be covered over without the approval of the department authorized by the State Council.

Article 32. With regard to mineral products stipulated by the State Council for unified procurement by a designated unit, no other unit may procure them nor may miners sell them to nondesignated units.

Article 33. With regard to the exploitation of mineral resources within nationality autonomous areas, the state should show regard for the interests of the nationality autonomous areas and make arrangements beneficial to the economic construction of the nationality autonomous areas with reference to the production and living conditions of the minority nationality masses in the area.

The autonomous organs of the nationality autonomous areas should enjoy priority, in accordance with laws and regulations and the state's unified plan, with regard to the rational exploitation and utilization of mineral resources which the areas can develop themselves.

CHAPTER V. RURAL COLLECTIVE MINING ENTERPRISES AND INDIVIDUAL MINERS

Article 34. The state exercises a policy of active support, rational planning, correct guidance, and strengthened management with regard to rural collective mining enterprises and individual miners; encourages rural collective mining enterprises to exploit mineral resources within the scope designated by the state; and allows individuals to exploit small, scattered deposits, sand, stone, and clay suitable for use only as common construction materials, and small quantities of minerals for their own domestic use.

The state guides and assists rural collective mining enterprises and individual miners to continuously upgrade their technological level, resource utilization rate, and economic efficiency.

Departments in charge of geology and mining, geological work units, and state mining enterprises should provide rural collective mining enterprises and individual miners with geological data and technical assistance in accordance with the principles of active support and mutual support on a compensation basis.

Article 35. Preexisting rural collective mining enterprises located within mining enterprise mineholdings whose opening has been approved by the State Council and the State Council's departments in charge should be closed or moved to designated sites elsewhere for mining, with the mine construction unit providing rational compensation and making proper arrangements for the masses' living conditions. They may also undertake joint operations in accordance with the unified arrangements of the (state) mining enterprise.

Article 36. Under the unified arrangements of the state mining enterprise and with the approval of the department in charge of the state mining enterprise at the next higher level, rural collective mining enterprises may exploit marginal, scattered mineral deposits within the area of the state mining enterprise's mineholding. However, they must apply for mining permits in accordance with regulations.

Article 37. Rural collective mining enterprises and individual miners should upgrade their levels of technology and mineral resource recovery rates. Mining in a reckless fashion, poaching, and causing damage to mineral resources is prohibited.

Rural collective mining enterprises must draw contrast maps of conditions above and below the shafts.

Article 38. The people's governments at and above the county level should guide and assist rural collective mining enterprises and individual miners to undertake technological renovation, improve their operational management, and strengthen on the job safety.

CHAPTER VI. LEGAL RESPONSIBILITY

Article 39. Whosoever in violation of the provisions of this law engages in unauthorized mining by himself without obtaining a mining permit; trespasses upon and engages in unauthorized mining on a state planned mineholding, a mineholding of major value to the national economy, or other mineholding; or engages in the unauthorized mining of minerals specially designated by the state for conservation-oriented mining, shall be ordered to cease mining and to pay compensation for damages, the mineral products that they have extracted and their illegal gains shall be confiscated, and they may also be fined. Criminal responsibility shall be investigated for anyone who is directly responsible for a refusal to cease mining and causes damage to mineral resources, in accordance with the stipulations of Article 156 of the Criminal Law.

Article 40. Whosoever engages in mining outside the area of their approved mineholdings shall be ordered to resume mining within the perimeter of their original mineholding and to pay compensation for damages, the mineral products and the illegal gains extracted from beyond the boundaries of their mineholdings shall be confiscated, and they may also be fined. Anyone who is directly responsible for a refusal to resume mining within the perimeter of the original mineholding and causing damage to mineral resources shall have their mining permits voided, and their criminal responsibility shall be investigated in accordance with Article 156 of the Criminal Law.

Article 41. The criminal responsibility of anyone who steals or robs the mining products or other property of mining enterprises or prospecting units, damages mining or prospecting facilities, or undermines production and work order in mineholdings or prospecting areas, shall be separately investigated in accordance with the relevant stipulations of the Criminal Law. In less serious cases, violators shall be fined in accordance with the various stipulations of the Articles of Punishment for the Management of Public Security.

Article 42. Whosoever buys and sells, rents, or by other means transfers mineral resources shall have their illegal gains confiscated and shall be fined.

Whosoever buys and sells or rents mining permits or pledges mining permits as collateral shall have their illegal gains confiscated, shall be fined, and shall have their mining permits voided.

Article 43. Whosoever in violation of this law buys and sells mineral products subject to unified procurement by the state shall have their mineral products and illegal gains confiscated, and they also may be fined. In serious cases, their criminal responsibility shall be investigated in accordance with Articles 117 and 118 of the Criminal Law.

Article 44. Whosoever in violation of this law exploits mineral resources with destructive mining methods causing serious damage to mineral resources shall be ordered to pay compensation for damages and shall be fined. In serious cases, their mining permits may also be voided.

Article 45. The administrative punishments stipulated in Articles 39, 40, and 42 of this law shall be decided by the municipal and county people's governments. The administrative punishments stipulated in Article 43 shall be decided by the branches of the industrial and commercial administration. The administrative punishments stipulated in Article 44 shall be decided by the geology and mining departments in charge of the people's governments of the provinces, autonomous regions, and municipalities directly under the central government. Punishment of mining enterprises whose opening was approved by the State Council and the State Council's relevant departments in charge by the voiding of mining permits must be reported to the people's governments of the provinces, autonomous regions, and municipalities directly under the central government for their approval.

Article 46. If a party contests an administrative punishment decision, he may file suit in the people's court within fifteen days of receipt of the notification of punishment. The organ that decided the punishment may ask the people's court for compulsory enforcement if the violator does not file suit in the people's court within the prescribed time period and does not comply with the administrative punishments involving fines and the confiscation of illegal gains.

Article 47. Disputes among mining enterprises involving mineholdings shall be resolved by the parties concerned through consultations. If the consultations are unsuccessful, then the local people's government at or above the county level shall resolve the dispute in accordance with the lawfully demarcated areas of the mineholdings. Disputes involving mineholdings that transcend (the boundaries of) provinces, autonomous regions, and municipalities directly under the central government shall be resolved through consultation among the relevant governments of the provinces, autonomous regions, and municipalities directly under the central government. If the consultations prove unsuccessful, the State Council shall resolve the dispute.

CHAPTER VII. SUPPLEMENTARY PROVISIONS

Article 48. Detailed provisions for this law shall be stipulated by the State Council.

Article 49. This law shall come into force on October 1, 1986.

Article 50. During the period before this law comes into force, any procedures that have not undergone approval, any boundaries of mineholdings that have not been demarcated, and any exploitation of mineral resources without a mining permit should be examined and their procedures supplemented in accordance with the relevant provisions of this law.

Appendix Z

Land Management Law (June 25, 1986)

GGB, no. 505 (July 10, 1986), pp. 531–39.

CHAPTER I. GENERAL PRINCIPLES

Article 1. This law is specially stipulated to strengthen land management, strengthen the socialist public land ownership system, protect and develop land resources, rationally utilize the land, earnestly conserve arable land, and meet the needs for the building of socialist modernization.

Article 2. The People's Republic of China practices the socialist public land ownership system, that is, the system of ownership by the whole people and the system of collective ownership by the laboring masses.

No unit or individual may occupy, buy and sell, rent, or illegally transfer land through other means.

The state may lawfully requisition collectively owned land to meet the needs of public interests.

Article 3. The people's governments at all levels must implement the policy of fully cherishing and rationally utilizing the land, do overall planning, strengthen management, protect and develop land resources, and halt the occupation of arable land and the misuse of land.

Article 4. Units and individuals with outstanding achievements in protecting and developing land resources, rationally utilizing the land, and conducting relevant scientific research should be rewarded by the people's governments at various levels.

Article 5. The State Council's land management department is in charge of unified land management work throughout the country.

The land management departments of the local people's governments at and above the county level are in charge of unified land management work within their respective areas of administration, with the organizational arrangements to be decided by the provinces, autonomous regions, and municipalities directly under the central government in accordance with actual conditions.

The people's governments at the township level are responsible for land management work within their respective areas of administration.

CHAPTER II. LAND OWNERSHIP AND USAGE RIGHTS

Article 6. Land within the urban districts of municipalities belongs to ownership by the whole people, that is, state ownership.

Land in the villages and in the suburban districts of municipalities belongs to collective ownership, except for that portion which belongs to state ownership according to law and regulation. Homesites, private plots, and private hills belong to collective ownership.

Article 7. State-owned land may definitely be lawfully assigned to units owned by the whole people or collectively owned units for their use, and state-owned and collectively owned land may definitely be assigned to individuals for their use. The units and individuals using the land have the obligation of protecting, managing, and rationally utilizing the land.

Article 8. According to law, collectively owned land belongs to the collective ownership of the village peasants and is managed by agricultural collective economic organizations, like agricultural production cooperatives, or by the village councils. Land that already belongs to township (or town) peasant collective economic organizations may belong to the collective ownership of the township (or town) peasants.

Land that is collectively owned by the village peasants which already belongs to two or more separate agricultural collective economic organizations within the village may belong to the peasants' collective ownership in the respective agricultural collective economic organizations.

Article 9. Collectively owned land shall be registered and recorded by the county-level people's governments, which shall conduct examinations and issue certificates recognizing ownership rights.

State-owned land that is lawfully utilized by units owned by the whole people, collectively owned units, and individuals shall be registered and recorded by the local people's governments at or above the county level which shall conduct examinations and issue certificates recognizing usage rights.

The recognition of ownership and usage rights for forestland and grassland and the recognition of usage rights for water surfaces and beaches shall be handled separately in accordance with the relevant stipulations of the Forestry Law, Grasslands Law, and Fisheries Law.

Article 10. Whenever land ownership or usage rights are lawfully changed, the procedures for handling changes in land rights must be followed, and certificates must be exchanged.

Article 11. Land ownership and usage rights are protected by law and may not be infringed upon by any unit or individual.

Article 12. Collectively owned and state-owned land used by units of the whole people or by collectively owned units may be contracted to collectives or individuals to engage in management for agricultural, forestry, animal husbandry, or fisheries production.

Collectives and individuals that contract to manage land are obligated to protect and, in accordance with the uses stipulated in the contract, rationally utilize the land.

Contract land management rights are protected by law.

Article 13. Disputes involving land ownership and usage rights shall be resolved by the parties concerned through consultation. If the consultations are unsuccessful, then the local people's government shall resolve the dispute.

Disputes involving land ownership and usage rights among units owned by the whole people, among collectively owned units, or between units owned by the whole people and collectively owned units shall be resolved by the people's government at or above the county level.

Disputes involving land usage rights among individuals, or between individuals and units owned by the whole people or collectively owned units, shall be resolved by the people's government at the township or county level.

If a party contests the decision of the relevant people's government, he may file suit within thirty days of receipt of the notification of the resolution decision.

Prior to the resolution of a dispute involving land ownership or usage rights, no party may alter the existing conditions of the land or damage items attached to the land.

CHAPTER III. LAND UTILIZATION AND PROTECTION

Article 14. The state shall establish a land survey and statistics system. Land surveys and statistics shall be conducted by the land management departments of the people's governments at and above the county level in conjunction with relevant departments.

Article 15. The people's governments at various levels shall compile land usage master plans. The land usage master plans of the local people's governments shall be implemented following approval by higher level people's governments.

Article 16. City plans and land usage master plans should be coordinated. Within city planning areas, land usage should conform to the city plans.

Within river and lake safety districts, land usage should conform to the river and lake comprehensive development and utilization plans.

Article 17. The development of state-owned waste hills, wasteland, and beaches for agricultural, forestry, animal husbandry, and fisheries production shall be approved by the people's governments at or above the county level and may definitely be assigned to the development units for their use.

Article 18. With regard to land that may be restored after mining or excavation, the unit or individual using the land should be responsible for its reclamation and restoring its utility.

Article 19. With regard to any of the following circumstances involving the usage of state-owned land, the land management departments shall report to the people's governments at or above the county level for permission to revoke the land usage permits of the units using the land and cancel their land usage permits:

1. The unit using the land has since been dissolved or relocated.
2. The land has not been utilized for two consecutive years without the consent of the organization that granted the original approval.
3. The land has been used for unapproved purposes.
4. Highways, airfields, and mines have since been declared obsolete.

Article 20. The people's governments at all levels should adopt measures to conserve arable land, safeguard irrigation projects and facilities, improve the soil, increase land productivity, control desertification, salinization, and soil erosion, and halt behavior that lays the land waste and damages arable land.

State construction and township (or town) and village construction must make economical use of land. Arable land may not be occupied when wasteland can be utilized, and good land may not be occupied when marginal land can be utilized.

CHAPTER IV. THE USE OF LAND FOR STATE CONSTRUCTION

Article 21. When the state must requisition collectively owned land or make use of state-owned land to undertake economic, cultural, or national defense construction or to operate socialist public utilities, it shall be conducted in accordance with the stipulations of this chapter.

Article 22. In accordance with state regulations with regard to state construction projects that have been incorporated in the state fixed capital investment plan or have been allowed to be built, the construction units may apply for the use of land only after approval (of the project) has been granted.

Article 23. With regard to the requisition of land for state construction, the construction units must abide by the approved design work statement or other approval document issued by the State Council's department in charge or by the local people's government at or above the county level in accordance with the sequence of procedures for state capital construction and submit an application to the land management department of the local people's government at or above the county level. After the local people's government at or above the county level has made a survey and issued its approval, the land management department shall allocate land.

With regard to land requisitioned for state construction, the unit whose land has been requisitioned should comply with state requirements and may not impose obstacles.

Article 24. With regard to collectively owned land that has been requisitioned for state construction, the ownership rights belong to the state while the unit using the land only acquires usage rights.

Article 25. The State Council shall approve all requisitions of arable land of 1,000 *mu* or larger, or 2,000 *mu* or larger of other land.

Land to be requisitioned within provinces and autonomous regions shall be approved by the provincial and autonomous region people's governments. The requisition of arable land of less than 3 *mu*, or less than 10 *mu* of other land, shall be approved by the county people's governments. The standing committees of the people's congresses of the provinces and autonomous regions shall decide the limits of approval authority for the people's governments of the municipalities and autonomous districts directly under the provincial governments.

Land to be requisitioned within the area of administration of the municipalities directly under the central government shall be approved by the people's governments of the municipalities directly under the central government. The standing committees of the people's congresses of the municipalities directly under the central government shall decide the limits of approval authority for the people's governments of the districts and counties within the municipalities directly under the central government.

Article 26. Land required for use in a construction project should be applied for and approved in conjunction with the overall design (of the construction project), preventing the whole process from being reduced to an empty letter. Projects to be built in stages may not requisition all land in advance and leave it idle. Land required for the needs of railways, highways, oil pipelines, and aqueducts may be applied for and approved in stages following land requisition procedures.

Article 27. With regard to land requisitioned for state construction, the unit that is to make use of the land shall pay a land compensation fee. The compensation fee for the requisition of arable land shall be three to six times the average annual output value of the arable land during the three years prior to requisition. The principles for setting compensation fees for the requisition of other types of land shall be stipulated by the provinces, autonomous regions, and municipalities directly under the central government in accordance with the principles for arable land requisition compensation fees.

The provinces, autonomous regions, and municipalities directly under the central government shall stipulate the principles for compensation involving structures and seedlings attached to the land to be requisitioned.

When land being used for growing vegetables in suburban areas is requisitioned, the unit that is to make use of the land should provide construction funds for the development of new land for growing vegetables in accordance with relevant state regulations.

Article 28. With regard to land requisitioned for state construction, in addition to compensation fees, the unit that is to make use of the land should pay a placement subsidy to those who are to be displaced.

The placement subsidy for arable land that is to be requisitioned shall be calculated according to the size of the agricultural population requiring placement. The size of the agricultural population requiring placement shall be calculated by dividing the amount of arable land to be requisitioned by the per capita arable land holdings of the unit to be requisitioned prior to requisition. The principle for setting placement fees for the agricultural population requiring placement shall be two to three times the average annual output value per *mu* of the arable land during the three years prior to requisition. However, the maximum per *mu* placement fee for arable land to be requisitioned may not exceed ten times the average annual output value during the three years prior to requisition. The principles for setting placement fees for the requisition of other types of land shall be stipulated by the provinces, autonomous regions, and municipalities directly under the central government in accordance with the principles for placement fees regarding the requisition of arable land.

Article 29. With regard to the payment of land compensation fees and placement fees according to the stipulations in Articles 27 and 28 of this law, placement fees may be increased for those peasants who remain unable to maintain their previous living standards with the approval of the people's governments of the provinces, autonomous regions, and municipalities directly under the central government. However, the combined total of land compensation fees and placement fees may not exceed twenty times the average annual output value of the land to be requisitioned during the three years prior to requisition.

Article 30. With regard to the various forms of compensation fees and placement fees paid during the requisition of land for state construction, with the exception of compensation fees paid to individuals for individually owned structures and seedlings attached to the land, the fees shall be expended by the unit whose land is to be requisitioned to develop production, to arrange employment for members of the labor force made redundant by the land requisition, and to subsidize the living expenses of members unable to work. These fees may not be devoted to other purposes, and no unit or individual may seize them.

Article 31. With regard to members of the labor force made redundant by land requisition, the land management departments of the local people's governments at and above the county level shall organize the units whose land is to be requisitioned, the units that are to make use of the land, and other relevant units to make additional placements through the development of agricultural and sideline production and by starting township (or town) and village enterprises. With regard to instances where placement remains incomplete, they can arrange employment for those members who satisfy the criteria of the units to make use of the land or other collectively owned or state-owned units and redirect a suitable portion of the placement fees to the units absorbing the labor force.

With regard to units whose land is to be completely requisitioned, following survey and approval by the people's governments of the provinces, autonomous regions, and municipalities directly under the central government, the formerly agricultural households may be reclassified as nonagricultural households. With regard to the former collectives, their property, together with the compensation and placement fees that they have received, shall be disposed of through consultations between the people's governments at or above the county level and the relevant townships (or towns) and villages and is to be used to organize production and subsidize the living expenses of those members unable to work and may not be divided up among individuals.

Article 32. The State Council shall make separate stipulations with regard to the principles for setting compensation fees and the procedures for resettling people who are displaced by the requisition of land for the construction of large- and medium-sized water conservancy and hydroelectric projects.

Article 33. With regard to land required for storage sites, transportation routes, and other temporary facilities associated with construction activities, arrangements should be made to the fullest extent within the area of the land to be requisitioned. In cases where additional land for temporary uses is absolutely necessary, the construction unit shall apply to the organ that approved the project's land usage, specifying the area and time period for which the land is to be used. Following approval, the construction unit shall negotiate a temporary land use agreement with the agricultural collective economic organizations, and provide compensation according to the average annual output value during the preceding three years. Permanent structures may not be erected on land intended for temporary usage. When the usage period has expired, the construction unit should restore production conditions and return the land in a timely manner.

Land that is temporarily required for building roads, laying underground pipelines, building other below ground projects, or geological prospecting shall be approved by the people's governments at the county level where the projects are located, and compensation shall be paid in accordance with the aforementioned stipulations.

When selecting construction sites, the construction units must conduct land surveys and should obtain the consent of the people's governments at the county level where the projects are located. If damages occur, they should pay suitable compensation.

Article 34. With regard to state-owned wasteland, waste hills, and state-owned land being utilized by other units that is to be used for state construction, the land shall be allocated after approval has been issued in accordance with the sequence of procedures for the requisition of state-owned land and the limits of approval authority. State-owned wasteland and waste hills that are to be utilized shall be allocated without the payment of compensation. With regard to the usage of state-owned land that is being utilized by other units, if the unit formerly using the land suffers harm, the construction unit should provide suitable compensation. The construction unit should assume responsibility for relocating units that formerly used the land which require relocation.

Article 35. Construction undertaken by urban collectively owned units that requires the usage of land shall be handled in accordance with the stipulations of this chapter.

Article 36. With regard to shared investment joint enterprises formed by enterprises owned by the whole people or urban collective enterprises with agricultural collective economic organizations that require collectively owned land for usage; they must uphold the design work statements or other approval documents that must undergo approval by the State Council's department in charge or the local people's governments at or above the county level in accordance with the sequence of procedures for approving state capital construction; an application must be submitted to the land management of the local people's government at or above the county level; and, in accordance with the limits of authority for land requisition for state construction, approval must be received from the people's government at or above the county level. Land that has been approved may be requisitioned in accordance with the stipulations on land requisition for state construction, or the land usage rights may be offered by the agricultural collective economic organizations for joint management in accordance with the agreement.

CHAPTER V. THE REQUISITION OF LAND FOR CONSTRUCTION IN TOWNSHIPS (OR TOWNS)

Article 37. Construction in townships (or towns) and villages should be planned in accordance with the principles of rational distribution and conservation of usable land, and the plans should be implemented following their approval by the people's governments at the county level. Construction plans for townships (or towns) and villages within city planning districts should be implemented following approval by the municipal people's governments.

Housing construction for villagers, the construction of township (or town) and village enterprises, and township (or town) and village construction of public facilities and public utilities should be conducted in conjunction with the township (or town) and village construction plans.

Article 38. Housing construction for village residents should make use of existing housing sites or empty lots in the villages. When arable land is to be utilized, it shall first be reviewed by the people's government at the township level and then reported to the people's government at the county level for its approval. The people's government at the township level shall approve the usage of existing housing sites, empty lots within villages, and other land.

The land to be used to build housing for village residents may not exceed the standards stipulated by the provinces, autonomous regions, and municipalities directly under the central government.

After a house has been sold or rented, applications for (additional) housing sites shall not be approved.

Article 39. With regard to the usage of land required for the construction of township (or town) and village enterprises: the design work statement or other approval document must be approved by the local people's government at or above the county level; application must be made to the land management department of the people's government at the county level; and approval shall be issued by the local people's government at or above the county level in accordance with the limits of authority for approval stipulated by the provinces, autonomous regions, and municipalities directly under the central government.

There must be strict control over the usage of land for the construction of township (or town) and village enterprises. The provinces, autonomous regions, and municipalities directly under the central government may stipulate different standards for land usage in terms of industry and scale of operations in accordance with variations among township (or town) and village enterprises.

In cases where the construction of township (or town) and village enterprises makes use of villagers' collectively owned land, the units whose land is to be requisitioned should be given suitable compensation and appropriate arrangements should be made for the peasants' production and living conditions in accordance with the stipulations of the provinces, autonomous regions, and municipalities directly under the central government.

Chinese-foreign joint cooperative management enterprises, and foreign investment enterprises.

Article 56. In accordance with this law, the State Council's land management department shall stipulate rules for implementation, submit them to the State Council for approval, and then implement them. The standing committees of the people's congresses of the provinces, autonomous regions, and municipalities directly under the central government shall stipulate procedures for implementation in accordance with this law.

Article 57. This law shall come into force on January 1, 1987, at which time the State Council's Regulations Governing the Management of Land Used for Housing Construction in Villages and Towns of February 13, 1982, and the State Council's Regulations Governing the Requisition of Land for State Construction of May 14, 1982, shall be repealed.

Part Seven
Charts

ENVIRONMENTAL CONTROL ADMINISTRATIVE STRUCTURE[4]

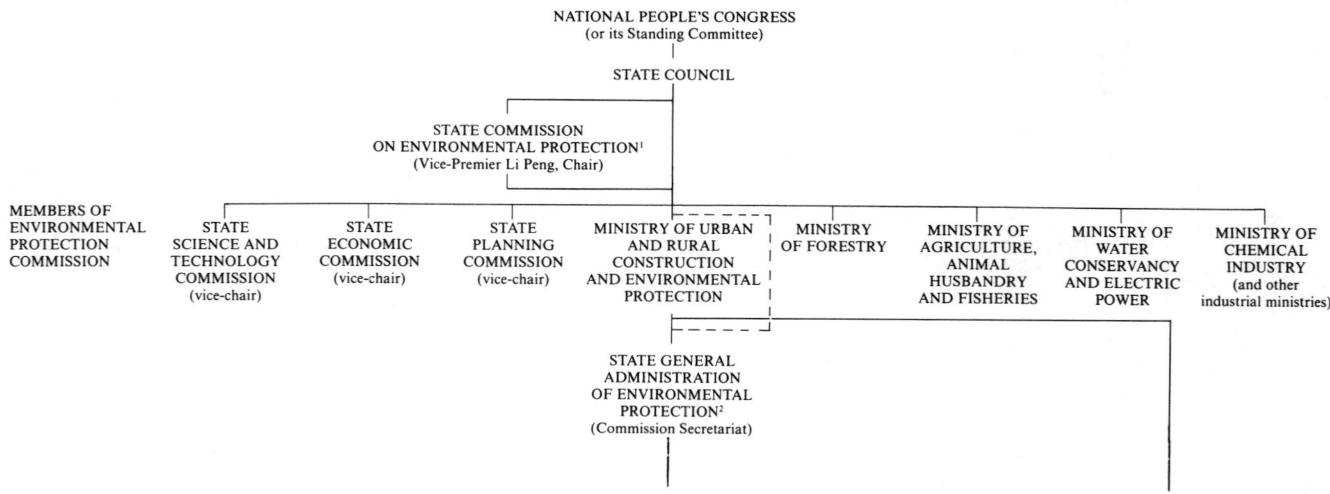

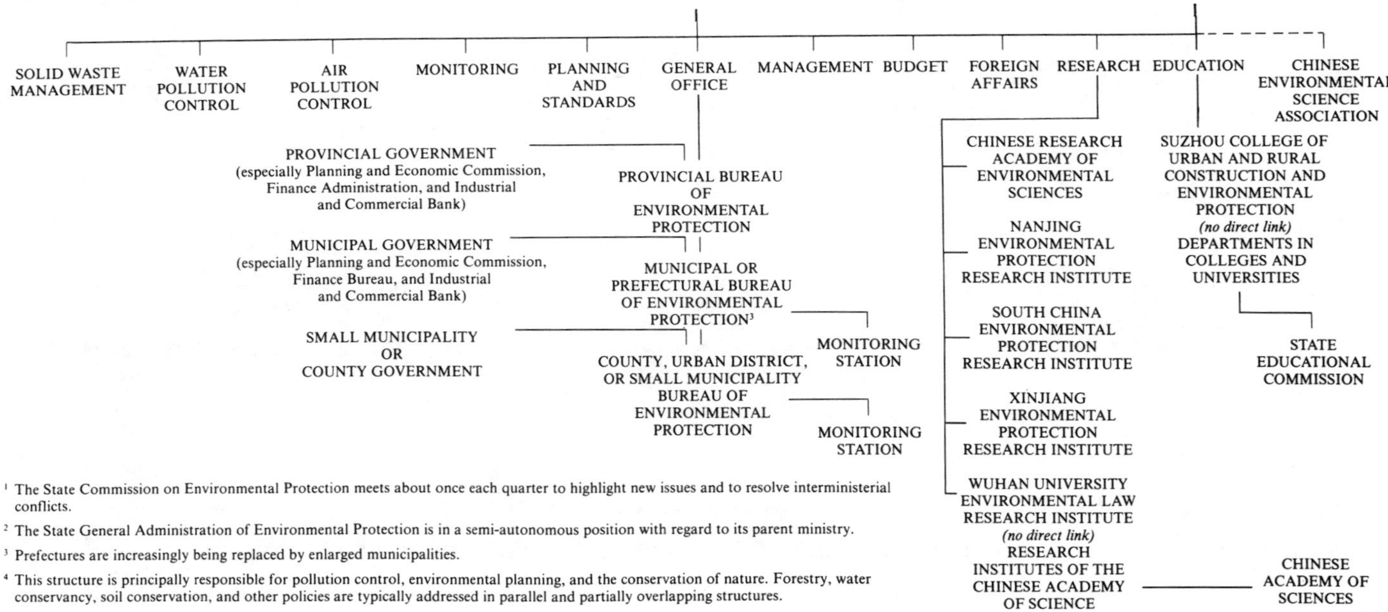

[1] The State Commission on Environmental Protection meets about once each quarter to highlight new issues and to resolve interministerial conflicts.

[2] The State General Administration of Environmental Protection is in a semi-autonomous position with regard to its parent ministry.

[3] Prefectures are increasingly being replaced by enlarged municipalities.

[4] This structure is principally responsible for pollution control, environmental planning, and the conservation of nature. Forestry, water conservancy, soil conservation, and other policies are typically addressed in parallel and partially overlapping structures.

ORGANIZATION OF ENVIRONMENTAL LEGISLATIVE SCHEME

STATE CONSTITUTION (1982)

(especially Articles 26, 9, and 22)

BASIC LAW

Environmental Protection Law (for trial implementation) (1979), currently under revision

SPECIALIZED LAWS

Laws for the Prevention and Control of Pollution and Other Natural Hazards

- Air Pollution Control Law (ip)
- Water Pollution Prevention and Control Law (1984)
- Noise and Vibration Control Law (ip)
- Solid Wastes Disposal Law (ip)
- Toxic Materials Management Law (ip)
- Radiation Control Law (ip)
- etc.

Laws for the Conservation of Natural Resources

- Forestry Law (1984)
- Grasslands Law (1985)
- Fisheries Law (1986)
- Land Use Law (1986)
- Wildlife Conservation Law (ip)
- Mineral Resources Law (1986)
- Marine Environmental Protection Law (1983)
- etc.

Laws for the Protection of the Cultural Environment

- Nature Preserves Law (ip)
- Law for the Protection of Scenic and Historical Sites (ip)
- etc.

ADMINISTRATIVE DECREES

Approved by the National People's Congress: such as the Regulations on Strengthening Environmental Protection Work in the Economic Readjustment Period (1981); Regulations on the Assessment of Effluent Fees (1982); Regulations on Integrating Technical Renovation and Pollution Control in the Industrial Sector (1982); and the Regulations on Strengthening the Management of Environmental Protection in Rural and Street Enterprises (1984).

LOCAL LAWS

Local laws approved by provincial and lower level people's congresses to adapt national statutes to local conditions.

REGULATIONS

Issued by national ministries and bureaus like the State Administration of Environmental Protection: such as the Regulations for the Registration of Agricultural Pesticides; Procedures for the Management of Environmental Protection on Construction Projects; Procedures Concerning the Retention of Profits by Industrial and Mining Enterprises from Products Derived from the Recovery of Waste Materials and Other Pollution Control Measures; and Procedures for the Management of Environmental Protection Standards.

LOCAL REGULATIONS

Issued by local level administrative agencies.

STATE STANDARDS

Ambient Standards

Ambient Air Quality Standards (GB 3095-82)
Public Health Standards for Drinking Water (TJ 20-76)
etc.

Emissions Standards

Emmissions Standards for Industrial Pollutants (GB 4200 series)

MINISTERIAL STANDARDS

Involve measurement procedures, equipment performance, and other technical criteria: such as forestry (LY) series, buidling materials (JC) series, and metallurgical industry (YB) series, communications or transportation (JT) series, railway (TD) series.

LOCAL STANDARDS

Primarily involve the setting of geographical boundaries for ambient and environmental quality standards.

NOTES: ip refers to laws in preparation. The entire organization of legislation is subject to the higher authority of the Communist Party. Moreover, all of the items listed above are subject to the relevant provisions of other basic laws like the Criminal Law, Law of Civil Procedure, etc.

SOURCES: Wen Boping, *The Principles of Environmental Law.* Beijing: Qunzhong chubanshe (1982); Wang Weimin (1985) "The Organization of Chinese Environmental Law is Being Put Together," *Chinese Environmental News,* January 12, p. 3; and Cui Kejing, "The Organization of Environmental Law," *Chinese Environmental News* March 9, p. 3.

Selected Bibliography

LEGISLATION

Japan

Air Pollution Control Law (1968)
Fundamental Pollution Control Law (1967)
Kawasaki Municipal Public Hazard Prevention Ordinance (1972)
Law Governing Criminal Responsibility in Public Hazard Cases (1970)
Osaka Municipal Public Hazard Prevention Ordinance (1971)
Tokyo Municipal Public Hazard Prevention Ordinance (1969)
Waste Disposal and Treatment Law (1970)

People's Republic of China

Act for Security Administration Punishment (1957)
Act for the Punishment of Counterrevolution (1951)
Bureau of Legal Affairs of the State Council (1955–63) *FGHB*. Beijing: Falü Chubanshe.
Collection of Laws and Regulations of China Concerning Foreign Economic and Trade Regulations (1983). Sydney: David Syme and Co., Ltd.
Constitution (1975)
Constitution (1978)
Constitution (1982)
Criminal Law (1979)
Documents of the First Session of the Fifth National People's Congress of the People's Republic of China (1978). Beijing: Foreign Languages Press.
Experimental Measures for the Inspection of Domestically Grown Plants for Contagious Diseases (1957)
Fang Chun-i, et al. (1982) *Laws and Regulations of the People's Republic of China*. Hong Kong: Kingsway Publishers.
GGB (1979–86)
Government Affairs Council (1949–54) *FLHB*. Beijing: Falü Chubanshe.
Law of Civil Procedure (for trial implementation) (1982)
Marine Transportation Safety Law (1983).
Measures Governing Land Requisition for National Construction (1953)
Ministry of Public Security, Office of Policy and Legal Research (1980) *Gongan Fagui*

Huibian, 1950–1979 (Compendium of Laws and Decrees on Public Security). Beijing: Qunzhong Chubanshe.

Ministry of Urban and Rural Construction, Office of Environmental Protection (1983) *BFWH*. Beijing: Zhongguo Huanjing Kexue Chubanshe.

Ministry of Urban and Rural Construction, Policy Research Office (1984) *Cheng Xiang Jianshe Huanjing Baohu Fagui Huibian* (Compendium of Laws and Regulations on Urban and Rural Construction and Environmental Protection). Beijing: Zhongguo Jianshe Gongye Chubanshe.

"1983 Marine Pollution Regulations" (January 13, 1984) *Zhongguo Fazhi Bao* (China Legal System Newspaper), p. 3.

Order on Trawler Fishing in Forbidden Areas in the Bohai, Huanghai, and Donghai Seas (1955)

Organic Law of the People's Courts

Provisional Measures on Highway Afforestation (1956)

Provisional Program for Water and Soil Conservation (1957)

Provisional Regulations on the Encouragement of Foreign Investment (1986)

Provisional Regulations on the Prevention of Pollution of Coastal Waters (1974)

Regulations Concerning Environmental Protection and Improvement (tentative draft) (1973)

Regulations Governing the Safety of Drinking Water (1959)

Regulations Governing the Transport of Dangerous Freight (1972)

Regulations on the Control of Foreign Ships (1979)

Regulations on Forest Protection (1963)

Regulations on Protecting the Breeding of Aquatic Resources (1979)

Regulations on the Supervision and Control of Ships Carrying Dangerous Freight (1981)

Resolutions Regarding the Revision of the Constitution and the Setting Up of a Committee to Revise the Constitution (1980)

Some Regulations on Combining Technological Upgrading with the Prevention and Control of Industrial Pollution (1983)

Zhongguo Huanjing Baohu Fagui Huibian (Compendium of China's Environmental Protection Laws and Regulations) (1985). Beijing: Zhongguo Huanjing Kexue Chubanshe.

Republic of China

Air Pollution Prevention and Control Act (1975, amended 1982)

Forestry Law (1932, last amended 1972)

Ministry of Communications Executive Order Governing Marine Pollution (1981)

Resource Control Law (1980)

Waste Materials Clean Up Law (1974, amended 1980)

Water Conservation Law (1942, last amended 1974)

Water Pollution Prevention and Control Act (1974, amended 1983)

Soviet Union and Eastern Europe

Decree of the Soviet Union on the Intensification of Nature Conservation and the Improved Utilization of Natural Resources (1972)

Environmental Protection Law of Rumania (1973)

Law of Hungary on the Protection of the Environment (1976)
Nature Protection Law of Bulgaria (1976)

United Kingdom

Alkali Act (1863)
Clean Air Act (1956)
Noise Abatement Act (1960)
Public Health Smoke Abatement Act (1926)
Refuse Act (1958)
Rivers Pollution Prevention Act (1876)
Water Resources Act (1963)

United States

Clean Air Act
Clean Water Act
Environmental Protection Act of the State of Michigan
Federal Noise Control Act
Internal Revenue Code
National Environmental Policy Act
National Labor Relations Act
Norris–La Guardia Act
Occupational Safety and Health Act of 1970
Railway Labor Act
Resource Recovery Act
Resource Conservation and Recovery Act
Solid Waste Disposal Act

Other Countries

CCW
Law of Italy on the Collection, Transport, and Disposal of Solid Waste (1941)
Solid Waste Disposal Law of the Federal Republic of Germany (1977)

International

Convention for the Prevention of Marine Pollution by Dumping from Ships and Aircraft (1972)
Convention for the Prevention of Pollution from Ships (1973, modified by protocol 1978 and 1983)
Convention on the High Seas (1958)
Convention on the Territorial Sea and the Contiguous Zone (1958)
European Human Rights Treaty
International Convention for the Prevention of Pollution of the Sea by Oil (1954)
International Convention Relating to Civil Liability for Pollution Damage (1969)

International Convention Relating to Intervention on the High Seas in Cases of Oil Pollution and Casualities (1969)

The Law of the Sea: United Nations Convention on the Law of the Sea with Index and Final Act of the Third United Nations Conference on the Law of the Sea (1983). United Nations Publications Sales No. E83.V.5. New York.

Third United Nations Conference on the Law of the Sea, Official Records, 15 vols. (1975–83). U.N. Pub. Sales Nos. E75.V.3, 4, 5, 10; E76.V.8; E77.V.2; E78.V.3, 4; E80.V.6, 12; E81.V.5; E82.V.2; E83.V.4. New York.

United Nations Declaration on the Human Environment (1972)

Third United Nations Convention on the Law of the Sea (1982)

Vienna Convention of the Law of Treaties (opened for signature May 23, 1969)

CASES

Adler v. American Standard Corp. 432 A.2d 434 (1981).

Attorney General v. P.Y.A. Quarries, Ltd., (1957) 2 Q.B. 169, (1957) 1 All E.R. 894.

The Caroline, in Moore, 2 *Digest of International Law* 412 (1906).

Gateway Coal Co. v. United Mine Workers, 414 U.S. 368 (1974).

Griggs v. Allegheny County, 264 U.S. 84 (1961).

National Labor Relations Board v. Washington Aluminum Co., 370 U.S. 9 (1962).

Papachristou v. City of Jacksonville, 405 U.S. 156 (1972).

Rylands v. Fletcher L.R. 3, H.L. 330 (1868).

Staggs v. Blue Cross of Maryland, Inc., 486 A.2d 798 (1985).

Union Oil v. Oppen, 501 F.2d 558 (1974).

United States v. Cadiff, 344 U.S. 174 (1952).

United States v. Causby 328 U.S. 256 (1956).

Whirlpool Corp. v. Marshall, 446 U.S. 1 (1980).

BOOKS

All China Federation of Trade Unions, State General Bureau of Labor and the Ministry of Public Health, eds. (1980) *Laodong Baohu Wenjian Xuanbian* (Selected Documents in Labor Protection). Beijing: Gongren Chubanshe.

Barnett, A. Doak (1981) *China's Economy in a Global Perspective*. Washington: Brookings Institution.

Baumol, William J., and Wallace E. Oates (1979) *Economics, Environmental Policy, and the Quality of Life*. Englewood Cliffs, N.J.: Prentice-Hall.

Bowman, M. J., and D. J. Harris (1984) *Multilateral Treaties: Index and Current Status*. London: Butterworth.

Butler, W. E., ed. (1983) *The Legal System of the Chinese Soviet Republic*. Dobbs Ferry, N.Y.: Transnational Publishers.

Caldwell, Lynton Keith (1984) *International Environmental Policy: Emergence and Dimensions*. Durham, N.C.: Duke University Press.

Cheng, Chu-yuan (1982) *China's Economic Development: Growth and Structural Change*. Boulder, Colo.: Westview Press.

Chinese Research Academy of Environmental Sciences (1983) *HBYWX*. Beijing: Falü Chubanshe.

Chinese Society of International Law (1983) *Zhongguo Guoji Fa Niankan* (Chinese Yearbook of International Law), vol. 2. Beijing: Zhongguo Duiwai Fanyi Chubanshe.

Chiu, Hungdah, ed. (1983) *Chinese Yearbook of International Law and Affairs*, vol. 3. Baltimore: Occasional Papers/Reprints in Contemporary Asian Studies.

Cohen, Jerome A. (1968) *The Criminal Process in the People's Republic of China*. Cambridge, Mass.: Harvard University Press.

——— (1983) *Legal Aspects of Doing Business in China*. New York: Practicing Law Institute.

Cohen, Jerome A., and Hungdah Chiu (1974) *People's China and International Law*. Princeton, N.J.: Princeton University Press.

Cohen, Jerome A., Timothy Gelatt and Florence Li (1984) *The Criminal Law and the Criminal Procedure Law of China*. Beijing: Foreign Languages Press.

Crandall, Robert W. (1983) *Controlling Industrial Pollution: The Economics and Politics of Clean Air*. Washington: Brookings Institution.

Dong Lou (1983) *Minfa Yuanze* (The Principles of Civil Law). Beijing: Falü Chubanshe.

Eckstein, Alexander (1977) *China's Economic Revolution*. Cambridge: Cambridge University Press.

Economic Law Editing Group (1983) *Jingji Faxue* (The Study of Economic Law). Beijing: Qunzhong Chubanshe.

Editorial Committee for the Atlas of Cancer Mortality (1979) *Atlas of Cancer Mortality in the People's Republic of China*. Beijing: China Map Press.

Falü Wenda Bianxie Zu (1983) *Xingshi Falu Wenda* (Questions and Answers on Criminal Law). Shanghai: Zhishi Chubanshe.

Feng Ertai (1984) *Falü Wenda Sibai Ti* (Four Hundred Questions and Answers on the Law). Shanghai: Xuelin Chubanshe.

Freeman, A. Myrick, III (1979) *The Benefits of Air and Water Pollution Control: A Review and Synthesis of Recent Estimates*. Prepared for the Council on Environmental Quality.

Gao Minxuan (1983) *Xingfa Xue* (The Study of Criminal Law). Beijing: Falü Chubanshe.

Greenfield, Jeannette (1979) *China and the Law of the Sea, Air, and Environment*. Germantown, Md.: Sijthoff and Noordhoff.

Gresser, Julian (1981) *Environmental Law in Japan*. Cambridge, Mass.: MIT Press.

Guo Liai, ed. (1985) *Jianzhu Sheji Weisheng Shencha* (An Examination of Public Health Considerations in Architecture and Design). Harbin: Heilongjiang Kexue Jishu Chubanshe.

Gustafson, Thane R. (1982) *Reform in Soviet Politics—Lessons of Recent Policies on Land and Water*. London: Cambridge University Press.

Harrison, Selig S. (1977) *China, Oil and Asia, Conflict Ahead?* New York: Columbia University Press.

Henkin, Louis, et al. (1980) *International Law: Cases and Materials*. St. Paul, Minn.: West Publishing Co.

Hess, Wilmot N., ed. (1978) *NOAA/EPA Special Report: The AMOCO CADIZ Oil Spill*. Washington: U.S. Government Printing Office.

Hsiung, James C., and Samuel S. Kim (1980) *China in the Global Community*. New York: Praeger Publishers.

Huanjing Fa Cankao Ziliao Xuanbian (Selection of Reference Materials in Environmental

Law), vols. 1–5 (1982). Beijing: Chinese Environmental Management, Economics and Law Society.

Jackson, David C., ed. (1983) *World Shipping Laws*. Dobbs Ferry, N.Y.: Ocean Publications, Inc.

Jiang Bikun, and Guo Rui, eds. (1980) *Huanjing Baohu Fa Jianghua* (A Discussion on Environmental Protection Law). Zhangjiakou: Falü Chubanshe.

Johnson, W. (1979) *The T'ang Code*. Princeton, N.J.: Princeton University Press.

Johnston, D. M., ed. (1981) *The Environmental Law of the Sea*. Berlin: Erich Schmidt Verlag.

Kelman, Steven (1981) *What Price Incentives? Economists and the Environment*. Cambridge: Auburn House.

Kim, Samuel S. (1979) *China, the United Nations and World Order*. Princeton, N.J.: Princeton University Press.

Knight, Gary (1980) *The Law of the Sea: Cases, Documents, and Readings*. Baton Rouge, La.: Claitor's Publishing Division.

Lave, Lester B., and Gilbert S. Omenn (1981) *Cleaning the Air: Reforming the Clean Air Act*. Washington: Brookings Institution.

Legal Dictionary Editing Commission, ed. (1979) *Faxue Cidian* (Dictionary of Legal Terminology). Shanghai: Cishu Chubanshe.

Legislative Bureau of the Ministry of Justice (1983) *Zhonghua Renmin Fagui Mulu* (Catalogue Listing of Laws and Regulations of the People's Republic of China). Beijing: Falü Chubanshe.

Leng, Shao-chuan, and Hungdah Chiu (1985) *Criminal Justice in Post-Mao China*. Albany, N.Y.: SUNY Press.

Li Haopei, trans. (1981) *Guoji Fa* (International Law). Beijing: Shangwu Yinshuguan.

Lillich, Richard B., and John Norton Moore (1980) *U.S. Naval War College International Law Studies*, vol. 61. Newport, R.I.: Naval War College Press.

Liu Fenming (1982) *Xiandai Guoji Fa Gangyao* (A General Outline of Contemporary International Law). Beijing: Qunzhong Chubanshe.

Lundqvist, Lennart J. (1980) *The Hare and the Tortoise: Clean Air Policies in the United States and Sweden*. Ann Arbor: University of Michigan Press.

Ma Xiangcong (1983) *Huanjing Baohu Fa Jiben Wenti* (Basic Problems in the Law of Environmental Protection). Beijing: Zhongguo Shehui Kexueyuan Chubanshe.

Ma Ying-jeou (1984) *Legal Problems of Seabed Boundary Delimitation in the East China Sea*. Baltimore: Occasional Papers/Reprints Series in Contemporary Asian Studies.

M'Gonigle, R. Michael and Mark W. Zacher (1979) *Pollution, Politics and International Law*. Berkeley and Los Angeles: Unversity of California Press.

Ministry of Urban and Rural Construction and Environmental Protection (1984) *Environmental Work Bulletin Compendium* (in Chinese). Beijing: Zhongguo Huanjing Kexue Chubanshe.

Moore, John Basset (1906) *Digest of International Law*, vol. 8. Washington: U.S. Government Printing Office.

Moser, Michael J., ed. (1987) *Trade, Foreign Investment and the Law in the People's Republic of China*, 2d ed. Hong Kong and London: Oxford University Press.

National Environmental Protection Conference Secretariat, ed. (1973) *Huanjing Baohu Jingyan Xuanbian* (Selected Experiences in Environmental Protection). Beijing: Renmin Chubanshe.

National Environmental Protection Conference Small Group Office (1973) *Gongye "San-*

fei'' Paifang Shixing Biaojun (Provisional Standards for Industrial ''Three Wastes'' Emissions). Beijing: Zhongguo Jianzhu Gongye Chubanshe.

O'Connell, Daniel Patrick (1982) *The International Law of the Sea*, vols. 1–2. Oxford: Clarendon Press.

Park, Choon-ho (1983) *East Asia and the Law of the Sea*. Seoul: Seoul National University Press.

Perkins, Dwight (1984) *Rural Development in China*. Baltimore: Johns Hopkins University Press.

Prybyla, Jan (1981) *China's Economy: Problems and Policies*, Columbia: University of South Carolina Press.

Pye, Lucian (1981) *The Dynamics of Chinese Politics*. Boston: Oelgeschlager, Gunn & Hain.

Ross, Lester (1988) *Environmental Policy in China*. Bloomington: Indiana University Press.

Salem, David (1983) *The People's Republic of China, International Law and Arms Control*. Baltimore: Occasional Papers/Reprints Series in Contemporary Asian Studies.

Shuihudi Qin Mu Zhujian Zhengli Xiaozu (1978) *Shuihudi Qin Mu Zhujian* (Bamboo Writings from the Qin Tombs at Shuihudi). Beijing: Wenwu Chubanshe.

Sigurdson, Jon (1977) *Rural Industrialization in China*. Cambridge, Mass.: Harvard University Press.

Smil, Vaclav (1984) *The Bad Earth: Environmental Degradation in China*. Armonk, N.Y.: M. E. Sharpe.

Sohn, Louis B., and Kristen Gustafson (1984) *The Law of the Sea in a Nutshell*. St. Paul, Minn.: West Publishing Co.

Starke, Joseph Gabriel (1977) *An Introduction to International Law*. London: Butterworth.

Staunton, Sir George Thomas (1966) *Ta Tsing Leu Lee*. Taipei: Ch'eng Wen Publishing Co. (reprint).

Swannack-Nunn, Susan (1979) *Environmental Protection in the People's Republic of China*. Washington: National Council for U.S.-China Trade.

Timagenis, G. J. (1980) *International Control of Marine Pollution*, vols. 1–2. Dobbs Ferry, N.Y.: Oceana Publications, Inc.

Wang Tieya, and Chen Tiqiang, trans. (1981) *Aubenhai Guoji Fa* (Oppenheim's International Law). Beijing: Shangwu Yinshuguan.

Wang Xuan, et al. (1981) *Xiandai Guoji Fa Gailun* (An Introduction to Modern International Law). Beijing: Zhongguo Shehui Kexue Yuan Chubanshe.

Wen Boping (1982) *Huanjing Baohu Fa Gailun* (An Introduction to Environmental Protection Law). Beijing: Qunzhong Chubanshe.

Woodard, Kim (1980) *The International Energy Relations of China*. Palo Alto, Calif.: Stanford University Press.

World Bank (1983) *China, Socialist Economic Development*, vols. 1–3. Washington: World Bank.

Yang Jinsen, et al. (1983) *Zhonghua Renmin Gongheguo Haiyang Huanjing Baohu Fa Qianshuo* (Talks on the Marine Environmental Protection Law of the People's Republic of China). Beijing: Falü Chubanshe.

Yu Guangyuan, et al., eds. (1980) *Lun Huanjing Guanli* (On Environmental Management). Taiyuan: Shanxi Renmin Chubanshe.

Zhang Shangzhuo (1981) *Zhonghua Renmin Gongheguo Xingfa Gailun* (The Essentials of the Criminal Law of the People's Republic of China). Beijing: Falü Chubanshe.

Zhang Youyu and Wang Shuwen (1979) *Faxue Jiben Zhishi Jianghua* (Lectures on Basic Knowledge in Law). Beijing: Falü Chubanshe.

Zhonggong Yuanshi Ziliao Bianji Weiyuanhui (1983) *Zhonggong Xianfa* (The Communist Chinese Constitutions). Taipei: Zhonggong Yanjiu Zazhishe.

Zhongguo Daibiaotuan Chuxi Lianhe Guo Youguan Huiyi Wenjianji (A Collection of Statements by the Chinese Delegation at the United Nations), vols. 1–6 (1982). Beijing: Shijie Zhishi Chubanshe.

Zhongguo Jianzhu Gongye Chubanshe, ed. (1975) *Huanjing Baohu Wenxian* (Essays on Environmental Protection). Beijing.

Zhongyang Zhengfu Ganbu Xuexiao, Xingfa Xingshi Susong Fa Jiaoyan Shi (1980) *Zhonghua Renmin Gongheguo Xingfa Zongze Jiangyi* (Lectures on the Principles of the Criminal Law of the People's Republic of China). Beijing: Qunzhong Chubanshe.

Zhou Gengsheng (1981) *Guoji Fa* (International Law). Beijing: Shangwu Yingshuguan.

Zhou Ziya, ed. (1982) *Guoji Gongfa* (Public International Law). Shanghai: Zhishi Chubanshe.

Zhu Qiwu, et al. (1983) *Guoji Fa Jichu* (The Basis of International Law). Beijing: Zhongguo Renmin Daxue Chubanshe.

ARTICLES

"A Thorough Marine Environmental Protection Law to Protect China's Marine Environment" (1982) *Guangming Ribao* (Enlightenment Daily), (August 25):2.

Amsterdam, A. (1960) "The Void-for-Vagueness Doctrine in the Supreme Court," *University of Pennsylvania Law Review* 109:1:67–116.

Bangongting (1982) "Joint Circular 225 on 25 City Water Conservation Conference," *GGB* 392, 14:795–99.

Bethill, Charles D. (1974) "People's China and the Law of the Sea," *International Lawyer* 8:4:724–51.

"Bidding for Offshore Petroleum Exploration" (1982) *Beijing Review* 25:8:5–6.

Bower, Blair T., et al. (1977) "Incentives for Managing the Environment," *Environmental Science & Technology* 11:3 (March):250–54.

Boxer, Baruch (1980) "Environmental Science." In Leo A. Orleans, ed., *Science and Contemporary China*. Palo Alto, Calif.: Stanford University Press, 463–74.

Cai Hanquan (1984) "Wei Shenmo Guangzhou Jinjiao Turang Wuran Yanzhong" (Why Has Polluted Soil Become a Problem in the Suburbs of Guangzhou?), *H* (September):20–21.

Cai Shouqiu (1981) "On the Character of the Law of Environmental Protection," *Faxue Yanjiu* (Studies in Law) 3:15–18.

——— (1985) "On Environmental Protection in the Special Economic Zones and Open Zones," *Huanjing Fa* (Environmental Law) 2:1–13.

Cao Fenglin (1982) "Qianzhule Huanjing Guanli Gongzuo de Niu Bizi" (Grabbing the Bull's Nose in Environmental Management Work), *H* (January):2–3.

Chen Lihu (1984) "Creating a Body of Local Environmental Civil Law," *H* (May):5:28–29.

Chen Ren (1984) "Zenyang Zhengque Duidai he Chuli Chang Qun Maodun" (How to

Properly Address and Resolve Contradictions between Factories and the Masses), *H* (May):21.

Cheng Yaping (1983) "She Dui Gongye de Fazhan Bixu Jianchi Jingji Xiaoyi yu Huanjing Xiaoyi de Tongyi" (The Development of Collective Industry Must Uphold the Unity of Economic and Environmental Interests), *HB* (May):28–29.

Cheng Zhengkang (1984) "The Abuse of Rights and Self Defense in Environmental Pollution Cases," *ZHK* 6:11–15.

"China Accedes to Marpol" (1983) *China Report* (December):71.

"China Implements MEPL" (1983) FBIS-*CHI* (March 2):14–15.

"China's Ten Cardinal Principles on Amending the 'Declaration on the Human Environment,' " (1972) *Peking Review* 15:32:12–18.

Chiu, Hungdah (1980) "China and the Law of the Sea Conference." In James C. Hsiung and Samuel S. Kim, eds., *China in the Global Community*. New York: Praeger Publishers, 187–215.

——— (1982) "Chinese Law and Justice: Trends over Three Decades," *Occasional Papers/Reprints in Contemporary Asian Studies*, no. 7.

——— (1984) "1982 United Nations Convention on the Law of the Sea and the Settlement of China's Maritime Boundary Dispute." In T. Buergenthal, ed. *Contemporary Issues in International Law: Essays in Honors of B. Sohn*. Arlington, Va: N. P. Engel, 189–208.

——— (1983) "The People's Republic of China and the Third United Nations Conference on the Law of the Sea," *International Property Investment Journal* 1:545–98.

——— (1975) "People's Republic of China on the Question of the Territorial Sea." *International Trade Law Journal* 1:1:29–78.

——— (1982) "Socialist Legalism: Reform and Continuity in Post-Mao People's Republic of China," *Occasional Papers/Reprints Series in Contemporary Asian Studies*, no. 1.

——— (1981) "Structural Changes in Organization and Operation in China's Criminal Justice System," *Occasional Papers/Reprints Series in Contemporary Asian Studies*, no. 1.

Chongqing Environmental Protection Bureau (1985) "An Environmental Pollution Conflict under Special Circumstances," *Zhongguo Huanjing Guanli* (Environmental Management in China) 1:39.

Coase, Ronald H. (1980) "The Problem of Social Cost," *Journal of Law and Economics* 3:1:1–44.

Cohen, Jerome A., Timothy Gelatt and Florence Li (1982) "The Criminal Law of the People's Republic of China," *Journal of Criminal Law and Criminology* 73:138–70.

Conway, M. (1970) "Asia: The Unnatural Rape," *Far Eastern Economic Review* (April 23):21.

Crandall, Robert W., and Paul R. Portney (1984) "Environmental Policy." In Portney, ed., *Natural Resources and the Environment*. Washington: Urban Institute Press, 47–81.

Dellapenna, Joseph W., and Ar-Young Wang (1984) "Protecting the Republic of China from Oil Pollution in the Sea: Accounting for Damages from Oil Spills," *Texas International Law Journal* 19:33:115–39.

Deng Jianxu (1983) "Guanyu Jianli Huan Bao Zhongcai Jigou de Jige Wenti" (Some

Questions on Establishing Conflict Arbitration Organizations for Environmental Protection), *HB* (April):11–12.

——— (1983) ''Some Questions on Establishing Conflict Arbitration Organizations,'' *H* (April):11–12.

''Develop the Ocean, Protect the Ocean'' (1982) *Renmin Ribao* (People's Daily), (August 25):2.

Dicks, Anthony (1982) ''A Legal Opinion,'' *China Trade Report* (July):13.

Dong Dingxun (1984) ''Organize and Coordinate the Strength of All Sectors to Open a New Vista in Environmental Protection Work,'' *Huanjing Guanli* 1:41.

Dong Lisheng (1984) ''New Law Bolsters Environment Protection,'' *China Daily* (May 12):1.

Earney, Fillmore C. F. (1981) ''China's Offshore Petroleum Frontiers,'' *Resources Policy* 7:118–28.

Enderton, Catherine E. (1985) ''Nature Preserves and Protected Wildlife in the People's Republic of China.'' In Clifton W. Pannell and Christopher R. Sulter, eds., *China Geographer*, no. 12 (Environment). Boulder, Colo.: Westview Press.

Epstein, Edward J. (1983) ''China's New Pollution Laws,'' *Petroleum News* (March):11.

——— (1984) ''A Legal Opinion,'' *China Trade Report* (July):13.

——— (1984) ''Pollution Law Laid Down,'' *China Trade Report* (March):4–5.

Fa, Jyh-pin (1983) ''Legislation and Constitutional Interpretations of Human Rights in the Republic of China, 1982–1983: An Overview.'' In Hungdah Chiu, ed., *Chinese Yearbook of International Law and Affairs* 3:87–103.

Fan Ming and Liu Bochun (1983) ''The Foundation and Direction of Environmental Management,'' *Huanjing Guanli* (Environmental Management) 2:3–6.

Fang Weizhong (1984) ''Jianshe You Zhongguo Tese de Jihua Guanli Zhidu he Jihua Jingjixue'' (Establish an Economic Planning System and Planning Economics with Chinese Characteristics), *HQ* 9:26–30.

Fountain, Kevin (1980) ''The Development of Chinese Offshore Oil,'' *China Business Review* 7:23–36.

''Further on Marine Law'' (1982) FBIS-*CHI* (August 20):5–6.

Gao Fengxiang (1973) ''Chong Zhi Wuran Jianghe, Huishou Bianwei Caifu'' (Halt Stream Pollution, Recover Wastes, and Transform Them into Treasures). In Quanguo Huanjing Baohu Huiyi Mishuchu, ed., *Huanjing Baohu Jingyan Xuanbian* (Selected Experiences in Environmental Protection). Beijing: Renmin Chubanshe.

Gao Yusheng (1981) ''Ruhe Genghao de Ba Huanjing Baohu Naru Guojiamin Jingji Jihua'' (How to Better Incorporate Environmental Protection in the National Economic Plan), *HB* (May):1–3.

Ge Dalu (1985) ''This Lawsuit Was Not Fair'' *H* (January):24–25.

Gold, Thomas B. (1984) '' 'Just in Time!' China Battles Spiritual Pollution on the Eve of 1984,'' *Asian Survey* 24:9 (September):947–74.

Goodwin, Robert C., Jr. (1983) ''The Evolving Legal Framework,'' *China Business Review* 10:42.

——— (1983) ''New Marine Environmentalal Protection Law Will Affect Oil Exploration and Development,'' *East Asian Executive Report* 5:3:9–11.

Gresser, Julian (1983) ''The Principle of Multiple Use in Chinese Environmental Law.'' In Jerome Cohen, ed., *Legal Aspects of Doing Business in China*. New York: Practicing Law Institute, 449–591.

Guangzhou Environmental Protection Office (1985) ''Strengthen Environmental Management in Accordance with the Law, and Promote the Opening of Cities to Foreign Investment,'' *Huanjing Fa* (Environmental Law) 2:28–31.

Guo Huan (1974) ''Accent on Environmental Protection,'' *Peking Review* 17:45 (November 8): 9–11.

——— (1974) ''Zhongshi Huanjing Baohu Gongzuo'' (Focus on Environmental Protection Work), *HQ* (September):11–15.

Guo Jicai, Li Jiling and Wang Zhenshao (1982) ''The Four Modernizations and Enactments for Environmental Protection,'' *Faxue* (August):36–46.

Hanson, Jaydee R. (1980) ''China's Fisheries: Scaling Up to Production,'' *China Business Review* 7:3:25–30.

Hardin, Garrett (1968) ''The Tragedy of the Commons,'' *Science* 162 (December 13):1243–48.

Harrison, Selig S. (1983) ''Conflicting Offshore Oil Boundary Claims,'' *China Business Review* 10:3:51–52.

He Ge (1983) ''Legal Responsibility Issues in the Marine Environmental Protection Law,'' *Zhongguo Fazhi Bao* (China Legal System Newspaper), (March 18):3.

Hou Jianqiu (1984) ''Huan Bao Gongzuo de Jige Renshi Wenti'' (Some Fundamental Questions regarding Environmental Protection Work), *H* (January):2–5.

Hua Guofeng (1978) ''The Report on the Work of the Government,'' *Peking Review* 21:10.

Hua Qingyuan (1971) ''Zonghe Liyong Yao Xingli Quhai'' (Comprehensive Utilization Requires Us to Promote the Good and Discard the Harmful), *HQ* (October):54–59.

''Huge Oil Slick Perils Pacific Area Off Coast'' (1969) *New York Times* (January 31):50.

Jiang De and Qin Liwen (1983) ''Chang Jiang Shipping Administrative Bureau Learns Lesson: Strong Emphasis on Environmental Protection Brings Preliminary Results,'' *Zhongguo Fazhi Bao* (China Legal System Newspaper), (February 25):1.

Jiang Yingguang (1983) ''On Several Theoretical Questions of Eco-economics'' (in Chinese), *JY* (October):56–60.

Kinzelbach, Wolfgang K. H. (1983) ''China: Energy and Environment,'' *Environmental Management* 7:4:303–10.

——— (1981) ''Environmental Problems in the People's Republic of China,'' presented at the Third International Conference on Energy Use Management, West Berlin, October 26–30.

Lan, H. D. (1984) ''Some Reflections on the Changes in Moral Atmosphere Brought on by the Rural Reforms,'' *Guangming Ribao* (Enlightenment Daily), (November 19):3.

''Legislation to Protect Marine Environment'' (1983) FBIS-*CHI* (March 2):15.

Leng, Shao-chuan (1977) ''The Role of Law in the People's Republic of China as Reflecting Mao Tse-tung's Influence,'' *Journal of Criminal Law and Criminology* 68:356–74.

Li Chaobo (1980) ''Huanjing Baohu Ying Naru Jingji Jihua'' (Environmental Protection Should Be Included in the State Plan), *HB* (April):1–2.

''Li Chaobo Explains Environment Protection Law at NPC Session.'' (1979) FBIS-*CHI* (September 13):L1.

Li Jinchang (1984) ''Dajia Guanzhu Huanjing Zhanlue'' (Everyone Should Be Concerned about Environmental Strategy), *HB* (January):5–7.

——— (1984) ''Guanyu 'Sansheng' Zonghe Liyong Zhibiao Tixi de Yidian Shexiang''

(Some Thoughts on a Comprehensive Indicator System for the "Three Livings' "), *HB* (May):2–4ff.

——— (1983) "Zhongshi Huanjing Baohu Wenti de Dingliang Fenxi" (Focus on Analyzing the Actual Magnitude of Environmental Problems), *HB* (July):2–4.

Li Kaiwang (1984) "A Discussion on the Object and Task of Socialist Environmental Economics" (in Chinese), *HK* 5:2 (April):67–70.

"Li Ximing on the MEPL (draft) at the 24th Session of the 5th NPC Standing Committee" (1982) *Renmin Ribao* (People's Daily) (August 20):1.

Li Yangming (1984) "Ruhe Shixian Woguo Huanjing Baohu de Zhanlue Mubiao" (How to Attain the Strategic Aims of Environmental Protection in China), *HB* (February):2–3.

——— (1982) "Tigao Renshi, Jin Yi Bu Tuidong Huanjing Baohu Gongzuo" (Raise Our Knowledge and Propel Environmental Protection Work Forward), *HB* (August):2–5.

Liu Honglin (1985) "Some Issues that Should be Addressed When Handling Environmental Pollution Disputes," *Faxue Jikan* (Jurisprudence Quarterly) 3:37–39.

Liu Wen (1980) "Some Remarks on Environmental Economics." In Yu Guangyuan, et al., ed., *Lun Huanjing Guanli* (On Environmental Economics):68–72.

Long Dehuai (1984) "Kongqi Wuran Daigei Nin Neixie Sunhai" (What Harm Can Air Pollution Cause You), *H* (November):6–7.

Lu Qi (1984) "Energy Conservation and Its Prospects," *Beijing Review* 27:46 (November 12):20–23.

Lu Shengwu (1981) "Problems Concerning the Law of the Sea," *Faxue Yanjiu* (Studies in Law), 1:41–48.

Luo Dianrong and Deng Jianxu (1981) "Economic Law and Environmental Protection," *ZHK* 3:6–9.

——— (1982) "The Necessity of Establishing a Trial Court System for Environmental Protection," *HB* (January):3–4.

Ma Xiangcong (1979) "Preliminary Discussion on the Law of Environmental Protection," *Faxue Yanjiu* (Studies in Law) 2:40–43.

——— (1979) "A Study of the Legal System of Environmental Protection," *ZHK* 1:23–27.

Ma Xiangcong and Chen Zhenguo (1983) "On the Marine Environmental Protection Law," *Faxue Yanjiu* (Studies in Law) 2:51–56.

Mao Yushi (1982) "Three Fundamental Problems in Environmental Economics" (in Chinese) *JY* (July):60–63.

"Marine Environmental Law Readied" (1983) FBIS-*CHI* (January 24):19–20.

"Marine Environmental Protection Law" (1983) *China Report* (June):53–54.

"Marine Environmental Regulations Promulgated" (1984) FBIS-*CHI* (January 11):19–20.

"Marine Protection Law Explained" (1982) FBIS-*CHI* (August 20):5.

Meng Qingnan (1983) " 'International Rules and Standards' and the 'Competent International Organization' Concerning Prevention, Reduction, and Control of Marine Pollution from Vessels in the U.N. Convention on the Law of the Sea." *Chinese Yearbook of International Law* 2:230–62.

"New Law Protects Sea Life" (1983) *Beijing Review* 26:13:5.

"New Pollution Law Aims to Clean Up Inland Waterways" (1984) *China Daily* (May 23):1.

"New Pollution Rules" (1984) *China Trade Report* (March):75.

"New Rules in Drive to Reduce Sea Pollution" (1984) *China Daily* (January 13):1.

Noll, Roger (1982) "Leasing the Air: An Alternative Approach to Regulation?" *Engineering & Science* 46:1 (September):12–17.

"Oil Slick Spreads, but Leak Slows" (1969) *New York Times* (February 1):32.

Oksenberg, Michel (1982) "Economic Policy-Making in China: Summer 1981," *China Quarterly* 90 (June):165–94.

Orleans, Leo A., and Richard P. Suttmeier (1970) "The Mao Ethic and Environmental Quality" *Science* 170:3962:1173–76.

Ouyang Xin (1984) "The International Marine Control of Dumping," *Faxue Yanjiu* (Studies in Law), 4:90–95.

Qiu Guotang (1985) "Some Issues Involving the Strengthening of the Environmental Legal System in the Special Economic Zones," *Huanjing Fa* (Environmental Law) 2:14–22.

Qu Geping (1982) "Qianghua Huanjing Guanli de Jiandu Zhineng" (Strengthen the Supervisory Capability of Environmental Management), *HB* (August):6–8ff.

Reidel, Steven (1981) "The Incredible Journey: A Forester's Perception of China" *American Forest* (May):22.

"Ren Zhonglin on the MEPL (draft) at the 24th Session of the 5th NPC Standing Committee" (1982) *Renmin Ribao* (People's Daily) (August 24):1.

Robinson, Nicholas A. (1980) "Environmental Law Begins in China," *New York Law Journal* (April 22):1.

Ross, Lester (1983) "Changes in Water Policy in the People's Republic of China" *Water Resources Bulletin* 19:1 (February):69–72.

——— (1983) "Flood Control Policy in China: The Policy Consequences of Natural Disasters," *The Journal of Public Policy* 3:2 (May):209–32.

——— (1982) "The Implementation of Environmental Policy in China: A Comparative Perspective" *Administration & Society* 15:4 (February):489–516.

——— (1986) "Market Reform and Collective Action in China" *Comparative Political Studies* 19:2 (July):217–32.

——— (1987) "Obligatory Tree Planting: The Role of Campaigns in Policy Implementation in Post-Mao China." In David M. Lampton, ed., *Policy Implementation in Post-Mao China*. Berkeley and Los Angeles: University of California Press.

Ross, Lester, and Mitchell A. Silk (1985) "Post-Mao China and Environmental Protection: The Effects of Legal and Politico-Economic Reform" *UCLA Pacific Basic Law Journal* 4:1–2 (Spring):63–89.

——— (1987) "Curbing Environmental Pollution," *China Business Review* 14:2 (March/April):51–53.

'Sea Patrols to Enforce Law" (1983) FBIS-*CHI* (March 2):16.

Shabad, A. (1985) "5 Jailed for '83 Soviet Disaster," *New York Times* (July 17):A10.

Shen Xin (1984) "Preliminary Discussion of the Administration of the Special Management Law" (in Chinese), *ZHK* 4:2 (April):29–32.

Shi Ehou et al. (1984) "Seawater Pollution on the Northshore of China," *ZHK* 4:71–75.

Silk, Mitchell A. (1985) "China's Marine Environmental Protection Law: The Dragon Creeping in Murky Waters," *Review of Socialist Law* 11:249–73. Revised in *Occasional Paper/ Reprints Series in Contemporary Asian Studies*, No. 6 (1986). Baltimore: University of Maryland School of Law.

——— (1985) "The Crime of Dissent in China," *Problems of Communism* 34:4:61–68.

——— (1987) "Investing and Doing Business in China: The Environmental Implications." In Michael J. Moser, ed., *Trade, Foreign Investment, and the Law in the People's Republic of China*. Hong Kong and London: Oxford University Press.

Smil, Vaclav (1981) "Energy Development in China," *Energy Policy* 9:113–26.

——— (1983) "Rivers of Waste," *China Business Review* 10:4:18–20.

Solinger, Dorothy (1982) "The Fifth National People's Congress and the Process of Policymaking: Reform, Readjustment and the Opposition," *Asian Survey* 22:12:1238–75.

Song Qiping and Shao Boding (1984) "A Brief Talk on the Status and Fundamental Principles of the Environmental Protection Law in China," *ZHK* 4:45–49.

Special Commentator (1984) "Lun Woguo Huanjing Baohu Gongzuo de Jingyan he Jiaoxun" (On Lessons and Experiences from China's Environmental Protection Work), *HB* (January):2–4.

State Council (1984) "Guanyu Huanjing Baohu Gongzuo de Jueding" (Decisions on Environmental Protection Work), May 8. In *GGB* 431 (May 30):319–22.

——— (1981) "Guanyu Zai Guomin Jingji Tiaozheng Shiqi Jiaqiang Huanjing Baohu Gongzuo de Jueding" (Decision on Strengthening Environmental Protection Work in the Economic Readjustment Period), February 24. In *GGB* 351 (April 25):103-7.

"Strengthen the Legal System, Protect the Ocean" (1983) *Renmin Ribao* (People's Daily) (March 1):2.

Sun Xiangming (1984) "Jei Shi 'Fangeming Pohuai Shijian' Ma?" (Is This "An Incident of Counterrevolutionary Destruction?"), *H* (October):24–25.

Tai Qisheng (1984) "Beijing Shi Jumin Kongqi Wuran Wu: Zongjie Yongliang Ji Qi Luodi Duice" (Atmospheric Pollutants and Beijing's Populace: Their Ultimate Consequences and Ways to Reduce Them), HB (June):16–19.

Tang Ke (1972) "China's Stand on the Question of Human Environment," *Peking Review* 15:24 (June 16):5–8ff.

Tian Chunsheng (1984) "Preliminary Analysis of Ground Water Characteristics and Trends in Quality in China" (in Chinese), *ZHK* 4:2 (April):34–40.

Tuan T. (1970) "Our Treatment of the Environment in Ideal and Actuality," *American Scientist* 58:74–79.

Tung Shih-chung (1981) "The Policy of China in the Third United Nations Conference on the Law of the Sea" (unpublished thesis). Geneva: The Graduate Institute of International Studies.

Utton, Albert E. (1968) "Protective Measures and the Torrey Canyon," *Boston College Industrial and Commercial Law Review* 9:3:613–32.

Vallouskas, Charles C., and Bruce C. Ottley (1981) "China's Developing Environmental Law: Policies, Practices and Legislation," *Boston College International and Comparative Law Review* 6:1:81–131.

——— (1981) "Recent Developments in Environmental Protection in China," *Review of Socialist Law* 7:1:35–51.

Walmsley, David J. (1972) "Oil Pollution Problems Arising out of Exploitation of the Continental Shelf: The Santa Barbara Disaster." *San Diego Law Review* 9:3:514–69.

Wan Li (1983) "Tigao Renshi, Jiaqiang Lingdao, Zhazha Shishi Tigao Hao Yiwu Zhishu" (Raise Our Knowledge, Strengthen Leadership, and Resolutely Do Obligatory Tree Planting Well), *ZL* (February):3–5.

Wang Weimin (1980) "Paiwu Shoufei Cujin Huanjing Baohu Gongzuo" (Effluent Fees Advance Environmental Protection Work), *HB* (May):26–27.

"Water Pollution Law Adopted." (1984) FBIS-*CHI* (May 14):K1.

Weil, Martin (1981) "Cleaning Up China's Environment," *China Business Review* 8:1:50–54.

Weisskopf, Michael (1983) "To Save Junk Is To Serve Socialism," *Washington Post* (October 22).

Wen Boping (1980) "Notes on China's Law of Environmental Protection," *Faxue Yanjiu* (Studies in Law) 1:21–25.

Willums, Jan-Oluf (1977) "China's Offshore Petroleum," *China Business Review* 4:4:6–14.

Wolfe, Douglas A., et al., (1983–84) "Marine Pollution in China," *Oceanus* 26:40–46.

Wu Jingcheng (1984) "Brief Comments on Environmental Legislation and Juridicature of China," *Faxue Yanjiu* (Studies in Law) 4:56–60.

Ya Ping (1984) "Yong Falü Shouduan Baohu Hao Shui Ziyuan" (Use Legal Measures to Protect Water Resources), *HB* (December):31–32.

Ye Yuhui (1984) "Ziran Ziyuan de Heli Liyong Yingdang Shi Jingji Xiaoyi de Zhongyao Neirong" (The Rational Utilization of Natural Resources Ought to Be an Important Element in Economic Return), *JY* (April):77–79.

Yeh, K. C. (1984) "Macroeconomic Changes in the Chinese Economy during the Readjustment," *China Quarterly* 100:691–716.

Yu Hong (1970) "Zhuyi Zonghe Liyong" (Stress Multiple Utilization), *HQ* (April):22–26.

Yuan, Paul C. (1983) "China's Jurisdiction Over Its Offshore Petroleum Resources." *Ocean Development and International Law* 12:3:191–208.

——— (1983) "China's Offshore Oil Development: Legal and Geo-Political Perspectives," *Texas International Law Journal* 18:1:107–26.

Zhao Zongliu (1981) "Economic Readjustment and Environment Protection" (in Chinese), *JY* (May):67–73.

Zheng, D. R., and R. Salib (1982) "AQCS For Coal Field Plants in the People's Republic of China." In S. W. Yuan, ed., *Energy Resources and Environment: Papers Presented at the First U.S.-China Conference on Energy, Resources and Environment 7–12 November 1982, Beijing, China*. New York: Pergamon, 121–31.

Zhou Fuxiang (1982) "Jiejue Huanjing Baohu Wenti Yu Jingji Zhengce" (Economic Policy and the Solution of Problems in Environmental Protection), *HQ* 13:27–30.

Zhu Qinfang (1984) "Major Economic and Social Achievements (II)," *Beijing Review* 27:41 (October 8):28–31.

Index

About the Authors

LESTER ROSS, currently an assistant professor of political science at Purdue University, is a specialist in comparative politics and public policy, with emphasis on environmental and regulatory politics and policy. He spent over a year in China conducting research on environmental policy sponsored by the National Academy of Sciences. He is the author of *Environmental Policy in China* and has published widely on Chinese politics and policy in major journals such as *Asian Survey*, *China Business Review*, *Comparative Political Studies*, *Environment*, *Journal of Public Policy*, *UCLA Pacific Basin Law Journal*, and *Water Resources Bulletin*.

MITCHELL A. SILK is a research consultant in the East Asian Legal Studies Program at the University of Maryland Law School. At present he is on a National Academy of Sciences fellowship conducting research and teaching at the Department of Law, Beijing University, and is associated with the Beijing office of Coudert Brothers. He has published extensively on China's legal system and Chinese perspectives on international law in such forums as the *American Journal of International Law*, *China Business Review*, *Far Eastern Economic Review*, *Problems of Communism*, *Review of Socialist Law*, *UCLA Pacific Basin Law Journal*, and the *Chinese Yearbook of International Law and Affairs*.